The Interpersonal Communication Book

FIFTEENTH EDITION

Joseph A. DeVito

Hunter College of the City University of New York

Director, Portfolio Management: Karon Bowers
Content Producer: Barbara Cappuccio
Content Developer: Angela Kao
Portfolio Manager Assistant: Dea Barbieri
Product Marketer: Christopher Brown
Field Marketer: Kelly Ross
Content Producer Manager: Melissa Feimer
Content Development Manager: Sharon Geary
Managing Editor: Maggie Barbieri
Content Developer, Learning Tools: Amy Wetzel
Designer: Kathryn Foot
Digital Studio Course Producer: Amanda Smith
Full-Service Project Manager: SPi Global
Compositor: SPi Global
Printer/Binder: LSC Communications, Inc.
Cover Printer: Phoenix Color/Hagerstown
Cover Designer: Lumina Datamatics, Inc.
Cover Images: 4x6/GettyImages; drbimages/GettyImages

Acknowledgments of third party content appear on pages 398–400, which constitutes an extension of this copyright page.

Library of Congress Cataloging-in-Publication Data

Names: DeVito, Joseph A., author.
Title: The interpersonal communication book / Joseph A. DeVito, Hunter
  College of the City University of New York.
Description: 15th edition. | Boston : Pearson Education, Inc., 2017. |
  Includes bibliographical references and index.
Identifiers: LCCN 2017037905 | ISBN 9780134623108 | ISBN 013462310X
Subjects: LCSH: Interpersonal communication.
Classification: LCC BF637.C45 D49 2017 | DDC 302.2--dc23 LC record available at https://lccn.loc.gov/2017037905

1   18

Instructor's Review Copy:
ISBN-10:   0-13-462446-7
ISBN-13: 978-0-13-462446-4

Access Code Card:
ISBN 10:   0-13-462444-0
ISBN 13: 978-0-13-462444-0

à la carte Edition:
ISBN-10:   0-13-462439-4
ISBN-13: 978-0-13-462439-6

Student Rental Edition:
ISBN 10:   0-13-462310-X
ISBN 13: 978-0-13-462310-8

Brief Contents

Contents

Specialized Contents

Welcome to *The Interpersonal Communication Book*

FIFTEENTH EDITION

It's a rare privilege for an author to present the fifteenth edition of a book. With each revision, I've been able to update and fine tune the presentation of interpersonal communication so that it is current—accurately reflecting what we currently know about the subject—and as clear, interesting, involving, and relevant to today's college students as it can be.

Like its predecessors, this fifteenth edition provides in-depth coverage of interpersonal communication, blending theory and research on the one hand, and practical skills on the other. The book's philosophical foundation continues to be the concept of *choice*. Choice is central to interpersonal communication, as it is to life in general. As speaker and listener, you're regularly confronted with choice points at every stage of the communication process: What do you say? When do you say it? How do you say it? Through what channel should you say it? And so on. In large part, the choices you make will determine the effectiveness of your messages and your relationships. The role of this text, then, is threefold:

1. to identify and explain the choices you have available to you in a vast array of interpersonal situations;
2. to explain the theory and research evidence that bears on these choices—enabling you to identify your available choices and to select more reasoned, reasonable, and effective communication choices;
3. to provide you with the skills needed to communicate your choices effectively.

The Interpersonal Communication Book is available in both print and digital formats. The flexibility of these options encourages students to make choices about their own learning style preferences in order to become more engaged and involved in the learning process.

What's New in This Fifteenth Edition?

Revel™
Educational technology designed for the way today's students read, think, and learn

Revel is an interactive learning environment that deeply engages students and prepares them for class. Media and assessment integrated directly within the authors' narrative lets students read, explore interactive content, and practice in one continuous learning path. Thanks to the dynamic reading experience in Revel, students come to class prepared to discuss, apply, and learn from instructors and from each other.

Learn more about Revel

www.pearson.com/revel

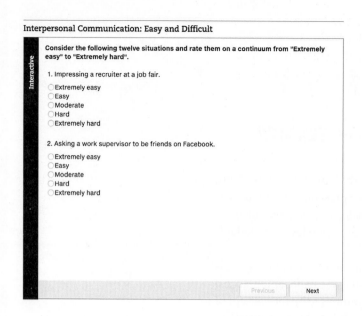

Rather than simply offering opportunities to read about and study interpersonal communication, Revel facilitates deep, engaging interactions with the concepts that matter most. For example, when learning about assertiveness in Chapter 4, students are presented with a self-assessment that rates their own communication behaviors, allowing them to examine their level of assertiveness and consider how they could improve on it. By providing opportunities to read about and practice communication at the same time, Revel engages students directly and immediately, which leads to a better understanding of course material. A wealth of student and instructor resources and interactive materials can be found within Revel. Interactive materials include the following:

- **Integrated Experiences** These interactive exercises allow students to analyze their own communication behavior, enabling them to learn and grow over the duration of the course. A variety of question styles are offered, including fill-in-the-blank, True or False, and numerical ratings.

- **Videos and Video Self-Checks** Short video clips showcase interviews with working professionals, examples of face-to-face scenarios, and concept reviews to boost mastery of content. All videos are bundled with correlating self-checks, enabling students to test their understanding immediately after watching the clip.

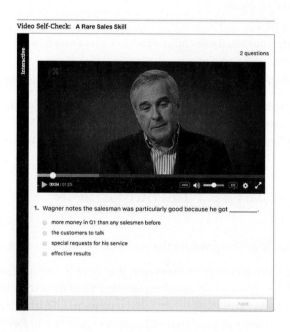

- **Dialogue Examples** Examples of effective and ineffective dialogue are enhanced with audio demonstrations, which add the dimensions of inflection, tone, and volume to enhance the learning experience.

- *Interactive Figures* Interactive figures (such as Figure 1.1: A Model of Interpersonal Communication) allow students to interact with the illustrations, increasing their ability to grasp difficult concepts. By allowing students to examine specific parts of a model, with either additional explanation or real-life examples, broad and theoretical concepts are easier to understand.

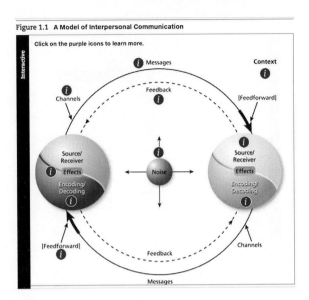

- *Interactive Tables* Two-stage interactive tables (such as Table 1.2: In a Nutshell – The Elements of Interpersonal Communication) allow students to first study and review the information in the original presentation, and then, when ready, assess their memory and understanding of the concepts by removing and then dragging content back to the correct position.

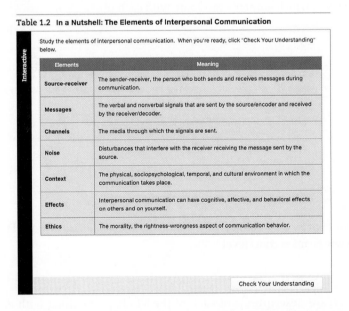

- *Interactive Cultural Maps* These maps recall major cultural differences discussed in Chapter 2 (such as ambiguity tolerance, masculine or feminine orientation, and high-or-low context) and describe how these differences may impact communication around the world. In Revel, readers are given the opportunity to manipulate the maps.

- *Integrated Writing Opportunities* To help students connect chapter content with personal meaning, each chapter offers two varieties of writing prompts: the journal prompt (structured around the concept of interpersonal choice making), eliciting a free-form, topic-specific response addressing topics at the module level; and the Shared Writing Prompt, eliciting a focused, brief response, addressing topics at the chapter level, which students can share with each other.

Journal 1.3: Interpersonal Choice Point - Reducing Relationship Ambiguity

You've gone out with someone for several months. At this point, you want to reduce ambiguity about the future of the relationship and discover your partner's level of commitment. But you don't want to scare your partner. *What would you do to reduce this ambiguity?*

The response entered here will appear in the performance dashboard and can be viewed by your instructor.

Submit

To access your own Revel account for *The Interpersonal Communication Book*, Fifteenth Edition, go to www.pearson.com/revel.

Updated Coverage

Here, in brief, are descriptions of each of the 12 chapters along with examples of what's new in this fifteenth edition.

- **Chapter 1, Foundations of Interpersonal Communication**, covers the elements and principles of interpersonal communication. *New material in this chapter* includes a reorganization of the chapter into three parts ("The Nature of Interpersonal Communication" and "Principles of Interpersonal Communication" are now combined under "Principles"), and inclusion of a new section on "Effects" in the model of interpersonal communication. The Revel version of this chapter includes a variety of new interactive tables that offer low-stakes assessment opportunities for review and retention purposes, and a new integrated exercise "Interpersonal Communication: Easy and Difficult" that offers students the opportunity to consider and learn from their own communication experiences. Two new videos with accompanying Self-Checks offer enhanced examples to illustrate this foundational content: one in which a working professional describes the value of good communication skills, and a concept review about ethical communication.

- **Chapter 2, Culture and Interpersonal Communication**, covers the nature of culture, and the major cultural differences that impact interpersonal communication, with some suggestions on how to make intercultural communication more effective. *New material in this chapter* includes additional figures and a new Cultural Map about internet access. The concept of ethnic identity has been clarified and a new nutshell table summarizes important concepts. The Revel version of this chapter also includes two new interactive figures (2.1 Factors Contributing to the Importance of Culture in Interpersonal Communication and 2.3 Some Steps to Effective Intercultural Communication), a variety of new assessment tables, and two videos with accompanying Self-Checks about culture and communication, and diversity and communication.

- **Chapter 3, Perception of the Self and Others**, covers the essential concepts of the self, the stages of perception, and impression formation and management. The Cultural Map in this chapter deals with ambiguity tolerance. *New material in this chapter* includes a brief section on improving accuracy in perception, and two new figures: 3.5 The Stages of Perception and 3.6 Impression Management Goals. The Revel version includes new interactive activities linked to the new figures and integrated exercises that deal with personality theory and consistency, as well as two videos with accompanying Self-Checks. The first video is about perception barriers, and the second is a brief lecture about impression management and networking basics.

- **Chapter 4, Verbal Messages**, covers the principles of verbal messages, confirmation and disconfirmation, and verbal message effectiveness. The Cultural Map in this chapter deals with high- and low-context cultures. *New material in this chapter* includes a revised organization (the chapter is now in three parts instead of two), two integrated exercises created out of text from the fourteenth edition, a slight expansion of coverage on cultural identifiers, and two new figures: 4.1 The Abstraction Ladder and 4.2 Effective Verbal Messaging. The Revel version of this chapter includes new interactive activities linked to the new figures, and two videos with accompanying Self-Checks: the first video is a concept review about assertive communication, and the second is an ABC News clip that shows racist interactions.

- **Chapter 5, Nonverbal Messages**, covers the principles of nonverbal communication, the ten major channels or codes, and nonverbal competence in encoding and decoding. The Cultural Map in this chapter deals with time orientation. *New material in this chapter* includes an expansion of the benefits from studying nonverbal communication, more coverage of nonverbal communication competence (summarized by a new nutshell table), and a new figure 5.1 The Power of Nonverbal Messages. The Revel version of this chapter includes interactivity linked to the new figures and tables, two new interactive exercises "Estimating Heights" and "Facial Management Techniques," and a multimedia gallery illustrating the five major meaning of touch. There are two videos with accompanying Self-Checks: the first video is an ABC News feature about the body language of politicians, and the second is a concept review of nonverbal messages.

- **Chapter 6, Listening**, covers the stages and styles of listening, as well as cultural and gender differences. The Cultural Map in this chapter deals with politeness. *New material in this chapter* includes a discussion on critical listening, a revision and reconceptualization of the styles of listening, the inclusion of hearing impairment as a potential barrier to listening, a new integrated exercise on empathy, and an enhanced section on politeness and the mobile phone. The Revel version includes a new interactive figure (6.2 Four Listening Styles), as well as two videos. The first video shows a family dinner in which parents and children fail to listen to one another, and the second features a businesswoman describing how she learned to be a better listener when she transferred from a company based in Ireland to one based in Japan.

- **Chapter 7, Emotional Messages**, covers the principles of emotional communication, some obstacles to communicating emotions, and emotional competence. The Cultural Map in this chapter deals with indulgent and restraint orientation. *New material in this chapter* includes an integrated exercise on expressing emotions effectively, a discussion on "emotional labor" (with display rules), and the inclusion of emotional happiness. The Revel version includes a new interactive exercise and new interactive figure (7.1 The Principles of Emotions and Emotional Expressions), as well as two videos with accompanying Self-Checks. The first video features a British backgammon champion explaining the importance of controlling her emotions under pressure, and the second shows Sheryl Sandberg describing how she dealt with the grief of losing her husband.

- **Chapter 8, Conversational Messages**, covers the principles of conversation, self-disclosure, and some everyday conversational encounters. The Cultural Map in this chapter deals with apologies. *New material in this chapter* includes a discussion on how to ask for a favor, along with three new figures that preview some of the major concepts in this chapter. In addition, the discussion of the conversation process has been reduced in length. The Revel version of this chapter includes activities related to the new figures: 8.1 The Principles of Conversation, 8.3 The Maxims of Conversation, and 8.4 The Maxims of Politeness. There are a host of new interactive tables with low-stakes assessment opportunities, as well as two videos, both of which show examples of face-to-face conversations. In the first video, three counselors try to discuss the best way to help a struggling student, and in the second, a manager tries to draw out an employee at a company party.

- **Chapter 9, Interpersonal Relationship Stages, Communication, and Theories**, covers the stages of relationships, the communication that takes place at these different stages, and some of the major theories that explain how relationships grow and deteriorate. *New material in this chapter* includes a reorganization that places "Relationship Communication" immediately after "Relationship Stages," and coverage of social penetration with the discussion on intimacy, rather than with the theories. The Revel version of this chapter includes two new interactive exercises on the advantages and disadvantages of interpersonal relationships, a new interactive figure (9.5 Relationship Theories), as well as two videos with accompanying Self-Checks. The first video is about friendship and social media, and the second shows how a student juggles classes, childcare, and work.

- **Chapter 10, Interpersonal Relationship Types**, covers friendship, love, family, and workplace relationships; and two of their dark sides: jealousy and violence. The Cultural Map in this chapter deals with masculine and feminine orientation. *New material in this chapter* includes nutshell tables and a tightening and updating of the narrative. The Revel version of this chapter includes a new multimedia gallery that illustrates relationship types, new preview figure (10.1 Types of Love), and a new interactive exercise on love styles and personality. Two new videos with accompanying Self-Checks include an overview of family relationships, and interviews with students about their own experiences with jealousy.

- **Chapter 11, Interpersonal Conflict and Conflict Management**, covers the nature and principles of conflict and the strategies of effective conflict management. The Cultural Map in this chapter deals with masculine and feminine orientation. The Cultural Map in this chapter deals with success. *New material in this chapter* includes a restructuring of the principles of conflict (the principles of content and relationship conflict and conflict can occur in all forms are now covered under conflict issues), and a refocused and rewritten section on conflict management is presented as a multistep process. The Revel version includes a new interactive figure (11.3 Conflict Management Strategies), and two videos. The first video is a concept review of conflict and communication, and the second shows students talking about their own relationship conflicts.

- **Chapter 12, Interpersonal Power and Influence**, covers the principles of power and influence; power in the relationship, person, and message; and the misuses of power (sexual harassment, bullying, and power plays). The Cultural Map in this chapter deals with high- and low-power distance. *New material in this chapter* includes a major section on prosocial communication, which now concludes this chapter and the book. The Revel version of this chapter includes an interactive Cultural Map on high- and low-power distance, a new multimedia gallery about the different types of power, and a new interactive figure: 12.1 Six Principles of Power. The two videos are both about communication in the workplace: one in which a professional describes two very different managers and another in which a professional explains how she dealt with bullying from a co-worker.

Features

This text is a complete learning package that will provide students with the opportunity to learn about the theories and research in interpersonal communication, and to acquire and practice the skills necessary for effective interpersonal interaction.

Learning Objectives

Learning objectives are presented in the chapter opener, repeated in the text with each major head, and iterated again in the summary. This feature helps focus attention on the key concepts and principles discussed, and how this learning can be demonstrated.

Preview Figures and Nutshell Summary Tables

Throughout the text, visuals preview the content of the sections, and Nutshell summary tables at the end of the sections help students review the content and fix it more firmly in memory.

Interpersonal Choice Points and ViewPoints

Interpersonal Choice Points—brief scenarios that require you make an interpersonal communication choice—encourage students to apply the material in the chapter to varied specific interactions. They are designed to encourage the application of the research and theory discussed in the text to real-life situations. These appear throughout the text in the margins.

ViewPoints appear as captions to all the interior photos and ask you to consider a wide variety of issues in interpersonal communication. These are designed to encourage students to explore significant communication issues discussed in the chapter from a more personal point of view.

Balance of Theory/Research and Skills

While a great deal of new research is integrated throughout the book, much of it is from the past five years, this text recognizes the practical importance of skill development and so gives considerable attention to mastering interpersonal skills. But it bases these skills on theory and research, which are discussed throughout the text. The boxes on Understanding Interpersonal Theory & Research from the previous edition have been integrated into the text narrative to give them a clearer context and the chapters greater continuity.

Like theory and research, interpersonal skills are discussed throughout this text. In addition, each chapter contains an Understanding Interpersonal Skills box. These boxes are designed to highlight some of the most important skills of interpersonal communication: Mindfulness, Cultural Sensitivity, Other-Orientation, Openness, Metacommunication, Flexibility, Expressiveness, Empathy, Supportiveness, Equality, and Interaction Management.

Culture and Interpersonal Communication

As our knowledge of culture and its relevance to interpersonal communication grows, so must culture's presence in an interpersonal communication textbook and course. The text stresses the importance of culture to all aspects of interpersonal communication.

An entire chapter devoted to culture (Chapter 2, Culture and Interpersonal Communication) is presented as one of the foundation concepts for understanding interpersonal communication. This chapter covers the relationship of culture and interpersonal communication, the ways in which cultures differ, and the strategies to make intercultural communication more effective. In addition to this separate chapter, here are some of the more important discussions that appear throughout the text:

- the cultural dimension of context; and culture in complementary and symmetrical relationships, in the principle of adjustment, and in ethical questions (Chapter 1)
- the role of culture in the development of self-concept, accurate perception, implicit personality theory, the self-serving bias, and uncertainty (Chapter 3)
- listening, culture, and gender (Chapter 4)
- cultural and gender differences in politeness, directness, and assertiveness; and cultural identifiers, sexism, heterosexism, racism, and ageism in language and in listening (Chapter 5)
- culture and gesture, facial expression, eye communication, color, touch, paralanguage, silence, and time (Chapter 6)
- the influences of culture on emotions, and cultural customs as an obstacle to the communication of emotions (Chapter 7)
- conversational maxims, culture, and gender; culture and expressiveness; and the influence of culture on self-disclosure (Chapter 8)
- the influences of culture on interpersonal relationships and the stages of relationships (Chapter 9)
- cultural differences in friendship and loving, and culture and the family (Chapter 10)
- cultural influences on conflict and conflict management (Chapter 11)
- the cultural dimension of power (Chapter 12)

The Cultural Map feature returns to the basic cultural differences discussed in Chapter 2 and connects these concepts with the content of the various chapters.

People with disabilities may also be viewed from a cultural perspective, and in this edition, three special tables offer suggestions for more effective communication between people with and people without disabilities. These tables provide tips for communication between people with and without visual impairments (Table 5.4 in Chapter 5); with and without hearing difficulties (Table 6.3 in Chapter 6); and between people with and without speech and language disorders (Table 8.1 in Chapter 8).

Politeness

Politeness in interpersonal communication is stressed throughout this text as one of the major features of effective interaction. Some of the major discussions include:

- politeness strategies for increasing attractiveness (Chapter 3)
- message politeness (Chapter 4)

- polite listening (Chapter 6)
- conversational politeness (Chapter 8)
- politeness theory of relationships (Chapter 9)
- politeness in conflict management (Chapter 11)

Social Media

The ways and means of social media are integrated throughout the text. For example, the principle of anonymity in interpersonal communication is included as a basic principle because of its increasing importance due to social media. The ubiquity of the cell phone and texting has changed interpersonal communication forever and is recognized throughout the text. Likewise, dating, keeping in touch with family and friends, making friends, and engaging in conflict—and much more—is viewed in a world dominated by (not simply a world that includes) social media.

In-Text Application

In print as well as in Revel, this text includes a variety of features that encourage interaction and self-exploration.

- *New to this edition*, integrated exercises appear throughout the text in every chapter. These exercises are part of the text narrative but require you to interact with and respond to the text material. Some of these are brand new and some of them have been revised and reconfigured from material in the previous edition.
- Interpersonal Choice Points that appear in the margins encourage you to apply the principles and skills of the text to specific interpersonal situations.
- ViewPoints captions encourage you to explore the implications of a variety of communication theories and research findings.
- Understanding Interpersonal Skills boxes ask for personal involvement that enables you to actively engage with these important skills.
- Ethics in Interpersonal Communication boxes present ethical issues and ask what you would do in each of the presented scenarios.

End of Chapter

Each chapter has a two-part ending: (1) Summary, a numbered propositional summary of the major concepts that are discussed in the chapter, organized by major topic headings. Each topic heading also contains the learning objective. (2) Key Terms, a list of key terms that are used in the chapter (and included in the "Glossary of Interpersonal Communication Concepts" at the end of the text).

Instructor and Student Resources

Key instructor resources include an Instructor's Manual (ISBN 0-13-462440-8), TestBank, (ISBN 0-13-462438-6), and PowerPoint Presentation Package (ISBN 0-13-462449-1). These supplements are available on the catalog page for this text on Pearson.com/us (instructor login required). MyTest online test-generating software (ISBN 0-13-462442-4) is available at www.pearsonmytest.com (instructor login required). For a complete list of the instructor and student resources available with the text, please visit the Pearson Communication catalog at www.pearson.com/communication.

Pearson MediaShare

Pearson's comprehensive media upload tool allows students to post videos, images, audio, or documents for instructor and peer viewing, time-stamped commenting, and assessment. MediaShare is an easy, mobile way for students and professors to interact and engage with speeches, presentation aids, and other files. MediaShare gives professors the tools to provide contextual feedback to demonstrate how students can improve their skills.

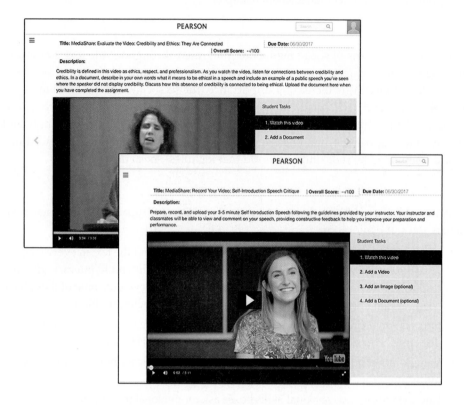

The best of MediaShare's functionality, including student video submissions with grading and video quizzes, is now available to use and assign *within Revel*, making Revel an even more complete solution for Communication courses. By placing the key components of MediaShare within Revel, students have an all-inclusive space to practice and have their performance assessed, while actively learning through interactive course content. Revel with MediaShare is an unparalleled immersive learning experience for the Communication curriculum.

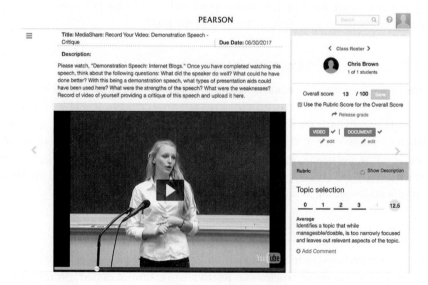

- Use MediaShare to assign or view speeches, video-based assignments, role-playing, and more in a variety of formats including video, Word, PowerPoint, and Excel.
- Assess students using customizable, Pearson-provided rubrics, or create your own around classroom goals, learning outcomes, or department initiatives.

- Set up assignments for students with options for full-class viewing and commenting, or private comments between you and the student.
- Record video directly from a tablet, phone, or other webcam.
- Embed video from YouTube via assignments to incorporate current events into the classroom experience.

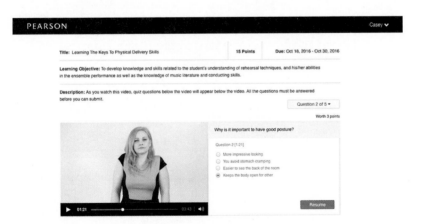

- Set up quiz questions on video assignments to ensure students master concepts and interact and engage with the media.
- Import grades into most learning management systems.
- Ensure a secure learning environment for instructors and students through robust privacy settings.

Acknowledgments

I wish to express my appreciation to the many specialists who carefully reviewed this text. Your comments resulted in a large number of changes; I'm extremely grateful. Thank you:

Cynthia Langham, University of Detroit Mercy

Gretchen Arthur, Lansing Community College

Karl Babij, DeSales University

Martin Mehl, California Poly State University SLO

Ellie Leonhardt, Rogue Community College

Rachel Reznik, Elmhurst College

Stacie Williams, Portland Community College

Diane Ferrero-Paluzzi, Iona College

In addition, I wish to express my appreciation to the people at Pearson who contributed so heavily to this text, especially Karon Bowers, Portfolio Manager of Communication, English, and Languages; Maggie Barbieri, Managing Editor; Angela Kao, Development Editor; Dea Barbieri, Editorial Assistant; Kelly Ross, Field Marketer; Christopher Brown, Product Marketer; Barbara Cappuccio, Content Producer; Annemarie Franklin and Raja Natesan, SPi Editorial Project Managers; and Beth Brenzel, Photo Researcher at SPi. I thank them all for making me—and this book—look so good.

Joseph A. DeVito

Foundations of Interpersonal Communication

Effective and satisfying interpersonal communication rests on a solid foundation of knowledge and skills. *Resolve to build a really strong foundation for your own communication.*

Chapter Topics

The Benefits of Studying Interpersonal Communication

The Elements of Interpersonal Communication

The Principles of Interpersonal Communication

Learning Objectives

1.1 Identify the personal and professional benefits of studying interpersonal communication.

1.2 Define *interpersonal communication* and its essential elements including *source–receiver, messages, channels, noise, context, effects,* and *ethics*.

1.3 Paraphrase the principles of interpersonal communication.

This chapter introduces the study of interpersonal communication and explains why interpersonal communication is so important, examines the essential elements of this unique form of communication, and describes its major principles.

The Benefits of Studying Interpersonal Communication

1.1 Identify the personal and professional benefits of studying interpersonal communication.

Fair questions to ask at the beginning of this text and this course are "What will I get out of this?" and "Why should I study interpersonal communication?" One very clear answer is given by the importance of interpersonal communication: it's a major part of human existence that every educated person needs to understand. Much as you need to understand history, science, geography, and mathematics, for example, you need to understand how people interact (how people communicate interpersonally) and how people form relationships—both face-to-face and online. On a more practical level, you'll learn the skills that will yield both personal and professional benefits.

Personal Benefits

Your personal success and happiness depend largely on your effectiveness as an interpersonal communicator. Close friendships and romantic relationships are developed, maintained, and sometimes destroyed largely through your interpersonal interactions. Likewise, the success of your family relationships depends heavily on the interpersonal communication among members. For example, in a survey of 1,001 people over 18 years of age, 53 percent felt that a lack of effective communication was the major cause of marriage failure—significantly greater than money (38 percent) and in-law interference (14 percent) (How Americans Communicate, 1999).

Likewise, your success in interacting with neighbors, acquaintances, and people you meet every day depends on your ability to engage in satisfying conversation—conversation that's comfortable and enjoyable.

Professional Benefits

The ability to communicate interpersonally is widely recognized as crucial to professional success (Morreale & Pearson, 2008; Satell, 2015; Morreale, Valenzano, & Bauer, 2016). From the initial interview at a college job fair to interning, to participating in and then leading meetings, your skills at interpersonal communication will largely determine your success.

Employers want graduates who can communicate orally and in writing (Berrett, 2013). This ability is even considered more important than job-specific skills, which employers feel could be learned on the job. For example, one study found that among the 23 attributes ranked as "very important" in hiring decisions, "communication and interpersonal skills," noted by 89 percent of the recruiters, was at the top of the list. This was a far higher percentage of recruiters than the percentage who noted "content of the core curriculum" (34 percent) or "overall value for the money invested in the recruiting effort" (33 percent) (Alsop, 2004). Interpersonal skills offer an important advantage for persons in finance (Messmer, 1999), play a significant role in preventing workplace violence (Parker, 2004), reduce medical mishaps and improve doctor–patient communication (Smith, 2004; Sutcliffe, Lewton, & Rosenthal, 2004), are one of six areas that define the professional competence of physicians and trainees (Epstein & Hundert, 2002), and contribute greatly to maintaining diversity in the workplace, team building, and employee morale (Johnson, 2017). In a survey of employers who were asked what colleges should place more emphasis on, 89 percent identified "the ability to effectively communicate orally and in writing" as the highest of any skill listed (Hart

Research Associates, 2010). And in that same survey, the largest number of employers (84 percent), when asked what would prepare college students for success, identified "communication skills." In still another survey of women and leadership, the ability to communicate and to build relationships—the essential of interpersonal communication—were noted among the competencies exemplified by top leaders (Goleman, 2013b). The importance of interpersonal communication skills extends over the entire spectrum of professions.

Clearly, interpersonal skills are vital to both personal and professional success. Understanding the theory and research in interpersonal communication and mastering its skills go hand in hand (Greene & Burleson, 2003). The more you know about interpersonal communication, the more insight and knowledge you'll gain about what works and what doesn't work. The more skills you have within your arsenal of communication strategies, the greater your choices for communicating in any situation. Put differently, the greater your knowledge and the greater the number of communication choices at your disposal, the greater the likelihood that you'll be successful in achieving your interpersonal goals. You might look at this text and this course as aiming to enlarge your interpersonal communication choices and give you a greater number of options for communicating effectively than you had before this exposure to the study of interpersonal communication.

Because of the importance of choice—after all, your interpersonal messages and relationships are the result of the choices you make in any given situation—you'll find boxes labelled *Interpersonal Choice Point* throughout the text. **Choice points** are simply moments when you need to make a choice, a decision, about your interpersonal communication—for example, about whom you communicate with, what you say, what you don't say, how you phrase what you want to say, the photos you want to post and those you don't, and so on. Some of the questions about choices will prove easy to answer while others will prove to be more difficult. This variation in difficulty mirrors real-life interpersonal communication; getting your meanings and feelings across is easy sometimes and very difficult at others. Let's look first at the easy-difficult dimension and then at a choice point.

Consider the following situations and rate them on a continuum from easy to difficult (use 1 for extremely easy and 5 for extremely difficult).

_____ **1.** Impressing a recruiter at a job fair.

_____ **2.** Asking a work supervisor to be friends on Facebook.

_____ **3.** Breaking up a two-year romantic relationship because you've fallen out of love with your partner.

_____ **4.** Responding to a compliment about the way you dress.

_____ **5.** Reconnecting with a long-lost friend by phone.

_____ **6.** Voicing an opinion about religion in class that is contrary to the opinions of all others in the class.

_____ **7.** Crying at a movie you're attending with three or four same-sex friends.

_____ **8.** Asking a relative to lie for you so you can get out of a family gathering.

_____ **9.** Introducing yourself to a group of people who are culturally very different from you.

_____ **10.** Asking an instructor for an extension on your term paper.

_____ **11.** Making small talk with someone you don't know in an elevator.

_____ **12.** Meeting someone face-to-face with whom you've interacted romantically online.

If you have the opportunity to compare your continuum with those of others, you'll probably find both similarities and differences. Reflecting on the easy-to-difficult interpersonal interactions will help you identify the skills you'd want to acquire or enhance as you make your varied interpersonal choices. Take a look at the first Interpersonal Choice Point which also explains the feature's purpose and format.

INTERPERSONAL CHOICE POINT
Communicating an Image

The *Interpersonal Choice Point* feature is designed to help you apply the text material to real-life situations by first considering your available choices and then making a communication decision. For each choice point, try to identify, as specifically as possible, the advantages and disadvantages of your available choices. Of all your choices, ask yourself which response is likely to work best for you.

You're taking a course in interpersonal communication at a new college and you want to be liked by your fellow students. *What might you do to appear likeable and be accepted as an approachable person? What would you be sure to avoid doing?*

a. smile and make eye contact

b. compliment others frequently even for no reason

c. dress a level above the average student

d. speak in class—regularly asking and answering questions

e. other

The Elements of Interpersonal Communication

1.2 Define *interpersonal communication* and its essential elements including *source–receiver*, *messages*, *channels*, *noise*, *context*, *effects*, and *ethics*.

Although this entire text is, in a sense, a definition of interpersonal communication, a working definition is useful at the start. **Interpersonal communication** is *the verbal and nonverbal interaction between two (or sometimes more than two) interdependent people.* This relatively simple definition implies a variety of elements which we discuss in this section. But, first, let's look at some of the myths about interpersonal communication that can get in the way of a meaningful understanding and mastery of this area.

Examine your beliefs about interpersonal communication by responding to the following questions with T if you believe the statement is usually true or F if you believe the statement is usually false.

_____ **1.** Good communicators are born, not made.

_____ **2.** The more you communicate, the better you will be at it.

_____ **3.** In your interpersonal communication, a good guide to follow is to be as open, empathic, and supportive as you can be.

_____ **4.** When communicating with people from other cultures, it's best to ignore the differences and treat the other person just as you'd treat members of your own culture.

_____ **5.** Fear of meeting new people is detrimental and must be eliminated.

_____ **6.** When there is conflict, your relationship is in trouble.

As you probably figured out, all six statements are generally false. As you read this text, you'll discover not only why these beliefs are false but also the trouble you can get into when you assume they're true. For now, and in brief, here are some of the reasons each of the statements is generally false:

1. Effective communication is a learned skill; although some people are born brighter or more extroverted, everyone can improve their abilities and become more effective communicators.

2. It's not the amount of communication people engage in but the quality that matters; if you practice bad habits, you're more likely to grow less effective than more effective, so it's important to learn and follow the principles of effectiveness (Greene, 2003; Greene & Burleson, 2003).

3. Each interpersonal situation is unique, and therefore the type of communication appropriate in one situation may not be appropriate in another.

4. This assumption will probably get you into considerable trouble because people from different cultures often attribute different meanings to a message; members of different cultures also follow different rules for what is and is not appropriate in interpersonal communication.

5. Many people are nervous meeting new people, especially if these are people in authority; managing, not eliminating, the fear will enable you to become effective regardless of your current level of fear.

6. All meaningful relationships experience conflict; relationships are not in trouble when there is conflict, though dealing with conflict ineffectively can often damage the relationship.

The model presented in Figure 1.1 is designed to reflect the circular nature of interpersonal communication; both persons send messages simultaneously rather than in a linear sequence, where communication goes from Person 1 to Person 2 to Person 1 to Person 2 and on and on.

Each of the concepts identified in the model and discussed here may be thought of as a universal of interpersonal communication in that it is present in all interpersonal interactions: (1) **source–receiver** (including competence, encoding–decoding, and code-switching), (2) messages (and the metamessages of feedback and feedforward), (3) channels, (4) noise, (5) contexts, (6) effects, and (7) ethics (though not indicated in the diagram), is an overriding consideration in all interpersonal communication.

Interpersonal Metaphors

Metaphors—figures of speech in which two unlike things are compared—are useful for providing different perspectives on interpersonal communication; they help you to look at interpersonal communication from different perspectives and help highlight different aspects of the interpersonal process. *How would you explain interpersonal communication in terms of metaphors such as a seesaw, a ball game, a television sitcom, a recliner, the weather, an opera, a good book, or a tug of war?*

Source–Receiver

Interpersonal communication involves at least two people. Each individual performs source functions (formulates and sends messages) and also performs receiver functions (perceives and comprehends messages). The term source–receiver emphasizes that both

Figure 1.1 A Model of Interpersonal Communication

After you read the section on the elements of interpersonal communication, you may wish to construct your own model of the process. In constructing this model, be careful that you don't fall into the trap of visualizing interpersonal communication as a linear or simple left-to-right, static process. Remember that all elements are interrelated and interdependent. *After completing your model, consider, for example: (1) Could your model also serve as a model of intrapersonal communication (communication with oneself)? Is the model applicable to both face-to-face and online communication? (2) What elements or concepts other than those noted here might be added to the model?*

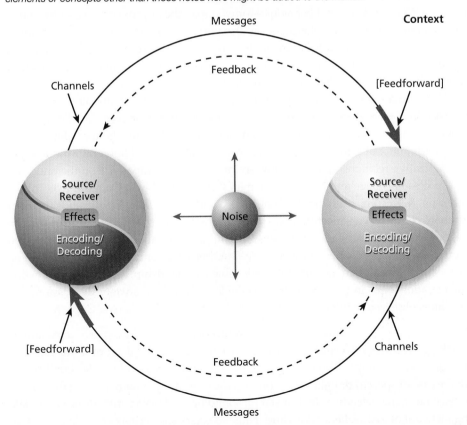

functions are performed by each individual in interpersonal communication. This, of course, does not mean that people serve these functions equally. As you've no doubt witnessed, some people are (primarily) talkers and some people are (primarily) listeners. And some people talk largely about themselves and others participate more in the give and take of communication. In an interesting analysis of Twitter messages, two major types of users were identified (Bersin, 2013; Dean, 2010a):

- *Informers* were those who shared information and also replied to others; these made up about 20 percent.
- *Meformers* were those who mainly gave out information about themselves; these made up about 80 percent.

Who you are, what you know, what you believe, what you value, what you want, what you have been told, and what your attitudes are all influence what you say, how you say it, what messages you receive, and how you receive them. Likewise, the person you're speaking to and the knowledge that you think that person has greatly influences your interpersonal messages (Lau, Chiu, & Hong, 2001). Each person is unique; each person's communications are unique.

To complicate matters just a bit, we need to recognize that although interpersonal communication may take place between two close friends, for example, there is generally what might be called a **remote audience**. For example, you update your status on Facebook for your friends (your intended audience) to see. This is your intended audience and the audience to whom you're directing your message. But, it's likely (even probable) that your prospective employers will also see this as will others who may receive it from a member of your intended audience. These are your remote audiences. The important practical implication is to be aware of both your audiences and know that the dividing line between your intended and your remote audiences is getting thinner every day.

Interpersonal Competence   Your ability to communicate effectively (as source and receiver) is your interpersonal **competence** (Spitzberg & Cupach, 1989; Wilson & Sabee, 2003). Your competence includes, for example, the knowledge that, in certain contexts and with certain listeners, one topic is appropriate and another isn't. Your knowledge about the rules of nonverbal behavior—for example, the appropriateness of touching, vocal volume, and physical closeness—is also part of your competence. In short, interpersonal competence includes knowing how to adjust your communication according to the context of the interaction, the person with whom you're interacting, and a host of other factors discussed throughout this text.

You learn communication competence much as you learn to eat with a knife and fork—by observing others, by explicit instruction, and by trial and error. Some individuals learn better than others, though, and these are generally the people with whom you find it interesting and comfortable to talk. They seem to know what to say and how and when to say it.

A positive relationship exists between interpersonal competence on the one hand and success in college and job satisfaction on the other (Rubin & Graham, 1988; Wertz, Sorenson, & Heeren, 1988). So much of college and professional life depends on interpersonal competence—meeting and interacting with other students, teachers, or colleagues; asking and answering questions; presenting information or argument—that you should not find this connection surprising. Interpersonal competence also enables you to develop and maintain meaningful relationships in friendship, love, family, and work. Such relationships, in turn, contribute to the lower levels of anxiety, depression, and loneliness observed in interpersonally competent people (Spitzberg & Cupach, 1989).

Encoding–Decoding   **Encoding** refers to the act of producing messages—for example, speaking or writing. **Decoding** is the reverse and refers to the act of understanding messages—for example, listening or reading. By sending your ideas via sound waves (in the case of speech) or light waves (in the case of writing), you're putting these ideas into a code, hence *en*coding. By translating sound or light waves into ideas, you're taking them out of a code, hence *de*coding. Thus, speakers and writers are called encoders, and listeners and readers are called decoders. The term *encoding–decoding* is used to emphasize that the two activities are performed in combination by each participant. For interpersonal communication to occur, messages must be encoded and decoded. For example, when a parent talks to a child whose eyes are closed and whose ears are covered by stereo headphones, interpersonal communication does not occur because the messages sent are not being received.

Code-Switching Technically, code switching refers to using more than one language in a conversation, often in the same sentence (Bullock & Toribio, 2012; Thompson, 2013; Esen, 2016). And so a native Spanish speaker might speak most

VIEWPOINTS

On-Screen Competence

What characters in television sitcoms or dramas do you think demonstrate superior interpersonal competence? What characters demonstrate obvious interpersonal incompetence? What specifically do they say or do—or don't say or don't do—that leads you to judge them as being or not being interpersonally competent?

of a sentence in English and then insert a Spanish term or phrase. More popularly, however, **code-switching** refers to using different language styles depending on the situation. For example, you probably talk differently to a child than to an adult—in the topics you talk about and in the language you use. Similarly, when you text or tweet, you use a specialized language consisting of lots of abbreviations and acronyms that you discard when you write a college term paper or when you're interviewing for a job.

The ability to code-switch serves at least two very important purposes. First, it identifies you as one of the group; you are not an outsider. It's a way of bonding with the group. Second, it often helps in terms of making your meaning clearer; some things seem better expressed in one language or code than in another.

Code switching can create problems, however. When used to ingratiate yourself or make yourself seem one of the group when you really aren't—and that attempt is obvious to the group members—code switching is likely to work against you. You risk being seen as an interloper, as one who tries to gain entrance to a group to which one really doesn't belong. The other case where code switching creates problems is when you use the code appropriate to one type of communication in another where it isn't appropriate, for example, when you use your Facebook or Twitter grammar during a job interview. Communication competence, then, involves the ability to code-switch when it's appropriate—when it makes your message clearer and when it's genuine.

Messages

Messages are signals that serve as stimuli for a receiver and are received by one of our senses—auditory (hearing), visual (seeing), tactile (touching), olfactory (smelling), gustatory (tasting), or any combination of these senses. You communicate interpersonally by gesture and touch as well as by words and sentences. The clothes you wear communicate to others and, in fact, to yourself as well. The way you walk communicates, as does the way you shake hands, tilt your head, comb your hair, sit, smile, or frown. Similarly, the colors and types of cell phones, the wallpaper and screen savers on your computer, and even the type and power of your computer communicate messages about you. The photo and background theme you choose for your Twitter page reveals something about yourself beyond what your actual tweets reveal. Tweeters with the generic white bird photo and standard background communicate something quite different from the Tweeters who customize their pages with clever photos, original backgrounds, and sidebars. The same is true of Facebook pages. All of these signals are your interpersonal communication messages.

Interpersonal communication can take place by phone, through prison cell walls, through webcams, or face-to-face. Increasingly, it's taking place through computers, through Facebook and Twitter. Some of these messages are exchanged in real time. This is **synchronous communication**; the messages are sent and received at the same time, as in face-to-face and phone messages. Other messages do not take place in real time. This is **asynchronous communication**; the messages are sent at one time and received at another and perhaps responded to at still another time. For example, you might poke someone on Facebook today, but that person may not see it until tomorrow and may not poke you back until the next day. Similarly, you might find a tweet or a blog post today that was actually written weeks or even years ago.

Messages may be intentional or unintentional. They may result from the most carefully planned strategy as well as from the unintentional slip of the tongue, lingering body odor, or nervous twitch. Messages may refer to the world, people, and events as well as to other messages (DeVito, 2003a).

Messages that are about other messages are called **metamessages** and represent many of your everyday communications; they include, for example, "Do you understand?," "Did I say that right?," "What did you say?," "Is it fair to say that . . . ?," "I want to be honest," "That's not logical." Two particularly important types of metamessages are feedback and feedforward.

Feedback Messages Throughout the interpersonal communication process, you exchange feedback—messages sent back to the speaker concerning reactions to what is said (Sutton, Hornsey, & Douglas, 2012). **Feedback** tells the speaker what effect she or he is having on listeners. On the basis of this feedback, the speaker may adjust, modify, strengthen, deemphasize, or change the content or form of the messages.

Feedback may come from yourself or from others. When you send a message—say, in speaking to another person—you also hear yourself. That is, you get feedback from your own messages: You hear what you say, you feel the way you move, you see what you write. In addition to this self-feedback, you get feedback from others. This feedback can take many forms. A frown or a smile, a yea or a nay, a pat on the back or a punch in the mouth are all types of feedback.

Feedback, of course, has significant effects on the receiver. For example, in one study, positive feedback on social networking sites, complimenting, say, the photo or profile, enhanced self-esteem and the sense of well-being whereas negative feedback (criticism, for example) resulted in a decrease in self-esteem and well-being (Valkenburg, Peter, & Schouten, 2006).

Sometimes feedback is easy to identify, but sometimes it isn't (Skinner, 2002). Part of the art of effective communication is to discern feedback and adjust your messages on the basis of that feedback.

Feedforward Messages **Feedforward** is information you provide before sending your primary message (Richards, 1968). Feedforward reveals something about the message to come. Examples of feedforward include the preface or table of contents of a book, the opening paragraph of a chapter or post, movie previews, magazine covers, e-mail subject headings, and introductions in public speeches. Feedforward may serve a variety of functions. For example, you might use feedforward to express your wish to chat a bit, saying something like "Hey, I haven't

Feedback and Relationships

If we were to develop a feedback theory of relationships, it would hold that satisfying friendships, romantic relationships, or workplace relationships may be characterized by feedback that is positive, person-focused, immediate, low in monitoring (not self-censored), and supportive—and that unsatisfying relationships are characterized by feedback that is negative, self-focused, non-immediate, high in monitoring, and critical. *How effective is this "theory" in explaining the relationships with which you're familiar?*

seen you the entire week; what's been going on?" Or you might give a brief preview of your main message by saying something like "You'd better sit down for this; you're going to be shocked." Or you might ask others to hear you out before they judge you.

Channel

The communication **channel** is the medium through which messages pass. It's a kind of bridge connecting source and receiver. Communication rarely takes place over only one channel; two, three, or four channels are often used simultaneously. For example, in face-to-face interaction, you speak and listen (vocal–auditory channel), but you also gesture and receive signals visually (gestural–visual channel), and you emit odors and smell those of others (chemical–olfactory channel). Often you communicate through touch (cutaneous–tactile channel). When you communicate online, you often send photo, audio, or video files in the same message or links to additional files and sites. In most situations, a variety of channels are involved.

Another way to think about channels is to consider them as the means of communication: for example, face-to-face contact, telephone, e-mail and snail mail, Twitter, instant messaging, news postings, Facebook, film, television, radio, smoke signals, or fax—to name only some.

Note that the channel imposes different restrictions on your message construction. For example, in e-mail you can pause to think of the right word or phrase, you can go on for as short or as long a time as you want without any threat of interruption or contradiction, and you can edit your message with ease. In face-to-face communication, your pauses need to be relatively short. You don't have the time to select just the right word or to edit, though we do edit a bit when we review what we said and put it in different words.

In this text, face-to-face communication and online/social media communication are integrated for a number of important reasons:

1. **It's the way we communicate today.** We interact face-to-face and online. Some interactions are likely exclusively face-to-face, while others are exclusively online. Increasingly, our interactions are with people with whom we communicate both online and offline.

2. **Online and offline communication are related.** The research and theory discussed here on face-to-face and on online communication inform each other. Most of the interpersonal theories discussed here were developed for face-to-face interaction but have much to say about online relationships as well.

3. **Employers expect employees to have both offline and online communication skill sets.** The ability to communicate orally and in writing (both online and offline) is consistently ranked among the most important qualities employers are looking for in new employees. For example, your employability will depend, in great part, on how effectively you communicate in your e-mails, in your phone conferences, in your Skype interviews, and in your in-person interviews.

4. **Both forms of communication are vital to current-day communication.** We increasingly develop, and maintain, relationships online with many of them moving to face-to-face interactions if the online interaction proves satisfying. And increasingly, relationships are dissolved through email and Facebook and Twitter posts.

Throughout this text, face-to-face and online communication are discussed, compared, and contrasted. Table 1.1 presents a brief summary of some communication concepts and some of the ways in which these two forms of communication are similar and different.

INTERPERSONAL CHOICE POINT
Channels

You want to ask someone for a date and are considering how you might go about this. You regularly communicate with this person on Facebook as well as face-to-face at school. *How would you ask for a date?*

a. on Facebook
b. face-to-face
c. phone
d. e-mail
e. other

Table 1.1 Face-to-Face and Online Communication

	Face-to-Face Communication	Online Communication
Sender		
• Presentation of self and impression management	• Personal characteristics (sex, approximate age, race, etc.) are open to visual inspection; receiver controls the order of what is attended to; disguise is difficult.	• Personal characteristics are hidden and are revealed when you want to reveal them; anonymity is easy.
• Speaking turn	• You compete for the speaker's turn and time with the other person(s); you can be interrupted.	• It's always your turn; speaker time is unlimited; you can't be interrupted.
Receiver		
• Number	• One or a few who are in your visual field.	• Virtually unlimited.
• Opportunity for interaction	• Limited to those who have the opportunity to meet; often difficult to find people who share your interests.	• Unlimited.
• Third parties	• Messages can be overheard by or repeated to third parties but not with complete accuracy.	• Messages can be retrieved by others or forwarded verbatim to a third party or to thousands.
• Impression formation	• Impressions are based on the verbal and nonverbal cues the receiver perceives.	• Impressions are based on text messages and posted photos and videos.
Context		
• Physical	• Essentially the same physical space.	• Can be in the next cubicle or separated by miles.
• Temporal	• Communication is synchronous; messages are exchanged at the same (real) time.	• Communication may be synchronous (as in chat rooms) or asynchronous (where messages are exchanged at different times, as in e-mail).
Channel		
	• All senses participate in sending and receiving messages.	• Visual (for text, photos, and videos) and auditory.
Message		
• Verbal and nonverbal	• Words, gestures, eye contact, accent, vocal cues, spatial relationships, touching, clothing, hair, etc.	• Words, photos, videos, and audio messages.
• Permanence	• Temporary unless recorded; speech signals fade rapidly.	• Messages are relatively permanent.

Noise

Technically, **noise** is anything that distorts a message—anything that prevents the receiver from receiving the message as the sender sent it. At one extreme, noise may prevent a message from getting from source to receiver. A roaring noise or line static can easily prevent entire messages from getting through to your receiver. At the other extreme, with virtually no noise interference, the message of the source and the message received are almost identical. Most often, however, noise distorts some portion of the message a source sends as it travels to a receiver. Four types of noise (**physical noise**, **physiological noise**, **psychological noise**, and **semantic noise**) are especially relevant and will help you identify sources of noise you'd want to lessen.

- **Physical noise** is interference that is external to both speaker and listener; it impedes the physical transmission of the signal or message. Examples include the screeching of passing cars, the hum of a computer, sunglasses, extraneous messages, illegible handwriting, blurred type or fonts that are too small or difficult to read, misspellings and poor grammar, and pop-up ads. Still another type of physical noise is extraneous information that makes what you want to find more difficult, for example, spam or too many photos on Facebook.
- **Physiological noise** is created by barriers within the sender or receiver, such as visual impairments, hearing loss, articulation problems, and memory loss.
- **Psychological noise** is mental interference in the speaker or listener and includes preconceived ideas, wandering thoughts, biases and prejudices, closed-mindedness, and extreme emotionalism. You're likely to run into psychological noise when you talk with someone who is closed-minded or who refuses to listen to anything he or she doesn't already believe.

- **Semantic noise** is interference that occurs when the speaker and listener have different meaning systems; examples include language or dialectical differences, the use of jargon or overly complex terms, and ambiguous or overly abstract terms whose meanings can be easily misinterpreted. You see this type of noise regularly in the medical doctor who uses "medicalese" without explanation or in the insurance salesperson who speaks in the jargon of the insurance industry.

A useful concept in understanding noise and its importance in communication is **signal-to-noise ratio**. **Signal** refers to information that you find useful; *noise* refers to information that is useless (to you). For example, a blog post that contains lots of useful information would be high on signal and low on noise; messages that contain lots of useless information are high on noise and low on signal. Spam, pop-ups, and advertisements for products you're not interested in are good examples. When you do an online search for information, the advertisements and the irrelevant sites are noise; the information you're looking for is the signal.

All communications contain noise. Noise cannot be totally eliminated, but its effects can be reduced. Making your language more precise, sharpening your skills for sending and receiving nonverbal messages, and improving your listening and feedback skills are some ways to combat the influence of noise.

VIEWPOINTS

Signal and Noise Online

Social media users are advised to be brief in their profiles and even in responding (Conniff & Nicks, 2014). Similarly, recruiters find that too much information on, say, Facebook, detracts from the candidate's résumé (Bersin, 2013). *How would you explain this in terms of* signal *and* noise?

Context

Communication always takes place in a **context** or environment that influences the form and content of your messages. At times this context isn't obvious or intrusive; it seems so natural that it's ignored—like background music. At other times the context dominates, and the ways in which it restricts or stimulates your messages are obvious. Compare, for example, the differences among communicating in a funeral home, football stadium, formal restaurant, and a rock concert. The context of communication has at least four dimensions, all of which interact with and influence each other.

Physical Dimension The *physical dimension* is the tangible or concrete environment in which communication takes place—the room, hallway, or park; the boardroom; or the family dinner table. The size of the space, its temperature, and the number of people present in the physical space are also part of the physical dimension. In print media, such as magazines or newspapers, context includes the positioning of stories and news articles; an article on page 37 is identified as less important than an article on page 1 or 2. Twitter's restriction of messages to 140 characters or fewer is an especially good example of the physical dimension influencing the message; Twitter requires you to abbreviate your message, while having coffee at Starbucks seems to encourage the opposite.

Temporal Dimension The *temporal dimension* has to do not only with the time of day and moment in history but also with where a particular message fits into the sequence of communication events. For example, a joke about illness told immediately after the disclosure of a friend's sickness will be received differently than the same joke told in response to a series of similar jokes. Also, some channels (for example, face-to-face, chat rooms, and instant messaging) allow for synchronous communication in which messages are sent and received simultaneously. Other channels (for example, letter writing, e-mail, and social networking postings) are asynchronous; messages are sent and received at different times.

Social–Psychological Dimension The *social–psychological dimension* includes, for example, status relationships among the participants; roles and games that people play; norms of the society or group; and the friendliness, formality, or gravity of the situation. Social networks such as Facebook are informal and largely for fun communication; LinkedIn and Plaxo, on the other hand, are primarily for serious, business-oriented communication.

THE CULTURAL MAP

Because of the importance of culture in all aspects of interpersonal communication, we return to culture and especially cultural differences in "The Cultural Map" feature. Consider these as reminders of the tremendous influence of culture on all aspects of interpersonal communication.

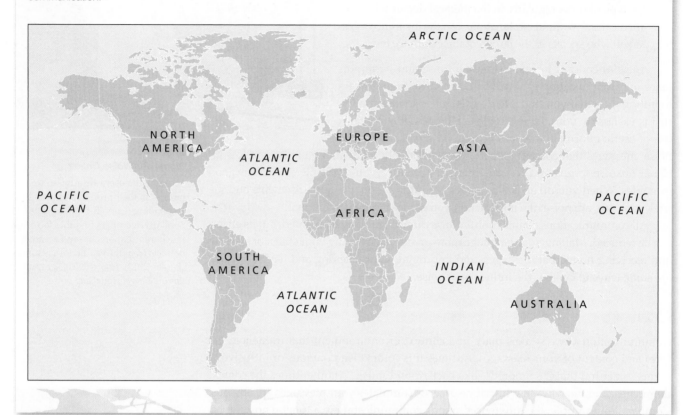

Cultural Dimension   The *cultural context* includes the cultural beliefs and customs of the people communicating. When you interact with people from different cultures, you may each follow different rules of communication. This can result in confusion, unintentional insult, inaccurate judgments, and a host of other miscommunications. Similarly, communication strategies or techniques that prove satisfying to members of one culture may prove disturbing or offensive to members of another. In fact, research shows that you lose more information in an intercultural situation (approximately 50 percent) than in an intracultural situation (approximately 25 percent) (Li, 1999).

Effects

Interpersonal communication always has some **effect** on one or more persons involved in the communication act. For every interpersonal interaction, there is some consequence, some effect. Generally, three types of effects are distinguished.

- *Cognitive effects* Cognitive effects are changes in your thinking. When you acquire information from a friend's Facebook post about the time of the concert, for example, the effect is largely intellectual.

- *Affective effects* Affective effects are changes in your attitudes, values, beliefs, and emotions. Thus, when you become frightened hearing about the increase in gun violence, its effect is largely affective. Similarly, after a great experience with, say, a person of another culture, your feelings about that culture may change. Again, the effect is largely affective (but perhaps also intellectual).

- *Behavioral effects* Behavioral effects are changes in behaviors such as, for example, learning new dance movements, to throw a curve ball, to paint a room, or to use different verbal and nonverbal behaviors.

These effects are not separate; rather, they interact. In many cases, a single message—say, a conversation on homelessness—may inform you (intellectual effect), move you to feel differently (affective effect), and lead you to be more generous when you come upon a homeless person (behavioral effect).

In addition to effects on others, your interpersonal communications also have effects on you. Part of this effect is from your self-evaluation; you might smile after posting a really clever comment or feel bad after criticizing a friend. In addition, however, the reactions of others will have effects on you. For example, your clever comment may be retweeted 30 or 40 times (which is likely to have effects on your self-esteem and perhaps on your future tweeting) and your criticism of your friend may result in a broken relationship (which will have affective and behavioral effects).

Ethics

Largely because interpersonal communication has effects on others, it also involves questions of **ethics**, the study of good and bad, of right and wrong, of moral and immoral. Ethics is concerned with actions, with behaviors; it's concerned with distinguishing between behaviors that are moral (ethical, good, and right) and those that are immoral (unethical, bad, and wrong). There's an ethical dimension to any interpersonal communication act (Neher & Sandin, 2007; Bok, 1978).

Consider some of the popular beliefs about ethics, perhaps one or more of which you hold personally. For each of the following statements, place a T (for true) if you feel the statement accurately explains what ethical behavior is and an F (for false) if you feel the statement does not accurately explain what ethical behavior is.

_____ **1.** My behavior is ethical when I feel (in my heart) that I'm doing the right thing.

_____ **2.** My behavior is ethical when it is consistent with my religious beliefs.

_____ **3.** My behavior is ethical when it is legal.

_____ **4.** My behavior is ethical when the majority of reasonable people would consider it ethical.

_____ **5.** My behavior is ethical when the effect of the behavior benefits more people than it harms.

These statements are based on responses given to the question, "What does ethics mean to you?" discussed on the website of the Santa Clara University's Markkula Center for Applied Ethics. The following "answers" are intended to stimulate discussion and the formation of your own ethical code for interpersonal communication; they are not "answers" in the traditional sense. All five of these statements are (generally) false; none of them state a useful explanation of what is and what is not ethical.

- Statement 1 is false simply because people often do unethical things they feel are morally justified. Jack the Ripper killing prostitutes is a good historical example, but there are many current ones such as stalking (*I'm so in love I need to be with this person.*) or insurances scams (*My family needs the money more than the insurance company.*). Even though Jack, the stalker, and the scam artist may feel justified in their own minds, it doesn't make their behavior moral or ethical.
- Statement 2 must be false when you realize that different religions advocate very different kinds of behavior, often behaviors that contradict one another. Examples abound in almost every issue of a daily newspaper.
- Statement 3 must be false when you realize so much discrimination against certain people is perfectly legal in many parts of the world, and, in many countries, war (even "preemptive" war) is legal.
- Statement 4 is false because the thinking of the majority changes with the times and has often proven to be extremely immoral. The burning of people supposed to be witches or of those who spoke out against majority opinion (as in the Inquisition) are good examples.

- Statement 5 comes the closest to being possibly and sometimes true, but it's more generally false. The reason it's more false than true is that the burning of witches, for example, was in the interest of the majority, as was slavery and discrimination against gay men and lesbians, certain religions, or different races. But despite this majority interest, we'd readily recognize these actions as immoral.

So, when is behavior ethical, and when is it unethical? Lots of people have come up with lots of theories. If you take an *objective view,* you'd claim that the ethical nature of an act—any act—depends on standards that apply to all people in all situations at all times. If lying, advertising falsely, using illegally obtained evidence, and revealing secrets, for example, are considered unethical, then they'd be considered unethical regardless of the circumstances surrounding them or of the values and beliefs of the culture in which they occur.

If you take a *subjective view,* you'd claim that the morality of an act depends on a specific culture's values and beliefs as well as on the particular circumstances. Thus, from a subjective position, you would claim that the end might justify the means—a good result can justify the use of unethical means to achieve that result. You would further argue that lying is wrong to win votes or to sell cigarettes but that lying can be ethical if the end result is positive (such as trying to make someone who is unattractive feel better by telling them they look great or telling a critically ill person that they'll feel better soon).

In addition to this introductory discussion, ethical dimensions of interpersonal communication are presented in each chapter in Ethics in Interpersonal Communication boxes.

ETHICS IN INTERPERSONAL COMMUNICATION

Ethical Standards

Each field of study defines what is not ethical to its concerns. Here are just a few to highlight some communication-oriented codes:

- The National Communication Association Ethical Credo
- Blogger's Ethics
- The Twitter Rules
- Online Journalism
- Radio-Television News Directors Association and Foundation Code of Ethics and Professional Conduct

Ethical Choice Point

You'll also find it interesting to look up the code of ethics for the profession you're in or planning on entering. Before you do so, however, think about what you consider ethical communication. *What ethical standards do you follow in your own communication (online and face-to-face)? What ethical principles do you, even if only rarely, violate?*

Table 1.2 presents a brief summary of the essential elements of interpersonal communication.

Table 1.2 In a Nutshell The Elements of Interpersonal Communication

Elements	Meaning
Source–receiver	The sender–receiver, the person who both sends and receives messages during communication.
Messages	The verbal and nonverbal signals that are sent by the source/encoder and received by the receiver/decoder.
Channels	The media through which the signals are sent.
Noise	Disturbances that interfere with the receiver receiving the message sent by the source.
Context	The physical, social-psychological, temporal, and cultural environment in which the communication takes place.
Effects	Interpersonal communication can have cognitive, affective, and behavioral effects on others and on yourself.
Ethics	The morality, the rightness-wrongness aspect of communication behavior.

UNDERSTANDING *INTERPERSONAL SKILLS*

Mindfulness: A State of Mental Awareness

Mindfulness is a state of mental awareness; in a mindful state, you're conscious of your reasons for thinking or communicating in a particular way. You're conscious of the uniqueness of the situation and of the many choices you have for interacting (Beard, 2014). And, especially important in interpersonal communication, you become aware of your choices. You act with an awareness of your available choices.

Its opposite, **mindlessness**, is a lack of conscious awareness of your thinking or communicating (Langer, 1989). To apply interpersonal skills appropriately and effectively, you need to be mindful of the unique communication situation you're in, of your available communication options or choices, and of the reasons why one option is likely to prove better than the others. You can look at this text and this course in interpersonal communication as a means of awakening your mindfulness about the way you engage in interpersonal communication. After you complete this course and this text, you should be much more mindful about all your interpersonal interactions (Carson, Carson, Gil, & Baucom, 2004; Sagula & Rice, 2004). In addition, mindfulness has been found to improve scores on verbal reasoning texts, increase short-term memory, and decrease mind wandering (Mrazek, Franklin, Phillip, Baird, & Schooler, 2013). It has also been found to reduce depression in adolescents (Raes, Griffith, Van der Gucht, & Williams, 2013).

None of this is to argue that you should be mindful always and everywhere. Certainly, there are times when mind wandering may help you develop a great idea (Hurley, 2014). But, generally, it's mindfulness that needs to be practiced.

Communicating with Mindfulness

To increase mindfulness in general, try the following suggestions (Langer, 1989; Burgoon, Berger, & Waldron, 2000):

- **Create and re-create categories.** Learn to see objects, events, and people as belonging to a wide variety of categories. Try to see, for example, your prospective romantic partner in a variety of roles—child, parent, employee, neighbor, friend, financial contributor, and so on. Avoid storing in memory an image of a person with only one specific label; if you do, you'll find it difficult to re-categorize the person later.

- **Be open to new information and points of view,** even when these contradict your most firmly held stereotypes. New information forces you to reconsider what might be outmoded ways of thinking. New information

can help you challenge long-held but now inappropriate beliefs and attitudes. Be willing to see your own and others' behaviors from a variety of viewpoints, especially from the perspective of people very different from yourself.

- **Beware of relying too heavily on first impressions** (Langer, 1989; Beard, 2014). Treat your first impressions as tentative—as hypotheses that need further investigation. Be prepared to revise, reject, or accept these initial impressions.

- **Be aware of possible misinterpretations in the message.** Make sure it's interpreted correctly. For example, you can paraphrase or restate the message in different ways or you can ask the person to paraphrase.

- **Become conscious of unproductive communication patterns.** For example, in a conflict situation, one common pattern is that each person brings up past relationship injustices. If you notice this happening, stop and ask yourself if this pattern is productive. If not, consider what you can do to change it. For example, in this conflict example, you can refuse to respond in kind and thereby break the cycle.

- **Remind yourself of the uniqueness of this communication situation.** Consider how you can best adapt your messages to this unique situation. For example, you may want to be especially positive to a friend who is depressed but not so positive to someone who betrayed a confidence.

- **Identify and evaluate your communication choices.** Especially in delicate situations (for example, when expressing anger or communicating commitment messages), it's wise to pause, think over the situation mindfully, and identify and evaluate your choices (DeVito, 2003b).

Working with Mindfulness

As you think about mindfulness, reflect on your own tendencies to communicate mindlessly and mindfully. *Do you regularly examine your choices before you send your message? In which situations are you more apt to communicate mindlessly? For example, when compared to face-to-face communication, are you more or less mindful when communicating on Facebook, Twitter, or other social network sites? If there is a difference, why do you suppose it exists? Do you communicate mindfully with certain people and mindlessly with others?*

The Principles of Interpersonal Communication

1.3 Paraphrase the principles of interpersonal communication.

Now that the nature of interpersonal communication and its elements are clear, we can explore some of the more specific axioms or principles that are common to all or most interpersonal encounters. These principles are the work of a wide variety of researchers (Watzlawick, Beavin, & Jackson, 1967; Watzlawick, 1977, 1978; Watzlawick, Weakland, & Fisch, 2011).

Interpersonal Communication Exists on a Continuum

Interpersonal communication exists along a continuum that ranges from relatively impersonal to highly personal (Miller, 1978, 1990). At the impersonal end of the spectrum, you have simple conversation between people who really don't know each other—the server and the customer, for example. At the highly personal end is the communication that takes place between people who are intimately interconnected—a father and son, two longtime lovers, or best friends, for example. A few characteristics distinguish the impersonal from the personal forms of communication.

- *Social role versus personal information.* Notice that, in the impersonal example, the individuals are likely to respond to each other according to the *roles* they are currently playing; the server treats the customer not as a unique individual but as one of many customers. And the customer, in turn, acts toward the server not as a unique individual but as he or she would act with any server. The father and the son, however, react to each other as unique individuals. They act on the basis of *personal information*.

- *Societal versus personal rules.* Notice too that the server and the customer interact according to the *rules of society* governing the server–customer interaction. The father and the son, on the other hand, interact on the basis of *personally established rules*. The way they address each other, their touching behavior, and their degree of physical closeness, for example, are unique to them and are established by them rather than by society.

- *Social versus personal messages.* Still another difference is found in the messages exchanged. The messages that the server and customer exchange, for example, are themselves *impersonal*; there is little personal information exchanged and there is little emotional content in the messages they exchange. In the father–son example, however, the messages may run the entire range and may at times be *highly personal*, with lots of personal information and lots of emotion.

Figure 1.2 depicts one possible interpersonal continuum.

Figure 1.2 An Interpersonal Continuum

Here is one possible interpersonal continuum. Other people would position the relationships differently. What would your interpersonal continuum look like? Try constructing one for both your face-to-face and online relationships.

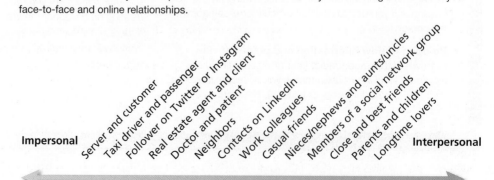

Interpersonal Communication Involves Interdependent Individuals

Interpersonal communication is the communication that takes place between people who are in some way "connected." Interpersonal communication thus includes what takes place between a son and his father, an employer and an employee, two sisters, a teacher and a student, two lovers, two friends, and so on. Although largely dyadic (two-person) in nature, interpersonal communication is often extended to include small intimate groups such as the family or group of friends. Even within a family, however, the communication that takes place is often dyadic—mother to child, father to mother, daughter to son, and so on.

Not only are the individuals simply "connected"—they are also interdependent: What one person does has an impact on the other person. The actions of one person have consequences for the other person. In a family, for example, a child's trouble with the police affects the parents, other siblings, extended family members, and perhaps friends and neighbors.

In much the same way that Facebook may have changed the definition of friendship, it may also have changed the definition of interpersonal communication. Sending a message to your closest 15 friends who then respond to you and the others would be considered interpersonal communication by some theorists and not by others. Online chats and phone and Skype conferences, on the other hand, are also considered interpersonal by some and not by others. Still another issue is the blurring of the lines between what is interpersonal and what is public. When you send a message to a friend on any of the social media sites, that message is, potentially at least, a public message. Although your intended message may be interpersonal—between you and a close friend, say—that message can (and often does) become a public one—between you and people with whom you have absolutely no connection.

Interpersonal Communication Is Inherently Relational

Because of this interdependency, interpersonal communication is inevitably and essentially relational in nature. Interpersonal communication takes place within a relationship—it has an impact on the relationship; it defines the relationship.

The communication that takes place in a relationship is in part a function of that relationship. That is, the way you communicate is determined in great part by the kind of relationship that exists between you and the other person. You interact differently with your interpersonal communication instructor and your best friend; you interact with a sibling in ways very different from the ways in which you interact with a neighbor, a work colleague, or a casual acquaintance. You interact on Facebook and Twitter in ways very different from the way you interact in a face-to-face situation.

But also notice that the way you communicate, the way you interact, influences the kind of relationship you develop. If you interact with a person in friendly ways, you're likely to develop a friendship. If you regularly exchange hateful and hurtful messages, you're likely to develop an antagonistic relationship. If you regularly express respect and support for each other, a respectful and supportive relationship is likely to develop. This is surely one of the most obvious observations you can make about interpersonal communication. And yet many people seem not to appreciate this very clear relationship between what they say and the relationships that develop (or deteriorate).

At the same time that interpersonal communication is relational, it also says something about you. Regardless of what you say, you are making reference, in some way, to yourself—to who you are and to what you're thinking and feeling, to what you value. Even your "likes" on Facebook, research shows, can reveal, for example, your sexual orientation, age, intelligence, and drug use; and photos—depending on the smile—can communication your level of personal well-being (Entis, 2013).

Interpersonal Communication Is a Transactional Process

A **transactional perspective** views interpersonal communication as (1) a process with (2) elements that are *inter*dependent and (3) participants who are mutually influential. Figure 1.3 visually explains this transactional view and distinguishes it from an earlier, linear view of how interpersonal communication works.

Interpersonal Communication Is a Process   Interpersonal communication is best viewed as an ever-changing, circular process. Everything involved in interpersonal communication is in a state of flux: you're changing, the people you communicate with are changing, and your environment is changing. Sometimes these changes go unnoticed and sometimes they intrude in obvious ways, but they're always occurring.

One person's message serves as the stimulus for another's message, which serves as a stimulus for the first person's message, and so on. Throughout this circular process, each person serves simultaneously as a speaker *and* a listener, an actor *and* a reactor. Interpersonal communication is a mutually interactive process.

This circular process seems more true of face-to-face interactions than of social media interactions. For example, in an analysis of tweets, one researcher found that a full 80 percent of users simply sent out information about themselves (Dean, 2010a). Only 20 percent replied to the tweets of others. In face-to-face interactions, you have to respond in some way—even if you choose to say nothing.

Elements are Interdependent   In interpersonal communication, not only are the individuals interdependent, as noted earlier, but the varied elements of communication are also interdependent. Each element—each part—of interpersonal communication is intimately connected to the other parts and to the whole. For example, there can be no source without a receiver; there can be no message without a source; there can be no feedback without a receiver. Because of interdependency, a change in any one element causes changes in the others. For example, you're talking with a group of fellow

Figure 1.3   The Linear and Transactional Views of Interpersonal Communication

The top figure represents a linear view of communication in which the speaker speaks and the listener listens. The bottom figure represents a transactional view, the view favored by most communication theorists, in which each person serves simultaneously as speaker and listener; at the same time that you send messages, you also receive messages from your own communications as well as from the reactions of the other person(s).

Linear View

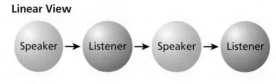

Transactional View

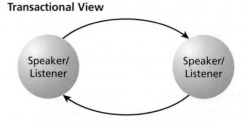

students about a recent examination, and your professor joins the group. This change in participants leads to other changes—perhaps in the content of what you say, perhaps in the manner in which you express it. But regardless of what change is introduced, other changes result.

Mutual Influence   In a transaction process, each individual influences the other, to some extent. For example, in face-to-face conversation, what you say influences what the other person says, which influences what you say, and so on. This mutual influence is the major characteristic distinguishing traditional media from social media. In traditional media—for example, newspapers, magazines, television, and film—the communication goes in one direction—from the media to you, as depicted in Figure 1.4(a). It's basically a linear view of communication, which was depicted in Figure 1.3. In social media—for example, photo and video sharing, social networks such as Facebook and LinkedIn, and wikis—the communication goes in both directions, as depicted in Figure 1.4(b). Over the last decade or so, traditional media—most notably television—have been moving in the direction of social media, of mutual interaction with, for example, news shows inviting tweets and reading them on air, voting for your favorite couple on *Dancing with the Stars*, or rating movies on Netflix. Of course, you can interact—but to a very limited extent—with traditional media such as newspapers and magazines by, for example, writing letters to the editor, asking for advice from columnists such as Dear Abby, or renewing or not renewing your subscription. With the move of newspapers and magazines (and textbooks) to a digital platform, traditional media will come to resemble—to a large extent—social media.

Interpersonal Communication Serves a Variety of Purposes

Interpersonal communication, whether face-to-face or online, is purposeful and serves a variety of purposes. Five such purposes can be identified: to learn, to relate, to influence, to play, and to help.

To Learn   Interpersonal communication enables you to learn, to better understand the external world—the world of objects, events, and other people. When you read the tweets from your followers, you're learning about them but also about the world they live in—whether it's down the road or across an ocean. Although a great deal of

Figure 1.4   Traditional and Social Media

In traditional media (a), the messages flow from the media to the individual with little opportunity for interaction. In social media (b), the messages go in both directions: from the media to the individual and from the individual to the media.

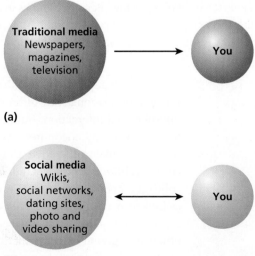

information comes from the media, you probably discuss and ultimately learn or internalize information through interpersonal interactions. In fact, your beliefs, attitudes, and values are probably influenced more by interpersonal encounters than by the media or even by formal education.

Most important, however, interpersonal communication helps you learn about yourself. By talking about yourself with others, you gain valuable feedback on your feelings, thoughts, and behaviors. Through these communications, you also learn how you appear to others—who likes you, who dislikes you, and why. This function, you'll note, is written into the very fabric of Facebook, Twitter, and blogs, where commenting, recommending, and liking for a post can be indicated so easily.

To Relate Interpersonal communication helps you relate. You communicate your friendship or love through your interpersonal communication; at the same time, you react and respond to the friendship and love messages of others. When you poke someone on Facebook, you're indicating your desire to relate to that person, to communicate with him or her. Such communication is at the heart of one of the greatest needs people have: to establish and maintain close relationships. You want to feel loved and liked, and in turn you want to love and like others. Such relationships help to alleviate loneliness and depression, enable you to share and heighten your pleasures, and generally make you feel more positive about yourself.

To Influence Very likely, you influence the attitudes and behaviors of others in your interpersonal encounters. You may wish others to vote a particular way, try a new diet, buy a new book, listen to a record, see a movie, take a specific course, think in a particular way, believe that something is true or false, or value some idea—the list is endless. A good deal of your time is probably spent in interpersonal persuasion. Some researchers, in fact, would argue that all communication is persuasive and that all our communications seek some persuasive goal.

This influencing function is seen on social media sites in at least two different ways: (1) direct influence attempts (advertisements or friends urging you to sign up for a cause or to join a group) and (2) indirect influence attempts (reading that your friends have seen a particular movie and enjoyed it, or a newsfeed announcing that one of your friends has joined a cause or bought a ticket to a play or concert, or is signing up for a particular group or cause).

To Play Talking with friends about your weekend activities, discussing sports or dates, telling stories and jokes, tweeting, and posting a clever joke or photo on some social media site and in general just passing the time are play functions. Far from frivolous, this extremely important purpose gives your activities a necessary balance and your mind a needed break from all the seriousness around you. In online communication, perhaps the most obvious forms of play are the interactive games in a real or virtual reality environment. In the process, players develop useful skills such as the ability to take the perspective of another person (Tynes, 2007). And even certain forms of cyberflirting may be viewed as play (Whitty, 2003b).

To Help Therapists of various kinds serve a helping function professionally by offering guidance through interpersonal interaction. But everyone interacts to help in everyday encounters: you console a friend who has broken off a love affair, counsel another student about courses to take, or offer advice to a colleague about work. Social media websites such as LinkedIn and Plaxo and even Facebook and Twitter are used extensively for securing the help of others and giving help to others. Success in accomplishing this helping function, professionally or

otherwise, depends on your knowledge and skill in interpersonal communication.

Interpersonal Communication Is Ambiguous

An ambiguous message is a message that can be interpreted as having more than one meaning. Sometimes **ambiguity** occurs because people use words that can be interpreted differently. Informal time language offers good examples; for example, the expressions *soon, right away, in a minute, early,* and *late,* can easily be interpreted very differently by different people.

Some degree of ambiguity exists in all interpersonal communication: all messages are ambiguous to some degree. When you express an idea, you never communicate your meaning exactly and totally; rather, you communicate your meaning with some reasonable accuracy—enough to give the other person a reasonably clear idea of what you mean. Sometimes, of course, you're less accurate than you anticipated. Perhaps your listener "gets the wrong idea" or "gets offended" when you only meant to be humorous, or the listener "misunderstands your emotional meaning." Because of this inevitable uncertainty, you may qualify what you're saying, give an example, or ask, "Do you know what I mean?" These additional explanations help the other person understand your meaning and reduce uncertainty (to some degree).

This quality of ambiguity makes it extremely important to resist jumping to conclusions about the motives of a speaker. For example, if someone doesn't poke you back, it may mean that the person is not interested in communicating with you, or it may be a function of information overload or a lack of knowledge in how to poke back or being away from the computer. Similarly, if someone stops following you on Twitter or unfriends you on Facebook, it may simply be a mistake. Meaning is in the person, not in the words or in the photos posted.

> ### INTERPERSONAL CHOICE POINT
> Reducing Relationship Ambiguity
>
> You've gone out with someone for several months. At this point, you want to reduce ambiguity about the future of the relationship and discover your partner's level of commitment. But you don't want to scare your partner. *What would you do to reduce this ambiguity?*
>
> **a.** ask the person directly
>
> **b.** ask a mutual friend
>
> **c.** just act as if the relationship were at the level you desire
>
> **d.** make a joke about it by saying something like: "So, when do we get married?"
>
> **e.** other

All relationships contain uncertainty. Consider one of your own close interpersonal relationships and answer the following questions; use a 6-point scale, with 1 meaning that you are completely or almost completely uncertain about the answer and 6 meaning that you are completely or almost completely certain of the answer.

_____ 1. What can or can't you say to each other in this relationship?

_____ 2. Do you and this person feel the same way about each other? How closely would your descriptions match?

_____ 3. How would you and this person describe this relationship?

_____ 4. What is the future of the relationship? Do you both see the relationship's future in the same way?

It's very likely that you were not able to respond with sixes for all four questions, and equally likely that the same would be true for your relationship partner. Your responses to these questions—adapted from a relationship uncertainty scale (Knoblock & Solomon, 1999)—and similar other questions illustrate that you probably experience some degree of uncertainty about (1) the norms that govern your relationship communication (question 1), (2) the degree to which you and your partner see the relationship in similar ways (question 2), (3) the definition of the relationship (question 3), and (4) the relationship's future (question 4).

A different kind of ambiguity—called **strategic ambiguity**—is used when you want to be ambiguous, and it is seen in a variety of situations (Eisenberg, 2007). The interviewer who compliments you on your interview (without actually offering you the job) may be acting strategically ambiguous to keep you interested in the position while the

Relationship Ambiguity

How would you describe the ambiguity that exists in your friendships or romantic relationships? Are there some things you'd like to be more certain about? Are there some things you'd like to remain ambiguous?

company interviews more and perhaps better candidates. The romantic partner who avoids moving in together but who professes a desire to do so may be giving ambiguous signals in order to leave open both possibilities—to move in together or not.

Interpersonal Relationships May Be Symmetrical or Complementary

Interpersonal relationships can be described as either symmetrical or complementary (Bateson, 1972; Watzlawick, Beavin, & Jackson, 1967). In a **symmetrical relationship**, the two individuals mirror each other's behavior (Bateson, 1972). If one member nags, the other member responds in kind. If one member is passionate, the other member is passionate. If one member expresses jealousy, the other member also expresses jealousy. If one member is passive, so is the other. The relationship is one of equality, with the emphasis on minimizing the differences between the two individuals.

Note the problems that can arise in this type of relationship. Consider the situation of a couple in which both members are very aggressive. The aggressiveness of one person fosters aggressiveness in the other, which fosters increased aggressiveness in the first individual. As this cycle escalates, the aggressiveness can no longer be contained and the relationship is consumed by the aggression.

In a **complementary relationship**, the two individuals engage in different behaviors. The behavior of one serves as the stimulus for the other's complementary behavior. In complementary relationships, the differences between the parties are maximized. The people occupy different positions, one superior and the other inferior, one passive and the other active, one strong and the other weak. At times, cultures establish such relationships—for example, the complementary relationship between teacher and student or between employer and employee.

Interpersonal Communication Refers to Content and Relationship

Messages may refer to the real world (content messages); for example, to the events and objects you see before you. At the same time, however, they also may refer to the relationship between the people communicating (relationship messages). For example, a judge may say to a lawyer, "See me in my chambers immediately." This simple message has both a content aspect, which refers to the response expected (namely, that the lawyer will see the judge immediately), and a relationship aspect, which says something about the relationship between the judge and the lawyer and, as a result of this relationship, about how the communication is to be dealt with. Even the use of the simple command shows that there is a status difference between the two parties. This difference can perhaps be seen most clearly if you imagine the command being made by the lawyer to the judge. Such a communication appears awkward and out of place because it violates the normal relationship between judge and lawyer.

In any two communications, the **content dimension** may be the same, but the relationship aspect may be different, or the relationship aspect may be the same and the content dimension different. For example, the judge could say to the lawyer, "You had better see me immediately." or "May I please see you as soon as possible?" In both cases, the content is essentially the same; that is, the message about the expected response is the same. But the **relationship dimension** is quite different. The first message signifies a definite superior–inferior relationship; the second signals a more equal relationship, one that shows respect for the lawyer.

At times the content is different but the relationship is essentially the same. For example, a daughter might say to her parents, "May I go away this weekend?" or "May I use the car tonight?" The content of the two questions is clearly very different. The relationship dimension, however, is the same. Both questions clearly reflect a superior–inferior relationship in which permission to do certain things must be secured.

Problems between people can easily result from the failure to recognize the distinction between the content and relationship dimensions of communication. Consider the following interchange:

Dialogue	*Comments*
He: I'm going bowling tomorrow. The guys at the plant are starting a team.	He focuses on the content and ignores any relationship implications of the message.
She: Why can't we ever do anything together?	She responds primarily on a relationship level, ignores the content implications of the message, and expresses her displeasure at being ignored in his decision.
He: We can do something together anytime; tomorrow's the day they're organizing the team.	Again, he focuses almost exclusively on the content.

This example reflects research findings that men generally focus more on the content while women focus more on the relationship dimensions of communication (Ivy & Backlund, 2000; Pearson, West, & Turner, 1995; Wood, 1994). Once you recognize this difference, you may be better able to remove a potential barrier to communication between the sexes by being sensitive to the orientation of the opposite sex. Here is essentially the same situation but with added sensitivity:

Dialogue	*Comments*
He: The guys at the plant are organizing a bowling team. I'd sure like to be on the team. Would it be a problem if I went to the organizational meeting tomorrow?	Although focused on content, he is aware of the relationship dimensions of his message and includes both in his comments—by acknowledging their partnership, asking if there would be a problem, and expressing his desire rather than his decision.
She: That sounds great, but I was hoping we could do something together.	She focuses on the relationship dimension but also acknowledges his content orientation. Note, too, that she does not respond as though she has to defend her emphasis on relationship aspects.
He: How about you meet me at Joe's Pizza, and we can have dinner after the organizational meeting?	He responds to the relationship aspect—without abandoning his desire to join the bowling team—and incorporates it.
She: That sounds great. I'm dying for pizza.	She responds to both messages, approving of his joining the team and their dinner date.

Arguments over the content dimension are relatively easy to resolve. Generally, you can look up something in a book or ask someone what actually took place. It is relatively easy to verify disputed facts. Arguments on the relationship level, however, are much more difficult to resolve, in part because you may not recognize that the argument is in fact a relational one. Once you realize that it is, you can approach the dispute appropriately and deal with it directly.

Social Media, Content, and Relationship

If you looked at social media in terms of content and relationship messages, Twitter and blogs would probably be more content-oriented and Facebook would be more relationship-oriented (Dean, 2010a). *How would you classify the other social media you use in terms of their content and relationship focus?*

Interpersonal Communication Is a Series of Punctuated Events

Communication events are continuous transactions. There is no clear-cut beginning and no clear-cut end. As participants in or observers of the communication act, you segment this continuous stream of communication into smaller pieces. You label some of these pieces causes or stimuli and others effects or responses.

Consider an example. A married couple is in a restaurant. The husband is flirting with another woman, and the wife is texting her sister. Both are scowling at each other and are obviously in a deep nonverbal argument. Recalling the situation later, the husband might observe that the wife texted, so he innocently flirted with the other woman. The only reason for his behavior (he says) was his anger over her texting when they were supposed to be having dinner together. Notice that he sees his behavior as a response to her behavior. In recalling the same incident, the wife might say that she texted her sister when he started flirting. The more he flirted, the longer she texted. She had no intention of calling anyone until he started flirting. To her, his behavior was the stimulus and hers was the response; he caused her behavior. Thus, the husband sees the sequence as going from texting to flirting, and the wife sees it as going from flirting to texting. This example is depicted visually in Figure 1.5 and is supported by research showing that, among married couples at least, the individuals regularly see their partner's behavior as the cause of conflict (Schutz, 1999).

This tendency to divide communication transactions into sequences of stimuli and responses is referred to as **punctuation** (Watzlawick, Beavin, & Jackson, 1967). Everyone punctuates the continuous sequences of events into stimuli and responses for convenience. As the example of the husband and wife illustrates, punctuation usually is done in ways that benefit the self and are consistent with a person's self-image.

Understanding how another person interprets a situation, how he or she punctuates, is a crucial step in interpersonal understanding. It is also essential in achieving empathy (feeling what the other person is feeling). In all communication encounters, but especially in conflicts, try to see how others punctuate the situation.

Interpersonal Communication Is Inevitable, Irreversible, and Unrepeatable

Interpersonal communication cannot be prevented (is inevitable), cannot be reversed (is irreversible), and cannot be repeated (is unrepeatable). Let's look briefly at each of these qualities and their implications.

Inevitability   Often communication is thought of as intentional, purposeful, and consciously motivated. In many instances, it is. But the **inevitability** principle means that, in many instances, you're communicating even though you might not think you are or might not even want to be. Consider, for example, the new editorial assistant sitting at the desk with an "expressionless" face, perhaps staring out the window. Although this assistant might say that she or he is not communicating with the manager, the manager may derive any of a variety of messages from this behavior—for example, that the assistant lacks interest, is bored, or is worried about something. In any event, the manager is receiving messages even though the assistant might not intend to communicate. In

Figure 1.5   Punctuation and the Sequence of Events

(a) Shows the actual sequence of events as a continuous series of actions with no specific beginning or end. Each action (texting and flirting) stimulates another action, but no initial cause is identified. (b) Shows the same sequence of events as seen by the wife. She sees the sequence as beginning with the husband's flirting and her texting behavior as a response to that stimulus. (c) Shows the same sequence of events from the husband's point of view. He sees the sequence as beginning with the wife's texting and his flirting as a response to that stimulus. Try using this three-part figure, discussed in the text, to explain what might go on when a supervisor complains that workers are poorly trained for their jobs and when the workers complain that the supervisor doesn't know how to supervise.

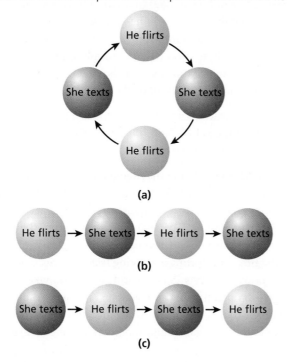

an interactional situation, all behavior is potentially communication. Any aspect of your behavior may communicate if the other person gives it message value. On the other hand, if the behavior (for example, the assistant's looking out the window) goes unnoticed, then no communication has taken place.

When you are in an interactional situation, your responses all have message value. For example, if you notice someone winking at you, you must respond in some way. Even if you don't respond openly, that lack of response is itself a response and it communicates (assuming it is perceived by the other person).

Irreversibility   Interpersonal communication is irreversible. This quality of **irreversibility** means that what you have communicated remains communicated; you cannot *un*communicate. Although you may try to qualify, negate, or somehow reduce the effects of your message, once it has been sent and received, the message itself cannot be reversed. In interpersonal interactions (especially in conflict), you need to be especially careful that you don't say things you may wish to withdraw later. Similarly, commitment messages, such as "I love you," must be monitored lest you commit yourself to a position you may be uncomfortable with later.

Face-to-face communication is evanescent; it fades after you have spoken. There is no trace of your communications outside the memories of the parties involved or of those who overheard your conversation. In computer-mediated communication, however, the messages are written and may be saved, stored, and printed. Both face-to-face and computer-mediated messages may be kept confidential or revealed publicly. But computer messages may be made public more easily and spread more quickly than face-to-face messages. Also, in communicating on Facebook, for example, it's relatively easy to intend to send a message to one person but actually send it to an entire group. Written messages provide clear evidence of what you have said and when you said it.

Because electronic communication is often permanent, you may wish to be cautious when you're e-mailing, posting your profile, or posting a message. Consider the following:

- **Electronic messages are virtually impossible to destroy and can easily be made public.** Your post on your blog or on a social networking site can be sent to anyone. And even e-mails you thought you deleted or a post you wrote in anger will remain on servers and workstations and may be retrieved by a clever hacker or may simply be copied and distributed to people you'd rather not have seen what you wrote.

- **Electronic messages can be used against you.** Electronic messages are not privileged communication; they can easily be accessed by others and be used against you. Your rant about a former employer may reach a prospective employer, who may see you as a complainer and reject your job application. In fact, employers regularly search such sites for information about job candidates. And you'll not be able to deny saying something; it will be there in black and white.

Despite these frequent warnings and despite the fact that online users are aware of the privacy issues, they still disclose (and often overdisclose) online, revealing things that may eventually affect them negatively (Taddicken, 2013).

Unrepeatability   In addition to being inevitable and irreversible, interpersonal communication is unrepeatable. The reason for this quality of **unrepeatability** is simple: everyone and everything is constantly changing. As a result, you can never recapture the exact same situation, frame of mind, or relationship dynamics that defined a previous interpersonal act. For example, you can never repeat the experience of meeting a particular person for the first time, comforting a grieving friend, or resolving a specific conflict. And, as you surely know, you never get a second chance to make a first impression.

You can, of course, try again, as when you say, "I'm sorry I came off so forward; can we try again?" But notice that even when you say this, you don't erase the initial impression. Instead, you try to counteract the initial (and perhaps negative) impression by going through the motions once more. In doing so, you try to create a more positive impression, which you hope will lessen the original negative effect—and which often does.

Table 1.3 summarizes the major principles of interpersonal communication and their basic ideas.

Table 1.3   In a Nutshell   Some Principles of Interpersonal Communication

Principle	Basic Idea
Interpersonal communication exists on a continuum	Interpersonal communication can range from relatively impersonal to extremely intimate.
Interpersonal communication involves interdependent individuals	In interpersonal communication, the behavior of one person has an impact on the other person.
Interpersonal communication is inherently relational	Interpersonal communication takes place within a relationship.
Interpersonal communication is a transactional process	The elements in communication are (1) always changing and (2) interdependent (each influences the other), (3) communication messages depend on the individual for their meaning and effect, and (4) each person is both speaker and listener.
Interpersonal communication serves a variety of purposes	Communication may serve a variety of purposes, for example, to learn, to relate, to help, to influence, to play.
Interpersonal communication is ambiguous	All messages and all relationships contain some uncertainty, some ambiguity.
Interpersonal relationships may be symmetrical or complementary	In some relationships, individuals mirror each other's behavior and in others, they engage in different behaviors.
Interpersonal communication refers to content and relationship	Messages may refer to the real world, to something external to both speaker and listener (the content), *and* to the relationships between the parties.
Interpersonal communication is a series of punctuated events	Communication events are continuous transactions, divided into causes and effects for convenience.
Interpersonal communication is inevitable, irreversible, and unrepeatable	Messages are (almost) always being sent, cannot be uncommunicated, and are always unique (one-time) occurrences.

Summary

This chapter introduced the importance and benefits of interpersonal communication, its elements, and some of its major principles.

The Benefits of Studying Interpersonal Communication

1.1 Identify the personal and professional benefits of studying interpersonal communication.

1. Personal benefits include a deeper understanding of yourself and others and of relationships.

2. Professional benefits include the increased ability to interact effectively in the work environment, from interviewing for the job to interacting with those from all levels of the organization.

The Elements of Interpersonal Communication

1.2 Define *interpersonal communication* and its essential elements including *source–receiver, messages, channels, noise, context, effects,* and *ethics*.

3. The source–receiver concept emphasizes that you send and receive interpersonal messages simultaneously through encoding and decoding (the processes of putting meaning into verbal and nonverbal messages and deriving meaning from the messages you receive from others), with competence and code-switching.

4. Messages are the signals that serve as stimuli for a receiver; metamessages are messages about other messages. Feedback messages are messages that are sent back by the receiver to the source in response to the source's messages. Feedforward messages are messages that preface other messages and ask that the listener approach future messages in a certain way.

5. Channels are the media through which messages pass and which act as a bridge between source and receiver; for example, the vocal–auditory channel used in speaking or the cutaneous–tactile channel used in touch.

6. Noise is the inevitable physical, physiological, psychological, and semantic interference that distorts messages.

7. Context is the physical, social–psychological, temporal, and cultural environment in which communication takes place.

8. Interpersonal communication always has effects which may be cognitive, affective, and/or behavioral.

9. Ethics is the moral dimension of communication, the study of what makes behavior moral or good as opposed to immoral or bad.

The Principles of Interpersonal Communication

1.3 Paraphrase the principles of interpersonal communication.

10. Interpersonal communication exists on a continuum ranging from mildly connected to intimately connected.

11. Interpersonal communication involves interdependent people; one person's behavior influences the other's behavior.

12. Interpersonal communication is inherently relational; the individuals are connected.

13. Interpersonal communication is a transactional process. Interpersonal communication is a process, an ongoing event, in which the elements are interdependent; communication is constantly occurring and changing. Don't expect clear-cut beginnings or endings or sameness from one time to another.

14. Interpersonal communication is purposeful. Five purposes may be identified: to learn, relate, influence, play, and help.

15. Interpersonal communication is ambiguous. All messages are potentially ambiguous; different people will derive different meanings from the "same" message. There is ambiguity in all relationships.

16. Interpersonal relationships may be symmetrical or complementary; interpersonal interactions may stimulate similar or different behavior patterns.

17. Interpersonal communication refers both to content and to the relationship between the participants.

18. Interpersonal communication is punctuated; that is, everyone separates communication sequences into stimuli and responses on the basis of his or her own perspective.

19. Interpersonal communication is inevitable, irreversible, and unrepeatable. When in an interactional situation, you cannot not communicate, you cannot uncommunicate, and you cannot repeat exactly a specific message.

Key Terms

These are the key terms discussed in this chapter. If you're in doubt about the definition of any of these terms, review the concept in this chapter, look up the definitions in the glossary at the end of the book, or search the term in the index.

ambiguity
asynchronous communication
channel
choice points
code-switching
competence
complementary relationship
content dimension
context
decoding
effect
encoding
ethics

feedback
feedforward
inevitability
interpersonal communication
irreversibility
messages
metamessages
metaphors
mindfulness
mindlessness
noise
physical noise
physiological noise

psychological noise
punctuation
relationship dimension
remote audience
semantic noise
signal
signal-to-noise ratio
source–receiver
strategic ambiguity
symmetrical relationship
synchronous communication
transactional perspective
unrepeatability

CHAPTER TWO

Culture and Interpersonal Communication

You live and interact in a multicultural world. *Being mindful of that will make interpersonal interactions and relationships a lot easier.*

Chapter Topics

Culture

Cultural Differences

Principles for Effective Intercultural Communication

Learning Objectives

2.1 Define *culture*, *enculturation*, and *acculturation* and explain the relevance of culture to interpersonal communication.

2.2 Explain the seven cultural differences identified here and how these impact on interpersonal communication.

2.3 Define *intercultural communication* and explain the principles for making intercultural communication more effective.

This chapter discusses one of the foundation concepts of interpersonal communication, culture—an often-misunderstood concept. More specifically, this chapter explains the nature of culture and its relationship to interpersonal communication, the major differences among cultures and how these differences affect interpersonal communication, and the ways you can improve your own intercultural communication.

Culture

2.1 Define *culture*, *enculturation*, and *acculturation* and explain the relevance of culture to interpersonal communication.

Culture may be defined as (1) the relatively specialized lifestyle of a group of people (2) that is passed on from one generation to the next through communication, not through genes.

Included in "culture" is everything that members of that group have produced and developed—their values, beliefs, artifacts, and language; their ways of behaving; their art, laws, religion; and, of course, communication theories, styles, and attitudes.

Culture is passed from one generation to the next through communication, not through genes. Culture is not synonymous with race or nationality. The term *culture* does not refer to skin color or the shape of one's eyes because these characteristics are passed on through genes, not communication. Of course, because members of a particular ethnic or national group are often taught similar beliefs, attitudes, and values, it's possible to speak of "Hispanic culture" or "African American culture." It's important to realize, however, that within any large group—especially a group based on race or nationality—there will be enormous differences. The Kansas farmer and the Wall Street executive may both be, say, German American, but they may differ widely in their attitudes, beliefs, and lifestyles. In many ways, the Kansas farmer may be closer in attitudes and values to a Chinese farmer than to the New York financier.

Sex and *gender*, although often used synonymously, are quite different. **Sex** refers to the biological distinction between male and female; sex is determined by genes, by biology. **Gender**, on the other hand, refers to the beliefs, attitudes, and behaviors that a culture assigns to *masculine* and to *feminine*. Gender (masculinity and femininity) is what boys and girls learn from their culture; it's the ways of behaving, communicating, and relating to one another that boys and girls learn as they grow up. It is from these teachings that you develop a **gender identity**, a concept of who you are, whether masculine, feminine, both, or neither. In any one individual, sex and gender may be the same or different. When sex and gender are the same, the person is referred to as **cisgender**. When sex and gender are different, the person is referred to as **transgender**.

Although sex is transmitted genetically and not by communication, gender may be considered a cultural variable—largely because cultures teach boys and girls different attitudes, beliefs, values, and ways of communicating and relating to others. Thus, you act like a man or a woman in part because of what your culture has taught you about how men and women should act. This does not, of course, deny that biological differences also play a role in the differences between male and female behavior. In fact, research continues to uncover biological roots of male/female differences we once thought were entirely learned (McCroskey, 1998).

An interesting perspective on culture can be gained by looking at some of the popular metaphors for culture. Table 2.1 identifies seven metaphors for culture which provide other ways of looking at the nature of culture. These insights are taken from a variety of sources (Hall, 1976; Hofstede, Hofstede, & Minkov, 2010; and the websites of Culture at Work and Culturally Teaching: Education across Cultures).

The Importance of Cultural Awareness

Because of (1) demographic changes, (2) increased sensitivity to cultural differences, (3) economic and political interdependence, (4) advances in communication technology, and (5) the culture-specific nature of interpersonal communication (what works in one culture does not necessarily work in another), it's impossible to communicate effectively without being aware of how culture influences human communication (Figure 2.1).

Table 2.1 Seven Metaphors of Culture

Metaphor	Metaphor's Claim/Assumption
Salad	Cultures are made up of many individual components, yet they work together with other cultures to produce an even better combination.
Iceberg	It may be that only a small part of culture is visible in a person's behavior and communication; but other facets of culture and its influences are hidden below the surface of a person's outward presentation.
Tree	Different cultures may originate from a strong trunk with branches and leaves, but the root system, which gives the tree its structure and function, is hidden from view.
Melting pot	When different cultures encounter one another, they can blend into one amalgam and lose their individuality, but the blend is often better than any one of the ingredients.
Software	A person's reactions and behavior can be "programmed" by their cultural upbringing. People are taught, often without awareness, how they should think and behave by their culture.
Organism	Culture, like a living thing, grows and changes with the environment and other cultural influences.
Mosaic	Culture is made up of pieces of different shapes, sizes, and colors; the whole, the combination, can be a piece of art more beautiful than any individual piece.

Figure 2.1 **Factors Contributing to the Importance of Culture in Interpersonal Communication**

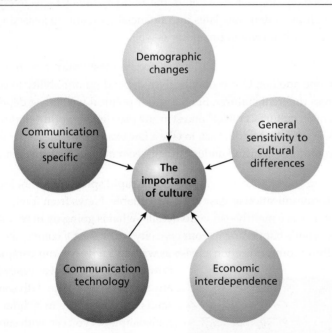

Demographic Changes   Perhaps the most obvious reason for the importance of culture is the vast demographic changes taking place throughout the United States. At one time, the United States was a country largely populated by Europeans, but it's now a country greatly influenced by the enormous number of new citizens from Latin and South America, Africa, and Asia. The same demographic shift is noticeable on college campuses. These changes have brought different interpersonal customs and the need to understand and adapt to new ways of communicating.

Internet dating encourages dating diversity, largely because it enables you to meet people outside of your immediate circle or daily life and because so many people around the world are now online (Dean, 2010b). Not surprisingly, interracial and inter-ethnic marriages are increasing. In 1970, fewer than 1 percent of the marriages in the

United States were interracial. In 1980, that percentage climbed to 6.7 percent; and, in 2010, 14.6 percent of the marriages were interracial (Passel, Wang, & Taylor, 2010; Wang, 2015). In 2010, 24 percent of the people surveyed thought that marriages among different races was a good thing for society; in 2014, the percentage rose to 37 percent. So, although a majority of people still interact with (and marry) those who are similar to them in race and religion, the number of interracial relationships and the positive attitudes toward them are growing.

Corporations are recognizing that a culturally diverse workforce is beneficial to their bottom line and are moving in the direction of greater diversity. Understanding the role of culture in interpersonal communication will enable you to function more effectively in this newly diverse environment (Hewlett, Marshall, & Sherbin, 2013).

Sensitivity to Cultural Differences As a people, we've become increasingly sensitive to cultural differences. American society has moved from an assimilationist attitude (people should leave their native culture behind and adapt to their new culture—a process known as **cultural assimilation**) to a perspective that values cultural diversity (people should retain their native cultural ways). We have moved from the metaphor of the melting pot, in which different cultures blended into one, to a metaphor of a tossed salad, in which there is some blending but specific and different tastes and flavors still remain. In this diverse society, and with some notable exceptions—hate speech, racism, sexism, homophobia, and classism come quickly to mind—we are more concerned with saying the right thing and ultimately with developing a society where all cultures coexist and enrich one another. As a bonus, the ability to interact effectively with members of other cultures often translates into financial gain and increased employment opportunities and advancement prospects as well.

Cultural Imperialism

The theory of cultural imperialism claims that certain developed countries, such as those of North America and Western Europe, impose their cultural values—largely through the use of their products; exposure to their music, films, and television; and their Internet dominance—on other cultures. *What do you think of the influence that media and the Internet are having on native cultures throughout the world? How do you evaluate this trend?*

Economic and Political Interdependence Today, most countries are economically dependent on one another. Our economic lives depend on our ability to communicate effectively across different cultures. Similarly, our political well-being depends in great part on that of other cultures. Political unrest in any place in the world—South Africa, Eastern Europe, Asia, and the Middle East, to take a few examples—affects our own security. Intercultural communication and understanding seem more crucial now than ever before.

Advances in Communication Technology The rapid spread of technology has made intercultural communication as easy as it is inevitable. News from foreign countries is commonplace. You see nightly—in vivid detail—what is going on in remote countries, just as you see what's happening in your own city and state. Of course, the Internet has made intercultural communication as easy as writing a note on your computer. You can now communicate just as easily by e-mail or any social network site with someone thousands of miles away in a different country, for example, as you can with someone living a few blocks away or in the next dorm room.

Culture-Specific Nature of Interpersonal Communication Still another reason why culture is so important is that interpersonal competence is culture-specific; what proves effective in one culture may prove ineffective in another. Many Asians, for example, often find that the values they were taught—values that promote cooperation and face-saving but discourage competitiveness and assertiveness—work against them in cultures that value competition

THE CULTURAL MAP Internet Access

The widespread use of the Internet in much of the Western world and in the United States (89% of the population has Internet access)—as a means of communication and as a means for learning about and engaging with the world—should not lead us to think that such access is global; it isn't.

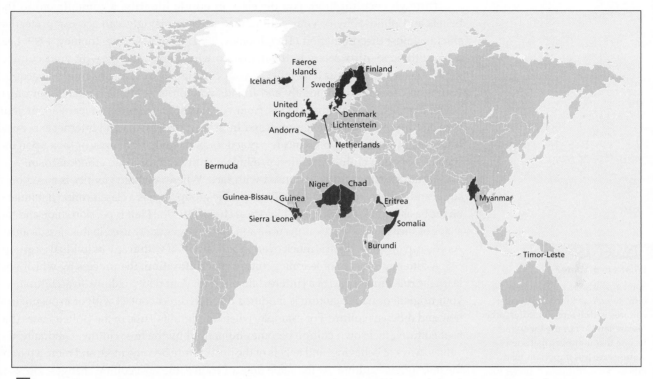

■ In these countries with lower numbers of internet users, less than 4 percent of the populations have access to the internet.

■ In these countries with higher numbers of internet users, at least 92 percent of the populations have access to the internet.

What are some of the interpersonal communication differences that you might predict would exist between those cultures with widespread Internet access and those with little?

and outspokenness (Cho, 2000). The same would be true for executives from the United States working in Asia. An example of these differences can be seen in business meetings. In the United States, corporate executives get down to business during the first several minutes of a meeting. In Japan, business executives interact socially for an extended period and try to find out something about one another. Thus, the communication principle influenced by U.S. culture would advise participants to get down to the meeting's agenda during the first five minutes. The principle influenced by Japanese culture would advise participants to avoid dealing with business until everyone has socialized sufficiently and feels well enough acquainted to begin negotiations.

Another example involves cultural differences based on religious beliefs. Giving a birthday gift to a close friend would be appreciated by many, but Jehovah's Witnesses would frown on this act because they don't celebrate birthdays (Dresser, 2005). Neither principle is right, neither is wrong. Each is effective within its own culture and ineffective outside its own culture.

The Transmission of Culture

Culture is transmitted from one generation to another through **enculturation**, the process by which you learn the culture into which you're born (your native culture). Parents, peer groups, schools, religious institutions, and government agencies are your main teachers of culture.

Through enculturation, you develop an **ethnic identity,** a commitment to the beliefs and philosophy of your culture that, not surprisingly, can act as a protective shield against discrimination (Ting-Toomey, 1981; Chung & Ting-Toomey, 1999; Lee, 2005). Ethnic identity refers to the degree to which you identify with your cultural group and see yourself as a member of your culture. As you can imagine, you acquire your ethnic identity from family and friends who observe ethnic holidays, patronize ethnic parades, and eat ethnic foods; from your schooling where you learn about your own culture and ethnic background; and from your own media and Internet exposure. If you begin looking at your culture's practices as the only right ones or look upon the practices of other cultures as inferior, ethnic identity can turn into ethnocentrism.

Ethnic identity is often confused with race. Whereas ethnic identity is based on a social and cultural identification with a specific group, **race** is a classification of humans on the basis of their physical and biological characteristics. Hair type, skin color, and the shape of such facial features as the nose and lips were generally used in this classification. As you can imagine, there is much overlap and variation within any individual or group.

A different process of learning culture is **acculturation**, the process by which you learn the rules and norms of a culture different from your native culture. In acculturation, your original or native culture is modified through direct contact with or exposure to a new and different culture. For example, when immigrants settle in the United States (the host culture), their own culture becomes influenced by the host culture. Gradually, the values, ways of behaving, and beliefs of the host culture become more and more a part of the immigrants' culture. At the same time, of course, the host culture changes, too, as it interacts with the immigrants' cultures. Generally, however, the culture of the immigrant changes more. The reasons for this are that the host country's members far outnumber the immigrant group and that the media are largely dominated by and reflect the values and customs of the host cultures (Kim, 1988).

New citizens' acceptance of the new culture depends on many factors (Kim, 1988). Immigrants who come from cultures similar to the host culture will become acculturated more easily. Similarly, those who are younger and better educated become acculturated more quickly than do older and less educated people. Personality factors also play a part. Persons who are risk takers and open-minded, for example, have greater acculturation potential. Also, persons who are familiar with the host culture before immigration—through interpersonal contact or through media exposure—will be acculturated more readily.

The Aim of a Cultural Perspective

Because culture permeates all forms of communication, it's necessary to understand its

influences if you're to understand how communication works and master its skills. As illustrated throughout this text, culture influences communications of all types (Jandt, 2016; Moon, 1996). It influences what you say to yourself and how you talk with friends, lovers, and family in everyday conversation (for example, Shibazaki & Brennan, 1998). It influences how you interact in groups and how much importance you place on the group versus the individual. It influences the topics you talk about and the strategies you use in communicating information or in persuading. It influences how you use the media and the credibility you attribute to them.

Consider attitudes toward age. If you were raised in the United States, you probably grew up with a youth bias (young is good, old is not so good)—an attitude the media reinforce daily—and might well assume that this preference for youth would be universal across all cultures. But this preference isn't universal, and if you assume it is, you may be in for intercultural difficulties. A good example is the case of the American journalist in China who remarked that the government official he was talking with was probably too young to remember a particular event—a comment that would be taken as a compliment by most youth-oriented Americans. But to the Chinese official, the comment appeared to be an insult, a suggestion that the official was too young to deserve respect (Smith, 2002).

You need cultural understanding to communicate effectively in a wide variety of intercultural situations. Success in interpersonal communication—at your job and in your social and personal life—depends in great part on your understanding of, and your ability to communicate effectively with, persons who are culturally different from yourself. The media bombard you daily with evidence of racial tensions, religious disagreements, sexual bias, and the problems caused when intercultural communication fails.

This emphasis on culture does not imply that you should accept all cultural practices or that all cultural practices will necessarily be equal in terms of your own values and beliefs (Hatfield & Rapson, 1996). Nor does it imply that you have to accept or follow all of the practices of your own culture. For example, even if the majority of the people in your culture find cockfighting acceptable, you need not agree with or follow the practice. Nor need you consider this practice equal to a cultural practice in which animals are treated kindly. You can reject capitalism or communism or socialism regardless of the culture in which you were raised. Of course, going against your culture's traditions and values is often very difficult. But it's important to realize that culture influences, it does not determine, your values or behavior. Often personality factors (your degree of assertiveness, extroversion, or optimism, for example) will prove more influential than culture (Hatfield & Rapson, 1996).

As demonstrated throughout this text, cultural differences exist throughout the interpersonal communication spectrum—from the way you use eye contact to the way you develop or dissolve a relationship (Chang & Holt, 1996). Culture even influences your level of happiness, which in turn influences your attitudes and the positivity and negativity of your messages (Kirn, 2005). But these differences should not blind you to the great number of similarities existing among even the most widely separated cultures. When discussing differences, remember that they are usually matters of degree rather than all-or-nothing situations. For example, most cultures value honesty, but some cultures give it greater emphasis than others. In addition, advances in media and technology and the widespread use of the Internet are influencing cultures and cultural change, and they are perhaps homogenizing different cultures to some extent, lessening differences and increasing similarities.

ETHICS IN INTERPERSONAL COMMUNICATION

Culture and Ethics

One of the most shocking revelations to come to world attention after the events of September 11, 2001, was the way in which women were treated under Taliban rule in Afghanistan. Females could not be educated or even go out in public without a male relative escort, and when in public, they had to wear garments that covered their entire body.

Throughout history there have been cultural practices that today would be judged unethical. Sacrificing virgins to the gods, burning people who held different religious beliefs, and sending children to fight religious wars are obvious examples. But even today there are practices woven deep into the fabric of different cultures that you might find unethical. Here are a few examples:

- Bronco riding, bullfighting, and fox hunting that involve inflicting pain and even causing the death of animals
- Same sex relationships, in some countries, are punishable by long prison sentences and even death.
- The belief and practice that a woman must be subservient to her husband's will or a legal system that allows only husbands to initiate divorce

Ethical Choice Point

You're talking with new work colleagues who are discussing one of these practices with great approval. Your colleagues argue that each culture has a right to its own practices and beliefs. *Given your own beliefs about these issues and about cultural diversity, what ethical obligations do you have to speak your mind without—you hope—jeopardizing your new position?*

UNDERSTANDING *INTERPERSONAL SKILLS*

Cultural Sensitivity: Responsiveness to Cultural Variation

Cultural sensitivity is an attitude and way of behaving in which you're aware of and acknowledge cultural differences; it's crucial for global goals such as world peace and economic growth as well as for effective interpersonal communication (Franklin & Mizell, 1995). Without cultural sensitivity, there can be no effective interpersonal communication between people who are different in gender or race or nationality or affectional orientation. So be mindful of the cultural differences between yourself and the other person. The techniques of interpersonal communication that work well with European Americans may not work well with Asian Americans; what proves effective in Japan might not in Mexico. The close physical distance that is normal in Arab cultures may seem too familiar or too intrusive in much of the United States and northern Europe. The empathy that most Americans welcome may be uncomfortable for most Koreans, Japanese, or Chinese.

Communicating with Cultural Sensitivity

This chapter has identified many guidelines for more effective intercultural communication, and among them are recommendations that constitute the best advice for achieving cultural sensitivity:

- **Prepare yourself.** Read about and listen carefully for culturally influenced behaviors.
- **Recognize your fears.** Recognize and face your own fears of acting inappropriately toward members of different cultures.
- **Recognize differences.** Be mindful of the differences between yourself and those from other cultures.
- **Recognize differences within the group.** At the same time that you recognize differences between yourself and others, recognize that there are often enormous differences within any given cultural group.
- **Recognize differences in meaning.** Words don't always have the same meaning to members of different cultures.
- **Be rule-conscious.** Become aware of and think mindfully about the cultural rules and customs of others.

Working with Cultural Sensitivity

How would you rate your own cultural sensitivity? Try to recall situations in which you were, and situations in which you weren't, culturally sensitive. What happened in each? Can you identify one situation that could have been improved with the addition of cultural sensitivity?

Table 2.2 In a Nutshell The Nature of Culture

Cultural Concept	Cultural Concepts Explained
Culture	A relatively specialized lifestyle of a group of people that is passed from one generation to the next through communication, not genes.
The Importance of Cultural Awareness	As the population in the U.S. reflects more and more demographic changes, the importance of cultural awareness and sensitivity has grown. Because nations around the world are economically and politically interdependent, and because technology enables interpersonal communication across oceans, understanding the rules for effective interpersonal communication across cultures is crucial. Communication techniques that work in one culture may not work in another.
Transmission of Culture	Through enculturation you develop an ethnic identity (a commitment to your culture's beliefs and values). Acculturation, in contrast, refers to the process through which you learn a culture other than the one into which you were born.
Aim of a Cultural Perspective	Culture is emphasized here simply because it's crucial to the effectiveness of interpersonal communication.

Table 2.2 offers a brief summary of these foundation concepts.

Cultural Differences

2.2 Explain the seven cultural differences identified here and how these impact on interpersonal communication.

For effective interpersonal communication to take place in a global world, goodwill and good intentions are helpful—but they are not enough. If you want to be an effective communicator, you need to know how cultures differ and how these differences influence communication. Research supports several major cultural distinctions that have an impact on communication: (1) individualist or collectivist orientation, (2) emphasis on context (whether high or low), (3) power structure, (4) masculinity–femininity, (5) tolerance for ambiguity, (6) long- and short-term orientation, and (7) indulgence and restraint. Each of these dimensions of difference has a significant impact on all forms of communication (Gudykunst, 1994; Hall & Hall, 1987; Hofstede, Hofstede, & Minkov, 2010). Following the major researchers in this area, these differences are discussed in terms of countries, even though in many cases different nations have very similar cultures (and so we often speak of Hispanic culture, which would include a variety of countries). In other cases, the same country includes various cultures; for example, in Canada, French Quebec has a different culture than, say, Toronto and in New Zealand there are the culture of the Maori and the culture of the British New Zealanders (Hofstede, Hofstede, & Minkov, 2010; Jandt, 2016).

As you read about these cultural differences ask yourself two crucial questions to help personalize this discussion and make it more useful:

1. What is your own cultural orientation? For example, are you more of an individualist or more of a collectivist and so on with the other dimensions to be discussed?

2. How do these cultural teachings influence your goals and your behavior?

Once you become aware of the influences of culture on your own behavior, you'll be better able to understand such influences on the behavior of others—essential skills for effective interpersonal and intercultural communication.

Before reading about these dimensions, respond to the following questions. For each of the items below, select either *a* or *b*. In some cases, you may feel that neither *a* nor *b* describes yourself accurately; in these cases, simply select the one that is closer to your feeling. As you'll see when you read this next section, these are not either/or preferences, but more-or-less preferences.

1. Success, to my way of thinking, is better measured by

   a. the extent to which I surpass others.

   b. my contribution to the group effort.

2. My heroes are generally

   a. people who stand out from the crowd.

   b. team players.

3. If I were a manager, I would likely

   a. reprimand a worker in public if the occasion warranted.

   b. always reprimand in private regardless of the situation.

4. In communicating, it's generally more important to be

   a. polite rather than accurate or direct.

   b. accurate and direct rather than polite.

5. As a student (and if I feel well informed), I feel

   a. comfortable challenging a professor.

   b. uncomfortable challenging a professor.

6. In choosing a life partner or even close friends, I feel more comfortable

   a. with just about anyone, not necessarily one from my own culture and class.

   b. with those from my own culture and class.

7. In a conflict situation, I'd be more likely to

   a. confront conflicts directly and seek to win.

   b. confront conflicts with the aim of compromise.

8. If I were a manager of an organization, I would stress

   a. competition and aggressiveness.

   b. worker satisfaction.

9. As a student, I'm more comfortable with assignments in which

   a. there is freedom for interpretation.

   b. there are clearly defined instructions.

10. Generally, when approaching an undertaking with which I've had no experience, I feel

    a. comfortable.

    b. uncomfortable.

11. Generally,

    a. I save money for the future.

    b. I spend what I have.

12. My general belief about child rearing is that

    a. children should be cared for by their mothers.

    b. children can be cared for by others.

13. For the most part,

    a. I believe I'm in control of my own life.

    b. I believe my life is largely determined by forces out of my control.

14. In general,

    a. I have leisure time to do what I find fun.

    b. I have little leisure time.

- Items 1–2 refer to the *individualist–collectivist orientation; a* responses indicate an individualist orientation, and *b* responses indicate a collectivist orientation.
- Items 3–4 refer to the *high- and low-context* characteristics; *a* responses indicate a high-context focus, and *b* responses indicate a low-context focus.
- Items 5–6 refer to the *power distance* dimension; *a* responses indicate greater comfort with a low power distance, and *b* responses indicate comfort with a high-power distance.

- Items 7–8 refer to the *masculine–feminine* dimension; *a* responses indicate a masculine orientation; *b* responses indicate a feminine orientation.
- Items 9–10 refer to the *tolerance for ambiguity* or uncertainty; *a* responses indicate a high tolerance, and *b* responses indicate a low tolerance.
- Items 11–12 refer to a *long- or short-term orientation; a* responses indicate a long-term orientation, and *b* responses indicate a short-term orientation.
- Items 13–14 refer to *indulgent and restraint orientation; a* responses indicate indulgent, and *b* responses indicate restraint.

Of course, two questions are far too few to identify your cultural orientation; they were presented here simply to help you personalize these orientations. Understanding your preferences in a wide variety of situations as culturally influenced (at least in part) is a first step to controlling them and to changing them should you wish to do so. This understanding also helps you modify your behavior as appropriate for greater effectiveness in certain situations. The remaining discussion in this section further explains these orientations and their implications.

Individual and Collective Orientation

Cultures differ in the way in which they promote individualist versus collectivist thinking and behaving (Hofstede, Hofstede, & Minkov, 2010; Singh & Pereira, 2005). An **individualist culture** teaches members the importance of individual values such as power, achievement, hedonism, and stimulation. Examples include the cultures of the United States, Australia, the United Kingdom, the Netherlands, Canada, New Zealand, Italy, Belgium, Denmark, and Sweden. A **collectivist culture**, on the other hand, teaches members the importance of group values such as benevolence, tradition, and conformity. Examples of such cultures include Guatemala, Ecuador, Panama, Venezuela, Colombia, Indonesia, Pakistan, China, Costa Rica, and Peru.

One of the major differences between these two orientations is the extent to which an individual's goals or the group's goals are given greater importance. Of course, these goals are not mutually exclusive—you probably have both individualist and collectivist tendencies. For example, you may compete with other members of your basketball team for the most baskets or most valuable player award (and thus emphasize individual goals). In a game, however, you act in a way that benefits the entire team (and thus emphasize group goals). In actual practice, both individual and collective tendencies help you and your team each achieve your goals. Yet most people and most cultures have a dominant orientation. In an individualist culture, members are responsible for themselves and perhaps their immediate family. In a collectivist culture, members are responsible for the entire group.

Success in an individualist culture is measured by the extent to which you surpass other members of your group; you take pride in standing out from the crowd. And your heroes—in the media, for example—are likely to be those who are unique and who stand apart. In a collectivist culture, success is measured by your contribution to the achievements of the group as a whole, and you take pride in your similarity to other members of your group. Your heroes are more likely to be team players who don't stand out from the rest of the group's members.

Distinctions between in-group members and out-group members are extremely important in collectivist cultures. In individualistic cultures, which prize each person's individuality, the distinction is likely to be less

important. In fact, closely related to individualism and collectivism is universalism and exclusionism (Hofstede, Hofstede, & Minkov, 2010). A universalist culture (highly correlated with individualism) is one in which people are treated as individuals rather than in terms of the groups (racial, sexual, national, for example) to which they belong. A universalist orientation teaches a respect for other cultures, other beliefs, and other ways of doing things. An exclusionist orientation (highly correlated with collectivism) fosters a strong in-group affiliation with much less respect for out-group members. Special privileges are reserved for in-group members, while indifference, impoliteness, and in some cases even hostility are directed at members of other cultures.

High- and Low-Context Cultures

Cultures also differ in the extent to which information is made explicit, on the one hand, or is assumed to be in the context or in the persons communicating, on the other. In a **high-context culture**, much of the information in communication is in the context or in the person—for example, information that was shared through previous communications, through assumptions about each other, and through shared experiences. The information is thus known by all participants, but it is not explicitly stated in the verbal message. In a **low-context culture**, most of the information is explicitly stated in the verbal message; in formal transactions, it will be stated in written (or contract) form.

High-context cultures are also collectivist cultures (Gudykunst & Kim, 1992; Gudykunst, Ting-Toomey, & Chua, 1988). These cultures place great emphasis on personal relationships and oral agreements (Victor, 1992). Examples of high-context cultures include Japanese, Arabic, Latin American, Thai, Korean, Apache, and Mexican. Low-context cultures are also individualist cultures. These cultures place less emphasis on personal relationships and more emphasis on verbalized, explicit explanation—for example, on written contracts in business transactions. Examples of low-context cultures include German, Swedish, Norwegian, and American.

A frequent source of intercultural misunderstanding that can be traced to the distinction between high- and low-context cultures is seen in face-saving (Hall & Hall, 1987). People in high-context cultures place a great deal more emphasis on face-saving, on avoiding one's own or another's possible embarrassment. For example, they're more likely to avoid argument for fear of causing others to lose face, whereas people in low-context cultures (with their individualist orientation) are more likely to use argument to make a point. Similarly, in high-context cultures criticism should take place only in private. Low-context cultures may not make this public–private distinction. Low-context managers who criticize high-context workers in public will find that their criticism causes interpersonal problems—and does little to resolve the difficulty that led to the criticism in the first place (Victor, 1992).

Members of high-context cultures are reluctant to say no for fear of offending and causing the other person to lose face. For example, it's necessary to understand when the Japanese executive's yes means yes and when it means no. The difference is not in the words used but in the way in which they're used. It's easy to see how the low-context individual may interpret this reluctance to be direct—to say no when you mean no—as a weakness or as an unwillingness to confront reality.

Power Distance

Power distance refers to how power is distributed in a society. In some cultures, power is concentrated in the hands of a few, and there's a great difference between the power held by these people and the power of the ordinary citizen. These are called

---

INTERPERSONAL CHOICE POINT
Saving Face

You accidentally refer to your best friend's current romantic partner with the name of your friend's ex-partner. From both their expressions you can tell your friend never mentioned the ex. *What can you say to get your friend out of the trouble you just created?*

a. "Wow, I guess you don't know about the infamous EX."

b. "Did I say something wrong?"

c. "Sorry, about that; I was thinking of someone else."

d. Say nothing and just continue the conversation.

e. Other

high-power-distance cultures. The ten countries with the highest power distance are Malaysia, Slovakia, Guatemala, Panama, the Philippines, Russia, Romania, Serbia, Suriname, and Mexico (Hofstede, Hofstede, & Minkov, 2010; Singh & Pereira, 2005). In a **low-power-distance culture**, power is more evenly distributed throughout the citizenry. The ten countries with the lowest power distance are Austria, Israel, Denmark, New Zealand, Switzerland, Ireland, Sweden, Norway, Finland, and Great Britain (Hofstede, Hofstede, & Minkov, 2010; Singh & Pereira, 2005). In a list of 76 countries, the United States ranks 59th (58 nations are higher in power distance). These differences affect communication in numerous ways. For example, in high-power-distance cultures, there's a great power distance between students and teachers; students are expected to be modest, polite, and totally respectful. In low-power-distance cultures (and you can see this clearly in U.S. college classrooms), students are expected to demonstrate their knowledge and command of the subject matter, participate in discussions with the teacher, and even challenge the teacher—something many high-power-distance culture members wouldn't even think of doing.

Friendship and dating relationships are also influenced by the power distance between groups (Andersen, 1991). In India, for example, such relationships are expected to take place within your cultural class. In Sweden, a person is expected to select friends and romantic partners not on the basis of class or culture but on the basis of individual factors such as personality, appearance, and the like.

Low-power-distance cultures expect you to confront a friend, partner, or supervisor assertively; in these cultures, there is a general feeling of equality that is consistent with assertive behavior (Borden, 1991). High-power-distance cultures, on the other hand, view direct confrontation and assertiveness negatively, especially if directed at a superior.

Masculine and Feminine Cultures

Especially important for self-concept is the culture's attitude about gender roles, that is, about how a man or woman should act. In fact, a popular classification of cultures is in terms of their masculinity and femininity (Hofstede, Hofstede, & Minkov, 2010). When denoting cultural orientations, the terms *masculine* and *feminine* should not be interpreted as perpetuating stereotypes but as reflecting some of the commonly held assumptions of a sizable number of people throughout the world. Some intercultural theorists note that equivalent terms would be *achievement* and *nurturance,* but because research is conducted under the terms *masculine* and *feminine* and because these are the terms you'd use to search the electronic databases, we use these terms here (Lustig & Koester, 2018).

A highly **masculine culture** values aggressiveness, material success, and strength. A highly **feminine culture** values modesty, concern for relationships and the quality of life, and tenderness. The 10 countries with the highest masculinity score are (beginning with the highest) Japan, Austria, Venezuela, Italy, Switzerland, Mexico, Ireland, Jamaica, Great Britain, and Germany. The 10 countries with the highest femininity score are (beginning with the highest) Sweden, Norway, the Netherlands, Denmark, Costa Rica, Yugoslavia, Finland, Chile, Portugal, and Thailand. Of the 53 countries ranked, the United States ranks 15th most masculine (Hofstede, Hofstede, & Minkov, 2010).

Masculine cultures emphasize success and so socialize their members to be assertive, ambitious, and competitive. For example, members of masculine cultures are more likely to confront conflicts directly and to fight out any differences competitively; they're more

likely to emphasize conflict strategies that enable them to win and ensure that the other side loses (win–lose strategies). Feminine cultures emphasize the quality of life and so socialize their members to be modest and to highlight close interpersonal relationships. Feminine cultures, for example, are more likely to utilize compromise and negotiation in resolving conflicts; they're more likely to seek solutions in which both sides win (win–win strategies).

High-Ambiguity-Tolerant and Low-Ambiguity-Tolerant Cultures

Levels of **ambiguity tolerance** vary widely among cultures. In some cultures, people do little to avoid uncertainty, and they have little anxiety about not knowing what will happen next. In some other cultures, however, uncertainty is strongly avoided and there is much anxiety about uncertainty.

High-Ambiguity-Tolerant Cultures   Members of high-ambiguity-tolerant cultures don't feel threatened by unknown situations: uncertainty is a normal part of life, and people accept it as it comes. The 10 countries with highest tolerance for ambiguity are Singapore, Jamaica, Denmark, Sweden, Hong Kong, Ireland, Great Britain, Malaysia, India, and the Philippines; the United States ranks 11th.

Because high-ambiguity-tolerant culture members are comfortable with ambiguity and uncertainty, they minimize the importance of rules governing communication and relationships (Hofstede, Hofstede, & Minkov, 2010; Lustig & Koester, 2018). People in these cultures readily tolerate individuals who don't follow the same rules as the cultural majority, and may even encourage different approaches and perspectives.

Students from high-ambiguity-tolerant cultures appreciate freedom in education and prefer vague assignments without specific timetables. These students want to be rewarded for creativity and readily accept an instructor's lack of knowledge.

Low-Ambiguity-Tolerant Cultures   Members of low-ambiguity-tolerant cultures do much to avoid uncertainty and have a great deal of anxiety about not knowing what will happen next; they see uncertainty as threatening and as something that must be counteracted. The 10 countries with the lowest tolerance for ambiguity are Greece, Portugal, Guatemala, Uruguay, Belgium, Malta, Russia, El Salvador, Poland, and Japan (Hofstede, Hofstede, & Minkov, 2010).

Low-ambiguity-tolerant cultures create clear-cut rules for communication that must not be broken. For example, students from strong-uncertainty-avoidance cultures prefer highly structured experiences with little ambiguity; they prefer specific objectives, detailed instructions, and definite timetables. An assignment to write a term paper on "anything" would be cause for alarm; it would not be clear or specific enough. These students expect to be judged on the basis of the right answers and expect the instructor to have all the answers all the time (Hofstede, Hofstede, & Minkov, 2010).

Long- and Short-Term Orientation

Another interesting distinction is the one between long- and short-term orientation. Some cultures teach a **long-term orientation**, an orientation that promotes the importance of future rewards; members of these cultures are more apt to save for the future and to prepare for the future academically (Hofstede, Hofstede, & Minkov, 2010). The most long-term oriented countries are South Korea, Taiwan, Japan, China, Ukraine, Germany, Estonia, Belgium, Lithuania, and Russia. The United States ranks 69th out of 93 countries, making it less long-term than most countries. In these cultures, marriage is a practical arrangement rather than one based on sexual or emotional arousal, and living with extended family (for example, in-laws) is common and considered quite normal. These cultures believe that mothers should be at home with their children, that humility is a virtue for both men and women, and that old age should be a happy time of life.

Cultures fostering a **short-term orientation** (Puerto Rico, Ghana, Egypt, Trinidad, Nigeria, Dominican Republic, Colombia, Iran, Morocco, and Zimbabwe are the top 10) look more to the past and the present. Instead of saving for the future, members of this culture spend their resources for the present and want quick results from their efforts. These cultures believe and teach that marriage is a moral arrangement, living with in-laws causes problems, children do not have to be cared for by their mothers (others can do that), humility is a virtue only for women (not men), and old age is an unpleasant time of life.

These cultures also differ in their view of the workplace. Organizations in long-term-oriented cultures look to profits in the future. Managers or owners and workers in such cultures share the same values and work together to achieve a common good. Organizations in short-term-oriented cultures, on the other hand, look to more immediate rewards. Managers and workers are very different in their thinking and in their attitudes about work.

Even in educational outlook there are significant differences. Students in long-term cultures will attribute their success or failure in school to their own efforts, while students in short-term cultures will attribute their success or failure to luck or chance.

Another perspective on this difference is offered by a study that asked Asian (long-term cultures) and American (short-term culture) executives to rank-order those values they considered most important in the workplace. The top six responses are presented in Table 2.3 and show a dramatic difference between the two cultural groups. Notice that the value of "hard work" makes both lists but in very different positions (Hofstede, Hofstede, & Minkov, 2010).

Indulgence and Restraint

Cultures also differ in their emphasis on indulgence or restraint (Hofstede, Hofstede, & Minkov, 2010). Cultures high in **indulgence** emphasize the gratification of desires; they focus on having fun and enjoying life. Venezuela, Mexico, Puerto Rico, El Salvador, Nigeria, Colombia, Trinidad, Sweden, New Zealand, and Ghana are the top 10 in indulgence; the United States ranks 15th out of 93 countries, making it considerably more indulgent than most countries. These cultures have more people who are happy, which depends on two major factors:

- *Life control.* This is the feeling that you may do as you please (at least to a significant degree), that you have freedom of choice to do or not do what you want.
- *Leisure.* This is the feeling that you have leisure time to do what you find fun.

In addition, members of indulgent cultures have more positive attitudes, greater optimism, and are more likely to remember positive emotions. They also have a more satisfying family life and loose gender roles (for example, household tasks are shared by both partners).

Table 2.3 Values of the Workplace

Values Selected by Asian (Long-Term-Oriented) Executives	Values Selected by American (Short-Term-Oriented) Executives
Hard work	Freedom of expression
Respect for learning	Personal freedom
Honesty	Self-reliance
Openness to new ideas	Individual rights
Accountability	Hard work
Self-discipline	Personal achievement

VIEWPOINTS

Health and Cultural Orientation

One difference between restrained and indulgent cultures is the finding that death rates from cardiovascular diseases are significantly higher in restrained than in indulgent cultures, and significantly more indulgent culture members describe their health as "very good" (Hofstede, Hofstede, & Minkov, 2010). *Why do you think this is so?*

Cultures high in **restraint** (Pakistan, Egypt, Latvia, Ukraine, Albania, Belarus, Lithuania, Bulgaria, Estonia, and Iraq are the top 10), on the other hand, are those that foster the curbing of such gratification and its regulation by social norms. Restraint cultures have more people who are unhappy: people who see themselves as lacking control of their own lives and with little or no leisure time to engage in fun activities. In contrast to indulgent cultures, members of cultures high in restraint are more cynical, pessimistic, and less likely to remember positive emotions. They have less satisfying family lives, rigid gender roles, and an unequal distribution of household tasks.

As you might expect, indulgent cultures do not place great value on thrift; instead the value is on spending to gratify one's needs. Restrained cultures place a great value on thrift. Also predictable is the finding that indulgent cultures place great importance on friendship and having lots of friends, whereas restrained cultures place less importance on friendships. Although there are no studies offering evidence, it's likely that the Facebook pages of indulgent culture members have a lot more friends than do those of members of restrained cultures.

Table 2.4 presents a brief summary of these seven cultural differences.

Table 2.4 In a Nutshell Cultural Differences

Cultural Dimensions	Cultural Differences
Individual and collective	The extent to which the individual is emphasized versus the group.
High- and low-context	The extent to which information is in the surrounding context versus explicitly stated in the message.
High- and low-power distance	The extent to which power is concentrated in the hands of a few versus being more equally distributed throughout the population.
Masculine and feminine	The extent to which a culture views men as strong, assertive, and focused on success and women as modest, tender, and focused on the quality of life versus viewing men and women more similarly.
High-ambiguity-tolerant and low- ambiguity-tolerant	The extent to which individuals within a culture can tolerate uncertainty and live comfortably with ambiguity.
Long- and short-term	The extent to which cultures promote the importance of future rewards versus more immediate rewards.
Indulgence and restraint	The extent to which cultures emphasize the gratification of desires and having fun versus the curbing and regulation of pleasures and fun.

Principles for Effective Intercultural Communication

2.3 Define *intercultural communication* and explain the principles for making intercultural communication more effective.

Intercultural communication refers to communication between persons who have different cultural beliefs, values, or ways of behaving. The model in Figure 2.2 illustrates this concept. The circles represent the cultures of the individual communicators. The inner circles identify the communicators (the sources and receivers). In this model, each communicator is a member of a different culture. In some instances, the cultural differences are relatively slight—say, between persons from Toronto and New York. In other instances, the cultural differences are great—say, between persons from Borneo and France, or between persons from rural Nigeria and industrialized Germany.

Regardless of your own cultural background, you will surely come into close contact with people from a variety of other cultures—people who speak different languages, eat different foods, practice different religions, and approach work and relationships in very different ways. It doesn't matter whether you're a longtime resident or a newly arrived immigrant: you are or soon will be living, going to school, working, and forming relationships with people who are from very different cultures. Your day-to-day interpersonal interactions on social media have become increasingly intercultural as have your face-to-face interactions.

Drawing on the work of numerous intercultural researchers, let's consider several guidelines designed to increase the chances for effective intercultural communication (Barna, 1997; Lustig & Koester, 2018; Ruben, 1985; Spitzberg, 1991; Jandt, 2016). See Figure 2.3.

Figure 2.2   A Model of Intercultural Communication

This model of intercultural communication illustrates that culture is part of every communication act. More specifically, it illustrates that the messages you send and the messages you receive are influenced by your cultural beliefs, attitudes, and values. Note also that the circles overlap to some degree, illustrating that no matter how different the cultures of the two individuals are, there will always be some commonalities, some similarities, along with differences.

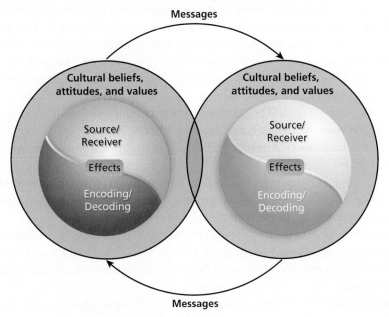

Figure 2.3 Some Steps to Effective Intercultural Communication

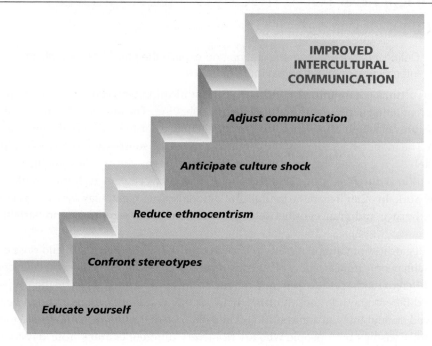

Educate Yourself

There's no better preparation for intercultural communication than learning about the other culture. Fortunately, there are numerous sources to draw on. View a documentary or movie that presents a realistic view of the culture. Read material about the culture by persons from that culture as well as by outsiders (e.g., Foster, 2004). Scan magazines and websites from the culture. Talk with members of the culture. Chat in international chat rooms. GeoSurf™ from your Facebook page or from your browser. Another fun way to educate yourself is with geotagging, which enables you to access tweets from the part of the world you're interested in to see what the people are doing and thinking about. Another way is to join a Facebook group focusing on the culture in which you're interested. Read materials addressed to people who need to communicate with those from other cultures.

Another part of this preparation is to recognize and face your own fears, which can stand in the way of effective intercultural communication (Gudykunst, 1994; Shelton & Richeson, 2005; Stephan & Stephan, 1985). For example, you may fear for your self-esteem. You may become anxious about your ability to control the intercultural situation, or you may worry about your own level of discomfort. You may fear saying something that will be considered politically incorrect or culturally insensitive and thereby losing face.

You may fear that you'll be taken advantage of by a member of another culture. Depending on your own stereotypes, you may fear being lied to, financially duped, or ridiculed. You may fear that members of this other group will react to you negatively. You may fear, for example, that they will not like you or may disapprove of your attitudes or beliefs or perhaps even reject you as a person. Conversely, you may fear negative reactions from members of your own group. For example, they might disapprove of your socializing with people who are culturally different.

Some fears, of course, are reasonable. In many cases, however, such concerns are groundless. Either way, they need to be assessed logically and their consequences weighed carefully. Then you'll be able to make informed choices about your communications.

Research shows that Internet daters typically develop more intercultural relationships than do those who meet face-to-face, though the preference for most people is to stick with members of their own race, nationality, and religion (Dean, 2010b). Internet dating is growing, so it is likely that more and more people will be dating interculturally. This is a good example of where your interactions will help educate both members. And the same is true for developing online friendships. Most of you very likely have friends or followers from different cultures on Facebook, Google+, Twitter, or Pinterest. Invariably your interactions will prove educational.

Recognize Differences

To communicate interculturally, you need to recognize the differences between yourself and people from other cultures; the differences within the other cultural group; and the numerous differences in meaning, and in dialect and accent.

Differences Between Yourself and the Culturally Different   A common barrier to intercultural communication occurs when you assume that similarities exist and that differences do not. This is especially true of values, attitudes, and beliefs. You might easily accept different hairstyles, clothing, and foods. In basic values and beliefs, however, you may assume that deep down all people are really alike. They aren't. When you assume similarities and ignore differences, you'll fail to notice important distinctions; when communicating, you will convey to others that your ways are the right ways and that their ways are not important to you. Consider this example. An American invites a Filipino coworker to dinner. The Filipino politely refuses. The American is hurt and feels that the Filipino does not want to be friendly. The Filipino is hurt and concludes that the invitation was not extended sincerely. Here, it seems, both the American and the Filipino assume that their customs for inviting people to dinner are the same when, in fact, they aren't. A Filipino expects to be invited several times before accepting a dinner invitation. When an invitation is given only once, it's viewed as insincere.

Differences within the Culturally Different Group   Within every cultural group there are vast and important differences. As all Americans are not alike, neither are all Indonesians, Greeks, Mexicans, and so on. When you ignore these differences—when you assume that all persons covered by the same label (in this case, a national or racial label) are the same—you're guilty of stereotyping. A good example of this is seen in the use of the term *African American*. The term stresses the unity of Africa and of those who are of African descent, and is analogous to *Asian American* or *European American*. At the same time, it ignores the great diversity within the African continent when, for example, it's used as analogous to *German American* or *Japanese American*. More analogous terms would be *Nigerian American* or *Ethiopian American*. Within each culture there are smaller cultures that differ greatly from each other and from the larger culture.

Differences in Meaning   Meaning exists not in words but in people. Consider, for example, the differences in meaning that exist for words such as *religion* to a born-again Christian and an atheist, and *lunch* to a Chinese rice farmer and a Madison Avenue advertising executive. Even though the same word is used, its meanings will vary greatly depending on the listeners' cultural definitions.

The same is true of nonverbal messages. For example, a child who avoids eye contact with an adult may be seen in one culture as deferent (the child is showing respect for the older person) and in another as disrespectful or even defiant (the child is indicating a lack of concern for what the older person is saying).

Differences in Dialect and Accent   **Dialects** are variations in a language, mainly in grammar and semantics. The difference between *language* and *dialect*—at least as viewed by most linguists—is that different languages are mutually *un*intelligible; different dialects are mutually intelligible. For example, a person who grew up with only the English language would not be able to understand Russian, and vice versa. But people speaking different dialects of English (say, Southern and Northern) would be able to understand each other.

It's interesting to note that the Southerner, for example, will perceive the New Englander to speak with an accent but will not perceive another Southerner to have an accent. Similarly, the New Englander will perceive the Southerner to have an accent but not another New Englander. Actually, linguists would argue that everyone speaks a dialect; it's just that we don't perceive speech like ours to be a dialect. We only think of speech different from ours as being a dialect.

Some dialects are popularly (but not scientifically) labeled standard and some are labeled nonstandard. Standard dialect would be the language that is recommended by dictionaries and that is covered in the English handbooks you've likely already experienced. A nonstandard dialect would be any variation from this. This concept of dialect can be extended easily and logically to texting and social media language. Today, the abbreviated texting style would be considered nonstandard; tomorrow, attitudes may be different.

Linguistically, all dialects are equal. Although no one dialect is linguistically superior to any other dialect, it is equally true that judgments are made on the basis of dialect. For example, you would be advised to use standard dialect in applying to the traditional conservative law firm and to write your e-mails to them in Standard English, the kind recommended by the English handbooks. On the other hand, when you're out with friends or texting, you may feel more comfortable using nonstandard forms.

When differences in speech are differences in pronunciation, we refer to them as **accents**, the emphasis or stress you place on various syllables. Just as everyone speaks with a particular dialect, everyone also speaks with a particular accent. Again, we notice accents that are different from our own and, in fact, don't think of speech that sounds like ours as having any accent at all. But all speakers speak with an accent. The "accents" that we probably notice most often are those that occur in speakers who learned the language in their teens or later. The second language is spoken through a kind of filter created by the original language.

Linguistically, everyone speaks with an accent; it's simply a fact of life. In terms of communication, however, we need to recognize that accents are often used by people to pigeonhole and stereotype others; for example, in some people's minds, certain accents are associated with lower class and others with upper class. Some accents are perceived as more credible, more knowledgeable, and more educated than others.

Confront Your Stereotypes

Stereotypes, especially when they operate below the level of conscious awareness, can create serious communication problems (Lyons & Kashima, 2003). Originally, the word *stereotype* was a printing term that referred to the plate that printed the same image over and over. A sociological or psychological **stereotype** is a fixed impression of a group of people. Everyone has attitudinal stereotypes—images of national groups, religious groups, or racial groups or perhaps of criminals, prostitutes, teachers, or plumbers. Consider, for example, if you have any stereotypes of, say, bodybuilders, the opposite sex, a racial group different from your own, members of a religion very different from your own, hard drug users, or college professors. It is very likely that you have stereotypes of several or perhaps even all of these groups. Although we often think of stereotypes as negative ("They're lazy, dirty,

Gender Stereotypes

The stereotype of the male generally defines him as logical, decisive, aggressive, insensitive, unemotional, nonnurturing, talented mechanically, and impatient. The stereotype of the female generally defines her as illogical, variable, nurturing, emotional, sensitive, and untalented mechanically (Cicarelli & White, 2017). *Do your acquaintances maintain any of these stereotypes? What are the short- and long-term effects of such stereotypes?*

and only interested in getting high"), stereotypes also may be positive ("They're smart, hardworking, and extremely loyal").

One researcher has pointed out that stereotypes have enabled criminals to escape or delay capture (Desar, 2013). For example, Boston mobster James Bulger likely escaped detection when on the run because he was significantly older than what stereotypes tell us about the age of mobsters. And Frank Abagnale (portrayed by Leonardo DiCaprio in *Catch Me If You Can*) likely escaped capture because he presented himself as a high-status person, and our stereotypes of high-status people is that they are honest.

If you have these fixed impressions, you may, on meeting a member of a particular group, see that person primarily as a member of that group. Initially this may provide you with some helpful orientation. However, it creates problems when you apply to that person all the characteristics you assign to members of that group without examining the unique individual. If you meet a politician, for example, you may have a host of characteristics for politicians that you can readily apply to this person. To complicate matters further, you may see in the person's behavior the manifestation of various characteristics that you would not see if you did not know that the person was a politician. Because there are few visual and auditory cues in online communications, it's not surprising to find that people form impressions of online communication partners with a heavy reliance on stereotypes (Jacobson, 1999).

Consider, however, another kind of stereotype: you're driving along a dark road and are stopped at a stop sign. A car pulls up beside you and three teenagers jump out and rap on your window. There may be a variety of possible explanations. Perhaps they need help or they want to ask directions. Or they may be about to engage in carjacking. Your self-protective stereotype may help you decide on "carjacking" and lead you to pull away and drive to the safety of a busy service station. In doing that, of course, you may have escaped being carjacked—or you may have failed to help people who needed assistance.

Stereotyping can lead to two major barriers. The tendency to group a person into a class and to respond to that person primarily as a member of that class can lead you to perceive that a person possesses certain qualities (usually negative) that you believe characterize the group to which he or she belongs. Then you will fail to appreciate the multifaceted nature of all people and all groups. For example, consider your stereotype of someone who is deeply into computers. Very likely your image is quite different from the research findings on such individuals, which show that in fact they are as often female as male and are as sociable, popular, and self-assured as their peers who are not into heavy computer use (Schott & Selwyn, 2000).

Stereotyping can also lead you to ignore the unique characteristics of an individual. In this instance, you may fail to benefit from the special contributions each person can bring to an encounter.

Reduce Your Ethnocentrism

Ethnocentrism is the tendency to see others and their behaviors through your own cultural filters, often as distortions of your own behaviors. It's the tendency to evaluate the values, beliefs, and behaviors of your own culture as superior and those of other cultures as inferior instead of different. It often leads you to see your own culture as more positive, logical, and natural than those of other cultures. For example, highly ethnocentric individuals think that other cultures should be more like theirs, that people from other cultures often don't know what's good for them, that the lifestyles of people in other countries are not as good as theirs, and that people from other cultures are not as smart or trustworthy as people from their own culture (Neuliep & McCroskey, 1997). To achieve effective interpersonal communication, you need to see yourself and others as different but as neither inferior nor superior. You need to become aware of the potential

blinders that ethnocentrism might impose—admittedly, not a very easily accomplished task.

Ethnocentrism exists on a continuum (see Figure 2.4). People aren't either ethnocentric or not ethnocentric; rather, most are somewhere between these polar opposites. Of course, your degree of ethnocentrism varies, depending on the group on which you focus. For example, if you're Greek American, you may have a low degree of ethnocentrism when dealing with Italian Americans but a high degree when dealing with Turkish Americans or Japanese Americans. Most important for our purposes is that your degree of ethnocentrism (and we are all ethnocentric to at least some degree) will influence your interpersonal interactions.

VIEWPOINTS

Ethnocentrism

What other suggestions would you offer for decreasing ethnocentrism, increasing cultural awareness and sensitivity, and making intercultural communication more satisfying and more productive?

Recognize Culture Shock

Culture shock is the psychological reaction you experience when you're in a culture very different from your own (Ward, Bochner, & Furnham, 2001; Wan, 2004). Culture shock is normal; most people experience it when entering a new and different culture. Nevertheless, it can seem unpleasant and frustrating when you lack knowledge of the rules and customs of the new society. You may not know basic things such as how to ask

Figure 2.4   The Ethnocentric Continuum

This figure summarizes some of the interconnections between ethnocentrism and communication. In this figure, five areas along the ethnocentrism continuum are identified; in reality, there are as many degrees as there are people. The "communication distances" are general terms that highlight the attitude that dominates that level of ethnocentrism. Under "communications" are some of the major ways people might interact given their particular degree of ethnocentrism. This figure draws on the research of several intercultural researchers (Lukens, 1978; Gudykunst & Kim, 1992; Gudykunst, 1991).

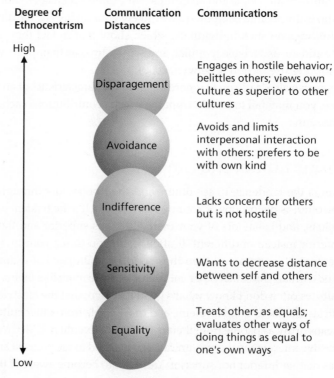

Degree of Ethnocentrism	Communication Distances	Communications
High	Disparagement	Engages in hostile behavior; belittles others; views own culture as superior to other cultures
	Avoidance	Avoids and limits interpersonal interaction with others: prefers to be with own kind
	Indifference	Lacks concern for others but is not hostile
	Sensitivity	Wants to decrease distance between self and others
Low	Equality	Treats others as equals; evaluates other ways of doing things as equal to one's own ways

someone for a favor, pay someone a compliment, how to extend or accept an invitation for dinner, or how early or how late to arrive for an appointment.

Culture shock occurs in four stages (Oberg, 1960). These stages are useful for examining many encounters with the new and the different. Going away to college, moving in with a romantic partner, or joining the military, for example, can also result in culture shock.

- *Stage One: The Honeymoon* At first you experience fascination, even enchantment, with the new culture and its people.
- *Stage Two: The Crisis* Here, the differences between your own culture and the new setting create problems. Feelings of frustration and inadequacy come to the fore. This is the stage at which you experience the actual shock of the new culture.
- *Stage Three: The Recovery* During this period you gain the skills necessary to function effectively. You learn the language and ways of the new culture. Your feelings of inadequacy subside.
- *Stage Four: The Adjustment* At this final stage, you adjust to and come to enjoy the new culture and the new experiences. You may still experience periodic difficulties and strains, but on the whole, the experience is pleasant.

People may also experience culture shock when they return to their original culture after living in a foreign culture, a kind of reverse culture shock (Jandt, 2016). Consider, for example, Peace Corps volunteers who work in rural and economically deprived areas. On returning to Las Vegas or Beverly Hills, they too may experience culture shock. A sailor who serves long periods aboard ship and then returns to an isolated farming community may experience culture shock. In these cases, however, the recovery period is shorter and the sense of inadequacy and frustration is less.

Among the ways recommended to manage the inevitable culture shock are to (1) familiarize yourself with the host nation, (2) form friendship networks to assist you in adjusting, (3) interact with members of the culture and your hosts, and (4) be open to seeking professional help in adjusting to cultural problems (Constantine, Anderson, Berkel, Caldwell, & Utsey, 2005; Britnell, 2004; Chapdelaine & Alexitch, 2004).

Adjust Your Communication

Intercultural communication (in fact, all interpersonal communication) takes place only to the extent that one person can understand the meanings of the words and nonverbal cues of the other—that is, only to the extent that the two individuals share the same system of symbols. Because no two people share the identical meaning system for symbols, each person needs to adjust in all interpersonal interactions, but especially, perhaps, in intercultural interactions. Figure 2.5 illustrates the connection between degrees of cultural difference and the degree of adjustment that is necessary for successful communication.

As you adjust your communications, recognize that each culture has its own rules and customs for communicating (Barna, 1997; Ruben, 1985; Spitzberg, 1991). These rules identify what is appropriate and what is inappropriate (Serewicz & Petronio, 2007). Thus, in American culture, for example, you would call a person you wished to date three or four days in advance; in certain Asian cultures you might call the person's parents weeks or even months in advance. In American culture, you say, as a general friendly gesture and not as a specific invitation, "Come over and pay us a visit." To members of other cultures, this comment is sufficient for the listeners actually to visit at their convenience.

INTERPERSONAL CHOICE POINT
Misusing Linguistic Privilege

You enter a group of racially similar people who are using terms normally considered offensive to refer to themselves. In an effort to fit in and be one of the crowd, you too use such terms. But, contrary to your expectations, you are met with extremely negative nonverbal feedback. *What might you say in response to these reactions?*

- **a.** "Sorry, that was really inappropriate."
- **b.** "Why the negative reaction? You use these terms all the time."
- **c.** "Well, I guess I'm not really one of the group. Thanks for letting me know."
- **d.** Say nothing.
- **e.** Other

Figure 2.5 Cultural Differences and Interpersonal Adjustment

As you can see from this diagram, the greater the cultural differences, the greater the communication adjustment you'll need to make in order to accomplish your interpersonal goal. Try identifying a specific interpersonal encounter in which little adjustment would be necessary and another in which a great deal of adjustment would be necessary. *In what ways are these situations different?*

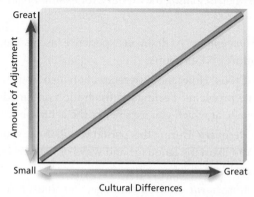

Parents and children, for example, not only have different vocabularies but also, even more important, have different meanings for some of the terms they have in common. People in close relationships—either as intimate friends or as romantic partners—realize that learning the other person's signals takes a long time and often great patience. If you want to understand what another person means—by smiling, by saying "I love you," by arguing about trivial matters, by self-deprecating comments—you have to learn his or her system of signals.

This principle is especially important in intercultural communication—largely because people from different cultures use different signals and/or use the same signals to signify quite different things. As previously mentioned, focused eye contact means honesty and openness in much of the United States. But in Japan and in many Hispanic cultures, that same behavior may signify arrogance or disrespect if it occurs between a youngster and someone significantly older.

An interesting theory focusing on adjustment is the *communication accommodation theory.* This theory holds that speakers adjust to or accommodate the speaking style of their listeners to gain, for example, social approval and greater communication efficiency (Giles, 2008; Giles & Ogay, 2007). For example, research shows that when two people have a similar speech rate, they're attracted more to each other than to people with dissimilar rates (Buller, LePoire, Aune, & Eloy, 1992). Another study found that roommates who had similar communication competence and were both low in verbal aggressiveness were highest in roommate liking and satisfaction (Martin & Anderson, 1995). People even accommodate in their e-mail. For example, responses to messages that contained politeness cues were significantly more polite than responses to e-mails that did not contain such cues (Bunz & Campbell, 2004).

Table 2.5 summarizes these guidelines for more effective intercultural communication.

Table 2.5 In a Nutshell Improving Intercultural Communication

General Guidelines	Specific Strategies
Educate yourself	Read about, view images and videos, and interact with culturally different individuals.
Recognize differences	Observe and respect the differences in meaning, dialect, and accent that exist between yourself and individuals from other cultures. At the same time, don't fail to notice what you also have in common with each other.
Confront your stereotypes	Recognize generalizations that prevent you from seeing an individual as a whole person.
Reduce your ethnocentrism	Recognize your own cultural filters and understand that different behaviors are not distortions of your own, but the product of different cultural upbringings.
Recognize culture shock	When traveling abroad, familiarize yourself with the host nation, form friendship networks, learn from your hosts, and be open to seeking help in adjusting.
Adjust your communication	Understanding the meanings that others have for gestures or for interpersonal interactions will help you change the way you communicate your own messages.

Summary

This chapter explored the nature of culture, identified some key concepts, and offered some principles for more effective intercultural communication.

Culture

2.1 Define *culture*, *enculturation*, and *acculturation* and explain the relevance of culture to interpersonal communication.

1. Culture is the relatively specialized lifestyle (values, beliefs, artifacts, ways of behaving) of a group of people that is passed from one generation to the next by means of communication, not through genes.

2. Enculturation is the process through which you learn the culture into which you're born. Ethnic identity is a commitment to the ways and beliefs of your culture. Acculturation is the process by which you learn the rules and norms of a culture that is different from your native culture and that modifies your original or native culture.

3. An individual's cultural beliefs and values influence all forms of interpersonal communication and therefore need to be considered in any full communication analysis.

4. Culture is especially relevant today because of the demographic changes, increased sensitivity to cultural variation, economic interdependency among nations, advances in communication technology that make intercultural communication easy and inexpensive, and the fact that communication effectiveness in one culture may not be effective in another.

Cultural Differences

2.2 Explain the seven cultural differences identified here and how these impact on interpersonal communication.

5. Individualist cultures emphasize individual values such as power and achievement, whereas collectivist cultures emphasize group values such as cooperation and responsibility to the group.

6. In high-context cultures, much information is in the context or the person; in low-context cultures, information is expected to be made explicit.

7. In high-power-distance cultures, there are large differences in power between people; in low-power-distance cultures, power is more evenly distributed throughout the population.

8. Masculine cultures emphasize assertiveness, ambition, and competition; feminine cultures emphasize compromise and negotiation.

9. High-ambiguity-tolerant cultures feel little threatened by uncertainty; it's accepted as it comes. Low-ambiguity-tolerant cultures feel uncomfortable with uncertainty and seek to avoid it.

10. Long-term-oriented cultures promote the importance of future rewards, whereas short-term-oriented cultures look more to the past and the present.

11. Cultures high in indulgence emphasize the gratification of desires and having fun; cultures high in restraint emphasize the curbing and regulation of pleasures and fun.

Principles for Effective Intercultural Communication

2.3 Define *intercultural communication* and explain the principles for making intercultural communication more effective.

12. Intercultural communication is communication between people who have different cultures, beliefs, values, and ways of behaving.

13. Some intercultural communication guidelines include educating yourself, recognizing differences (between yourself and others, within the culturally different group, in meanings, and in dialects and accents), confronting your stereotypes, reducing your ethnocentrism, recognizing culture shock, and adjusting your communication.

Key Terms

accent	cultural assimilation	ethnic identity
acculturation	culture	ethnocentrism
ambiguity tolerance	culture shock	feminine culture
cisgender	dialect	gender
collectivist culture	enculturation	gender identity

high-context culture

high-power-distance culture

individualist culture

indulgence

intercultural communication

long-term orientation

low-context culture

low-power-distance culture

masculine culture

power distance

race

restraint

sex

short-term orientation

stereotype

transgender

CHAPTER THREE

Perception of the Self and Others

Accurate perception is often difficult. *Learning the strategies for increasing accuracy will help.*

Chapter Topics

The Self in Interpersonal Communication

Perception in Interpersonal Communication

Impression Formation

Impression Management: Goals and Strategies

Learning Objectives

3.1 Define *self-concept, self-awareness,* and *self-esteem,* and identify the suggestions for increasing awareness and esteem.

3.2 Explain the five stages of perception and how they influence how you receive messages.

3.3 Define the major impression formation processes and the ways to increase accuracy in perception.

3.4 Explain the impression management strategies that may help you to be liked, to be believed, to excuse failure, to secure help, to hide faults, to be followed, and to confirm your self-image.

This chapter discusses two interrelated topics—the self (including self-concept, self-awareness, and self-esteem) and the nature of perception. Then these concepts are applied by looking at the ways in which you form impressions of others and how you manage the impressions of yourself that you convey to others.

The Self in Interpersonal Communication

3.1 Define *self-concept*, *self-awareness*, and *self-esteem* and identify the suggestions for increasing awareness and esteem.

Let's begin this discussion by focusing on several fundamental aspects of the self: self-concept (the way you see yourself), self-awareness (your insight into and knowledge about yourself), and self-esteem (the value you place on yourself). In these discussions, you'll see how these dimensions influence and are influenced by the way you communicate.

Self-Concept

You no doubt have an image of who you are; this is your **self-concept**. It consists of your feelings and thoughts about your strengths and weaknesses, your abilities and limitations, and your aspirations and worldview (Black, 1999). Your self-concept develops from at least four sources: (1) the image of you that others have and that they reveal to you, (2) the comparisons you make between yourself and others, (3) the teachings of your culture, and (4) the way you interpret and evaluate your own thoughts and behaviors (previewed in Figure 3.1).

Figure 3.1   The Sources of Self-Concept

This diagram depicts the four sources of self-concept, the four contributors to how you see yourself: (1) others' images of you; (2) social comparisons; (3) cultural teachings; and (4) your own observations, interpretations, and evaluations. As you read about self-concept, consider the influence of each factor throughout your life. *Are the influences of each factor likely to change with age? For example, do the same factors influence you in the same way they did when you were a preteen? Which will likely influence you the most 25 or 30 years from now?*

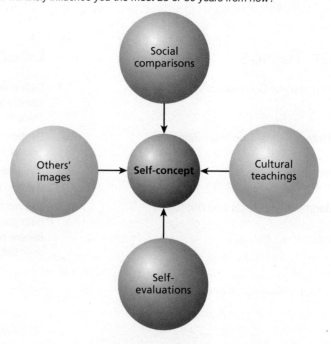

Others' Images   According to Charles Horton Cooley's (1922) concept of the *looking-glass self,* when you want to discover, say, how friendly or how assertive you are, you look at the image of yourself that others reveal to you through the way they treat you and react to you (Hensley, 1996). You look especially to those who are most significant in your life. As a child, for example, you look to your parents and then to your teachers. As an adult, you may look to your friends, romantic partners, and colleagues at work. If these important others think highly of you, you'll see this positive image of yourself reflected in their behaviors; if they think little of you, you'll see a more negative image.

Social Comparisons   Another way you develop self-concept is by comparing yourself with others, most often with your peers (Festinger, 1954). For example, after an exam, you probably want to know how you performed relative to the other students in your class. This gives you a clearer idea of how effectively you performed. If you play on a baseball team, it's important to know your batting average in comparison with the batting averages of others on the team. You gain a different perspective when you see yourself in comparison to your peers. And social networks have provided a great opportunity to engage in comparisons. This seems especially true for women, who, research finds, use social media sites to compare themselves to others. Men, on the other hand, use social media more to look at the profiles of others and to search for additional friends (Haferkamp, Eimler, Papadakis, & Kruck, 2012).

For good or ill, social media have provided you with the tools (all very easy to use) to compare yourself to others and thus to estimate your individual worth or make you feel better about yourself. Here are a half dozen ways social media enable you to find out where you stand.

- *Search engine reports*   Type in your name on Google, Bing, or Yahoo!, for example, and you'll see the number of websites on which your name (and similarly named others) appears. Type in a colleague's name and you get his or her "score," which, you're no doubt hoping, is lower than yours.

- *Network spread*   Your number of friends on Facebook or your contacts on LinkedIn or Plaxo is in some ways a measure of your potential influence, a practice that seems to encourage friend-collecting behavior. Look at a friend's profile and you have your comparison. And you can easily find websites that will surf the Internet to help you contact more social network friends. Recently, for example, the State Department spent some $630,000 to attract friends and followers to its Facebook and Twitter accounts (McKelway, 2013).

- *Online influence*   Network sites such as Klout and Peer Index provide you with a score (from 0 to 100) of your online influence. Your Klout score, for example, is a combination of your "true reach"—the number of people you influence, "amplification"—the degree to which you influence them, and "network"—the influence of your network. Postrank Analytics, on the other hand, provides you with a measure of engagement—the degree to which people interact with, pay attention to, read, or comment on what you write.

- *Twitter activities*   The number of times you tweet might be one point of comparison but more important is the number of times you are tweeted about or your tweets are repeated (retweets). Twitalyzer can provide you with a three-part score (an impact score, a Klout score, and a Peer Index score) and can also enable you to search the "twitter elite" for the world as well as for any specific area (you can search by zip code). Assuming your Twitter score is what you'd like it to be, a single click enables you to post this score on your own Twitter page.

- *Blog presence*   Your blog presence is readily available from your "stats" tab, where you can see how many people visited your blog since inception or over the past year, month, week, or day. And you'll also see a map of the world indicating where people who are visiting your blog come from.

- *References to written works*   Google Scholar, for example, enables you to see how many other writers have cited your works (and how many cited the works of the

Social Comparisons

Consider the ways in which you engage in social comparisons. *Do you engage more in downward social comparison (comparing yourself to those you know are inferior to you in some way) or in upward social comparison (comparing yourself to those who you think are better than you)? How do you feel about yourself when making these two very different comparisons?*

person you're comparing) and the works in which you were cited. And, of course, Amazon and other online book dealers provide rankings of your books along with a star system based on reviewers' comments.

Cultural Teachings Through your parents, teachers, and the media, your culture instills in you a variety of beliefs, values, and attitudes—about success (how you define it and how you should achieve it); about your religion, race, or nationality; and about the ethical principles you should follow in business and in your personal life. These teachings provide benchmarks against which you can measure yourself. For example, achieving what your culture defines as success contributes to a positive self-concept. A perceived failure to achieve what your culture promotes (for example, not being in a permanent relationship by the time you're 30) may contribute to a negative self-concept.

Self-Evaluations Much in the way others form images of you based on what you do, you also react to your own behavior; you interpret and evaluate it. These interpretations and evaluations help to form your self-concept. For example, let us say that you believe lying is wrong. If you lie, you will evaluate this behavior in terms of your internalized beliefs about lying. You'll thus react negatively to your own behavior. You may, for example, experience guilt if your behavior contradicts your beliefs. In contrast, let's say that you tutor another student and help him or her pass a course. You will probably evaluate this behavior positively; you will feel good about this behavior and, as a result, about yourself.

Self-Awareness

Your **self-awareness** represents the extent to which you know yourself, your strengths and your weaknesses, your thoughts and feelings, and your personality tendencies. Understanding how your self-concept develops is one way to increase your self-awareness: The more you understand about why you view yourself as you do, the more you will understand who you are. Additional insight is gained by looking at self-awareness through the Johari model of the self, or your four selves (Luft, 1984).

Your Four Selves Self-awareness is neatly explained by the model of the four selves—the Johari window. This model, presented in Figure 3.2, has four basic areas, or quadrants, each of which represents a somewhat different self: the **open self**, the **blind self**, the **hidden self**, and the **unknown self**. The Johari model emphasizes that the several aspects of the self are not separate pieces but are interactive parts of a whole. Each part is dependent on each other part. Like that of interpersonal communication, this model of the self is transactional. Each person's Johari window is different, and each individual's window varies from one time to another and from one interpersonal situation to another. Figure 3.3, for example, illustrates two possible configurations.

- The *open self* represents all the information about you—behaviors, attitudes, feelings, desires, motivations, and ideas—that you and others know. The type of information included here might range from your name, skin color, and sex to your age, political and religious affiliations, and financial situation. Your open self varies in size depending on the situation you're in and the person with whom you're interacting. Some people, for example, make you feel comfortable and supported; to them, you open yourself wide, but to others you may prefer to leave most of yourself closed.

Figure 3.2 The Johari Window

Visualize this model as representative of yourself. The entire model is of constant size, but each section can vary from very small to very large. As one section becomes smaller, one or more of the others grows larger. Similarly, as one section grows, one or more of the others must get smaller. For example, if you reveal a secret and thereby enlarge your open self, this shrinks your hidden self. This disclosure may in turn lead to a decrease in the size of your blind self (if your disclosure influences other people to reveal what they know about you but that you have not known). *How would you draw your Johari window to show yourself when interacting with your parents? With your friends on Facebook or another social media site? With your college instructors?* The name *Johari*, by the way, comes from the first names of the two people who developed the model, Joseph Luft and Harry Ingham.

SOURCE: *Group Processes: An Introduction to Group Dynamics*, 3d ed. by Joseph Luft, 1984, p. 60. Reprinted by permission of Mayfield Publishing Company, Mountain View, CA.

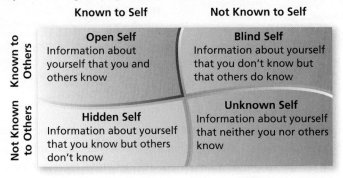

- The *blind self* represents all the things about you that others know but of which you're ignorant. These may include relatively insignificant habits like saying "You know," gestures like rubbing your nose when you get angry, or traits such as a distinct body odor; they may also include details as significant as defense mechanisms, fight strategies, or repressed experiences.

- The *hidden self* contains all that you know of yourself that you keep secret. In any interaction, this area includes everything you don't want to reveal, whether it's relevant or irrelevant to the conversation. At the extremes of the hidden-self spectrum, we have the overdisclosers and the underdisclosers. The overdisclosers tell all. They tell you their marital difficulties, their children's problems, their financial status, and just about everything else. The underdisclosers tell nothing. They talk about you but not about themselves.

- The *unknown self* represents truths about yourself that neither you nor others know. Sometimes this unknown self is revealed through temporary changes brought about by special experimental conditions such as hypnosis or sensory deprivation. Sometimes this area is revealed by certain projective tests or dreams. Mostly, however, it's revealed by the fact that you're constantly learning things about yourself that you didn't know before (things that were previously in the unknown self)—for example, that you become defensive when someone asks you a question or voices disagreement, or that you compliment others in the hope of being complimented back.

Growing in Self-Awareness   Here are five ways you can increase your self-awareness:

- *Ask yourself about yourself.* One way to ask yourself about yourself is to take an informal "Who Am I?" test (Bugental & Zelen, 1950; Grace & Cramer, 2003). Title a piece of paper "Who Am I?" and write 10, 15, or 20 times "I am . . ." Then complete each of the sentences. Try not to give only positive or socially acceptable responses; just respond with what comes to mind first. Take another piece of paper and divide it into two columns; label one column "Strengths" and the other column "Weaknesses." Fill in each column as quickly as possible. Using these first two tests as a base, take a third piece of paper, title it "Self-Improvement Goals," and complete the statement "I want to improve my . . ." as many times as you can in five minutes. Because you're constantly changing, these self-perceptions and goals also change, so update them frequently.

Figure 3.3   Johari Windows of Different Structures

Notice that as one self grows, one or more of the other selves shrink. Assume that these models depict the self-awareness and self-disclosure of two different people. *How would you describe the type of communication (especially self-disclosure) that might characterize each of these two people?*

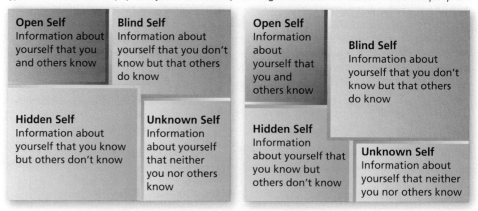

- *Listen to others.* You can learn a lot about yourself by seeing yourself as others do. In most interpersonal interactions—whether they be face-to-face or online, people comment on you in some way—on what you do, what you say, how you look. Sometimes these comments are explicit; most often they're found in the way others look at you, in what they talk about, in what they tweet, in the pictures they post, in their interest in what you say or post. Pay close attention to this verbal and nonverbal information.

- *Actively seek information about yourself.* Actively seek out information to reduce your blind self. You need not be so obvious as to say, "Tell me about myself" or "What do you think of me?" But you can use everyday situations to gain self-information: "Do you think I was assertive enough when asking for the raise?" Or "Would I be thought too forward if I invited myself for dinner?" Do not, of course, seek this information constantly; your friends would quickly find others with whom to interact.

- *See your different selves.* Each person with whom you have an interpersonal relationship views you differently; to each, you're a somewhat different person. Yet you are really all of these selves, and your self-concept is influenced by each of these views as they are reflected back to you in everyday interpersonal interactions. For starters, visualize how you're seen by your mother, your father, your teachers, your best friend, the stranger you sat next to on the bus, your employer, your neighbor's child. The experience will give you new and valuable perspectives on yourself.

- *Increase your open self.* When you reveal yourself to others and increase your open self, you also reveal yourself to yourself. At the very least, you bring into clearer focus what you may have buried within. As you discuss yourself, you may see connections that you had previously missed, and with the aid of feedback from others you may gain still more insight. Also, by increasing the open self, you increase the likelihood that a meaningful and intimate dialogue will develop, which will enable you to get to know yourself better.

Self-Esteem

Self-esteem is a measure of how valuable you think you are. If you have high self-esteem, you think highly of yourself; if you have low self-esteem, you tend to view yourself negatively. Self-esteem includes cognitive or thinking, affective or emotional, and behavioral components (Reasoner, 2010).

- *Cognitive self-esteem* refers to your thinking about your strengths and weaknesses, about who you are versus who you'd like to be. What is your ideal self? How close are you to achieving this ideal self?

- *Affective self-esteem* refers to your feelings about yourself in light of your analysis of your strengths and weaknesses. For example, do you feel pleased with yourself? Does your analysis lead you to feel dissatisfied and perhaps depressed?
- *Behavioral self-esteem* refers to verbal and nonverbal behaviors such as your disclosures, your assertiveness, your conflict strategies, your gestures. Do you assert yourself in group situations? Do you allow others to take advantage of you? Are you confident enough to disclose who you really are?

Before reading further about this topic, think about your self-esteem by considering the following six statements. Respond with T for true if the statement describes you at least some significant part of the time, or with F for false if the statement describes you rarely or never.

____ 1. Generally, I feel I have to be successful in all things.

____ 2. Several of my acquaintances are often critical or negative of what I do and how I think.

____ 3. Despite outward signs of success, I still feel unsuccessful.

____ 4. I often tackle projects that I know are impossible to complete to my satisfaction.

____ 5. When I focus on the past, I focus more often on my failures than on my successes and on my negative rather than on my positive qualities.

____ 6. I make little effort to improve my personal and social skills.

True responses to the questions generally suggest ways of thinking that can get in the way of building positive self-esteem. False responses indicate that you are thinking much like a self-esteem coach would want you to think. The following discussion elaborates on these six statements/beliefs and illustrates why each of them creates problems for the development of healthy self-esteem.

The basic idea behind self-esteem is that when you feel good about yourself—about who you are and what you're capable of doing—you will perform better. When you think you're a success, you're more likely to act like you're a success. Conversely, when you think you're a failure, you're more likely to act like you're a failure. When you reach for the phone to ask the most popular student in the school for a date and you visualize yourself being successful and effective, you're more likely to give a good impression. If, on the other hand, you think you're going to forget what you want to say or stutter or say something totally stupid, you're less likely to be successful.

Low self-esteem is learned (Lancer, 2013). Somewhere, somehow you learned that your feelings are not justified or that you aren't capable of doing this or that. And because it's learned behavior, it's possible to change this, although it's not an easy process (Gross, 2006). Here are six suggestions for increasing self-esteem that parallel the questions in the self-test (also see Figure 3.4).

Attack Self-Destructive Beliefs Challenge **self-destructive beliefs**—ideas you have about yourself that are unproductive or that make it more difficult for you to achieve your goals (Einhorn, 2006; Butler, 1981; Gross, 2006). Often, these self-destructive beliefs tell you that you *should* be able to achieve unrealistic goals. Here, for example, are some beliefs that are likely to prove self-destructive:

- I *should* be liked by everyone.
- I *should* be successful in everything I do.
- I *should* always win.
- I *should* be totally in control of my life.
- I *should* always be productive.

These beliefs set unrealistically high standards, and therefore almost always end in failure. As a result, you may develop a negative self-image, seeing yourself as

Figure 3.4 Climbing to Higher Self-Esteem

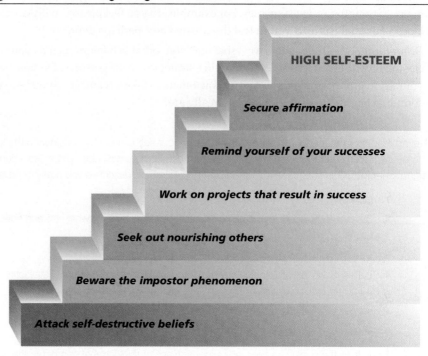

HIGH SELF-ESTEEM

Secure affirmation

Remind yourself of your successes

Work on projects that result in success

Seek out nourishing others

Beware the impostor phenomenon

Attack self-destructive beliefs

someone who constantly fails. So replace these self-destructive beliefs with more productive ones, such as these:

- It would be nice to be loved by everyone, but it isn't necessary to my happiness.
- It's nice to be successful but impossible to be successful at everything.
- It would be nice if I always won but no one can always win. And I don't have to win all the time to be happy. I can deal with losing.
- I can't possibly control everything that has an impact on my life. Only some things are under my control.
- There is a limit on what one person can do; it's okay if I do what I can do and don't do the rest.

Seek out Nourishing People Psychologist Carl Rogers (1970) drew a distinction between noxious and nourishing people. Noxious people criticize and find fault with just about everything. Nourishing people, on the other hand, are positive and optimistic. Most important, they reward us, they stroke us, they make us feel good about ourselves. To enhance your self-esteem, seek out these people. At the same time, avoid noxious people—those who make you feel negatively about yourself. Seek to become more nourishing yourself so that you can build up others' self-esteem.

Identification with people similar to yourself also seems to increase self-esteem. For example, deaf people who identified with the larger deaf community had greater self-esteem than those who didn't so identify (Jambor & Elliott, 2005). Similarly, identification with your cultural group also seems helpful in fostering positive self-esteem (McDonald, McCabe, Yeh, Lau, Garland, & Hough, 2005).

Beware the Impostor Phenomenon The **impostor phenomenon** refers to the tendency to disregard outward signs of success and to consider yourself an "impostor," a fake, a fraud, one who doesn't really deserve to be considered successful (Cuddy, 2015; Clance, 1985; Harvey & Katz, 1985). Even though others may believe you are a success, you "know" that they are wrong. As you might expect, this tendency is more likely in new situations—a new job, say. One of the dangers of this belief is that it may prevent you from seeking advancement in your profession, believing you won't be up to the task. Becoming aware that such beliefs are not uncommon and that they are not necessarily permanent should help relieve some of these misperceptions. Another useful aid is to develop a relationship with an honest and knowledgeable mentor who will not only teach you the ropes but will let you know that you are successful. At the same time, be careful of the Lake Wobegon effect—a concept taken from Garrison Keillor's novel, *Lake Wobegon*, in which everyone in the town was above average; it refers to the tendency to see ourselves as better, more competent, and more intelligent than our peers without any real evidence or reason.

Work on Projects that will Result in Success   Some people want to fail (or so it seems). Often, they select projects that result in failure simply because these projects are impossible to complete. Avoid this trap and select projects that result in success. Each success helps to build your self-esteem. Each success, too, will make the next success a little easier. If a project does fail, recognize that this does not mean that you're a failure. Everyone fails somewhere along the line. Failure is something that happens to you; it's not something you've created, and it's not something inside you. Failing once does not mean that you will fail the next time. Learn to put failure in perspective.

Remind Yourself of Your Successes   Some people have a tendency to focus on and to exaggerate their failures, their missed opportunities, their social mistakes. However, others witnessing these failures give them much less importance (Savitsky, Epley, & Gilovich, 2001). If your objective is to correct what you did wrong or to identify the skills that you need to correct these failures, then focusing on failures can have some positive value. But if you focus only on failure without forming any plans for correction, then you're probably just making life more difficult for yourself and limiting your self-esteem. To counteract the tendency to recall failures, remind yourself of your successes. Recall these successes both intellectually and emotionally. Realize why they were successes, and relive the emotional experience when you sank that winning basketball, or aced that test, or helped that friend overcome personal problems. And while you're at it, recall your positive qualities.

Secure Affirmation   An affirmation is simply a statement asserting that something is true. In discussions of self-concept and self-awareness, the word **affirmation** is used to refer to positive statements about yourself, statements asserting that something good or positive is true of you. It's frequently recommended that you remind yourself of your successes with affirmations—that you focus on your good deeds; on your positive qualities, strengths, and virtues; and on your productive and meaningful relationships with friends, loved ones, and relatives (Aronson, Cohen, & Nail, 1998; Aronson, Wilson, Akert, & Sommers, 2016).

One useful way to look at self-affirmation is in terms of "I am," "I can," and "I will" statements (www.coping.org).

- *"I am" statements* focus on your self-image—on how you see yourself—and might include, for example, "I am a worthy person," "I am responsible," "I am capable of loving," and "I am a good team player."

VIEWPOINTS

Self-Esteem and Facebook

The difference between those with high and those with low self-esteem is even shown in how they post on social media (Nie & Sundar, 2013). Those with high self-esteem post information about their family, work, and education. Those with low self-esteem do this less and spend much of their social media time monitoring their wall and deleting any posts or photos that may reflect on them negatively. *How do you see the relationship between self-esteem and posting to social media?*

VIEWPOINTS

The Gift Economy

In one experiment, three types of "invitations" to use a flower delivery service were offered: Group 1 users were offered $10 to invite friends to use the service; Group 2 users were offered the chance to give a $10 discount to someone they invited, but they received no money themselves; and Group 3 users and invitees were each offered $5. Which group of users do you think sent their friends more invitations? The answer is that Groups 2 and 3 generated more "sends" than did Group 1 (Aral, 2013). The researcher notes that this conforms to the notion of a gift economy, where being generous increases one's status. *Have you seen examples of this gift economy in your own social media experiences? How does this gift economy relate to self-esteem?*

- *"I can" statements* focus on your abilities and might include, for example, "I can accept my past but also let it go," "I can learn to be a more responsive partner," "I can assert myself when appropriate," and "I can control my anger."
- *"I will" statements* focus on useful and appropriate goals you want to achieve and might include, for example, "I will get over my guilty feelings," "I will study more effectively," "I will act more supportively," and "I will not take on more responsibility than I can handle."

The idea behind this advice is that the way you talk to yourself influences what you think of yourself. If you affirm yourself—if you tell yourself that you're a friendly person, that you can be a leader, that you will succeed on the next test—you will soon come to feel more positively about yourself. Before reading on, reflect on your nine statements. How did writing these and thinking about them make you feel?

Some researchers, however, argue that such affirmations—although extremely popular in self-help books—may not be very helpful. These critics contend that if you have low self-esteem, you're not going to believe your self-affirmations because you don't have a high opinion of yourself to begin with (Paul, 2001). According to this view, the alternative to self-affirmation is securing affirmation from others. You do this by, for example, becoming more interpersonally competent and interacting with more positive people. In this way, you'd get more positive feedback from others—which, these researchers argue, is more helpful than self-talk in raising self-esteem.

Table 3.1 summarizes these basic concepts of the self that are at the heart of all interpersonal communication.

Table 3.1 In a Nutshell The Self Concept

	Definition
Self-concept	the image you have of who you are, derived from others' images of you, social comparisons, cultural teachings, and self-evaluations
Self-awareness	the extent to which you know yourself and the information in your open, blind, hidden, and unknown self
Self-esteem	the extent to which you value yourself which can be increased through, for example, attacking self-destructive beliefs, being aware of the impostor phenomenon, seeking out nourishing others, working on successful projects, reminding yourself of your successes, and securing affirmation

Perception in Interpersonal Communication

3.2 Explain the five stages of perception and how they influence how you receive messages.

Perception is the process by which you become aware of objects, events, and especially people through your senses: sight, smell, taste, touch, and hearing. Perception is an active, not a passive, process. Your perceptions result both from what exists in the outside world and from your own experiences, desires, needs and wants, loves, and hatreds. Among the reasons perception is so important in interpersonal communication is that it influences your communication choices. The messages you send and listen to

Figure 3.5 The Stages of Perception

Perception occurs in stages. Understanding how perception works will help you make your own perceptions (of yourself and of others) more accurate.

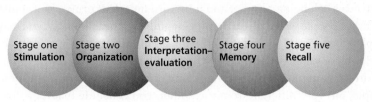

depend on how you see the world, on how you evaluate specific situations, and on what you think of yourself and of the people with whom you interact.

Interpersonal perception is a continuous series of processes that blend into one another. For convenience of discussion, we can separate interpersonal perception into five stages: (1) You sense, you pick up some kind of stimulation; (2) you organize the stimuli in some way; (3) you interpret and evaluate what you perceive; (4) you store it in memory; and (5) you retrieve it when needed (Figure 3.5).

Stage One: Stimulation

At this first stage of perception, your sense organs are stimulated—you hear a new song, see a friend, smell someone's perfume, taste an orange, receive an instant message, feel another's sweaty palm. Change and newness seem to be particularly stimulating and often get your attention. This is one of the reasons that changing your profile photo gets you more attention; you "look new" (Roper, 2014). Contrast also seems to prove especially stimulating and attention-getting; if there are six or seven similar items and one different, you're likely to focus on the different one.

It's especially important to understand that at this first stage you perceive selectively; you engage in what is called **selective perception**, a general term that includes selective attention and selective exposure:

- In **selective attention**, you attend to those things that you anticipate will fulfill your needs or will prove enjoyable. For example, when daydreaming in class, you don't hear what the instructor is saying until your name is called. Your selective attention mechanism then focuses your senses on your name. As you can appreciate from searching the web and especially social media sites, selective attention is made more difficult by the enormity of information available on every computer screen and the varied ways in which it comes at you, for example, with pop-up images and videos and advertisements you're forced to listen to.

- Through **selective exposure**, you expose yourself to people or messages that confirm your existing beliefs, contribute to your objectives, or prove satisfying in some way. For example, after you buy a car, you're more apt to read and listen to advertisements for the car you just bought because these messages tell you that you made the right decision. At the same time, you are likely to avoid advertisements for the cars that you considered but eventually rejected because these messages would tell you that you made the wrong decision.

Stage Two: Organization

At the second stage, you organize the information your senses pick up. Three interesting ways in which people organize their perceptions are by rules, by schemata, and by scripts. Let's look at each briefly.

Organization by Rules In the organization of perceptions by rules, one frequently used is the **rule of proximity** or physical closeness: Things that are physically close to each other are perceived as a unit. Thus, using this rule, you tend to perceive people who are often together, or messages spoken one immediately after the other, as units, as belonging together.

Another is the **rule of similarity**: Things that are physically similar (they look alike) are perceived as belonging together and forming a unit. This principle of similarity may lead you to see people who dress alike as belonging together. Similarly, you may assume that people who work at the same jobs, who are of the same religion, who live in the same building, or who talk with the same accent belong together.

The **rule of contrast** is the opposite of similarity: When items (people or messages, for example) are very different from each other, you conclude that they don't belong together; they're too different from each other to be part of the same unit. If you're the only one who shows up at an informal gathering dressed unlike anyone else in the group, you'll be seen as not belonging to the group because you contrast too much with the other people present.

Organization by Schemata Another way you organize material is by creating **schemata**, mental templates that help you organize the millions of items of information you come into contact with every day (as well as those you already have in memory). *Schemata*, the plural of **schema** (though *schemas* is used in many texts), may thus be viewed as general ideas about people (e.g., about Pat and Chris, Japanese people, Baptists, Texans), about yourself (your qualities, abilities, liabilities), or about social roles (the characteristics of a police officer, professor, multibillionaire CEO).

You develop schemata from your own experience—actual as well as via television, reading, the Internet, and hearsay. You might have a schema for college athletes, for example, and this might include an image of college athletes as strong, ambitious, academically weak, and egocentric.

Organization by Scripts A **script** is really a type of schema, but because it's a different type, it's given a different name. A script is an organized body of information about some action, event, or procedure. It's a general idea of how some event should play out or unfold; it's the rules governing events and their sequence. For example, you probably have a script for eating in a restaurant, with the actions organized into a pattern something like this: Enter, take a seat, review the menu, order from the menu, eat your food, ask for the bill, leave a tip, pay the bill, and exit the restaurant. Similarly, you probably have scripts for how you do laundry, how an interview is to be conducted, the stages you go through in introducing someone to someone else, and the way you ask for a date.

As you can appreciate, rules, schemata, and scripts are useful shortcuts to simplify your understanding, remembering, and recalling information about people and events. They also enable you to generalize, make connections, and otherwise profit from previously acquired knowledge. If you didn't have these shortcuts, you'd have to treat every person or action differently from each other person or action. This would make every experience a new one, totally unrelated to anything you already know. As you'll see in the next stage, however, these shortcuts may mislead you; they may contribute to your remembering things that are consistent with your schemata (even if they didn't occur) and to your distorting or forgetting information that is inconsistent.

Stage Three: Interpretation–Evaluation

The **interpretation–evaluation** step in perception (a combined term because the two processes cannot be separated) is greatly influenced by your experiences; needs; wants; values; beliefs about the way things are or should be; expectations; physical and emotional state; and so on. Your interpretation–evaluation is influenced by your rules, schemata, and scripts as well as by your gender; for example, women have been found to view others more positively than men (Winquist, Mohr, & Kenny, 1998).

For example, on meeting a new person who is introduced to you as Ben Williams, a college football player, you're likely to apply your schema for athletes to this person and view him as strong, ambitious, academically weak, and egocentric. You will, in other words, see this person through the filter of your schema and evaluate him according to your schema for college athletes. Similarly, when viewing someone performing some series of actions (say, eating in a restaurant), you apply your script to this event and view the event through the script. You will interpret the actions of the diner as appropriate or inappropriate depending on your script for this behavior and the ways in which the diner performed the sequence of actions.

Judgments about members of other cultures are often ethnocentric. Because your schemata and scripts are created on the basis of your own cultural beliefs and experiences, you can easily (but inappropriately) apply these to members of other cultures. And so it's easy to infer that when members of other cultures do things that conform to your own scripts, they're right; and when they do things that contradict your scripts, they're wrong—a classic example of ethnocentric thinking. This tendency can easily contribute to intercultural misunderstandings.

Stage Four: Memory

Your perceptions and their interpretations–evaluations are put into memory; they're stored so that you may retrieve them at some later time. So, for example, you have in memory your schema for college athletes and the fact that Ben Williams is a football player. Ben Williams is then stored in memory with "cognitive tags" that tell you that he's strong, ambitious, academically weak, and egocentric. Despite the fact that you've not witnessed Ben's strength or ambitions and have no idea of his academic record or his psychological profile, you still may store your memory of Ben along with the qualities that make up your schema for "college athletes."

Now let's say that at different times you hear that Ben failed Spanish I, normally an A or B course at your school; that Ben got an A in chemistry, normally a tough course; and that Ben is transferring to Harvard as a theoretical physics major. Schemata act as filters or gatekeepers; they allow certain information to get stored in relatively objective form, much as you heard or read it, and may distort other information or prevent it from getting stored. As a result, these three pieces of information about Ben may get stored very differently in your memory.

For example, you may readily store the information that Ben failed Spanish because it's consistent with your schema; it fits neatly into the template you have of college athletes. Information that's consistent with your schema—as in this example—strengthens your schema and makes it more resistant to change (Aronson, Wilson, Akert, & Sommers, 2016). Depending on the strength of your schema, you may also store in memory (even though you didn't hear it) that Ben did poorly in other courses as well. The information that Ben got an A in chemistry, because it contradicts your schema (it just doesn't seem right), may easily be distorted or lost. The information that Ben is transferring to Harvard, however, is a bit different. This information is also inconsistent with your schema, but it is so drastically inconsistent that you begin to look at this mindfully and may even begin to question your schema or perhaps view Ben as an exception to the general rule. In either case, you're going to etch Ben's transferring to Harvard very clearly in your mind.

Stage Five: Recall

The **recall** stage of perception involves accessing the information you have stored in memory. Let's say that at some later date you

> ### INTERPERSONAL CHOICE POINT
> Reversing a First Impression
>
> You made a really bad first impression in your interpersonal communication class. You meant to be sarcastically funny but came off as merely sarcastic. *What might you say to lessen the impact of this first impression?*
>
> **a.** "I'm sorry, I meant to be funny but I see it didn't come off as I thought it would."
> **b.** "This really isn't me; I don't know why I said that."
> **c.** "Why the negative reaction? You probably feel the same way but just don't say it."
> **d.** Say nothing.
> **e.** Other

want to retrieve your information about Ben because he's the topic of discussion among you and a few friends. But your memory isn't *reproductive;* you don't simply reproduce what you've heard or seen. Rather, you *reconstruct* what you've heard or seen into a whole that is meaningful to you—depending in great part on your schemata and scripts. It's this reconstruction that you store in memory. When you want to retrieve this information, you may recall it with a variety of inaccuracies:

- You're likely to recall information that is consistent with your schema; in fact, you may not even be recalling the specific information (say, about Ben) but may actually just be recalling your schema (which contains information about college athletes and, because of this, also about Ben).
- You may fail to recall information that is inconsistent with your schema; you have no place to put that information, so you easily lose it or forget it.
- You may recall information that drastically contradicts your schema because it forces you to think about (and perhaps rethink) your schema and its accuracy; it may even force you to revise your schema for college athletes in general.

Table 3.2 summarizes these five stages of interpersonal perception.

Table 3.2 In a Nutshell The Stages of Perception

Stage	Action
Stimulation	your sense organs pick up some signal
Organization	you put these signals into some kind of organized pattern, by rules, schemata, or scripts
Interpretation–evaluation	you give these signals some kind of meaning
Memory	you store this meaning for later retrieval
Recall	you access this information that you've stored in memory

UNDERSTANDING *INTERPERSONAL SKILLS*

Other-Orientation: A Focus on the Other Person and that Person's Perspective

Other-orientation is a quality of interpersonal effectiveness that highlights the focus on the other person rather than on the self (Spitzberg & Hecht, 1984; Dindia & Timmerman, 2003). The more you focus on the other person, the more accurately you're likely to understand this person and the more effectively you'll be able to adapt your own messages to them. Other-orientation involves communicating attentiveness to and interest in the other person and in what the person says.

Communicating with Other-Orientation

You'll recognize the following behaviors in those with whom you enjoy talking. As you read these suggestions, you'll note that these are also likely to serve the impression formation function of being liked.

- *Show consideration.* Demonstrate respect; for example, ask if it's all right to tell your troubles to someone before doing so, or ask if your phone call comes at a good time.
- *Acknowledge the other person's feelings as legitimate.* Expressions such as "You're right" or "I can understand why you're so angry" help focus the interaction on the other person and confirm that you're listening.

- *Acknowledge the other person.* Recognize the importance of the other person. Ask for suggestions, opinions, and clarification. This ensures that you understand what the other person is saying from that person's point of view.
- *Focus your messages on the other person.* Use open-ended questions to involve the other person in the interaction (as opposed to questions that merely ask for a yes or no answer), and make statements that directly address the person. Use focused eye contact and appropriate facial expressions; smile, nod, and lean toward the other person.
- *Grant permission.* Let the other person know that it's okay to express (or not to express) her or his feelings. A simple statement such as "I know how difficult it is to talk about feelings" opens up the topic of feelings and gives the other person permission either to pursue such a discussion or to say nothing.

Working with Other-Orientation

How you would rate your general other-orientation? Can you identify situations in which you are especially likely to forget other-orientation? In what ways might you become more other-oriented?

Impression Formation

3.3 Define the major impression formation processes and the ways to increase accuracy in perception.

Impression formation (sometimes referred to as *person perception*) consists of a variety of processes that you go through in forming an impression of another person. Each of these perception processes has pitfalls and potential dangers.

Before reading about these processes that you use in perceiving other people, examine your perception strategies by responding to the following statements with T if the statement is usually or generally true (accurate in describing your behavior), or with F if the statement is usually or generally false (inaccurate in describing your behavior).

_____ 1. I make predictions about people's behaviors that generally prove to be true.

_____ 2. When I know some things about another person, I can pretty easily fill in what I don't know.

_____ 3. Generally, my expectations are borne out by what I actually see; that is, my later perceptions usually match my initial expectations.

_____ 4. I base most of my impressions of people on the first few minutes of our meeting.

_____ 5. I generally find that people I like possess positive characteristics and people I don't like possess negative characteristics.

_____ 6. I generally take credit for the positive things that happen and deny responsibility for the negative things.

_____ 7. I generally attribute people's attitudes and behaviors to their most obvious physical or psychological characteristic.

_____ 8. When making judgments about others, I emphasize looking to their personality rather than to the circumstances or context.

These questions were designed to raise questions to be considered in this chapter. All the statements refer to perceptual processes that many people use but that often get people into trouble because they lead us to form inaccurate impressions. The questions refer to several processes to be discussed below: the self-fulfilling prophecy (statement 1), personality theory (2), perceptual accentuation (3), primacy–recency (4), and consistency (5). Statements 6, 7, and 8 refer to the barriers we encounter as we attempt to determine motives for other people and even our own behaviors: self-serving bias, overattribution, and the fundamental attribution error.

As you read this chapter, think about these processes and consider how you might use them more accurately and not allow them to get in the way of accurate and reasonable people perception. At the same time, recognize that situations vary widely and that strategies for clearer perception will prove useful most of the time but not all of the time.

Impression Formation Processes

The way in which you perceive another person, and ultimately come to some kind of evaluation or interpretation of this person, is not a simple logical sequence. Instead, your perceptions seem to be influenced by a variety of processes. Here we consider some of the more significant: the self-fulfilling prophecy, personality theory, perceptual accentuation, primacy–recency, consistency, and attribution of control.

Self-Fulfilling Prophecy   A **self-fulfilling prophecy** (identified in statement 1 in the previous self-test) is a prediction that comes true because you act on it as if it were true. Put differently, a self-fulfilling prophecy occurs when you act on your schema as if it were true and in doing so make it true. Self-fulfilling prophecies occur in

VIEWPOINTS

The Pygmalion Effect

Findings such as those on the Pygmalion effect have led one researcher to suggest that companies apply these insights to improve worker productivity—by creating in supervisors positive attitudes about employees and by helping employees to feel that their supervisors and the organization as a whole value them highly (McNatt, 2001). *In what ways might this Pygmalion effect be applied at your own workplace?*

widely different situations such as parent–child relationships, educational settings, and business (Merton, 1957; Rosenthal, 2002; Madon, Guyll, & Spoth, 2004; Tierney & Farmer, 2004). There are four basic steps in the self-fulfilling prophecy:

1. You make a prediction or formulate a belief about a person or a situation. For example, you predict that Pat is friendly in interpersonal encounters.

2. You act toward that person or situation as if that prediction or belief were true. For example, you act as if Pat were a friendly person.

3. Because you act as if the belief were true, it becomes true. For example, because of the way you act toward Pat, Pat becomes comfortable and friendly.

4. You observe your effect on the person or the resulting situation, and what you see strengthens your beliefs. For example, you observe Pat's friendliness and this reinforces your belief that Pat is in fact friendly.

The self-fulfilling prophecy can also be seen when you make predictions about yourself and fulfill them. For example, suppose you enter a group situation convinced that the other members will dislike you. Almost invariably you'll be proved right; the other members will appear to you to dislike you. What you may be doing is acting in a way that encourages the group to respond to you negatively. In this way, you fulfill your prophecies about yourself.

Self-fulfilling prophecies can short-circuit critical thinking and influence others' behavior (or your own) so that it conforms to your prophecies. As a result, you may see what you predicted rather than what is really there (for example, you may perceive yourself as a failure because you have predicted it rather than because of any actual failures).

A widely-known example of the self-fulfilling prophecy is the **Pygmalion effect** (Rosenthal & Jacobson, 1992). In a classic research study, experimenters told teachers that certain pupils were expected to do exceptionally well—that they were late bloomers. And although the experimenters selected the "late bloomers" at random, the students who were labeled "late bloomers" performed at higher levels than their classmates. These students became what their teachers thought they were. The Pygmalion effect has also been studied in varied contexts such as the courtroom, the clinic, the work cubicle, management and leadership practices, athletic coaching, and stepfamilies (Eden, 1992; Solomon et al., 1996; Einstein, 1995; McNatt, 2001; Rosenthal, 2002).

Personality Theory   Each person has a personality theory that says which characteristics of an individual go with other characteristics (statement 2 in the self-test). Most often these theories are subconscious or implicit, but they can be brought to consciousness.

Consider, for example, the following brief statements. Note the word in parentheses that you think best completes each sentence.

- Emma is energetic, eager, and (intelligent, unintelligent).
- Daniel is bold, defiant, and (extroverted, introverted).
- Sophie is bright, lively, and (thin, heavy).
- Nicholas is attractive, intelligent, and (likeable, unlikeable).
- Isabella is cheerful, positive, and (outgoing, shy).
- William is handsome, tall, and (friendly, unfriendly).

What makes some of these choices seem right and others wrong is your **personality theory**, the system of rules that tells you which characteristics go together. Your theory may, for example, have told you that a person who is energetic and eager is also intelligent, not unintelligent—although there is no logical reason why an unintelligent person could not be energetic and eager.

Another type of personality theory that many hold is that you are what your friends are. It's a simple theory based on the assumption that friends are generally similar to each other. If your friends are cool, so must you be. If your friends are dull (as demonstrated in their photos and in their posts), you'll be seen as dull too. Social media users, for example, are seen to be more attractive when they have attractive friends than when their friends are less attractive (Walther et al., 2008).

The widely-documented **halo effect** is a function of personality theory (Dion, Berscheid, & Walster, 1972; Riggio, 1987; Gunaydin, Selcuk, & Zayas, 2017; Dean, 2016a). If you believe a person has some positive qualities, you're likely to infer that she or he also possesses other positive qualities. There is also a **reverse halo effect** (or "horns" effect): If you know a person possesses several negative qualities, you're more likely to infer that the person also has other negative qualities. For example, you're more likely to perceive attractive people as more generous, sensitive, trustworthy, and interesting than those less attractive. And the reverse halo effect leads you to perceive those who are unattractive as mean, dishonest, antisocial, and sneaky (Katz, 2003).

The ambiguity of the message tends to increase your reliance on your personality theory in making judgments. This is especially important in online communication, which is often more ambiguous than face-to-face communication. When you read or view something on some social media site that is ambiguous, you'll resolve the ambiguity according to your personality theory. For example, you know that Joe is an honest and positive person who always sees the best in people; when you read an ambiguous comment from Joe, you'll resolve it so that Joe retains your image of him as an honest and positive person.

In using personality theories, apply them carefully and critically to avoid perceiving qualities in an individual that your theory tells you should be present but aren't, or seeing qualities that are not there (Plaks, Grant, & Dweck, 2005).

Perceptual Accentuation When poor and rich children were shown pictures of coins and later asked to estimate their size, the poor children's size estimates were much greater than the rich children's. Similarly, hungry people need fewer visual cues to perceive food objects and food terms than do people who are not hungry. This process, called **perceptual accentuation**, leads you to see what you expect or want to see (statement 3 in the self-test). You see people you like as better looking and smarter than those you don't like. You magnify or accentuate what will satisfy your needs and desires: The thirsty person sees a mirage of water; the sexually deprived person sees a mirage of sexual satisfaction.

Perceptual accentuation can lead you to perceive what you need or want to perceive rather than what is really there and can lead you to fail to perceive what you don't want to perceive. For example, you may not perceive signs of impending relationship problems because you're only seeing what you want to see. Another interesting distortion created by perceptual accentuation is that you may perceive certain behaviors as indicative that someone likes you simply because you want to be liked. For example, you view general politeness and friendly behavior used as a persuasive strategy (say, by a salesperson) as an indication that the person genuinely likes you.

Primacy–Recency Assume for a moment that you're enrolled in a course in which half the classes are extremely dull and half are extremely exciting. At the end of the semester, you evaluate the course and the instructor. Will your evaluation be more favorable if the dull classes occurred in the first half of the semester and the exciting classes in the second? Or will it be more favorable if the order is reversed? If what comes first exerts the most influence, you have a **primacy effect** (statement 4 in the self-test). If what comes last (or most recently) exerts the most influence, you have a **recency effect**.

In the classic study on the effects of **primacy–recency** in interpersonal perception, college students perceived a person who was described as "intelligent, industrious, impulsive, critical, stubborn, and envious" more positively than a person described as "envious, stubborn, critical, impulsive, industrious, and intelligent" (Asch, 1946). Notice that the descriptions are identical; only the order was changed. Clearly, we have a tendency to use early information to get a general idea about a person and to use later information to make this impression more specific. The initial information helps us form a schema for the person. Once that schema is formed, we're likely to resist information that contradicts it.

One interesting practical implication of primacy–recency is that the first impression you make is likely to be the most important—and is likely to be made very quickly (Sunnafrank & Ramirez, 2004; Willis & Todorov, 2006). When you form an initial impression based on a photograph, that initial impression will influence impressions you form even after meeting face-to-face—a factor to keep in mind when posting photos on dating sites (Gunaydin, Selcuk, & Zayas, 2017). A violation of trust, for example, that occurs early in a relationship can do permanent damage to a relationship even after you've tried to make amends (Lount, Zhong, Sivanathan, & Murnighan, 2008). The reason is that the schema that others form of you functions as a filter to admit or block additional information about you. If the initial impression or schema is positive, others are likely to (1) remember additional positive information readily because it confirms this original positive image or schema, (2) forget or distort negative information easily because it contradicts this original positive schema, and (3) interpret ambiguous information as positive. You win in all three ways—if the initial impression is positive.

Consistency   The tendency to maintain balance among perceptions or attitudes is called **consistency** (statement 5 in the self-test). People expect certain things to go together and other things not to go together.

On a purely intuitive basis, for example, respond to the following sentences by noting your expected response:

1. I expect a person I like to (like, dislike) me.
2. I expect a person I dislike to (like, dislike) me.
3. I expect my friend to (like, dislike) my friend.
4. I expect my friend to (like, dislike) my enemy.
5. I expect my enemy to (like, dislike) my friend.
6. I expect my enemy to (like, dislike) my enemy.

According to most consistency theories, your expectations would be as follows: You would expect a person you liked to like you (1) and a person you disliked to dislike you (2). You would expect a friend to like a friend (3) and to dislike an enemy (4). You would expect your enemy to dislike your friend (5) and to like your other enemy (6). All these expectations are intuitively satisfying.

You would also expect someone you liked to possess characteristics you liked or admired and would expect your enemies not to possess characteristics you liked or admired. Conversely, you would expect people you liked to lack unpleasant characteristics and those you disliked to possess unpleasant characteristics.

Uncritically assuming that an individual is consistent can lead you to ignore or distort perceptions that are inconsistent with your picture of the whole person. For example, you may misinterpret Karla's unhappiness because your image of Karla is "happy, controlled, and contented."

Attribution of Control   Still another way in which you form impressions is through the **attribution of control**. For example, suppose you invite your friend Desmond to dinner for 7:00 p.m. and he arrives at 9:00. Consider how you would respond to each of these reasons:

> Reason 1:   "I just couldn't tear myself away from the beach. I really wanted to get a great tan."
>
> Reason 2:   "I was driving here when I saw some young kids mugging an old couple. I broke it up and took the couple home. They were so frightened that I had to stay with them until their children arrived. Their phone was out of order and my cell battery died, so I had no way of calling to tell you I'd be late."
>
> Reason 3:   "I got in a car accident and was taken to the hospital."

Depending on the reason, you would probably attribute very different motives to Desmond's behavior. With reasons 1 and 2, you'd conclude that Desmond was in control of his behavior (the reasons were internal). With reason 3, you'd conclude that he was not in control of his behavior (the reason was external and not under Desmond's control). You would probably respond negatively to reason 1 (Desmond was selfish and inconsiderate) and positively to reason 2 (Desmond was a Good Samaritan). Because Desmond was not in control of his behavior in reason 3, you would probably not attribute either positive or negative motivation to his behavior. Instead, you would probably feel sorry that he got into an accident.

You probably make similar judgments based on control in numerous situations. Consider, for example, how you would respond to the following situations:

- Doris fails her history midterm exam.
- Sidney's car is repossessed because he failed to keep up the payments.
- Margie has developed high blood pressure and is complaining that she feels awful.
- Thomas' wife has just filed for divorce and he is feeling depressed.

You would most likely be sympathetic to each of these people if you felt that he or she was not in control of what happened; for example, if the examination was unfair, if Sidney lost his job because of employee discrimination, if Margie's blood pressure was caused by some inherited physiological problem, and if Thomas' wife wanted to leave him for a wealthy drug dealer. On the other hand, you probably would not be sympathetic if you felt that these people were in control of what happened; for example, if Doris partied instead of studying, if Sidney gambled his payments away, if Margie ate nothing but salty junk food and refused to exercise, and if Thomas had been repeatedly unfaithful and his wife finally gave up trying to reform him.

In perceiving, and especially in evaluating, other people's behavior, you frequently ask if they were in control of the behavior. Generally, research shows that if you feel a person was in control of negative behaviors, you'll come to dislike him or her. If you believe the person was not in control of negative behaviors, you'll come to feel sorry for and not blame the person.

In your attribution of control—or in attributing motives on the basis of any other reasons (for example, hearsay or observations of the person's behavior) beware of several potential errors: (1) the **self-serving bias**, (2) **overattribution**, and (3) the **fundamental attribution error**.

1. You exhibit the **self-serving bias** when you take credit for the positive and deny responsibility for the negative (statement 6 in the self-test). For example, you're more likely to attribute your positive outcomes (say, you get an A on an exam) to

internal and controllable factors—to your personality, intelligence, or hard work. And you're more likely to attribute your negative outcomes (say, you get a D) to external and uncontrollable factors—to the exam's being exceptionally difficult or to your roommate's party the night before (Bernstein, Stephan, & Davis, 1979; Duval & Silva, 2002).

2. **Overattribution** is the tendency to single out one or two obvious characteristics of a person and attribute everything that person does to this one or these two characteristics (statement 7 in the self-test). For example, if a person is blind or was born into great wealth, there's often a tendency to attribute everything that person does to such factors. And so you might say, "Alex overeats because he's blind," or "Lillian is irresponsible because she has never had to work for her money." To avoid overattribution, recognize that most behaviors and personality characteristics result from lots of factors. You almost always make a mistake when you select one factor and attribute everything to it.

3. The **fundamental attribution error** occurs when you assess someone's behavior but overvalue the contribution of internal factors (for example, a person's personality) and undervalue the influence of external factors (for example, the context or situation the person is in). This fundamental attribution error (statement 8 in the self-test) leads you to conclude that people do what they do because that's the kind of people they are, not because of the situation they're in. When Pat is late for an appointment, for example, you're more likely to conclude that Pat is inconsiderate or irresponsible than to attribute the lateness to a bus breakdown or a traffic accident.

Increasing Accuracy in Impression Formation

Successful interpersonal communication depends largely on the accuracy of the impressions you form of others and that others form of you. So, your objective needs to be to eliminate or reduce the barriers to accurate perception and to use some effective tools to increase accuracy.

Avoid Processing Errors   Recall that each of the six perceptual processes discussed above can lead you to make inaccurate perceptions. So, remember:

*   The self-fulfilling prophecy may lead you to influence what you see.
*   Personality theories are not always accurate.
*   Perceptual accentuation may create inaccurate perceptions by leading you to see what you want to see instead of what is really there.
*   Primacy–recency may lead you to give undue emphasis to what comes first even when more important information is added later.
*   Consistency may lead you to see what is consistent instead of the inconsistencies that really exist.
*   In attributing control, be aware of the self-serving bias, overattribution, and the fundamental attribution error.

Analyze Impressions   Subject your perceptions to logical analysis, to critical thinking. Here are two suggestions:

*   *Recognize your own role in perception.*   Your emotional and physiological state influences the meaning you give to your perceptions. A movie may seem hysterically funny when you're in a good mood but just plain stupid when you're in a bad mood. Understand your own biases; for example, do you tend to perceive only the positive in people you like and only the negative in people you don't like?

- *Avoid early conclusions.* On the basis of your observations of behaviors, formulate hypotheses to test against additional information and evidence; avoid drawing conclusions that you then look to confirm. Look for a variety of cues pointing in the same direction. The more cues point to the same conclusion, the more likely your conclusion is correct. Be especially alert to contradictory cues that seem to refute your initial hypotheses. At the same time, seek validation from others. Do others see things in the same way you do? If not, ask yourself if your perceptions may be distorted in some way.

Check Perceptions **Perception checking** is another way to reduce uncertainty and to make your perceptions more accurate. The goal of perception checking is to further explore the thoughts and feelings of the other person, not to prove that your initial perception is correct. With this simple technique, you lessen your chances of misinterpreting another's feelings. At the same time, you give the other person an opportunity to elaborate on his or her thoughts and feelings. In its most basic form, perception checking consists of two steps:

1. *Describe what you see or hear,* recognizing that descriptions are not really objective but are heavily influenced by who you are, your emotional state, and so on. At the same time, you may wish to describe what you think is happening. Try to do this as descriptively as you can, without evaluating what is happening. Sometimes you may wish to offer several possibilities.

   - You've called me from work a lot this week. You seem concerned that everything is all right at home.
   - You've not wanted to talk with me all week. You say that my work is fine, but you don't seem to want to give me the same responsibilities that other research assistants have.

2. *Seek confirmation.* Ask the other person if your description is accurate. Avoid mind reading; that is, don't try to read the thoughts and feelings of another person just from observing his or her behaviors. Regardless of how many behaviors you observe and how carefully you examine them, you can only guess what is going on in someone's mind. A person's motives are not open to outside inspection; you can only make assumptions based on overt behaviors. So be careful that your request for confirmation does not sound as though you already know the answer. Avoid phrasing your questions defensively; for example, "You really don't want to go out, do you? I knew you didn't when you turned on that lousy television." Instead, ask for confirmation in as supportive a way as possible:

   - Would you rather watch TV?
   - Are you worried about me or the kids?
   - Are you displeased with my work? Is there anything I can do to improve my job performance?

Reduce Uncertainty Every interpersonal situation has some degree of uncertainty. A variety of strategies can help reduce uncertainty (Berger & Bradac, 1982; Gudykunst, 1993; Brashers, 2007).

- *Observe other people.* Observing another person while he or she is engaged in an active task, preferably interacting with others in an informal social situation, often reveals a great deal about the person because people are less apt to monitor their behaviors and are more likely to reveal their true selves in informal situations.
- *Prepare for different situations.* You can sometimes manipulate situations to observe the person in more specific and revealing contexts. Employment interviews, theatrical auditions, and student teaching are good examples of situations arranged to provide an accurate view of the person in action.

- *Learn about different online groups before you engage.* When you log on to a social media site and lurk, reading the exchanges between the other group members before saying anything yourself, you're learning about the people in the group and about the group itself, thus reducing uncertainty. When uncertainty is reduced, you're more likely to make contributions that are appropriate to the group and less likely to violate the group's norms.

- *Gather information by talking to others.* Learn about a person through asking others. You might inquire of a colleague if a third person finds you interesting and might like to have dinner with you.

- *Interact with the individual.* For example, you can ask questions: "Do you enjoy sports?" "What did you think of that computer science course?" "What would you do if you got fired?" You also gain knowledge of another by revealing information about yourself, which encourages the other person to also talk about him- or herself.

Beware the Just-World Hypothesis   Many people believe that the world is just: Good things happen to good people and bad things happen to bad people (Aronson, Wilson, Akert, & Sommers, 2016; Hunt, 2000). Put differently, you get what you deserve! Even when you mindfully dismiss this assumption, you may use it mindlessly when perceiving and evaluating other people. Consider a particularly vivid example: In certain cultures (for example, in Bangladesh, Iran, or Yemen), if a woman is raped, she is considered by many in that culture (certainly not all) to have disgraced her family and to be deserving of severe punishment—in many cases, even death. And although you may claim that this is unfair, much research shows that even in the United States many people do, in fact, blame the victim for being raped, especially if the victim is male (Adams-Price, Dalton, & Sumrall, 2004; Anderson, 2004). The belief that the world is just distorts your perception by leading you to deemphasize the influence of situational factors and to overemphasize the influence of internal factors in your attempts to explain the behaviors of other people or even your own behaviors.

Increase Cultural Sensitivity   **Cultural sensitivity**—recognizing and being sensitive to cultural differences—helps increase your accuracy in perception. For example, Russian or Chinese artists such as ballet dancers often applaud their audience by clapping. Americans seeing this may easily interpret this as egotistical. Similarly, a German man enters a restaurant before the woman in order to see if the place is respectable enough for the woman to enter. This simple custom can easily be interpreted as rude when viewed by people from cultures in which it's considered courteous for the woman to enter first (Axtell, 2007).

Within every cultural group are wide and important differences. As all Americans are not alike, neither are all Indonesians, Greeks, or Mexicans. When you make assumptions that all people of a certain culture are alike, you're thinking in stereotypes. Recognizing differences between another culture and your own, and among members of the same culture, helps you perceive situations more accurately.

Cultural sensitivity helps counteract the difficulty most people have in understanding the nonverbal messages of people from other cultures. For example, it's easier to interpret the facial expressions of members of your own culture than those of members of

---

INTERPERSONAL CHOICE POINT
Relationship Uncertainty

You've been dating someone casually over the last few months and want to take this to the next level. But you first want to find out if your partner feels the same way. You don't want to be embarrassed by a refusal. *What are some of the things you can do to reduce this relationship uncertainty?*

a. Ask a mutual friend.

b. Come right out and ask directly.

c. Talk about other people who have made a commitment and watch the reactions.

d. Wait until your partner signals a desire to move the relationship forward.

e. Other

THE CULTURAL MAP   Ambiguity Tolerance

Ambiguity tolerance refers to the degree to which members of a culture are accepting of uncertainty; high-ambiguity tolerant cultures are comfortable with not knowing exactly what will happen next, whereas low-ambiguity tolerant cultures resist uncertainty and, in many cases, are stressed out by it.

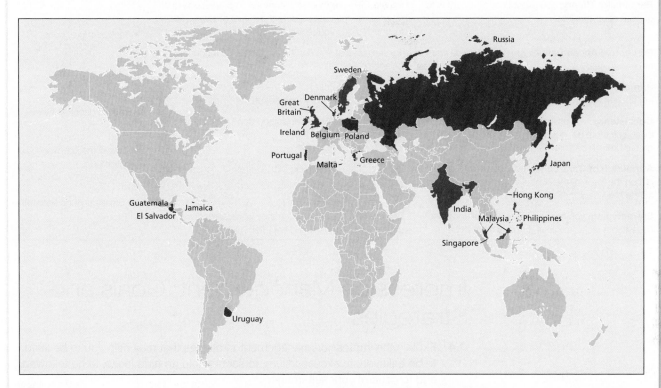

In these high-ambiguity tolerant cultures (generally, the top 10 countries are highlighted in these cultural maps), uncertainty is considered normal and expected. High ambiguity tolerant people are comfortable in uncertain situations and with unfamiliar tasks and assignments. They are also tolerant of ethnic differences and diversity and are generally positive to foreigners.

In these low-ambiguity tolerant cultures, members try to avoid uncertainty, because uncertainty is typically uncomfortable and anxiety provoking for them. Members of these cultures are also more prejudiced toward other ethnic groups and would not be welcoming to immigrants.

How do you feel when an instructor gives an ambiguous assignment? Do you see the lack of specific direction as stressful or as an opportunity to get creative and think of different ways you might approach the assignment?

other cultures (Weathers, Frank, & Spell, 2002). This "in-group advantage" assists your perceptional accuracy for members of your own culture but often hinders your accuracy for members of other cultures (Elfenbein & Ambady, 2002).

The suggestions for improving intercultural communication offered in popular and academic discussions are applicable to increasing your cultural sensitivity in perception. For example, educate yourself, reduce uncertainty, recognize differences (between yourself and people from other cultures, among members of other cultures, and between your meanings and the meanings that people from other cultures may have), confront your stereotypes, and adjust your communication.

A summary of impression formation processes, the cautions to be observed, and some suggestions for increasing perceptual accuracy are presented in Table 3.3. Stereotyping, discussed in Chapter 2, is included in this table because it is also one of the processes used in impression formation.

Table 3.3 In a Nutshell Impression Formation

Impression Formation Processes	Cautions to Observe	Increasing Accuracy in Perception
Self-Fulfilling Prophecy: you act on your predictions as if they were true, and they become true.	Beware of your predictions that come true; you may be influencing them in that direction.	
Personality Theory: you expect certain qualities to go with other qualities.	Personalities are much too complex to predict one quality easily on the basis of others; beware of always finding fault with those you dislike or good with those you like.	• Avoid processing errors.
Perceptual Accentuation: you see what you want to or need to see	Try seeing what you don't want to see (as a counterbalance measure).	• Analyze impressions.
Primacy–Recency: you are most influenced by what occurs first and by what occurs last.	Basing your impressions on the basis of early or late information may bias your perceptions.	• Check perceptions.
Consistency: you assume that people are consistent; if you see them as "good people," then the things they do are likely to be seen as good.	People are not always consistent; don't expect them to be.	• Reduce uncertainty.
Attribution of Control: you evaluate what a person did on the basis of the control you perceive this person to have had on his or her behavior.	Beware of the self-serving bias, overattribution, and the fundamental attribution error.	• Beware the just-world hypothesis.
Stereotyping: you form an impression of someone based on a racial, religious, or other stereotype.	Beware of stereotypes; often they were learned without conscious awareness and are often misleading.	• Increase cultural sensitivity.

Impression Management: Goals and Strategies

3.4 Explain the impression management strategies that may help you to be liked, to be believed, to excuse failure, to secure help, to hide faults, to be followed, and to confirm your self-image.

Impression management (some writers use the term *self-presentation* or *identity management*) has to do with the processes you go through to communicate the image of yourself that you want others to have of you. The impression you make on others is largely the result of the messages you communicate. In the same way that you form impressions of others largely on the basis of how they communicate, verbally and nonverbally, you also convey an impression of yourself through what you say (your verbal messages), the photos you post, and how you act and dress, as well as how you decorate your office or apartment (your nonverbal messages). Communication messages, however, are not the only means for impression formation and management. For example, you also communicate your self-image by the people with whom you associate (and judge others the same way); if you associate with A-list people, then surely you must be A-list yourself, the theory goes. Also, as illustrated in the discussion of stereotypes, you may form an impression of someone on the basis of that person's age, gender, or ethnic origin. Or you may rely on what others have said about the person and form impressions that are consistent with these comments. And, of course, others may do the same in forming impressions of you.

Part of the art and skill of interpersonal communication is to understand and be able to manage the impressions you give to others; mastering the art of impression management enables you to present yourself as you want others to see you— at least to some extent. Social media has made impression management a lot easier than it would

be in only face-to-face encounters. You have more control over the information that you send out in your posts and in your photos than you do when presenting yourself in a face-to-face situation (Dean, 2007; Gibbs, Ellison, & Heino, 2006; DeVito, 2012).

The strategies you use to achieve this desired impression depend on your specific goal. Here is an interpersonal typology of seven major communication goals and strategies of impression management (previewed in Figure 3.6). As you read about these goals and strategies, and about how these strategies can backfire, consider your own attempts to communicate the "right" impression to others and what you do (that is, the strategies you use) to achieve this unique kind of communication. Consider, for example, how you might use these strategies in writing your online profile for, say, eHarmony or OK Cupid or for one of the many apps such as How About We, Hinge, or Tinder (also see Table 3.4, which identifies some popular profile writing suggestions).

To Be Liked: Affinity-Seeking and Politeness Strategies

If you want to be liked—say, you're new at school or on the job and you want to be well liked, to be included in the activities of other students or work associates, and to be thought of highly by these other people—you'll likely use these two sets of strategies: affinity-seeking strategies and politeness strategies.

Affinity-Seeking Strategies   As you can see from examining the list of **affinity-seeking strategies** that follows, the use of these techniques is likely to increase your chances of being liked (Bell & Daly, 1984). Such strategies are especially important in initial interactions, and their use by teachers has even been found to increase student motivation (Martin & Rubin, 1998; Myers & Zhong, 2004; Wrench, McCroskey, & Richmond, 2008).

- Be of help to the other person.
- Present yourself as comfortable and relaxed when with another person.
- Follow the cultural rules for polite, cooperative conversation with others.

Figure 3.6   Impression Management Goals

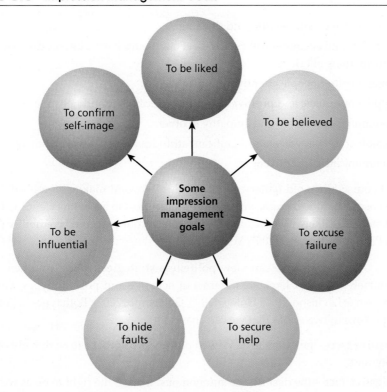

Table 3.4 12 Guidelines for Writing Your Online Profile

Guideline	To Explain
Say something meaningful.	Depending on the site, this might include your education and career, your entrepreneurial spirit, or your athleticism. Stress your uniqueness.
Post a flattering photo, the most important part of your dating profile.	Select a photo that's appealing, colorful, and recent. Don't Photoshop, especially if you plan a face-to-face meeting. Some social media watchers suggest a full body shot. Avoid photos that can call up stereotypes, for example, the man with the muscle car or the woman with the cat. Selfies are generally okay for women—both straight and lesbian—but popular men used them significantly less often (Roper, 2014).
Be positive, friendly, open, optimistic, active, and truthful.	These characteristics are universally appreciated. We want friends who are positive and friendly, and others do as well. We also prefer those who like active sports such as surfing, skiing, and biking more than spectator sports such as basketball and baseball (Roper, 2014).
Be honest about what you want and don't want—what you must have.	Honesty helps focus your search and others' search for you.
Avoid information that is too personal or that you don't want to share with everyone.	People can easily get scared off, feeling this is too early for intimate disclosures.
Avoid unappealing details especially in your profile but generally at the start of relationships.	Details are best appreciated (and tolerated) after getting to know someone.
Secure feedback and listen to it.	Before posting, get some feedback. Send it to a trusted friend in e-mail and ask for honest feedback.
Avoid turnoff terms, those that bring negative thoughts to mind.	Some examples are *prison, death, illness, debts*, and vulgar or gross terms.
Avoid badmouthing past relationships or jobs.	Some fear this negativity will one day be directed at them, which is likely to turn people off.
Rewrite and edit. And be brief.	Don't try to write your profile in one shot. Instead, write and rewrite and edit your profile, then copy and paste it into the site.
Examine other profiles.	Read a variety of profiles and identify the characteristics that you could adapt to your own unique profile.
Start from the general to the specific.	Give the reader an overview and then begin to fill in the relevant details.

SOURCE: These suggestions were drawn from a variety of websites, such as those of eHarmony and Ask, and from research: Alpert (2013) and Conniff & Nicks (2014).

- Appear active, enthusiastic, and dynamic.
- Stimulate and encourage others to talk about themselves; reinforce disclosures and contributions of others.
- Listen to other people attentively and actively.
- Appear optimistic and positive rather than pessimistic and negative.
- Communicate warmth and empathy to others.
- Demonstrate that you share significant attitudes and values with others.
- Communicate supportiveness.

And, of course, plain old flattery goes a long way toward making you liked. Flattery has also been found to increase your chances for success in a job interview, increase the tip a customer is likely to leave, and even increase your perceived credibility (Varma, Toh, & Pichler, 2006; Seiter, 2007; Vonk, 2002).

Politeness Strategies We can view **politeness strategies**, which are often used to make ourselves appear likeable, in terms of negative and positive types (Goffman, 1967; Brown & Levinson, 1987; Holmes 1995; Goldsmith, 2007). Both types of politeness are responsive to two needs that we each have:

1. **Positive face**—the desire to be viewed positively by others, to be thought of favorably, and

2. **Negative face**—the desire to be autonomous, to have the right to do as we wish.

Politeness in interpersonal communication, then, refers to behavior that allows others to maintain both positive and negative face; impoliteness refers to behaviors that attack either positive face (for example, you criticize someone) or negative face (for example, you make demands on someone).

To help another person maintain positive face, speak respectfully to and about the person, give the person your full attention, say "excuse me" when appropriate. In short, treat the person as you want to be treated. In this way, you allow the person to maintain positive face through what is called positive politeness. You attack the person's positive face when you speak disrespectfully about the person, ignore the person or the person's comments, and fail to use the appropriate expressions of politeness such as "thank you" and "please." It is attacks on positive face—sometimes called face-threatening acts (FTAs)—that the term *dissing* is meant to capture. Introduced in the 1980s in rap music, the term refers to a form of impoliteness in which you criticize, act rudely, insult, put down, offend, or disrespect another person verbally and/or nonverbally. It attacks a person's positive face needs, the need to be approved of, to be respected.

To help another person maintain negative face, respect the person's right to be autonomous; thus, request rather than demand that he or she does something; say, "Would you mind opening a window" rather than "Open that window!" You might also give the person the option of saying no when you make a request; say, "If this is a bad time, please tell me, but I'm really strapped and could use a loan of $100" rather than "You have to lend me $100." If you want a recommendation, you might say, "Would it be possible for you to write me a recommendation for graduate school?" rather than "You have to write me a recommendation for graduate school." In this way, you enable the person to maintain negative face through what is called negative politeness.

Of course, we do this almost automatically, and asking for a favor without any consideration for the person's negative face needs would seem totally insensitive. In most situations, however, this type of attack on negative face often appears in more subtle forms. For example, your mother saying "Are you going to wear that?"—to use Deborah Tannen's (2006) example—attacks negative face by criticizing or challenging your autonomy. This comment also attacks positive face by questioning your ability to dress properly.

Like all the strategies discussed here, politeness, too, may have negative consequences. Overpoliteness, for example, is likely to be seen as phony and is likely to be resented. Overpoliteness may also be resented if it's seen as a persuasive strategy.

To Be Believed: Credibility Strategies

Let's say you're a politician and you want people to vote for you or to support a particular proposal you're advancing. In this case, you'll probably use **credibility strategies**—a concept that goes back some 2300 years, to the ancient Greek and Roman rhetoricians. Credibility strategies are supported by contemporary research; they seek to establish your competence, character, and charisma. For example, to establish your competence, you may mention your great educational background or the courses you took that qualify you as an expert. To establish that you're of good character, you may mention how fair and honest you are or speak of your concern for enduring values or your concern for others. And to establish your charisma—your take-charge, positive personality—you may demonstrate enthusiasm, be emphatic, or focus on the positive while minimizing the negative.

Of course, if you stress your competence, character, and charisma too much, you risk being perceived as too eager—as someone who is afraid of being exposed as lacking the very qualities that you seek to present to others. For example, people who are truly competent generally need say little directly about their own competence; their knowledgeable, insightful, and logical messages reveal their competence.

ETHICS IN INTERPERSONAL COMMUNICATION

The Ethics of Impression Management

Impression-management strategies may also be used unethically. For example, people may use affinity-seeking strategies to get you to like them so that they can extract favors from you. Politicians frequently portray themselves as credible (when they are not) in order to win votes. The same could be said of the stereotypical used-car salesperson or insurance agent trying to make a sale. Some people use self-handicapping strategies or self-deprecating strategies to get you to see their behavior from a perspective that benefits them rather than you. Self-monitoring strategies are often deceptive and are designed to present a more polished image than the one you might see without this self-monitoring. And, of course, influence strategies have been used throughout history in deception as well as in truth. Even image-confirming strategies can be used to deceive, as when people exaggerate their positive qualities (or make them up) and hide their negative ones.

Ethical Choice Point

You're interviewing for a job you really want and you need to be perceived as credible and likeable. *What are your ethical choices for presenting yourself as both credible and likeable?*

To Excuse Failure: Self-Handicapping Strategies

If you were about to tackle a difficult task and were concerned that you might fail, you might use what are called **self-handicapping strategies** (Koklitz & Arkin, 1982). In the more extreme type of self-handicapping strategy, you actually set up barriers or obstacles to make the task impossible so that when you fail, you won't be blamed or thought ineffective—after all, the task was impossible. Let's say that you aren't prepared for your interpersonal communication exam and you feel you're going to fail. Using this extreme type of self-handicapping strategy, you might go out and party the night before so that when you do poorly on the exam, you can blame it on the all-night party rather than on your intelligence or knowledge. The less extreme type involves manufacturing excuses for failure and having them ready if you do fail. "The exam was unfair" is one popular excuse. Or you might blame a long period without a date on your being too intelligent or too shy or too poor, or blame a poorly cooked dinner on your defective stove.

Using self-handicapping strategies too often may lead people to see you as incompetent or foolish—after all, partying late into the night before an exam for which you are already unprepared doesn't make a whole lot of sense. This type of behavior can reflect negatively on your overall competence.

Self-Deprecating Humor

Self-deprecating humor has been found to increase attractiveness of high-status men and women but not for lower-status individuals. It has also been found to be used more by men than by women (Greengross & Miller, 2008). *Do you find these findings intuitively satisfying? What explanation might you offer to account for these findings?*

To Secure Help: Self-Deprecating Strategies

If you want to be taken care of and protected or simply want someone to come to your aid, you might use **self-deprecating strategies**. Confessions of incompetence and inability often bring assistance from others. And so you might say, "I just can't fix that drain and it drives me crazy; I just don't know anything about plumbing," with the hope that the other person will offer help.

But be careful: using self-deprecating strategies may convince people that you are in fact as incompetent as you say you are. Or people may see you as someone who doesn't want to do something and so confesses incompetence to get others to do it for you. This is not likely to get you help in the long run.

To Hide Faults: Self-Monitoring Strategies

Much impression management is devoted not merely to presenting a positive image but to suppressing the negative via **self-monitoring strategies**. Here you carefully monitor (self-censor) what you say or do. You avoid your normal slang to make your colleagues think more highly of you; you avoid chewing gum so you don't look juvenile or unprofessional. While you readily disclose favorable parts of your experience, you actively hide the unfavorable parts. And, of course, you can self-monitor nonverbally, as you might when you fake a smile, a technique many have mastered (Dean, 2010b).

But if you self-monitor too often or too obviously, you risk being seen as unwilling to reveal your true self, perhaps because you don't trust others enough to feel comfortable disclosing your weaknesses as well as your strengths. In more extreme cases, you may be seen as dishonest or as trying to fool other people.

To Be Followed: Influencing Strategies

In many instances, you'll want to get people to see you as a leader, as someone to be followed in thought and perhaps in behavior. Here you can use a variety of **influencing strategies**. Perhaps the most common influencing strategies are those of persuasion and persuasive communication. Here is just a small sample:

- *Use logic.* Use facts, evidence, and argument to support whatever you want others to do. When people are persuaded by logic, they are more likely to remain persuaded over time and are more likely to resist attempts at counter-persuasion that may come up in the future (Petty & Wegener, 1998).
- *Stress similarity.* Identify with the other person. Demonstrate that you and the other person share important attitudes, beliefs, and values. Be aware, however, that insincere or dishonest identification is likely to backfire and create problems. So avoid even implying similarities between yourself and others that don't exist.
- *Stress agreement.* If you can secure an initial yes response, you'll improve your chances of influencing others on related matters (Goldstein, Martin, & Cialdini, 2008). Agreement encourages agreement.
- *Provide positive social proof.* Demonstrate that others are doing what you want your listener to do, and he or she will be more likely to follow (Cialdini, 2013; Surowiecki, 2005). This herd instinct is a powerful impulse.

Influencing strategies, too, can easily backfire. If your influence attempts fail—for whatever reason—you will lose general influence. That is, if you try but fail to influence someone, you'll be seen to have less power than before you tried the failed influence attempt. And, of course, if you're perceived as trying to influence others for self-gain, your persuasive attempts are likely to be rejected, and perhaps seen as self-serving and be resented.

To Confirm Self-Image: Image-Confirming Strategies

Sometimes you communicate to confirm your self-image. For example, if you see yourself as the life of the party, you'll tell jokes and try to amuse people. In doing so you'd be using **image-confirming strategies**. Your behaviors confirm your own self-image.

INTERPERSONAL CHOICE POINT
From Online to Face-to-Face

You've been communicating with Pat on one of the dating sites and you've finally decided to meet for coffee. You really want Pat to like you and perhaps to see you as a potential long-term romantic partner. *What might you do to increase your likeability index?*

- **a.** Stimulate and encourage Pat to talk.
- **b.** Reveal significant information about yourself.
- **c.** Demonstrate shared attitudes and beliefs.
- **d.** Present yourself as freethinking and independent.
- **e.** Other

Accents

There is some evidence that we attribute less credibility to people who have accents than we do to people who don't (Lev-Ari & Keysar, 2010). *Does your experience support this finding? Can you think of exceptions? For example, might the chef who speaks with a French accent (assuming you hold French cooking in high esteem) be seen as having more credibility than one without such an accent?*

By engaging in image-confirming behaviors, you also let others know that this is who you are and this is how you want to be seen. At the same time that you reveal aspects of yourself that confirm your desired image, you probably suppress revealing aspects of yourself that would disconfirm this image.

If you use image-confirming strategies too frequently, however, you risk being seen as "too perfect to be for real." If you try to project an all-positive image, it's likely to turn people off—people want to see their friends and associates as having some faults, some imperfections. Also recognize that image-confirming strategies invariably involve you talking about yourself; with that comes the risk of appearing self-absorbed.

Knowledge of these impression-management strategies and the ways in which they are effective and ineffective gives you a greater number of choices for achieving widely diverse goals such as being liked, being believed, excusing failure, securing help, hiding faults, being followed, and confirming your self-image.

A summary of the strategies of impression management appears in Table 3.5.

Table 3.5 In a Nutshell Impression-Management Strategies

Strategies	Goal to Achieve
Affinity-seeking and politeness strategies	to be liked, to be thought of highly, to be seen in the right light
Credibility strategies	to be seen as competent, of good character, and dynamic
Self-handicapping strategies	to excuse actual or possible future failure
Self-deprecating strategies	to secure help by making yourself seem unable to do the task
Self-monitoring strategies	to hide faults, to emphasize the positive and minimize the negative
Influencing strategies	to be persuasive, to be in control, to be followed, to be the leader
Image-confirming strategies	to seek reassurance of one's self-image; to be recognized for who you are

Summary

This chapter looked at the ways in which you perceive yourself and other people and how you manage the perception of yourself that you communicate to others.

The Self in Interpersonal Communication

3.1 Define *self-concept*, *self-awareness*, and *self-esteem* and identify the suggestions for increasing awareness and esteem.

1. Self-concept is the image you have of who you are. Sources of self-concept include others' images of you, social comparisons, cultural teachings, and your own interpretations and evaluations.

2. Self-awareness is your knowledge of yourself—the extent to which you know who you are. A useful way of looking at self-awareness is through the Johari window, which consists of four parts. The open self holds information known to the self and others; the blind self holds information known only to others; the hidden self holds information known only to the self; and the unknown self holds information known to neither the self nor others.

3. To increase self-awareness, ask yourself about yourself, listen to others, actively seek information about yourself, see your different selves, and increase your open self.

4. Self-esteem is the value you place on yourself—your perceived self-worth.

5. To increase self-esteem, try attacking your self-destructive beliefs, seeking affirmation, seeking out nourishing people, and working on projects that result in success.

Perception in Interpersonal Communication

3.2 Explain the five stages of perception and how they influence how you receive messages.

6. Perception is the process by which you become aware of objects and events in the external world.

7. Perception occurs in five stages: (1) stimulation, (2) organization, (3) interpretation–evaluation, (4) memory, and (5) recall.

Impression Formation

3.3 Define the major impression formation processes and the ways to increase accuracy in perception.

8. Seven important processes influence the way you form impressions: Self-fulfilling prophecies may influence the behaviors of others; personality theory allows you to conclude that certain characteristics go with certain other characteristics; perceptual accentuation may lead you to perceive what you expect to perceive instead of what is really there; primacy–recency may influence you to give extra importance to what occurs first (a primacy effect) and may lead you to see what conforms to this judgment and to distort or otherwise misperceive what contradicts it; the tendency to seek and expect consistency may influence you to see what is consistent and not to see what is inconsistent; and attributions, through which you try to understand the behaviors of others, are made in part on the basis of your judgment of control. (And, stereotyping, discussed in Chapter 2, provides often inaccurate shortcuts to impression formation.)

9. Among the major errors of attribution are the self-serving bias, overattribution, and the fundamental attribution error.

10. To increase your accuracy in impression formation, avoid common processing errors, analyze your impressions and recognize your role in perception, check your impressions, reduce uncertainty; and become culturally sensitive by recognizing the differences between you and others and also the differences among people from other cultures.

Impression Management: Goals and Strategies

3.4 Explain the impression management strategies that may help you to be liked, to be believed, to excuse failure, to secure help, to hide faults, to be followed, and to confirm your self-image.

11. Among the goals and strategies of impression management are to be liked (affinity-seeking and politeness strategies), to be believed (credibility strategies that establish your competence, character, and charisma), to excuse failure (self-handicapping strategies), to secure help (self-deprecating strategies), to hide faults (self-monitoring strategies), to be followed (influencing strategies), and to confirm your self-image (image-confirming strategies).

12. Each of these impression-management strategies can backfire and give others negative impressions. Also, each of these strategies may be used to reveal your true self or to present a false self and deceive others in the process.

Key Terms

affinity-seeking strategies
affirmation
attribution of control
blind self
consistency
credibility
cultural sensitivity
fundamental attribution error
halo effect
hidden self
image-confirming strategies
impostor phenomenon
impression formation
impression management
influencing strategies
interpretation–evaluation
negative face

open self
other-orientation
overattribution
perception
perception checking
perceptual accentuation
personality theory
politeness strategies
positive face
primacy effect
primacy–recency
Pygmalion effect
recall
recency effect
reverse halo effect ("horns" effect)
rule of contrast
rule of proximity

rule of similarity
schema
schemata
script
selective attention
selective exposure
selective perception
self-awareness
self-concept
self-deprecating strategies
self-destructive beliefs
self-esteem
self-fulfilling prophecy
self-handicapping strategies
self-monitoring strategies
self-serving bias
unknown self

Verbal Messages

Verbal messages come in different forms. *Using the right forms in the right situations can make a big difference.*

Chapter Topics

Principles of Verbal Messages

Confirmation and Disconfirmation

Guidelines for Using Verbal Messages Effectively

Learning Objectives

4.1 Paraphrase the principles of verbal messages.

4.2 Distinguish between confirmation and disconfirmation; define *racism, ageism, heterosexism,* and *sexism;* and provide examples of appropriate cultural identifiers.

4.3 Explain the guidelines for avoiding the major misuses of verbal language: intensional orientation, allness, fact–inference confusion, indiscrimination, polarization, and static evaluation.

As you communicate, you use two major signal systems—the verbal and the nonverbal. **Verbal messages** are those sent with words. The word *verbal* refers to words, not to orality; verbal messages consist of both oral and written words. Verbal messages do not include laughter; vocalized pauses you make when you speak, such as "er," "um," and "ah"; or responses you make to others that are oral but don't involve words, such as "ha-ha," "aha," and "ugh!" These sounds are considered nonverbal—as are, of course, facial expressions, eye movements, gestures, and so on. This chapter focuses on verbal messages; the next focuses on nonverbal messages.

Principles of Verbal Messages

4.1 Paraphrase the principles of verbal messages.

To clarify the nature of verbal messages and the meanings they create in the minds of listeners, let's examine some specific principles: (1) messages are packaged, (2) meanings are in people, (3) meanings are denotative and connotative, (4) messages vary in abstraction, (5) messages vary in politeness, (6) messages can be onymous or anonymous, (7) messages can deceive, and (8) messages vary in assertiveness. Throughout this discussion you'll find lots of useful suggestions for more effective interpersonal communication.

Messages Are Packaged

Both verbal and nonverbal signals occur simultaneously. Usually, verbal and nonverbal behaviors reinforce or support each other. For example, you don't usually express fear with words while the rest of your body relaxes. You don't normally express anger verbally while your face smiles. Your entire being works as a whole—verbally and nonverbally—to express your thoughts and feelings. This blending of verbal and nonverbal signals seems also to help you think and remember (Iverson & Goldin-Meadow, 1999). Social networking sites enable you to package your messages with simple clicks of the mouse—combining photos and videos with your verbal posts. Even in the text-only Twitter, you can post the URLs to photos, videos, and sites (for example a blog post or a website) where you elaborate on your 140-character tweet.

You often fail to notice this "packaging" in others' messages because it seems so natural. But when the nonverbal messages of someone's posture or face contradict what is said verbally, you take special notice. For example, the person who says, "I'm so glad to see you," but avoids direct eye contact and looks around to see who else is present is sending contradictory messages. You also see contradictory or mixed messages when couples say they love each other but seem to go out of their way to hurt each other nonverbally—for example, being late for important dates, flirting with others, or avoiding touching each other.

An awareness of the packaged nature of communication thus suggests a warning against the too-easy interpretation of another's meaning, especially as revealed in nonverbal behaviors. Before you identify or guess the meaning of any bit of behavior, look at the entire package or cluster of which it is a part, the way in which the cluster is a response to its context, and the role of the specific nonverbal behavior within that cluster. That attractive person winking in your direction may be giving you the come-on—but don't rule out the possibility of ill-fitting contact lenses.

Message Meanings Are in People

Meaning depends not only on the packaging of messages (the combined verbal and nonverbal elements) but also on the interaction of these messages and the

receiver's own thoughts and feelings. You don't "receive" meaning; you create meaning. You construct meaning out of the messages you receive combined with your own social and cultural perspectives (beliefs, attitudes, and values, for example) (Berger & Luckmann, 1980; Delia, 1977; Delia, O'Keefe, & O'Keefe, 1982). Words don't mean; people mean.

For example, if you wanted to know the meaning of the word *love,* you'd probably turn to a dictionary. There you'd find such definitions as "attraction for another person" and "deep affection for another." But where would you turn if you wanted to know what Pedro means when he says, "I'm in love"? Of course, you'd turn to Pedro to discover his meaning. It's in this sense that meanings are not in words but in people. Consequently, to uncover meaning, you need to look into people and not merely into words.

Also recognize that as you change, you also change the meanings you create. That is, although the message sent may not have changed, the meanings you created from it yesterday and the meanings you create today may be quite different. Yesterday, when a special someone said, "I love you," you created certain meanings. But today, when you learn that the same "I love you" was said to three other people, or when you fall in !ove with someone else, you drastically change the meanings you draw from those three words.

Because meanings are in people—and each person is unique and different from every other person—no word or message will mean the same thing to two different people. And this is why, for example, the same message (for example, "Will you get me a cup of coffee," may be perceived as controlling by one person and as a simple request by another. As you can appreciate, this type of misunderstanding can easily lead to interpersonal conflict if you fail to recognize that the meaning is not in the words; it's in the person. As a result, check your perceptions of another's meanings by asking questions, echoing what you perceive to be the other person's feelings or thoughts, and seeking elaboration and clarification.

Meanings Are Denotative and Connotative

Consider a word such as *death.* To a doctor, this word may mean the moment at which the heart stops beating. This is denotative meaning—a rather objective description of an event. To a mother whose son has just died, however, the word means much more. It recalls the son's youth, his ambitions, his family, his illness, and so on. To her, the word is emotional, subjective, and highly personal. These emotional, subjective, and personal associations are the word's connotative meaning. The **denotation** of a word is its objective definition; the **connotation** is its subjective or emotional meaning. Take another example: compare the term *migrant* (to designate Mexicans coming into the United States to better their economic condition) with the term *settlers* (to designate Europeans who came to the United States for the same reason) (Koppelman, 2005). Although both terms describe essentially the same activity (and are essentially the same denotatively), one is often negatively evaluated and the other is more often positively valued, and so these terms differ widely in their connotations.

Now consider a simple nod of the head in answer to the question, "Do you agree?" This gesture is largely denotative and simply says yes. But what about a wink, a smile, or an overly rapid speech rate? These nonverbal expressions are more connotative; they express your feelings rather than objective information. The denotative meaning of a message is universal; most people would agree with the denotative meanings and would give similar definitions. Connotative meanings, however, are extremely personal, and few people would agree on the precise connotative meaning of a word or nonverbal behavior.

Snarl words and *purr words* may further clarify the distinction between denotative and connotative meaning (Hayakawa & Hayakawa, 1989; Hoffmann, 2005). Snarl words are highly negative ("She's an idiot," "He's a pig," "They're a bunch of losers"). Sexist, racist, and heterosexist language and hate speech provide lots of other examples. Purr words are highly positive ("She's a real sweetheart," "He's a dream," "They're the greatest"). Although they may sometimes seem to have denotative meaning and refer to the "real world," snarl and purr words are actually connotative in meaning. They don't describe people or events; rather, they reveal the speaker's feelings about these people or events.

Similarly, the meaning of a given signal depends on the other behavior it accompanies or is close to in time. Pounding a fist on the table during a speech in support of a politician means something quite different from that same gesture in response to news of a friend's death. Divorced from the context, both the denotative and the connotative meanings of messages can be hard to determine. Of course, even if you know the context in detail, you still may not be able to decipher the meaning of the message as the speaker intended. But understanding the context helps and also raises the chances of our understanding the speaker's message accurately.

Understanding the distinction between denotation and connotation should encourage you to clarify connotative meanings (or ask for clarification) when you anticipate potential misunderstandings; misunderstandings are almost always centered on connotative differences.

Messages Vary in Abstraction

Messages vary greatly in **abstraction**, the degree to which they are general or specific. Figure 4.1 illustrates that messages and individual words exist on different levels of abstraction.

At the top of the list is the general or abstract term *entertainment*. Note that *entertainment* includes all the items on the list plus various others—television, novels, drama, comics, and so on. *Film* is more specific and concrete. It includes all of the items below it as well as various other items, such as Indian film or Russian film. It excludes, however, all entertainment that is not film. *American film* is again more specific and excludes all films that aren't American. *Classic American film* further limits American film to a relatively small group of highly acclaimed films. *Classic American Western film* is still more specific, limiting *film* to those that are classic, American, and Western. And *Shane* specifies concretely the one item to which reference is made.

The more general term—in this case, *entertainment*—conjures up many different images. One person may focus on television, another on music, another on comic books,

Figure 4.1   The Abstraction Ladder

Try creating an abstraction ladder of four or five levels for an abstract term such as *food, building, asset,* or any other abstract term. *What do you see as the major differences between the most abstract and the most concrete terms?*

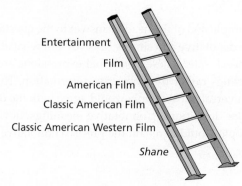

and still another on radio. To some, the word *film* may bring to mind the early silent films. To others, it brings to mind high-tech special effects. To still others, it recalls Disney's animated cartoons. *Shane* guides the listener still further—in this case to one film. But note that even though *Shane* identifies one film, different listeners are likely to focus on different aspects of the film: perhaps its character development, perhaps its love story, perhaps its financial success.

Effective verbal messages include words at many levels of abstraction. At times, an abstract, general term may suit your needs best; at other times, a more concrete, specific term may serve better. Generally, however, the specific term will prove the better choice. As you get more specific—less abstract—you guide the images that will come into your listeners' minds more effectively. In much the same way that you use specific terms to direct your face-to-face listeners' attention to exactly what you want them to focus on, you also use specific terms to direct an Internet search engine to narrow its focus to just those items you want to access (ideally).

Messages Vary in Politeness

One of the best ways to look at **politeness** (consideration, respect, etc.) in interpersonal communication is in terms of both positive and negative politeness. Both of these forms of politeness are responsive to two needs that each person has: (1) the need to be viewed positively by others, to be thought of favorably (that is, to maintain **positive face**) and (2) the need to be autonomous, to have the right to do as we wish (that is, to maintain **negative face**). Politeness in interpersonal communication, then, involves behavior that allows others to maintain both positive and negative face.

Politeness is considered a desirable trait across most cultures (Brown & Levinson, 1987). Cultures differ, however, in how they define politeness. For example, among English speakers, politeness involves showing consideration for others and presenting yourself with confidence and polish. For Japanese speakers, it involves showing respect, especially for those in higher-status positions, and presenting yourself with modesty (Haugh, 2004). Cultures also vary in how important they consider politeness as compared with, say, openness or honesty. And, of course, cultures differ in the rules for expressing politeness or impoliteness and in the punishments for violating the accepted rules (Mao, 1994; Strecker, 1993). For example, members of Asian cultures, especially those of China and Japan, are often singled out because they emphasize politeness and mete out harsher social punishments for violations than would people in the United States or Western Europe (Fraser, 1990).

In the business world, politeness is recognized as an important part of interpersonal interactions. In one study, some 80 percent of employees surveyed believed that they did not get respect at work, and 20 percent felt they were victims of weekly incivility (Tsiantar, 2005). In another study, workers were 33 percent less creative when they were exposed to impolite/uncivil behavior and four times less helpful to others (Lapowsky, 2014). Rudeness in the workplace, it's been argued, reduces performance effectiveness, hurts creativity, and leads to increased worker turnover—all of which is costly for the organization.

Of course, culture is not the only factor influencing politeness. Your personality and your professional training influence your degree of politeness and how you express politeness (Edstrom, 2004). And the context of communication influences politeness; formal situations in which there is considerable power difference call for greater politeness than informal circumstances in which the power differences are minimal (Mullany, 2004).

Politeness and Directness Messages that support or attack face needs (the latter are called face-threatening acts [FTAs]) are often discussed in terms of direct and indirect language. Directness is usually less polite and may infringe on a person's need to maintain negative face—"Write me the recommendation." "Lend me $100." Indirectness

THE CULTURAL MAP   High- and Low-Context Cultures

Context refers to the extent to which information is made explicit or left implicit (because it's known from past experiences or just assumed). In low-context cultures information is made explicit (as in contracts and signed agreements); the communication is direct. In high-context cultures, much of the information is in the context or in what each person already knows from previous experiences; the communication is often indirect.

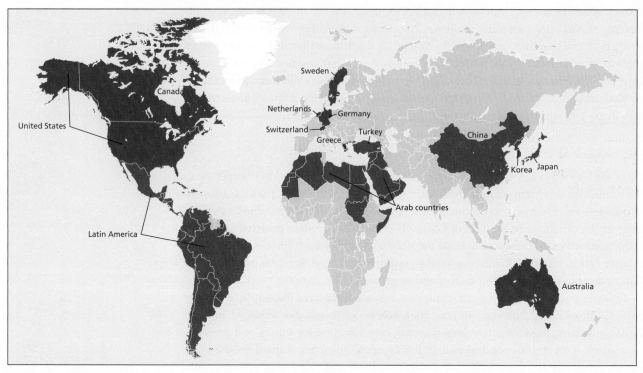

In high context cultures such as these, much meaning is encoded through facial, eye, and other nonverbal movements. The context is more important than the actual words.

In low-context cultures such as these, meaning is encoded largely in verbal form; little is left to chance. The words are more important than the context.

Using the concepts of high and low context, how would you compare your posts on Facebook or Twitter to writing an email to your instructor?

allows the person to maintain autonomy (negative face) and provides an acceptable way for the person to refuse your request. "Would it be possible for you to write me a recommendation?" "Do you happen to have a spare $100 that I might borrow?"

Indirect messages also allow you to express a desire or preference without insulting or offending anyone; they allow you to observe the rules of polite interaction. So instead of saying, "I'm bored with this group," you say, "It's getting late and I have to get up early tomorrow," or you look at your watch and pretend to be surprised by the time. Instead of saying, "This food tastes like cardboard," you say, "I just started my diet" or "I just ate."

Women are more polite in their speech and use more indirect statements when making requests than do men. This difference seems to have both positive and negative implications. Indirect statements, in being more polite, are generally perceived positively, yet they may also be perceived negatively if they are seen as being weaker and less authoritative than more direct statements. Partly for cultural reasons, indirect statements also may be seen as manipulative or underhanded, whereas direct statements may be seen as straightforward and honest.

Politeness in Inclusion and Exclusion Another perspective on politeness can be seen in messages of inclusion and exclusion. Inclusive messages include all people present, acknowledge the relevance of others, and are normally considered polite. Exclusive messages shut out specific people or entire cultural groups and are normally considered impolite.

You see messages of exclusion in the use of in-group language in the presence of an out-group member. When doctors get together and discuss medicine, there's no problem. But when they get together with someone who isn't a doctor, they often fail to adjust to this new person. Instead, they may continue with discussions of procedures, symptoms, medications, and so on, excluding others present. Excluding talk also occurs when people of the same nationality get together within a larger, more heterogeneous group and use the language of their nationality. Similarly, references to experiences not shared by all (experiences such as having children, exotic vacations, and people we know) can serve to include some and exclude others. The use of these terms and experiences can exclude outsiders from full participation in the communication act (Sizemore, 2004).

VIEWPOINTS

Directness

How would you describe the level of directness you use when talking face-to-face versus the level you use in social networking? If you notice differences, what are they (specifically) and to what do you attribute these differences?

Politeness Online The Internet has very specific rules for politeness, called netiquette or, in the case of Twitter, twittiquette. Much as the rules of etiquette provide guidance in communicating in face-to-face social situations, the rules of netiquette and twittiquette provide guidance for communicating politely online (McFedries, 2010). These rules not only make online communication more pleasant and easier but also improve your personal efficiency. Here are some key guidelines:

- *Familiarize yourself with the site before contributing.* Before asking questions about the system, read the Frequently Asked Questions (FAQs).
- *Be brief.* Communicate only the information that is needed; communicate clearly, briefly, and in an organized way.
- *Be gentle.* Refuse a request for friendship gently or ignore it.
- *Don't shout.* WRITING IN CAPS IS PERCEIVED AS SHOUTING.
- *Be discreet.* Don't use social networking information outside the network.
- *Don't spam or flame.* Don't send unsolicited mail, repeatedly send the same mail, or post the same message (or irrelevant messages) to lots of newsgroups. Don't make personal attacks on other users.
- *Avoid offensive language.* Refrain from expressions that would be considered offensive to others, such as sexist or racist terms.
- *Be considerate.* Avoid asking to be friends with someone you suspect may have reason for not wanting to admit you.
- *Don't advertise.* Don't market a product, yourself, or your services on Twitter; it's permissible on Facebook but do it discreetly.
- *Don't plagiarize.* Give credit to others for the ideas you post and certainly any direct quotations.
- *Don't brag.* The norm for social networking is modesty, at least as most social networkers think about it.

Messages Can Be Onymous or Anonymous

Some messages are **onymous** or "signed"; that is, the author of the message is clearly identified, as it is in your textbooks, news-related editorials, feature articles, and, of course, when you communicate face-to-face and, usually, by phone or chat. In many cases, you have the opportunity to respond directly to the speaker/writer and voice your opinions, for example, your agreement or disagreement. Other messages are **anonymous**: the author is not identified. For example, on faculty evaluation questionnaires and on RateMyProfessor.com, the ratings and the comments are published anonymously.

The Internet has made anonymity extremely easy and there are currently a variety of websites that offer to send your e-mails to your boss, your ex-partner, your secret crush, your noisy neighbors, or your inadequate lawyer—all anonymously. Thus, your message gets sent but you are not identified with it. For good or ill, you don't have to deal with the consequences of your message.

One obvious advantage of anonymity is that it allows people to voice opinions that may be unpopular and may thus encourage greater honesty. In the case of RateMyProfessor.com, for example, anonymity ensures that the student writing negative comments about an instructor will not be penalized. An anonymous e-mail to a sexual partner informing him or her about your having an STD and suggesting testing and treatment might never get said in a face-to-face or phone conversation. The presumption is that anonymity encourages honesty and openness.

Anonymity also enables people to disclose their inner feelings, fears, hopes, and dreams with a depth of feeling that they may be otherwise reluctant to do. A variety of websites that enable you to maintain anonymity are available for these purposes. And in these cases, not only are you anonymous but the people who read your messages are also anonymous, a situation that is likely to encourage a greater willingness to make disclosures and to make disclosures that are at a deeper level than people would otherwise employ.

An obvious disadvantage is that anonymity might encourage people to go to extremes—to voice opinions that are outrageous—because there are no consequences to the message. This in turn can easily spark unproductive and unnecessary conflict. With anonymous messages, you can't evaluate the credibility of the source. Advice on depression, for example, may come from someone who knows nothing about depression and may make useless recommendations.

Messages Can Deceive

It comes as no surprise that some messages are truthful and some are deceptive. Although we operate in interpersonal communication on the assumption that people tell the truth, some people do lie. High school students, for example, reported lying about four times in the last 24 hours (Levine, Serota, Carey, & Messer, 2013). College students seem to lie less, about twice per day (DePaulo, et al, 2003). Other research puts the figure a bit lower, from .6 to 1.6 lies per day (George & Robb, 2008). In fact, many view lying as common, whether in politics, business, or interpersonal relationships (Amble, 2005; Knapp, 2008). Lying also begets lying; when one person lies, the likelihood of the other person lying increases (Tyler, Feldman, & Reichert, 2006). Furthermore, people like people who tell the truth more than they like people who lie. So lying needs to be given some attention in any consideration of interpersonal communication.

Lying refers to the act of (1) sending messages (2) with the intention of giving another person information you believe to be false. (1) Lying involves sending some kind of verbal and/or nonverbal message (and remember the absence of facial expression or the absence of verbal comment also communicates); it also requires reception by another person. (2) The message must be sent to deceive intentionally. If you give false information to someone but you believe it to be true, then you haven't lied. You do lie when you send information that you believe to be untrue and you intend to mislead the other person.

INTERPERSONAL CHOICE POINT
Making an Excuse

Your friend is very upset over a recent breakup and wants to patch things up and so asks to borrow your car. You don't think your friend is in any position to drive. *What might you say to refuse this request— a request you've always complied with on previous occasions?*

a. "No, you're not in any shape to drive."

b. "I need the car myself, sorry."

c. "Wouldn't it be better to wait and calm down first?"

d. "I'll drive you."

e. Other

As with other interpersonal topics, cultural differences exist with lying—in the way lying is defined and in the way lying is treated. For example, as children get older, Chinese and Taiwanese (but not Canadians) see lying about the good deeds that they do as positive (as we would expect for cultures that emphasize modesty), but taking credit for these same good deeds is seen negatively (Lee et al., 2002).

Some cultures consider lying to be more important than others—in one study, for example, European Americans considered lies less negatively than did Ecuadorians. Both, however, felt that lying to an out-group member was more acceptable than lying to an in-group member (Mealy, Stephan, & Urrutia, 2007).

Types of Lies Lies vary greatly in type; each lie seems a bit different from every other lie (Bhattacharjee, 2017). Here we discuss one useful system that classifies lies into four types (McGinley, 2000).

Prosocial Deception: To Achieve Some Good These lies are designed to benefit the person lied to or lied about. For example, praising a person's effort to give him or her more confidence or to tell someone they look great to simply make them feel good would be examples of prosocial lies. Many of these lies are taught by the culture (Talwar, Murphy, & Lee, 2007). For example, adults might teach children about Santa Claus and the tooth fairy on the theory that these beliefs somehow benefit the child.

ETHICS IN INTERPERSONAL COMMUNICATION

Lying

Lies have ethical implications. In fact, one of the earliest cultural rules children are taught is that lying is wrong. At the same time, children also learn that in some cases lying is effective—in gaining some reward or in avoiding some punishment.

Some prosocial, self-enhancement, and selfish-deception lies are considered ethical (for example, publicly agreeing with someone you really disagree with to enable the person to save face, saying that someone will get well despite medical evidence to the contrary, or simply bragging about your accomplishments). Some lies are considered not only ethical but required (for example, lying to protect someone from harm or telling the proud parents that their child is beautiful). Other lies (largely those in the antisocial category) are considered unethical (for example, lying to defraud investors or to accuse someone falsely).

However, a large group of lies are not that easy to classify as ethical or unethical, as you'll see in the Ethical Choice Points.

Ethical Choice Points

- *Is it ethical to lie to get what you deserve but can't get any other way? For example, would you lie to get a well-earned promotion or raise? Would it matter if you hurt a colleague's chances of advancement in the process?*
- *Is it ethical to lie to your relationship partner to avoid a conflict and perhaps splitting up? In this situation, would it be ethical to lie if the issue was a minor one (you were late for an appointment because you wanted to see the end of the football game) or a major one (say, continued infidelity)?*
- *Is it ethical to lie to get yourself out of an unpleasant situation? For example, would you lie to get out of an unwanted date, an extra office chore, or a boring conversation?*
- *Is it ethical to lie about the reasons for breaking up a relationship to make it easier for you and the other person? For example, would you conceal that you've fallen in love with another person (or that you're simply bored with the relationship or that the physical attraction is gone) in your breakup speech?*
- *Is it ethical to exaggerate the consequences of an act in order to discourage it? For example, would you lie about the bad effects of marijuana in order to prevent your children or your students from using it?*
- *Is it ethical to lie about yourself in order to appear more appealing—for example, saying you were younger or richer or more honest than you really are? For example, would you lie in your profile on Facebook or Google+ or on a dating website to increase your chances of meeting someone really special?*

Some prosocial lies are expected and not to lie would be considered impolite. For example, it would be impolite to tell parents that their child is ugly (even if you firmly believe that the child is ugly). The only polite course is to lie. Still another type of prosocial lie is when you lie to someone who would harm others: you would lie to an enemy or to someone intending to hurt another person. These lies too would be expected and not to lie would likely brand you as contributing to any harm done as a result of your telling the truth. Children learn prosocial lying early in life and it remains the major type of lie children (and likely adults as well) tell (McGinley, 2000).

Self-Enhancement Deception: To Make Yourself Look Good   Not all self-enhancement involves deception. For example, impression-management strategies may be used simply to highlight what is already true about you and that others may not see at first glance. And so, you might mention your accomplishments to establish your credibility. If these accomplishments are true, then this impression-management effort is not deception.

At the same time, however, each of the impression-management strategies may also involve self-enhancement deception. For example, you might mention your good grades but omit the poorer ones; you might recount your generous acts and omit any selfish ones; or you might embellish your competence, lie about your financial situation, or present yourself as a lot more successful than you really are. And, of course, some simply lie in the attempt to enhance the self. For example, in a study of online Taiwanese teen daters, some 70 percent admitted to lying (Huang & Yang, 2013).

Selfish Deception: To Protect Yourself   These lies are designed to protect yourself. Sometimes it's something as simple as not answering the phone because you are busy. In this case, no one really gets hurt. But some selfish deception strategies may involve hurting others. For example, you might imply that you did most of the work for the report—protecting yourself but also hurting the reputation of your colleague. Or you might conceal certain facts to protect yourself—previous failed relationships, an unsavory family history, or being fired. Hiding an extra-relational affair is perhaps the classic example of selfish deception.

Sometimes selfish deception is designed to protect the relationship and so, for example, you might lie about a one-time infidelity to protect yourself (and perhaps your partner as well) but also to protect and maintain the relationship.

Antisocial Deception: To Harm Someone   These lies are designed to hurt another person. Such lies might include spreading false rumors about someone you dislike or falsely accusing an opposing candidate of some wrongdoing (something you see regularly in political debates). Fighting parents may falsely accuse each other of a variety of wrongdoing to gain the affection and loyalty of a child. Falsely accusing another person of a wrong you did yourself would be perhaps the clearest example of antisocial deception.

Messages Vary in Assertiveness

If you disagree with other people in a group, do you speak your mind? Do you allow others to take advantage of you because you're reluctant to say what you want? Do you feel uncomfortable when you have to state your opinion in a group? Questions such as these speak to your degree of **assertiveness**.

Lying Reasons

Most often people lie to gain some benefit or reward (for example, to increase closeness in a desirable relationship, to protect their self-esteem, or to obtain money) or to avoid punishment. In an analysis of 322 lies, researchers found that 75.8 percent benefited the liar, 21.7 percent benefited the person who was told the lie, and 2.5 percent benefited a third party (Camden, Motley, & Wilson, 1984). *Do you think you'd find similar percentages if this study were done today? How would the figures for face-to-face lies differ from the figures for lying in social media?*

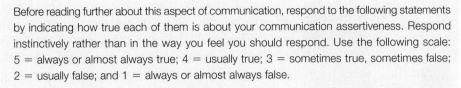

Before reading further about this aspect of communication, respond to the following statements by indicating how true each of them is about your communication assertiveness. Respond instinctively rather than in the way you feel you should respond. Use the following scale: 5 = always or almost always true; 4 = usually true; 3 = sometimes true, sometimes false; 2 = usually false; and 1 = always or almost always false.

_____ **1.** I would express my opinion in a group even if my view contradicted the opinions of others.

_____ **2.** When asked to do something that I really don't want to do, I can say no without feeling guilty.

_____ **3.** I can express my opinion to my superiors on the job.

_____ **4.** I can start a conversation with a stranger on a bus or at a business gathering without fear.

_____ **5.** I voice objection to people's behavior if I feel it infringes on my rights.

All five items identify characteristics of assertive communication. So high scores (say, about 20 and above) indicate a high level of assertiveness. Low scores (say, about 10 and below) indicate a low level of assertiveness. The discussion in this section clarifies the nature of assertive communication and offers guidelines for increasing your own assertiveness and, at the same time, reducing any aggressive tendencies when appropriate.

Assertive people operate with an "I win, you win" philosophy; they assume that both parties can gain something from an interpersonal interaction, even from a confrontation. Assertive people are more positive and score lower on measures of hopelessness than do nonassertive people (Velting, 1999). Assertive people are willing to assert their rights. Unlike their aggressive counterparts, however, they don't hurt others in the process. Assertive people speak their minds and welcome others to do likewise.

Do realize that, as with many other aspects of communication, there are wide cultural differences when it comes to assertiveness. For example, the values of assertiveness are more likely to be extolled in individualist cultures than in collectivist cultures. Assertiveness is valued more by those cultures that stress competition, individual success, and independence. It is valued much less by those cultures that stress cooperation, group success, and the interdependence of all members on one another. American students, for example, are found to be significantly more assertive than Japanese or Korean students (Thompson, Klopf, & Ishii, 1991; Thompson & Klopf, 1991). Thus, for some situations, assertiveness may be an effective strategy in one culture but may create problems in another. Assertiveness with an elder in many Asian and Hispanic cultures may be seen as insulting and disrespectful.

Most people are nonassertive in certain situations; if you're one of these people and if you wish to increase your assertiveness, consider the suggestions in the following subsections (Bower & Bower, 2005; Windy & Constantinou, 2005). (If you are always nonassertive and are unhappy about this, then you may need to work with a therapist to change your behavior.)

Analyze Assertive Communications The first step in increasing your assertiveness skills is to understand the nature of assertive communications. Observe and analyze the messages of others. Learn to distinguish the differences among assertive, aggressive, and nonassertive messages. Focus on what makes one behavior assertive and another behavior nonassertive or aggressive. After you've gained some skills in observing the behaviors of others, turn your analysis to yourself. Analyze situations in which you're normally assertive and situations in which you're more likely to act nonassertively or aggressively. What characterizes these situations? What do the situations in which you're normally assertive have in common? How do you speak? How do you communicate nonverbally?

Assertiveness and Leadership

There is some evidence that the extremes of assertiveness—being too assertive or not assertive enough—are seen as weaknesses in organizational leadership (Santora, 2007). *How would you describe an effective leader's level of assertiveness? How does this compare with your own level of assertiveness?*

Rehearse Assertive Communications One way to rehearse assertiveness is to use desensitization techniques (Dwyer, 2005; Wolpe, 1958). Select a situation in which you're normally nonassertive. Build a hierarchy that begins with a relatively nonthreatening message and ends with the desired communication. For example, let's say that you have difficulty voicing your opinion to your supervisor at work. The desired behavior then is to tell your supervisor your opinions. To desensitize yourself, construct a hierarchy of visualized situations leading up to this desired behavior. Such a hierarchy might begin with visualizing yourself talking with your boss. Visualize this scenario until you can do it without any anxiety or discomfort. Once you have mastered this visualization, visualize a step closer to your goal, such as walking into your boss's office. Again, do this until your visualization creates no discomfort. Continue with these successive visualizations until you can visualize yourself telling your boss your opinion. As with the other visualizations, do this until you can do it while totally relaxed. This is the mental rehearsal. You might add a vocal dimension to this by actually acting out (with voice and gesture) telling your boss your opinion. Again, do this until you experience no difficulty or discomfort. Next, try doing this in front of a trusted and supportive friend or group of friends. Ideally this interaction will provide you with useful feedback. After this rehearsal, you're probably ready for the next step.

Communicate Assertively This step is naturally the most difficult but obviously the most important. Here's a generally effective pattern to follow in communicating assertively:

1. *Describe the problem.* Don't evaluate or judge it. "We're all working on this advertising project together. You're missing half our meetings, and you still haven't produced your first report."

2. *State how this problem affects you.* Tell the person how you feel. "My job depends on the success of this project, and I don't think it's fair that I have to do extra work to make up for what you're not doing."

3. *Propose solutions that are workable.* Propose solutions that allow the person to save face. Describe or visualize the situation if your solution were put into effect. "If you can get your report to the group by Tuesday, we'll still be able to meet our deadline. I could give you a call on Monday to remind you."

4. *Confirm understanding.* "It's clear that we can't produce this project if you're not going to pull your own weight. Will you have the report to us by Tuesday?"

Keep in mind that assertiveness is not always the most desirable response. Assertive people are assertive when they want to be, but they can be nonassertive if the situation calls for it. For example, you might wish to be nonassertive in a situation in which assertiveness might emotionally hurt the other person. Let's say that an older relative wishes you to do something for her or him. You could assert your rights and say no, but in doing so you would probably hurt this person; it might be better simply to do as asked. Of course, limits should be observed. You should be careful in such a situation that you're not hurt instead.

A note of caution should be added to this discussion. It's easy to visualize a situation in which, for example, people are talking behind you in a movie and, with your newfound enthusiasm for assertiveness, you tell them to be quiet. It's also easy to see yourself getting smashed in the teeth as a result. In applying the principles of assertive communication, be careful that you don't go beyond what you can handle effectively.

Table 4.1 provides a summary of the principles of verbal messages and some implications for speaking and listening more effectively.

Table 4.1 In a Nutshell Principles of Verbal Messages

Principle	Verbal Message Strategies
Messages are packaged.	Look for the combination of verbal and nonverbal messages working together or against each other.
Message meanings are in people.	Look not only to the words used but to the person using the words.
Meanings are both denotative and connotative.	Look at both the objective meaning and the subjective meaning expressed.
Messages vary in abstraction.	Use both general and specific terms.
Messages vary in politeness.	Use messages that reflect positively on others and allow them to be autonomous.
Messages can be onymous or anonymous.	Use ownership of a message as one factor in evaluating messages.
Messages can deceive.	Acting with a truth bias is usually appropriate, but realize that in some situations, messages may be false and may be purposely designed to mislead you.
Meanings vary in assertiveness.	Acting assertively is most often the preferred mode of communication, but attitudes toward assertiveness vary greatly with culture.

UNDERSTANDING *INTERPERSONAL SKILLS*

Metacommunication: The Ability to Talk about Your Talk

Metacommunication refers to communication about communication. Messages may refer to the objects and events in the world (in what is called *object language*) but also to itself—you can talk about your talk, write about your writing, and this is metacommunication. (The prefix *meta-* can mean a variety of things, but as used in communication, philosophy, and psychology, its meaning is best translated as *about*. Thus, *metacommunication* is communication *about* communication, *metalanguage* is language *about* language, and a *metamessage* is a message *about* a message.)

Actually, you use this distinction every day, perhaps without realizing it. For example, when you send someone an e-mail with a seemingly sarcastic comment and then put a smiley face at the end, the smiley face communicates about your communication; it says something like this: "This message is not to be taken literally; I'm trying to be humorous." The smiley face is a metamessage; it's a message about a message. When you say, in preface to some comment, "I'm not sure about this, but . . . ," you're communicating a message about a message; you're commenting on the message you're about to send and asking that it be understood with the qualification that you may be wrong. When you conclude a comment with "I'm only kidding," you're metacommunicating; you're communicating about your communication. In relationship communication, you often talk in metalanguage and say things like, "You're too critical" or "I love when you tell me how much I mean to you."

Metalanguage is especially important when you want to clarify the communication patterns between yourself and another person: "I'd like to talk about the way you talk about me to our friends" or "I think we should talk about the way we talk about sex."

And, of course, you can also use nonverbal messages to metacommunicate. You can wink at someone to indicate that you're only kidding or roll your eyes after saying "Yeah, that was great," with your eye movement contradicting the literal meaning of the verbal message.

Communicating with Metacommunication

Here are a few suggestions for increasing your metacommunication effectiveness:

- *Explain the feelings* that go with your thoughts. For example, if your comments are, say, harsher than usual, you might note that you are angry or frightened.
- *Give clear feedforward* to help the other person get a general picture of the messages that will follow.
- *Paraphrase* your own complex messages to clarify your meaning even further. Similarly, check on your understanding of another's message by paraphrasing what you think the other person means.
- *Ask for clarification* if you have doubts about another's meaning.

Working With Metacommunication

As you continue reading this chapter, think about the role of metacommunication in your everyday communication. *In what ways do you normally metacommunicate? Are these generally productive? What kinds of metacommunication messages do you wish other people would use more often?*

Confirmation and Disconfirmation

4.2 Distinguish between confirmation and disconfirmation; define *racism*, *ageism*, *heterosexism*, and *sexism;* and provide examples of appropriate cultural identifiers.

The language behaviors known as confirmation and disconfirmation have to do with the extent to which you acknowledge another person. Consider this situation: You've been living with someone for the last six months and you arrive home late one night. Your partner, Pat, is angry and complains about your being so late. Of the following responses, which are you most likely to give?

1. Stop screaming. I'm not interested in what you're babbling about. I'll do what I want, when I want. I'm going to bed.

2. What are you so angry about? Didn't you get in three hours late last Thursday when you went to that office party? So knock it off.

3. You have a right to be angry. I should have called to tell you I was going to be late, but I got involved in a serious debate at work and I couldn't leave until it was resolved.

In response 1, you dismiss Pat's anger and even indicate dismissal of Pat as a person. In response 2, you reject the validity of Pat's reasons for being angry, although you do not dismiss either Pat's feelings of anger or of Pat as a person. In response 3, you acknowledge Pat's anger and the reasons for being angry. In addition, you provide some kind of explanation and, in doing so, show that both Pat's feelings and Pat as a person are important and that Pat has the right to know what happened. The first response is an example of disconfirmation, the second of rejection, and the third of confirmation.

Psychologist William James once observed that "no more fiendish punishment could be devised, even were such a thing physically possible, than that one should be turned loose in society and remain absolutely unnoticed by all the members thereof." In this often-quoted observation, James identifies the essence of disconfirmation (Veenendall & Feinstein, 1995; Watzlawick, Beavin, & Jackson, 1967).

Disconfirmation is a communication pattern in which you ignore a person's presence as well as that person's communications. You say, in effect, that the person and what she or he has to say aren't worth serious attention. Disconfirming responses often lead to loss of self-esteem (Sommer, Williams, Ciarocco, & Baumeister, 2001).

Note that disconfirmation is not the same as rejection. In **rejection**, you disagree with the person; you indicate your unwillingness to accept something the other person says or does. In disconfirming someone, however, you deny that person's significance; you claim that what this person says or does simply does not count.

Confirmation is the opposite of disconfirmation. In **confirmation**, you not only acknowledge the presence of the other person but also indicate your acceptance of this person, of this person's definition of self, and of your relationship as defined or viewed by this other person. Confirming responses often lead to gains in self-esteem and have been shown to reduce student apprehension in the classroom and indirectly to increase motivation and learning (Ellis, 2004). You can communicate both confirmation and disconfirmation in a wide variety of ways; Table 4.2 identifies some specific confirming and disconfirming differences. As you review this table, try to imagine a specific illustration for

Hate Speech

Hate speech is speech that is hostile, offensive, degrading, or intimidating to a particular group of people because of their race, nationality, age, affectional orientation, or sex. *How do you respond when you hear other students using hate speech?*

Table 4.2 Confirmation and Disconfirmation

Disconfirmation	Confirmation
Ignores the presence or contributions of the other person; expresses indifference to what the other person says.	**Acknowledges** the presence and the contributions of the other person by either supporting or taking issue with what he or she says.
Makes no nonverbal contact; avoids direct eye contact; avoids touching and general nonverbal closeness.	**Makes nonverbal contact** by maintaining direct eye contact and, when appropriate, touching, hugging, kissing, and otherwise demonstrating acknowledgment of the other.
Monologues; engages in communication in which one person speaks and one person listens; there is no real interaction; there is no real concern or respect for each other.	**Dialogues;** communication in which both persons are speakers and listeners; both are involved; both are concerned with and have respect for each other.
Jumps to interpretation or evaluation rather than working at understanding what the other person means.	**Demonstrates understanding** of what the other person says and means and reflects understanding in what the other person says; when in doubt asks questions.
Discourages, interrupts, or otherwise makes it difficult for the other person to express him- or herself.	**Encourages** the other person to express his or her thoughts and feelings by showing interest and asking questions.
Avoids responding or responds tangentially by acknowledging the other person's comment but shifts the focus of the message in another direction.	**Responds directly** and exclusively to what the other person says.

each of the ways of communicating disconfirmation and confirmation (Galvin, Braithwaite, & Bylund, 2015; Pearson, 1993).

You can gain insight into a wide variety of offensive language practices by viewing them as types of disconfirmation—as language that alienates and separates. We'll explore this important principle by looking at racism, ageism, heterosexism, and sexism.

Racism

Racist language is language that denigrates an ethnic or racial group; it is language that expresses racist attitudes. It also, however, contributes to the development of racist attitudes in those who use or hear the language. Even when racism is subtle, unintentional, or even unconscious, its effects are systematically damaging (Dovidio, Gaertner, Kawakami, & Hodson, 2002).

Racism exists on both individual and institutional levels—distinctions made by educational researchers and used throughout this discussion (Koppelman, 2005). Individual racism involves the negative attitudes and beliefs that people hold about specific races. The assumption that certain races are intellectually inferior to others or that certain races are incapable of certain achievements are clear examples of individual racism. Prejudice against groups such as American Indians, African Americans, Hispanics, and Arabs have been with us throughout history and is still a part of many people's lives. Such racism is seen in the negative terms people use to refer to members of other races and to disparage their customs and accomplishments.

Institutionalized racism is seen in patterns—such as de facto school segregation, companies' reluctance to hire members of minority groups, and banks' unwillingness to extend mortgages and business loans to members of some races or tendency to charge higher interest rates.

Examine your own language for:

- Derogatory terms for members of a particular race.
- Maintaining stereotypes and interacting with members of other races based on those stereotypes.
- Including reference to race when it's irrelevant, as in "the [racial name] surgeon" or "the [racial name] athlete."
- Attributing an individual's economic or social problems to the individual's race rather than to, say, institutionalized racism or general economic problems that affect everyone.

Ageism

Although used mainly to refer to prejudice against older people, the word **ageism** can also refer to prejudice against other age groups. For example, if you describe all teenagers as selfish and undependable, you're discriminating against a group purely because of their age and thus are ageist in your statements. In some cultures—some Asian and some African cultures, for example—the old are revered and respected. Younger people seek them out for advice on economic, ethical, and relationship issues.

Individual ageism is seen in the general disrespect many show toward older people and in negative stereotypes about older people. Institutional ageism is seen in mandatory retirement laws and age restrictions in certain occupations (as opposed to requirements based on demonstrated competence). In a survey by AARP, 48 percent of those age fifty and over said that they experienced or witnessed age discrimination at work (AARP, 2014). In less obvious forms, ageism is seen in the media's portrayal of old people as incompetent, complaining, and (perhaps most clearly evidenced in both television and films) without romantic feelings. Rarely, for example, does a TV show or film show older people working productively, being cooperative and pleasant, and engaging in romantic and sexual relationships.

Popular language is replete with examples of **ageist language**; "little old lady," "old hag," "old-timer," "over the hill," "old coot," and "old fogy" are a few examples. As with sexism, qualifying a description of someone in terms of his or her age demonstrates ageism. For example, if you refer to "a quick-witted 75-year-old" or "an agile 65-year-old" or "a responsible teenager," you're implying that these qualities are unusual in people of these ages and thus need special mention.

You also communicate ageism when you speak to older people in overly simple words or explain things that don't need explaining. Nonverbally, you demonstrate ageist communication when, for example, you avoid touching an older person but touch others, when you avoid making direct eye contact with the older person but readily do so with others, or when you speak at an overly high volume (suggesting that all older people have hearing difficulties).

One useful way to avoid ageism is to recognize and avoid the illogical stereotypes that ageist language is based on and examine your own language to see if you do any of the following:

- Talk down to a person because he or she is older. Older people are not mentally slow; most people remain mentally alert well into old age.
- Refresh an older person's memory each time you see the person. Older people can and do remember things.
- Imply that romantic relationships are no longer important. Older people continue to be interested in relationships.
- Speak at an abnormally high volume. Being older does not mean being hard of hearing or being unable to see; most older people hear and see quite well, sometimes with hearing aids or glasses.
- Avoid engaging older people in conversation as you would wish to be engaged. Older people are interested in the world around them.

Even though you want to avoid ageist communication, you may sometimes wish to make adjustments when talking with someone who does have language or communication difficulties. The American Speech and Hearing Association website offers several useful suggestions:

- Reduce as much background noise as you can.
- Ease into the conversation by beginning with casual topics and then moving into more familiar topics. Stay with each topic for a while; avoid jumping too quickly from one topic to another.

- Speak in relatively short sentences and questions.
- Give the person added time to respond. Some older people react more slowly and need extra time.
- Listen actively.

Heterosexism

Heterosexism also exists on both an individual and an institutional level. Individual heterosexism consists of attitudes, behaviors, and language that disparage gay men and lesbians and includes the belief that all sexual behavior that is not heterosexual is unnatural and deserving of criticism and condemnation. These beliefs are at the heart of antigay violence and "gay bashing." Individual heterosexism also includes beliefs such as the notions that gay men or lesbians are more likely to commit crimes than are heterosexuals (there's actually no difference) and to molest children than are heterosexuals (actually, child molesters are overwhelmingly heterosexual, married men) (Abel & Harlow, 2001; Koppelman, 2005). It also includes the belief that gay men and lesbians cannot maintain stable relationships or effectively raise children, beliefs that contradict research evidence (Fitzpatrick, Jandt, Myrick, & Edgar, 1994; Johnson & O'Connor, 2002).

Institutional heterosexism is easy to identify. For example, the ban on gay marriage in most states and the fact that at this time only a handful of states allow gay marriage is a good example of institutional heterosexism. Other examples include the Catholic Church's ban on gay priests and the many laws prohibiting adoption of children by gay men or lesbians. In some cultures (for example, in India, Malaysia, Pakistan, and Singapore), same-sex relations are illegal; penalties range from a misdemeanor charge in Liberia to life in jail in Singapore and death in Pakistan.

Heterosexist language includes derogatory terms used for lesbians and gay men. For example, surveys in the military showed that 80 percent of those surveyed heard "offensive speech, derogatory names, jokes or remarks about gays" and that 85 percent believed that such derogatory speech was "tolerated" (*The New York Times*, March 25, 2000, p. A12). You also see heterosexism in more subtle forms of language usage, for example, when you qualify a professional—as in "gay athlete" or "lesbian doctor"—and, in effect, say that athletes and doctors are not normally gay or lesbian.

Still another form of heterosexism is the presumption of heterosexuality. Usually, people assume the person they're talking to or about is heterosexual. And usually they're correct because most people are heterosexual. At the same time, however, this presumption denies the lesbian or gay identity a certain legitimacy. The practice is very similar to the presumptions of whiteness and maleness that we have made significant inroads in eliminating.

Examine your own language for possible heterosexism and consider, for example, if you do any of the following:

- Use offensive nonverbal mannerisms that parody stereotypes when talking about gay men and lesbians. Do you avoid the "startled eye blink" with which some people react to gay couples (Mahaffey, Bryan, & Hutchison, 2005)?
- "Compliment" gay men and lesbians by saying that they "don't look it." To gay men and lesbians, this is not a compliment. Similarly, expressing disappointment that a person is gay—often thought to be a compliment, as in comments such as "What a waste!"—is not really a compliment.

Gay Homophobes

Anecdotal evidence supports a commonly held idea that those who are most outspokenly homophobic may themselves be gay (and very closeted), based perhaps on the behaviors of people like Ted Haggard, Larry Craig, Glenn Murphy Jr., and Dennis Hastert, all of whom were outspoken critics of same-sex rights. Now, however, there is also academic research supporting this connection (Ryan & Ryan, 2012). *How do you feel about this?*

- Make the assumption that every gay or lesbian knows what every other gay or lesbian is thinking. It's very similar to asking a Japanese person why Sony is investing heavily in the United States.
- Stereotype—saying things like "Lesbians are so loyal" or "Gay men are so open with their feelings," which ignore the reality of wide differences within any group and are potentially insulting to all groups.
- Overattribute—the tendency to attribute just about everything a person does, says, and believes to the fact that the person is gay or lesbian. This tendency helps to activate and perpetuate stereotypes.
- Forget that relationship milestones are important to all people. Ignoring anniversaries or birthdays of, say, a relative's partner is resented by everyone.
- The failure to acknowledge the relationship status of gay and lesbian relatives, for example, not referring to your mother's brother's partner as *uncle*.

As you think about heterosexism, recognize not only that heterosexist language creates barriers to communication but also that its absence fosters more meaningful communication: greater comfort, an increased willingness to disclose personal information, and a greater willingness to engage in future interactions (Dorland & Fisher, 2001).

Sexism

Individual sexism consists of prejudicial attitudes and beliefs about men or women based on rigid beliefs about gender roles. These might include beliefs such as the idea that women should be caretakers, should be sensitive at all times, and should acquiesce to a man's decisions concerning political or financial matters. Sexist attitudes also include the beliefs that men are insensitive, interested only in sex, and incapable of communicating feelings.

Institutional sexism, on the other hand, results from customs and practices that discriminate against people because of their gender. Clear examples in business and industry are the widespread practice of paying women less than men for the same job and the discrimination against women in upper levels of management. Another clear example of institutionalized sexism is the courts' practice of automatically or nearly automatically granting child custody to the mother rather than to the father.

A subtle form of sexism is seen in the attitudes, concerns, and expectations of parents (Stephens-Davidowitz, 2014). For example, of the Google searches asking whether a child is overweight, there are 17 requests about a girl for every 10 requests about a boy. On the other hand, there are 25 requests about whether a son is gifted for every 10 about a daughter. More Google searches are asked about a boy's intelligence and leadership abilities, whereas more searches are asked about a girl's attractiveness.

Parents are apparently more concerned about a girl's weight than a boy's, perhaps reinforcing the "girls must be attractive" stereotype. Apparently, parents are more concerned about a son being gifted (and ultimately being successful) than a daughter, perhaps reinforcing the stereotype that boys must succeed by their wits.

Of particular interest here is **sexist language**: language that puts down someone because of his or her gender (a term usually used to refer to language derogatory toward women). The National Council of Teachers of English (NCTE) has proposed guidelines for nonsexist (gender-free, gender-neutral, or sex-fair) language. These guidelines concern the use of the generic word *man*, the use of

---

INTERPERSONAL CHOICE POINT
Putting Your Foot in Your Mouth

During a discussion in class you make some remarks you thought were funny but that you soon discovered were considered homophobic and that clearly violated the classroom norms for polite and unbiased talk. *What might you say to make this situation a little less awkward?*

a. "It's homophobic, but it's funny, don't you think?"

b. "Don't get so uptight. It was meant to be humorous."

c. "That was really stupid of me to say. Please ignore that stupid comment."

d. Say nothing.

e. Other

generic *he* and *his,* and sex-role stereotyping (Penfield, 1987). Consider your own communication behavior. Examine your own language for examples of sexism such as these:

- **Use of *man* generically.** Using the term to refer to humanity in general emphasizes maleness at the expense of femaleness. Gender-neutral terms can easily be substituted. Instead of "mankind," say "humanity," "people," or "human beings." Similarly, the use of terms such as *policeman* or *fireman* that presume maleness as the norm—and femaleness as a deviation from this norm—are clear and common examples of sexist language.

- **Use of *he* and *his* as generic.** Instead, you can alternate pronouns or restructure your sentences to eliminate any reference to gender. For example, the NCTE Guidelines (Penfield, 1987) suggest that instead of saying, "The average student is worried about his grades," you say, "The average student is worried about grades." You can also use the plural form that avoids sex identification and say "Students worry about their grades."

- **Use of sex-role stereotyping.** When you make the hypothetical elementary school teacher female and the college professor male, or refer to doctors as male and nurses as female, you're sex-role stereotyping, as you are when you include the sex of a professional with terms such as "woman doctor" or "male nurse."

The Spread of Sexism

Research finds that when a man makes sexist remarks to a particular woman, other women (bystanders who overhear the remarks) also experience reactions such as anxiety, depression, and a general negative attitude toward men (Nauert, 2015). *How do you respond when you hear sexist comments?*

Cultural Identifiers

Recognizing that messages vary in cultural sensitivity is a great step toward developing confirming and avoiding disconfirming messages. Perhaps the best way to develop nonracist, nonheterosexist, nonageist, and nonsexist language is to examine the preferred **cultural identifiers** to use in talking to and about members of different groups. Keep in mind, however, that preferred terms frequently change over time, so keep in touch with the most current preferences. The preferences and many of the specific examples identified here are drawn largely from the findings of the Task Force on Bias-Free Language of the Association of American University Presses (Schwartz, 1995, 2005; Faigley, 2009; the GLAAD Media Reference Guide (2016)); and the numerous educational and governmental websites devoted to bias-free language.

Race and Nationality Generally, most African Americans prefer *African American* to *black* (Hecht, Jackson, & Ribeau, 2003), although *black* is often used with *white,* as well as in a variety of other contexts (for example, Department of Black and Puerto Rican Studies, the *Journal of Black History*, and Black History Month). The American Psychological Association recommends that both terms be capitalized, but the *Chicago Manual of Style* (the manual used by most newspapers and publishing houses) recommends using lowercase. The terms *Negro* and *colored,* although used in the names of some organizations (for example, the United Negro College Fund and the National Association for the Advancement of Colored People), are no longer used outside these contexts. *People of color*—a literary-sounding term appropriate perhaps to public speaking but awkward in most conversations—is preferred to *nonwhite,* which implies that whiteness is the norm and nonwhiteness is a deviation from that norm.

White is generally used to refer to those whose roots are in European cultures and usually does not include Hispanics. Analogous to African American (which itself is based on a long tradition of terms such as Irish American and Italian American) is the phrase *European American*. Few European Americans, however, call themselves that; most prefer their national origins emphasized, as in, for example, German American or Greek American.

Generally, the term *Hispanic* refers to anyone who identifies as belonging to a Spanish-speaking culture. *Latina* (female) and *Latino* (male) refer to persons whose roots are in one of the Latin American countries, such as Haiti, the Dominican Republic, Nicaragua, or Guatemala. *Hispanic American* refers to U.S. residents whose ancestry is in a Spanish culture; the term includes people from Mexico, the Caribbean, and Central and South America. In emphasizing a Spanish heritage, however, the term is really inaccurate because it leaves out the large numbers of people in the Caribbean and in South America whose origins are African, Native American, French, or Portuguese. *Chicana* (female) and *Chicano* (male) refer to persons with roots in Mexico, although it often connotes a nationalist attitude (Jandt, 2004) and is considered offensive by many Mexican Americans. *Mexican American* is generally preferred.

Inuk (plural *Inuit*), also spelled with two *n*'s (*Innuk* and *Innuit*), is preferred to *Eskimo* (the term the U.S. Census Bureau uses), which was applied to the indigenous peoples of Alaska and Canada by Europeans and literally means "raw meat eaters."

The word *Indian* technically refers only to someone from India, not to members of other Asian countries or to the indigenous peoples of North America. *American Indian* or *Native American* is preferred, even though many Native Americans do refer to themselves as *Indians* and *Indian people.* The word *squaw,* used to refer to a Native American woman and still used in the names of some places in the United States and in some textbooks, is clearly a term to be avoided; its usage is almost always negative and insulting (Koppelman, 2005).

In Canada, indigenous people are called *first people* or *first nations.* The term *native American* (with a lowercase *n*) is most often used to refer to persons born in the United States. Although technically the term could refer to anyone born in North or South America, people outside the United States generally prefer more specific designations, such as *Argentinean, Cuban,* or *Canadian.* The term *native* describes an indigenous inhabitant; it is not used to indicate "someone having a less developed culture."

Muslim (rather than the older *Moslem*) is the preferred form to refer to a person who adheres to the religious teachings of Islam. *Quran* (rather than *Koran*) is the preferred spelling for the scriptures of Islam. *Jewish people* is often preferred to *Jews,* and *Jewess* (a Jewish female) is considered derogatory. Finally, the term *non-Christian* is to be avoided: it implies that people who have other beliefs deviate from the norm.

When history was being written from a European perspective, Europe was taken as the focal point and the rest of the world was defined in terms of its location relative to that continent. Thus, Asia became the East or the Orient, and *Asians* became *Orientals*—a term that is today considered inappropriate or "Eurocentric." Thus, people from Asia are *Asians*, just as people from Africa are *Africans* and people from Europe are *Europeans.*

Age   *Older person* is preferred to *elder, elderly, senior,* or *senior citizen* (which

technically refers to someone older than 65). Usually, however, terms designating age are unnecessary. Sometimes, of course, you will need to refer to a person's age group, but most of the time age is irrelevant—in much the same way that racial or affectional orientation terms are usually irrelevant.

Affectional Orientation   Generally, *gay* is the preferred term to refer to a man who has an affectional orientation toward other men, and *lesbian* is the preferred term for a woman who has an affectional orientation toward other women. ("Lesbian" means "gay woman," so the term *lesbian woman* is redundant.) *Homosexual* refers to both gay men and lesbians, and describes a same-sex sexual orientation but is generally considered derogatory because it implies a total focus on sex; *lesbian* and *gay man* are preferred (GLAAD, 2016). The definitions of *gay* and *lesbian* go beyond sexual orientation and refer to a self-identification as a gay man or lesbian. *Gay* as a noun, although widely used, may be offensive in some contexts, as in "We have two gays on the team." *Gay* is best used only as an adjective.

Straight meaning *heterosexual* is generally accepted as in "he's gay and he's straight." The problem with the word *straight* is that its opposite is not *gay* but *crooked* or *bent* which would be derogatory. But, the jury is out on this one.

Queer is used by many gay and lesbian people but is not thought appropriate by others. Some major newspapers such as the *The Washington Post* and the *The New York Times* will not use the term while *The Huffington Post* has a section called "queer voices" where GLBTQ news and opinions are reported. So, again, there is no universal agreement. The best advice to give with this one is, if you're GLBTQ, use it as you wish; if you're straight, avoid it.

Because most scientific thinking holds that sexuality is not a matter of choice, the terms *sexual orientation* and *affectional orientation* are preferred to *sexual preference* or *sexual status* (which is also vague). In the case of same-sex marriages, there are two husbands or two wives. In a male-male marriage, each person is referred to as husband and in the case of female-female marriage, each person is referred to as wife. Some same-sex couples prefer the term *partner* or *lover*.

Sex and Gender   Generally, the term *girl* should be used only to refer to very young females and is equivalent to *boy*. In online dating, it is okay for women to refer to themselves as girls but men need to use the word *woman* (Roper, 2014). *Boy* is never used to refer to people in blue-collar positions, as it once was. *Lady* is negatively evaluated by many because it connotes the stereotype of the prim and proper woman. *Woman* or *young woman* is preferred. The term *ma'am*, originally an honorific used to show respect, is probably best avoided because today it's often used as a verbal tag to comment (indirectly) on the woman's age or marital status (Angier, 2010). Transgendered people (people who identify themselves as members of the sex opposite to the one they were assigned at birth and who may be gay or straight, male or female) are addressed according to their self-identified sex. Thus, if the person identifies as a woman, then the feminine name and pronouns are used—regardless of the person's biological sex. If the person identifies as a man, then the masculine name and pronouns are used. **Transgender** is the opposite of **cisgender** which refers to people whose self-identification corresponds to the sex assigned at birth.

Transvestites (people who prefer at times to dress in the clothing of the sex other than the one they were assigned at birth and who may be gay or straight, male or female) are addressed on the basis of their clothing. If the person is dressed as a woman—regardless of the birth-assigned sex—she is referred to and addressed with feminine pronouns and feminine name. If the person is dressed as a man—regardless of the birth-assigned sex—he is referred to and addressed with masculine pronouns and masculine name.

Table 4.3 provides a brief summary of confirming and disconfirming messages.

Table 4.3 In a Nutshell Confirmation and Disconfirmation

Confirming Messages	Disconfirming Messages
Those messages that • accept • support • acknowledge the importance and contributions of the other person	Those messages that ignore the presence and the contributions of the other person and that put down others such as • racism • heterosexism • ageism • sexism

Guidelines for Using Verbal Messages Effectively

4.3 Explain the guidelines for avoiding the major misuses of verbal language: intensional orientation, allness, fact–inference confusion, indiscrimination, polarization, and static evaluation.

Our examination of the principles governing the verbal messages system has suggested a wide variety of ways to use language more effectively. Here are some additional guidelines for making your own verbal messages more effective and a more accurate reflection of the world in which we live. We'll consider six such guidelines: (1) Extensionalize: avoid intensional orientation; (2) see the individual: avoid allness, (3) distinguish between facts and inferences: avoid fact–inference confusion, (4) discriminate among: avoid indiscrimination, (5) talk about the middle: avoid polarization, and (6) update messages: avoid static evaluation (previewed in Figure 4.2).

Extensionalize: Avoid Intensional Orientation

The term **intensional orientation** refers to a tendency to view people, objects, and events in terms of how they're talked about or labeled rather than in terms of how they actually exist. **Extensional orientation** is the opposite: it's a tendency to look first at

Figure 4.2 Effective Verbal Messaging

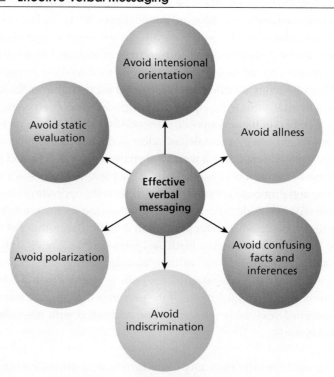

the actual people, objects, and events and then at the labels—a tendency to be guided by what you see happening rather than by the way something or someone is talked about or labeled.

Intensional orientation occurs when you act as if the words and labels were more important than the things they represent—as if the map were more important than the territory. In its extreme form, intensional orientation is seen in the person who is afraid of dogs and who begins to sweat when shown a picture of a dog or when hearing people talk about dogs. Here the person is responding to a label as if it were the actual thing. In its more common form, intensional orientation occurs when you see people through your schemata instead of on the basis of their specific behaviors. For example, it occurs when you think of a professor as an unworldly egghead before getting to know the specific professor.

The corrective to intensional orientation is to focus first on the object, person, or event and then on the way in which the object, person, or event is talked about. Labels are certainly helpful guides, but don't allow them to obscure what they're meant to symbolize.

See the Individual: Avoid Allness

The world is infinitely complex, and because of this you can never say all there is to say about anything—at least not logically. This is particularly true when you are dealing with people. You may think you know all there is to know about certain individuals or about why they did what they did, yet clearly you don't know all. You can never know all the reasons you do something, so there is no way you can know all the reasons your parents, friends, or enemies did something. When you assume you can say all or have said all that can be said, you are into the pattern of illogical thinking called **allness**.

Suppose, for example, you go on a first date with someone who, at least during the first hour or so, turns out to be less interesting than you would have liked. Because of this initial impression, you may infer that this person is dull, always and everywhere. Yet it could be that this person is simply ill at ease or shy during first meetings. The problem here is that you run the risk of judging a person on the basis of a very short acquaintanceship. Further, if you then define this person as dull, you're likely to treat the person as dull and fulfill your own prophecy.

Famed British Prime Minister Benjamin Disraeli once said that "to be conscious that you are ignorant is a great step toward knowledge." This observation is an excellent example of a nonallness attitude. If you recognize that there is more to learn, more to see, more to hear, you leave yourself open to this additional information, and you'll be better prepared to assimilate it.

A useful extensional device that can help you avoid allness is to end each statement, sometimes verbally but always mentally, with an "et cetera"—a reminder that there is more to learn, know, and say, that every statement is inevitably incomplete. To be sure, some people overuse the "et cetera." They use it as a substitute for being specific, which defeats its purpose. It should be used to mentally remind yourself that there is more to know and more to say.

Distinguish between Facts and Inferences: Avoid Fact–Inference Confusion

Language enables us to form statements of facts and inferences without making any linguistic distinction between the two. Similarly, when we listen to such statements, we often don't make a clear distinction between statements of fact and statements of inference. Yet there are great differences between the two. Barriers to clear thinking can be created when inferences are treated as facts—a hazard called **fact–inference confusion**.

INTERPERSONAL CHOICE POINT
Confronting a Lie

You ask about the previous night's whereabouts of your romantic partner of two years and are told something that you're convinced is false. You don't want to break up the relationship over this, but you do want your partner to be truthful and you want an opportunity to resolve the problems that contributed to this situation. *What might you say to achieve your purposes?*

a. "Is that the truth?"

b. "Let's be honest with each other; I can deal with the truth."

c. "You're lying now like you always lie."

d. Say nothing.

e. Other

For example, you can make statements about objects and events that you observe, and you can make statements about objects and events that you have not observed. In form or structure, these statements are similar; they cannot be distinguished from each other by any grammatical analysis. For example, you can say, "She is wearing a blue jacket" as well as "She is harboring an illogical hatred." If you diagrammed these sentences, they would yield identical structures, and yet you know that they're different types of statements. In the first sentence, you can observe the jacket and the blue color; the sentence constitutes a *factual statement*. But how do you observe "illogical hatred"? Obviously, this is not a descriptive statement but an *inferential statement*, a statement that you make not solely on the basis of what you observe but on the basis of what you observe plus your own conclusions.

There's no problem with making inferential statements; you must make them if you're to talk about much that is meaningful. The problem arises when you act as though those inferential statements are factual statements.

The differences between factual and inferential statements are highlighted in Table 4.4 and are based on the discussions of William Haney (1973) and Harry Weinberg (1959). As you go through this table, consider how you would classify such statements as: "God exists," "Democracy is the best form of government," and "This paper is white." Distinguishing between these two types of statements does not imply that one type is better than the other. Both types of statements are useful; both are important. The problem arises when you treat an inferential statement as if it were fact. Phrase your inferential statements as tentative. Recognize that such statements may be wrong. Leave open the possibility of other alternatives.

You may wish to test your ability to distinguish facts from inferences by carefully reading the following account, modeled on a report developed by William Haney (1973), and the observations based on it. Indicate whether you think the observations are true, false, or doubtful on the basis of the information presented in the report. Circle T if the observation is definitely true, F if the observation is definitely false, and ? if the observation may be either true or false. Judge each observation in order. Don't reread the observations after you have indicated your judgment, and don't change any of your answers.

A world-renowned scientist had just printed out the final results to the experiment, and turned out the lights in the lab, when a broad figure appeared and demanded the printout. The researcher opened the drawer. Everything in the drawer was picked up. The individual ran down the hall. The chief medical officer was notified immediately.

1. The thief was tall and broad.

2. The researcher turned off the lights.

3. A broad figure demanded the printout.

4. The printout was picked up by someone.

Table 4.4 Differences between Factual and Inferential Statements

Inferential Statements	Factual Statements
May be made at any time	May be made only after observation
Go beyond what has been observed	Are limited to what has been observed
May be made by anyone	May be made only by the observer
May be about any time—past, present, or future	May be about only the past or the present
Involve varying degrees of probability	Approach certainty
Are not subject to verifiable standards	Are subject to verifiable, scientific standards

5. The printout was picked up by the thief.

6. A tall figure appeared after the researcher turned off the lights in the lab.

7. The man who opened the drawer was the researcher.

8. The broad figure ran down the hall.

9. The drawer was never actually opened.

10. Three persons are referred to in this story.

For each statement, ask yourself, "How can I be absolutely certain that the statement is true or false?" You should find that only statement 3 can be clearly identified as true and only statement 9 as false; the remaining eight statements should be marked "?." This brief experience was designed to trap you into making inferences and thinking of them as facts. Statement 3 is true (it's in the report) and statement 9 is false (the drawer was opened). But all other statements are inferences and should have been marked "?". Review the remaining eight statements to see why you cannot be certain that any of them are either true or false.

Discriminate Among: Avoid Indiscrimination

Nature seems to abhor sameness at least as much as vacuums because nowhere in the universe can you find identical entities. Everything is unique. Language, however, provides common nouns—such as *teacher, student, friend, enemy, war, politician, liberal,* and the like—that may lead you to focus on similarities. Such nouns can lead you to group together all teachers, all students, and all friends and perhaps divert attention from the uniqueness of each individual, object, and event.

The misevaluation known as **indiscrimination**—a form of stereotyping—occurs when you focus on classes of individuals, objects, or events and fail to see that each is unique and needs to be looked at individually. Indiscrimination can be seen in statements such as these:

- He's just like the rest of them: lazy, stupid, a real slob.
- I really don't want another ethnic on the board of directors. One is enough for me.
- Read a romance novel? I read one when I was 16. That was enough to convince me.

A useful antidote to indiscrimination is the extensional device called the *index,* a mental subscript that identifies each individual in a group as an individual, even though all members of the group may be covered by the same label. For example, when you think and talk of an individual politician as just a "politician," you may fail to see the uniqueness in this politician and the differences between this particular politician and other politicians. However, when you think with the index—when you think not of politician but of $politician^1$ or $politician^2$ or $politician^3$—you're less likely to fall into the trap of indiscrimination and more likely to focus on the differences among politicians. The same is true with members of cultural, national, or religious groups; when you think of $Iraqi^1$ and $Iraqi^2$, you'll be reminded that not all Iraqis are the same. The more you discriminate among individuals covered by the same label, the less likely you are to discriminate against any group.

Talk about the Middle: Avoid Polarization

Polarization, often referred to as the fallacy of either/or, is the tendency to look at the world and to describe it in terms of extremes—good or bad, positive or negative, healthy or sick, brilliant or stupid, rich or poor, and so on. Polarized statements come in many forms; for example:

- After listening to the evidence, I'm still not clear who the good guys are and who the bad guys are.
- Well, are you for us or against us?
- College had better get me a good job. Otherwise, this has been a big waste of time.

Most people exist somewhere between the extremes of good and bad, healthy and sick, brilliant and stupid, rich and poor. Yet there seems to be a strong tendency to view only the extremes and to categorize people, objects, and events in terms of these polar opposites.

You can easily demonstrate this tendency by filling in the opposites for each of the following words:

		Opposite
tall	___:___:___:___:___:___:___	_____
heavy	___:___:___:___:___:___:___	_____
strong	___:___:___:___:___:___:___	_____
happy	___:___:___:___:___:___:___	_____
legal	___:___:___:___:___:___:___	_____

Filling in the opposites should have been relatively easy and quick. The words should also have been fairly short. Further, if various different people supplied the opposites, there would be a high degree of agreement among them. Now try to fill in the middle positions with words meaning, for example, "midway between tall and short," "midway between heavy and light," and so on. Do this before reading any further.

These midway responses (compared to the opposites) were probably more difficult to think of and took you more time. The responses should also have been long words or phrases of several words. And different people would probably agree less on these midway responses than on the opposites.

This exercise clearly illustrates the ease with which we can think and talk in opposites and the difficulty we have in thinking and talking about the middle. But recognize that the vast majority of cases exist between extremes. Don't allow the ready availability of extreme terms to obscure the reality of what lies in between (Read, 2004).

In some cases, of course, it's legitimate to talk in terms of two values. For example, either this thing you're holding is a book or it isn't. Clearly, the classes "book" and "not-book" include all possibilities. There is no problem with this kind of statement. Similarly, you may say that a student either will pass this course or will not, as these two categories include all the possibilities.

You create problems, however, when you use this either/or form in situations in which it's inappropriate; for example, "The supervisor is either for us or against us." The two choices simply don't include all possibilities: The supervisor may be for us in some things and against us in others, or he or she may be neutral. Right now there is a tendency to group people into pro- and antiwar, for example—and into similar pro- and anti- categories on abortion, taxes, and just about every important political or social issue. Similarly, you see examples of polarization in opinions about the Middle East, with some people entirely and totally supportive of one side and others entirely and totally supportive of the other side. But clearly these extremes do not include all possibilities, and polarized thinking actually prevents us from entertaining the vast middle ground that exists on all such issues.

Update Messages: Avoid Static Evaluation

Language changes very slowly, especially when compared to the rapid pace at which people and things change. When you retain an evaluation of a person, despite the inevitable changes in the person, you're engaging in **static evaluation**.

Alfred Korzybski (1933) used an interesting illustration in this connection: In a tank there is a large fish and many small fish that are its natural food source. Given freedom in the tank, the large fish will eat the small fish. After some time, the tank is partitioned, with the large fish on one side and the small fish on the other, divided only by glass. For a time, the large fish will try to eat the small fish but will fail; each time it tries, it will knock into the glass partition. After some time it will learn that trying to eat the small fish means difficulty, and it will no longer go after them. Now, however, the partition is removed, and the small fish swim all around the big fish. But the big fish does not eat them and in fact will die of starvation while its natural food swims all around. The large fish has learned a pattern of behavior, and even though the actual territory has changed, the map remains static.

While you would probably agree that everything is in a constant state of flux, the relevant question is whether you act as if you know this. Do you act in accordance with the notion of change instead of just accepting it intellectually? Do you treat your little sister as if she were 10 years old, or do you treat her like the 20-year-old woman she has become? Your evaluations of yourself and others need to keep pace with the rapidly changing real world. Otherwise you'll be left with attitudes and beliefs—static evaluations—about a world that no longer exists.

To guard against static evaluation, use an extensional device called the date: mentally date your statements and especially your evaluations. Remember that Gerry Smith^{2015} is not Gerry Smith^{2019}; academic abilities^{2015} are not academic abilities^{2019}. T. S. Eliot, in *The Cocktail Party*, said that "what we know of other people is only our memory of the moments during which we knew them. And they have changed since then . . . at every meeting we are meeting a stranger."

These six guidelines, which are summarized in Table 4.5, will not solve all problems in verbal communication—but they will help you to align your language more accurately with the real world, the world of words and not words; infinite complexity; facts and inferences; sameness and difference; extremes and middle ground; and, perhaps most important, constant change.

Table 4.5 In a Nutshell Essential Verbal Message Guidelines

Effective	Ineffective
Extensionalize: distinguish between the way people, objects, and events are talked about and what exists in reality; the word is not the thing.	**Intensionalize:** treat words and things as the same; respond to things as they are talked about rather than as they exist.
Avoid allness: no one can know or say all about anything; always assume there is more to be said, more to learn.	**Commit allness:** assume you know everything that needs to be known or that all that can be said has been said.
Distinguish between facts and inferences and respond to them differently.	**Confuse facts and inferences:** respond to inferences as if they were facts.
Discriminate among items covered by the same label.	**Indiscriminately treat** all items (people, objects, and events) covered by the same label similarly.
Talk about the middle, where the vast majority of cases exist.	**Polarize:** view and talk about only the extremes; ignore the middle.
Recognize change: regularly update your messages, meanings, evaluations, and beliefs.	**Statically evaluate:** fail to recognize the inevitable change in things and people.

Summary

This chapter introduced the verbal message system and identified some basic principles concerning how the verbal message system works and how it can be used more effectively.

Principles of Verbal Messages

4.1 Paraphrase the principles of verbal messages.

1. Messages are packaged; verbal and nonverbal signals interact to produce one (ideally) unified message. Six major ways nonverbal messages can interact with verbal messages are to (1) accent, or emphasize a verbal message; (2) complement, or add nuances of meaning; (3) contradict, or deny the verbal message; (4) control, or manage the flow of communication; (5) repeat, or restate the message; and (6) substitute, or take the place of a verbal message.

2. Message meanings are in people—in people's thoughts and feelings, not just in their words.

3. Meanings are both denotative and connotative. Denotation is the dictionary meaning of a word or sentence. Connotation is the personal meaning of a word or sentence. Denotative meaning is relatively objective; connotative meaning is highly subjective.

4. Messages vary in abstraction; they vary from very specific and concrete to highly abstract and general.

5. Messages vary in politeness—from rude to extremely polite—and may be viewed in terms of maintaining positive and negative face. Variations in what is considered polite among cultures are often great.

6. Messages can be onymous, in which the sender is identified, or anonymous, in which the sender is unidentified.

7. Messages can deceive; some messages are lies.

8. Messages vary in assertiveness. Standing up for one's own rights without infringing on the rights of others is the goal of most assertive communication.

Confirmation and Disconfirmation

4.2 Distinguish between confirmation and disconfirmation; define *racism*, *ageism*, *heterosexism*, and *sexism*; and provide examples of appropriate cultural identifiers.

9. Disconfirmation is communication that ignores another, that denies the other person's definition of self. Confirmation expresses acknowledgment and acceptance of others and avoids racist, ageist, heterosexist, and sexist expressions that are disconfirming.

10. Appropriate cultural identifiers are essential for effective interpersonal communication.

Guidelines for Using Verbal Messages Effectively

4.3 Explain the guidelines for avoiding the major misuses of verbal language: intensional orientation, allness, fact–inference confusion, indiscrimination, polarization, and static evaluation.

11. Extensionalize: the word is not the thing. Avoid intensional orientation, the tendency to view the world in the way it's talked about or labeled. Instead, respond to things first; look for the labels second.

12. See the individual; avoid allness, our tendency to describe the world in extreme terms that imply we know all or are saying all there is to say. To combat allness, remind yourself that you can never know all or say all about anything; use a mental and sometimes verbal "et cetera."

13. Distinguish between facts and inferences, and act differently depending on whether the message is factual or inferential.

14. Discriminate among. Avoid indiscrimination, the tendency to group unique individuals or items because they're covered by the same term or label. To combat indiscrimination, recognize uniqueness, and mentally index each individual in a group (teacher[1], teacher[2]).

15. Talk with middle terms; avoid polarization, the tendency to describe the world in terms of extremes or polar opposites. To combat polarization, use middle terms and qualifiers.

16. Update messages regularly; nothing is static. Avoid static evaluation, the tendency to describe the world in static terms, denying constant change. To combat static evaluation, recognize the inevitability of change; date statements and evaluations, realizing, for example, that Gerry Smith[2013] is not Gerry Smith[2020].

Key Terms

abstraction	denotation	onymous messages
ageism	disconfirmation	polarization
ageist language	extensional orientation	politeness
allness	fact–inference confusion	positive face
anonymous messages	heterosexist language	racist language
assertiveness	indiscrimination	rejection
cisgender	intensional orientation	sexist language
confirmation	lying	static evaluation
connotation	metacommunication	transgender
cultural identifiers	negative face	verbal messages

CHAPTER FIVE

Nonverbal Messages

Nonverbal messages come in different forms. *Learn to use and respond to them for greater interpersonal effectiveness.*

Chapter Topics

Principles of Nonverbal Communication

Channels of Nonverbal Communication

Nonverbal Communication Competence

Learning Objectives

5.1 Explain the principles of nonverbal messages.

5.2 Explain the channels through which nonverbal messages are sent and received.

5.3 Identify the competencies for effectively encoding and decoding nonverbal messages.

A good way to begin the study of **nonverbal communication**, which we define simply as communication without words, is to consider your own beliefs about nonverbal communication. Which of the following statements do you believe are true?

1. Nonverbal communication conveys more meaning than verbal communication.
2. Understanding nonverbal communication will enable you to tell what people are thinking, "to read a person like a book."

3. Studying nonverbal communication will enable you to detect lying.

4. Unlike verbal communication, the meanings of nonverbal signals are universal throughout the world.

5. When verbal and nonverbal messages contradict each other, it's wise to believe the nonverbal.

Actually, all of these statements are popular myths about nonverbal communication. Briefly, (1) in some instances, nonverbal messages may communicate more meaning than verbal messages, but, in most cases, it depends on the situation. You won't get very far discussing complex theories and historical events nonverbally, for example. (2) This is an impossible task; you may get ideas about what someone is thinking, but you really can't be certain on the basis of nonverbal behaviors alone. (3) Lie detection is a far more difficult process than any chapter or even series of courses could accomplish. (4) Although some nonverbal behaviors may be universal in meaning, many signals communicate very different meanings in different cultures. (5) People can be deceptive verbally as well as nonverbally; it's best to look at the entire group of signals before making a judgment, but even then it won't be an easy or sure thing.

Studying nonverbal communication and developing your nonverbal competence will yield a variety of benefits.

- It improves your understanding of people, those from your own culture as well as those from cultures very different from your own. Increased accuracy in understanding others will yield obvious benefits in social and workplace situations—from understanding the coy smile of a romantic interest to the meaning of a supervisor's gestures.

- It increases your effectiveness in a variety of interpersonal situations, including close relationships, workplace relationships, teacher–student relationships, intercultural communication, courtroom communication, politics, and health care (DeVito, 2014; Knapp, 2008; Richmond, McCroskey, & Hickson, 2012; Riggio & Feldman, 2005).

- It increases your own perceived attractiveness; the greater your ability to send and receive nonverbal signals, the higher your popularity and psychosocial well-being are likely to be (Burgoon, Guerrero, & Floyd, 2010).

- It enables you to make a more effective self-presentation. For example, when you meet someone for the first time—at least in face-to-face meetings—you form impressions of the person largely on the basis of his or her nonverbal messages. Being able to more effectively understand and manage your nonverbal messages will enable you to present yourself in the way you want to be perceived.

You communicate nonverbally when you gesture, smile or frown, widen your eyes, move your chair closer to someone, wear jewelry, touch someone, raise your vocal volume, or even when you say nothing. The crucial aspect of nonverbal communication is that the message you send is in some way received by one or more other people. If you gesture while alone in your room and no one is there to see you, then, most theorists would argue, communication has not taken place. The same, of course, is true of verbal messages: if you recite a speech and no one hears it, then interpersonal communication has not taken place.

Principles of Nonverbal Communication

5.1 Explain the principles of nonverbal messages.

Perhaps the best way to begin the study of nonverbal communication is to examine several principles that, as you'll see, also identify the varied functions that nonverbal messages serve (Afifi, 2007; Burgoon & Bacue, 2003; Burgoon & Hoobler, 2002; DeVito, 2014). These will also demonstrate the power of nonverbal communication. Figure 5.1 provides a preview of these principles.

Nonverbal Messages Interact with Verbal Messages

Verbal and nonverbal messages interact with each other in six major ways: to accent, to complement, to contradict, to control, to repeat, and to substitute for each other.

- *Accent* Nonverbal communication is often used to accent or emphasize some part of the verbal message. You might, for example, raise your voice to underscore a particular word or phrase, bang your fist on the desk to stress your commitment, or look longingly into someone's eyes when saying, "I love you."

- *Complement* Nonverbal communication may be used to complement, to add nuances of meaning not communicated by your verbal message. Thus, you might smile when telling a story (to suggest that you find it humorous) or frown and shake your head when recounting someone's deceit (to suggest your disapproval).

- *Contradict* You may deliberately contradict your verbal messages with nonverbal movements, for example, by crossing your fingers or winking to indicate that you're lying.

- *Control* Nonverbal movements may be used to control, or to indicate your desire to control, the flow of verbal messages, as when you purse your lips, lean forward, or make hand movements to indicate that you want to speak. You might also put up your hand or vocalize your pauses (for example, with "um") to indicate that you have not finished and aren't ready to relinquish the floor to the next speaker.

Figure 5.1 The Power of Nonverbal Messages

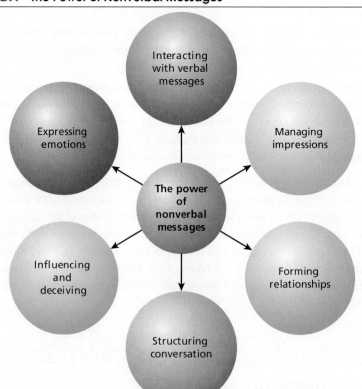

- *Repeat* You can repeat or restate the verbal message nonverbally. You can, for example, follow your verbal "Is that all right?" with raised eyebrows and a questioning look, or you can motion with your head or hand to repeat your verbal "Let's go."
- *Substitute* You may also use nonverbal communication to substitute for verbal messages. You can, for example, signal "okay" with a hand gesture. You can nod your head to indicate yes or shake your head to indicate no.

When you communicate electronically, of course, your message is communicated by means of typed letters without facial expressions or gestures that normally accompany face-to-face communication and without the changes in rate and volume that are part of normal telephone communication. To compensate for this lack of nonverbal behavior, the **emoticon** or **smiley**, and their more sophisticated counterparts, the **emoji**, were created. Originally—and it's still widely in use—an emoticon or smiley was a symbol typed with regular computer keys. And so :-) represented a smile and ;-) represented a wink. Even here there was cultural variation. For example, because it's considered impolite for a Japanese woman to show her teeth when she smiles, the Japanese emoticon for a woman's smile is (∧ . ∧), where the dot signifies a closed mouth. A man's smile is written (∧ - ∧), signifying a more open mouth smile. Now, emoticons and emoji are more often inserted into written messages from pull down menus and, of course, are provided as comment options on social media.

Nonverbal Messages Help Manage Impressions

It is largely through the nonverbal communications of others that you form impressions of them. Based on a person's body size, skin color, and dress, as well as on the way the person smiles, maintains eye contact, and expresses him- or herself facially, you form impressions—you judge who the person is and what the person is like.

And, at the same time that you form impressions of others, you are also managing the impressions they form of you, using different strategies to achieve different impressions. Of course, many of these strategies involve nonverbal messages. For example:

- *To be liked*, you might smile, pat another on the back, and shake hands warmly. See Table 5.1 for some additional ways in which nonverbal communication may make you seem more attractive and more likeable (Andersen, 2004; Riggio & Feldman, 2005).
- *To be believed*, you might use focused eye contact, a firm stance, and open gestures.
- *To excuse failure*, you might look sad, cover your face with your hands, and shake your head.
- *To secure help*, by indicating helplessness, you might use open hand gestures, a puzzled look, and inept movements.
- *To hide faults*, you might avoid self-touching.
- *To be followed*, you might dress the part of a leader or display your diploma or awards where others can see them.
- *To confirm your self-image and to communicate it to others*, you might dress in certain ways or decorate your apartment with items that reflect your personality.

Nonverbal Messages Help Form Relationships

Much of your relationship life is lived nonverbally. You communicate affection, support, and love, in part at least, nonverbally (Floyd & Mikkelson, 2005). At the same time, you also communicate displeasure, anger, and animosity through nonverbal signals.

Table 5.1 Ten Nonverbal Messages and Attractiveness

Attractive	Unattractive
Gesture to show liveliness and animation in ways that are appropriate to the situation and to the message.	Gesture for the sake of gesturing or gesture in ways that may prove offensive to members of other cultures.
Nod and lean forward to signal that you're listening and are interested.	Go on automatic pilot, nodding without any connection to what is said, or lean so far forward that you intrude on the other's space.
Smile and facially show your interest, attention, and positivity.	Overdo it; inappropriate smiling is likely to be perceived negatively.
Make eye contact in moderation.	Stare, ogle, glare, or otherwise make the person feel that he or she is under scrutiny.
Touch in moderation when appropriate. When in doubt, avoid touching another.	Touch excessively or too intimately.
Use vocal variation in rate, rhythm, pitch, and volume to communicate your animation and involvement in what you're saying.	Fall into a pattern in which, for example, your voice goes up and down without any relationship to what you're saying.
Use appropriate facial reactions, posture, and back-channeling cues to show that you're listening.	Listen motionlessly or in ways that suggest you're listening only halfheartedly.
Stand reasonably close to show connectedness.	Invade the other person's comfort zone.
Present a pleasant smell—and be careful to camouflage the onions, garlic, or smoke that you're so used to you can't smell.	Overdo the cologne or perfume.
Dress appropriately to the situation.	Wear clothing that's uncomfortable or that calls attention to itself.

Greetings

The social or cheek kiss is fast replacing the handshake in the workplace, perhaps because of the Latin influence or perhaps because of growing informality in the business world (Olson, 2006). But because the practice is in transition, it's often difficult to know how to greet people. *What nonverbal signals would you look for in deciding whether someone expects you to extend a hand or pucker your lips?*

You also use nonverbal signals to communicate the nature of your relationship to another person, and you and that person communicate nonverbally with each other. These signals that communicate your relationship status are known as tie signs: they indicate the ways in which your relationship is tied together (Afifi & Johnson, 2005; Goffman, 1967; Knapp, Hall, & Horgan, 2014.). Tie signs are also used to confirm the level of the relationship; for example, you might hold hands to see if this is responded to positively. Of course, tie signs are often used to let others know that the two of you are tied together.

Tie signs vary in intimacy and may extend from the relatively informal handshake through more intimate forms—such as hand-holding and arm linking—to very intimate contact—such as full mouth kissing (Andersen, 2004).

You also use nonverbal signals to communicate your relationship dominance and status (Dunbar & Burgoon, 2005; Knapp, Hall, & Horgan, 2014). The large corner office with the huge desk communicates high status, just as the basement cubicle communicates low status.

Nonverbal Messages Structure Conversation

When you're in conversation, you give and receive cues—signals that you're ready to speak, to listen, to comment on what the speaker just said. These cues regulate and structure the interaction. These turn-taking cues may be verbal (as when you say, "What do you think?" and thereby give the speaking turn over to the listener). Most often, however, they're nonverbal; a nod of the head in the direction of someone else, for example, signals that you're ready to give up your speaking turn and want this other person to say something. You also show that you're listening and that you want the conversation to continue (or that you're not listening and want the conversation to end) largely through nonverbal signals of posture and eye contact (or the lack thereof).

Nonverbal Messages Can Influence and Deceive

You can influence others not only through what you say but also through your nonverbal signals. A focused glance that says you're committed; gestures that further explain what you're saying; appropriate dress that says, "I'll easily fit in with this organization"—these are just a few examples of ways in which you can exert nonverbal influence.

Gesturing even seems to help learning and memory (Dean, 2010c). For example, children increase their learning when they gesture (Stevanoni & Salmon, 2005) and, among adults, those who gestured while solving a problem were quicker to solve the problem the second time (Beilock & Goldin-Meadow, 2010). Apparently, gesturing helps reinforce the message or activity in one's memory.

And with the ability to influence, of course, comes the ability to deceive—to mislead another person into thinking something is true when it's false or that something is false when it's true. One common example of nonverbal deception is using your eyes and facial expressions to communicate a liking for other people when you're really interested only in gaining their support in some endeavor. Not surprisingly, you also use nonverbal signals to detect deception in others. For example, you may well suspect a person of lying if he or she avoids eye contact, fidgets, and conveys inconsistent verbal and nonverbal messages.

Research shows that it's very difficult to detect when a person is lying or telling the truth. The hundreds of research studies conducted on this topic find that, in most instances, people judge lying accurately in less than 60 percent of the cases, only slightly better than chance (Knapp, 2008). And these percentages are even lower when you try to detect lying in a person from a culture very different from your own (Sabourin, 2007).

Some evidence shows that lie detection is even less accurate in long-standing relationships, where it is expected that each person will tell the truth (Guerrero, Andersen, & Afifi, 2007). One of the most important reasons for this is the **truth bias**: you assume that the person is telling the truth. There are also situations where there is a **deception bias**. For example, in prison, where lying is so prevalent and where lie detection is a crucial survival skill, prisoners and prison guards often operate with a lie bias and assume that what the speaker is saying is a lie (Knapp, 2008).

With these cautions in mind, and from a combination of research studies, the following behaviors were found to accompany lying most often (Andersen, 2004; Burgoon, 2005; DePaulo et al., 2003; Knapp, 2008; Leathers & Eaves, 2008):

- *Liars hold back.* They speak more slowly, take longer to respond to questions, and generally give less information and elaboration.
- *Liars leak.* Slight facial and eye movements may reveal the person's real feelings, a process referred to as leakage. Often this is the result of what has come to be called "duping delight"—the pleasure you get when you feel you're putting over a lie.
- *Liars make less sense.* Liars' messages contain more discrepancies, more inconsistencies.

INTERPERSONAL CHOICE POINT
Smiling to Bad Effect

Sally smiles almost all the time. Even when she criticizes or reprimands a subordinate, she ends with a smile, and this dilutes the strength of her message. As Sally's supervisor, you need her to realize what she's doing and to change her nonverbals. *What are some of the things you can say to Sally that will not offend her but at the same time get her to realize that her nonverbals are not consistent with her verbal message?*

a. Give Sally a book on nonverbal communication.

b. Tell Sally directly.

c. Catch her smiling and then call it to her attention.

d. Say nothing.

e. Other

- *Liars give a more negative impression.* Generally, liars are seen as less willing to be cooperative, smile less than truth-tellers, and are more defensive.
- *Liars are tense.* The tension may be revealed by their higher-pitched voices and their excessive body movements.
- *Liars exhibit greater pupil dilation, more eye blinks, and more gaze aversion.*
- *Liars speak with a higher vocal pitch.* Their voices often sound as if they were under stress.
- *Liars make more errors and use more hesitations in their speech.* They pause more and for longer periods of time.
- *Liars make more hand, leg, and foot movements.*
- *Liars engage in more self-touching movements.* For example, liars touch their face or hair more and touch more objects, for example, playing with a coffee cup or pen.

Nonverbal Messages Are Crucial for Expressing Emotions

Although people often explain and reveal emotions verbally, nonverbal signals communicate a great part of your emotional experience. For example, you reveal your level of happiness or sadness or confusion largely through facial expressions. Of course, you also reveal your feelings by posture (for example, whether tense or relaxed), gestures, eye movements, and even the dilation of your pupils. Nonverbal messages often help people communicate unpleasant messages that they might feel uncomfortable putting into words (Infante, Rancer, & Avtgis, 2010). For example, you might avoid eye contact and maintain large distances between yourself and someone with whom you didn't want to interact or with whom you want to decrease the intensity of your relationship.

You also use nonverbal messages to hide your emotions. You might, for example, smile even though you feel sad to avoid dampening the party spirit. Or you might laugh at someone's joke even though you think it is silly.

At the same time that you express emotions nonverbally, you also use nonverbal cues to decode or decipher the emotions of others. Of course, emotions are internal and a person can use emotional expression to deceive, so you can only make inferences about another's emotional state. Not surprisingly, scientists working in a field called affective computing are developing programs that decode a person's emotions by analyzing voices, facial movements, and style of walking (Savage, 2013).

Table 5.2 summarizes these several principles of nonverbal communication.

Table 5.2 In a Nutshell The Principles of Nonverbal Communication

Principles	Examples
Nonverbal messages interact with verbal messages.	To accent, complement, contradict, control, repeat, substitute.
Nonverbal messages help you manage the impressions you want to give.	To be believed, to excuse failure, to secure help, to hide faults, to be followed, to confirm self-image.
Nonverbal messages help form relationships.	To help develop and maintain (and even dissolve) relationships.
Nonverbal messages structure conversations.	To signal speaking and listening turns.
Nonverbal messages can influence and deceive.	To strengthen or change attitudes, beliefs, and values.
Messages are crucial for expressing emotions.	To communicate varied emotions and their strength.

Channels of Nonverbal Communication

5.2 Explain the channels through which nonverbal messages are sent and received.

Nonverbal communication involves a variety of channels. Here we look at: (1) body messages, (2) facial communication, (3) eye communication, (4) touch communication, (5) paralanguage, (6) silence, (7) spatial messages and territoriality, (8) artifactual communication, (9) olfactory messages, and (10) temporal communication. As you'll see, nonverbal messages are heavily influenced by culture (Matsumoto, 2006; Matsumoto & Yoo, 2005; Matsumoto, Yoo, Hirayama, & Petrova, 2005; Jandt, 2016).

Body Messages

In much interpersonal interaction, it's the person's body that communicates most immediately. Here we look at body gestures and body appearance—two main ways the body communicates.

Body Gestures An especially useful classification in **kinesics**—or the study of communication through body movement—identifies five types: emblems, illustrators, affect displays, regulators, and adaptors (Ekman & Friesen, 1969).

Emblems **Emblems** are substitutes for words; they're body movements that have rather specific verbal translations, such as the nonverbal signs for "okay," "peace," "come here," "go away," "who, me?" "be quiet," "I'm warning you," "I'm tired," and "it's cold." Emblems are as arbitrary as any words in any language. Consequently, your present culture's emblems are not necessarily the same as your culture's emblems of 300 years ago or the same as the emblems of other cultures. For example, the sign made by forming a circle with the thumb and index finger may mean "nothing" or "zero" in France, "money" in Japan, and something sexual in certain southern European cultures.

Illustrators **Illustrators** accompany and literally illustrate verbal messages. Illustrators make your communications more vivid and help to maintain your listener's attention. They also help to clarify and intensify your verbal messages. In saying, "Let's go up," for example, you probably move your head and perhaps your finger in an upward direction. In describing a circle or a square, you more than likely make circular or square movements with your hands. Research points to another advantage of illustrators: they increase your ability to remember. People who illustrated their verbal messages with gestures remembered some 20 percent more than those who didn't gesture (Goldin-Meadow, Nusbaum, Kelly, & Wagner, 2001).

We are aware of illustrators only part of the time; at times, they may have to be brought to our attention. Illustrators are more universal than emblems; illustrators are recognized and understood by members of more different cultures than are emblems.

Affect Displays **Affect displays** are the movements of the face that convey emotional meaning—the expressions that show anger and fear, happiness and surprise, eagerness and fatigue. They're the facial expressions that give you away when you try to present a false image and that lead people to say, "You look angry. What's wrong?" We can, however, consciously control affect displays, as actors do when they play a role. Affect displays may be unintentional (as when they give you away) or intentional (as when you want to show anger, love, or surprise). A particular kind of affect display is the poker player's "tell," a bit of nonverbal behavior that communicates bluffing; it's a nonverbal cue that tells others that a player is lying. In much the same way that you may want to conceal certain feelings from friends or relatives, the poker player tries to conceal any such tells.

Regulators **Regulators** monitor, maintain, or control the speaking of another individual. When you listen to another, you're not passive; you nod your head, purse your lips, adjust your eye focus, and make various paralinguistic sounds such as "uh-huh" or "tsk." Regulators are culture-bound: each culture develops its own rules for the regulation of conversation. Regulators also include broad movements such as shaking your head to show disbelief or leaning forward in your chair to show that you want to hear more. Regulators communicate what you expect or want speakers to do as they're talking, for example, "Keep going," "Tell me what else happened," "I don't believe that. Are you sure?" "Speed up," and "Slow down." Speakers often receive these nonverbal signals without being consciously aware of them. Depending on their degree of sensitivity, speakers modify their speaking behavior in accordance with these regulators.

Adaptors   **Adaptors** satisfy some need and usually occur without conscious awareness; they're unintentional movements that usually go unnoticed. Nonverbal researchers identify three types of adaptors based on their focus, direction, or target: self-adaptors, alter-adaptors, and object-adaptors (Burgoon, Guerrero, & Floyd, 2010).

- *Self-adaptors* usually satisfy a physical need, generally serving to make you more comfortable; examples include scratching your head to relieve an itch, moistening your lips because they feel dry, or pushing your hair out of your eyes.
- *Alter-adaptors* are the body movements you make in response to your interactions. Examples include crossing your arms over your chest when someone unpleasant approaches or moving closer to someone you like.
- *Object-adaptors* are movements that involve your manipulation of some object. Frequently observed examples include punching holes in or drawing on a Styrofoam coffee cup, clicking a ballpoint pen, or chewing on a pencil. Object-adaptors are usually signs of negative feelings; for example, you emit more adaptors when feeling hostile than when feeling friendly (Burgoon, Guerrero, & Floyd, 2010).

Table 5.3 summarizes and provides examples of these five types of movements.

Gestures and Cultures   There is much variation in gestures and their meanings among different cultures (Axtell, 2007). Consider a few common gestures that you may often use without thinking but that could easily get you into trouble if you used them in another culture (also see Figure 5.2):

- Folding your arms over your chest would be considered defiant and disrespectful in Fiji.
- Waving your hand would be insulting in Nigeria and Greece.
- Gesturing with the thumb up would be rude in Australia.
- Tapping your two index fingers together would be considered an invitation to sleep together in Egypt.
- Pointing with your index finger would be impolite in many Middle Eastern countries.

Table 5.3   Five Types of Body Movements

	Movement and Function	Examples
	Emblems directly translate words or phrases.	"Okay" sign, "Come here" wave, hitchhiker's sign.
	Illustrators accompany and literally "illustrate" verbal messages.	Circular hand movements when talking of a circle, hands far apart when talking of something large.
	Affect displays communicate emotional meaning.	Expressions of happiness, surprise, fear, anger, sadness, disgust, contempt, and interest.
	Regulators monitor, maintain, or control the speaking of another.	Facial expressions and hand gestures indicating "Keep going," "Slow down," or "What else happened?"
	Adaptors satisfy some need.	Scratching head, chewing on pencil, adjusting glasses.

Figure 5.2 Some Cultural Meanings of Gestures

Cultural differences in the meanings of nonverbal gestures are often significant. The over-the-head clasped hands that signify victory to an American may signify friendship to a Russian. To an American, holding up two fingers to make a V signifies victory or peace. To certain South Americans, however, it is an obscene gesture that corresponds to an American's extended middle finger. This figure highlights some additional nonverbal differences. *Can you identify others?*

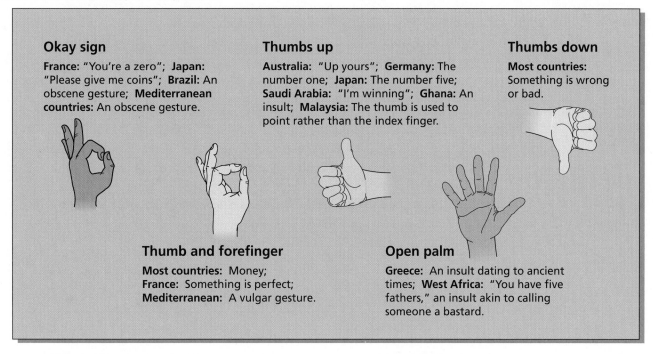

Okay sign

France: "You're a zero"; **Japan:** "Please give me coins"; **Brazil:** An obscene gesture; **Mediterranean countries:** An obscene gesture.

Thumbs up

Australia: "Up yours"; **Germany:** The number one; **Japan:** The number five; **Saudi Arabia:** "I'm winning"; **Ghana:** An insult; **Malaysia:** The thumb is used to point rather than the index finger.

Thumbs down

Most countries: Something is wrong or bad.

Thumb and forefinger

Most countries: Money; **France:** Something is perfect; **Mediterranean:** A vulgar gesture.

Open palm

Greece: An insult dating to ancient times; **West Africa:** "You have five fathers," an insult akin to calling someone a bastard.

- Bowing to a lesser degree than your host would be considered a statement of your superiority in Japan.
- Inserting your thumb between your index and middle finger in a clenched fist would be viewed as a wish that evil fall on the person in some African countries.
- Resting your feet on a table or chair would be insulting and disrespectful in some Middle Eastern cultures.

Body Appearance   Of course, the body communicates even without movement. For example, others may form impressions of you from your general body build; from your height and weight; and from your skin, eye, and hair color. Assessments of your power, attractiveness, and suitability as a friend or romantic partner are often made on the basis of your body appearance (Sheppard & Strathman, 1989). Your body also reveals your race, through skin color and tone, and also may give clues about your more specific nationality. Your weight in proportion to your height communicates messages to others, as do the length, color, and style of your hair. Your hair, for example, may communicate a concern for being up-to-date, a desire to shock, or perhaps a lack of concern for appearances. Men with long hair are generally judged as less conservative than men with shorter hair. And, research finds, women perceive men with full beards better prospects for long-term relationships while stubble seems preferred for short-term relationships (Dixon, Sulikowski, Gouda-Vossos, Rantala, & Brooks, 2016; Dean, 2016a).

Your general attractiveness is also part of body communication. Attractive people have the advantage in just about every activity you can name. They get better grades in school, are more valued as friends and lovers, and are preferred as coworkers (Burgoon, Guerrero, & Floyd, 2010). Although we normally think that attractiveness is culturally determined—and to some degree it is—research seems to indicate that definitions of attractiveness are becoming universal (Brody, 1994). That is, a person rated as attractive in one culture is likely to be rated as attractive in other cultures—even in cultures whose people are widely different in appearance.

Height is an especially important part of body appearance. Before reading about this, try estimating the heights of the following famous people whom you've probably read about or heard about (but probably not seen in person) by circling the guessed height. In each of these examples, one of the heights given is correct.

1. Baby Face Nelson (bank robber and murderer in the 1930s): 5′5″, 5′11″, 6′2″
2. Ludwig Van Beethoven (influential German composer): 5′6″, 6′0″, 6′5″
3. Kim Kardashian (media personality): 5′2″, 5′5″, 5′8″
4. Buckminster Fuller (scientist, credited with inventing the geodesic dome): 5′2″, 5′10″, 6′3″
5. Bruno Mars (singer): 5′5″, 5′8″, 5′10″
6. Mahatma Gandhi (Indian political leader whose civil disobedience led to India's independence from British rule): 5′3″, 5′8″, 6′0″
7. Jada Pinkett Smith (actor): 5′0″, 5′6″, 5′9″
8. Joan of Arc (military leader, burned for heresy at age 19, and declared a saint) 4′11″, 5′4″, 5′10″
9. T. E. Lawrence of Arabia (adventurer and British army officer) 5′5″, 6′0″, 6′5″
10. Salma Hayek (actor): 5′2″, 5′5″, 5′8″

This exercise was designed to see if you would overestimate the heights of a number of these people. Fame seems to be associated with height, and so most people would think these people were taller than they really were. The specific heights for all are the shortest heights given above.

Height has been shown to be significant in a wide variety of situations (Keyes, 1980; Knapp, Hall, & Horgan, 2014). For example, when corporate recruiters were shown identical résumés for people some of whom were noted as being 5′5″ and others as being 6′1″—everything else being the same—the taller individual was chosen significantly more often than were the shorter individuals.

In another study, it was found that the salaries of those between 6′2″ and 6′4″ were more than 12 percent higher than the salaries of those shorter than 6 feet. Tall presidential candidates have a much better record of winning elections than do their shorter opponents.

In an investigation of height and satisfaction, it was found that boys were less satisfied with their heights than were girls. Fifty percent of the boys surveyed indicated that they wanted to be taller, 2 percent said they wanted to be shorter, and 48 percent indicated satisfaction. Only 20 percent of the girls indicated that they wanted to be taller, 13 percent said they wanted to be shorter, and 67 percent indicated they were satisfied. Perhaps because of the perceived importance of height, this is one of the things that men lie about in their Internet dating profiles, making themselves appear a bit taller. Women, on the other hand, present themselves as weighing a bit less (Toma, Hancock, & Ellison, 2008; Dean, 2010b).

Facial Communication

Throughout your interpersonal interactions, your face communicates—especially signaling your emotions. In fact, facial movements alone seem to communicate the degree of pleasantness, agreement, and sympathy a person feels; the rest of the body doesn't provide any additional information. For other aspects—for example, the intensity with which an emotion is felt—both facial and bodily cues are used (Graham & Argyle, 1975; Graham, Bitti, & Argyle, 1975).

Some nonverbal communication researchers claim that facial movements may communicate at least the following eight emotions: happiness, surprise, fear, anger, sadness, disgust, contempt, and interest (Ekman, Friesen, & Ellsworth, 1972). Others propose that, in addition, facial movements may communicate bewilderment and determination (Leathers & Eaves, 2008). And, to complicate matters just a bit, biological researchers, from an analysis of the 42 facial muscles and their expressions, argue that there are four basic emotions (anger, fear, happiness, and sadness) and that other emotions are combinations of these four (Jack, Garrod, & Schyns, 2014; Dean, 2014a).

Of course, some emotions are easier to communicate and to decode than others. For example, in one study, happiness was judged with an accuracy ranging from 55 percent to 100 percent, surprise from 38 percent to 86 percent, and sadness from 19 percent to 88 percent (Ekman, Friesen, & Ellsworth, 1972). Research finds that women and girls are more accurate judges of facial emotional expression than are men and boys (Argyle, 1988; Hall, 1984).

As you've probably experienced, you may interpret the same facial expression differently depending on the context in which it occurs. For example, in a classic study, when a smiling face was presented looking at a glum face, the smiling face was judged to be vicious and taunting. But when the same smiling face was presented looking at a frowning face, it was judged peaceful and friendly (Cline, 1956).

The Smile   The smile is likely to be the first thing you think about when focusing on facial communication. Because it is largely a social behavior, the smile is important in just about any relationship you can imagine. Although you may smile when spotting a cute photo or joke you read even when alone, most smiling occurs in response to social situations. Most often you smile at other people rather than at yourself (Andersen, 2004).

Nonverbal communication researchers distinguish between two kinds of smiles: the real and the fake. The real smile, known as the **Duchenne smile**, is genuine; it's an unconscious movement that accurately reflects your feelings at the time. It is a smile that spreads across your face in about one-half second. The fake smile, on the other hand, is conscious. It takes about one-tenth of a second to spread across the face (Dean, 2011b). Distinguishing between these two is crucial in a wide variety of situations. For example, you distinguish between these smiles when you make judgments about whether someone is genuinely pleased at your good fortune or is really jealous. You distinguish between these smiles when you infer that the person really likes you or is just being polite. In each of these cases, you're making judgments about whether someone is lying; you're engaging in deception detection. Not surprisingly, then, Duchenne smiles are responded to positively and fake smiles—especially if they are obvious—are responded to negatively. Computer programs for facial recognition are becoming more and more proficient. For example, one recent study reported in *Science Digest.com* found that smiles of delight and smiles of aggravation were distinguished by the computer, whereas human observation was unable to detect the difference (Hogue, McDuff, & Picard, 2012).

People who smile are judged to be more likable and more approachable than people who don't smile or people who pretend to smile (Gladstone & Parker, 2002; Kluger, 2005; Woodzicka & LaFrance, 2005). Profile photos in which the person smiled (and showed teeth) were much more highly valued than any other expressions. Fifty-four percent of the photos judged the hottest showed the person smiling with teeth; the percentage drops to 13 for smiles without teeth (Roper, 2014). And women perceive men who are smiled at by other women as being more attractive than men who are not smiled at. But men—perhaps being more competitive—perceive men whom women

Smiling and Trust

Research finds that people trust those who smile more than they trust those who don't smile (Mehl, et al. 2007; Dean, 2011b). People who smile are also rated higher on generosity. *Are these findings consistent with your own experiences? What reasons can you advance to account for these findings?*

smile at as being less attractive than men who are not smiled at (Jones, DeBruine, Little, Burriss, & Feinberg, 2007).

Smiling is usually an expression of enjoyment and pleasure; it's a happy reaction and seems to be responded to positively in almost all situations. One study, for example, found that participants rated people who smile as more likeable and more approachable than people who don't smile or who only pretend to smile (Gladstone & Parker, 2002). In another study, men and women signaled that they wanted to hitchhike (this study was done in France, where it's legal and common to hitchhike) to some 800 motorists. Motorists stopped more often for the smiling women than for those who didn't smile. Smiling had no effect on whether motorists would stop for men (Guéguen & Fischer-Lokou, 2004). Smiling female servers earned more tips than those who didn't smile (Tidd & Lockard, 1978; Dean 2011b). Research also shows that women in a bar or club are seen as more attractive and are approached by men more when they smile. Oddly enough that doesn't work for men; smiling men are not seen as more attractive (Dean, 2011b; Tracy & Beall, 2011; Walsh & Hewitt, 1985).

Women smile significantly more than men—regardless of whether women are talking with women or men (Hall, 1984; Helgeson, 2009). This is a difference that can even be observed in very young girls and boys.

Facial Management   As you learned the nonverbal system of communication, you also learned certain facial management techniques that enable you to communicate your feelings to achieve the effect you want—for example, to hide certain emotions and to emphasize others.

Consider your own use of such facial management techniques. As you do so, think about the types of interpersonal situations in which you would use each of these facial management techniques (Malandro, Barker, & Barker, 1989; Metts & Planalp, 2002). Would you:

- **intensify** to exaggerate your surprise when friends throw you a party to make your friends feel better? Yes/No
- **deintensify** to cover up your own joy in the presence of a friend who didn't receive such good news? Yes/No
- **neutralize** to cover up your sadness to keep from depressing others? Yes/No
- **mask** to express happiness in order to cover up your disappointment at not receiving the gift you expected? Yes/No
- **simulate** to express an emotion you don't feel? Yes/No

These facial management techniques help you display emotions in socially acceptable ways. For example, when someone gets bad news in which you may secretly take pleasure, the display rule dictates that you frown and otherwise signal your sorrow nonverbally. If you place first in a race and your best friend barely finishes, the display rule requires that you minimize your expression of pleasure in winning and avoid any signs of gloating. If you violate these display rules, you'll be judged as insensitive. Although facial management techniques may be deceptive, they're also expected—and, in fact, required—by the rules of polite interaction.

Facial Feedback   The **facial feedback hypothesis** holds that your facial expressions influence your physiological arousal (Lanzetta, Cartwright-Smith, & Kleck, 1976; Zuckerman, Klorman, Larrance, & Spiegel, 1981). For example, in one study, participants held a pen in their teeth simulating a sad expression and then rated a series of photographs. Results showed that mimicking sad expressions actually increased the degree of sadness the subjects reported feeling when viewing the photographs (Larsen, Kasimatis, & Frey, 1992).

Generally, research finds that facial expressions can produce or heighten feelings of sadness, fear, disgust, and anger. But this effect does not occur with all emotions; smiling, for example, won't make you feel happier. And if you're feeling sad, smiling is not likely to replace your sadness with happiness. A reasonable conclusion seems to be that your facial expressions can influence some feelings but not all of them (Burgoon & Bacue, 2003).

Culture and Facial Communication   The wide variations in facial communication that we observe in different cultures seem to reflect which reactions are publicly permissible rather than a fundamental difference in the way emotions are facially expressed. In one study, for example, Japanese and American students watched a film of a surgical operation (Ekman, 1985). The students were video-recorded both during an interview about the film and alone while watching the film. When alone, the students showed very similar reactions, but in the interview, the American students displayed facial expressions indicating displeasure, whereas the Japanese students did not show any great emotion. Similarly, it's considered "forward" or inappropriate for Japanese women to reveal broad smiles, so many Japanese women hide their smile, sometimes with their hands (Ma, 1996). Women in the United States, on the other hand, have no such restrictions and so are more likely to smile openly. Thus, the difference may not be in the way different cultures express emotions but rather in the society's **cultural display rules**, or rules about the appropriate display of emotions in public (Aune, 2005; Matsumoto, 1991). For example, the well-documented finding that women smile more than men is likely due, at least in part, to display rules that allow women to smile more than men (Hall, 2006).

Eye Communication

Oculesics is the study of the messages communicated by the eyes, which vary depending on the duration, direction, and quality of the eye behavior. For example, in every culture there are rather strict, though unstated, rules for the proper duration for eye contact. In much of England and the United States, for example, the average length of gaze is 2.95 seconds. The average length of mutual gaze (two persons gazing at each other) is 1.18 seconds (Argyle, 1988; Argyle & Ingham, 1972). When the duration of eye contact is shorter than 1.18 seconds, you may think the person is uninterested, shy, or preoccupied. When the appropriate amount of time is exceeded, you may perceive this as showing high interest.

In much of the United States, direct eye contact is considered an expression of honesty and forthrightness. But the Japanese often view eye contact as a lack of respect. The Japanese glance at the other person's face rarely and then only for very short periods (Axtell, 2007). In many Hispanic cultures, direct eye contact signifies a certain equality and so should be avoided by, say, children when speaking to a person in authority. Try visualizing the potential misunderstandings that **eye communication** alone could create when people from Tokyo, San Francisco, and San Juan try to communicate.

The direction of the eye also communicates. Generally, in communicating with another person, you glance alternatively at the other person's face, then away, then again at the face, and so on. When these directional rules are broken, different meanings are communicated—abnormally high or low interest, self-consciousness, nervousness over the interaction, and so on. The quality of the gaze—how wide or how narrow your eyes get during interaction—also communicates meaning, especially interest level and emotions such as surprise, fear, and disgust.

Eye Contact   You use eye contact to serve several important functions (Knapp, Hall, & Horgan, 2014; Malandro, Barker, & Barker, 1989; Richmond, McCroskey, & Hickson, 2012):

- *To monitor feedback*   When you talk with others, you look at them and try to understand their reactions to what you're saying. You try to read their feedback, and on this basis, you adjust what you say. As you can imagine, successful readings of feedback help considerably in your overall effectiveness when it comes to communication.

- *To secure attention*   When you speak with two or three other people, you maintain eye contact to secure the attention and interest of your listeners. When someone fails to pay you the attention you want, you probably increase your eye contact, hoping that this will increase attention. When online dating profile photos were analyzed, those women who made eye contact with the camera received significantly more responses than did those who looked away. Men, on the other hand, did better when they looked away from the camera (Dean, 2010b).

- *To regulate the conversation*   Eye contact helps you regulate, manage, and control the conversation. With eye movements, you can inform the other person that she or he should speak. A clear example of this occurs in the college classroom, where the instructor asks a question and then locks eyes with a student. This type of eye contact tells the student to answer the question.

- *To signal the nature of the relationship*   Eye communication can also serve as a tie sign or signal of the nature of the relationship between two people—for example, to indicate positive or negative regard. Depending on the culture, eye contact may communicate your romantic interest in another person, or eye avoidance may indicate respect. Some researchers note that eye contact serves to enable gay men and lesbians to signal their orientation and perhaps their interest in someone—an ability referred to as "gaydar" (Nicholas, 2004).

- *To signal status*   Eye contact is often used to signal status and aggression. Among many younger people, prolonged eye contact from a stranger is taken to signify aggressiveness and frequently prompts physical violence—merely because one person looked perhaps a little longer than was considered normal in that specific culture (Matsumoto, 1996).

- *To compensate for physical distance*   Eye contact is often used to compensate for increased physical distance. By making eye contact, you overcome, psychologically, the physical distance between yourself and another person. When you catch someone's eye at a party, for example, you become psychologically closer even though you may be separated by considerable physical distance.

Eye Avoidance   The eyes, sociologist Erving Goffman observed in *Interaction Ritual* (1967), are "great intruders." When you avoid eye contact or avert your glance, you allow others to maintain their privacy. You probably do this when you see a couple arguing in the street or on a bus. You turn your eyes away, as if to say, "I don't mean to intrude; I respect your privacy," a type of behavior called **civil inattention** (Goffman, 1967).

Eye avoidance can also signal lack of interest—in a person, a conversation, or some visual stimulus. At times, like the ostrich, we hide our eyes to try to cut off unpleasant stimuli. Notice, for example, how quickly people close their eyes in the face of some extreme unpleasantness. Even if the unpleasantness is auditory, we tend to shut it out by closing our eyes. At other times, we close our eyes to block out visual stimuli and thus to heighten our other senses; for example, we often listen to music with our eyes closed. Lovers often close their eyes while kissing, and many prefer to make love in a dark or dimly lit room.

The research and theory discussed above is, of course, based on people without visual impairment. People vary greatly in their visual abilities: some are totally blind, some are partially sighted, and some have unimpaired vision. Ninety percent of people who are "legally blind" have some vision. All people, however, have the same need for communication and information. Here are some tips for making communication better between those who have visual impairments and those without such difficulties. Table 5.4 addresses this imbalance and identifies some suggestions for communicating between people with and people without visual impairment.

Pupil Dilation   In the fifteenth and sixteenth centuries, Italian women used to put drops of belladonna (which literally means "beautiful woman") into their eyes to enlarge the pupils so that they would look more attractive. Research in the field of pupillometrics supports the intuitive logic of these women: dilated pupils are in fact judged more attractive than constricted ones (Hess, 1975; Marshall, 1983).

In one study, for example, photographs of women were retouched (Hess, 1975). In one set of photographs the pupils were enlarged, and in the other they were made smaller. Men were then asked to judge the women's personalities from the photographs. The photos of women with small pupils drew responses such as cold, hard, and selfish; those with dilated pupils drew responses such as feminine and soft. However, the male observers could not verbalize the reasons for the different perceptions. Both pupil dilation itself and people's reactions to changes in the pupil size of others seem to function below the level of conscious awareness.

Pupil size also reveals your interest and level of emotional arousal. Your pupils enlarge when you're interested in something or when you're emotionally aroused. In one study, gay men and heterosexuals were shown pictures of nude bodies; the gay men's pupils dilated more when viewing same-sex bodies, whereas the heterosexuals'

Table 5.4 Interpersonal Communication between People with and People without Visual Impairments

If you're the person without visual impairment and are talking with a visually impaired person:

Generally	Specifically
Identify yourself.	Don't assume the visually impaired person recognizes your voice.
Face your listener; you'll be easier to hear.	Don't shout. Most people who are visually impaired are not hearing impaired. Speak at your normal volume.
Encode into speech all the meanings you wish to communicate.	Remember that your gestures, eye movements, and facial expressions cannot be seen by the visually impaired.
Use audible turn-taking cues.	When you pass the role of speaker to a person who is visually impaired, don't rely on nonverbal cues; instead, say something like "Do you agree with that, Joe?"
Use normal vocabulary and discuss topics that you would discuss with sighted people.	Don't avoid terms like *see* or *look* or even *blind*. Don't avoid discussing a television show or the way your new car looks; these are normal topics for all people.

If you are a person with visual impairment and are talking with a person without visual impairment:

Help the sighted person meet your special communication needs.	If you want your surroundings described, ask. If you want the person to read the road signs, ask.
Be patient with the sighted person.	Many people are nervous talking with people who are visually impaired for fear of offending. Put them at ease in a way that also makes you more comfortable.
Demonstrate your comfort.	When appropriate, let the other person know that you're comfortable with the interaction, verbally or nonverbally.

SOURCE: These suggestions were drawn from a variety of sources, including the websites of the Cincinnati Association for the Blind and Visually Impaired, the Association for the Blind of WA, the National Federation of the Blind, and the American Foundation for the Blind, all accessed February 23, 2017.

Gender Differences

Research on nonverbal gender differences (Burgoon, Guerrero, & Floyd, 2010; Gamble & Gamble, 2014; Guerrero & Hecht, 2008; Krolkke & Sørensen, 2006; Stewart, Cooper, & Stewart, 2003) finds that: (1) women smile more than men; (2) women stand closer to each other than do men and are generally approached more closely than men; (3) women (and also men), when speaking, look at men more than at women; (4) women both touch and are touched more than men; (5) men extend their bodies more, taking up greater areas of space, than do women. Examine the photos on one of your social media sites. *Can you see these differences in the photos?*

pupils dilated more when viewing opposite-sex bodies (Hess, Seltzer, & Schlien, 1965). These pupillary responses are unconscious and are even observed in persons with profound mental retardation (Chaney, Givens, Aoki, & Gombiner, 1989). Perhaps we find dilated pupils more attractive because we judge them as indicative of a person's interest in us. That may be why models, Beanie Babies, and Teletubbies, for example, have exceptionally large pupils.

Although belladonna is no longer used, the cosmetics industry has made millions selling eye enhancers—eye shadow, eyeliner, false eyelashes, and tinted contact lenses that change eye color. These items function (ideally, at least) to draw attention to these most powerful communicators.

Culture and Eye Communication   Eye messages vary with both culture and gender. Americans, for example, consider direct eye contact an expression of honesty and forthrightness, but the Japanese often view this as showing a lack of respect. A Japanese person will glance at the other person's face rarely, and then only for very short periods (Axtell, 2007). Interpreting another's eye contact messages according to your own cultural rules is a risky undertaking; eye movements that you may interpret as insulting may have been intended to show respect.

Women make eye contact more and maintain it longer (both in speaking and in listening) than do men. This holds true whether women are interacting with other women or with men. This difference in eye behavior may result from women's greater tendency to display their emotions (Wood, 1994). When women interact with other women, they display affiliative and supportive eye contact, whereas when men interact with other men, they avert their gaze (Gamble & Gamble, 2003).

Cultural differences also exist in the ways people decode the meanings of facial expressions. For example, American and Japanese students judged the meaning of a smiling and a neutral facial expression. The Americans rated the smiling face as more attractive, more intelligent, and more sociable than the neutral face. In contrast, the Japanese rated the smiling face as more sociable but not as more attractive—and they rated the neutral face as more intelligent (Matsumoto & Kudoh, 1993).

Touch Communication

Tactile communication, or communication by touch, also referred to as **haptics**, is perhaps the most primitive form of communication. Developmentally, touch is probably the first sense to be used; even in the womb, the child is stimulated by touch. Soon after birth, the infant is fondled, caressed, patted, and stroked. In turn, the child explores its world through touch. In a very short time, the child learns to communicate a wide variety of meanings through touch. Not surprisingly, touch also varies with your relationship stage. In the early stages of a relationship, you touch little; in intermediate stages (involvement and intimacy), you touch a great deal; and at stable or deteriorating stages, you again touch little (Guerrero & Andersen, 1991).

The Meanings of Touch   Touch may communicate at least five major meanings (Jones, 2005; Jones & Yarbrough, 1985):

- *Emotions* Touch often communicates emotions, mainly between intimates or others who have a relatively close relationship. Among the most important of these positive emotions are support, appreciation, inclusion, sexual interest or intent, and affection. Additional research found that touch communicated positive feelings such as composure, immediacy, trust, similarity and equality, and informality (Burgoon, 1991). In one study, people were able to identify emotions such as fear, disgust, anger, sympathy, love, and gratitude from a simple touch on the forearm, even when the person doing the touching could not be seen (Dean, 2011a; Hertenstein et al., 2009). Touch also has been found to facilitate self-disclosure (Rabinowitz, 1991). And, not surprisingly, those who touch are perceived more positively (more sincere, honest, and friendly) than those who don't touch (Erceau & Gueguen, 2007).

- *Playfulness* Touch often communicates a desire to play, either affectionately or aggressively. When touch is used in this manner, the playfulness deemphasizes the emotion and tells the other person that it's not to be taken seriously. Playful touches lighten an interaction.

- *Control* Touch also may seek to control the behaviors, attitudes, or feelings of the other person. Such control may communicate various different kinds of messages. To ask for compliance, for example, we touch the other person to communicate, "Move over," "Hurry," "Stay here," or "Do it." In one study people were asked to complete a questionnaire; those who were touched twice on the upper arm complied more than did those who were touched once who, in turn, complied more than those who weren't touched at all (Willis & Hamm, 1980; Vaidis & Hamimi-Falkowicz, 2008; Dean, 2011a). Touching to control may also communicate status and dominance (DiBaise & Gunnoe, 2004; Henley, 1977). The higher-status and dominant person, for example, initiates touch. In fact, it would be a breach of etiquette for the lower-status person to touch the person of higher status.

- *Ritual* Much touching centers on performing rituals, for example, in greetings and departures. Shaking hands to say hello or goodbye is perhaps the clearest example of ritualistic touching, but we might also hug, kiss, or put an arm around another's shoulder.

- *Task-related* Touching is often associated with the performance of a function, such as removing a speck of dust from another person's face, helping someone out of a car, or checking someone's forehead for fever. Task-related touching seems generally to be regarded positively. In studies on the subject, for example, book borrowers had a more positive attitude toward the library and the librarian when touched lightly, and customers gave larger tips when lightly touched by the waitress (Marsh, 1988). Similarly, diners who were touched on the shoulder or hand when being given their change in a restaurant tipped more than diners who were not touched (Crusco & Wetzel, 1984; Guéguen & Jacob, 2004; Stephen & Zweigenhaft, 1986).

As you can imagine, touching can also get you into trouble. For example, touching that is too intimate too early in a relationship may send the wrong signals. Similarly, playing too roughly or holding someone's arm to control their movements may be resented. Using ritualistic touching incorrectly or in ways that may be culturally insensitive may likewise get you into difficulty.

Touch Avoidance Much as we have a need and desire to touch and be touched by others, we also have a tendency to avoid touch from certain people or in certain circumstances (Andersen, 2004; Andersen & Leibowitz, 1978). Among the important findings is that **touch avoidance** is positively related to communication apprehension, or fear or anxiety about communicating: people who fear oral communication also score high on touch avoidance. Touch avoidance is also high among those who self-disclose little; touch and self-disclosure are intimate forms of communication, and people who are reluctant to get close to another person by self-disclosure also seem reluctant to get close through touch.

Older people have higher touch avoidance scores for opposite-sex persons than do younger people. Apparently, as we get older, we are touched less by members of the opposite sex, and this decreased frequency of touching may lead us to avoid touching. Males

INTERPERSONAL CHOICE POINT
Touching

Your supervisor touches just about everyone. You don't like it and want it to stop—at least as far as you're concerned. *What are some ways you can nonverbally show your aversion to this unwanted touching?*

a. Move away.

b. Scowl.

c. Remove your supervisor's hand with a verbal comment of disapproval.

d. Avoid eye contact and smiling at your supervisor.

e. Other

score higher than females on same-sex touch avoidance. This accords well with our stereotypes: men avoid touching other men, but women may and do touch other women. Women, it is found, have higher touch avoidance scores for opposite-sex touching than do men.

Culture and Touch   The several functions and examples of touching discussed earlier in this chapter were based on studies in North America; in other cultures, these functions are not served in the same way. In some cultures, for example, some task-related touching is viewed negatively and is to be avoided. Among Koreans it is considered disrespectful for a store owner to touch a customer in, say, handing back change; it is considered too intimate a gesture. A member of another culture who is used to such touching may consider the Korean's behavior cold and aloof. Muslim children are socialized not to touch members of the opposite sex; their behavior can easily be interpreted as unfriendly by American children who are used to touching one another (Dresser, 2005).

Some cultures—including many in southern Europe and the Middle East—are contact cultures; others are noncontact cultures, such as those of northern Europe and Japan. Members of contact cultures maintain close distances, touch one another in conversation, face each other more directly, and maintain longer and more focused eye contact. Members of noncontact cultures maintain greater distance in their interactions, touch each other rarely (if at all), avoid facing each other directly, and maintain much less direct eye contact. As a result of these differences, problems may occur. For example, northern Europeans and Japanese may be perceived as cold, distant, and uninvolved by southern Europeans—who may in turn be perceived as pushy, aggressive, and inappropriately intimate.

Paralanguage

Paralanguage is the vocal but nonverbal dimension of speech. It has to do with the manner in which you say something rather than with what you say. An old exercise used to increase a student's ability to express different emotions, feelings, and attitudes was to have the student say the following sentence while accenting or stressing different words: "Is this the face that launched a thousand ships?" (This sentence, by the way, comes from Greek mythology where Helen of Troy, considered the most beautiful of all women, was abducted by Paris [some accounts say they eloped] and began the ten-year Trojan War and the "launching of a thousand ships.") Significant differences in meaning are easily communicated, depending on where the stress is placed.

Consider, for example, the following variations; try to paraphrase each of these questions, giving special attention and emphasis to the italicized word:

1. Is *this* the face that launched a thousand ships?

Out of all the possible faces, are you sure that this face is the one that started the war? It might be a way of implying that she's not that beautiful.

2. Is this the *face* that launched a thousand ships?

Was it really her face that started this war? It might be a way of saying that there had to be other reasons.

3. Is this the face that launched a *thousand ships*?

Were there really a thousand ships? It might be a way of questioning the number of ships.

Each of these three sentences communicates something different. Each, in fact, asks a totally different question, even though the words used are identical. All that distinguishes the sentences is variation in stress, one of the aspects of paralanguage.

In addition to stress, paralanguage includes vocal characteristics such as **rate** and **volume**. Paralanguage also includes the vocalizations that we make when laughing, yelling, moaning, whining, and belching; vocal segregates—sound combinations that aren't words—such as "uh-uh" and "shh"; and **pitch**, the highness or lowness of vocal tone (Argyle, 1988; Trager, 1958, 1961).

Paralanguage and People Perception   When listening to people—regardless of what they're saying—we form impressions based on their paralanguage about what kind of people they are. It does seem that certain voices are symptomatic of certain personality types or problems and, specifically, that the personality orientation gives rise to the vocal qualities. Our impressions of others from paralanguage cues span a broad range and consist of physical impressions (perhaps about body type and certainly about gender and age), personality impressions (they sound shy, they appear aggressive), and evaluative impressions (they sound like good people, they sound evil and menacing, they have vicious laughs). And men are found to be more attracted to women who vary their paralanguage to make their voice sound sexier, though it doesn't work the other way around: women do not find men who try to make their voice sound sexier more attractive (Hughes, Mogilski, & Harrison, 2014; Dean, 2016a).

One of the most interesting findings on voice and personal characteristics is that listeners can accurately judge the socioeconomic status (high, middle, or low) of speakers after hearing a 60-second voice sample. In fact, many listeners reported that they made their judgments in less than 15 seconds. It has also been found that the speakers judged to be of high status were rated as being of higher credibility than those rated of middle or low status.

It's interesting to note that listeners agree with one another about the personality of the speaker even when their judgments are in error. Listeners have similar stereotyped ideas about the way vocal characteristics and personality characteristics are related, and they use these stereotypes in their judgments.

Paralanguage and Persuasion   The rate of speech is the aspect of paralanguage that has received the most research attention—because speech rate is related to persuasiveness. Therefore, it's of interest to the advertiser, the politician, and anyone else who wants to convey information or to influence others orally—especially when time is limited or expensive. The research on rate of speech shows that in one-way communication situations, persons who talk fast are more persuasive and are evaluated more highly than those who talk at or below normal speeds (MacLachlan, 1979). This greater persuasiveness and higher regard holds true whether the person talks fast naturally or the speech is sped up electronically (as in time-compressed speech).

In one experiment, subjects were asked to listen to recorded messages and then to indicate both the degree to which they agreed with the message and their opinions about how intelligent and objective they thought the speaker was (MacLachlan, 1979). Rates of 111, 140 (the average rate), and 191 words per minute were used. Subjects agreed most with the fastest speech and least with the slowest speech. Further, they rated the fastest speaker as the most intelligent and objective, and the slowest speaker as the least intelligent and objective. Even in experiments in which the speaker was known to have something to gain personally from persuasion (as would, say, a salesperson), the speaker who spoke at the fastest rate was the most persuasive. Research also finds that faster speech rates increase listeners' perceptions of speaker competence and dominance (Buller, LePoire, Aune, & Eloy, 1992).

Although generally research finds that a faster than normal speech rate lowers listener comprehension, a rapid rate may still have the advantage in communicating information (Jones, Berry, & Stevens, 2007; MacLachlan, 1979). For example, people who listened to speeches at 201 words per minute (140 is average) comprehended 95 percent of the message, and those who listened to speeches at 282 words per minute (that is, double the normal rate) comprehended 90 percent. Even though the rates increased dramatically, the comprehension rates fell only slightly. These 5 percent and 10 percent losses

are more than offset by the increased speed and thus make the faster rates much more efficient in communicating information. If the speech speeds are increased more than 100 percent, however, listener comprehension falls dramatically. But, with small children, a rate slower than normal, is more effective in learning difficult or new tasks (Haake, Hansson, Gulz, Schötz, Sahlén, 2013). A slower rate would also likely make comprehension easier for those new to a language or those who have some cognitive impairment.

Culture and Paralanguage   Cultural differences also need to be taken into consideration when we evaluate the results of the studies on speech rate because different cultures view speech rate differently. For example, investigators found that Korean male speakers who spoke rapidly were given unfavorable credibility ratings, unlike Americans who spoke rapidly (Lee & Boster, 1992). Researchers have suggested that in individualist societies, a rapid-rate speaker is seen as more competent than a slow-rate speaker, whereas in collectivist cultures, a speaker who uses a slower rate is judged more competent.

Silence

"Speech," wrote Thomas Mann, "is civilization itself. The word, even the most contradictory word, preserves contact; it's silence which isolates." But philosopher Max Picard noted that "silence is nothing merely negative; it's not the mere absence of speech. It's a positive, a complete world in itself." The one thing on which these two contradictory observations agree is that **silence** communicates. Your silence communicates just as intensely as anything you verbalize (Jaworski, 1993; Richmond, McCroskey, & Hickson, 2012).

The Functions of Silence   Like words and gestures, silence serves several important communication functions:

- *To provide time to think* Silence allows you *time to think*, time to formulate and organize your verbal communications.
- *To hurt* Some people use silence as a weapon *to hurt* others. We often speak of giving someone the silent treatment. After a conflict, for example, one or both individuals may remain silent as a kind of punishment.

ETHICS IN INTERPERSONAL COMMUNICATION

Interpersonal Silence

Remaining silent is at times your right. For example, you have the right to remain silent to avoid incriminating yourself. You have a right to protect your privacy—to withhold information that has no bearing on the matter at hand. For example, your previous relationship history, affectional orientation, or religion is usually irrelevant to your ability to function in a job and thus may be kept private in most job-related situations. On the other hand, these issues may be relevant when, for example, you're about to enter a more intimate phase of a relationship; then there may be an obligation to reveal information about yourself that ethically could have been kept hidden at earlier relationship stages.

You do not have the right to remain silent and to refuse to reveal information about crimes you've seen others commit. However, psychiatrists, clergy members, and lawyers—fortunately or unfortunately—are often exempt from the requirement to reveal information about criminal activities when the information had been gained through privileged communication with clients.

Ethical Choice Point

Pat is HIV positive and engages only in safe sex. *Does Pat have an obligation to reveal the HIV status to any potential sexual partner? Does this obligation change if Pat is in a long-term relationship? At what point in a relationship does Pat incur an obligation to reveal this HIV status (if at all)?*

- *To respond to personal anxiety* Sometimes silence is used as a response to personal anxiety, shyness, or threats. You may feel anxious or shy among new people and prefer to remain silent.

- *To prevent communication* Silence may be used to prevent communication of certain messages. In conflict situations, silence is sometimes used to prevent certain topics from surfacing or to prevent one or both parties from saying things they may later regret.

- *To communicate emotions* Like the eyes, face, or hands, silence can also be used to communicate emotions (Ehrenhaus, 1988; Lane, Koetting, & Bishop, 2002). Sometimes silence communicates a determination to be uncooperative or defiant; by refusing to engage in verbal communication, you defy the authority or the legitimacy of the other person's position.

- *To achieve specific effects* Silence may also be used strategically, to achieve specific effects. The pause before making what you feel is an important comment or after hearing about some mishap may be strategically positioned to communicate a desired impression—to make your idea stand out among others or perhaps to give others the impression that you care a lot more than you really do. Generally, research finds that people use silence strategically more with strangers than they do with close friends (Hasegawa & Gudykunst, 1998).

VIEWPOINTS

Nonverbal Communication and Ethics

In addition to silence, other dimensions of nonverbal communication appear to be related to ethics. For example, there is some evidence to show that people are more ethical in the morning than in the afternoon or evening. People are less apt to lie or cheat early in the day than they are later in the day (Kouchakil & Smith, 2013). And people are more apt to lie or cheat when they are sitting in chairs that allow for expansion and are more moral when seated in chairs that are more restrictive (Yap et al., 2013). *What other dimensions of nonverbal communication might have ethical implications?*

The Spiral of Silence   The **spiral of silence** theory offers a somewhat different perspective on silence. When this theory (originally developed to explain the media's influence on opinion) is applied to the interpersonal context, it argues that you're more likely to voice agreement than disagreement (Noelle-Neumann, 1973, 1980, 1991; Scheufele & Moy, 2000; Severin & Tankard, 2001). The theory claims that when a controversial issue arises, you estimate the opinions of others and figure out which views are popular and which are not. In face-to-face conversations—say, with a group of five or six people—you'd have to guess about their opinions or wait until they're voiced. In social media communication, on the other hand, you're often provided statistics on opinions that eliminate the guesswork. You also estimate the rewards and the punishments you'd likely get from expressing popular or unpopular positions. You then use these estimates to determine which opinions you'll express and which you won't. Some research on the spiral of silence theory, applied to online communication, indicates that people support issues held by the minority in the offline world but not issues held by the minority in the online community (Yun & Park, 2011).

Generally, you're more likely to voice your opinions when you agree with the majority than when you disagree. And there's evidence to show that this effect is stronger for minority group members (Bowen & Blackmon, 2003). You may do this to avoid being isolated from the majority or for fear of being proved wrong or being disliked, for example. Or you may simply assume that the majority, because they're a majority, must be right.

As people with minority views remain silent, the majority position gets stronger (because those who agree with it are the only ones speaking); as the majority position becomes stronger and the minority position becomes weaker, the situation becomes an ever-widening spiral. The Internet (blogs and social network sites, especially) may in some ways act as a counteragent to the spiral of silence because Internet discussions provide so many free ways for you to express minority opinions (anonymously if you wish) and to find like-minded others quickly (McDevitt, Kiousis, & Wahl-Jorgensen, 2003).

Culture and Silence   Not all cultures view silence as functioning in the same way (Vainiomaki, 2004). In the United States, for example, people often interpret silence negatively. At a business meeting or even in an informal social group, others may wonder if the silent member is not listening, has nothing interesting to add, doesn't understand the issues, is insensitive, or is too self-absorbed to focus on the messages of others.

Other cultures, however, view silence more positively. In many situations in Japan, for example, silence is a response that is considered more appropriate than speech (Haga, 1988). And in the United States, the traditional Apache regard silence very differently than do European Americans (Basso, 1972). Among the Apache, mutual friends do not feel the need to introduce strangers who may be working in the same area or on the same project. The strangers may remain silent for several days. This period enables people to observe one another and to come to a judgment about the other individuals. Once this assessment is made, the individuals talk. When courting, especially during the initial stages, Apache couples remain silent for hours; if they do talk, they generally talk very little. Only after a couple has been dating for several months will they have lengthy conversations.

Spatial Messages and Territoriality

Space is an especially important factor in interpersonal communication, although we seldom think about it. Edward T. Hall (1959, 1963, 1966), who pioneered the study of spatial communication, called this area **proxemics**. We can examine this broad area by looking at proxemic distances, the theories about space, and territoriality.

Proxemic Distances   Four **proxemic distances**, the distances we maintain between each other in our interactions, correspond closely to the major types of relationships. They are intimate, personal, social, and public distances, as depicted in Table 5.5. Note that these four distances can be further divided into close and far phases and that the far phase of one level (say, personal) blends into the close phase of the next level (social). Do your relationships also blend into one another? Or are your personal relationships totally separate from your social relationships?

Intimate Distance   In intimate distance, ranging from actual touching to 18 inches, the presence of the other individual is unmistakable. Each person experiences the sound, smell, and feel of the other's breath. You use intimate distance for lovemaking, comforting, and protecting. This distance is so short that most people do not consider it proper in public.

Table 5.5   In a Nutshell Relationships and Proxemic Distances

Relationship		Distance	
	Intimate relationship	Intimate distance 0 _____ 18 inches close phase ___ far phase	
	Personal relationship	Personal distance $1\frac{1}{2}$ _____ 4 feet close phase ___ far phase	
	Social relationship	Social distance 4 _____ 12 feet close phase ___ far phase	
	Public relationship	Public distance 12 _____ 25+ feet close phase ___ far phase	

Personal Distance   You carry a protective bubble defining your **personal distance**, which allows you to stay protected and untouched by others. Personal distance ranges from 18 inches to about 4 feet. In the close phase, people can still hold or grasp each other but only by extending their arms. You can then take into your protective bubble certain individuals—for example, loved ones. In the far phase, you can touch another person only if you both extend your arms. This far phase is the extent to which you can physically place your hands on others; hence, it defines, in one sense, the limits of your physical control over others. At times, you may detect breath odor, but generally at this distance, etiquette demands that you direct your breath to some neutral area.

Social Distance   At the **social distance**, ranging from 4 to 12 feet, you lose the visual detail you had at the personal distance. The close phase is the distance at which you conduct impersonal business or interact at a social gathering. The far phase is the distance at which you stand when someone says, "Stand away so I can look at you." At this distance, business transactions have a more formal tone than they do when conducted in the close phase. In the offices of high officials, the desks are often positioned so that clients are kept at least this distance away. Unlike the **intimate distance**, where eye contact is awkward, the far phase of the social distance makes eye contact essential—otherwise, communication is lost. The voice is generally louder than normal at this level. This distance enables you to avoid constant interaction with those with whom you work without seeming rude.

Public Distance   **Public distance** ranges from 12 to more than 25 feet. In the close phase, a person seems protected by space. At this distance, you're able to take defensive action should you feel threatened. On a public bus or train, for example, you might keep at least this distance from a drunk. Although you lose the fine details of the face and eyes, you're still close enough to see what is happening.

At the far phase, you see others not as separate individuals but as part of the whole setting. People automatically establish a space of approximately 30 feet around important public figures, and they seem to do this whether or not there are guards preventing their coming closer. The far phase is the distance by which actors on stage are separated from their audience; consequently, their actions and voices have to be somewhat exaggerated.

Theories about Space   Researchers studying nonverbal communication have offered numerous explanations about why people maintain the distances they do. Prominent among these explanations are protection theory, equilibrium theory, and expectancy violation theory—rather complex names for simple and interesting concepts.

Protection theory holds that you establish a body buffer zone around yourself as protection against unwanted touching or attack (Dosey & Meisels, 1976). When you feel that you may be attacked, your body buffer zone increases; you want more space around you. For example, if you found yourself in a dangerous neighborhood at night, your body buffer zone would probably expand well beyond what it would be if you were in familiar and safe surroundings. If someone entered this buffer zone, you would probably feel threatened and seek to expand the distance by walking faster or crossing the street. In contrast, when you're feeling secure and protected, your buffer zone becomes much smaller. For example, if you're with a group of close friends and feel secure, your buffer zone shrinks, and you may welcome close proximity and mutual touching.

Equilibrium theory holds that intimacy and interpersonal distance vary together: the greater the intimacy, the closer the distance; the lower the intimacy, the greater the distance. This theory says that you maintain close distances with those with whom you have close interpersonal relationships and that you maintain greater distances with those with whom you do not have close relationships (Argyle & Dean, 1965; Bailenson, Blascovich, Beall, & Loomis, 2001).

Expectancy violations theory explains what happens when you increase or decrease the distance between yourself and another in an interpersonal interaction (Burgoon, Guerrero, & Floyd, 2010). The theory assumes that you have expectancies for the distance people are to maintain in their conversations. When these expectancies are violated, you try to explain to yourself why this violation occurred and it brings into focus the nature of your relationship. Perhaps the most interesting conclusion to emerge from this theory is that the meaning you give to the violation depends on whether you like the person. If you like the person who violated your expectancies by, say, standing too close, you'll like the person even more as a result of this violation—probably because you'll interpret this added closeness as an indication that the person likes you. If, on the other hand, you do not like the person, you'll like the person even less as a result of the violation—perhaps because you'll interpret this added closeness as threatening or being overly forward.

Territoriality   Another type of communication having to do with space is **territoriality**, the possessive reaction to an area or to particular objects. You interact basically in three types of territories: **primary territories** or **home territories**, **secondary territories**, and **public territories** (Altman, 1975):

- *Primary territories*, or *home territories*, are areas that you might call your own; these areas are your exclusive preserve and might include your room, your desk, or your office.
- *Secondary territories* are areas that don't belong to you but that you have occupied; thus, you're associated with them. Secondary territories might include the table in the cafeteria that you regularly eat at, your classroom seat, or your neighborhood turf.
- *Public territories* are areas that are open to all people; they may be owned by some person or organization, but they are used by everyone. Examples include a movie house, a restaurant, or a shopping mall.

When you operate in your own primary territory, you have an interpersonal advantage, often called the **home field advantage**. In their own home or office, people take on a kind of leadership role: they initiate conversations; fill in silences; assume relaxed and comfortable postures; and, in conversations, maintain their positions with greater conviction. Because the territorial owner is dominant, you stand a better chance of getting your raise, having your point accepted, or getting a contract resolved in your favor if you're in your own territory (your office, your home) rather than in someone else's (your supervisor's office, for example) (Marsh, 1988).

Like animals, humans mark both their primary and secondary territories to signal ownership. Some people—perhaps because they can't own territories—use markers to indicate pseudo-ownership or appropriation of someone else's space or of a public territory for their own use (Childress, 2004). Graffiti and the markings of gang boundaries come quickly to mind as examples. If you think about your own use of markers, you'll probably be able to identify three different types of **markers: central markers**, **boundary markers**, and **ear markers** (Goffman, 1971):

- *Central markers* are items you place in a territory to reserve it for you—for example, a coffee cup on the table, books on your desk, or a sweater over a library chair.
- *Boundary markers* set boundaries that divide your territory from that of others. In the supermarket checkout line, the bar that is placed between your groceries and those of the person behind you is a boundary marker, as are fences, the armrests separating chairs in a movie theater, and the contours of the molded plastic seats on a bus.
- *Ear markers* a term taken from the practice of branding animals on their ears—are identifying marks that indicate your possession of a territory or object. Trademarks, nameplates, and monograms are all examples of ear markers.

Markers are important in giving you a feeling of belonging. For example, students in college dormitories who marked their rooms by displaying personal items stayed in school longer than did those who didn't personalize their spaces (Marsh, 1988).

Again, like animals, humans use territory to signal their status. For example, the size and location of your territory (your home or office, say) indicates something about your status. Status is also signaled by the unwritten law granting the right of invasion, or **territorial encroachment**. Higher-status individuals have a "right" to invade the territory of lower-status persons, but the reverse is not true. The boss of a large company, for example, can barge into the office of a junior executive, but the reverse would be unthinkable. Similarly, a teacher may invade a student's personal space by looking over her or his shoulder as the student writes, but the student cannot do the same to the teacher.

At times, you may want to resist the encroachment on your territory. If so, you can react in several ways: **withdrawal**, **turf defense**, **insulation**, and **linguistic collusion** (Lyman & Scott, 1967; Richmond, McCroskey, & Hickson, 2012):

- In *withdrawal* you simply leave the scene, whether the country, home, office, or social media site.
- In *turf defense* you defend the territory against the encroachment. This may mean doing something as simple as saying, "This is my seat," or you may start a fight, as nations do.
- *Insulation* involves erecting barriers between yourself and those who would encroach on your territory. Putting up a fence around your property or surrounding your desk with furniture so that others can't get close are common examples of insulation.
- *Linguistic collusion* means speaking in a language or jargon that the "invaders" don't understand and thus excluding them from your interactions.

Artifactual Communication

Artifactual communication consists of messages conveyed by objects that are made by human hands. Thus, aesthetics, color, clothing, jewelry, and hairstyle, as well as scents such as perfume, cologne, or incense, all are considered artifactual. Here are a few examples.

Space Decoration   That the decoration or surroundings of a place exert influence on perceptions should be obvious to anyone who has ever entered a hospital, with its sterile walls and furniture, or a museum, with its imposing columns, glass-encased exhibits, and brass plaques.

And, of course, the way you decorate your private spaces communicates something about who you are. The office with a mahogany desk, bookcases, and oriental rugs communicates importance and status within the organization, just as a metal desk and bare floor communicate a status much farther down in the hierarchy. At home, the cost of your furnishings may communicate your status and wealth, and their coordination may communicate your sense of style. The magazines may communicate your interests. The arrangement of chairs around a television may reveal how important watching television is. Bookcases lining the walls reveal the importance of reading. In fact, there is probably little in your home that does not send messages to others and that others do not use for making inferences about you. Computers, wide-screen televisions, well-equipped kitchens, and oil paintings of great-grandparents, for example, all say something about the people who own them.

Pygmalion Gifting

The "Pygmalion gift" is a gift designed to change the recipient into what the donor wants that person to become. For example, the parent who gives a child books or science equipment may be asking the child to be a scholar or a scientist. *What messages have you recently communicated in your gift-giving behavior? What messages do you think others have communicated to you by the gifts they gave you?*

Likewise, the absence of certain items communicates something about you. Consider, for example, what messages you would get from a home in which there was no television, computer, or books.

People form opinions about your personality on the basis of room decorations. Research, for example, finds that people make judgments about your openness to new experiences (distinctive decorating usually communicates this, as do different types of books and magazines and travel souvenirs) and about your conscientiousness, emotional stability, degree of extroversion, and agreeableness. Not surprisingly, bedrooms prove more revealing than offices (Gosling, Ko, Mannarelli, & Morris, 2002).

Color Communication   When you're in debt, you speak of being "in the red"; when you make a profit, you're "in the black." When you're sad, you're "blue"; when you're healthy, you're "in the pink"; when you're covetous, you're "green with envy." To be a coward is to be "yellow," and to be inexperienced is to be "green." When you talk a great deal, you talk "a blue streak." When you're angry, you "see red." As revealed through these timeworn clichés, language abounds in color symbolism.

Color communication takes place on many levels. For example, there is some evidence that colors affect us physiologically. Respiratory movements increase in the presence of red light and decrease in the presence of blue light. Similarly, eye blinks increase in frequency when eyes are exposed to red light and decrease when exposed to blue. This seems consistent with our intuitive feelings that blue is more soothing and red more provocative. At the same time, blue light has been found to increase alertness (Rahman, et al., 2014; Dean, 2014b).

Color also seems to influence the expectation of taste sensation (Srivastava & More, 2010). For example, people expect pink pills to be sweeter than red pills, yellow pills to be salty, white and blue pills to be bitter, and orange pills to be sour.

Colors vary greatly in their meanings from one culture to another. To illustrate this cultural variation, Table 5.6) lists some of the many meanings communicated by popular colors in different cultures (Dresser, 2005; Dreyfuss, 1971; Hoft, 1995; Singh & Pereira, 2005). As you read this section, you may want to consider your own meanings for these colors and where your meanings came from.

Table 5.6   Color and Meaning across Cultures

- **Red:** In China, red signifies prosperity and rebirth, and is used for festive and joyous occasions. In France and the United Kingdom, red indicates masculinity; in many African countries, blasphemy or death; and in Japan, anger and danger. Red ink, especially among Korean Buddhists, is used only to write a person's name at the time of death or on the anniversary of the person's death; this can create problems when American teachers use red ink to mark homework.

- **Green:** In the United States, green signifies capitalism, a signal to go ahead, and envy; in Ireland, patriotism; among some Native Americans, femininity; to the Egyptians, fertility and strength; to the Japanese, youth and energy.

- **Black:** In Thailand, black signifies old age; in parts of Malaysia, courage; in much of Europe, death.

- **White:** In Thailand, white signifies purity; in many Muslim and Hindu cultures, purity and peace; in Japan and other Asian countries, death and mourning.

- **Blue:** In Iran, blue signifies something negative; in Ghana, joy; for the Cherokee, it signifies defeat; in Egypt, virtue and truth; in Greece, national pride.

- **Yellow:** In China, yellow signifies wealth and authority; in the United States, caution and cowardice; in Egypt, happiness and prosperity; in many countries throughout the world, femininity.

- **Purple:** In Latin America, purple signifies death; in Europe, royalty; in Egypt, virtue and faith; in Japan, grace and nobility; in China, barbarism; in the United States, nobility and bravery.

And, of course, colors are often associated with gender, beginning with pink for baby girls and blue for baby boys in the United States. Even as adults, women are allowed great choice in clothing color. Men, on the other hand, have a more restricted palette from which to choose.

Clothing and Jewelry   Clothing serves a variety of functions. It protects you from the weather and, in sports like football, from injury. It helps you conceal parts of your body and so serves a modesty function. In the business world, it may communicate your position within the hierarchy and your willingness and desire to conform to the clothing norms of the organization. It may also communicate your professionalism, which seems to be the reason why some organizations favor dress codes (Smith, M. H., 2003). Clothing also serves as a form of **cultural display** (Morris, 2002). It communicates your cultural and subcultural affiliations. In the United States, where there are so many different ethnic groups, you regularly see examples of dress that indicate what country the wearers are from.

Today, wearable technology has added a new dimension of the messages clothing communicates. Google glasses, watches that function as computers, and cameras built into ties or jewelry are among the "clothing" that communicates something about who you are and, perhaps, where you're going.

The very poor and the very rich don't dress in the same way, nor do white- and blue-collar workers or the young and the old (Lurie, 1983). People dress, in part at least, to identify with the groups of which they are or want to be members. At the same time, they dress to manage the impressions they give to others (Frith & Gleeson, 2004; Keating, 2006). For example, you're likely to dress conservatively if you're interviewing for a job at a conservative firm, to indicate that you share the values of the firm of which you want to be a part. On the other hand, you'd dress very differently if you are going clubbing at one of the trendy hot spots.

You probably make judgments about your college instructors on the basis of the way they dress, especially on the first day. In one study, college students perceived an instructor dressed informally as friendly, fair, enthusiastic, and flexible, and the same instructor dressed formally as prepared, knowledgeable, and organized (Malandro, Barker, & Barker, 1989). Perceptions naturally vary with the fashions of the time and the expectations of what's appropriate and what's inappropriate. Today, with websites such as Rate My Professor, students may come into the class with a pretty firm picture of the instructor, and clothing is likely to prove less important.

Clothing also seems to influence your own behavior and the behavior of groups. For example, it has been argued that people who dress casually act more informally (Morand, 1995). Therefore, meetings with such casually dressed people are more likely to involve a freer exchange of thoughts and ideas, which in turn may stimulate creativity. This casual attire seems to work well in companies that must rely heavily on creative development, such as computer software companies. And many technology companies, like Google, Yahoo!, and Apple, encourage a more informal, casual style of dress. But banks and insurance companies, which traditionally have resisted change, may prefer more formal attire that creates distance between workers as well as between employees and customers.

Your jewelry, too, communicates messages about you. Wedding and engagement rings are obvious examples of jewelry designed to communicate very specific messages. College rings and political buttons also communicate specific information. If you wear a Rolex watch or large precious stones, others are likely to infer that you're rich. Men with earrings will be judged differently from men without earrings. And the number and type of buttons you display on your Facebook page also communicate something about you, your sense of humor, your passions, and your values.

Tattoos and Rings   Today body piercings are popular, especially among the young. Nose and nipple rings and tongue and belly-button jewelry send a variety of messages.

Dress Implications

A popular defense tactic in sex crimes against women, gay men, lesbians, and transgender individuals is to blame the victim by referring to the way the victim was dressed and implying that the victim, by wearing certain clothing, provoked the attack. *What do you think of this tactic? Is it likely to be effective? Is it ethical?*

Although people wearing such jewelry may wish to communicate meanings of their own, those interpreting these messages seem to infer that the wearer is communicating an unwillingness to conform to social norms and a willingness to take greater risks than those without such piercings (Forbes, 2001). It's worth noting that in a study of employers' perceptions, applicants with eyebrow piercings were rated and ranked significantly lower than those without such piercings (Acor, 2001). In another study, nose-pierced job candidates were given lower scores on measures of credibility, such as character and trust, as well as sociability and job suitability (Seiter & Sandry, 2003). Tattoos—temporary or permanent—likewise communicate a variety of messages, often the name of a loved one or some symbol of allegiance or affiliation. Tattoos also communicate to the wearers themselves. For example, tattooed students see themselves (and perhaps others do as well) as more adventurous, creative, individualistic, and risk-prone than those without tattoos (Drews, Allison, & Probst, 2000). Another study found that 30% of tattooed Americans felt it made them sexier. And women do find men with tattoos sexy (Brooks, 2014). Men who display tattoos in their profile photos get more attention than those without tattoos, though the same is not true for women (Roper, 2014). However, tattoos and piercings may also communicate undesirable traits, such as impulsiveness, unpredictability, and a tendency toward recklessness or violence (Rapsa & Cusack, 1990; Smith, M. H., 2003).

Attitudes toward tattoos are changing quickly. For example, 64 percent of Americans over 65 said the increase in tattoos was a change for the worse, while only 22 percent of those 18 to 29 said this (Brooks, 2014). Nevertheless, business experts continue to note the negative effects in terms of getting a job and suggest hiding tattoos during job interviews (Ingegneri, 2008; Varenik, 2010).

Olfactory Messages

Smell is a peculiar aspect of nonverbal communication and is discussed in widely different ways by different writers. Here, because the emphasis is on using scents (for example, perfume or cologne), it's grouped with artifactual communication. But recognize that body odor also communicates, and perhaps that part of smell is best thought of as a form of body communication. In fact, some research argues that body odor is a significant factor in influencing why some relationships develop and some don't (Comstock, 2012). You also use smells to make yourself feel better. When the smells are pleasant, you feel better about yourself; when the smells are unpleasant, you feel less good about yourself. In fact, research finds that smells can influence your body's chemistry, which, in turn, influences your emotional state. For example, the smell of chocolate results in the reduction of theta brain waves, which produces a sense of relaxation and a reduced level of attention (Martin, 1998).

Olfactory communication, or olfactics, is extremely important in a wide variety of situations. Scientists estimate that you can smell some 10,000 different odors (Angier, 1995a). People are able to identify relatives from their smells, fear and stress in others, and even illness and relative age (Comstock, 2012; Mitro, Gordon, Olsson, & Lundström, 2012). There is some evidence, though not conclusive, showing that the smell of lemon contributes to a perception of health, the smells of lavender and eucalyptus seem to increase alertness, and the smell of rose oil seems to reduce blood pressure. Findings such as these have contributed to the growth of aromatherapy and to the profession of aromatherapist (Furlow, 1996). Some of the most important messages that scent seems to communicate involve attraction, taste, memory, and identification.

- **To attract others** In many animal species, the female gives off a scent that draws males, often from far distances, and thus ensures the continuation of the species. Humans, too, emit sexual attractants called sex pheromones, body secretions that arouse sexual desire (Kluger, 2008). Humans, of course, supplement pheromones with perfumes, colognes, after-shave lotions, powders, and the like, to enhance attractiveness and sexuality and, at the same time, to cover up any unpleasant body odor. And if we can judge from the advertisements and the space devoted to such products, men seem to be catching up with women in the number and diversity of such products. Women, research finds, prefer the scent of men who bear a close genetic similarity to themselves—a finding that may account in part for our attraction to people much like ourselves (Ober, et al., 1997; Wade, 2002). And the Associated Press reports (June 23, 2012) that pheromone sniffing parties, in which members submit a slept-in T-shirt to be smelled by others in an attempt to meet eligible singles, have been held in New York City and Los Angeles and are planned for other cities as well. The idea is that singles bring a slept-in T-shirt, coded for identification purposes, to a party. Others smell it and if they like the smell, they get together. It's seen by some as an alternative to online dating.

- **To aid taste** Without smell, taste would be severely impaired. For example, it would be extremely difficult to taste the difference between a raw potato and an apple without the sense of smell. Street vendors selling hot dogs, sausages, and similar foods are aided greatly by the smells that stimulate the appetites of passersby.

- **To aid memory** Smell is a powerful memory aid; you can often recall situations from months and even years ago when you happen upon a similar smell. One reason smell can help you recall a previous situation so effectively is that it's often associated with significant emotional experiences (Rubin, Groth, & Goldsmith, 1984; Malandro, Barker, & Barker, 1989).

- **To create an image** Smell is often used to create an image or an identity for a product. Advertisers and manufacturers spend millions of dollars each year creating scents for cleaning products and toothpastes, for example. These scents have nothing to do with the products' cleaning power. Instead, they function solely to help create product images or identities. There is also evidence that we can identify specific significant others by smell. For example, infants find their mothers' breasts through smell, mothers can identify their newborns solely through smell, and children are able to identify the T-shirts of their brothers and sisters solely on the basis of smell (Porter & Moore, 1981; Angier, 1995a).

Temporal Communication

The study of **temporal communication**, known technically as **chronemics**, concerns the use of time—how you organize it, react to it, and communicate messages through it (Bruneau, 1985, 1990, 2009/2010). Here we'll look at psychological, interpersonal, and cultural time.

Psychological Time   Before reading about **psychological time**, consider your time orientation.

For each of the following statements, indicate which is true (T) and which is false (F) in terms of your general attitude and behavior.

_____ **1.** I often turn to the past for guidance in the present.

_____ **2.** Old people have wisdom that I can learn from.

_____ **3.** I enjoy learning about and from the past.

_____ **4.** Knowing about the past helps me in the present.

_____ **5.** I enjoy life as it comes.

____ **6.** I avoid looking too far ahead.

____ **7.** I frequently put off work to enjoy the moment.

____ **8.** I look for immediate payoffs and rewards.

____ **9.** I work hard today basically because of tomorrow's expected rewards.

____ **10.** I enjoy planning for tomorrow and the future generally.

____ **11.** I'm willing to endure difficulties if there's a payoff and/or reward at the end.

____ **12.** I prepare "to do" lists fairly regularly.

These questions were designed to raise the issue of time orientation, whether you focus more on the past, the present, or the future. [The idea for this test and the insights on psychological time owe their formulation to Gonzalez and Zimbardo (1985).]

- In a *past orientation*, you have special reverence for the past. You relive old times and regard the old methods as the best. You see events as circular and recurring, so the wisdom of yesterday is applicable also to today and tomorrow. Past-oriented individuals would (as you can tell from the questions) respond with true (T) to questions 1–4 and with either true (T) or false (F) for the remaining statements.
- In a *present orientation*, you live in the present: for now, not tomorrow. Present-oriented individuals respond with true (T) to questions 5–8, false (F) to questions 9–12, and either true (T) or false (F) to questions 1–4.
- In a *future orientation*, you look toward and live for the future. You save today, work hard in college, and deny yourself luxuries because you're preparing for the future. Future-oriented individuals respond with true (T) to questions 9–12, false (F) to questions 5–8, and either true (T) or false (F) to questions 1–4.

As you'll see, your time orientation has important implications for both your college and your professional career.

The time orientation you develop depends to a great extent on your socioeconomic class and your personal experiences (Gonzalez & Zimbardo, 1985). For example, parents with unskilled and semiskilled occupations are likely to teach their children a present-oriented fatalism and a belief that enjoying yourself is more important than planning for the future. Parents who are teachers, managers, or other professionals tend to teach their children the importance of planning and preparing for the future, along with other strategies for success. In the United States, not surprisingly, future income is positively related to future orientation; the more future-oriented you are, the greater your income is likely to be.

Different time perspectives also account for much intercultural misunderstanding because different cultures often teach their members drastically different time orientations. For example, people from some Latin cultures would rather be late for an appointment than end a conversation abruptly or before it has come to a natural end. So the Latin cultures may see an individual's lateness as a result of politeness. But others may see the lateness as impolite to the person with whom the individual had the appointment (Hall & Hall, 1987).

Similarly, the future-oriented person who works for tomorrow's goals frequently sees the present-oriented person as lazy and poorly motivated for enjoying today and not planning for tomorrow. In turn, the present-oriented person may see those with strong future orientations as obsessed with amassing wealth or rising in status. Some cultures—individualistic cultures in particular—seem to emphasize a future orientation; members work hard today for a better future and without much regard for the past, for example. Collectivist cultures, on the other hand, have greater respect for the past; the past is often looked to for guidance for the present. According to some intercultural researchers, many Asian cultures (Japanese and Chinese) place great value on the past, Latinos and Native Americans place more emphasis on the present, and European Americans emphasize the future (Lustig, Koester, & Halualani, 2018).

As you read more about time and nonverbal communication generally, consider how these time orientations work for or against you. For example, will your time orientation help you achieve your social and professional goals? If not, what might you do about changing these attitudes and behaviors? Time and its effective management are important, and Table 5.7 offers some suggestions for effective time management.

Interpersonal Time **Interpersonal time** refers to a wide variety of time-related elements that figure into interpersonal interaction. Here are several of the more important (Burgoon, Guerrero, & Floyd, 2010; Andersen & Bowman, 1999; DeVito, 2014):

- *Punctuality* refers to being on time for a variety of occasions—for company meetings, class, teacher-student appointments, a ballgame, a movie or television show, and completing assignments, to name just a few examples.
- *Wait time* refers to the amount of time it's considered appropriate to wait for someone. Generally, the rule is that you'd wait longer for higher-status people than for lower-status people. You'd wait a long time if your supervisor is late, but you may wait only a few minutes for a colleague.
- *Duration* refers to the length of time that a particular interaction will take. When you go to the doctor or dentist, you're likely given a specific amount of time. If you use a consultant, lawyer, or accountant, you may be charged for the length of time you interact and the length of time he or she works on your project. Appropriately enough, the practice is referred to as being "on the clock."
- *Talk time* refers, for example, to who initiates and who terminates a conversation, who talks more, who selects and directs the topics for discussion. As with so many such factors, status plays an important role here. It's the higher-status person who makes the decisions. But perhaps the best example of high status and talk time is the privilege to interrupt.
- *Work time* refers to the time schedule of your working life. If you're a low-level employee, you may have to punch a clock. And you're probably paid per unit of time, per hour or per day. You need to arrive on time and not leave before the workday is finished. And you need to wait for your lunch break to eat even if you have been hungry for the last two hours. If you're a high-level employee or the boss, you may actually spend more time at work, but it will be of your own choosing. You won't have to punch a time clock; get permission to arrive late or leave early; and, of course, you don't have to wait for your lunch break to eat.
- *Relationship time* is similar to work time but refers to the time one gives or should give to the various people with whom he or she has a relationship. In our culture,

Table 5.7 Ten Principles of Time Management

Principle	Suggestion
Understand your use of time.	Take a look at what takes up most of your time. In a 24-hour day, what takes up the largest block of time (aside from sleeping)? Once you know how you spend your time, you'll be able to see what can be and should be cut back.
Attack your time-wasters.	Begin by getting rid of the one time-waster that you can do without most easily.
Avoid procrastination.	It's highly unlikely that you will do a better job when you're rushed.
Use tools.	Everyone needs help and you can't keep everything in short-term memory. Twitter can easily be used for jogging your memory, as can the various online calendars.
Prioritize.	Put some order into your list.
Break up large tasks.	Most large tasks can be divided into small steps to accomplish during the workday.
Set realistic time limits.	It often helps to set time limits, especially when the task is unpleasant, like doing your income taxes or reading a boring but important textbook.
Reward yourself.	Rewarding yourself after completing a unit of work often makes unpleasant tasks a bit easier to accomplish.
Do things once rather than twice.	For example, one of the popular rules for time management is to look only once at a piece of paper, act on it, and then file or get rid of it.
Avoid distractions.	Minimize whatever distractions you can control. You're not going to be able to control all of them.

THE CULTURAL MAP Long-Term Versus Short-Term Orientation

Long-term-oriented cultures teach the importance of future rewards, whereas short-term-oriented cultures teach their members to appreciate the rewards of the past and the present.

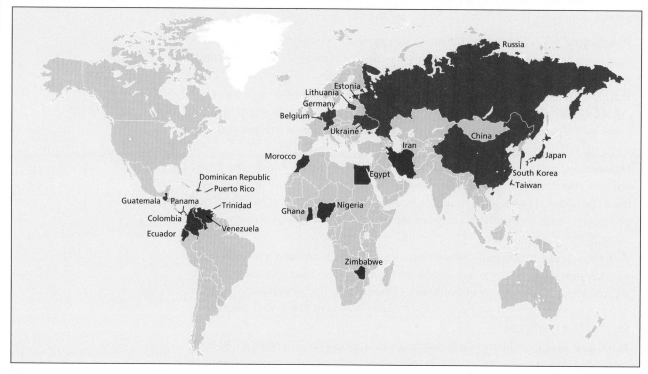

■ These countries are associated with long-term orientation and emphasize the importance of future rewards. Work now to benefit later is a shared belief. A good education and planning for the future are strongly valued in these countries.

■ These countries are associated with short-term orientation and emphasize the importance of present rewards. Benefit now because you may not benefit later. Spending resources now and getting quick results are strongly valued in these countries.

How might the differences between long- and short-term orientation influence interpersonal communication? Do you think long- and short-term oriented cultural members would use social media in the same way? For example, would their posted photos be similar? Different?

committed romantic couples normally spend a considerable amount of time together and when that time is abbreviated (and considered too little by one of the partners), the relationship may be headed for trouble. Even long-distance relationships normally have relationship time—whether on the phone, through periodic visits, or via Skype.

- *Response time* refers to the time it takes you to respond. Response time is observed in both synchronous and asynchronous communication. For example, in face-to-face communication, the response time to some statements and questions must be immediate. There should be very little response lag between one's person's "Will you marry me?" and the other's "Yes." When the response time is inappropriately long, you may sense some kind of disagreement or lack of certainty. An article in *The Week* (June 1, 2012, p. 12) gave a perfect example of inappropriate response time. An Indian woman filed a motion for divorce from her husband of two months because he took too long to change his relationship status on Facebook to "married." Her reasoning was that this was an indication that he was probably cheating; the judge didn't agree and ordered them to undergo counseling.

All of these types of interpersonal time are influenced by a variety of factors involved in the interpersonal communication process. Status differences, as already illustrated, influence significantly the way in which interpersonal time is treated. But other factors also come into play. For example, your personality likely influences your punctuality, how long you wait for someone, whether you interrupt others, and your response time to invitations. Similarly, the context and purpose of the communication influence how you'll treat interpersonal time. For example, if you're interviewing for the job of a lifetime and the interviewer is late, you'll no doubt wait. But if you're simply meeting someone to walk to classes with and the person is late, you'd be more likely to move on.

Cultural Time   Here we look at three types of cultural time: monochronism and polychronism, formal and informal time, and the social clock.

Monochronism and Polychronism   Another important distinction is that between **monochronic time orientation** and **polychronic time orientation** (Hall, 1959, 1976; Hall & Hall, 1987). Monochronic people or cultures—such as those of the United States, Germany, Scandinavia, and Switzerland—schedule one thing at a time. In these cultures, time is compartmentalized and there is a time for everything. On the other hand, polychronic people or cultures—such as those of Latin America, the Mediterranean, and Arabic cultures—schedule multiple things at the same time. Eating, conducting business with several different people, and taking care of family matters all may occur at the same time.

It's interesting to note that social network sites enable you to do (or at least appear to do) more things at one time by enabling you to schedule your tweets or the sending of birthday cards. So you can be skiing down the slopes at the same time your tweets are posted or your cards are sent.

No culture is entirely monochronic or polychronic; rather, these are general tendencies that are found across a large part of the culture. Some cultures combine both time orientations; for example, both orientations are found in Japan and in parts of American culture. Table 5.8 identifies some of the distinctions between these two time orientations. As you read this table, which is based on Hall and Hall (1987), note the potential for miscommunication that these differences may create when monochronic-time and polychronic-time people interact. Have any of these differences ever created interpersonal misunderstandings for you?

Formal and Informal Time   Days are astronomically determined by the earth's rotation on its axis, months by the moon's movement around the earth, and years by the earth's rotation around the sun. But the rest of our time divisions are cultural (largely religious) in origin.

Formal time divisions in the United States and in most of the world include seconds, minutes, hours, days, weeks, months, and years. Some cultures, however, may use seasons or phases of the moon to demarcate their most important time periods. In the United States, if your college is on the semester system, your courses are divided into 50- or 75-minute periods that meet two or three times a week for 14-week periods. Eight semesters of 15 or 16 periods per week equal a college education. As these examples illustrate, formal time units are arbitrary. The culture establishes them for convenience.

VIEWPOINTS

Time Management

What factors determine how long you'll wait for someone who is late for an appointment?

Table 5.8   Monochronic and Polychronic Time

The Monochronic-Time Person	The Polychronic-Time Person
Does one thing at a time.	Does several things at once.
Treats time schedules and plans very seriously; feels they may be broken only for the most serious of reasons.	Treats time schedules and plans as useful (not sacred) tools; feels they may be broken for a variety of causes.
More often have short term relationships.	More often have long term, even life-time, relationships.
Considers the job the most important part of life, ahead of even family.	Considers the family and interpersonal relationships more important than the job.
Considers privacy extremely important; seldom borrows or lends to others; works independently.	Is actively involved with others; works in the presence of and with lots of people at the same time.

Informal time divisions are more general, more ambiguous, and involve informal time terms such as *forever, immediately, soon, right away, as soon as possible*. This type of time communication creates the most problems because informal terms have different meanings for different people. This is especially true when these terms are used interculturally. For example, what does *late* mean when applied to a commuter train that is not on time? Apparently, it depends on your culture. In the United States (the New York area specifically), *late* means arriving six minutes or more after the scheduled time; in Britain, it means five minutes or more. But in Japan, it means one minute.

Not only in concepts of lateness but in other respects as well, attitudes toward time vary from one culture to another. In one study, for example, researchers measured the accuracy of clocks in six cultures—in Japan, Indonesia, Italy, England, Taiwan, and the United States. Japan had the most accurate and Indonesia had the least accurate clocks. The investigators also measured the speed at which people in these six cultures walked; results showed that the Japanese walked the fastest, the Indonesians the slowest (LeVine & Bartlett, 1984).

The Social Clock   Your culture maintains a *social clock*—a time schedule for the right time to do various important things, such as starting to date, finishing college, buying your own home, or having a child. The social clock tells you if you're keeping pace with your peers, are ahead of them, or are falling behind (Greene, 2003; Neugarten, 1979). On the basis of this social clock, which you learned as you grew up, you evaluate your own social and professional development. If you're keeping pace with the rest of your peers (for example, you started dating at the "appropriate" age or you're finishing college at the "appropriate" age), you'll feel well-adjusted, competent, and part of the group. If you're late, you'll probably experience feelings of dissatisfaction. Although today the social clock is becoming more flexible and more tolerant of deviations from the acceptable timetable than it was in past decades, it still exerts pressure on each of us to keep pace with our peers (Peterson, 1996).

Understanding these culturally different perspectives on time should make intercultural communication a bit easier, especially if these time differences are discussed in a culturally sensitive atmosphere. After all, one view of time is not any more correct than any other. However, like all cultural differences, these different time orientations have consequences. For example, members of future-oriented cultures are more likely to succeed in competitive markets like the United States, but they may be viewed negatively by members of cultures that stress living in, and enjoying, the present.

Table 5.9 summarizes the 10 channels of communication discussed here.

Table 5.9 In a Nutshell Ten Channels of Nonverbal Communication

Channel	Key Concepts
Body messages include body gestures and body appearance (also known as kinesics).	Five types of gestures: emblems, illustrators, affect displays, regulators, and adaptors; general body build, height, and weight.
Facial communication.	Facial management, facial feedback.
Eye communication (also known as occulesis).	Eye contact, eye avoidance, pupil dilation.
Touch communication (also known as tactile communication, haptics).	Touch communicates a variety of emotions as does touch avoidance.
Paralanguage.	The rate, pitch, volume of your speech.
Silence.	Silence is functional; spiral of silence.
Spatial messages and territoriality (also known as proxemics).	Proxemic distances (intimate, personal, social, public) and territories (primary, secondary, public).
Artifactual communication.	Items made or arranged by the person, for example, space decoration, colors, clothing and body adornment, and scent.
Olfactory messages.	Scent can be used to attract others, to aid taste, to aid memory, and to create an image.
Temporal communication (also known as chronemics).	Psychological, interpersonal, cultural, and biological time.

Understanding *Interpersonal Skills*

Immediacy: Interpersonal Closeness and Togetherness

Immediacy is the creation of closeness, a sense of togetherness, a oneness between speaker and listener. When you communicate immediacy, you convey a sense of interest and attention, a liking for, and an attraction to, the other person. You communicate immediacy with both verbal and nonverbal messages.

Not surprisingly, people respond to communication that is immediate more favorably than to communication that is not. People like people who communicate immediacy. You can increase your interpersonal attractiveness, the degree to which others like you and respond positively toward you, by using immediacy behaviors. In addition, there is considerable evidence to show that immediacy behaviors are also effective in workplace communication, especially between supervisors and subordinates (Richmond, McCroskey, & Hickson, 2012). For example, when a supervisor uses immediacy behaviors, he or she is seen by subordinates as interested and concerned; subordinates are therefore likely to communicate more freely and honestly about issues that can benefit the supervisor and the organization. Also, workers who have supervisors who communicate immediacy have higher job satisfaction and motivation.

Not all cultures or all people respond in the same way to immediacy messages. For example, in the United States, immediacy behaviors are generally seen as friendly and appropriate. In other cultures, however, the same immediacy behaviors may be viewed as overly familiar—as presuming that a relationship is close when only an acquaintanceship exists. Similarly, recognize that some people may take your immediacy behaviors as indicating a desire for increased intimacy in the relationship. Although you may be trying to signal a friendly closeness, the other person may perceive a romantic invitation. Also, recognize that because immediacy behaviors prolong and encourage in-depth communication, they may not be responded to favorably by persons who are fearful about communication and/or who want to get the interaction over with as soon as possible (Richmond, McCroskey, & Hickson, 2012).

Communicating with Immediacy

Here are a few suggestions for communicating immediacy verbally and nonverbally (Mottet & Richmond, 1998; Richmond, McCroskey, & Hickson, 2012).

- *Self-disclose.* Reveal something significant about yourself. But remember the cautions.
- *Refer to the other person's good qualities* of, say, dependability, intelligence, or character—"you're always so reliable." Be complimentary.
- *Express your positive view* of the other person and of your relationship—"I'm so glad you're my roommate; you know everyone."
- *Talk about commonalities*, things you and the other person have done together or share.
- *Demonstrate your responsiveness* by giving feedback cues that indicate you want to listen more and that you're interested—"And what else happened?"
- *Express psychological closeness and openness* by, for example, maintaining physical closeness and arranging your body to exclude third parties.
- *Maintain appropriate eye contact* and limit looking around at others.
- *Smile* and express your interest in the other person.
- *Focus on the other person's remarks.* Make the speaker know that you heard and understood what was said, and give the speaker appropriate verbal and nonverbal feedback.

At the same time that you want to demonstrate these immediacy messages, try also to avoid nonimmediacy messages, such as speaking in a monotone, looking away from the person you're talking to, frowning while talking, maintaining a tense body posture, or avoiding gestures.

Working with Immediacy

How would other people rate you on immediacy? How would you rate yourself? In what situations might you express great immediacy? In what situations might you express little immediacy?

Nonverbal Communication Competence

5.3 Identify the competencies for effectively encoding and decoding nonverbal messages.

Throughout the discussion of nonverbal communication, you've probably deduced a number of suggestions for improving your own nonverbal communication. Here we bring together some suggestions for both receiving and sending nonverbal messages.

Perhaps the most general skill that applies to both receiving and sending is to become mindful of nonverbal messages—those of others as well as your own. Observe those whose nonverbal behavior you find particularly effective and those you find ineffective and try to identify exactly what makes one effective and one ineffective. Consider this chapter a brief introduction to a lifelong study. In addition to mindfulness, general suggestions can be offered for encoding (or sending) nonverbal messages and for decoding (or interpreting) nonverbal messages. Putting these skills into practice will help you improve your nonverbal communication.

Encoding Skills

In using nonverbal messages to express your meanings, consider these suggestions:

1. *Identify choices.* Identify your choices for your nonverbal communication just as you do for your verbal messages. Identify and think mindfully about the choices you have available for communicating what you want to communicate. For example, when you post a photo on Facebook, you are telling others something about yourself; is your message positive or negative?

2. *Be consistent.* Keep your nonverbal messages consistent with your verbal messages; avoid sending verbal messages that say one thing and nonverbal messages that say something else—at least not when you want to be believed.

3. *Self-monitor.* Monitor your own nonverbal messages with the same care that you monitor your verbal messages. If it's not appropriate to say "this meal is terrible," then it's not appropriate to have a negative expression when you're asked if you want seconds.

4. *Avoid extremes and monotony.* Too little nonverbal communication or too much are likely to be responded to negatively. Similarly, always giving the same nonverbal message—say, continually smiling and nodding your head when listening to a friend's long story—is likely to be seen as insincere.

5. *Analyze the situation.* Take the situation into consideration. Effective nonverbal communication is situational; to be effective, adapt your nonverbal messages to the specific situation. Nonverbal behavior appropriate to one situation may be totally inappropriate in another.

6. *Maintain eye contact with the speaker.* Whether at a meeting, in the hallway, or on an elevator make eye contact; it communicates politeness and says that you are giving the person the consideration of your full attention. Eye contact that is too focused and too prolonged is likely to be seen as invasive and impolite.

7. *Avoid certain adaptors in public.* For example, combing your hair, picking your teeth, or putting your pinky in your ear are likely to be seen as impolite. And, not surprisingly, the greater the formality of the situation, the greater the perception of impoliteness is likely to be. So, for example, combing your hair while sitting with two or three friends would probably not be considered impolite (or perhaps only mildly so), but in a classroom or at a company meeting, it would be considered inappropriate.

8. *Avoid strong cologne or perfume.* While you may enjoy the scent, those around you may find it unpleasant and intrusive. Much like others do not want to hear your cell messages, they probably don't want to have their sense of smell invaded, either.

9. *Be careful with touching.* Touching may or may not be considered appropriate or polite depending on the relationship you have with the other person and in the context in which you find yourselves. The best advice to give here is to avoid touching unless it's part of the culture of the group or organization.

INTERPERSONAL CHOICE POINT
Dealing with Unpleasant Nonverbals

Your colleague in the next cubicle wears extremely strong cologne that you find horrendous. You can't continue smelling this horrible scent any longer. *What might you do to correct this situation?*

a. Cough repeatedly when passing your colleague, who you hope will get the hint.

b. Say something to the office manager.

c. Say something to your colleague.

d. Say nothing; bear it.

e. Other

As a type of conclusion to this section, consider the findings of one nonverbal expert for nonverbal behaviors that you should avoid because they often create negative impressions (Smith, 2014). But, because each situation is different, it's best to look at these nonverbal behaviors as creating negative impressions under certain circumstances but, certainly, not in all situations:

- Crossing your arms across your chest can signal defensiveness.
- Leaning forward too much or too quickly can indicate aggressiveness.
- Breaking your eye contact too early in the interaction might indicate a lack of concern or focus.
- Putting your hands on your hips when standing can indicate aggressiveness.
- Taking a step or two back when asked a question or for a decision may lead people to see you as defensive and unwilling to be honest.
- Putting your hands behind your back or in your pockets can make you look overly stiff.
- Nodding more than usual can make you look less than serious.

Decoding Skills

When you make judgments or draw conclusions about another person on the basis of her or his nonverbal messages, consider these suggestions:

1. **Be tentative.** Resist the temptation to draw immediate conclusions from nonverbal behaviors. Instead, develop hypotheses (educated guesses) about what is going on, and test the validity of your hypotheses on the basis of other evidence.

2. **Mindfully seek alternatives when making judgments.** Your first judgment may be in error, and one good way to test it is to consider alternative judgments. When your romantic partner creates a greater-than-normal distance between you, it may signal an annoyance with you, but it can also signal that your partner needs some space to think something out.

3. **See messages as multi-channeled.** Notice that messages come from lots of different channels and that reasonably accurate judgments can only be made when multiple channels are taken into consideration. Although textbooks (like this one) must present the areas of nonverbal communication separately, the various elements all work together in actual communication situations.

4. **Consider the possibility that you are incorrect.** Even after you've explored the different channels, consider the possibility that you are somehow mistaken; that you've misevaluated the situation. This is especially true when you make a judgment that another person is lying based on, say, avoidance or long pauses. These nonverbal signals may mean lots of things (as well as the possibility of lying).

5. **Interpret your judgments and conclusions against a cultural context.** Consider, for example, if you interpret another's nonverbal behavior through its meaning in your own culture. So, for example, if you interpret someone's "overly close" talking distance as pushy or intrusive because that's your culture's interpretation, you may miss the possibility that this distance is simply standard in the other person's culture or it's a way of signaling closeness and friendliness.

VIEWPOINTS

Nonverbal Skills

Research shows that women are perceived to be, and in reality are, more skilled at both encoding and decoding nonverbal messages (Briton & Hall, 1995; Burgoon, Guerrero, & Floyd, 2010). Do you notice this in your own interactions? Do these differences give women an advantage in conversations? In negotiation? In conflict resolution? In serving on a jury?

6. **Consider the multitude of factors.** A wide variety of factors can influence the way a person behaves nonverbally; for example, a person's physical condition, personality, or particular situation may all influence a person's nonverbal communication. A sour stomach may be more influential in unpleasant expressions than any interpersonal factor. A low grade in an exam may make your normally pleasant roommate scowl and grumble. Without knowing these factors, it's difficult to make an accurate judgment.

7. **Measure behaviors against a baseline.** In judging the meaning of another's behavior, you need to know how this person behaves ordinarily so you can tell what's a deviation and what's normal for this person. For example, if Pat is normally shy and reticent to talk and you observe Pat being the life of the party, it's more meaningful than if you observed Pat being shy and reticent. Nonverbal behavior is most revealing when it deviates from the baseline.

Table 5.10 summarizes these guidelines for increasing your own nonverbal communication competence.

Table 5.10 In a Nutshell Nonverbal Communication Competence

Guidelines for Encoding Competence	Guidelines for Decoding Competence
Identify choices.	Be tentative.
Be consistent.	Mindfully seek alternatives when making judgments.
Self-monitor.	See messages as multi-channeled.
Avoid extremes and monotony.	Consider the possibility that you are incorrect.
Analyze the situation.	Interpret your judgments and conclusions against a cultural context.
Maintain eye contact with the speaker.	Consider the multitude of factors.
Avoid certain adaptors in public.	Measure behaviors against a baseline.
Avoid strong cologne or perfume.	
Be careful with touching	

Summary

This chapter explored nonverbal communication and identified the major principles of nonverbal communication, the varied channels of nonverbal communication, and suggestions for increasing competence in encoding and decoding.

Principles of Nonverbal Communication

5.1 Explain the principles of nonverbal messages.

1. Nonverbal messages interact with verbal messages in six major ways: to accent, to complement, to contradict, to control, to repeat, and to substitute for each other.

2. Nonverbal messages help manage impressions. It is largely through the nonverbal communications of others that you form impressions of them and through your nonverbals that they draw impressions of you.

3. Nonverbal messages help you form relationships. You communicate affection, support, and love, and also displeasure, anger, and animosity through nonverbal signals.

4. Nonverbal messages structure conversation. When you're in conversation, you exchange nonverbal signals indicating that you're ready to speak, to listen, or to comment on what the speaker just said.

5. Nonverbal messages can influence and deceive. You can influence (and deceive) others not only through what you say but also through your nonverbal signals.

6. Nonverbal messages are crucial for emotional expression. Although people often explain and reveal emotions verbally, nonverbal signals communicate a great part of the emotional experience.

Channels of Nonverbal Communication

5.2 Explain the channels through which nonverbal messages are sent and received.

7. Nonverbal messages are communicated through a variety of channels and their meanings are greatly influenced by culture.

8. Among body gestures are emblems, illustrators, affect displays, regulators, and adaptors.

9. General body appearance (e.g., height, weight, and eye and skin colors) can communicate a person's power, level of attractiveness, and suitability as a friend or romantic partner.

10. Facial movements express emotions such as happiness, surprise, fear, anger, sadness, disgust/contempt, interest, bewilderment, and determination. Some facial movements manage the meanings being communicated by means of intensifying, deintensifying, neutralizing, masking, and simulating.

11. Through eye contact, we monitor feedback, maintain interest/attention, signal conversational turns, signal the nature of relationships, signal status, and compensate for physical distance. Through eye avoidance we may give others privacy, signal disinterest, cut off unpleasant stimuli, or heighten other senses. Pupil dilation indicates interest/arousal and increases attractiveness.

12. Among the meanings touch can communicate are positive affect, playfulness, control, ritual functions, and task-relatedness.

13. Paralanguage cues help people form impressions; identify emotional states; and make judgments of speakers' credibility, intelligence, and objectivity.

14. Silence can communicate varied meanings (for example, the desire to hurt, to prevent communication, or to achieve special effects). The spiral of silence theory offers an interesting perspective on the influence of silence.

15. The major types of distance that correspond to types of relationships are intimate distance (touching to 18 inches), personal distance (18 inches to 4 feet), social distance (4 to 12 feet), and public distance (12 or more feet).

16. Theories about space include protection theory (you maintain spatial distance to protect yourself), equilibrium theory (you regulate distance according to the intimacy level of your relationship), and expectancy violations theory (increasing or decreasing the expected distance between yourself and another can send important messages).

17. Your territories may be identified as primary (areas you own), secondary (areas that you occupy regularly), and public (areas open to everyone). Like animals, humans often mark their territories with central, boundary, and ear markers as proof of ownership. Your territory (its appearance and the way it's used) also communicates status.

18. Among the artifactual nonverbal cues are space decoration, color, clothing, and body adornment.

19. Olfactory messages include those designed to attract others, to aid taste and memory, and to create images and recollections.

20. Three main time orientations can be distinguished: past, present, and future. These orientations influence a wide variety of behaviors, such as your willingness to plan for the future, your tendency to party, and even your potential income.

Nonverbal Communication Competence

5.3 Identify the competencies for effectively encoding and decoding nonverbal messages.

21. You can increase your nonverbal encoding competence by considering your choices for communicating, being consistent in your messages, monitoring your nonverbal choices, avoiding extremes, being aware of the situation, maintaining eye contact, avoiding adaptors, avoiding strong and potentially unpleasant scents, and being cautious about touching.

22. You can increase your nonverbal decoding competence by mindfully seeking alternative judgments, being tentative, attending to all nonverbal channels, considering that you might be wrong, being sensitive to the cultural context, and considering the vast array of factors that can influence what a person does or says.

Key Terms

adaptors
affect displays
artifactual communication
boundary markers
central marker
chronemics
civil inattention
color communication
cultural display rules
cultural display
deception bias
Duchenne smile
ear marker
emblems
emoji
emoticon
equilibrium theory
expectancy violations theory
eye avoidance
eye communication
facial feedback hypothesis
formal time

haptics
home field advantage
home territories
illustrators
immediacy
informal time
insulation
interpersonal time
intimate distance
kinesics
linguistic collusion
markers
monochronic time orientation
nonverbal communication
oculesics
olfactory communication
paralanguage
personal distance
polychronic time orientation
primary territories
protection theory
proxemic distances

proxemics
psychological time
public distance
public territories
rate
regulators
secondary territories
silence
smiley
social distance
spiral of silence
tactile communication
temporal communication
territorial encroachment
territoriality
touch avoidance
truth bias
turf defense
volume
withdrawal

CHAPTER SIX

Listening

Listening isn't always easy. *A variety of skills can make it more effective and more comfortable.*

Chapter Topics

The Process and Skills of Listening

Listening Barriers

Styles of Effective Listening

Culture, Gender, and Listening

Learning Objectives

6.1 Define *listening*, describe its five stages, and identify some of the skills for improving listening at each stage.

6.2 Explain the major barriers to effective listening.

6.3 Define the four styles of listening and explain how each may be used effectively.

6.4 Describe some of the cultural and gender differences in listening.

There can be little doubt that you listen a great deal. On waking, you listen to the radio or television. On the way to school, you listen to friends, people around you, screeching cars, singing birds, or falling rain. In school, you listen to the instructors, to other students, and to yourself. You listen to friends at lunch and return to class to listen to more instructors. You arrive home and again listen to family and friends. Perhaps you listen to music on your phone,

news on the radio or your computer, or dramas and sitcoms on television. All in all, you listen for a good part of your waking day.

And there can be little doubt that listening is significant both professionally and personally. In today's workplace, listening is regarded as a crucial skill.

Whether a temporary intern or a high-level executive, you need to listen if you're going to function effectively in today's workplace. If you're not convinced of this, take a look at the many websites that talk about the skills needed for success in today's workplace and you will find that listening consistently ranks among the most important skills. Job searching website, *The Balance*, identifies listening as the most important of the 10 communication skills for success in the workplace (Doyle, 2016).

Personally, we want partners who listen to us; we seek them out in good times and bad to share our thoughts and feelings. Without someone to listen to us, our lives would be a lot less fulfilling.

In this chapter, we look at the nature of the listening process, the barriers to effective listening, the varied styles of listening you might use in different situations, and some cultural and gender differences in listening. Throughout this chapter, we'll identify ways to avoid the major barriers to listening and provide guidelines for more effective listening.

The Process and Skills of Listening

6.1 Define *listening*, describe its five stages, and identify some of the skills for improving listening at each stage.

Traditionally, the study of listening has focused on spoken messages (Emmert, 1994; Brownell, 2013, Worthington & Fitch-Hauser, 2012). However, in light of Facebook, Twitter, wikis, and blogs, we need to expand the traditional definition of listening as the receiving and processing of auditory signals. If posting messages on social media sites is part of interpersonal communication (which it surely is), then the reading of these messages must also be part of interpersonal communication and most logically part of listening. **Listening**, then, may be defined as *the process of receiving, understanding, remembering, evaluating, and responding to verbal [spoken or written] and/or nonverbal messages.*

You can look at listening as a process occurring in five stages: (1) receiving (hearing and attending to the message), (2) understanding (deciphering meaning from the message you hear), (3) remembering (retaining what you hear in memory), (4) evaluating (thinking critically about and judging the message), and (5) responding (answering or giving feedback to the speaker). This five-step process is visualized in Figure 6.1.

All five listening stages overlap; when you listen, you're performing all five processes at essentially the same time. For example, when listening in conversation, you're not only remaining attentive to what the other person is saying but also critically evaluating what he or she just said and perhaps giving feedback.

Listening is never perfect. There are lapses in attention, misunderstandings, lapses in memory, inadequate critical thinking, and inappropriate responding. The goal is to reduce these obstacles as best you can.

Note that the listening process is circular. The responses of Person A serve as the stimuli for Person B, whose responses in turn serve as the stimuli for Person A, and so on. As will become clear in the following discussion of the five steps, listening is not a process of transferring an idea from the mind of a speaker to the mind of a listener. Rather, it is a process in which speaker and listener work together to achieve a common understanding.

Figure 6.1 emphasizes that listening involves a collection of skills for improving: attention and concentration (receiving), learning (understanding), memory (remembering), critical thinking (evaluation), and competence in giving feedback (responding). Listening can go wrong at any stage—but you can improve your listening ability by strengthening the skills needed at each step of the listening process. Consequently, suggestions for listening improvement are offered with each of the five stages.

Figure 6.1   A Five-Stage Model of Listening

Lapses occur at each stage of listening. For example, at the receiving stage, a listener receives part of the message but, because of noise and perhaps for other reasons, fails to receive other parts. Similarly, at the stage of understanding, a listener understands part of the message but, because of each person's inability to share another's meanings exactly, fails to understand other parts. The same is true for remembering, evaluating, and responding. This model draws on a variety of previous models that listening researchers have developed (for example, Worthington & Fitch-Hauser, 2012; Barker, 1990; and Brownell, 2013).

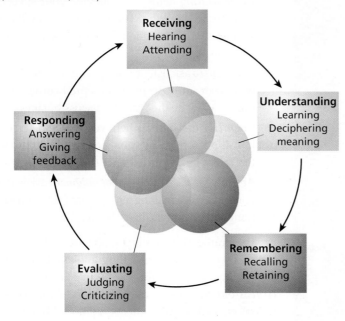

Stage One: Receiving

Listening begins with hearing, the process of receiving the messages the speaker sends. One of the great myths about listening is that it's the same as hearing. It isn't. Hearing is just the first stage of listening; it's equivalent to receiving. Hearing (and receiving) is a physiological process that occurs when you're in the vicinity of vibrations in the air and these vibrations impinge on your eardrum. Hearing is basically a passive process that occurs without any attention or effort on your part; hearing is mindless. Listening, as you'll see, is very different; listening is mindful.

At the **receiving** stage, you note not only what is said (verbally and nonverbally) but also what is omitted. You receive, for example, your boss's summary of your accomplishments as well as the omission of your shortcomings. To improve your receiving skills:

- *Focus your attention.* Focus your attention on the speaker's verbal and nonverbal messages, on what is said and on what isn't said. Avoid focusing your attention on what you'll say next; if you begin to rehearse your responses, you're going to miss what the speaker says next.

- *Avoid distractions.* Avoid distractions in the environment; if necessary, take the ear buds out of your ears or turn off your cell phone.

- *Maintain your role as listener.* Maintain your listening role and avoid interrupting as much as possible. It will only prevent you from hearing what the speaker is saying.

At times, you may wish to ask your listeners to receive your messages fairly and without prejudice, especially when you anticipate a negative reaction. For this purpose, you're likely to use **disclaimers**, statements that aim to ensure that your messages will be understood and will not reflect negatively on you. Disclaimers also lessen

Listening Attentively

What makes a person or a message deserving of your attentive listening? For example, would you find it more difficult to listen to someone who was overjoyed because of winning the lottery for $27 million or to someone who was overcome with sadness because of the death of a loved one? How easy would it be for you to listen to someone who was depressed because an expected bonus of $60,000 turned out to be only $45,000? Put differently, what types of people and what types of messages engage your listening attention?

any impression of what you're saying being an attack on face. Some of the more popular disclaimers follow (Hewitt & Stokes, 1975; McLaughlin, 1984):

- *Hedging* helps you to separate yourself from the message so that if your listeners reject your message, they need not reject you (for example, "I may be wrong here, but . . . ").
- *Credentialing* helps you establish your special qualifications for saying what you're about to say ("Don't get me wrong; I'm not homophobic" or "As someone who telecommutes, I . . . ").
- *Sin licenses* ask listeners for permission to deviate in some way from some normally accepted convention ("I know this may not be the place to discuss business, but . . . ").
- *Cognitive disclaimers* help you make the case that you're in full possession of your faculties ("I know you'll think I'm crazy, but let me explain the logic of the case").
- *Appeals for the suspension of judgment* ask listeners to hear you out before making a judgment ("Don't hang up on me until you hear my side of the story").

Generally, disclaimers are effective when you think you might offend listeners in telling a joke ("I don't usually like these types of jokes, but . . . "). In one study, for example, 11-year-old children were read a story about someone whose actions created negative effects. Some children heard the story with a disclaimer, and others heard the same story without the disclaimer. When the children were asked to indicate how the person should be punished, those who heard the story with the disclaimer recommended significantly lower punishments (Bennett, 1990).

Disclaimers, however, can also get you into trouble. For example, to preface remarks with "I'm no liar" may well lead listeners to think that perhaps you are lying. Also, if you use too many disclaimers, you may be perceived as someone who doesn't have any strong convictions or as someone who wants to avoid responsibility for just about everything. This seems especially true of hedges.

In responding to statements containing disclaimers, it's often necessary to respond to both the disclaimer and to the statement. By doing so, you let the speaker know that you heard the disclaimer and that you aren't going to view this communication negatively. Appropriate responses might be: "I know you're no sexist, but I don't agree that . . . " or "Well, perhaps we should discuss the money now even if it doesn't seem right."

Stage Two: Understanding

Understanding is the stage at which you learn what the speaker means—the stage at which you grasp both the thoughts and the emotions expressed. Understanding one without the other is likely to result in an unbalanced picture. Understanding is not an automatic process; it takes effort.

You can improve your listening understanding in a variety of ways:

1. *Avoid assuming you understand.* Avoid assuming that you already know what the speaker is going to say before he or she actually says it. Making assumptions can prevent you from accurately listening to what the speaker wants to say.

2. *See the speaker's messages from the speaker's point of view.* Make a special effort to see the messages from the point of view of the speaker. Avoid judging the message until you fully understand it as the speaker intended it.

3. *Ask questions.* Whenever in doubt, ask for clarification; ask for additional details or examples if they're needed. This shows not only that you're listening—which the speaker will appreciate—but also that you want to learn more. Material that is not clearly understood is likely to be easily lost.

4. *Paraphrase.* Paraphrase or rephrase the speaker's ideas in your own words. This can be done silently or aloud. If done silently, it will help you rehearse and learn the material; if done aloud, it also helps you confirm your understanding of what the speaker is saying.

Right now, a large part of your listening takes place in the classroom—listening to the instructor and to other students, essentially for understanding. Table 6.1 offers a few suggestions for listening effectively in the classroom.

Stage Three: Remembering

Effective listening depends on **remembering**. For example, when Susan says that she is planning to buy a new car, the effective listener remembers this and at a later meeting asks about the car. When Joe says that his mother is ill, the effective listener remembers this and asks about her health later in the week.

In some small-group and public speaking situations, you can augment your memory by taking notes or by recording the messages. In many work situations, taking notes is common and may even be expected. In most interpersonal communication situations, however, note taking is inappropriate—although you often do write down a telephone number, an appointment, or directions.

Perhaps the most important point to understand about memory is that what you remember is not what was said but what you remember was said. Memory for speech is not reproductive; you don't simply reproduce in your memory what the speaker said. Rather, memory is reconstructive; you actually reconstruct the messages you hear into a system that makes sense to you. Although this may seem obvious to you (reading a chapter on listening), in a survey of over 1,800 people, 63 percent thought that memory works like a video and accurately records what they hear and what they see (Simons & Chabris, 2011).

If you want to remember what someone says or the names of various people, this information needs to pass from your **short-term memory** (the memory you use, say, to remember a phone number just long enough to write it down) into long-term memory. Short-term memory is very limited in capacity—you can hold only a small amount of information there. **Long-term memory** is unlimited. To facilitate the passage

Table 6.1 Listening in the Classroom

General Suggestions	Specifically
Prepare to listen.	Sit up front where you can see your instructor and any visual aids clearly and comfortably. You listen with your eyes as well as your ears.
Avoid distractions.	Avoid daydreaming, and put away physical distractions like your laptop, smartphone, or newspaper.
Pay special attention to the introduction.	Listen for orienting remarks and for key words and phrases (often written on the board or on presentation slides), such as "another reason," "three major causes," and "first." Using these cues will help you outline the lecture.
Take notes in outline form.	Listen for key terms and use these as headings in your outline. When the instructor says, for example, "there are four kinds of noise," you have your heading and a numbered list of four kinds of noise.
Assume relevance.	Some information may eventually prove irrelevant (unfortunately), but if you listen with the assumption of irrelevancy, you'll never hear anything relevant.
Listen for understanding.	Avoid taking issue with what is said until you understand it fully. Generally, it's wise not to rehearse your arguments against a particular position. When you do this, you run the risk of missing additional explanation or qualification.

False Memories

The term *false memory syndrome* refers to a phenomenon in which you "remember" past experiences that never actually occurred (Loftus, 2004), a situation depicted here from the 1995 movie *Indictment: The McMartin Trial*. Most of the studies on false memory syndrome have centered on erroneous recollections of abuse and other traumatic experiences. Often these false memories are implanted by therapists and interviewers, whose persistent questioning over a period of time can create such a realistic scenario that you come to believe these things actually occurred (Porter, Brit, Yuille, & Lehman, 2000). *In what other ways can false memory syndrome occur and create problems?*

of information from short- to long-term memory, here are FOUR suggestions (**f**ocus, **o**rganize, **u**nite, **r**epeat):

1. ***Focus.*** Focus your attention on the central ideas. Even in the most casual of conversations, there are central ideas. Fix these in your mind. Repeat these ideas to yourself as you continue to listen. Avoid focusing on minor details that often lead to detours in listening and in conversation.

2. ***Organize.*** Organize what you hear; summarize the message in a more easily retained form, but take care not to ignore crucial details or qualifications. If you chunk the material into categories, you'll be able to remember more information. For example, if you want to remember 15 or 20 items to buy in the supermarket, you'll remember more if you group them into chunks—produce, canned goods, and meats.

3. ***Unite.*** Unite the new with the old; relate new information to what you already know. Avoid treating new information as totally apart from all else you know. There's probably some relationship and if you identify it, you're more likely to remember the new material.

4. ***Repeat.*** Repeat names and key concepts to yourself or, if appropriate, aloud. By repeating the names or key concepts, you in effect rehearse these names and concepts, and as a result they'll be easier to learn and remember. If you're introduced to Alice, you'll stand a better chance of remembering her name if you say, "Hi, Alice" than if you say just "Hi." Be especially careful that you don't rehearse your own anticipated responses; if you do, you're sure to lose track of what the speaker is saying.

Stage Four: Evaluating

Evaluating consists of judging the messages in some way. At times you may try to evaluate the speaker's underlying intentions or motives. Often this evaluation process goes on without much conscious awareness. For example, Elaine tells you that she is up for a promotion and is really excited about it. You may then try to judge her intention: perhaps she wants you to use your influence with the company president, or maybe she's preoccupied with the promotion and so she tells everyone, or possibly she's looking for a compliment.

In other situations, your evaluation is more in the nature of critical analysis. For example, in listening to proposals advanced in a business meeting, you may ask: Are the proposals practical? Will they increase productivity? What's the evidence? Is there contradictory evidence?

In evaluating, consider these suggestions:

1. ***Resist evaluation.*** Resist evaluation until you fully understand the speaker's point of view. This is not always easy, but it's almost always essential. If you put a label on the speaker (ultraconservative, bleeding-heart liberal), you'll hear the remainder of the messages through these labels.

2. ***Distinguish facts from opinions.*** Distinguish facts from the opinions and personal interpretations of the speaker. And, most important, fix these labels in mind with the information; for example, try to remember that *Jesse thinks Pat did XYZ*, not just that *Pat did XYZ*.

3. *Identify any biases.* Identify biases, prejudices, or self-interests that may lead the speaker to slant unfairly what is said. It's often wise to ask if the material is being presented fairly or if this person is slanting or spinning it in some way.

4. *Recognize fallacious forms of "reasoning."* Recognize the common fallacies of reasoning that speakers may employ, such as:

- *Name-calling:* applying a favorable or unfavorable label to color your perception—"democracy" and "soft on terrorism" are two currently popular examples.

- *Testimonial:* using positively or negatively viewed spokespersons to encourage your acceptance or rejection of something—such as a white-coated actor to sell toothpaste or a disgraced political figure associated with an idea the speaker wants rejected.

- *Bandwagon:* arguing that you should believe or do something because "everyone else does."

Stage Five: Responding

Responding occurs in two phases: responses you make while the speaker is talking (immediate feedback) and responses you make after the speaker has stopped talking (delayed feedback). These feedback messages send information back to the speaker and tell the speaker how you feel and what you think about his or her messages. When you nod or smile in response to someone you're interacting with face-to-face, you're responding with immediate feedback. When you comment on a blog post, poke a person on Facebook who has poked you, or say you like a photo or post on Facebook, you're responding with delayed feedback. The ease with which feedback can be given on social media (and e-mail and mobile communication) seems to have created an expectation for feedback. When you don't respond (or don't respond quickly enough), it may be interpreted as negative feedback, for example, that you don't like the new post or that you want to create more distance between you. This ease of responding and the expectation (and desire) for feedback may also be one of the reasons motivating the frequent status updates and the adding of new photos, at least for some social media users.

In face-to-face communication, supportive responses made while the speaker is talking are particularly effective; they acknowledge that you're listening and that you're understanding the speaker. These responses include what nonverbal researchers call *back-channeling cues*—comments such as "I see," "yes," "uh-huh," and similar signals.

Responses made after the speaker has stopped talking or after you read a post on a blog or on Facebook are generally more elaborate and might include expressing empathy ("I know how you must feel"), asking for clarification ("Do you mean that this new health plan is going to replace the old one?"), challenging ("I think your evidence is weak here"), agreeing ("You're absolutely right on this; I'll support your proposal"), or giving support ("Good luck"). Social networks make this type of feedback especially easy with comment buttons and the thumbs up icon.

Improving listening responding involves avoiding some of the destructive patterns and practicing more constructive patterns, such as the following five:

1. *Support the speaker.* Give the speaker support throughout the conversation by using and varying your listening cues, such as head nods and minimal responses, for example, "I see" or "uh-huh." Using the "like" or "love" icon, poking back on Facebook, and commenting on another's photos or posts on social networking sites also prove supportive.

INTERPERSONAL CHOICE POINT
Giving Anti-Listening Cues

One of your friends is a storyteller; instead of talking about the world and about people, he tells endless stories—about things that happened a long time ago that he finds funny (though no one else does). You just can't deal with this any longer. *What might you say to help you get out of these situations?*

a. "I've heard this before" and exit.

b. "You need to stop telling these stories over and over again."

c. "I'm sure your stories are interesting but not for me; I'd much rather hear about you, what's happening in your life."

d. Say nothing.

e. Other

The Skills of Listening

Thinking back to your last few face-to-face conversations, can you identify examples where the suggestions made here were or were not followed? How did the use or misuse of these suggestions influence the conversation?

2. *Own your responses.* Take responsibility for what you say. Instead of saying, "Nobody will want to do that" say something like "I don't think I'll do that." Use the anonymity that most social networks allow with discretion.

3. *Resist "responding to another's feelings" with "solving the person's problems."* Men are often accused of responding by trying to solve the person's problems. Generally, this is best avoided, unless, of course, you're asked for advice (Tannen, 1990).

4. *Focus on the other person.* Focus your attention on the other person. Avoid multitasking when you're listening. Show the speaker that he or she is your primary focus. Take off headphones; shut down the iPhone and the television; turn away from the computer screen. Instead of looking around the room, look at the speaker; the speaker's eyes should be your main focus.

5. *Avoid being a thought-completing listener.* Avoid completing the speaker's thoughts or what you think the speaker will say next. Instead, express respect by allowing the speaker to complete his or her thoughts. Completing someone's thoughts often communicates the message that nothing important is going to be said ("I already know it").

Table 6.2 provides a summary of effective listening at each of these five stages.

Table 6.2 In a Nutshell Effective Listening in Five Stages

Listening Stage	Effective Listening
Receiving: You note not only what is said (verbally and nonverbally) but also what is omitted.	**Focus your attention** on the speaker's verbal and nonverbal messages. **Avoid distractions** in the environment. **Maintain your role as listener** and avoid interrupting.
Understanding: You learn what the speaker means, the stage at which you grasp both the thoughts and the emotions expressed.	**Avoid assuming you understand** what the speaker is going to say before he or she actually says it. **See the speaker's messages from the speaker's point of view.** **Ask questions** for clarification. **Rephrase (paraphrase)** the speaker's ideas in your own words.
Remembering: You put the information into short-term memory and rehearse it so that it is stored in long-term memory.	**Focus** your attention on the central ideas. **Organize** what you hear. **Unite** the new with the old. **Rehearse;** repeat names and key concepts to yourself or, if appropriate, aloud.
Evaluating: You judge or evaluate the messages in some way.	**Resist evaluation** until you fully understand the speaker's point of view. **Distinguish facts from the opinions** and personal interpretations of the speaker. **Identify any biases,** self-interests, or prejudices in the speaker. **Recognize some of the popular but fallacious forms of "reasoning"** that speakers may employ, such as **name-calling, testimonial, and bandwagon.**
Responding: You may respond immediately as well as at some later time.	**Support the speaker.** **Own your responses.** **Resist "responding to another's feelings" with "solving the person's problems."** **Focus on the other person.** **Avoid being a thought-completing listener.**

Listening Barriers

6.2 Explain the major barriers to effective listening.

In addition to practicing the various skills for each stage of listening, consider some of the common general barriers to listening. Here are six such barriers and some suggestions for dealing with them as both listener and speaker—because both speaker and listener are responsible for effective listening.

Physical and Mental Distractions

Physical barriers to listening may include, for example, hearing impairment, a noisy environment, or loud music. Multitasking (watching TV while listening to someone with the aim of being supportive, say) simply doesn't work. As both listener and speaker, try to remove whatever physical barriers can be removed; for those that you can't remove, adjust your listening and speaking to lessen the effects as much as possible. As a listener, focus on the speaker; you can attend to the room and the other people later.

Mental distractions are in many ways similar to physical distractions; they get in the way of focused listening. Typical mental distractions, for example, are thinking about your upcoming Saturday night date, worrying about the unflattering photo your ex posted on Facebook, or becoming too emotional to think (and listen) clearly. In listening, recognize that you can think about your date later. In speaking, make what you say compelling and relevant to the listener.

Cell Conversations

Research indicates that overheard cell phone conversations are rated as more intrusive than overheard conversations between two people talking face-to-face (Monk, Fellas, & Ley, 2004). *Why do you think this is so?*

Biases and Prejudices

Biases and prejudices against groups, or against individuals who are members of such groups, will invariably distort listening. For example, a gender bias that assumes that only one sex has anything useful to say about certain topics will likely distort incoming messages that contradict this bias. As a listener, be willing to subject your biases and prejudices to contradictory information; after all, if they're worth having, they should stand up to differences of opinion. When you as a speaker feel that you may be facing bias, ask your listeners to suspend their attitude for the moment—*I know you don't like the Martins, and I can understand why. But, just listen to . . .*

Another type of bias is **closed-mindedness**, which is seen, for example, in the person who refuses to hear any feminist argument or anything about gay marriage. As a listener, assume that what the speaker is saying will be useful in some way. As a speaker, anticipate that many people will be closed-minded on a variety of issues, and remember that it often helps to simply ask for openness—*I know this is contrary to what many people think, but let's look at this logically.*

Racist, Heterosexist, Ageist, and Sexist Listening

Just as racist, heterosexist, ageist, and sexist attitudes influence your language, they can also influence your listening if you hear what speakers are saying through the stereotypes you hold. Prejudiced listening occurs when you listen differently to a person because of his or her gender, race, affectional orientation, or age, even though these characteristics are irrelevant to the message. As you can appreciate, this type of listening can present a major barrier to accurate listening.

Often you're asked by a speaker if he or she is getting through or making sense. It seems as if speakers doubt that you're listening. But, usually at least, you are. *What can you do to show people you're listening to them and interested in what they're saying?*

a. Maintain eye contact and face-to-face posture.

b. Smile and allow your face to express your feelings.

c. Give minimal response cues such as "Yes, I see that" or simple head nods of agreement and listening involvement.

d. Ask questions.

e. Other

Racist, heterosexist, ageist, and sexist listening occurs in many situations. For example, when you dismiss a valid argument—or attribute validity to an invalid argument—because the speaker is of a particular race, affectional orientation, age group, or gender, you're listening with prejudice.

Of course, there are many instances when these characteristics are relevant and pertinent to your evaluation of a message. For example, the sex of a person who is talking about pregnancy, fathering a child, birth control, or surrogate motherhood is, most would agree, probably relevant to the message. So, in these cases it is not sexist listening to take the sex of the speaker into consideration. It is sexist listening, however, to assume that only one sex can be an authority on a particular topic or that one sex's opinions are without value. The same is true in relation to listening through a person's race or affectional orientation.

Lack of Appropriate Focus

Focusing on what a person is saying is obviously necessary for effective listening. And yet there are many influences that can lead you astray. For example, listeners often get lost because they focus on irrelevancies, say, on an especially vivid example that conjures up old memories. As a listener, try not to get detoured from the main idea; don't get hung up on unimportant details. Try to repeat the idea to yourself and see the details in relation to this main concept. As a speaker, try to avoid language or examples that may divert attention from your main idea.

People sometimes listen only for information with an obvious relevance to them. But this type of listening only prevents you from expanding your horizons. After all, it's quite possible that information that you originally thought irrelevant will eventually prove helpful. Avoid interpreting everything in terms of what it means to you; see other perspectives. As a speaker, be sure to make what you say relevant to your specific listener.

Another mistake is for the listener to focus on the responses he or she is going to make while the speaker is still speaking. Anticipating how you're going to respond or what you're going to say (and perhaps even interrupting the speaker) just prevents you from hearing the message in full. Instead, make a mental note of something and then get back to listening. As a speaker, when you feel someone is preparing to argue with you, ask them to hear you out—*I know you disagree with this, but let me finish and we'll get back to that*.

One of the things that makes maintaining an appropriate focus difficult is the enormous amount of information that surrounds you. Consider the Facebook pages of some of your friends. They are often so cluttered with posts and photos and album covers and advertisements and much more that it's difficult to focus on what is important.

Premature Judgment

Perhaps the most obvious form of premature judgment is assuming you know what the speaker is going to say—so there's no need to really listen. Let the speaker say what he or she is going to say before you decide that you already know it. As a speaker, of course, it's often wise to assume that listeners will do exactly this, so it may be helpful to make clear that what you're saying will be unexpected.

A common listener reaction is to draw conclusions or judgments on incomplete evidence. Sometimes listeners stop listening after hearing a speaker, for example, express an attitude they disagree with or make some sexist or culturally insensitive remark. Instead, this is a situation that calls for especially concentrated listening so that you don't rush to judgment. Instead, wait for the evidence or argument; avoid making judgments before you gather all the information. Listen first; judge second. As a speaker, be aware of this tendency and when you feel this is happening, ask for a suspension of judgment. A simple "Hear me out" is often sufficient to prevent a too-early judgment on the part of listeners.

Hearing Impairment

Still another barrier is the physiological one of hearing impairment. People with hearing loss differ greatly in their hearing ability: Some are totally deaf and can hear nothing, others have some hearing loss and can hear some sounds, and still others have impaired hearing but can hear most speech. Although people with profound hearing loss can speak, their speech may appear labored and may be less clear than the speech of those with unimpaired hearing. Table 6.3 provides some suggestions for more effective communication between people who hear well and those who have hearing problems.

Table 6.4 provides a brief summary of these barriers.

Table 6.3 Improving Effective Communication between People with and without Hearing Difficulties

If you have unimpaired hearing:

Generally	Specifically
Avoid interference.	Make sure the visual cues from your speech are clearly observable; face the person squarely and avoid smoking, chewing gum, or holding your hand over your mouth.
Speak at an adequate volume.	But avoid shouting, which can distort your speech and may insult the person. Be careful to avoid reducing volume at the ends of your sentences.
Phrase ideas in different ways.	Because some words are easier to lip-read than others, it often helps if you can rephrase your ideas in different words.
Avoid overlapping speech.	In group situations, only one person should speak at a time. Similarly, direct your comments to the person with the hearing loss; don't talk to the person through a third party.
Use nonverbal cues.	Nonverbals can help communicate your meaning; gestures indicating size or location and facial expressions indicating feelings are often helpful.
Address the person.	Even if there's a sign language interpreter, address your comments to the person to whom you're speaking, not to the interpreter.

If you have impaired hearing:

Do your best to eliminate background noise.	Reduce the distance between yourself and the other person. Reduce background noise. Make sure the lighting is adequate.
Move closer to the speaker if this helps you hear better.	Alert the speaker that this closer distance will help you hear better.
Ask for adjustments.	If you feel the speaker can make adjustments, ask the speaker to repeat a message, to speak more slowly, or to increase volume.
Position yourself for best reception.	If you hear better in one ear than another, position yourself accordingly and, if necessary, clue the speaker in to this fact.
Ask for additional cues.	If necessary, ask the speaker to write down certain information, such as phone numbers or website addresses.

SOURCES: These suggestions were drawn from a variety of sources, including the websites of the Rochester Institute of Technology, the National Technical Institute for the Deaf, and the United States Department of Labor, and the suggestions of Professor Paul Siegel of the University of Hartford. All accessed February 25, 2017.

Table 6.4 In a Nutshell Listening Barriers

Barrier	Reasons
Distractions	Distractions can be both physical and mental and take your mind away from the message.
Biases and prejudices	These prevent you from listening openly and critically, especially to differences of opinion and belief.
Racism, heterosexism, ageism, and sexism	As with biases in general, these prejudices will serve as filters, preventing you from receiving accurate messages.
Lack of appropriate focus	Failure to focus on the essentials of the message and perhaps becoming diverted by small details often will waste your time.
Premature judgments	Premature judgments will lead you to hear the message you want to hear instead of the message as intended.
Hearing impairment	Hearing loss can distort or even prevent messages from being heard.

ETHICS IN INTERPERSONAL COMMUNICATION

Ethical Listening

As a listener, you have, at a minimum, these two ethical obligations:

1. You owe it to the speaker to give an honest hearing, without prejudgment, putting aside prejudices and preconceptions as best you can. At the same time, you owe the speaker your best effort at understanding emotionally as well as intellectually what he or she means.

2. You owe the speaker honest responses. Just as you should be honest with the listener when speaking, you should be honest with the speaker when listening. This means giving open and honest feedback, and also reflecting honestly on the questions that the speaker raises. This suggestion will appear insensitive or unacceptable in many cultures where polite responses are expected regardless of what you really think.

Ethical Choice Points

What would you do in each of these two situations?

(a) Your friend begins revealing deeply personal secrets—problems at home, a lack of money, no friends, and on and on. You don't want to hear all this; it depresses you. At the same time, however, you wonder if you have an ethical obligation to listen openly and respond honestly to your friend. *What would you do in this situation?*

(b) At work, you're listening to a colleague (who you know is lying) criticize another colleague. *What are your ethical obligations in a situation like this?*

Styles of Effective Listening

6.3 Define the four styles of listening and explain how each may be used effectively.

Listening is situational (Brownell, 2013). The way you listen should depend on the situation you're in. For example, you don't listen to a State of the Union address in the same way that you listen to Jimmy Fallon's monologue. You don't listen to a friend's relationship breakup story in the same way you listen to a person giving you directions for completing a task or to get to your desired destination.

At the least, you need to adjust your listening on the basis of (1) your purposes (for example, are you listening to learn? to give comfort? to judge?) and (2) your knowledge of and relationship to the other person (is this person prone to exaggeration? or does this person need support?) (Figure 6.2).

The following discussion identifies four styles of listening which will cover most listening situations. Select the style (or combination of styles) that best fit(s) your specific situation. The four styles are empathic, polite, critical, and active. Before doing so, take the following self-test to examine your own listening style. Respond to each statement using the following scale:

1 = always, **2** = frequently, **3** = sometimes, **4** = seldom, and **5** = never.

_____ 1. I listen actively, communicate acceptance of the speaker, and prompt the speaker to further explore his or her thoughts.

_____ 2. I listen to what the speaker is saying and feeling; I try to feel what the speaker feels.

_____ 3. I listen without judging the speaker.

_____ 4. I listen to the literal meanings that a speaker communicates; I don't look too deeply into hidden meanings.

_____ 5. I listen without active involvement; I generally remain silent and take in what the other person is saying.

_____ **6.** I listen objectively; I focus on the logic of the ideas rather than on the emotional meaning of the message.

_____ **7.** I listen politely even to messages that contradict my attitudes and beliefs.

_____ **8.** I'll interrupt a speaker when I have something really relevant to say.

_____ **9.** I listen critically, evaluating the speaker and what the speaker is saying.

_____ **10.** I look for the hidden meanings, the meanings that are revealed by subtle verbal or nonverbal cues.

These statements focus on the ways of listening discussed in this chapter. All of these ways are appropriate at some times but not at other times. It depends. So, the only responses that are really inappropriate are "always" and "never." Effective listening is listening that is tailored to the specific communication situation.

Consider how you might use these statements to begin to improve your listening effectiveness. A good way to do this is to review these statements and identify situations in which each statement would be appropriate and situations in which each statement would be inappropriate.

Empathic Listening

If you're going to understand what a person means and what a person is feeling, you need to listen with some degree of **empathy;** you need to engage in **empathic listening** (Rogers, 1970; Rogers & Farson, 1981). To empathize with others is to see the world as they see it, to feel what they feel. When you listen empathically as a neighbor tells of having her apartment burgled and all her prized possessions taken, you can share on some level the loss and emptiness she feels. Only when you achieve empathy can you fully understand another person's meaning. Empathic listening will also help you enhance your relationships (Barrett & Godfrey, 1988; Snyder, 1992).

One potential danger: over-empathizing with another's feelings can lead you to lose control over your own feelings (Stern & Divecha, 2015). It's important to remember that with effective empathy, you feel what the other is feeling but retain your own thoughts and feelings.

In empathic listening, keep the following recommendations in mind.

Figure 6.2   Four Listening Styles

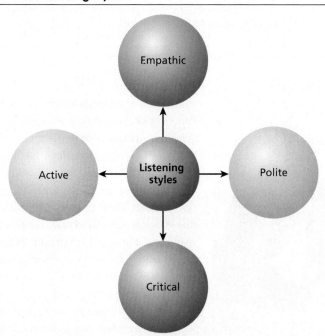

- *See from the speaker's point of view.* See the sequence of events as the speaker does, and try to figure out how this perspective can influence what the speaker says and does.
- *Engage in equal, two-way conversation.* To encourage openness and empathy, try to eliminate any physical or psychological barriers to equality. For example, step from behind the large desk separating you from your employees. Avoid interrupting the speaker—a sign that you think what you have to say is more important.
- *Seek to understand both thoughts and feelings.* Don't consider your listening task finished until you've understood what the speaker is feeling as well as what he or she is thinking.

Listening with empathy and especially responding with empathy are not always easy. Here, for example, are five possible responses to the "simple" statement, "I guess I'm feeling a little depressed." Assume that the two individuals are close friends—not best friends but more than acquaintances. Assume that they are two women, two men, or a woman and a man—select the genders as you wish. Read over each statement and consider why each is a non-empathic response. After reading these, try formulating your own empathic response.

Some Responses	Comments
Response 1: *I've been reading about depression and it's all in your head. This research—it was done at the University of Illinois—showed that the . . . .*	This statement is non-empathic because it depersonalizes the issue. It moves the conversation away from the person and the person's feelings by intellectualizing the person's feelings of depression.
Response 2: *You depressed? Have you talked to Pat? Now that's depression.*	The lack of empathy is shown here in minimizing or lessening the importance of what the person is thinking and feeling.
Response 3: *Well, then, you need to get out more; let's go and have some fun.*	This type of problem-solving response also minimizes the feelings of the person by offering a quick fix and does nothing to encourage the person to explore his or her feelings.
Response 4: *Me too. I don't know what it is but I woke up this morning and felt so depressed. I thought it was from a dream but I'm still feeling that way. Do you think I should see a counselor?*	This type of response refocuses the conversation and shifts the focus from the person speaking to oneself.
Response 5: *Are you? That's really serious; it's often a sign of suicide. Remember Pat? Got depressed after the breakup and jumped off the roof.*	This type of response is a good example of "catastrophizing" or "awfulizing," making the problem seem even worse than it probably is and likely increasing the person's depression.

VIEWPOINTS

Negative Empathy

There is some evidence to show that empathy can also have a negative side. For example, the more empathy you feel toward your own racial and ethnic group, the less empathy—possibly even the more hostility—you feel toward other groups. The same empathy that increases your understanding of your own group decreases your understanding of other groups (Angier, 1995b). *Have you ever experienced or witnessed these negative effects of empathy?*

Polite Listening

Politeness is often thought of as the exclusive function of the speaker, as solely an encoding or sending function. But politeness (or impoliteness) may also be signaled through listening (Fukushima, 2000).

Of course, there are times when you would not want to listen politely (for example, if someone is being verbally abusive or condescending or using racist or sexist language). In these cases, you might want to show your disapproval by showing that you're not even listening. But most often you'll want to listen politely, and you'll want to express this politeness through your listening behavior.

Here are a few suggestions for demonstrating that you are, in fact, listening politely. As you read these strategies, you'll notice that they are designed to be supportive of the speaker's positive and negative face needs:

- *Avoid interrupting the speaker.* Avoid trying to take over the speaker's turn. Avoid changing the topic. If you must say something in response to something the speaker said and can't wait until he or she finishes, then say it as briefly as possible and pass the speaker's turn back to the speaker.

- *Give supportive listening cues.* These might include nodding your head, giving minimal verbal responses such as "I see" or "yes, it's true," or moving closer to the speaker. Listen in a way that demonstrates that what the speaker is saying is important. In some cultures, polite listening cues must be cues of agreement (Japanese culture is often used as an example); in other cultures, polite listening cues are attentiveness and support rather than cues of agreement (much of United States culture is an example).

- *Show empathy with the speaker.* Demonstrate that you understand and feel the speaker's thoughts and feelings by giving responses that show this level of understanding—smiling or cringing or otherwise echoing the feelings of the speaker. If you echo the speaker's nonverbal expressions, your behavior is likely to be seen as empathic.

- *Maintain eye contact.* In much of the United States, this is perhaps the single most important rule. If you don't maintain eye contact when someone is talking to you, then you'll appear to be not listening and definitely not listening politely. This rule, however, does not hold true in all cultures. In some Latin and Asian cultures, polite listening would consist of looking down and avoiding direct eye contact when, for example, listening to a superior or much older person.

- *Give positive feedback.* Throughout the listening encounter and perhaps especially after the speaker's turn (when you continue the conversation as you respond to what the speaker has said), positive feedback will be seen as polite and negative feedback as impolite. If you must give negative feedback, then do so in a way that does not attack the person's negative face, for example, first mention areas of agreement or what you liked about what the person said and stress your good intentions. And, most important, do it in private. Public criticism is especially threatening and will surely be seen as a personal attack.

The ubiquity of the cell phone and texting has led to enormous increases in communication, but it has also created problems, many of which are problems of politeness. Because much use occurs in public spaces, people often are forced to listen to conversations that don't involve them or to lose your attention when you send or respond to a text message. Table 6.5 offers some suggestions for using cell phones politely.

Table 6.5   Cell Phone Etiquette

General Rule	Adjustments
Avoid using cell phones where inappropriate.	If you must make or take a call when in these various situations, excuse yourself and try to move to a less public area. ***Specifically:*** *Avoid calls in restaurants, hospitals, theaters, museums, commuter buses or trains, and the classroom.*
Avoid texting when in a group.	If the text is especially important, apologize for the inconvenience. ***Specifically:*** *Unless the text message concerns everyone and will be shared, avoid making everyone wait until you're finished.*
Silence your cell.	When you can't avoid taking a call, speak as quietly as possible and ask to call back at a better time. ***Specifically:*** *Put your phone on vibrate mode, or let your voicemail answer and take a message when your call might interfere with others.*
Avoid unwanted photo taking.	Of course, if there's an accident or incident such as robbery, you may want to photograph the events. ***Specifically:*** *Don't take pictures of people who aren't posing for you, and delete photos if the person you photographed requests it.*
Avoid extended talking when your reception is weak.	In an emergency, caution trumps politeness. ***Specifically:*** *Talking on your cell on a crowded street will probably result in poor reception, which is annoying to the other person.*
Consider the other person.	As with any phone call, it's wise to ask if this is a good time to call—a strategy that helps maintain the autonomy (negative face) of the person you're calling. ***Specifically:*** *It's easy to assume that when you have nothing better to do, the person you're calling also has nothing better to do.*

THE CULTURAL MAP Politeness

Politeness, in both speaking and in listening, refers to being civil to others, having consideration for others. It refers to being positive and kind and at the same time not imposing on people.

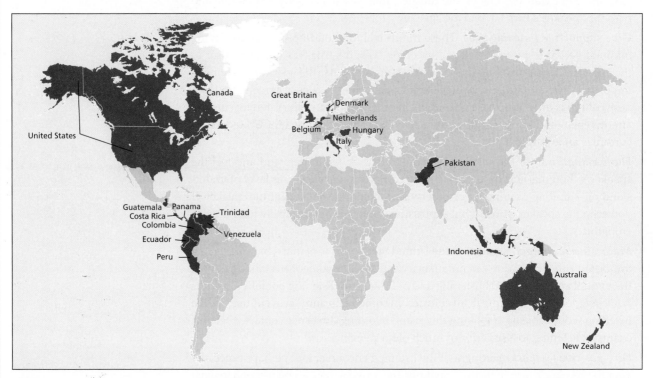

These countries are among the most strongly affiliated with high individualism, making politeness and face-saving less important, whether at school, at work, or at home, compared to collectivist cultures where interpersonal relationships are more valued and nurtured (often through politeness).

These countries are among the most strongly affiliated with high collectivism, making politeness and face saving very important. And not surprisingly, the social consequences and negative impressions will be greater for those being impolite in collectivist cultures.

If you were with a group of fellow students you just met and one of them made a factual error, would you offer a correction (believing that errors need to be corrected) or would you ignore it (believing it's more important to allow the other person to not be embarrassed, to save face)? Is your choice based on your cultural beliefs about relationships and politeness?

Critical Listening

In many listening situations, you'll need to exercise critical evaluation or judgment. When you engage in **critical listening**, you think logically and dispassionately about, for example, the stories your friends tell you or the sales pitch of the car dealer. Listening with an open mind will help you understand the messages better; listening with a critical mind will help you analyze and evaluate the messages. In listening critically, focus on the following guidelines:

• *Keep an open mind.* Avoid prejudging. Delay your judgments until you fully understand both the content and the intention the speaker is communicating. Avoid either positive or negative evaluation until you have a reasonably complete understanding. Even when a friend tells you he or she did something you disapprove of, keeping an open mind requires that you withhold making value judgments (in your mind as well as in your responses) that can get in the way of your understanding your friend.

- *Avoid filtering out or oversimplifying complex messages.* Similarly, avoid filtering out undesirable messages. Clearly, you don't want to hear that something you believe is untrue, that people you care for are unkind, or that ideals you hold are self-destructive. Yet it's important that you reexamine your beliefs by listening to these messages.

- *Recognize your own biases.* These may interfere with accurate listening and cause you to distort message reception through a process of assimilation—the tendency to integrate and interpret what you hear or think you hear according to your own biases, prejudices, and expectations.

- *Combat the tendency to sharpen*—to highlight, emphasize, and perhaps embellish one or two aspects of a message. Often the concepts that we tend to *sharpen* are incidental remarks that somehow stand out from the rest of the message. Be careful, therefore, about sharpening your blind date's "Thank you, I had a nice time" and assuming that the date was a big success—while ignoring the signs that it was just so-so, such as the lack of eye contact, the awkward silences, and the cell phone interruptions.

- *Focus on both verbal and nonverbal messages.* Recognize both consistent and inconsistent "packages" of messages, and use these as guides for drawing inferences about the speaker's meaning. Ask questions when in doubt. Listen also to what is omitted. Remember that speakers communicate by what they leave out as well as by what they include. When Jack says things will be okay now that his relationship is finally over but says it with downcast eyes, deep breathing, and clenched hands, consider the possibility that Jack is really hurting and that things are not okay.

- *Watch out for language fallacies.* Language is often used to serve less than noble purposes, to convince or persuade you without giving you any reasons, and sometimes to fool you. Table 6.6 presents four language fallacies that often get in the way of meaningful communication and need to be identified in critical listening. Often these fallacies are used to fool you; they are ways in which language can be used to serve less than noble purposes, to convince or persuade you without giving you any reasons. After reviewing this table, examine some of the commercial websites for clothing, books, music, or any such product you're interested in. You'll find lots of examples of these fallacies.

Active Listening

One of the most important communication skills you can learn is that of **active listening** (Gordon, 1975). Consider the following interaction. You're disappointed that you have to redo your entire budget report, and you say, "I can't believe I have to redo this entire

Table 6.6   Recognizing Fallacies of Language

Fallacy	Notes	Example
Weasel words are terms whose meanings are slippery and difficult to pin down (Hayakawa & Hayakawa, 1989).	Weasel words (and terms) include "help," "virtually," "as much as," "like" (as in "it will make you feel like new"), and "more economical." Ask yourself, "Exactly what is being claimed?" For example, "What does 'may reduce cholesterol' mean? What exactly is being asserted?"	A commercial claims that Medicine M works "better than Brand X" but doesn't specify how much better or in what respect Medicine M performs better. It's quite possible that it performs better in one respect but less effectively according to nine other measures.
Euphemisms make the negative and unpleasant appear positive and appealing.	Euphemisms often take the form of inflated language designed to make the mundane seem extraordinary, the common seem exotic. Don't let words get in the way of accurate firsthand perception.	An executive calls the firing of 200 workers "downsizing" or "reallocation of resources."
Jargon is the specialized language of a professional class.	Jargon prevents meaningful communication when it is used to intimidate or impress; for example when it is used around people who aren't members of the same profession. Don't be intimidated by jargon; ask questions when you don't understand.	A computer coder explains the HTML coding of a website to a philosophy student.
Gobbledygook is overly complex language that overwhelms the listener instead of communicating meaning.	Some people just normally speak in complex language. But others use complexity to confuse and mislead. Ask for simplification when appropriate.	An academic scholar speaks in long sentences, complex grammatical constructions, and rare or unfamiliar words.

report. I really worked hard on this project, and now I have to do it all over again." To this you get three different responses:

APOLLO: That's not so bad; most people find they have to redo their first reports. That's the norm here.

ATHENA: You should be pleased that all you have to do is a simple rewrite. Peggy and Michael both had to completely redo their entire projects.

DIANA: You have to rewrite that report you've worked on for the past three weeks? You sound really angry and frustrated.

All three listeners are probably trying to make you feel better. But they go about it in very different ways and, we can be sure, with very different results. Apollo tries to lessen the significance of the rewrite. This type of well-intended response is extremely common but does little to promote meaningful communication and understanding. Athena tries to give the situation a positive spin. With these responses, however, both these listeners are also suggesting that you should not be feeling the way you do. They're also implying that your feelings are not legitimate and should be replaced with more logical feelings.

Diana's response, however, is different from the others. Diana uses active listening. Active listening owes its development to Thomas Gordon (1975), who made it a cornerstone of his P-E-T (Parent Effectiveness Training) technique; it is a process of sending back to the speaker what you as a listener think the speaker meant—both in content and in feelings. Active listening, then, is not merely repeating the speaker's exact words but rather putting together into some meaningful whole your understanding of the speaker's total message.

Functions of Active Listening   Active listening serves several important functions. Perhaps the most obvious function is that active listening enables you to *check understanding*. It helps you as a listener check your understanding of what the speaker said and, more important, what he or she meant. Reflecting back perceived meanings to the speaker gives the speaker an opportunity to offer clarification and correct any misunderstandings.

A second function is to let the speaker know that you *acknowledge and accept his or her feelings*. In the sample responses given, the first two listeners challenged your feelings. Diana, the active listener, who reflected back to you what she thought you meant, accepted what you were feeling. In addition, she also explicitly identified your emotions; she commented that you sounded "angry and frustrated," allowing you an opportunity to correct her interpretation if necessary. Do be careful, however, to avoid sending what Gordon (1975) calls "solution messages." Solution messages tell the person how he or she *should* feel or what he or she *should* do. The four types of messages that send solutions and that you'll want to avoid in your active listening are (1) ordering messages—*Do this . . . , Don't touch that . . .*; (2) warning and threatening messages—*If you don't do this, you'll . . . , If you do this, you'll . . .*; (3) preaching and moralizing messages—*People should all . . . , We all have responsibilities . . .*; and (4) advising messages—*Why don't you . . . , What I think you should do is . . . .*

Remembering Names

Research finds that names are generally difficult to remember, more difficult than a person's job, hobbies, or home town (Dean, 2011c). *If you too have difficulty remembering names, why do you think this is so? And, more important, what can you do about it?*

A third function is to *encourage the speaker to explore his or her feelings and thoughts.* For example, Diana's response encourages you to elaborate on your feelings. This opportunity to elaborate also helps you deal with your feelings by talking them through.

Techniques of Active Listening   Three simple techniques may help you succeed in active listening:

- *Paraphrase the speaker's meaning.* Stating in your own words what you think the speaker means and feels can help ensure understanding and also shows interest in the speaker. Paraphrasing gives the speaker a chance to extend what was originally said. Thus, when Diana echoes your thoughts, you're given the opportunity to elaborate on why rewriting the budget report is so daunting to you. Be especially careful not to lead the speaker in the direction you think he or she should go. Also, be careful that you don't overdo it; only a very small percentage of statements need paraphrasing. Paraphrase when you feel there's a chance for misunderstanding or when you want to express support for the other person and keep the conversation going.

- *Express understanding of the speaker's feelings.* In addition to paraphrasing the content, echo the feelings the speaker expressed or implied ("You must have felt horrible"). This expression of feelings will help you further check your perception of the speaker's feelings. This also will allow the speaker to see his or her feelings more objectively—especially helpful when they're feelings of anger, hurt, or depression—and to elaborate on these feelings.

- *Ask questions.* Asking questions strengthens your own understanding of the speaker's thoughts and feelings and elicits additional information ("How did you feel when you read your job appraisal report?"). Ask questions to provide just enough stimulation and support so the speaker will feel he or she can elaborate on these thoughts and feelings. These questions should further confirm your interest and concern for the speaker but not pry into unrelated areas or challenge the speaker in any way.

Consider this dialogue and note the active listening techniques used throughout:

PAT: That jerk demoted me. He told me I wasn't an effective manager. I can't believe he did that, after all I've done for this place.

CHRIS: I'm with you. You've been manager for three or four months now, haven't you?

INTERPERSONAL CHOICE POINT
Listening Actively

Your 6-year-old nephew comes home from school crying. He says that his new teacher hates him and he hates her and that he doesn't want to go back to school ever again. *What can you say to help your nephew?*

a. "Are you sure you weren't making trouble?"

b. "You don't want to go back to school?"

c. "Everybody loves school. What's wrong with you?"

d. "How do you feel when you're in class?"

e. Other

PAT: A little over three months. I know it was probationary, but I thought I was doing a good job.

CHRIS: Can you get another chance?

PAT: Yes, he said I could try again in a few months. But I feel like a failure.

CHRIS: I know what you mean. It sucks. What else did he say?

PAT: He said I had trouble getting the paperwork done on time.

CHRIS: You've been late filing the reports?

PAT: A few times.

CHRIS: Is there a way to delegate the paperwork?

PAT: No, but I think I know now what needs to be done.

CHRIS: You sound as though you're ready to give that manager's position another try.

PAT: Yes, I think I am, and I'm going to let him know that I intend to apply in the next few months.

Even in this brief interaction, Pat has moved from unproductive anger and feelings of failure to a determination to correct an unpleasant situation. Note, too, that Chris didn't offer solutions but "simply" listened actively.

Table 6.7 presents a brief summary of the four styles of listening along with their goals and strategies.

Table 6.7   In a Nutshell   Listening Styles

Styles and Goals	Strategies
Empathic listening: to understand on an emotional level the meanings of the other person	• See the situation from the speaker's point of view. • Engage in equal, two-way conversation. • Seek to understand both thoughts and feelings.
Polite listening: to respect the other's positive face and his or her right to autonomy (negative face)	• Avoid interrupting the speaker. • Give supportive listening cues. • Maintain eye contact. • Give positive feedback.
Critical listening: to separate truth from falsehood, accuracy from inaccuracy	• Keep an open mind. • Avoid filtering out or oversimplifying complex messages. • Recognize your own biases. • Combat the tendency to sharpen. • Focus on both verbal and nonverbal messages. • Watch out for language fallacies.
Active listening: to check your understanding, to acknowledge your acceptance of the other person's feelings, and to stimulate the speaker to talk about things as needed	• Paraphrase the speaker's meaning. • Express understanding of the speaker's feelings. • Ask questions.

Culture, Gender, and Listening

6.4   Describe some of the cultural and gender differences in listening.

Listening is difficult in part because of the inevitable differences in communication systems between speaker and listener. Because each person has had a unique set of experiences, each person's meaning system is different from every other person's. When speaker and listener come from different cultures or are of different genders, these differences and their effects are naturally much greater. Consider culture first.

UNDERSTANDING *INTERPERSONAL SKILLS*

Openness: Willingness to Disclose and be Honest

Openness in interpersonal communication refers to your willingness to self-disclose—to reveal information about yourself as appropriate. Openness also includes a willingness to listen openly and to react honestly to the messages of others. This does not mean that openness is always appropriate. In fact, too much openness is likely to lead to a decrease in your relationship satisfaction (Dindia & Timmerman, 2003).

Openness is almost always appreciated and valued over closed-mindedness in both face-to-face and online communication. According to Match.com, those who showed openness had higher contact rates than those who didn't display openness (Roper, 2014).

Communicating with Openness

To communicate openness, consider these few ideas:

- *Self-disclose when appropriate.* Be mindful about whatever you say about yourself. There are benefits and dangers to this form of communication. And listen carefully to the disclosures of others; these reciprocal disclosures (or the lack of them) will help guide your own disclosures.
- *Listen mindfully.* And respond to those with whom you're interacting with spontaneity and with appropriate honesty—though also with an awareness of what you're saying and of what the possible outcomes of your messages might be.
- *Communicate a clear willingness to listen.* Let the other person know that you're open to listening to his or her thoughts and feelings.
- *Use active listening techniques.* Paraphrase, express understanding, ask questions.
- *Use nonverbal messages to signal interest.* Focus your eye contact, move closer, block out other nearby activities.
- *Use feedback cues.* Nod, give minimal listening cues such as "yes" or "I see what you mean," give facial and eye movement cues that say you understand.

Working with Openness

How would you describe your face-to-face communication and your social networking communication with casual friends or acquaintances in terms of openness? Are there significant differences in openness in your face-to-face versus online communication? If so, what might be the reasons?

Culture and Listening

In a global environment in which people from very different cultures work together, it's especially important to understand the ways in which cultural differences can influence listening. Three such factors may be singled out: (1) language and speech, (2) nonverbal behaviors, and (3) feedback.

Language and Speech   Even when speaker and listener speak the same language, they speak it with different meanings and, as noted earlier, with different dialects and accents. No two speakers speak exactly the same language. Speakers of the same language, at the very least, have different meanings for the same terms because they have had different experiences.

Speakers and listeners who speak different native languages and who may have learned English as a second language have even greater differences in meaning. Translations never fully capture the meaning in the other language. If your meaning for the word *house* was learned in a culture in which everyone lived in their own house with lots of land around it, then communicating with someone for whom the meaning of *house* was learned in a neighborhood of high-rise tenements is going to be difficult. Although you'll each hear the same word, the meanings you'll each develop will be drastically different. In adjusting your listening—especially in an intercultural setting—understand that the speaker's meanings may be very different from yours even though you're speaking in the same language.

In many classrooms throughout the world, there is a wide range of accents. Students whose native language is a tonal one (in which differences in pitch signal important meaning differences), such as Chinese, may speak other languages such as English with variations in pitch that may seem puzzling to others. Those whose native language

INTERPERSONAL CHOICE POINT
Listening without Judging

A classmate says to you, "I got a C on that paper. That's the worst grade I've ever received. I just can't believe that I got a C. This is my major. What am I going to do?" *What might be appropriate to say?*

a. "So what? I got a D and you don't hear me complaining."

b. "Grades don't matter in the real world."

c. "That professor is crazy; there's no logic to these grades."

d. "You got a C? That's insane; you're the best student in the class."

e. Other

is Japanese may have trouble distinguishing *l* from *r* in English, for example, because the Japanese language does not include this distinction. In these cases, the native language acts as a filter and influences the accent given to the second language.

Nonverbal Behaviors Speakers from different *cultures* have different **display rules**—cultural rules that govern what nonverbal behaviors are appropriate or inappropriate in a public setting. As you listen to other people, you also "listen" to their nonverbal cues. If nonverbals are drastically different from what you expect on the basis of the verbal message, you may experience them as a kind of noise or interference, or even as contradictory messages. Also, of course, different cultures may give very different meanings to the same nonverbal gesture. For example, the thumb and forefinger forming a circle means "okay" in most of the United States, but it means "money" in Japan, "zero" in some Mediterranean countries, and "I'll kill you" in Tunisia.

Feedback Members of some cultures give very direct and very frank feedback. Speakers from these cultures—the United States is a good example—expect feedback to be an honest reflection of what their listeners are feeling. In other cultures—Japan and Korea are good examples—it's more important to be positive than to be truthful, so people may respond with positive feedback (say, in commenting on a business colleague's proposal) even though they don't agree with what is being said. Listen to feedback, as you would all messages, with a full recognition that various cultures view feedback very differently.

Gender and Listening

Men and women learn different styles of listening, just as they learn different styles for using verbal and nonverbal messages. Not surprisingly, these different styles can create major difficulties in opposite-sex interpersonal communication.

Rapport and Report Talk According to Deborah Tannen (1990) in her best-selling *You Just Don't Understand: Women and Men in Conversation*, women seek to build rapport and establish closer relationships, and they use listening to achieve these ends. Men, on the other hand, emphasize their expertise and use it in dominating the interaction. They talk about things; they report. Women play down their expertise and are more interested in talking about feelings and relationships and in communicating supportiveness. Tannen argues that the goal of a man in conversation is to be given respect, so he seeks to show his knowledge and expertise. A woman, on the other hand, seeks to be liked, so she expresses agreement.

Listening Cues Men and women feed back to the speaker different types of listening cues and consequently show that they're listening in different ways. In conversation, a woman is more apt to give lots of listening cues—interjecting "yeah" or "uh-huh," nodding in agreement, and smiling. A man is more likely to listen quietly, without giving lots of listening cues as feedback. Women also make more eye

VIEWPOINTS

Gender Differences

What do you see as the major differences between the ways in which men and women listen? Consider, for example, men listening to men, men listening to women, women listening to men, and women listening to women.

contact when listening than do men, who are more apt to look around and often away from the speaker (Brownell, 2013). As a result of these differences, women seem to be more engaged in listening than do men.

Amount and Purposes of Listening   Tannen argues that men listen less to women than women listen to men. The reason, says Tannen, is that listening places the person in an inferior position, whereas speaking places the person in a superior position. Men may seem to assume a more argumentative posture while listening, as if getting ready to argue. They also may appear to ask questions that are more argumentative or that seek to puncture holes in your position as a way to play up their own expertise. Women are more likely to ask supportive questions and perhaps offer criticism that is more positive than men. Men and women act this way to both men and women; their customary ways of talking don't seem to change depending on whether the listener is male or female.

It's important to note that not all researchers agree that there is sufficient evidence to make the claims that Tannen and others make about gender differences (Goldsmith & Fulfs, 1999). Gender differences are changing drastically and quickly; it's best to take generalizations about gender as starting points for investigation and not as airtight conclusions (Gamble & Gamble, 2014). Further, as you no doubt have observed, gender differences—although significant—are far outnumbered by similarities between males and females. It's important to be mindful of both differences and similarities.

Table 6.8 provides a reminder of some of the topics that research has investigated in regard to cultural and gender differences in listening.

Table 6.8   In a Nutshell Culture and Gender

Cultural Differences	Gender Differences
Language and Speech: meanings vary from one language to another as well as from one dialect to another	**Rapport and Report:** women emphasize rapport, men emphasize report
Nonverbal Behaviors: different cultures assign different meanings to the same non-verbal behavior	**Listening Cues:** women give more
Feedback: cultures vary in the directness and honesty of feedback	**Amount and Purposes:** some evidence suggests men listen less as a way of asserting superiority

Summary

This chapter focused on the nature and process of listening and the relevant skills, the barriers to effective listening and how these might be lessened, the varied styles of listening and their relevant skills, and the influence of culture and gender on listening.

The Process of Listening

6.1 Define *listening*, describe its five stages, and identify some of the skills for improving listening at each stage.

1. Listening is an active process of receiving, understanding, remembering, evaluating, and responding to communications.

2. Listening enables you (1) to learn, to acquire information; (2) to relate, to help form and maintain relationships; (3) to influence, to have an effect on the attitudes and behaviors of others; (4) to play, to enjoy yourself; and (5) to help, to assist others.

Listening Barriers

6.2 Explain the major barriers to effective listening.

3. Both listener and speaker share in the responsibility for effective listening.

4. Among the obstacles to effective listening are physical and mental distractions; biases and prejudices; racist, heterosexist, ageist, and sexist listening; lack of appropriate focus; premature judgment, and hearing impairment.

Styles of Effective Listening

6.3 Define the four styles of listening and explain how each may be used effectively.

5. Listen empathically to understand on an emotional level the meanings of the other person.

6. Listen politely to be supportive and encourage the speaker to communicate.

7. Listen critically to separate truth from falsehood, accuracy from inaccuracy.

8. Listen actively to check your understanding, to acknowledge your acceptance of the other person's feelings, and to stimulate the speaker to talk about them as needed.

Culture, Gender, and Listening

6.4 Describe some of the cultural and gender differences in listening.

9. Members of different cultures vary on several communication dimensions that influence listening, among them speech and language, nonverbal behavioral differences, and approaches to feedback.

10. Men and women appear to listen differently; generally, women give more specific listening cues to show they're listening than do men.

Key Terms

active listening	empathic listening	receiving
closed-mindedness	empathy	remembering
critical listening	evaluating	responding
disclaimer	listening	short-term memory
display rules	long-term memory	understanding

CHAPTER SEVEN

Emotional Messages

The range of emotions is infinite. *Learn the strategies for expressing and responding to emotions for greater interpersonal effectiveness.*

Chapter Topics

Principles of Emotions and Emotional Messages

Obstacles to Communicating Emotions

Emotional Competence

Learning Objectives

7.1 Describe the principles of emotions and emotional expression.

7.2 Identify the major obstacles that could prevent the effective communication of emotions.

7.3 Summarize the guidelines for emotional competence in expressing and responding to emotions.

Can you choose the emotions you feel? Or do outside circumstances make you feel different emotions? It's a difficult question and theorists do not agree about whether you can choose the emotions you feel. Some argue that you can; others argue that you cannot.

You are, however, in control of whether you communicate your emotions and you're in control of the ways in which you express your emotions. Whether you choose to express your emotions depends on your own attitudes about emotional expression. You may wish to explore your attitudes about expressing feelings by responding to the following questions.

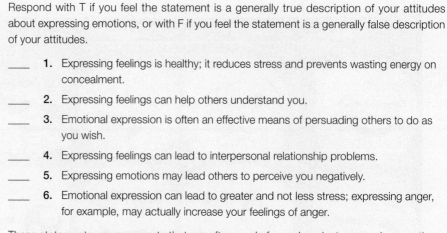

Respond with T if you feel the statement is a generally true description of your attitudes about expressing emotions, or with F if you feel the statement is a generally false description of your attitudes.

_____ 1. Expressing feelings is healthy; it reduces stress and prevents wasting energy on concealment.

_____ 2. Expressing feelings can help others understand you.

_____ 3. Emotional expression is often an effective means of persuading others to do as you wish.

_____ 4. Expressing feelings can lead to interpersonal relationship problems.

_____ 5. Expressing emotions may lead others to perceive you negatively.

_____ 6. Emotional expression can lead to greater and not less stress; expressing anger, for example, may actually increase your feelings of anger.

These statements are arguments that are often made for and against expressing emotions. Statements 1, 2, and 3 are arguments made in favor of expressing emotions; statements 4, 5, and 6 are arguments made against expressing emotions. You can look at your responses as revealing (in part) your attitude favoring or opposing the expression of feelings. "True" responses to statements 1, 2, and 3 and "false" responses to statements 4, 5, and 6 indicate a favorable attitude to expressing feelings. "False" responses to statements 1, 2, and 3 and "true" responses to statements 4, 5, and 6 indicate a negative attitude. There is evidence suggesting that expressing emotions can lead to all six outcomes, both positive and negative, and underscores the importance of critically assessing your options for emotional expression and being flexible, remembering that what will work in one situation will not work in another.

If you decide to communicate your feelings, you need to make several decisions. For example, you have to choose how to do so—face-to-face, letter, social media post, phone, e-mail, text message, or office memo. And you have to choose the specific emotions you will and will not reveal. Finally, you have to choose the words and nonverbals you'd use in expressing your emotions.

Some of the more difficult interpersonal communication situations are those that involve **emotions**, which we can define simply as _strong feelings_. This chapter addresses this crucial topic; it offers insight into the nature of emotions and emotional expression, discusses some of the obstacles to communicating emotions, and presents suggestions for communicating emotions and for responding to the emotions of others.

A useful backdrop to this discussion is to identify some of the reasons you communicate emotions—whether happy news (getting a large bonus or finding the love of your life) or sad news (the death of a loved one or getting fired). Here are just three (Rime, 2007; Dean, 2011b):

- You want/need to vent. You want catharsis, to reveal your feelings.
- You want/need attention, support, or advice. You want/need people to pay attention to you, to offer you consolation, or to give you suggestions for what you should do now.
- You want/need to bond—to strengthen your relationship—and so you might share similar emotional experiences to show your understanding and empathy.

Before reading about the principles for emotional expression and responding, consider the following five emotional statements. Are they effective expressions of emotions? Are they ineffective? Why? After reading this chapter, review these statements again but this time try to rephrase them into more effective emotional expressions.

1. You hurt me when you ignore me. Don't ever do that again.
2. I'll never forgive you. The hatred and resentment will never leave me.
3. Look. I really can't bear to hear about your problems of deciding whom to date tomorrow and whom to date the next day and the next. Give me a break. It's boring. Boring.
4. You did that just to upset me. You enjoy seeing me get upset, don't you?
5. Don't talk to me in that tone of voice. Don't you dare insult me with that attitude of yours.

Principles of Emotions and Emotional Messages

7.1 Describe the principles of emotions and emotional expression.

Communicating emotions, or feelings, is difficult. It's difficult because your thinking often gets confused when you're intensely emotional. It's also difficult because you probably weren't taught how to communicate emotions—and you probably have few effective models to imitate.

Communicating emotions is also important. Feelings constitute a great part of your meanings. If you leave your feelings out, or if you express them inadequately, you fail to communicate as well as you might. For example, consider what your communications would be like if you left out your feelings when talking about failing a recent test, winning the lottery, becoming a parent, getting engaged, driving a car for the first time, becoming a citizen, or being promoted to supervisor. Emotional expression is so much a part of communication that even in the cryptic e-mail message style, emoticons are becoming more popular.

So important is **emotional communication** that it is at the heart of what is now called emotional intelligence or social intelligence (Goleman, 1995a). One very important aspect of emotional intelligence is that it enables you to distinguish between those emotions that are relevant to your choices and those emotions that are irrelevant and thereby improve your decision making (Yip & Côté, 2013; Dean, 2013). This chapter is, in fact, a primer of emotional intelligence.

The inability to engage in emotional communication—as sender and as receiver—is part of the learning disability known as *dyssemia*, a condition in which individuals are unable to read appropriately the nonverbal messages of others or to communicate their own meanings nonverbally (Duke & Nowicki, 2005). Persons suffering from dyssemia, for example, look uninterested, fail to return smiles, and use facial expressions that are inappropriate to the situation and the interaction. As you can imagine, people who are poor senders and receivers of emotional messages likely have problems in developing and maintaining relationships. When interacting with such people, you're likely to feel uncomfortable because of their inappropriate emotional communication (Goleman, 1995a).

VIEWPOINTS

Emotions and Decision Making

It's been shown that without emotions, decision making is impaired and often rendered impossible (Damasio, 2005). *What other situations would be negatively affected by the lack of emotion?*

Figure 7.1 The Principles of Emotions and Emotional Expression

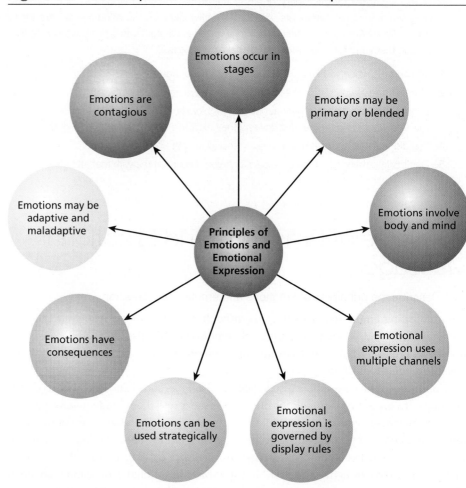

Let's look first at several general principles of emotions and emotional expression. These principles will establish a foundation for our consideration of the skills of emotional competence and are previewed in Figure 7.1.

Emotions Occur in Stages

Although there are conflicting theories about emotions, all agree that emotions occur in stages. Consider how you would describe what happens when you experience emotional arousal. Most people would identify these stages: (1) An event occurs. (2) You experience an emotion such as surprise, joy, or anger. (3) You respond physiologically; your heart beats faster, your face flushes, and so on. The process would go like this:

Psychologist William James and physiologist Carl Lange offered a different explanation to the previous "commonsense" theory. Their theory places the physiological arousal before the experience of the emotion. The sequence of events according to the **James–Lange theory** is: (1) An event occurs. (2) You respond physiologically. (3) You experience an emotion; for example, you feel joy or sadness. This process would look like this:

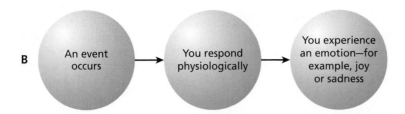

According to a third explanation, the **cognitive labeling theory**, you interpret the physiological arousal and, on the basis of this, experience the emotions of joy, sadness, or whatever (Reisenzein, 1983; Schachter, 1971). The sequence goes like this: (1) An event occurs. (2) You respond physiologically. (3) You interpret this arousal—that is, you decide what emotion you're experiencing. (4) You experience the emotion. Your interpretation of your arousal depends on the situation you're in. For example, if you experience an increased pulse rate after someone you've been admiring smiles at you, you may interpret this as joy. If three suspicious-looking strangers approach you on a dark street, however, you may interpret that same increased heartbeat as fear. It's only after you make the interpretation that you experience the emotion, for example, the joy or the fear. This process looks like this:

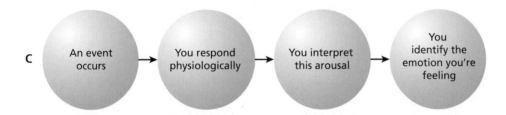

Our major concern in interpersonal communication is with the next step of the process. Each of these diagrams needs another stage, the stage of expression, the stage at which you make a choice about what to do and what to say.

Emotions May Be Primary or Blended

How would you feel in each of the following situations?

- You won the lottery.
- You got the job you applied for.
- Your best friend just died.
- Your parents tell you they're getting divorced.

You would obviously feel very differently in each of these situations. In fact, each feeling is unique and unrepeatable. Yet amid all these differences, there are some similarities. For example, most people would agree that the first two sets of feelings are more similar to each other than they are to the last two. Similarly, the last two are more similar to each other than they are to the first two.

To capture the similarities and differences among emotions, one researcher identifies the basic or **primary emotions** (Havlena, Holbrook, & Lehmann, 1989; Plutchik, 1980): joy, trust, fear, surprise, sadness, disgust, anger, and anticipation (Figure 7.2). This model of emotions is especially useful for viewing the broad scale of emotions,

Figure 7.2   A Model of the Emotions

Emotions that are close to each other on this wheel are also close to each other in meaning. For example, joy and anticipation are more closely related than are joy and sadness or trust and disgust. Emotions that are opposite each other on the wheel are also opposite each other in their meaning. For example, joy is the opposite of sadness; anger is the opposite of fear. *Do you agree with the basic assumptions of this model?*

Reprinted with permission from Annette deFerrari Design.

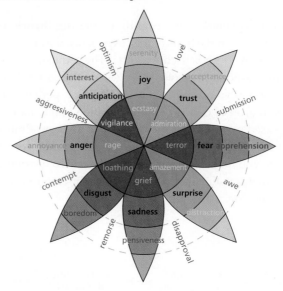

their relationships to each other, and their varied combinations. View it as a wheel spread out.

In this model, there are also blends. These **blended emotions** are combinations of the primary emotions. These are noted outside the emotion wheel. For example, according to this model, love is a blend of joy and trust. Remorse is a blend of disgust and sadness. Similar but milder emotions appear in lighter shades (for example, serenity is a milder joy) and stronger emotions appear in darker shades (for example, terror is a stronger fear).

Emotions Involve Both Body and Mind

Emotion involves both the body and the mind; when you experience emotion, you experience it both physically and mentally. Bodily reactions (such as blushing when you're embarrassed) and mental evaluations and interpretations (as in estimating the likelihood of getting a yes response when you propose) interact.

Bodily reactions are the most obvious aspect of our emotional experience because we can observe them easily. Such reactions span a wide range and include, for example, the blush of embarrassment, the sweating palms that accompany nervousness, and the gestures (such as playing with your hair or touching your face) that go with discomfort. When you judge people's emotions, you probably look to these nonverbal behaviors. You conclude that Ramon is happy to see you because of his smile and his open body posture. You conclude that Lisa is nervous from her damp hands, vocal hesitations, and awkward movements.

The mental or cognitive part of emotional experience involves the evaluations and interpretations you make on the basis of what you

THE CULTURAL MAP   Indulgent and Restraint Orientation

Culture influences the willingness and likelihood that its members will engage in fun activities. Some cultures emphasize the experience and expression of enjoyment (and its accompanying positive emotions) in the present, and some teach their members to delay such experiences and accompanying emotions. This is seen clearly in the distinction between indulgent and restraint cultures. *Indulgent cultures* are those that emphasize having fun and gratifying your desires without undue delay, whereas cultures high in *restraint* resist such gratification and, instead, focus on planning and saving for the future.

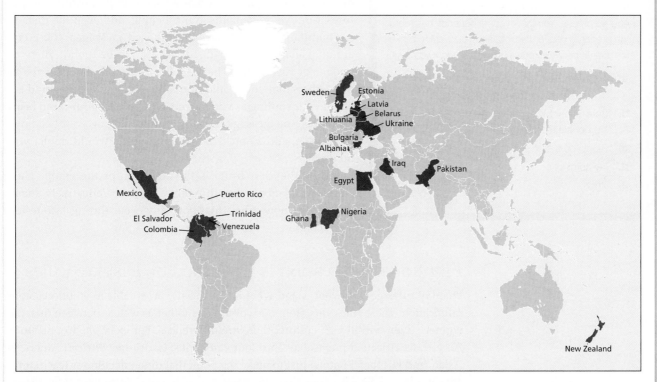

Citizens of indulgent cultures emphasize gratification of desires and are among the happiest cultures. They see themselves as having control over their lives and ample leisure time. These cultures also stress the importance of friendships and close relationships.

Citizens of restraint cultures curb personal gratification and are less happy than indulgent cultures. They see themselves as having little control over their lives and little leisure time. Friendships and close relationships are less important.

Would you guess that indulgent and restraint individuals have the same number of Facebook friends? The same number of close friends? How might their Twitter behaviors differ? Would their Pinterest boards or Instagram photos be different?

experience. For example, leading psychotherapist Albert Ellis (1988; Ellis & Harper, 1975), whose insights are used throughout this chapter, claims that your evaluations of what happens have a greater influence on your feelings than what actually happens. Let us say, for example, that your best friend, Sally, ignores you in the college cafeteria. The emotions you feel depend on what you think this behavior means. You may feel pity if you figure that Sally is depressed because her father died. You may feel anger if you believe that Sally is simply rude and insensitive and snubbed you on purpose. Or you may feel sadness if you believe that Sally is no longer interested in being friends with you.

Emotional Expression Uses Multiple Channels

As with most meanings, emotions are encoded both verbally and nonverbally. Your words, the emphasis you give them, and the gestures and facial expressions that accompany them all help to communicate your feelings. Conversely, you decode the emotional

INTERPERSONAL CHOICE POINT
Responding Emotionally (or Not)

Your supervisor seems to belittle your experience, which you thought was your strong point, constantly. Often your supervisor says that your experiences were "in school" or "with only a few people" or some such negative phrase. You think your experience has more than prepared you for this job, and you want to make sure your supervisor knows this. *What might you say?*

   a. "I have trouble when you belittle my experience; it's just makes my job more difficult."

   b. "Screw you. My experience is more than appropriate for this job."

   c. "Right you are."

   d. Say nothing.

   e. Other

messages of others on the basis of their verbal and nonverbal cues. And, of course, emotions, like all messages, are most effectively communicated when verbal and nonverbal messages reinforce and complement each other.

This principle has special implications for communication that's exclusively text-based. When we express emotions in a face-to-face situation, we express the emotions with our words but also with our facial expressions, our body posture and gestures, our eye movements, our touching, and even the distance we maintain from others. In text-based messages, these cues are unavailable and so substitutes need to be found. There are two major substitutes. The first is to use words that describe the nonverbals that you would normally express. And so you'd talk about your smiling as you looked at the photo, your rapid heartbeat when the message came in, your scratching your head over the puzzle, and so on. That is, your words would depict your nonverbals.

The other substitute is the emoticon or the emoji. These emotional symbols can, in many cases, very effectively substitute for the nonverbals that normally occur during face-to-face interaction.

Emotional Expression Is Governed by Display Rules

Display rules govern what is and what is not socially acceptable in emotional communication. These rules vary from one culture to another as well as between men and women. Even within U.S. culture, there are differences. For example, in one study, Americans classified themselves into four categories: Caucasian, African American, Asian, and Hispanic/Latino. Just to make the point that different cultures teach different rules for the display of emotions, here are a few of the study's findings (Matsumoto, 1994, 2009): (1) Caucasians found the expression of contempt more appropriate than did Asians; (2) African Americans and Hispanics felt that showing disgust was less appropriate than did Caucasians; (3) Hispanics rated public displays of emotion as less appropriate than did Caucasians; and (4) Caucasians rated the expression of fear as more appropriate than did Hispanics.

Gender display rules permit women to talk more about feelings and emotions and to display more emotional expression than they do for men (Barbato & Perse, 1992). Women also express themselves facially more than men. Even junior and senior high school students show this gender difference. Women are permitted to express "soft" emotions and to cry (in some situations but definitely not in others) while men may be criticized for doing similarly. Women are also more likely to express socially acceptable emotions than are men (Brody, 1985). For example, women smile significantly more than men. In fact, women smile even when smiling is not appropriate—for example, when reprimanding a subordinate. Men, on the other hand, are more likely than women to express anger and aggression (DePaulo, 1992; Fischer, 1993; Wade & Tavris, 2007). Similarly, women are more effective at communicating happiness, and men are more effective at communicating anger (Coats & Feldman, 1996). Women also cry more than men (Metts & Planalp, 2002). These differences are in large part due to the display rules that women and men learned as they were growing up. But, display rules change and, in the case of gender especially, are changing very rapidly; what seems logical today may not seem so tomorrow (Gamble & Gamble, 2014).

Closely related to the concept of display rules is that of **emotional labor** which refers to the effort it takes to manage your emotional expression. Commonly applied to the workplace and to face-to-face communication, emotional labor refers to the management of emotions between, say, customers and complaint department personnel or between a server and a diner (Hochschild, 1983).

Visualize yourself as a flight attendant dealing with passengers. Your smile, focused eye contact, and pleasant facial expression, all required by the airline, are examples of emotional labor. You have to work to express these emotions and also to conceal your voice of frustration, your expression of annoyance, and your scowling facial expression to hide the emotions you're feeling. Emotional labor is certainly not limited to the workplace; it's relevant to any and all interpersonal interactions whether face-to-face or online, whether verbal or nonverbal. In many (some might replace "many" with "all") of your interpersonal interactions, you manage your emotional expression so as to, for example, communicate a favorable image (you hide emotions to appear in control), to protect the feelings of another person (you give a thumbs-up to a friend's totally inane photo), and to comply with what is expected of you (you smile at the unreasonable customer).

The amount of emotional labor that you'll have to expend to manage your emotions would depend on, for example, the strength of your emotions. If, for example, you are feeling extremely annoyed but have to act pleasantly, it's going to be more difficult than if you are only mildly annoyed; strong emotions are more difficult to manage than weak emotions. The amount of labor will also depend on the display rules operating in the specific communicaton situation; some situations (whether workplace, family, friends, or strangers) are more accepting of the expression of negative emotions than are others. And, these display rules will be different for men and women, especially in a business setting. In many businesses, strong emotions—even negative ones—are more readily acceptable for men than for women. Crying, however, will be less acceptable for men than for women. These display rules are changing rapidly; in most cases, the changes are in the direction of increased sex-equality for emotional display.

VIEWPOINT

Emotional Labor

In dealing with emotional management, people employ one of two basic strategies (Hochschild, 1983). One strategy, called *surface acting*, is to control your outward display of emotions but continue to experience them internally. The other strategy, called *deep acting*, involves changing your feelings so that they are consistent with the emotional expressions that you're required to display. *What do you see as the advantages and disadvantages of each of theses strategies?*

Emotions Can Be Used Strategically

Although you may at first think of emotional expression as honest reflections of what a person is feeling, emotions can be and often are used strategically. In **strategic emotionality**, emotions (for example, crying, ranting, screaming, and threatening to commit self-harm) are used for one's personal ends. Such emotions can take a variety of forms and serve a variety of purposes. But the basic idea behind strategic emotionality is to control the situation or the other person. For example, in a conflict situation, emotions are often used to win. If someone cries enough and loud enough, the other person may just give in. It works for the baby who wants to be picked up, and it often works for the adult and enables the person to win the fight. This strategy is more likely to be used by members of individualist cultures that emphasize the winning of a conflict rather than compromise or negotiation (which would be more likely in collectivist cultures).

One frequent emotional strategy is **emotional blackmail** where there is a clear threat if the other person doesn't comply: *If you don't do as I say, you'll never see the kids again. If you see that person again, I'll kill myself.* Sometimes, the threat is never really stated but somehow you know that if your romantic breakup is not friendly, your social media contacts will all hear about it.

This strategy, which is essentially one of manipulation, often creates resentment and perhaps a desire to retaliate—neither of which is good for a relationship. Another negative outcome of this strategy is that the other person can never be sure how accurately his or her partner's emotional displays reflect the partner's true feelings, and this is likely to create communication problems whenever emotions are involved. The effect of this lack of transparency—of not knowing if one's partner is trying to manipulate or if she or he is expressing strong and honest feelings—is likely to be greatest in intimate relationships, where these expressions are likely to have long-term effects.

Earlier we considered the fundamental attribution error in which too much emphasis is placed on internal factors (for example, personality) and too little emphasis is placed on external factors (for example, the workload) in explaining a person's behavior. This is exactly what happens when the emotional behavior of men and women is "explained." Specifically, a woman's anger was most often attributed to her personality (she's unstable or out of control), whereas a man's anger was more often attributed to external factors (the report was inadequate or the work was late). As you can imagine, women's anger was seen as unjustified, whereas men's anger was judged justifiable (Kreamer, 2011).

Emotions Have Consequences

Like all communications, emotions and emotional expression have consequences and affect your relationships in important ways. By revealing your emotions, you may create close bonds with others. At the same time, you may also scare people with too much and too intimate disclosure.

Revealing your emotions communicates important information about who you are and how you feel about those with whom you are communicating. If you talk about your loneliness, then you're revealing important information about yourself and also expressing a confidence in the person with whom you're talking. It also tells people what's really important to you. Do realize that in revealing strongly felt emotions, you may be exposing vulnerabilities or weaknesses that conceivably could be used against you.

Emotions and emotional expression also affect your work life and, in fact, organizations are devoting energy to dealing with workers' emotion, trying to turn the negative into the positive. Among the most significant negative emotions experienced at work are frustration over feeling stuck in a rut; worry and anxiety over job security; anger over the actions or decisions of others; dislike of others you work with and for; and disappointment over your position, accomplishments, and prospects (Fisher, 1998). As you can see, all of these are unproductive from the point of view of management as well as for the individual.

Emotions May Be Adaptive and Maladaptive

Emotions are often adaptive; that is, they can help you adjust appropriately to situations. For example, if you feel anxious about not doing well on an exam, it may lead you to study harder. If you fear losing your partner, you may behave more supportively and lovingly. If you're worried that someone might not like you, your worry may motivate you to be especially nice to the person. If you feel suspicious of someone following you down a dark street, you may take safety precautions. All of these situations are examples of emotions aiding you in accomplishing useful goals.

At other times, however, emotions may be maladaptive and may get in the way of your accomplishing your goals. For example, you may be so anxious about a test that you stop thinking and do more poorly than you would have if you walked in totally cold. Or you may fear losing your partner and, as a result, may become suspicious and accusatory, making your relationship even less likely to survive. In extreme cases,

VIEWPOINTS

Crying On The Job

When workers cry on the job, the most frequent reason—for both men and women—is that stress from home spread into the workplace (Kreamer, 2011). *What other reasons might account for crying (or wanting to cry) on the job? Will these reasons be different for men and women? How do you evaluate the crying of your male and female coworkers?*

emotional upset may lead to inflicting harm on oneself (as in cutting) or even committing suicide. And, of course, computer programs are currently being designed to investigate the ways and means to detect extreme emotional distress from the words people use in their social media communication. Certain words seem to suggest an intent to commit suicide, for example (Innis, 2013).

Another way in which emotions may create problems is in a tendency that some theorists have cleverly called *catastrophizing* (or *awfulizing*): taking a problem—even a minor one—and making it into a catastrophe. For example, you may feel that "If I don't do well on this test, I'll never get into law school" or "If this relationship doesn't work, I'm doomed." As you convince yourself of these impending catastrophes, your emotional responses can easily get out of hand (Bach & Wyden, 1968; Willson & Branch, 2006).

The important point is that emotions can work for you or against you. And the same is true of emotional communication. Some of it is good and is likely to lead to positive outcomes (a more secure relationship or a more positive interaction, say). But some of it is bad and may aggravate a conflict, alienate friends, or lessen your relationship satisfaction. Or emotional communication may simply be thought inappropriate and thus give others a bad impression.

Emotions Are Contagious

Emotional messages are often contagious (Cappella & Schreiber, 2006). If you've ever watched an infant and mother interacting, you can readily see how quickly the infant mimics the emotional expressions of the mother. If the mother smiles, the infant smiles; if the mother frowns, the infant frowns. As children get older, they begin to pick up subtler expressions of emotions. For example, children quickly identify and often mimic a parent's anxiety or fear. Among college roommates, the depression of one roommate spread to the other over a period of just three weeks (Joiner, 1994). In short, in **emotional contagion**, emotions pass from one person to another. Women, research shows, are especially prone to this process (Cappella & Schreiber, 2006; Doherty, Orimoto, Singelis, Hatfield, & Hebb, 1995).

In conversation and in small groups, the strong emotions of one person can easily prove contagious to others present; this can be productive when the emotions are productive, or it can be unproductive when the emotions are unproductive. Emotional

ETHICS IN INTERPERSONAL COMMUNICATION

Motivational Appeals

Appeals to motives are commonplace. For example, if you want a friend to take a vacation with you, you're likely to appeal to motives such as the friend's desire for fun and excitement, and perhaps to the friend's hopes of meeting his or her true love. If you look at the advertisements for cruises and vacation packages, you'll see appeals to very similar motives. Fear appeals also are common: persons who want to censor the Internet may appeal to your fear of children's accessing pornographic materials; those who want to restrict media portrayals of violence may appeal to your fear of increased violence in your community. Advertisers appeal to your vanity and your desire for increased sexual attractiveness in selling you cosmetics and expensive clothing.

There can be no doubt that such motivational appeals are effective. But are they ethical?

Ethical Choice Point

Suppose you wanted to dissuade your teenage children from engaging in sexual relationships. *What would be some ethical ways of using motivational appeals? For example, would it be ethical to use emotional appeals to fear—to scare them so that they'd avoid such relationships? Would it be ethical to bribe them with money? Would it be ethical to threaten them with punishment?*

Positive And Negative Affect

People react positively to the positive expressions of others and negatively to negative expressions (Monahan, 1998; Sommers, 1984). But it's not always easy to determine how others will perceive an emotion; for example, jealousy, although a negative emotion, may be perceived positively, as a sign that you really care (Metts & Planalp, 2002). *What rule(s) do you follow in deciding whether to express your positive and your negative emotions?*

contagion applies to both happiness and depression; interacting with happy people is likely to increase your own happiness, and interacting with depressed people is likely to increase your own level of depression (Hamilton, 2011). Emotional contagion has even been proposed as a skill for both socializing and seduction (Amante, 2013).

One view of this process goes like this (Figure 7.3):

1. You perceive an emotional expression of another.
2. You mimic this emotional expression, perhaps unconsciously.
3. The feedback you get from expressing the emotion creates in you a replication of the other person's feelings.

Emotional contagion also occurs in online interactions (Jain, 2010). For example, you are more likely (52 percent more likely) to experience loneliness if you have a direct network connection (say, with a best friend) who is also lonely. If the connection is between you and a friend of a friend of a friend, your likelihood of experiencing loneliness is only 15 percent more.

You see another variant of intentional emotional contagion in attempts at persuasion that utilize **emotional appeals**. One popular appeal, which organizations use frequently in fund-raising for needy children, is to the emotion of pity. By showing you images of hungry and destitute children, these fund-raisers hope to get you to experience so much pity that you'll help finance their efforts. Similarly, people who beg for money often emphasize their difficulties in an effort to evoke pity and donations.

Emotional contagion also seems the goal of certain organizational display rules. For example, a company may require (or at least expect) that the sales force cheer enthusiastically as each new product is unveiled. This cheering is extremely useful and is likely to make the sales representatives more enthusiastic about and more emotionally committed to the product than if they didn't engage in this cheering.

Another popular appeal is to guilt. If someone does something for you, he or she may try to make you feel guilty unless you do something in return. Or someone may present him- or herself as in desperate need of money and make you feel guilty for having what you have and not sharing it. Sometimes people encourage others to feel guilty to make them more easily manipulated. If you can make a person feel guilty for having a great deal of money while others have little, you are on the road to persuading the person to give some of that money away.

Table 7.1 summarizes the principles of emotions and emotional communication. With these principles of emotions and emotional expression as a foundation, we can now look at some of the obstacles to effective emotional expression.

Figure 7.3 Emotional Contagion

This figure depicts the process of emotional contagion as explained in the text. Another view of emotional contagion, however, holds that the process is under more conscious control. That is, you look at others who are expressing emotions to see how you should be feeling—you take nonverbal cues from those you observe—and then feel the feeling you believe you should be feeling. *Which view seems more satisfying?*

Table 7.1 In a Nutshell Principles of Emotions and Emotional Expression

Principle	Comments
Emotions occur in stages.	Different theories have been offered to explain the stages.
Emotions may be primary or blended.	Primary emotions are joy, trust, fear, surprise, sadness, disgust, anger, and anticipation; blended emotions are combinations of these.
Emotions involve both body and mind.	You not only feel emotions bodily but you also think about them.
Emotional expression uses multiple channels.	Verbal and nonverbal channels all come into play here.
Emotional expression is governed by display rules.	Cultures prescribe rules for the expression of emotions.
Emotions can be used strategically.	Like any form of communication, emotional expression can be used strategically.
Emotions have consequences.	Emotions and emotional expression, like any message, has consequences.
Emotions may be adaptive and maladaptive.	Not all emotions are good; not all emotions are bad.
Emotions are contagious.	Emotions spread easily.

Obstacles to Communicating Emotions

7.2 Identify the major obstacles that could prevent the effective communication of emotions.

The expression of feelings is part of most meaningful relationships. Yet it's often very difficult. Four major obstacles stand in the way of effective emotional communication: (1) personality factors, (2) inadequate interpersonal skills, (3) society's rules and customs, and (4) fear. Let's look more closely at each of these barriers.

Personality Factors

Your personality influences the emotions you feel, the extent to which you feel them, and, perhaps most important for our purposes, the ways in which you express or conceal these emotions and the way you respond to the emotions of others. And, in some case, personality factors can set up obstacles for both expressing and responding to the emotions of others.

Extroverted people, for example, experience more positive emotions and are more competent in expressing the emotions than are those who are more introverted. Those who have neurotic tendencies are more likely to experience more negative emotions. Similarly, those who score high on openness to varied experiences, agreeableness, and conscientiousness (in addition to extroversion) are more effective in expressing and in responding to the emotions of others (Nawi, Redzuan, & Hamsan, 2012).

Another important factor is the degree to which you experience communication apprehension. Some people have little apprehension about communicating, say, in public speaking while others have a great deal. The same is true when it comes to emotions. Some people have little apprehension or anxiety about expressing their emotions while others experience a great deal of apprehension and anxiety.

Inadequate Interpersonal Skills

Perhaps the most important obstacle to effective emotional communication is lack of interpersonal skills. Many people simply don't know how to express their feelings. Some people, for example, can express anger only through violence or avoidance. Others can deal with anger only by blaming and accusing others. And many people cannot express love. They literally cannot say, "I love you."

Expressing negative feelings is doubly difficult. Many of us suppress or fail to communicate negative feelings for fear of offending the other person or making matters worse. But failing to express negative feelings will probably not help the relationship, especially if these feelings are concealed frequently and over a long time.

Both communicating your emotions and responding appropriately to the emotional expressions of others are as important as they are difficult (Burleson, 2003). And to complicate matters further, emotional expression can be good and also bad, as noted in the self-test earlier in this chapter. On the one hand, expressing emotions can be cathartic to you. And, if appropriate communication is used, emotional expression, even of negative emotions, may actually benefit a relationship (Bloch, 2013). Expressing emotions can also help you air dissatisfactions and perhaps reduce or even eliminate them. Through emotional expression, you can come to understand each other better, which may lead to a closer and more meaningful relationship.

On the other hand, expressing emotions may cause relationship difficulties. For example, expressing your dislike of a colleague's customary way of answering the phone may generate hostility; expressing jealousy when your partner spends time with friends may cause your partner to fear being controlled and losing autonomy.

Societal and Cultural Customs

If you grew up in the United States, you probably learned that many people frown on emotional expression. This attitude is especially prevalent in men and has been aptly called the "cowboy syndrome," after a pattern of behavior seen in old Westerns on film and television (Balswick & Peck, 1971). The cowboy syndrome characterizes the closed and unexpressive male. This man is strong but silent. He never feels any of the softer emotions (such as compassion, love, or contentment). He would never ever cry, experience fear, or feel sorry for himself.

Unfortunately, many men grow up trying to live up to this unrealistic image. It's a syndrome that prevents open and honest expression. Boys are taught early in life not to cry and not to be "babies" if hurt. All of this is not to suggest that men should communicate their emotions more openly. Unfortunately, there are many who will negatively evaluate men who express emotions openly and often; such men may be judged ineffective, insecure, or unmanly. In fact, some research shows that the reason men are reluctant to provide sensitive emotional support—to the degree that women do, for example—is that men don't want their behavior to be seen as feminine (Burleson, Holmstrom, & Gilstrap, 2005).

Nor are women exempt from restraints on emotional expression. At one time, our society permitted and encouraged women to express emotions openly. The tide now is turning, especially for women in executive and managerial positions. Today the executive woman is being forced into the same cowboy syndrome. She is not allowed to cry or to show any of the once acceptable "soft" emotions. She is especially denied these feelings while she is on the job. As noted earlier, gender display rules are changing rapidly.

And, of course, organizations have their own cultural norms for the expression of emotions. For example, in many organizations, employees are expected to pretend to be cheerful even when they are not and generally to display some emotions and to hide others. Differences between the emotions you feel and the emotions you express can create emotional dissonance, which in turn can lead to stress (Remland, 2006).

For both men and women, the best advice (as with any of the characteristics of communication effectiveness discussed in this text) is to express your emotions selectively. Carefully weigh the arguments for and against expressing your emotions. Consider the situation, the people you're with, the emotions themselves, and all of the elements that make up the communication act. And, most important, consider your choices for communicating emotions—not only what you'll say but also how you'll say it.

VIEWPOINTS

Expressiveness

Marie and Dave have been married for several years. Marie is extremely expressive, yelling one minute, crying the next. By comparison, Dave is nonexpressive. This difference is now causing problems. Dave feels Marie reacts impulsively without thinking her feelings through; Marie feels Dave is unwilling to share his emotional life with her. *What skills do Marie and Dave need to learn?*

Fear

A variety of types of fear stand in the way of emotional expression. This is true for both men and women but more so for men, who have greater difficulty expressing emotions (Zakowski et al., 2003). Emotional expression exposes a part of you that makes you vulnerable to attack. For example, if you express your love for another person, you risk being rejected. When you expose a weakness, you can more easily be hurt by uncaring or insensitive others. Of course, you may also fear hurting someone else by, say, voicing your feelings about past loves. Or you may be angry and want to say something but fear that you might hurt the person and then feel guilty yourself.

In addition, you may avoid revealing your emotions for fear of causing a conflict. Expressing your dislike for Pat's friends, for example, may create difficulties for the two of you, and you may not be willing to risk the argument and its aftermath. Because of fears such as these, you may deny to others and perhaps even to yourself that you have certain feelings. In fact, this kind of denial is the way many people were taught to deal with emotions.

As you can appreciate, fear can be adaptive; it may lead you to avoid saying things you may be sorry for later. It may lead you

---

INTERPERSONAL CHOICE POINT
Responding to Betrayal

A colleague at work has revealed to other workers personal information about your relationship problems that you confided in him and him alone. You're steaming as you pass a group of colleagues commenting on these relationship problems. *What might be an effective way of dealing with this situation?*

a. Say nothing now, but talk later to the one who betrayed you in private.

b. Confront the group, saying, for example, "Yes, I did XYZ, but I told Chris in confidence; it wasn't something I was comfortable with everyone knowing."

c. "Well, that's what happens when you trust someone with a confidence and are betrayed."

d. "Watch out; you're next on the betrayal list."

e. Other

UNDERSTANDING *INTERPERSONAL SKILLS*

Flexibility: The Ability to Change Communication Patterns to Suit the Situation

Before reading about flexibility, consider the extent to which you hold beliefs such as those in the list.

- People should be spontaneous in conversation.
- People who are angry should say nothing rather than say something they will be sorry for later.
- People should listen supportively.
- People in a long-term relationship should be totally honest.

Although each of these statements seems reasonable, a simple "sometimes" should preface each of them (Hart, Carlson, & Eadie, 1980; Martin & Rubin, 1994). For example, although you might want to be spontaneous with a group of friends, you might want more rehearsed responses when interviewing for a job. **Flexibility**, then, is a quality of interpersonal effectiveness that enables you to interact in different ways depending on the situation.

As you can appreciate, flexibility is especially important when communicating your feelings, be they positive or negative, because it's in times of emotional arousal that you're likely to forget the varied choices you have available. And, of course, this is exactly the time when you need to consider your choices. The greater your flexibility, the more likely you'll be to see the varied choices you do have for communicating in any situation.

Communicating with Flexibility

Here are a few ways to cultivate interpersonal flexibility.

- ***See uniqueness.*** Realize that no two situations or people are exactly alike; consider what is different about this situation or person and take these differences into consideration as you construct your messages.

- ***See the context.*** Recognize that communication always takes place in a context; discover what that unique context is and ask yourself how it might influence your messages. Communicating bad news during a joyous celebration, for example, needs to be handled quite differently from communicating good news.

- ***See change.*** Become aware of the constant change in people and in things. Everything is in a state of flux. Even if the way you communicated last month was effective, that doesn't mean it will be effective today or tomorrow. Realize too that sudden changes (the death of a lover or a serious illness) influence what are and what are not appropriate messages.

- ***See choices.*** Appreciate the fact that every situation offers you different options for communicating. Consider these options and try to predict the effects each option might have.

Working with Flexibility

Try applying the suggestions offered here to increase your flexibility in any of the following situations: (1) you're assisting a teacher in a ninth-grade class known for being especially difficult, (2) you're leading a work team designed to find ways to increase worker morale, or (3) you're responding to some negative comments on your Facebook wall.

Table 7.2 In a Nutshell Obstacles to Emotional Expression

Obstacles	Reasons
Personality	Your degree of extroversion and apprehension, for example, will often pose an obstacle.
Inadequate Interpersonal Skills	The lack of skills creates doubt about how to express emotions.
Social and Cultural Customs	Societies and cultures have different rules and customs for displaying emotions.
Fear	Fear of causing a conflict or of losing control can inhibit emotional expression.

to consider more carefully whether you should express yourself and how you might do it. But when it debilitates you and contradicts what logic and reason might tell you, then the fear becomes maladaptive.

Table 7.2 summarizes these varied obstacles to effective emotional communication.

Emotional Competence

7.3 Summarize the guidelines for emotional competence in expressing and responding to emotions.

Much as emotions are part of your psychological life, emotional expression is part of your interpersonal life; it is not something you could avoid even if you wanted to. In specific cases, you may decide to hide your emotions and not express them, but in other cases, you'll want to express your emotions and this calls for what we might call emotional competence, the skills for expressing your emotions and responding to the emotions of others.

Before expressing or responding to emotions, however, you'll want to increase your self-awareness about your feelings (Stein & Book, 2011; Joseph, 2013). Ask yourself a few pertinent questions:

- *"What am I feeling, and what made me feel this way?"* That is, understand your emotions. Think about your emotions as objectively as possible. Identify, in terms as specific as possible, the antecedent conditions that may be influencing your feelings. Try to answer the question, "Why am I feeling this way?" or "What happened to lead me to feel as I do?"

- *"What exactly do I want to communicate?"* Consider also whether your emotional expression will be a truthful expression of your feelings. When emotional expressions are faked—when, for example, you smile though feeling angry or say, "I forgive you" when you don't—you may actually be creating emotional and physical stress (Grandey, 2000). Remember, too, the irreversibility of communication; once you communicate something, you cannot take it back.

- *"What are my communication choices?"* Evaluate your communication options in terms of both effectiveness (what will work best and help you achieve your goal) and ethics (what is right or morally justified).

With this increased understanding let's consider the two essential parts of emotional communication: emotional expression and emotional responding.

Emotional Expression

Here are a few guidelines for this special type of communication and a special case illustration to clarify the role of emotional expression.

Guidelines for Emotional Expression Although each situation is different, the following guidelines should prove useful in most cases.

- *Be specific.* Consider, for example, the frequently heard, "I feel bad." Does it mean, "I feel guilty" (because I lied to my best friend)? "I feel lonely" (because I haven't had a date in the last two months)? "I feel depressed" (because I failed that last exam)? Specificity helps. Describe also the intensity with which you feel the emotion: "I feel so angry I'm thinking of quitting the job." "I feel so hurt I want to cry." Also describe any mixed feelings you might have. Very often feelings are a mixture of several emotions, sometimes even of conflicting emotions. Learn the vocabulary (as well as the usefulness of smiley faces and emoticons) to describe your emotions and feelings in specific and concrete terms.

- *Describe the reasons you're feeling as you are.* "I'm feeling guilty because I was unfaithful." "I feel lonely; I haven't had a date for the last two months." "I'm really depressed from failing that last exam." If your feelings were influenced by something the person you're talking to did or said, describe this also. For example, "I felt so angry when you said you wouldn't help me." "I felt hurt when you didn't invite me to the party."

- *Address mixed feelings.* If you have mixed feelings—and you really want the other person to understand you—then address these mixed or conflicting feelings. "I want so much to stay with Pat and yet I fear I'm losing my identity." Or "I feel anger and hatred, but at the same time I feel guilty for what I did."

- *In expressing feelings—inwardly or outwardly—try to anchor your emotions in the present.* Coupled with specific description and the identification of the reasons for your feelings, such statements might look like this: "I feel like a failure right now; I've erased this computer file three times today." "I felt foolish when I couldn't think of that formula." "I feel stupid when you point out my grammatical errors."

- *Ask for what you want.* Depending on the emotions you're feeling, you may want the listener to assume a certain role or just listen or offer advice. Let the listener know what you want. Use I-messages to describe what, if anything, you want the listener to do: "I'm feeling sorry for myself right now; just give me some space. I'll give you a call in a few days." Or, more directly: "I'd prefer to be alone right now." Or "I need advice." Or "I just need someone to listen to me."

- *Respect emotional boundaries.* Each person has a different level of tolerance for communication about emotions or communication that's emotional. Be especially alert to nonverbal cues that signal that boundaries are near to being broken. It's often useful simply to ask, "Would you rather change the subject?" At the same time, realize that you also have a certain tolerance for revealing your own feelings as well as for listening to and responding to the emotions of others.

- *Own your feelings; take personal responsibility for your feelings.* Consider the following statements: "You make me angry." "You make me feel like a loser." "You make me feel stupid." "You make me feel like I don't belong here." In each of these statements, the speaker blames the other person for the way he or she is feeling. Of course, you know, on more sober reflection, that no one can make you feel anything. Others may do things or say things to you, but it is you who interpret them and give them meaning. That is, you develop feelings as a result of the interaction between what people say and your own interpretations.

Table 7.3 presents a list of terms for describing your emotions verbally. As you can appreciate, the more accurate you are in describing your emotions, the better the chances are that you'll be understood as you want to be and the better the chances are that others will be able to respond appropriately. The table is based on the eight primary emotions identified by Plutchik and referred to in Figure 7.2. Notice that the terms included for each basic emotion provide you with lots of choices for expressing the intensity level you're feeling. For example, if you're extremely fearful, then *terror* or

Table 7.3 Verbal Expressions of Emotion

Basic Emotion	Synonyms	Antonyms
Joy	Happiness, bliss, cheer, contentment, delight, ecstasy, enchantment, enjoyment, felicity, rapture, gratification, pleasure, satisfaction, well-being	Anger, depression, gloom, misery, pain, sadness, sorrow, unhappiness, woe, grief, upset
Trust	Confidence, belief, hope, assurance, faith, reliance, certainty, credence, certitude, conviction	Distrust, disbelief, mistrust, uncertainty
Fear	Anxiety, apprehension, awe, concern, consternation, dread, fright, misgiving, phobia, trepidation, worry, qualm, terror	Courage, fearlessness, heroism, unconcern, bravery
Surprise	Amazement, astonishment, awe, bewilderment, eye-opener, incredulity, jolt, revelation, shock, unexpectedness, wonder, startle, catch off-guard, unforeseen	Expectation, assurance, confidence, intention, likelihood, possibility, prediction, surmise
Sadness	Dejection, depression, distress, grief, loneliness, melancholy, misery, sorrow, unhappiness	Happiness, gladness, joy, cheer, delight, enjoyment, pleasure, euphoria, gaiety
Disgust	Abhorrence, aversion, loathing, repugnance, repulsion, revulsion, sickness, nausea, offensiveness	Admiration, desire, esteem, fondness, liking, love, reverence, respect
Anger	Acrimony, annoyance, bitterness, displeasure, exasperation, fury, ire, irritation, outrage, rage, resentment, umbrage, wrath, hostility	Calmness, contentment, enjoyment, peace, joy, pleasantness
Anticipation	Contemplation, prospect, forward-looking, expectancy, hope, foresight, expectation, foreboding, forecast, forethought	Unreadiness, doubt, uncertainty, ambiguity, disinterest

dread might be appropriate, but if your fear is mild, then perhaps *apprehension* or *concern* might be a more appropriate term.

Owning feelings means acknowledging that your feelings are your feelings. The best way to own your statements is to use **I-messages**. With I-messages, the statement "you make me angry" and "you make me feel like a loser" would look more like these: "I get angry when you come home late without calling" and "I begin to think of myself as a loser when you criticize me in front of my friends." Or, "I feel so stupid when you use medical terms that I don't understand" and "When you ignore me in public, I feel like I don't belong here."

As you can see, I-messages differ greatly from *you*-messages in several important ways:

- *Description versus evaluation* I-messages describe your feelings, whereas *you*-messages evaluate (negatively) another's behavior.

- *Acknowledgment of responsibility versus blaming others* I-messages acknowledge responsibility for your feelings, whereas *you*-messages shift the responsibility to someone else, usually in a blaming kind of way.

- *Preserving versus attacking positive and negative face* I-messages preserve both positive and negative face, whereas *you*-messages attack the person for some wrongdoing (thus attacking positive face and the person's self-image) and also imply that this person needs to do something about it (thus attacking negative face and the person's autonomy). I-messages don't attack the person or demand that the person change his or her behavior.

- *Openness versus withdrawal* I-messages encourage openness, whereas *you*-messages encourage defensiveness and a withdrawal from interpersonal interaction. No one wants to be attacked, and withdrawal is a common response.

Table 7.4 provides a comparison of effective and ineffective emotional expression.

Handling Anger: A Special Case Illustration As a kind of summary of the guidelines for expressing your emotions, this section looks at anger. **Anger** is one of the eight basic emotions identified in Plutchik's model (Figure 7.2). It's also an emotion that can create considerable problems if not managed properly.

Table 7.4   Effective and Ineffective Emotional Expression

Ineffective Emotional Expression	Effective Emotional Expression
General; talks about emotions and feelings in general terms and without specifics.	**Specific;** talks about emotions with specific terms and with specific examples and behavioral references.
Ignores reasons; mindlessly accepts emotions without trying to discover their causes.	**Describes reasons;** seeks to understand the causes of emotions.
Ignores mixed feelings; is more strategic than open.	**Addresses mixed feelings;** is honest and open.
Past focused; concentrates on past feelings (perhaps as a way to avoid focusing on present feelings).	**Present focused;** concentrates on the here and now, on current feelings.
Expect mindreading; and then get angry when you're not read correctly.	**Asks for what you want,** but respects the other's need for positive and negative face.
Ignores or fails to see boundary signals.	**Respects boundaries** and doesn't burden those who may not be ready to hear these feelings.
Lacks ownership; attributes feelings to others—"You made me angry," "you hurt me," "you don't love me."	**Owns one's feelings** and their expressions, for example, "I feel angry," "I'm hurt," "I don't feel loved."

Anger varies from mild annoyance to intense rage; increases in pulse rate and blood pressure usually accompany these feelings. Of all the emotions, anger is the one most likely to go viral on the Internet (Fan, Zhao, Chen, & Xu, 2013; Popkin, 2013).

Anger is not always necessarily bad. In fact, anger may help you protect yourself, energizing you to fight or flee. Often, however, anger does prove destructive—as when, for example, you allow it to obscure reality or to become an obsession.

Anger doesn't just happen; you make it happen by your interpretation of events. Yet life events can contribute mightily. There are the road repairs that force you to detour so you wind up late for an important appointment. There are the moths that attack your favorite sweater. There's the water leak that ruins your carpet. People, too, can contribute to your anger: the driver who tailgates, the clerk who overcharges you, the supervisor who ignores your contributions to the company. But it is you who interpret these events and people in ways that stimulate you to anger.

Writing over 100 years ago, Charles Darwin observed in his *The Expression of the Emotions in Man and Animals* (1872), "The free expression by outside signs of an emotion intensifies it . . . the repression, as far as this is possible, of all outside signs softens our emotions. He who gives way to violent gestures will increase his rage." Popular psychology ignored Darwin's implied admonition in the 1960s and 1970s, when the suggested prescription for dealing with anger was to "let it all hang out" and "tell it like it is." Express your anger, many people advised, or risk its being bottled up and eventually exploding. This idea, called the **ventilation hypothesis**, holds that expressing emotions allows you to ventilate your negative feelings and that this has a beneficial effect on your physical health, your mental well-being, and even your interpersonal relationships (Kennedy-Moore & Watson, 1999; Spett, 2004).

Later thinking has returned to Darwin, however, and suggests that venting anger may not be the best strategy (Tavris, 1989). Expressing anger doesn't get rid of it but makes it grow: angry expression increases anger, which promotes more angry expression, which increases anger, and on and on. Some support for this idea that expressing emotions makes them stronger comes from a study that compared (a) participants who felt emotions such as happiness and anger with (b) participants who both felt and expressed these emotions. The results of the study indicated that people who felt *and expressed* the emotions became emotionally aroused faster than did those who only felt the emotion (Hess, Kappas, McHugo, et al., 1992). And, of course, this spiral of anger can make conflicts all the more serious and all the more difficult to manage.

Anger communication is not angry communication. In fact, it might be argued that the communication of anger ought to be especially calm and dispassionate. Here, then, are a few suggestions for communicating your anger in a nonangry way (DeVito, 2003b):

- *Get ready to communicate calmly and logically.* Relax. Breathe deeply. Think pleasant thoughts. Tell yourself to "take it easy," "think rationally," and "calm down." Get rid of any unrealistic ideas you may have that might contribute to your anger. For example, ask yourself if this person's revealing something about your past to a third party is really all that serious or was it really intended to hurt you.

- *Examine your communication choices.* In most situations, you'll have a range of choices. There are lots of different ways to express yourself, so don't jump to the first possibility that comes to mind. Assess your options for the form of the communication—should you communicate face-to-face? By e-mail? By telephone? Similarly, assess your options for the timing of your communication, for the specific words and gestures you might use, for the physical setting, and so on.

- *Consider the advantages of delaying the expression of anger.* For example, consider writing the e-mail but sending it to yourself, at least until the next morning. Then the options of revising it or not sending it at all will still be open to you.

- *Remember that different cultures have different display rules—* norms for what is and what is not appropriate to display. Assess the culture you're in as well as the cultures of the other people involved, especially these cultures' display rules for communicating anger.

- *Apply the relevant skills of interpersonal communication.* For example, be specific, use I-messages, avoid allness, avoid polarized terms, and in general communicate with all the competence you can muster.

- *Recall the irreversibility of communication.* Once you say something, you'll not be able to erase or delete it from the mind of the other person.

These suggestions are not going to solve the problems of road rage, gang warfare, or domestic violence. Yet they may help—a bit—in reducing some of the negative consequences of anger and perhaps even some of the anger itself.

A somewhat different view of emotional competence would be emotional happiness; after all, if you're emotionally competent, it should contribute to your individual happiness, a topic addressed in Table 7.5. The table offers a few "dos" (but with qualifications) for achieving emotional satisfaction, contentment, and happiness.

VIEWPOINTS

Displaying Strong Emotions

Some societies permit and even expect men (but not women) to show strong emotions such as anger. *What has your culture taught you about the expression of anger and particularly about gender differences in the expression of anger?*

Table 7.5 Emotional Happiness

Do	But
Think positively.	Don't be a Pollyanna; don't gloss over problems.
Associate with positive people.	Don't avoid others because they have different ideas or backgrounds; you'll miss out on a lot.
Do what you enjoy.	Don't forget your responsibilities or ignore obligations.
Talk about your feelings.	Don't substitute talk for action or talk too much.
Imagine yourself positively.	Don't become egotistical; after all, we all have faults and these need to be addressed if we're to improve.
Think logically; keep emotions in perspective.	Don't ignore the crucial role that emotions and emotional expression often play in interpersonal communication.

Emotional Responding

Expressing your feelings is only half of the process of emotional communication; the other half is listening and responding to the feelings of others. As with emotional expression, we first consider some general guidelines and then offer a specific case illustration.

Guidelines for Emotional Responding   Like emotional expression, each situation calling for emotional responding will be different from every other situation. Nevertheless, a few general principles should prove useful most of the time and in most situations.

- *Look at nonverbal cues to understand the individual's feelings.* For example, overly long pauses, frequent hesitations, eye contact avoidance, or excessive fidgeting may be a sign of discomfort that might be wise to talk about. Similarly, look for inconsistent messages, as when someone says, "Everything is okay" while expressing facial sadness; these are often clues to mixed feelings. But be sure to use any verbal or nonverbal cues as hypotheses, never as conclusions. Check your perceptions before acting on them. Treat inferences as inferences and not as facts.

- *Look for cues about what the person wants you to do.* Sometimes all the person wants is for someone to listen. Don't equate (as the stereotypical male supposedly does) "responding to another's feelings" with "solving the other person's problems." Instead, provide a supportive atmosphere that encourages the person to express his or her feelings.

- *Use active listening techniques.* These will encourage the person to talk should he or she wish to. Paraphrase the speaker. Express understanding of the speaker's feelings. Ask questions as appropriate.

- *Empathize.* See the situation from the point of view of the speaker. Don't evaluate the other person's feelings. For example, comments such as, "Don't cry; it wasn't worth it" or "You'll get promoted next year" can easily be interpreted to mean, "Your feelings are wrong or inappropriate."

- *Focus on the other person.* Interjecting your own similar past situations is often useful for showing your understanding, but it may create problems if it refocuses the conversation away from the other person. Show interest by encouraging the person to explore his or her feelings. Use simple encouragers like "I see" or "I understand." Or ask questions to let the speaker know that you're listening and that you're interested.

- *Remember the irreversibility of communication.* Whether expressing emotion or responding to the emotions of others, it's useful to recall the irreversibility of communication. You won't be able to take back an insensitive or disconfirming response. Responses to another's emotional expressions are likely to have considerable impact, so be especially mindful to avoid inappropriate responding.

Communicating with the Grief-Stricken: A Special Case Illustration   Communicating with people who are experiencing grief, a common but difficult type of communication interaction, requires special care (Zunin & Zunin, 1991). Consideration of this topic will also offer a useful recap of some of the principles of responding to the emotions of others.

A person may experience grief because of illness or death, the loss of a job or highly valued relationship (such as a friendship or romantic breakup), the loss of certain physical or mental abilities, the loss of material possessions (a house fire or stock losses), or the loss of some ability (for example, the loss of the ability to have children or to play the piano). Each situation seems to call for a somewhat different set of dos and don'ts.

VIEWPOINTS

Responding To Grief

Can you recall a situation in which you interacted with someone who was experiencing grief, but for some reason you didn't communicate very effectively? Did you violate any of the suggestions identified here? What would you do differently if this situation occurred today?

INTERPERSONAL CHOICE POINT
Spending Time

Your grandmother is dying and calls to ask you to spend some time with her. She says that she knows she is dying, that she wants you to know how much she has always loved you, and that her only regret in dying is not being able to see you anymore. You want her to feel comforted, and yet it's so emotional for you. *What might you say?*

a. "I love you, Granny."

b. "You've always been such an inspiration to me; I don't know what I'll do without you."

c. "I wish we could have more time together."

d. "Granny, I don't want you to die."

e. Other

When people experience grief, they normally go through five stages, identified by Elisabeth Kubler-Ross (1969) in *On Death and Dying*. This five-stage model is not necessarily followed by everyone, nor does everyone go through the five stages in neat order—there can be overlap in the stages. One stage doesn't necessarily end before the next stage occurs. Kubler-Ross developed this model from her work with cancer patients who were confronting their own impending deaths. But it has been applied more widely to anyone experiencing grief, whether because of one's own illness, because of the illness or death of a loved one, or to relationship breakups—to the loss of an important friendship or romantic partner (Kromberg, 2013).

Stage 1 *Denial* When someone close to you dies or is diagnosed with a life-threatening illness, a first reaction is often to deny what happened. Maybe there was a mistake in the diagnosis; maybe there is still hope.

Stage 2 *Anger* As the denial fades, you confront reality and become angry. The object of your anger varies—perhaps you become angry at the person who died for leaving you alone—an irrational belief but a common one nevertheless. Or you might direct your anger at the doctor or hospital for not detecting the illness at a stage when it could have been cured.

Stage 3 *Bargaining* For religious people, this stage often takes the form of making a deal with God—perhaps to stop drinking, perhaps to be more generous toward the poor, perhaps to contribute money for some religious purpose. Almost invariably it is a promise to be a better person and to do good works.

Stage 4 *Depression* Perhaps the stage you think about most often when you think of grief is depression—for the loss or impending loss of someone you love. Or you might feel sorry that you didn't spend more time with this person or didn't do what you could have to make the person's life a better one.

Stage 5 *Acceptance* At this stage you come to terms with your loss. You accept its inevitability and eventuality. This is not a stage of happiness or joy, just acceptance of reality.

Consider, for example, the following expression of sympathy:

I just heard that Harry died—I mean—passed away. Excuse me. I'm so sorry. We all are. I know exactly how you feel. But, you know, it's for the best. I mean the man was suffering. I remember seeing him last month; he could hardly stand up, he was so weak. And he looked so sad, so lonely, so depressed. He must have been in constant pain. It's better this way; believe me. He's at peace now. And you'll get over it. You'll see. Time heals all wounds. It was the same way with me and you know how close we were. I mean we were devoted to each other. Everyone said we were the closest pair they ever saw. And I got over it. So, how about we'll go to dinner tonight? We'll talk about old times. Come on. Come on. Don't be a spoilsport. I really need to get out. I've been in the house all week and you know what a drag that can be. So, do it for me; come to dinner. I won't take no for an answer; I'll pick you up at seven.

Obviously, this is not the way to talk to the grief-stricken. In fact, this paragraph was written to illustrate several popular mistakes that the following guidelines address. After you read these guidelines, you may wish to return to this "expression of sympathy," reanalyze it, and rework it into an effective expression of sympathy.

- *Confirm the other person and the person's emotions.* A simple, "You must be worried about finding another position" or "You must be feeling very alone right now" confirms the person's feelings. This type of expressive support lessens feelings of grief (Reed, 1993).

- *Choose the appropriate channel of communication.* Today, it's very easy to send a note of sympathy on Facebook or through email but, although quick and easy, this may not be the appropriate means of communication (Feiler, 2016). It really depends on the unique situation and especially on your relationship with the person. The closer you are to the grieving individual, the more intimate the form of communication should be. So, if you're close, a phone call or a face-to-face visit, for example, might be more appropriate than a simple post.

- *Give the person permission to grieve.* Let the person know that it's acceptable and okay with you if he or she grieves in the ways that feel most comfortable—for example, crying or talking about old times. Don't try to change the subject or interject too often. As long as the person is talking and seems to be feeling better for it, be supportive.

- *Avoid trying to focus on the bright side.* Avoid expressions such as, "You're lucky you have some vision left" or "It's better this way; Pat was suffering so much." These expressions may easily be seen as telling people that their feelings should be redirected, that they should be feeling something different.

- *Encourage the person to express feelings and talk about the loss.* Most people will welcome this opportunity. On the other hand, don't try to force people to talk about experiences or feelings they may not be willing to share.

- *Be especially sensitive to leave-taking cues.* Behaviors such as fidgeting or looking at a clock and statements such as "It's getting late" or "We can discuss this later" are hints that the other person is ready to end the conversation. Don't overstay your welcome.

- *Let the person know you care and are available.* Saying you're sorry is a simple but effective way to let the person know you care. Express your empathy; let the grief-stricken person know that you can feel (to some extent) what he or she is going through. But don't assume that your feelings, however empathic you are, are the same in depth or in kind. At the same time, let the person know that you are available—"If you ever want to talk, I'm here" or "If there's anything I can do, please let me know."

Even when you follow the principles and do everything according to the book, you may find that your comments are not appreciated or are not at all effective in helping the person feel any better. Use these cues to help you readjust your messages.

Table 7.6 provides a brief summary of the two competencies and their respective strategies.

Table 7.6 In a Nutshell Emotional Competence

Competencies	Strategies
Expressing	• Be specific.
	• Describe why you feel as you do.
	• Address any mixed feelings.
	• Focus on the present.
	• Ask for what you want.
	• Respect emotional boundaries.
	• Own your feelings.
Responding	• Pay attention to nonverbal cues.
	• Seek cues about what the person wants.
	• Listen actively.
	• Empathize.
	• Focus on the other person.
	• Remember the irreversibility of communication.

Summary

This chapter explored the nature and principles of emotions in interpersonal communication, the obstacles to meaningful emotional communication, and some guidelines that will help you communicate your feelings and respond to the feelings of others more effectively.

Principles of Emotions and Emotional Messages

7.1 Describe the principles of emotions and emotional expression.

1. Emotions occur in stages.

2. Emotions may be primary or blends. The primary emotions, according to Robert Plutchik, are joy, trust, fear, surprise, sadness, disgust, anger, and anticipation. Other emotions, such as love, awe, contempt, and aggressiveness, are blends of primary emotions.

3. Emotions consist of both a physical part (our physiological reactions) and a cognitive part (our interpretations of our feelings).

4. Emotions use multiple communication channels.

5. Emotional expression depends greatly on the display rules the individual is expected to follow.

6. Emotions may be used strategically.

7. Emotions and their expressions have consequences.

8. Emotions may be adaptive or maladaptive.

9. Emotions are often contagious.

Obstacles to Communicating Emotions

7.2 Identify the major obstacles that could prevent the effective communication of emotions.

10. Personality factors such as introversion and apprehension may prevent meaningful emotional communication.

11. Societal and cultural customs may have taught you that emotional expression is inappropriate.

12. Fear of exposing weaknesses or causing a conflict may inhibit your emotional expression.

13. Inadequate interpersonal skills may make you feel unsure or hesitant, so you might withdraw.

Emotional Competence

7.3 Summarize the guidelines for emotional competence in expressing and responding to emotions.

14. Understand what you are feeling and what made you feel this way.

15. Formulate a communication goal; what exactly do you want to accomplish when expressing emotions?

16. Identify your communication choices and evaluate them.

17. Describe your feelings as specifically as possible, identify the reasons for your feelings, address mixed feelings, anchor your feelings and their expression in the present time, ask for what you want, respect emotional boundaries, and own your feelings.

18. Look for cues to understand the person's feelings. Listen for what is said and not said; look at the nonverbals, especially those that don't match the verbals.

19. Look for cues about what the person wants you to do. Don't assume the person wants you to solve his or her problem.

20. Use active listening techniques. Paraphrase, express understanding, and ask questions as appropriate.

21. Empathize. See the situation from the other person's perspective. Ask yourself what the other person may be feeling.

22. Focus on the other person. Avoid interpreting the situation from your own experiences.

23. Remember the irreversibility of communication. Once said, messages can't be erased, mentally or emotionally.

Key Terms

anger communication
anger
blended emotions
cognitive labeling theory
display rules
emotional appeals
emotional blackmail

emotional communication
emotional contagion
emotional labor
emotions
flexibility
gender display rules
I-messages

James–Lange theory
owning feelings
primary emotions
strategic emotionality
ventilation hypothesis

CHAPTER EIGHT

Conversational Messages

Conversations vary greatly in purpose and form. *Understanding the different types of conversations will make for more satisfying interactions.*

Chapter Topics

Principles of Conversation

Conversational Disclosure

Everyday Conversations

Learning Objectives

8.1 Describe the major principles of conversation.

8.2 Define *self-disclosure*, its potential rewards and dangers, and the guidelines for disclosing, responding to disclosures, and resisting the pressure to disclose.

8.3 Identify the guidelines for small talk; making introductions, excuses, and apologies; asking a favor; and giving and receiving compliments and advice.

Conversation is an essential part of interpersonal communication and may be defined simply as informal social interaction (McLaughlin, 1984). Examining conversation provides an excellent opportunity to look at verbal and nonverbal messages as they're used in day-to-day communications, and thus serves as a useful culmination for this second part of the text.

This chapter explains the principles of conversation, the nature of self-disclosure (one of the most important forms of conversation), and some of your everyday conversational situations (such as small talk and apologizing). Guidelines are offered throughout the chapter for making conversation more satisfying and more effective.

Principles of Conversation

8.1 Describe the major principles of conversation.

Although conversation is an everyday process and one you seldom think about, it is, like most forms of communication, governed by several principles (Figure 8.1).

The Principle of Process

It's convenient to divide the process of conversation into chunks or stages and to view each stage as requiring a choice about what you'll say and how you'll say it. Here the sequence is divided into five steps: opening, feedforward, business, feedback, and closing (see Figure 8.2). These stages and the way people follow them vary depending on the personalities of the communicators, their culture, the context in which the conversation occurs, the purpose of the conversation, whether it's face-to-face or computer mediated, and the entire host of factors considered throughout this text.

When reading about the process of conversation, keep in mind that not everyone speaks with the fluency and ease that many textbooks often assume. Speech and language disorders, for example, can seriously disrupt the conversation process when some elementary guidelines aren't followed. Keep in mind that speech and language disorders vary widely in type and severity and include, for example, indistinct articulation, fluency problems (such as stuttering), and difficulty in finding the right word (aphasia). Table 8.1 offers some suggestions for making such conversations run more smoothly.

Opening   The first step is to open the conversation, usually with some kind of greeting: A "Hi, how are you?" or "Hello, this is Joe" or a comment on Facebook. The greeting is a good example of **phatic communication**: it's a message that establishes a connection between two people and opens up the channels for more meaningful interaction. When you send a friend a virtual gift of strawberry cheesecake, you're creating an opportunity for communication; you're saying that you're thinking of the person and want

Figure 8.1 The Principles of Conversation

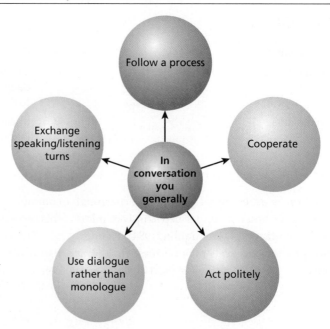

Figure 8.2 A Functional Five-Stage Model of Conversation

This model of the stages of conversation is best seen as a way of talking about conversation and not as a hard-and-fast depiction of stages all conversations follow. As you review the model, consider how accurately it depicts conversation as you experience it. *Can you develop a more accurate and more revealing model?*

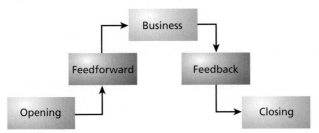

to communicate. A simple tweet or post likewise can serve as a conversation opener. Openings, of course, may be nonverbal as well as verbal. A smile or smiley face, kiss, or handshake may be as clear an opening as "Hello." Greetings are so common that they often go unnoticed. But when they're omitted—as when the doctor begins the conversation by saying, "What's wrong?"—you may feel uncomfortable and thrown off guard.

Feedforward   At the second step, you usually provide some kind of feedforward or preview, which gives the other person a general idea of the conversation's focus: "I've got to tell you about Jack," "Did you hear what happened in class yesterday?" or "We need to talk about our vacation plans." Feedforward also may identify the tone of the conversation ("I'm really depressed and need to talk with you") or the time required ("This will just take a minute") (Frentz, 1976; Reardon, 1987). Often the feedforward is combined with the opening, as when you see someone on campus, for example, and say, "Hey, listen to this" or when, in a work situation, someone says, "Well, folks, let's get the meeting going."

Table 8.1   Interpersonal Communication for People with and without Speech and Language Disorders

If you're the person without a speech or language disorder:

Generally	Specifically
Avoid finishing another's sentences.	Finishing the person's sentences may communicate the idea that you're impatient and don't want to spend the extra time necessary to interact effectively.
Avoid giving directions to the person with a speech disorder.	Saying "slow down" or "relax" will often seem insulting and will make further communication more difficult.
Maintain eye contact.	Show interest and at the same time avoid showing any signs of impatience or embarrassment.
Ask for clarification as needed.	If you don't understand what the person said, ask him or her to repeat it. Don't pretend that you understand when you don't.
Don't treat people who have language problems like children.	A person with aphasia, say, who has difficulty with names or nouns generally, is in no way childlike. Similarly, a person who stutters is not a slow thinker; in fact, stutterers differ from nonstutterers only in their oral fluency.

If you're the person with a speech or language disorder:

Generally	Specifically
Let the other person know what your special needs are.	If you stutter, you might tell others that you have difficulty with certain sounds and so they need to be patient.
Demonstrate your own comfort.	Show that you have a positive attitude toward the interpersonal situation. If you appear comfortable and positive, others will also.
Be patient.	For example, have patience with those who try to finish your sentences; they're likely just trying to be helpful.

SOURCES: These suggestions were drawn from a variety of sources, including the websites of the National Stuttering Association, the National Aphasia Association, the United States Department of Labor, and the American Speech and Hearing Association, all accessed March 7, 2017.

Business The third step is the business, the substance or focus of the conversation. The term *business* is used to emphasize that most conversations are goal-directed. That is, you converse to fulfill one or several of the general purposes of interpersonal communication: to learn, relate, influence, play, or help. The term is also sufficiently general to incorporate all kinds of interactions. The business is conducted through an exchange of speaker and listener roles. Brief, rather than long, speaking turns characterize most satisfying conversations. In the business stage, you talk about Jack, what happened in class, or your vacation plans. This is obviously the longest part of the conversation and the reason for the opening and the feedforward.

Feedback The fourth step is feedback, the reverse of the second step. Here you reflect on the conversation to signal that, as far as you're concerned, the business is completed: "So you want to send Jack a get-well card?" "Wasn't that the craziest class you ever heard of?" or "I'll call for reservations." The other half of the feedback equation is the person receiving the feedback (Robbins & Hunsaker, 2006). When you are the recipient of feedback, be sure to show your interest in feedback. This is vital information that will help you improve whatever you're doing. Encourage the feedback giver. Be open to hearing this feedback. Don't argue; don't be defensive.

Closing The fifth and last step, the opposite of the first step, is the closing, the goodbye, which often reveals how satisfied the persons were with the conversation: "I hope you'll call soon" or "Don't call us; we'll call you." The closing also may be used to schedule future conversations: "Give me a call tomorrow night" or "Let's meet for lunch at twelve." When closings are indefinite or vague, conversation often becomes awkward; you're not quite sure if you should say goodbye or if you should wait for something else to be said.

VIEWPOINTS

The Meanings Of Greetings

Greetings (whether face-to-face or computer-mediated) are a kind of feedforward and serve various functions. *What functions did your last three greetings serve?*

The Principle of Cooperation

During conversation, you probably follow the principle of **cooperation**; you and the other person implicitly agree to cooperate in trying to understand what each is saying (Grice, 1975; Lindblom, 2001). You cooperate largely by using four **conversational maxims**—principles that speakers and listeners in the United States and in many other cultures follow in conversation. Although the names for these maxims may be new, the principles themselves will be easily recognized from your own experiences (see Figure 8.3).

The Maxim of Quantity Be as informative as necessary to communicate the intended meaning. Thus, in keeping with the **quantity maxim**, include information that makes the meaning clear but omit what does not; give neither too little nor too much information. You see people violate this maxim when they try to relate an incident and digress to give unnecessary information. You find yourself thinking or saying, "Get to the point; so what happened?" This maxim is also violated when necessary information is omitted. In this situation, you find yourself constantly interrupting to ask questions: "Where were they?" "When did this happen?" "Who else was there?"

The Maxim of Quality Say what you know or assume to be true, and do not say what you know to be false. When you're in conversation, you assume that the other person's information is true—at least as far as he or she knows. When you speak with people who frequently violate the **quality maxim** by lying, exaggerating, or minimizing major problems, you come to distrust what such individuals are saying and wonder what is true and what is fabricated.

Figure 8.3   The Maxims Of Cooperation

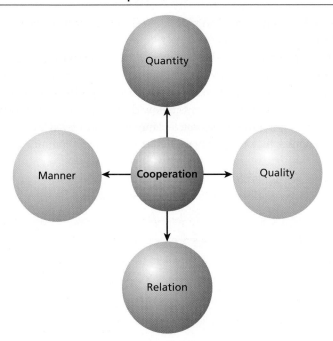

The Maxim of Relation   Talk about what is relevant to the conversation. Thus, the **relation maxim** states that, if you're talking about Pat and Chris and say, for example, "Money causes all sorts of relationship problems," it's assumed by others that your comment is somehow related to Pat and Chris. This principle is frequently violated by speakers who digress widely or frequently interject irrelevant comments, causing you to wonder how these comments are related to what you're discussing.

The Maxim of Manner   Be clear, avoid ambiguities, be relatively brief, and organize your thoughts into a meaningful sequence. Thus, in accordance with the **manner maxim**, use terms that the listener understands and clarify terms that you suspect the listener will not understand. When talking with a child, for example, simplify your vocabulary. Similarly, adjust your manner of speaking on the basis of the information you and the listener share. When talking to a close friend, for example, you can refer to mutual acquaintances and to experiences you've had together. When talking to a stranger, however, you'll either omit such references or explain them.

The four maxims just discussed aptly describe most conversations as they take place in much of the United States. Recognize, however, that maxims will vary from one culture to another. Here are two maxims appropriate in cultures other than that of the United States but are also appropriate to some degree throughout the United States:

- In Japanese conversations and group discussions, a maxim of preserving peaceful relationships with others may be observed (Midooka, 1990). For example, it would be considered inappropriate to argue and to demonstrate that another person is wrong. It would be inappropriate to contribute to another person's embarrassment or loss of face.

- The maxim of self-denigration, observed in the conversations of Chinese speakers, may require that you avoid taking credit for some accomplishment or make less of some ability or talent you have (Gu, 1990). To put yourself down in this way is a form of politeness that seeks to elevate the person to whom you're speaking.

The Principle of Politeness

Conversation is expected (at least in many cases) to follow the principle of politeness (previewed briefly in Figure 8.4).

Six maxims of politeness have been identified by linguist Geoffrey Leech (1983) and seem to encompass a great deal of what we commonly think of as conversational politeness. Before reading about these maxims, examine your **politeness** tendencies by indicating how closely each of the statements below describes your typical communication behavior. Avoid giving responses that you feel might be considered "socially acceptable"; instead, give responses that accurately represent your typical communication behavior.

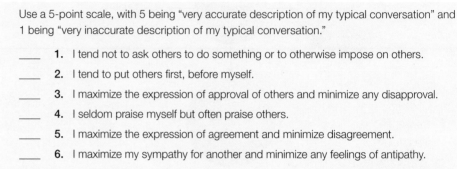

Use a 5-point scale, with 5 being "very accurate description of my typical conversation" and 1 being "very inaccurate description of my typical conversation."

_____ **1.** I tend not to ask others to do something or to otherwise impose on others.

_____ **2.** I tend to put others first, before myself.

_____ **3.** I maximize the expression of approval of others and minimize any disapproval.

_____ **4.** I seldom praise myself but often praise others.

_____ **5.** I maximize the expression of agreement and minimize disagreement.

_____ **6.** I maximize my sympathy for another and minimize any feelings of antipathy.

All six statements characterize politeness; thus, high numbers, say 4s to 5s, indicate politeness, whereas low numbers, say 1s and 2s, indicate impoliteness. As you read this material, personalize it with examples from your own interpersonal interactions and try to identify specific examples and situations in which increased politeness might have been more effective.

- The *maxim of tact* (Statement 1 in the self-test) helps to maintain the other's autonomy or negative face. Tact in your conversation would mean that you do not impose on others or challenge their right to do as they wish. For example, if you wanted to ask someone a favor, using the maxim of tact, you might say something

Figure 8.4 The Maxims of Politeness

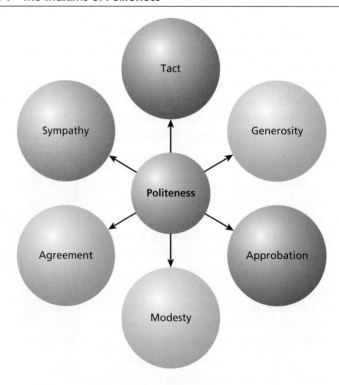

like, "I know you're very busy, but . . ." or "I don't mean to impose, but . . ." Not using the maxim of tact, you might say something like, "You have to lend me your car this weekend" or "I'm going to use your ATM card."

- The *maxim of generosity* (Statement 2) helps to confirm the other person's importance, the importance of the person's time, insight, or talent, for example. Using the maxim of generosity, you might say, "I'll walk the dog; I see you're busy." In violating the maxim, you might say, "I'm really busy. Why don't you walk the dog? You're not doing anything important."

- The *maxim of approbation* (Statement 3) refers to praising someone or complimenting the person in some way (for example, "I was really moved by your poem") and minimizing any expression of criticism or disapproval (for example, "For a first effort, that poem wasn't half bad").

- The *maxim of modesty* (Statement 4) minimizes any praise or compliments *you* might receive. At the same time, you might praise and compliment the other person. For example, using this maxim, you might say something like, "Well, thank you, but I couldn't have done this without your input; that was the crucial element." Violating this maxim, you might say, "Yes, thank you, it was one of my best efforts, I have to admit."

- The *maxim of agreement* (Statement 5) refers to your seeking out areas of agreement and expressing them ("That color you selected was just right; it makes the room exciting") and at the same time avoiding and not expressing (or at least minimizing) disagreements ("It's an interesting choice, very different"). In violation of this maxim, you might say "That color—how can you stand it?"

- The *maxim of sympathy* (Statement 6) refers to the expression of understanding, sympathy, empathy, supportiveness, and the like, for the other person. Using this maxim, you might say, "I understand your feelings; I'm so sorry." If you violated this maxim you might say, for example, "You're making a fuss over nothing" or "You get upset over the least little thing; what is it this time?"

The Principle of Dialogue

Often the term *dialogue* is used as a synonym for *conversation*. But, it's more than simple conversation; it's conversation in which there is genuine two-way interaction (Buber, 1958; McNamee & Gergen, 1999; Yau-fair Ho, Chan, Peng, & Ng, 2001). It's useful to distinguish the *ideal* dialogic (two-way) communicator from the opposite, the totally monologic (one-way) communicator.

In **dialogue**, each person is both speaker and listener, sender and receiver. It's a type of conversation in which there is deep concern for the other person and for the relationship between the two. The objective of dialogue is mutual understanding, supportiveness, and empathy. There is respect for the other person, not because of what this person can do or give but simply because this person is a human being and therefore deserves to be treated honestly and sincerely.

Monologue is the opposite side; it's communication in which one person speaks and the other listens—there's no real interaction between participants. The monologic communicator is focused only on his or her own goals and has no real concern for the listener's feelings or attitudes; this speaker is interested in the other person only insofar as that person can serve his or her purposes.

To increase dialogue and decrease monologue, try the following:

- *Demonstrate respect for the other person.* Allow that person the right to make his or her own choices without coercion, without the threat of punishment, and without fear or social pressure. A dialogic communicator believes that other people can make decisions that are right for them and implicitly or explicitly lets them know that whatever choices they make, they will still be respected as people.

- *Avoid negative criticism* ("I didn't like that explanation") and negative judgments ("You're not a very good listener, are you?"). Instead, practice using positive criticism ("I like those first two explanations best; they were really well reasoned").

- *Keep the channels of communication open* by displaying a willingness to listen. Give cues (nonverbal nods, brief verbal expressions of agreement, paraphrasing) that tell the speaker you're listening.

- *Acknowledge the presence and importance of the other person.* Ask for suggestions, opinions, and clarification. This will ensure that you understand what the other person is saying from that person's point of view and also signals a real interest in the person.

- *Avoid manipulating the conversation* to get the person to say something positive about you or to force the other person to think, believe, or behave in any particular way.

The Principle of Turn Taking

The defining feature of conversation is that the speaker and listener exchange roles throughout the interaction. You accomplish this through a wide variety of verbal and nonverbal cues that signal **conversational turns**—the changing (or maintaining) of the speaker or listener role during the conversation. In hearing people, turn taking is regulated by both audio and visual signals. Among blind speakers, turn taking is governed in larger part by audio signals and often touch. Among deaf speakers, turn-taking signals are largely visual and also may involve touch (Coates & Sutton-Spence, 2001). Combining the insights of a variety of communication researchers (Burgoon, Guerrero, & Floyd, 2010; Duncan, 1972; Pearson & Spitzberg, 1990), let's look more closely at conversational turns in terms of cues that speakers use and cues that listeners use.

Speaker Cues As a speaker, you regulate conversation through two major types of cues: turn maintaining and turn yielding. Turn-maintaining cues are designed to help you maintain the speaker's role. You can do this with a variety of cues, for example, by audibly inhaling to show that you have more to say, continuing a gesture or gestures to show that you have not completed the thought, avoiding eye contact with the listener so there's no indication that you're passing the speaking turn to him or her, sustaining your intonation pattern to indicate that you intend to say more, or vocalizing pauses ("er," "um") to prevent the listener from speaking and to show that you're still talking (Burgoon, Buller, & Woodall, 1996; Duncan, 1972). In most cases, speakers are expected to maintain relatively brief speaking turns and to turn over the speaking role willingly to the listener (when so signalled by the listener).

With turn-yielding cues, you tell the listener that you're finished and wish to exchange the role of speaker for that of listener. These cues tell the listener (sometimes a specific listener) to take over the role of speaker. For example, at the end of a statement you might add some paralinguistic cue such as "eh?" that asks one of the listeners to assume the role of speaker. You can also indicate that you've finished speaking by dropping your intonation, by prolonged silence, by making direct eye contact with a listener, by asking some general question, or by nodding in the direction of a particular listener.

In much the same way that you expect a speaker to yield the role of speaker, you also expect the listener to assume the speaking role willingly. Those who don't may be regarded as reticent or unwilling to involve themselves and take equal responsibility for the conversation. For example, in an analysis of turn-taking violations in the conversations of married people, the most common violation found was that of no response. Forty-five percent of the 540 violations identified involved a lack of response to an invitation to assume the speaker role. Of these "no response" violations, 68 percent were committed by men and 32 percent by women. Other turn-taking violations include interruptions, delayed responses, and inappropriately brief responses. From this, it's been argued that by means of these violations, all of which are committed more frequently by men, men often silence women in marital interactions (DeFrancisco, 1991).

Listener Cues As a listener, you can regulate the conversation by using a variety of cues. Turn-requesting cues let the speaker know that you'd like to take a turn as speaker. Sometimes you can do this by simply saying, "I'd like to say something," but often you do it more subtly through some vocalized "er" or "um" that tells the mindful speaker that you'd now like to speak. This request to speak is also often made with facial and mouth gestures. You can, for example, indicate a desire to speak by opening your eyes and mouth widely as if to say something, by beginning to gesture with your hand, or by leaning forward.

You can also indicate your reluctance to assume the role of speaker by using turn-denying cues. For example, intoning a slurred "I don't know" or a brief grunt signals you have nothing to say. Other ways to refuse a turn are to avoid eye contact with the speaker who wishes you to take on the role of speaker or to engage in some behavior that is incompatible with speaking—for example, coughing or blowing your nose.

Back-Channeling Cues **Back-channeling cues** are used to communicate various types of information back to the speaker *without* your assuming the role of speaker. Some researchers call these acknowledgment tokens—brief utterances such as "mm-hm," "uh-huh," and "yeah," the three most often used such tokens—that tell the speaker you're listening (Drummond & Hopper, 1993; Schegloff, 1982). Others call them overlaps to distinguish them from those interruptions that are aimed at taking over the speaker's turn (Tannen, 1994b). Back-channeling cues are generally supportive and confirming and show that you're listening and are involved in the interaction (Kennedy & Camden, 1988).

You can communicate a variety of messages with these back-channeling cues (overlaps, acknowledgment tokens); here are four of the most important messages (Burgoon, Guerrero, & Floyd, 2010; Pearson & Spitzberg, 1990).

- *To indicate agreement or disagreement.* Smiles, nods of approval, brief comments such as "right" and "of course," or a vocalization like "uh-huh" signal agreement. Frowning, shaking your head, or making comments such as "no" or "never" signal disagreement.

- *To indicate degree of involvement.* An attentive posture, forward leaning, and focused eye contact tell the speaker that you're involved in the conversation. An inattentive posture, backward leaning, and avoidance of eye contact communicate a lack of involvement.

- *To pace the speaker.* You ask the speaker to slow down by raising your hand near your ear and leaning forward or to speed up by repeatedly nodding your head. Or you may cue the speaker verbally by asking the speaker to slow down or to speed up.

- *To ask for clarification.* Puzzled facial expressions, perhaps coupled with a forward lean, or direct interjection of "who?" "when?" or "where?" signal your need for clarification.

Interruptions In contrast to back-channeling cues, **interruptions** are attempts to take over the role of the speaker. These are not supportive and are often disconfirming. Interruptions are often interpreted as attempts to change the topic to a subject that the interrupter knows more about or to emphasize the person's authority. Interruptions are seen as attempts to assert power and to maintain control. Superiors (bosses and supervisors) and those in positions of authority (police officers and interviewers), research finds, interrupt those in inferior positions more than the other way around (Ashcraft, 1998; Carroll, 1994). In fact, it would probably

---

INTERPERSONAL CHOICE POINT
Interrupting

One of your team members repeatedly interrupts you. Whenever you start to explain something, this member interrupts you to change the topic or to finish your thought—sometimes accurately but most often inaccurately. You need to do something about this and are wondering if you're actually encouraging interruptions by the way you express yourself. *What might you do in your own communication to discourage another's interruptions?*

- **a.** Explain why interrupting doesn't accomplish any useful purpose.
- **b.** Ignore the interruption; just keep talking.
- **c.** Criticize the person interrupting in private or during the meeting.
- **d.** At the next interruption, explain the problem the interruption is causing.
- **e.** Other

VIEWPOINTS

Interruptions

From your own interactions and observations, how would you describe conversational interruptions? For example, who interrupts whom? When are interruptions most likely to occur? Under what circumstances are interruptions appropriate? Inappropriate?

strike you as strange to see a worker repeatedly interrupting a supervisor or a student repeatedly interrupting a professor.

Another and even-more-often-studied aspect of interruption is that of gender difference. The popular belief is that men interrupt more than women. This belief, research finds, is basically accurate. Men interrupt both women and other men more than women do. For example, one analysis of 43 published studies on interruptions and gender differences showed that men interrupted significantly more than women (Anderson, 1998). In addition, the more male-like the person's gender identity—regardless of the person's biological sex—the more likely it is that the person will interrupt (Drass, 1986). Fathers, one research study shows, interrupt their children more than mothers do (Greif, 1980). These gender differences, however, are small. More important than gender in determining who interrupts is the specific type of situation; some contexts (for example, task-oriented situations) may call for more interruptions, whereas others (such as relationship discussions) may call for more back-channeling cues (Anderson, 1998).

The various turn-taking cues and how they correspond to the conversational wants of speaker and listener are illustrated in Figure 8.5.

Figure 8.5   Turn Taking and Conversational Wants

Each quadrant represents a different type of turn taking:

- Quadrant 1: the speaker wishes to continue speaking, using *turn-maintaining cues.*
- Quadrant 2: the speaker wishes to listen, using *turn-yielding cues.*
- Quadrant 3: the listener wishes to speak, using *turn-requesting cues.* Interruptions also appear in quadrant 3, though they're not so much cues that request a turn as takeovers of the speaker's position.
- Quadrant 4: the listener wishes to continue listening, using *turn-denying cues.* Back-channeling cues also appear in quadrant 4 because they are cues that listeners use while they continue to listen.

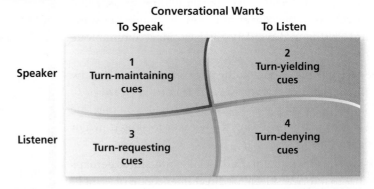

A summary of these principles of conversation appears in Table 8.2.

Table 8.2   In a Nutshell   A Summary of the Principles of Conversation

General Principle	Principle in Conversation
The principle of process	Conversation can be viewed as consisting of five stages: opening, feedforward, business, feedback, and closing.
The principle of cooperation	Conversation relies on the maxims of quantity, quality, relation, and manner.
The principle of politeness	Conversations generally follow the maxims of tact, generosity, approbation, modesty, agreement, and sympathy.
The principle of dialogue	Conversation relies on each person listening and responding as well as speaking.
The principle of turn taking	Conversation works best when messages are relatively short and easily exchanged.

Conversational Disclosure

8.2 Define *self-disclosure*, its potential rewards and dangers, and the guidelines for disclosing, responding to disclosures, and resisting the pressure to disclose.

One of the most important forms of interpersonal communication that you can engage in is talking about yourself, or self-disclosure.

Revealing Yourself

Self-disclosure means communicating information about yourself to another person. Although the term is often limited to revealing information that you normally keep hidden, it can also refer to information that you would share with just about anyone: your likes and comments (as you do on Facebook); your brief tweets that say something about what you like or don't like; what you're thinking about; or your preferences for foods, books, or music; and what you reveal when you post a photo on Pinterest or Instagram (Greene, Derlega, & Mathews, 2006). It may involve information about (1) your values, beliefs, and desires ("I believe in reincarnation"); (2) your behavior ("I shoplifted but was never caught"); or (3) your self-qualities or characteristics ("I'm dyslexic"). Overt and carefully planned statements about yourself as well as slips of the tongue would be classified as self-disclosing communications. Similarly, you could self-disclose nonverbally by, for example, wearing gang colors; a wedding ring; a shirt with slogans that reveal your political or social concerns, such as "Pro-Choice" or "Go Green"; or photos on Facebook. Self-disclosure also may involve your reactions to the feelings of others, for example, when you tell your friend that you're sorry she was fired.

Self-disclosure involves at least one other individual; it cannot be an *intra* personal communication act. To qualify as self-disclosure, the information must be received and understood by another person. In some cases, the disclosure would be received by hundreds or thousands on your Twitter, Facebook, or LinkedIn networks.

Self-disclosure can vary from the relatively insignificant ("I'm a Leo" or "I enjoy the soaps") to the highly revealing and deeply personal ("I'm currently in an abusive relationship" or "I was born a man").

Self-disclosure occurs in all forms of communication, not just interpersonal. It frequently occurs in small-group settings, in public speeches, on television talk shows such as *Maury* and *Jerry Springer*, and even on *Jimmy Fallon* or *Jimmy Kimmel* and such shows as *The Bachelor* or *The Bachelorette* and *Big Brother*. And self-disclosure can occur not only in face-to-face settings but also online. On social network sites such as Twitter or Facebook, for example, a great deal of self-disclosure goes on, as it does when people reveal themselves in personal e-mails, newsgroups, and blog posts. In fact, research finds that reciprocal self-disclosure occurs more quickly and at higher levels online than it does in face-to-face interactions (Joinson, 2001; Levine, 2000).

Some researchers have pointed to a **disinhibition effect** that occurs in online communication. We seem less inhibited in communicating in e-mail or in social media, for example, than we do face-to-face. Among the reasons for this seems to be the fact that, in online communication, there is a certain degree of anonymity and invisibility (Suler, 2004). Other research, however, finds less support for the importance of anonymity. In an examination of blog posts, those posts that were accompanied by a photograph of the author (making it onymous rather than anonymous) actually disclosed more than those posts that did not so identify the author (Hollenbaugh & Everett, 2013).

You probably self-disclose for a variety of reasons. Perhaps you feel the need for catharsis—a need to get rid of feelings of guilt or to confess some wrongdoing. You may

VIEWPOINTS

Disinhibition

In light of the contradictory research findings on online disinhibition, examine your own tendencies when you post on a blog, comment on Facebook, or tweet. *Are you more or less likely to disclose online than in face-to-face encounters? What factors influence the likelihood of your disclosing in online versus face-to-face encounters? Does your relative anonymity in online communication lead you to self-disclose differently than you do in face-to-face interactions?*

also disclose to help the listener, for example, to show the listener how you dealt with an addiction or succeeded in getting a promotion. Of course, you may self-disclose to encourage relationship growth, or to maintain or repair a relationship, or even as a strategy for ending a relationship.

Although self-disclosure may occur as a single message—for example, you tell a stranger on a train that you're thinking about getting a divorce—it's best viewed as a developing process in which information is exchanged between people over the period of their relationship (Spencer, 1993, 1994). In fact, the website for the University of California, Long Beach (http://web.csulb.edu/colleges/chhs/safe-zone/coming-out/), in their discussion of coming out as a GLBTQ person—an especially important kind of self-disclosure—note the developmental nature of coming out; it's a process rather than an event.

If you view it as a developing process, you can then appreciate how self-disclosure changes as the relationship changes; for example, as a relationship progresses from initial contact through involvement to intimacy, the self-disclosures increase. If the relationship deteriorates and perhaps dissolves, the disclosures decrease. Self-disclosure will also vary depending on the type of relationship you have with the person or persons to whom you'll disclose. You'll disclose differently, for example, depending on whether the other person is your friend, lover, parent, child, or counselor.

Thinking about your willingness to disclose the following types of information—and you can easily add other things about yourself that you would and would not disclose—should get you started examining your own self-disclosing behavior.

- Your happiest moments in life
- Your unhappiest moments in life
- Your personality characteristics that you do not like
- Your most embarrassing moment
- Your major weaknesses
- Your prejudices
- Your net worth
- Your sexual fantasies
- Your greatest fears
- Your ideal relationship partner

The remaining discussion of this important concept will be more meaningful if you first consider your own willingness to self-disclose. Consider the following disclosures and think about whether you'd disclose, to whom you'd disclose, and under what circumstances you might disclose?

Influences on Self-Disclosure

Many factors influence whether or not you disclose, what you disclose, and to whom you disclose. Among the most important factors are who you are, your culture, your gender, who your listeners are, and what your topic is.

- *You:* Highly sociable and extroverted people self-disclose more than those who are less sociable and more introverted. People who are apprehensive about talking in general also self-disclose less than do those who are more comfortable in communicating. Competent people and those with high self-esteem engage in self-disclosure more than less competent people and those with low self-esteem (Dolgin, Meyer, & Schwartz, 1991; McCroskey & Wheeless, 1976).
- *Your culture:* Different cultures view self-disclosure differently. People in the United States, for example, disclose more than do those in Great Britain, Germany, Japan, or Puerto Rico (Gudykunst, 1983). Americans also reported greater self-disclosure when communicating with other Americans than when communicating interculturally (Allen, Long, O'Mara, & Judd, 2003). In Japan, it's considered undesirable

for colleagues to reveal personal information, whereas in much of the United States, it's expected (Barnlund, 1989; Hall & Hall, 1987).

- *Your gender:* Research supports the popular belief that women disclose more than men (Stewart, Cooper, & Stewart, 2003). Women disclose more than men about their previous romantic relationships, their feelings about their closest same-sex friends, their greatest fears, and what they don't like about their partners (Sprecher, 1987). A notable exception occurs in initial encounters. Here men will disclose more intimately than women, perhaps "in order to control the relationship's development" (Derlega, Winstead, Wong, & Hunter, 1985).

- *Your listeners:* Because you disclose on the basis of the support you receive, you disclose to people you like (Collins & Miller, 1994; Derlega, Winstead, Greene, Serovich, & Elwood, 2004) and to people you trust and love (Wheeless & Grotz, 1977; Sprecher & Hendrick, 2004). You also come to like those to whom you disclose (Berg & Archer, 1983). You're more likely to disclose to people who are close to you in age (Parker & Parrott, 1995). You are also more likely to disclose when the other person has disclosed, a pattern referred to as **reciprocity**; you give back what you get. If someone reveals a past indiscretion to you, for example, you'd be more likely to reciprocate with revealing one of your own.

- *Your topic:* You're more likely to self-disclose about some topics than others; for example, you're more likely to disclose information about your job or hobbies than about your sex life or financial situation (Jourard, 1968, 1971). You're also more likely to disclose favorable than unfavorable information. Generally, the more personal and negative the topic, the less likely you'll be to self-disclose.

- *Your media:* The medium or channel through which you communicate also influences your disclosures. Some people disclose more in face-to-face situations, while others disclose more in, say, e-mail or snail mail or perhaps by phone. Many people seem to disclose a great deal—some would say that they overshare—on social media (Grant, 2013). Social media seems to have created a culture where sharing (and oversharing) are normal and in some cases expected. The permanency and the public nature of these messages do not seem to provide a deterrent to such disclosures.

Rewards and Dangers of Self-Disclosure

Research shows that self-disclosure has both significant rewards and dangers. In making choices about whether or not to disclose, consider both.

Rewards of Self-Disclosure   Self-disclosure may help increase self-knowledge, communication and relationship effectiveness, physiological well-being, and likeability.

Self-disclosure helps you gain greater self-knowledge: a new perspective on yourself, a deeper understanding of your own behavior. Through self-disclosure, you may bring to consciousness a great deal that you might otherwise keep from conscious analysis. Even self-acceptance is difficult without self-disclosure. You accept yourself largely through the eyes of others. Through self-disclosure and subsequent support, you'll see the positive responses to you; you'll see, for example, that others appreciate your sense of humor or ability to tell a good story or the values you espouse. And through these positive responses, you'll likely strengthen your positive self-concept.

Because you understand the messages of another person largely to the extent that you understand the person, self-disclosure is an essential condition for communication and relationship effectiveness. Self-disclosure helps you achieve a closer relationship with the person to whom you self-disclose and increases relationship satisfaction (Meeks, Hendrick, & Hendrick, 1998; Schmidt & Cornelius, 1987; Sprecher, 1987). Within a sexual relationship, self-disclosure increases sexual rewards and general relationship satisfaction; after all, it's largely through self-disclosure that you learn what another person likes and dislikes. These two benefits increase sexual satisfaction (Byers & Demmons, 1999). Self-disclosure has also been studied as it relates to psychological abuse;

Self-Disclosing

Self-disclosure sometimes occurs more in temporary than in permanent relationships—for example, between strangers on a train or plane, a kind of "in-flight intimacy" (McGill, 1985). In this situation, two people set up an intimate self-disclosing relationship during a brief travel period, but they don't pursue it beyond that point. In a similar way, you might set up a relationship with one or several people on the Internet and engage in significant disclosure. Perhaps knowing that you'll never see these other people and that they will never know where you live or work or what you look like makes it easier. *Do you engage in such disclosure? If so, why?*

research indicates that persons who engage in in-depth self-disclosure seem to experience less psychological abuse (Shirley, Powers, & Sawyer, 2007). The reason for this finding may be that people in abusive relationships tend to disclose less for fear that such disclosures will provide "reasons" for the abuse. Or it may be that freedom to disclose comes from a nonabusive, supportive, confirming relationship.

Related to this increase in communication and relationship effectiveness is the possibility (some would say probability) that in the absence of disclosure, people (even your romantic partner or best friend) may wonder about this or that and construct explanations that are worse than the secret (Isay, 2014). And, romantic partners and best friends, especially, will snoop to discover information that you've kept hidden. According to some research, approximately 44 percent of couples have at least one partner who snoops and 37 percent of the couples snooped on each other (Helsper & Whitty, 2010). In another study, over 60 percent of college students admitted to using Facebook to keep tabs on romantic partners and others (Stern & Willis, 2007). Snooping is so prevalent that dating websites such as eHarmony provide advice on whether or not to snoop.

Self-disclosure seems to have a positive effect on physiological health. People who self-disclose are less vulnerable to illnesses (Pennebacker, 1991). Health benefits also result from disclosing in e-mails (Sheese, Brown, & Graziano, 2004). For example, bereavement over the death of someone very close is linked to physical illness for those who bear this alone and in silence. But it's unrelated to any physical problems for those who share their grief with others.

In addition to these advantages, research finds that people who disclose intimacies of their lives are liked more than those who do not engage in such disclosure (Dean, 2007). Conversely, you come to like those to whom you disclose. So, disclosure seems to contribute to an increase in mutual liking (Collins & Miller, 1994). And, as you'd expect, online daters who engage in positive self-disclosure are more successful than those who do not (Gibbs, Ellison, & Heino, 2006).

Dangers of Self-Disclosure Self-disclosure comes with considerable potential personal, relational, and professional risks.

- *Personal risks* If you self-disclose aspects of your life that vary greatly from the values of those to whom you disclose, you incur personal risks; you may experience rejection from even your closest friends and family members. Men and women who disclose that they have cheated on their relationship partner, have stolen, or are suffering from protracted depression, for example, may find their friends and family no longer wanting to be quite as close as before. Girls (but not boys) who emphasize their attractiveness and who post lots of party pictures on Facebook run the risk of being labeled negatively (Bailey, Steeves, Burkell, & Regan, 2013). GLBTQ people who come out may not have predicted the degree of homophobia, even in family members and best friends. And, in some countries, even today, such disclosures can result in imprisonment or even death.

- *Relational risks* Even in close and long-lasting relationships, self-disclosure can pose relational risks (Bochner, 1984). Total self-disclosure may prove threatening to a relationship by causing a decrease in mutual attraction, trust, or any of the bonds holding the individuals together. Self-disclosures concerning infidelity, romantic fantasies, past indiscretions or crimes, lies, or hidden weaknesses and fears could easily have such negative effects.

- *Professional risks* Revealing political views or attitudes toward different religious or racial groups may open you to professional risks and create problems on the job, as may disclosing any health problems, such as being HIV positive (Fesko, 2001). Disclosures that go against organizational norms—for example, the disclosures are too personal or not job-related—carry additional risks (Rosh & Offermann, 2013). Teachers, for example, who disclose former or current drug use or cohabitation with students may find themselves denied tenure, teaching at undesirable hours, arrested, and/or victims of "budget cuts."

In making your choice between disclosing and not disclosing, keep in mind—in addition to the advantages and dangers already noted—the irreversible nature of communication. Regardless of how many times you may try to qualify something or take it back, once you have disclosed, you cannot undisclose. Nor can you erase the conclusions and inferences listeners have made on the basis of your disclosures.

Guidelines for Self-Disclosure

Because self-disclosure is so important and so delicate a matter, guidelines are offered here for (1) deciding whether and how to self-disclose, (2) responding to the disclosures of others, and (3) resisting pressures to self-disclose.

Guidelines for Making Self-Disclosures   The following guidelines will help you ask yourself the right questions before you make a choice that must ultimately be your own.

- *Disclose out of appropriate motivation.* Self-disclosure should be motivated by a concern for the relationship, for the others involved, and for yourself. Avoid disclosing to hurt the listener; for example, people who tell their parents that they hindered their emotional development may be disclosing out of a desire to hurt and punish rather than a desire to improve the relationship.

- *Disclose in the appropriate context.* Before making any significant self-disclosure, ask whether this is the right time and place. Could a better time and place be arranged? Ask, too, whether this self-disclosure is appropriate to the relationship. Generally, the more intimate the disclosures, the closer the relationship should be. It's probably best to resist intimate disclosures (especially negative ones) with nonintimates, with casual acquaintances, or in the early stages of a relationship. And, of course, ask yourself whether the forum for the disclosures is appropriate. Some disclosures may best be made in private with one person, while others can be broadcast on television or on any one of the social network sites. Social networks such as Twitter and Facebook have recognized this and instituted privacy controls, enabling you to monitor who can receive your posts (that is, disclosures) and who will be blocked.

- *Disclose gradually.* During your disclosures, give the other person a chance to reciprocate with his or her own disclosures. If reciprocal disclosures are not made, reassess your own self-disclosures. It may be a signal that for this person, at this time, and in this context, your disclosures are not welcome or appropriate. Disclosing gradually will also enable you to gauge reactions, enabling you to stop disclosing if the reactions are not what you wanted or expected.

- *Disclose without imposing burdens on yourself or others.* Carefully weigh the potential problems that you may incur as a result of your disclosure. Can you afford to lose your job if you disclose your arrest record? Is it wise to swear your in-laws to secrecy about your disclosures of infidelity?

You've dated someone three or four times, and each time you're pressured to self-disclose past experiences and personal information you're simply not ready to talk about—at least, not at this early stage of the relationship. *What can you say to resist this pressure to self-disclose?*

a. Ignore the request and change the subject.

b. Make a joke of it; for example, say "If I told you, I'd have to kill you."

c. Reveal your feelings about not disclosing at this stage in the relationship.

d. Give in and disclose.

e. Other

Guidelines for Facilitating and Responding to Self-Disclosures
When someone discloses to you, it's usually a sign of trust and affection. In serving this most important receiver function, keep the following guidelines in mind. These guidelines will also help you facilitate the disclosures of another person.

- *Practice the skills of effective and active listening.* The skills of effective listening are especially important when you are listening to self-disclosures: listen actively, listen for different levels of meaning, listen with empathy, and listen with an open mind. Express an understanding of the speaker's feelings to allow the speaker the opportunity to see them more objectively and through the eyes of another. Ask questions to ensure your own understanding and to signal your interest and attention.

- *Support and reinforce the discloser.* Express support for the person during and after the disclosures. Concentrate on understanding and empathizing with (rather than evaluating) the discloser. Make your supportiveness clear to the discloser through your verbal and nonverbal responses: maintain eye contact, lean toward the speaker, ask relevant questions, and echo the speaker's thoughts and feelings.

- *Be willing to reciprocate.* When you make relevant and appropriate disclosures of your own in response to the other person's disclosures, you're demonstrating your understanding of the other's meanings and at the same time showing a willingness to communicate on this meaningful level.

- *Keep the disclosures confidential.* When a person discloses to you, it's because she or he wants you to know the feelings and thoughts that are communicated. If you reveal these disclosures to others, negative outcomes are inevitable and your relationship is almost sure to suffer. And be sure not to use the disclosures against the person. Many self-disclosures expose some kind of vulnerability or weakness. If you later turn around and use disclosures against the person who made them, you betray the confidence and trust invested in you. Regardless of how angry you may get, resist the temptation to use disclosures as weapons.

Guidelines for Resisting Pressure to Self-Disclose   You may, on occasion, find yourself in a position where a friend, colleague, or romantic partner pressures you to self-disclose. In such situations, you may wish to weigh the pros and cons of self-disclosure and then make your decision about whether and what you'll disclose. Do realize that one of the consequences of the Internet and social media generally is that it's very difficult to keep lots of information hidden. And, although you may resist, say, revealing your age in your office, it can probably be found online easily. You may not want to reveal how much your house is worth but readily available real estate websites provide very accurate estimates. Nevertheless, there are occasions when you do not want to disclose and you're still being pressured, and you need to say something. Here are a few suggestions:

- *Don't be pushed.* Although there may be certain legal or ethical reasons for disclosing, generally, if you don't want to disclose, you don't have to. Don't be pushed into disclosing because others are doing it or because you're asked to.

- *Be assertive in your refusal to disclose.* Say, very directly, "I'd rather not talk about that now" or "Now is not the time for this type of discussion."

- *Delay a decision.* If you don't want to say no directly but still don't want to disclose, delay the decision. Say something like, "That's pretty personal; let me think about that before I make a fool of myself" or "This isn't really a good time (or place) to talk about this; I'll get back to you and we'll talk."

- *Be indirect and move to another topic.* Avoid the question and change the subject. This is a polite way of saying, "I'm not talking about it," and may be the preferred choice in certain situations. Most often people will get the hint and understand your refusal to disclose.

A summary of these guidelines is presented in Table 8.3.

Table 8.3 In a Nutshell Guidelines and Strategies for Self-Disclosure

Self Disclosure	Disclosure Strategies
Self-disclosing to another	• Consider the motivation, the appropriateness, and the specific disclosures of the other person.
	• Consider the possible burdens that self-disclosure might entail.
Facilitating and responding to the disclosures of others	• Practice the skills of effective and active listening.
	• Support and reinforce the discloser.
	• Be willing to reciprocate.
	• Keep the disclosures confidential.
	• Don't use the disclosures against the person.
Resisting pressure to self-disclose	• Don't be pushed.
	• Be indirect and move to another topic.
	• Be assertive in your refusal to disclose.

ETHICS IN INTERPERSONAL COMMUNICATION

The Ethics of Gossip

Gossip is social talk that involves making evaluations about persons who are not present during the conversation; it generally occurs when two people talk about a third party (Eder & Enke, 1991; Wert & Salovey, 2004). And sometimes it occurs when someone reveals a private disclosure. A large part of your conversation at work and in social situations is spent gossiping (Carey, 2005; Lachnit, 2001; Waddington, 2004). In fact, one study estimates that approximately two-thirds of people's conversation time is devoted to social topics, and that most of these topics can be considered gossip (Dunbar, 2004). Gossiping seems universal among all cultures (Laing, 1993); among some it's a commonly accepted ritual (Hall, 1993). And, of course, gossip occupies a large part of Internet communication, as demonstrated by the growing popularity of websites such as Juicy Campus (www.JuicyCampus.com), which links a variety of college campuses (Morgan, 2008).

As you might expect, gossiping often has ethical implications, and in many instances gossip is considered unethical. Such instances generally identified as unethical are (Bok, 1983):

- when gossip is used to hurt another person unfairly, for example, spreading gossip about an office romance or an instructor's past indiscretions.
- when you know that what you're saying is not true, for example, lying to make another person look bad.
- when no one has the right to such personal information, for example, revealing the income of neighbors to others or revealing a fellow student's poor grades to other students.
- when you have promised secrecy, for example, revealing something that you promised not to repeat to others.

Ethical Choice Point

Your best friend's romantic partner has come on to you on several occasions. *What is your ethical obligation to your friend? If you decide that it would be ethical to tell your friend, would it also be ethical to tell other mutual friends? At what point does revealing this become unethical gossip?*

UNDERSTANDING *INTERPERSONAL SKILLS*

Expressiveness: Communication of Genuine Involvement

Expressiveness is the skill of communicating genuine involvement in the conversation; it entails, for example, taking responsibility for your thoughts and feelings, encouraging expressiveness or openness in others, and providing appropriate feedback. These are the qualities that make a conversation exciting and satisfying. Expressiveness includes both verbal and nonverbal messages, and often involves revealing your emotions and your normally hidden self—bringing in a variety of interpersonal skills noted earlier.

Communicating with Expressiveness

Here are a few suggestions for communicating expressiveness.

- *Vary your vocal rate, pitch, volume, and rhythm.* This helps you convey involvement and interest. Vary your language; avoid clichés and trite expressions, which signal a lack of originality and personal involvement.
- *Use appropriate gestures.* Especially helpful are gestures that focus on the other person rather than yourself. Maintain eye contact and lean toward the person; at the same time, avoid self-touching gestures or directing your eyes to others in the room.
- *Give verbal and nonverbal feedback.* This helps show that you're listening. Such feedback promotes relationship satisfaction.

- *Smile.* Your smile is probably your most expressive feature and it will likely be much appreciated.
- *Communicate expressiveness in ways that are culturally sensitive.* Some cultures (Italian, for example) encourage expressiveness and teach children to be expressive. Other cultures (Japanese and Thai, for example) encourage a more reserved response style (Matsumoto, 1996). Some cultures (Arab and many Asian cultures, for example) consider expressiveness by women in business settings to be inappropriate (Lustig, Koester, & Halualani, 2018; Axtell, 2007; Hall & Hall, 1987).

Working with Expressiveness

Think about the people you know who are extremely popular (online and offline) and those who are significantly less popular. It's likely that one way the groups differ is in expressiveness. As you read about expressiveness, consider your own degree of expressiveness in various different situations, for example, in the classroom, face-to-face with a group of close friends or work colleagues, or with your social media friends and how this relates to interpersonal popularity.

Everyday Conversations

8.3 Identify the guidelines for small talk; making introductions, excuses, and apologies; asking a favor; and giving and receiving compliments and advice.

In this section we discuss a variety of everyday conversation situations: making small talk, making introductions, making excuses, apologizing, asking for a favor, and giving and receiving compliments and advice.

Before reading about this ever-present form of conversation, respond to the following situations to examine your small talk behavior by indicating what you would be most likely to do.

____ 1. On an elevator with three or four strangers, I'd be most likely to

    a. avoid interacting.

    b. respond to another but not initiate interaction.

    c. be the first to talk.

____ 2. When I'm talking with someone and I meet a friend who doesn't know the person I'm with, I'd be most apt to

    a. avoid introducing them.

    b. wait until they introduce each other.

    c. introduce them to each other.

____ **3.** At a party with people I've never met before, I'd be most likely to

   a. wait for someone to talk to me.

   b. nonverbally indicate that I am receptive to someone interacting with me.

   c. initiate interaction with others nonverbally and verbally.

____ **4.** When confronted with someone who doesn't want to end the conversation, I'd be most apt to

   a. just stick it out and listen.

   b. tune out the person and hope time goes by quickly.

   c. end it firmly myself.

____ **5.** When the other person monologues, I'd be most apt to

   a. listen politely.

   b. try to change the focus.

   c. exit as quickly as possible.

The *a* responses are unassertive, the *b* responses are indirect (not totally unassertive but not assertive either), and the *c* responses are direct and assertive. Very likely, if you answered with 4 or 5 *c* responses, you're comfortable and satisfied with your small talk experiences. Lots of *a* responses indicate some level of dissatisfaction and discomfort with the experience of small talk. If you had lots of *b* responses, then you probably experience both satisfaction and dissatisfaction with small talk. If your small talk experiences are not satisfying to you, read on. The entire body of interpersonal skills will prove relevant here, as will a number of suggestions unique to small talk.

Making Small Talk

Small talk is pervasive; all of us engage in small talk. Sometimes, you use small talk as a preface to big talk. For example, before a conference with your boss or even an employment interview, you're likely to engage in some preliminary small talk. *How are you doing? I'm pleased this weather has finally cleared up. That's a great looking jacket.* The purpose here is to ease into the major topic or the big talk.

Sometimes, small talk is a politeness strategy and a bit more extensive way of saying hello as you pass someone in the hallway or a neighbor you meet at the post office. And, so you might say, "Good seeing you, Jack. You're ready for the big meeting?" or "See you in Geology at 1."

Sometimes your relationship with another person revolves totally around small talk, perhaps with your barber or hair dresser, a colleague at work, your next-door neighbor, or a student you sit next to in class. In these relationships neither person makes an effort to deepen the relationship, and it remains on a small talk level.

The Topics and Contexts of Small Talk   The topics of small talk have one important characteristic: the topic must be noncontroversial in the sense that it must not be something that you and the other person are likely to disagree on. If a topic is likely to arouse deep emotions or different points of view, then it is probably not a small talk topic.

Most often the topics are relatively innocuous. The weather is perhaps the most popular small talk topic. "Trivial" news, for example, news about sports (although criticizing the other person's favorite team would not be considered noncontroversial by many), and movie or television stars are also popular small talk topics. Current affairs—as long as there is agreement—might also be used in small talk ("Did you see the headline in the news? Horrible, isn't it?"). Sometimes small talk grows out of the context; for example, waiting on line for tickets may prompt a comment to the person next to you about your feet hurting or if they know how long it will be until the tickets go on sale.

Gender Stereotypes

One of the stereotypes about gender differences in communication and widely reported in popular writing about gender is that women talk more than men. But one study of 396 college students found that women and men talk about the same number of words per day, about 16,000; more precisely, women spoke an average of 16,215 words while men spoke an average of 15,669 words, a difference that was statistically insignificant (Mehl, Vazire, Ramirez-Esparza, Slatcher, & Pennebaker, 2007). *Do your own experiences support the stereotype or do they support these research findings?*

Small talk is usually short in duration, a factor that helps make this talk noncontroversial. Because of the context in which small talk occurs—waiting on line to get into a movie or for a store to open—it allows for only a brief interaction.

Another popular occasion, which contradicts this short-duration characteristic, is sitting next to someone on a long plane or train ride. Here, the small talk—assuming you keep it to small talk—can last for many hours. Sometimes, this situation produces a kind of "in-flight intimacy" in which you engage in significant self-disclosure, revealing secrets you normally keep hidden, largely because you know you'll never see this person again.

Even though small talk is noncontroversial and brief, it serves important purposes. One obvious purpose is to pass the time more pleasantly than you might in silence. Another purpose is that it demonstrates that the normal rules of politeness are operating. In the United States, for example, you would be expected to smile and at least say hello to people on an elevator in your apartment building and perhaps at your place of work. It also demonstrates to others that all is well with you.

Guidelines for Effective Small Talk   Although "small," this talk still requires the application of the interpersonal communication skills for "big" talk. Keep in mind, as already noted, that the best topics are noncontroversial and that most small talk is relatively brief. Here are a few additional guidelines for more effective small talk:

- Be positive. No one likes a negative doomsayer.
- Be sensitive to leave-taking cues. Small talk is necessarily brief, but at times one person may want it to be a preliminary to the big talk and another person may see it as the sum of the interaction.
- Stress similarities rather than differences; this is a good way to ensure that this small talk is noncontroversial.
- Answer questions with enough elaboration to give the other person information that can then be used to interact with you. Let's say someone sees a book you're carrying and says, "I see you're taking interpersonal communication." If you say, simply yes, you've not given the other person anything to talk with you about. Instead, if you say, "Yes, it's a great course; I think I'm going to major in communication," then you have given the other person information that can be addressed. The more elaborate answer also signals your willingness to engage in small talk. Of course, if you do not want to interact, then a simple one-word response will help you achieve your goal.

Making Introductions

Making introductions of yourself or of others often creates difficulties which are compounded by the simple fact that all situations are unique. Nevertheless, a few general suggestions for making these introductions easier and more comfortable may be offered.

Introducing Yourself   Here are a few suggestions that will help you introduce yourself to others whether you're at a club, in the college cafeteria, or at a party. It's important to remember that first impressions are long lasting and highly resistant to change. When you introduce yourself to someone you're giving them a first impression that will influence your future interactions. So, although it is in many ways impersonal and brief, it's tremendously important.

Your first step is to make eye contact and smile so that the person notices. If the other person avoids making eye contact, then this person may not be open to meeting you. If the other person returns eye contact and perhaps a smile, it's likely that he or she is open to meeting you.

After this nonverbal contact, you can make verbal contact simply by saying hello and your first and last name (leave out any middle initials or name). In some situations—especially business situations—you might want to add your connection with the company or with the event, for example, "Hi, I'm Joe DeVito from the communication department."

In some situations, this would be followed by a handshake (see Table 8.4). In the United States, the handshake is the most essential gesture of the introduction and generally follows rather specific rules. In other cultures, different rules operate. For example, in Muslim cultures, people of the same sex hug, but people of the opposite sex do not. In Latin America, South America, and the Mediterranean, people are more likely to hug (and perhaps kiss on the cheek) than are Northern Europeans, Asians, and many from the United States. Given the great Hispanic influence on the United States today, it's probable that the hug-kiss will grow in general popularity. Asians are more reluctant to extend their hands and more often bow, with lower bows required when people of lower status meet someone of higher status.

At the same time that you shake hands, the other person will likely respond similarly, "I'm Carol Taylor from computer science." At this point, you would probably then talk about the event that you're both attending. If this is a potentially romantic situation, then this might be followed by a compliment, nothing too personal at this point, for example, "I saw you and thought there's a friendly face and someone I can relate to."

Throughout this brief introduction, continue to give your full attention to the other person. Be ready to listen more than speak and be ready to use all the other interpersonal skills discussed throughout this text.

Introducing Another Person   The other half of making introductions is to introduce one person to another. Let's say you're with Jack and bump into Jill who stops to talk. Because they don't know each other, it's your job to introduce them. Generally, it's best to do this simply but with enough detail to provide a context for further interaction. It might go something like this:

> Jill Williams, this is Jack Smith, who works with me at XYZ as marketing manager. I went to college with Jill and, if I'm not mistaken, she has just returned from Hawaii.

With this introduction, Jack and Jill can say something to each other based on the information provided in this brief (32-word) introduction. They can talk about working at XYZ, what it's like being a marketing manager, what Jill majored in, what Hawaii is like,

Table 8.4   Six Steps to an Effective Handshake

Dos	Don'ts
Make eye contact at the beginning and maintain it throughout the handshake.	Look away from the person or down at the floor or at your shaking hand.
Smile and otherwise signal positiveness.	Appear static or negative. You shake hands not just with your hands but with your whole body.
Extend your entire right hand.	Extend just your fingers or your left hand.
Grasp the other person's hand firmly but without discomforting pressure.	Grasp the other person's fingers as if you really don't want to shake hands but you're making a gesture to be polite.
Pump three times for about 3 to 4 seconds.	Give the person a "dead fish." Be careful that the other person's pumping doesn't lead you to withdraw your own pumping.
Release grasp while still maintaining eye contact.	Hold grasp for an overly long time or release too early.

what Jill did in Hawaii, and so on. If you simply said, "Jill, this is Jack" there would be almost nothing for Jack and Jill to talk about.

Also, if you know that the two people have something in common, you might mention this—for example, Jack is also a native New Yorker or Jill is also a marathon runner. This will help to ease the communication between Jack and Jill, and is likely to make the interaction more meaningful and satisfying. If you're unsure about what to reveal in your introduction, it's best to leave it out. The safest policy is to include only obviously public information. Avoid repeating things either of the individuals might have disclosed to you in confidence or that might be kept hidden from outsiders. Introducing Jack as "soon to be single" may reveal more than Jack would like.

When one of the people being introduced has a right hand that is disabled in some way, the general rule is that if one person shakes hands with other people in the group, he or she should also shake hands with the person who has a disability. The person with a disabled right hand is free to use the left hand in most cultures, although in some cultures the left hand is considered unclean.

As you can imagine, cultural differences may create intercultural difficulties and misunderstandings. For example, if you shake hands in a culture that hugs and kisses, you may appear standoffish. If you hug and kiss in a culture that is used to shaking hands, you may seem presumptuous and overly friendly.

Generally, a man is introduced to a woman rather than the woman to the man. Similarly, the lower ranking person—say, in a business organization, in the military, or in a police department—is introduced to the higher-ranking person. When the people are of opposite sex, rank trumps gender—the lower ranking person, regardless of gender, is introduced to the one of higher rank.

The best advice is to watch what the people of the culture you're in do and try to do likewise. At the same time, don't get upset if members of other cultures unknowingly "violate" your own culture's rituals. After all, one ritual is no more inherently logical or correct than any other.

Making Excuses

Excuses are explanations that are designed to reduce any negative reactions to what you've said or done; the objective is to maintain your positive image (Snyder, 1984; Snyder, Higgins, & Stucky, 1983). Excuses are especially appropriate when you say or are accused of saying something that runs counter to what is expected, sanctioned, or considered "right" by the people with whom you're in conversation. Ideally, you hope, the excuse will lessen the negative impact of your message.

The major motives for excuse making seem to be to maintain your self-esteem and to project a positive image of yourself to others. Excuses also represent an effort to reduce stress: you may feel that if you can offer an excuse—especially a good one that is accepted by those around you—it will reduce the negative reaction and the subsequent stress that accompanies a poor performance.

Excuses also may enable you to maintain effective interpersonal relationships after some negative behavior. For example, after criticizing a friend's behavior and observing his or her negative reaction to your criticism, you might offer an excuse such as, "I'm really exhausted. I'm just not thinking straight." Excuses enable you to place your messages—even your possible failures—in a more favorable light.

Types of Excuses   Different researchers have classified excuses into various categories (Cody & Dunn, 2007; Scott & Lyman, 1968). One of the best typologies classifies excuses into three main types (Snyder, 1984):

- *I didn't do it.* Here you deny that you have done what you're being accused of. You may then bring up an alibi to prove you couldn't have done it, or perhaps you may accuse another person of doing what you're being blamed for ("I never said that" or "I wasn't even near the place when it happened").

- *It wasn't so bad.* Here you admit to doing it but claim the offense was not really so bad or perhaps that there was justification for the behavior ("I only padded the expense account, and even then only modestly" or "Sure, I hit him, but he was asking for it").

- *Yes, but.* Here you claim that extenuating circumstances accounted for the behavior, for example, that you weren't in control of yourself at the time or that you didn't intend to do what you did ("I was too upset to think" or "I never intended to hurt him; I was actually trying to help").

Good and Bad Excuses   The most important question for most people is what makes a good excuse and what makes a bad excuse (Slade, 1995; Snyder, 1984). Good excuse makers use excuses in moderation; bad excuse makers rely on excuses too often. Good excuse makers accept responsibility for their failures and avoid blaming others, while bad excuse makers won't acknowledge their mistakes and are quick to pass the blame. Excuse makers who accept responsibility will be perceived as more credible, competent, and likeable than those who deny responsibility (Dunn & Cody, 2000).

What makes one excuse effective and another ineffective varies from one culture to another and depends on factors already discussed, such as the culture's individualism–collectivism, its power distance, the values it places on assertiveness, and various other cultural tendencies (Tata, 2000). At least in the United States, however, researchers seem to agree that the best excuses in interpersonal communication contain four or five elements (Coleman, 2002; Slade, 1995):

1. You demonstrate that you understand the problem and that your partner's feelings are legitimate and justified. Avoid minimizing the issue or your partner's feelings ("It was only $100; you're overreacting," "I was only two hours late," or "It was only one time").

2. You acknowledge your responsibility. If you did something wrong, avoid qualifying your responsibility ("I'm sorry *if* I did anything wrong") or expressing a lack of sincerity ("Okay, I'm sorry; it's obviously my fault—*again*"). On the other hand, if you can demonstrate that you had no control over what happened and therefore cannot be held responsible, your excuse is likely to be highly persuasive (Heath, Stone, Darley, & Grannemann, 2003).

3. You acknowledge your own displeasure at what you did; you make it clear that you're not happy with yourself for your actions.

4. You make it clear that your misdeed will never happen again.

5. Some researchers include a fifth step, which is actually an apology. Here you would express your sorrow or regret and perhaps ask forgiveness for what you did.

Apologizing

An **apology** is an expression of regret or sorrow for having said or done something that you shouldn't have. Often the apology is blended with the excuse—"I didn't realize how fast I was driving" (the excuse); "I'm really sorry" (the apology). The most basic of all apologies is simply, "I'm sorry." In popular usage, the apology includes some admission of wrongdoing on the part of the person making the apology. Sometimes the wrongdoing is acknowledged explicitly ("I'm sorry I lied") and sometimes only by implication ("I'm sorry you're so upset"). In many cases, the apology also includes a request for forgiveness and some assurance that the behavior won't be repeated ("Please forgive my lateness; it won't happen again").

According to the Harvard Business School Working Knowledge website (http://hbswk.hbs.edu/archive/3481.html), apologies are useful for two main reasons: (1) to help repair relationships and (2) to repair the reputation of the wrongdoer. If you do something wrong in your relationship, for example, an apology will help you

Apologizing

Research finds that women report apologizing more than do men (Schumann & Ross, 2010). Additional research finds that apologies by men are more effective than apologies by women (Walfisch, Van Dijk, & Kark, 2013). One reason for these differences seems to be that men feel that fewer things require an apology than do women and so apologize less. Therefore, when men do apologize, it's more effective because it happens less often. *What other possible explanations might you advance for these gender differences?*

repair the relationship with your partner and perhaps reduce the level of conflict. At the same time, however, realize that other people know about your behavior and an apology will help improve their image of you.

An effective apology, like an effective excuse, must be crafted for the specific situation. Effective apologies to a long-time lover, to a parent, or to a new supervisor are likely to be very different because the individuals and your relationships are different. Similarly, apologies vary greatly from one culture to another (Jandt, 2017). Therefore, the first rule of an effective apology is to take into consideration the uniqueness of the situation—the people, context, cultural rules, relationship, specific wrongdoing—for which you might want to apologize.

Some Dos for Effective Apologies   Here are some general guidelines for effective apologies. As with all communication guidelines, these need to be adjusted to the unique situation.

- *Admit wrongdoing.* Admit wrongdoing if indeed wrongdoing occurred. Accept responsibility. Own your own actions; don't try to pass them off as the work of someone else. Instead of "Smith drives so slow; it's a wonder I'm only 30 minutes late," say "I should have taken traffic into consideration." This admission of wrongdoing, research finds, is the most important component of an effective apology (Lewick, Polin, & Lount, 2016).
- *Be apologetic.* Say (and mean) "I'm sorry" or "What I did was wrong."
- *Be specific.* State in specific rather than general terms what you've done. Instead of "I'm sorry for what I did," say "I'm sorry for getting drunk at the party and flirting with everyone."
- *Express your understanding.* Express understanding of how the other person feels, and acknowledge the legitimacy of these feelings. For example, "You have every right to be angry; I should have called."
- *Express your regret.* Express your regret that this has created a problem for the other person: "I'm sorry I made you miss your appointment."
- *Offer to correct your behavior.* Offer to correct the problem (whenever this is possible), "I'm sorry I didn't clean up the mess I made; I'll do it now."
- *Give reassurance.* Give assurance that this will not happen again. Say, quite simply, "It won't happen again" or better and more specifically, "I won't be late again."

Some Don'ts for Effective Apologies   At the same time that you follow the suggestions for crafting an effective apology, try to avoid these common don'ts:

- *Don't apologize needlessly.* Don't apologize when it isn't necessary.
- *Don't try to justify your behavior.* Avoid trying to justify your behavior by mentioning that everyone does it, for example, "Everyone leaves work early on Friday."
- *Don't minimize your role.* Avoid minimizing your wrongdoing by saying that the other person has done something equally wrong. "So I play poker; you play the lottery."
- *Don't accuse others.* Don't accuse the other person of contributing to the problem. "I should have known you're overly anxious about receiving the figures exactly at 9 A.M."

- *Don't minimize other's feelings.* Avoid minimizing the hurt that this may have caused. Avoid comments such as "So the figures arrived a little late. What's the big deal?"
- *Don't include excuses with the apology.* Avoid combinations such as "I'm sorry the figures are late, but I had so much other work to do." An excuse often negates the apology by saying, in effect, "I'm really not sorry because there was good reason for what I did, but I'm saying 'I'm sorry' to cover all my bases and to make this uncomfortable situation go away."
- *Don't apologize via e-mail.* Generally, it's preferable to use a more personal mode of communication—face-to-face or phone, for example. It's more difficult, but it's more effective. (This rule applies *unless* the wrongdoing was originally committed in e-mail or if e-mail is your only or main form of communication).

Asking for a Favor

One of the most difficult of all conversational tasks is to ask someone for a favor. Of course, it depends on the favor and on the relationship you have with the person from whom you want the favor. If it's a close friend and the favor is relatively easy to perform, there is little difficulty and little conversational awkwardness. If the favor is to

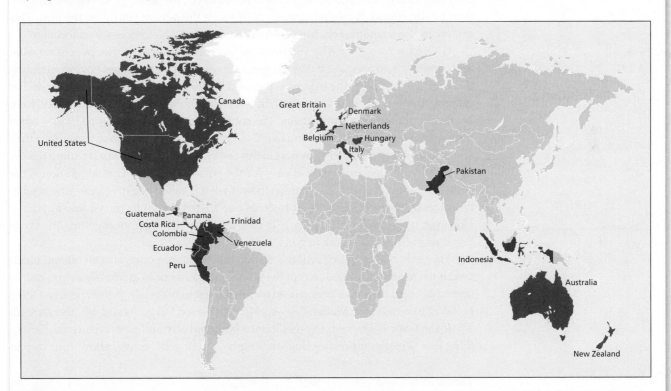

THE CULTURAL MAP Apologies

Apologies are admissions of responsibility for something you did and generally a request to be forgiven. The frequency with which people apologize, however, can depend on their culture.

These countries are among the most strongly affiliated with individualism, making apologies less important. High individualist cultures do not concern themselves with ill-feeling among the group as often as high collectivist cultures.

These countries are among the most strongly affiliated with collectivism, making apologies especially important in their emphasis on peaceful relationships, cohesiveness, and getting along with others.

How would you describe the last few apologies you heard or used yourself? Were they successful? If so, what made the apologies effective or ineffective? Were they culturally influenced?

a superior, say a work supervisor, and the favor would be difficult or time-consuming to perform, there would be much difficulty and much conversational awkwardness. Asking a total stranger poses still other problems.

Yet, despite these many differences, some general suggestions may be offered. So, how do you ask for a favor? Here are a few steps (also see Table 8.5).

- *Select an appropriate communication context.* Consider the time, place, and medium of communication—at the very least. Is this the appropriate time? Is this the appropriate place? Is this the most appropriate channel (email, Facebook, phone call, face to face)? Each has advantages and disadvantages.
- *Give appropriate feedforward.* Tell the person you need to ask for a favor. Avoid overly long feedforwards where you talk all around the intended favor but take too long to get to the point. Don't procrastinate.
- *Ask for the favor.* Be honest about what you're asking. Avoid the annoying ploy of asking for a small favor and then when that is granted ask for something more: for example, asking for a loan of $20, getting it, and then before you leave, asking if another $20 would be possible. This may actually be effective in getting you $40—perhaps even more effective than asking for the $40 right at the start. Yet, it seems a bit sneaky and underhanded and is not likely to work a second time.

Some writers would argue that somewhere along the process of asking for a favor, you compliment the potential favor-giver. Again, this is likely to prove effective. People respond very favorably to flattery, even when that flattery is perceived to be strategically motivated—in this case to get the favor. And yet, this strategy too seems a bit less than totally ethical. A related strategy is to touch the person gently on the arm. This gesture is also a compliment but one that communicates a closeness, a connection.

Give some reason for why you need the favor. This strategy works; people are more apt to comply with a request if they are given some reason for it. Studies have even shown that they will comply if the request is prefaced by a reason that doesn't make sense. For example, in one study a confederate of the researcher broke into a line of people who were waiting to photocopy various items. The confederate was offered less resistance when the request was phrased something like: *Can I get ahead; I have to photocopy something* than when no reason was offered—even, as in this case, when the reason wasn't really a reason.

Provide an easy exit; make it easy for the person to refuse. This suggestion is the polite way to go. It enables the person to save what is called negative face—the need to be autonomous, to have the right to do as one wishes, to not be forced into anything. However, it may well be ineffective. In fact, it's likely to hinder your getting the favor. Yet, it seems the ethical way to go.

The other half of this equation is responding to the response, also an often-difficult task. If the request is refused, accept the refusal graciously or as graciously as you can. In some cases, repeating your urgent need for this request may actually prove effective. Often, however, it damages the relationship—making one person feel guilty and the other rejected.

If the favor is granted, express thanks both verbally and nonverbally. Say something like "I really appreciate this" or simply "thank you," Smile, allow your face to

Table 8.5 Asking for a Favor

Conversation stage	For example:
Opening; you establish contact by phone, social media, face to face.	Hi, Pat, this is Chris. Hello, Pat. How you doing?
Feedforward; you state the need.	I need to ask a favor.
Business; you explain the reason for the favor.	You see, I lost at the tables, yada, yada, yada
Feedback, being especially careful to preserve the other's negative face so offer an out	If you can't do this, I totally understand.
Closing	Can you help me out?

express your satisfaction, and perhaps shake hands, hug, or kiss—depending on the request and your relationship.

In addition to expressing thanks you might also explain how this is going to help you. Something simple is best: *This will save me paying a large penalty* or *Now I'll be able to buy that program I need.*

If appropriate—as in the loan of money—a promise to pay it back should accompany the acceptance. It should also accompany the request, of course. If the favor is not one that involves a clear repayment, then it may help to offer to do the same on another occasion or in some way show that you are prepared and willing to reciprocate.

Express thanks again.

Complimenting

A **compliment** is a message of praise, flattery, or congratulations. The compliment functions like a kind of interpersonal glue; it's a way of relating to another person with positiveness and immediacy. It's also a conversation starter, "I like your watch; may I ask where you got it?"

Another important purpose of compliments is to influence the other person. An obvious case is when you give a person a compliment in expectation that you will also be complimented in turn. But compliments have also been shown to influence other types of behaviors. For example, when food servers complimented diners on their menu selections, they earned higher tips than when they didn't express such simple compliments (Seiter & Weger, 2010). In another study, young women who were complimented on their physical appearance complied with a young man's request to have a drink with him significantly more often than those who were not so complimented (Guéguen, Fischer-Lokou, & Lamy, 2013).

Compliments can be unqualified or qualified. The unqualified compliment is a message that is purely positive. "Your paper was just great, an A." The qualified message is not entirely positive: "Your paper was great, an A; if not for a few problems, it would have been an A+." You might also give a qualified compliment by qualifying your own competence; for example, "That song you wrote sounded great, but I really don't know anything about music."

A **backhanded compliment** is really not a compliment at all; it's usually an insult masquerading as a compliment. For example, you might give a backhanded compliment if you say, "That sweater takes away from your pale complexion; it makes you look less washed out" (it compliments the color of the sweater but criticizes the person's complexion), or "Looks like you've finally lost a few pounds; am I right?" (It compliments a slimmer appearance but points out that the person is overweight.) Compliments are sometimes difficult to give and even more difficult to respond to without discomfort or embarrassment. Fortunately, there are easy-to-follow guidelines.

Giving a Compliment   As with all of these everyday conversations, compliments need to be tailored to the specific situation. Nevertheless, here are a few suggestions for giving a compliment that should prove effective in a wide variety of circumstances:

- *Be real and honest.* Say what you mean and refrain from giving compliments you don't believe in. They'll likely sound insincere.
- *Compliment in moderation.* A compliment that is too extreme (say, for example, "That's the best decorated apartment I've ever seen in my life") may be viewed as dishonest. Similarly, don't compliment at every possible occasion; if you do, your compliments will seem too easy to win and not really meaningful.

- *Be totally complimentary.* Avoid qualifying your compliments. If you hear yourself giving a compliment and then adding a "but" or a "however," stop and rethink what you are going to say. Many people will remember the qualification rather than the compliment, and the qualified compliment will instead feel like a criticism.
- *Be specific.* Direct your compliment at something specific rather than something general. Instead of saying, "I liked your speech" you might say "I liked your speech—the introduction gained my attention immediately and you held it throughout." Avoid ambiguous comments that may be taken the wrong way (Whitbourne, 2013b).
- *Be personal.* Personalize the compliment by referring to your own feelings—"Your song really moved me; it made me recall so many good times"—but not personal about the other person—"Your hair looks so natural; is that a weave or a toupee?" At the same time, avoid any compliment that can be misinterpreted as overly sexual. Depending on your relationship with the person, you might use her or his name; people like to hear their name spoken and doubly so when it's associated with a compliment.
- *Compliment accomplishments.* Some interpersonal watchers recommend that you compliment people for their accomplishments rather than for who they are or for things over which they have no control. So, for example, you would compliment people for their clear reports, their poetry, their problem solving, their tact, and so on, and you would not compliment someone for being attractive or having beautiful green eyes.

Receiving a Compliment   In receiving a compliment, people generally take either one of two options: denial or acceptance. Many people deny the compliment ("It's nice of you to say, but I know I was terrible"), minimize it ("It isn't like I wrote the great American novel; it was just an article that no one will read"), change the subject ("So, where should we go for dinner?"), or say nothing. Each of these responses denies the legitimacy of the compliment. Accepting the compliment seems the much better alternative. An acceptance might consist simply of (1) a smile with eye contact (avoid looking at the floor); (2) a simple "thank you"; and (3) if appropriate, a personal reflection where you explain (very briefly) the meaning of the compliment and why it's important to you (for example, "I really appreciate your comments; I worked really hard on the project and it's great to hear it was effective").

Advising

Advice is best viewed as a process of giving another person a suggestion for thinking or behaving, usually to effect a change. In many cases, it will take the form of a suggestion to solve a problem. For example, you might advise a friend to change his or her way of looking at a broken love affair, a financial situation, or a career path. Or you might advise someone to do something such as start dating again, invest in certain stocks, or go back to school to complete a degree. Sometimes, the advice serves to encourage the person to stick with what she or he is currently thinking or doing—for example, to stay with Pat despite the difficulties, to hold the stocks the person already has, or to continue on his or her current career path.

One of the most important types of advice is what we might call **meta-advice**, advice about advice. At least three types of meta-advice can be identified:

- *To explore options and choices.* This type of meta-advice focuses on helping the person explore the available options. For example, if a friend asks what he or she should do about never having a date, you might help your friend explore the available options (such as dating websites, speed dating, or singles groups) and the advantages and disadvantages of each.
- *To seek expert advice.* If confronted with a request for advice about a subject you know little about, the best advice is often to seek advice from someone who is an

expert in the field. When a friend asks what to do about a persistent cough, the best advice seems to be the meta-advice to "talk to your doctor."

- *To delay a decision.* If asked for advice about a decision that doesn't have to be made immediately, one form of meta-advice would be to delay the decision while additional information is collected. For example, if your advice seeker has two weeks to decide on a whether or not to take a job with XYZ Company, meta-advice would suggest that the decision be delayed while the company is researched more thoroughly.

Meta-advice is one of the safest types of advice to give. When you meta-advise to explore options more thoroughly, you're not so much giving advice as helping the advice seeker to collect the information needed to make his or her own decision.

Giving Advice   The following are some suggestions for giving advice effectively:

- *Listen.* This is the first rule for advice giving. Listen to the person's thoughts and feelings to discern what he or she really wants. The person who says, for example, "I just don't know what to do" may be requesting support and active listening rather than advice. The person may simply want to vent in the presence of a friend. The person who says, "What do you think I can do to make the room look better?" might be looking for praise. Rather than advice about what to change, this person may want the response to be, "It's perfect as it is. I wouldn't touch a thing." If you're in doubt about what the person is seeking, ask.

- *Empathize.* Try to feel what the other person is feeling. Perhaps you might recall similar situations you were in or similar emotions you experienced. Think about the importance of the issue to the person and, in general, try to put yourself in his or her position.

- *Be tentative.* If you give advice, give it with the qualifications it requires. The advice seeker has a right to know how sure (or unsure) you are of the advice or what evidence (or lack of evidence) you have that the advice will work.

- *Offer options.* When appropriate, offer several options and give the pros and cons of each: "If you do X, then A and B are likely to follow." Even better, allow the advice seeker to identify the possible consequences of each option.

- *Ensure understanding.* Often people seeking advice are emotionally upset and may not remember everything in the conversation. Seek feedback after giving advice by saying, for example, "Does that make sense?" or "Is my suggestion workable?"

- *Keep the interaction confidential.* People often seek advice about very personal matters. It's best to keep such conversations confidential, even if you're not explicitly asked to do so.

- *Avoid* **should** *statements.* People seeking advice still ultimately have to make their own decisions. It's better to say, "You *might* do X" or "You *could* do Y" rather than "You *should* do Z." Avoid demanding—or even implying—that the person has to follow your advice. This attacks the person's negative face, his or her need for autonomy.

Receiving Advice   Here are a few suggestions for receiving advice:

- If you ask for advice, then accept what the person says. You owe it to the advice giver to listen to and consider the advice, even if you decide not to follow it.

INTERPERSONAL CHOICE POINT
Unwanted Advice

You want to explore some ideas you have for a new business venture and want to discuss some ideas with one of your close friends. Unfortunately, this close friend has the annoying habit of trying to give you advice that you don't want and only depresses you. *What would you do to deal with this problem?*

- **a.** Preface your remarks by explaining that you don't want advice.
- **b.** Explain the reasons for not wanting advice.
- **c.** "Let's avoid telling each other what we *should* or *should not* do."
- **d.** Explain the pattern of advice giving and ask that it stop.
- **e.** Other

- Resist the temptation to retaliate or criticize the advice giver, even if you didn't ask for advice. Instead of responding with "Well, your hair doesn't look that great either," consider if the advice has any merit. If you decide to reject the advice, ask yourself why someone would think you were in need of such advice in the first place.
- Interact with the advice. Talk about it with the advice giver. A process of asking and answering questions is likely to produce added insight into the problem.
- Express your appreciation for the advice. It's often difficult to give advice. Showing the advice giver some gratitude in return is a good idea.

Responding to Advice   Responding appropriately to advice is often a difficult process. Here are some suggestions for making receiving advice more effective:

- Thank the person for the advice. After all, it's not easy offering advice. This will also ensure that the person will not be reluctant to offer advice in the future.
- Let the other person know that you are thoughtfully considering their advice. Be careful not to indicate that you're rejecting the advice without due consideration.
- Use your active listening skills: paraphrase what the speaker has said, express understanding for what the speaker said, and ask questions (non-defensively) if there is anything you don't understand.
- Remember that you don't have to follow the advice, you just need to let the other person know that you appreciate the proposed help.

In each of these everyday conversations, you have choices in terms of what you say and in terms of how you respond. Consider these choices mindfully, taking into consideration the variety of influencing factors discussed throughout this text and their potential advantages and disadvantages. Once you lay out your choices in this way, you'll be more likely to select effective ones.

Table 8.6 offers a brief summary of the types of everyday conversations.

Table 8.6 In a Nutshell Effective Everyday Conversations

Everyday Conversations	Effectiveness Characteristics
Making small talk	Small talk about noncontroversial topics and be brief.
Making introductions	When introducing yourself, make eye contact and smile. When introducing others, the lower rank is introduced to the higher rank, the man to the woman.
Making excuses	Demonstrate understanding, responsibility, personal displeasure, and a commitment to it not happening again.
Apologizing	Be apologetic (really) and specific, express understanding and a commitment to it not happening again, omit excuses, and express the apology through the appropriate channel.
Asking a favor	Select the right channel, give appropriate feedforward, ask for the favor.
Complimenting	Be honest, compliment in moderation, avoid qualifying compliments, be specific and personal.
Advising	Listen, empathize, be tentative, ensure understanding, maintain confidentiality, and avoid *should*.

Summary

This chapter reviewed the principles of conversation, the nature of conversational disclosure, and some everyday conversations such as small talk, introducing people, making excuses, apologizing, asking for a favor, giving and receiving compliments, and giving and receiving advice.

Principles of Conversation

8.1 Describe the major principles of conversation.

1. The principle of process emphasizes that conversation is a process rather than an act; it's a process with an opening, feedforward, business, feedback, and closing.

2. The principle of cooperation emphasizes that conversation proceeds with the assumption that each person is cooperating in the process.

3. The principle of politeness is designed to emphasize that there is a politeness dimension to conversation; some, probably most, are polite; others not so much.

4. The principle of dialogue emphasizes that conversation involves two involved people.

5. The principle of turn taking points to the most obvious aspect of conversation, namely, that it's essentially a process of exchanging speaking and listening turns.

Conversational Disclosure

8.2 Define *self-disclosure*, its potential rewards and dangers, and the guidelines for disclosing, responding to disclosures, and resisting the pressure to disclose.

6. Self-disclosure is revealing information about yourself to others—usually information that is normally hidden.

7. Self-disclosure is influenced by a variety of factors: who you are, your culture, your gender, your listeners, and your topic and channel.

8. Among the rewards of self-disclosure are self-knowledge, ability to cope, communication effectiveness, meaningfulness of relationships, and physiological health. Among the dangers are personal risks, relational risks, professional risks, and the fact that communication is irreversible; once something is said, you can't take it back.

9. In self-disclosing, consider your motivation, the appropriateness of the disclosure to the person and context, the emergence (or absence) of reciprocal disclosure from the other person, and the possible burdens that the self-disclosure might impose on others and on yourself.

10. In responding to the disclosures of others, listen effectively, support and reinforce the discloser, keep disclosures confidential, and don't use disclosures as weapons.

11. In some situations, you'll want to resist self-disclosing by being determined not to be pushed into it, being assertive and direct, or being indirect.

Everyday Conversations

8.3 Identify the guidelines for small talk; making introductions, excuses, and apologies; asking a favor; and giving and receiving compliments and advice.

12. Small talk is pervasive, noncontroversial, and often serves as a polite way of introducing one's self or a topic.

13. In introducing people, the lower-ranking individual is introduced to the higher ranking.

14. Excuses are explanations designed to lessen any negative implications of a message.

15. Apologies are expressions of regret or sorrow for having done what you did or for what happened.

16. Asking for a favor involves selecting the right channel, giving appropriate feedforward, and asking.

17. A compliment is a message of praise, flattery, or congratulations and often enables you to interact with positiveness and immediacy.

18. Advice—telling another person what he or she should do—can be specific or general (meta-advice).

Key Terms

advice	dialogue	phatic communication
apology	disinhibition effect	politeness
back-channeling cues	excuse	quality maxim
backhanded compliment	expressiveness	quantity maxim
compliment	gossip	reciprocity
conversation	interruptions	relation maxim
conversational maxims	manner maxim	self-disclosure
conversational turns	meta-advice	small talk
cooperation	monologue	

Interpersonal Relationship Stages, Communication, and Theories

Relationships start, grow, and sometimes end in vastly different ways. *Understanding relationship stages and theories will help you guide relationships in the desired trajectory.*

Chapter Topics

Relationship Stages

Relationship Communication

Relationship Theories

Learning Objectives

9.1 Describe the process of relationship development—from contact through (possible) dissolution.

9.2 Explain the role of communication at the different relationship stages.

9.3 Summarize the major theories that explain relationship development, deterioration, and repair (attraction, relationship rules, relationship dialectics, social exchange, equity, and politeness).

Contact with other human beings is so important that when you're deprived of it for long periods, depression sets in, self-doubt surfaces, and you may find it difficult to manage even the basics of daily life. Research shows clearly that the most important contributor to happiness—outranking money, job, and sex—is a close relationship with one other person (Freedman, 1978; Laroche & deGrace, 1997; Lu & Shih, 1997). The desire for relationships is universal; interpersonal relationships are important to men and to women, to gay men and lesbians and to heterosexuals, to young and to old (Huston & Schwartz, 1995).

A good way to begin the study of interpersonal relationships is by examining your relationship advantages and disadvantages and by asking yourself what your relationships (past, present, or those you look forward to) do for you. What are the advantages and the disadvantages? Focus on your own relationships in general (friendship, romantic, family, and work), or on one particular relationship (say, your life partner or your child or your best friend), on one type of relationship (say, friendship) and respond to the following statements by indicating whether or not your relationship(s) serve each of these functions.

You may wish to do this twice—once for your face-to-face relationships and once for your online relationships.

_____ 1. My relationships help to lessen my loneliness.
_____ 2. My relationships help me gain in self-knowledge and in self-esteem.
_____ 3. My relationships help enhance my physical and emotional health.
_____ 4. My relationships maximize my pleasures and minimize my pains.
_____ 5. My relationships help me to secure stimulation (intellectual, physical, and emotional).

Let's elaborate just a bit on each of these commonly accepted advantages of interpersonal communication.

1. One of the major benefits of relationships is that they help to lessen loneliness (Rokach, 1998; Rokach & Brock, 1995). They make you feel that someone cares, that someone likes you, that someone will protect you, that someone ultimately will love you.

2. Through contact with others you learn about yourself and see yourself from different perspectives and in different roles—as a child or parent, as a coworker, as a manager, as a best friend, for example. Healthy interpersonal relationships help enhance self-esteem and self-worth. Simply having a friend or romantic partner (at least most of the time) makes you feel desirable and worthy.

3. Research consistently shows that interpersonal relationships contribute significantly to physical and emotional health (Goleman, 1995a; Pennebacker, 1991; Rosen, 1998; Rosengren, Orth-Gomer, Wedel, & Wilhelmsen, 1993) and to personal happiness (Berscheid & Reis, 1998). Without close interpersonal relationships, you're more likely to become depressed—and this depression, in turn, contributes significantly to physical illness. Isolation, in fact, contributes as much to mortality as high blood pressure, high cholesterol, obesity, smoking, or lack of physical exercise (Goleman 1995a).

4. The most general function served by interpersonal relationships, and the function that encompasses all the others, is that of maximizing pleasure and minimizing pain. Your good friends, for example, will make you feel even better about your good fortune and less hurt when you're confronted with hardships.

5. Just as plants are heliotropic and orient themselves to light, humans are stimulotropic and orient themselves to sources of stimulation (Davis, 1973). Human contact is one of the best ways to secure this stimulation—intellectual, physical, and emotional. Even an imagined relationship seems better than none.

Now, respond to these sentences as you did to the sentences above.

____ 6. My relationships put uncomfortable pressure on me to expose my vulnerabilities.

____ 7. My relationships increase my obligations.

____ 8. My relationships prevent me from developing other relationships.

____ 9. My relationships scare me because they may be difficult to dissolve.

____ 10. My relationships hurt me.

These statements express what most people would consider disadvantages of interpersonal relationships.

6. Close relationships put pressure on you to reveal yourself and to expose your vulnerabilities. While this is generally worthwhile in the context of a supporting and caring relationship, it may backfire if the relationship deteriorates and these weaknesses are used against you.

7. Close relationships increase your obligations to other people, sometimes to a great extent. Your time is no longer entirely your own. And although you enter relationships to spend more time with these special people, you also incur time (and perhaps financial) obligations with which you may not be happy.

8. Close relationships can lead you to abandon other relationships. Sometimes the other relationship involves someone you like, but your partner can't stand. More often, however, it's simply a matter of time and energy; relationships take a lot of both, and you have less to give to these other and less intimate relationships.

9. The closer your relationships, the more emotionally difficult they are to dissolve—a feeling which may be uncomfortable for some people. If a relationship is deteriorating, you may feel distress or depression. In some cultures, for example, religious pressures may prevent married couples from separating. And if lots of money is involved, dissolving a relationship can often mean giving up the fortune you've spent your life accumulating.

10. And, of course, your partner may break your heart. Your partner may leave you—against all your pleading and promises. Your hurt will be in proportion to how much you care and need your partner. If you care a great deal, you're likely to experience great hurt. If you care less, the hurt will be less—it's one of life's little ironies.

Relationship Stages

9.1 Describe the process of relationship development—from contact through (possible) dissolution.

It's useful to look at interpersonal relationships as created and constructed by the individuals. That is, in any interpersonal relationship—say, between Pat and Chris—there are actually several relationships: (1) the relationship that Pat sees, (2) the relationship as Chris sees it, (3) the relationship that Pat wants and is striving for, and (4) the relationship that Chris wants. And, of course, there are the many relationships that friends and relatives see and that they reflect back in their communications. For example, the relationship that Pat's mother, who dislikes Chris, sees and reflects in her communication with Pat and Chris is very likely to influence Pat and Chris in some ways. And then there's the relationship that a dispassionate researcher/observer would see. Viewed in this way, there are many interpersonal relationships in any interpersonal relationship.

This is not to say that there is no *real* relationship; it's just to say that there are many real relationships. And because of these differently constructed relationships, people often disagree about a wide variety of issues and evaluate the relationship very differently. Regularly, on *Jerry Springer* and *Maury,* you see couples who view their relationship very differently. The first guest thinks all is going well until the second guest comes on and explodes—often identifying long-held dissatisfactions and behaviors that shock the partner.

One of the most obvious characteristics of relationships is that they occur in stages, moving from initial contact to greater intimacy and sometimes to dissolution. You and another person don't become intimate friends immediately upon meeting. Rather, you build an intimate relationship gradually, through a series of steps or stages. The same is true of most relationships (Mongeau & Henningsen, 2008).

The six-stage model presented in Figure 9.1 describes the main stages in most relationships. As shown in the figure, the six stages of relationships are contact, involvement, intimacy, deterioration, repair, and dissolution, with each stage having an early and a late phase. The arrows represent the movements that take place

Figure 9.1 A Six-Stage Model of Relationships

Because relationships differ so widely, it's best to think of any relationship model as a tool for talking about relationships rather than as a specific map that indicates how you move from one relationship position to another. As you review this figure, consider, for example, if you feel that other steps or stages would further explain what goes on in relationship development.

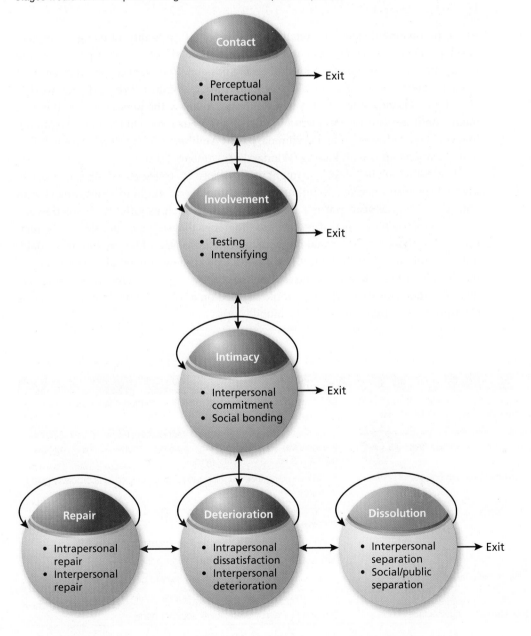

as relationships change. Let's first examine the six stages, and then we'll look at the types of relationship movements.

Contact

At the initial phase of the **contact** stage, there is some kind of *perceptual contact*—you see, hear, read a message from, view a photo or video, read a person's profile, or perhaps smell the person. From this you form a mental and physical picture—gender, approximate age, beliefs and values, height, and so on. After this perception, there is usually *interactional contact*. Here the contact is superficial and relatively impersonal. This is the stage at which you exchange basic information that is preliminary to any, more intense involvement ("Hello, my name is Joe"), or you might send someone a request to be a friend. Here you initiate interaction ("May I join you?") and engage in invitational communication ("Can I buy you a latté?"). The contact stage is the time of "first impressions." According to some researchers, it's at this stage—within the first four minutes of initial interaction—that you decide whether you want to pursue the relationship (Zunin & Zunin, 1972).

Involvement

At the **involvement** stage of a relationship, a sense of mutuality, of being connected, develops. Here you experiment and try to learn more about the other person. At the initial phase of involvement, a kind of *testing* goes on. You want to see whether your initial judgment proves reasonable. So you may ask questions: "Where do you work?" "What are you majoring in?" If you want to get to know the person even better, you might continue your involvement by intensifying your interaction and by beginning to reveal yourself, though in a preliminary way. Another way of testing the suitability of the relationship is with kissing (Wlodarski & Dunbar, 2013).

In a dating relationship, you might use a variety of strategies to help you move to the next stage and perhaps to intimacy. For example, you might increase contact with your partner; give your partner tokens of affection such as gifts, cards, or flowers; increase your own personal attractiveness; do things that suggest intensifying the relationship, such as flirting or making your partner jealous; and become more sexually intimate (Tolhuizen, 1989). Table 9.1 provides a look at a few nonverbal and verbal ways that people flirt face-to-face. Some cautions to observe are also included. Try rewriting these flirtatious messages as they would be used on a social media dating site such as eHarmony, OK Cupid, or any of the mobile apps.

Table 9.1 Nine Ways to Flirt

Flirtatious Messages	Cautions
Maintain an open posture; face the person; lean forward; tilt your head to one side (to get a clearer view of the person you're interested in).	Don't move so close that you make it uncomfortable for the other person.
Make eye contact and maintain it for a somewhat longer than normal time; raise your eyebrows to signal interest; blink and move your eyes more than usual; wink.	Be careful that your direct eye contact doesn't come off as leering or too invasive, and avoid too much blinking—people will think you have something wrong with your eyes.
Smile and otherwise display positive emotions with your facial expressions.	Avoid overdoing this; laughing too loud at lame jokes is probably going to appear phony.
Touch the person's hand.	Be careful that the touching is appropriate and not perceived as intrusive.
Mirror the other's behaviors.	Don't overdo it. It will appear as if you're mimicking.
Introduce yourself.	Avoid overly long or overly cute introductions.
Ask a question (most commonly, "Is this seat taken?").	Avoid sarcasm or joking; these are likely to be misunderstood.
Compliment ("great jacket").	Avoid any compliment that might appear too intimate.
Be polite; respect the individual's positive and negative face needs.	But don't be overly polite; it will appear phony.

Intimacy

At the **intimacy** stage, you commit yourself still further to the other person and establish a relationship in which this individual becomes your best or closest friend, lover, or companion. Both the quantity and the quality of your interpersonal exchanges increase (Emmers-Sommer, 2004) and, of course, you also talk more and in greater detail about the relationship (Knobloch, Haunani, & Theiss, 2006). You also come to share each other's social networks—a practice followed by members of widely different cultures (Gao & Gudykunst, 1995). Your relationship satisfaction also increases with the move to this stage (Siavelis & Lamke, 1992).

The intimacy stage usually divides itself into two phases. In the *interpersonal commitment* phase the two people commit themselves to each other in a private way. In the *social bonding* phase the commitment is made public—perhaps to family and friends, perhaps to the public at large. Here you and your partner become a unit, an identifiable pair. Commitment is especially strong when individuals are satisfied with their relationship; it grows weaker as individuals become less satisfied (Hirofumi, 2003). Three types of commitment are often distinguished and can be identified from your answers to the following questions (Johnson, 1973, 1982, 1991; Knapp & Taylor, 1994; Knapp, Vangelisti, & Cauglin, 2014; Kurdek, 1995):

- *Do I have a desire to stay in this relationship?* Do I have a desire to keep this relationship going? How strong is this desire?
- *Do I have a moral obligation to stay in this relationship?* Did I make promises that I should keep?
- *Do I have to stay in this relationship?* Is it necessary for me to stay in this relationship?

All relationships are held together, in part, by commitment based on desire, obligation, or necessity, or on some combination of these factors. And the strength of the relationship, including its resistance to possible deterioration, is related to your degree of commitment. When a relationship shows signs of deterioration and yet there's a strong commitment to preserving it, you may well surmount the obstacles and reverse the process. For example, couples with high relationship commitment will avoid arguing about minor grievances and also will demonstrate greater supportiveness toward each other than will those with lower commitment (Roloff & Solomon, 2002). Similarly, those who have great commitment are likely to experience greater jealousy in a variety of situations (Rydell, McConnell, & Bringle, 2004). When commitment is weak and the individuals doubt that there are good reasons for staying together, the relationship deteriorates faster and more intensely.

Deterioration

The **relationship deterioration** stage is characterized by a weakening of the bonds between friends or lovers. The first phase of deterioration is usually *intrapersonal dissatisfaction*: you begin to experience personal dissatisfaction with everyday interactions and begin to view the future with your partner more negatively. If this dissatisfaction grows, you pass to the second phase, *interpersonal deterioration*. You withdraw and grow further and further apart. You share less of your free time. When you're together, there are more awkward silences, fewer disclosures, less physical contact, and a lack of psychological closeness. Conflicts become more common and their resolution more difficult. On social

VIEWPOINTS

Culture and Sexual Relationships

Some cultures consider sexual relationships to be undesirable outside marriage; others see sex as a normal part of intimacy and chastity as undesirable (Hatfield & Rapson, 1996). *How have your cultural beliefs and values influenced what you consider appropriate relationship and sexual behavior?*

network sites, the deterioration stage is perhaps seen most clearly in the decline in frequency of comments, pokes, and thumbs-up liking. And, in fact, research shows that high levels of social media usage are associated with relational problems for relatively new relationships (Clayton, Nagurney, & Smith, 2012).

This is also the stage at which you consider dissolving the relationship. You consider the pros and cons, the advantages and disadvantages. And here you seek the counsel of your face-to-face friends and your social media friends. And if you're still not sure what to do, there are websites that offer you suggestions.

In addition to the problems caused by relationships not meeting the needs the relationship was developed to serve in the first place, Table 9.2 presents some additional reasons for relationship deterioration. The preventives noted should not be taken to mean that all relationship partners should stay together; there are many good reasons for breaking up.

Repair

Some relationship partners, sensing deterioration, may pursue the **relationship repair** stage. Others, however, may progress—without stopping, without thinking—to dissolution. At the repair stage, you try to mend the relationship, to bring it back to an earlier, happier stage.

At the first repair phase, *intrapersonal repair,* you may analyze what went wrong and consider ways of solving your relational difficulties. You might, at this stage, consider changing your behaviors or perhaps changing your expectations of your partner. You might also evaluate the rewards of your relationship as it is now and the rewards to be gained if your relationship ended.

Should you decide that you want to repair your relationship, you might discuss this with your partner at the *interpersonal repair* phase—you might talk about the problems in the relationship, the changes you want to see, and perhaps what you are willing to do and what you want your partner to do. This is the stage of negotiating new agreements and new behaviors. You and your partner might try to repair your relationship by yourselves, or you might seek the advice of friends or family or perhaps go for professional counseling.

Table 9.2 Some Causes of Relationship Deterioration

Problems	Reasons	Preventive Strategies
Poor communication	Communication that is excessively critical, unsupportive, or disconfirming creates dissatisfaction that can easily lead to a breakdown in friendship, love, or family relationships.	Talk about your communication; voice your expectations.
Third-party relationships	When a person's goals cease to be met within the relationship, a new relationship may be pursued; if this new relationship serves the goals better, then the original relationship is likely to deteriorate.	Talk about needs openly, explaining what you want from the relationship and listening to what the other person wants.
Relationship changes	The development of incompatible attitudes, vastly different intellectual interests and abilities, or major goal changes may contribute to relationship deterioration.	Discuss changes as they develop and consider changes in your partner. If appropriate and possible, participate in the changes of the other.
Sex- and work-related problems	Problems within the relationship (for example, sex) or outside the relationship (for example, work) can put a strain on a relationship with the frequent result that other, more supportive relationships may be sought.	Discussing these problems with each other and/or with a therapist can help prevent them from escalating.
Financial difficulties	Money (in part because of its close association with power and control) often proves to be a cause of major problems as people settle into their relationship.	Discuss your attitudes and beliefs about money before entering a relationship.
Beliefs about relationships	If you and your partner hold widely different beliefs about, say, gender or financial expectations, then your relationship is more likely to experience instability and interpersonal distancing (Goodwin & Gaines, 2004).	Try to be more open-minded and flexible; differences do not have to lead to deterioration.

Dissolution

At the **relationship dissolution** stage, the bonds between the individuals are broken. In the beginning, dissolution usually takes the form of *interpersonal separation,* in which you may move into separate apartments and begin to lead lives apart from each other. If this separation proves acceptable and if the original relationship isn't repaired, you enter the phase of *social or public separation.* If the relationship is a marriage, this phase corresponds to divorce. Avoidance of each other and a return to being "single" are among the primary characteristics of dissolution. On Facebook, this would be the stage where you defriend the person and/or block that person from accessing your profile.

Dissolution is also the stage during which the ex-partners begin to look upon themselves as individuals rather than halves of a pair. They try to establish a new and different life, either alone or with another person. Some people, it's true, continue to live psychologically with a relationship that has already been dissolved; they frequent old meeting places, reread old love letters, daydream about all the good times, and fail to extricate themselves from a relationship that has died in every way except in their memory.

In cultures that emphasize continuity from one generation to the next—as in, say, China—interpersonal relationships are likely to be long-lasting and permanent. Those who maintain long-term relationships tend to be rewarded, and those who break relationships tend to be punished. But in cultures in which change is seen as positive—as in, say, the United States—interpersonal relationships are likely to be more temporary (Moghaddam, Taylor, & Wright, 1993). The rewards for long-term relationships and the punishments for broken relationships will be significantly less.

> ### INTERPERSONAL CHOICE POINT
> Ending the Relationship
>
> You want to break up your eight-month online (but very intense) romantic relationship. *How would you do this?*
>
> **a.** Send a Facebook message.
> **b.** Change your Facebook status.
> **c.** Talk face-to-face.
> **d.** Phone your decision.
> **e.** Other

Movement among the Stages

Relationships are not static; we move from one stage to another largely as a result of our interpersonal interactions. Three general kinds of movement may be identified: stage movement, relationship turning points, and relationship license.

Stage Movement   The six-stage model shown in Figure 9.1 illustrates the kinds of movement that take place in interpersonal relationships. In the model, you'll note three types of arrows:

- *Exit arrows* The *exit arrows* show that each stage offers the opportunity to exit the relationship. After saying "Hello" you can say "Goodbye" and exit. And, of course, you can end even the most intimate of relationships.

- *Vertical arrows* The *vertical arrows* between the stages represent the fact that you can move to another stage: either to a stage that is more intense (say, from involvement to intimacy) or to a stage that is less intense (say, from intimacy to deterioration).

- *Self-reflexive arrows* The *self-reflexive arrows*—the arrows that return to the beginning of the same level or stage—signify that any relationship may become stabilized at any point. You may, for example, continue to maintain a relationship at the intimate level without its deteriorating or going back to the less intense stage of involvement. Or you may remain at the "Hello, how are you?" stage—the contact stage—without getting any further involved.

As you can imagine, movement from one stage to another depends largely on your communication skills—for example, your abilities to initiate a relationship; to present yourself as likeable; to express affection; to self-disclose appropriately; and, when necessary, to dissolve the relationship with the least possible amount of acrimony

Negative Turning Points

Turning points are often positive,
as the examples in the text indicate,
but they can also be negative. For
example, the first realization that
a partner has been unfaithful, lied
about past history, or revealed
a debilitating condition would
likely be significant turning points
for many romantic relationships.
*What have been your experiences with
negative relationship turning points?*

(Dindia & Timmerman, 2003). These issues are covered in the last section of this chapter, Relationship Communication.

Turning Points   Movement through the various stages takes place both gradually and in leaps. Often, you progress from one stage to another gradually. You don't jump from contact to involvement to intimacy; rather, you progress gradually, a few degrees at a time. In addition to this gradual movement are relationship **turning points** (Baxter & Bullis, 1986). These are significant relationship events that have important consequences for the individuals and the relationship, and may turn its direction or trajectory. For example, a relationship that is progressing slowly might experience a rapid rise after the first date, the first kiss, the first sexual encounter, or the first meeting with the partner's child.

Turning points vary with culture. In some cultures, the first sexual experience is a major turning point; in others it's a minor progression in the normal dating process.

What constitutes a turning point will also vary with your relationship stage. For example, an expensive and intimate gift may be a turning point at the involvement or the repair stage, an ordinary event if you're at the intimate stage and such gifts are exchanged regularly, and an inappropriate gift if given too early in the relationship.

Relationship License Changes   Movement of a somewhat different type can be appreciated by looking at what is called the **relationship license**—the license or permission to break some relationship rule as a result of your relationship stage. As the relationship develops, so does the relationship license; as you become closer and approach the intimacy stage, you have greater permission to say and do things that you didn't have at the contact or involvement stage. The license becomes broader as the relationship develops and becomes more restrictive as the relationship deteriorates. For example, long-term friends or romantic couples (say, at the intimacy stage) may taste each other's food in a restaurant or may fix each other's clothing or pat each other on the rear. These are violations of rules that normally hold for non-intimates, for casual acquaintances, or for people in the initial stages of a relationship. In relationships that are deteriorating, the licenses become more limited or may be withdrawn entirely.

In some relationships, the license is reciprocal; each person's license is the same. In other relationships, it's nonreciprocal; one person has greater license than the other. For example, perhaps one person has license to come home at any time, but the other is expected to stay on schedule. Or one person has license to spend the couple's money without explanation, but the other has no such right. Or one perhaps has the right to be unfaithful, but the other doesn't. For example, in some cultures, men are expected to have intimate relationships with many women, whereas women are expected to have relationship only with a legally approved partner. In this case, a nonreciprocal license is built into the culture's rules.

Part of the art of relationship communication—as you move through the various stages—is to negotiate the licenses that you want without giving up the privacy you want to retain. This negotiation is almost never made explicit; most often it is accomplished nonverbally and in small increments. The license to touch intimately, for example, is likely to be arrived at through a series of touches that increase gradually, beginning with touching that is highly impersonal.

Table 9.3 provides a brief summary of relationship stages and movements.

Table 9.3   In a Nutshell   Relationship Stages and Movements

Stages	Contact: perceptual and interactional	First impressions are templates through which future contacts will be viewed.
	Involvement: testing and intensifying	The time of this stage varies greatly from one person to another.
	Intimacy: interpersonal commitment and social bonding	Intimacy means different things to different people; it's good to understand each other's meaning.
	Deterioration: intrapersonal dissatisfaction and interpersonal deterioration	Some relationships turn less satisfying and no longer serve the purpose for which it was developed.
	Repair: intrapersonal repair and interpersonal repair	Reversing the deterioration process involves rebuilding the positives and lessening the negatives.
	Dissolution: interpersonal separation and social/public separation	When a relationship becomes more unpleasant than pleasant, many choose to dissolve it.
Movements	Stage movements	Here you move up, down, or stay put.
	Turning points	These can be positive (moving the relationship toward intimacy) or negative (moving the relationship toward deterioration).
	Relationship license	Increases and decreases occur in the relationship license depending on whether the move is toward intimacy or away from intimacy.

ETHICS IN INTERPERSONAL COMMUNICATION

Your Obligation to Reveal Yourself

If you're in a close relationship, your influence on your partner is considerable, so you may have an obligation to reveal certain things about yourself. Conversely, you may feel that the other person—because he or she is so close to you—has an ethical obligation to reveal certain information to you.

At what point in a relationship—if any—do you feel you would have an ethical obligation to reveal each of the 10 items of information listed here? Visualize a relationship as existing on a continuum, from initial contact at 1 to extreme intimacy at 10, and use the numbers from 1 to 10 to indicate at what point you would feel your romantic partner or friend would have a right to know each type of information about you. If you feel you would never have the obligation to reveal this information, use 0.

At what point do you have an ethical obligation to reveal the following information to a romantic partner (say, of a year or two) and a close friend?

Romantic Partner   **Friend**

_____   _____   Age

_____   _____   History of family genetic disorders

_____   _____   HIV status

_____   _____   Past sexual experiences

_____   _____   Marital history

_____   _____   Annual salary and net financial worth

_____   _____   Affectional orientation

_____   _____   Attitudes toward other races and nationalities

_____   _____   Religious beliefs

_____   _____   Past criminal activity or incarceration

Ethical Choice Point

You're in a romantic relationship and your partner presses you to reveal your past sexual experiences. You really don't want to (you're not very proud of your past); furthermore, you don't think it's relevant to your current relationship. Today, your partner asks you directly to reveal this part of your past. *What are your ethical obligations here? Are there certain aspects that you are ethically bound to reveal and other aspects that you are not ethically bound to reveal?*

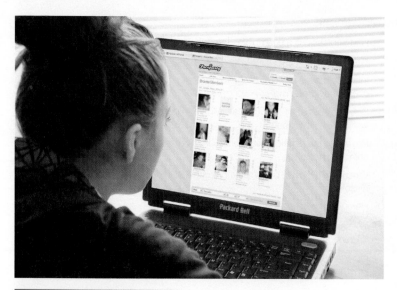

Meeting Online

One study found that people who met on the Internet and who communicated over a period of time before they met in person were more likely to stay together than couples who did not engage in much communication (Baker, 2002). *Based on your own experiences, how would you predict which couples who met online would stay together and which would break apart?*

Relationship Communication

9.2 Explain the role of communication at the different relationship stages.

Communication is the lifeblood of relationships—without communication, relationships could not exist. And without effective communication, effective relationships could not exist. With effective communication, however, you stand a much better chance of experiencing relationships that are productive, satisfying, supportive, open, and honest, and possess all the characteristics you want in a relationship. Here, we look at some of the communication patterns and guides to effectiveness in developing, deteriorating, and repairing relationships.

Communicating in Developing and Maintaining Relationships

Much research has focused on the communication that takes place as you make contact, become involved, and reach intimacy (Ayres, 1983; Canary & Stafford, 1994; Canary, Stafford, Hause, & Wallace, 1993; Dainton & Stafford, 1993; Dindia & Baxter, 1987; Guerrero, Eloy, & Wabnik, 1993).

As a relationship develops, both the breadth and the depth of the communication increase. This relationship is explained clearly in **social penetration theory** (Altman & Taylor, 1973). It describes relationships in terms of the number of topics that people talk about (the **breadth** of the relationship) and the degree of "personalness" of those topics (the **depth** of the relationship).

We can represent an individual as a circle and divide that circle into various parts, as in Figure 9.2. This figure illustrates different models of social penetration. Each circle in the figure contains eight topic areas to depict breadth (identified as A through H) and five levels of intimacy to depict depth (represented by the concentric circles). Note that in circle 1, only three topic areas are penetrated. Of these, one is penetrated only to the first level and two to the second. In this type of interaction, three topic areas are discussed, and only at rather superficial levels. This is the type of relationship you

Figure 9.2 Models of Social Penetration

How accurately do the concepts of breadth and depth express your communication in relationships of different intensities? Can you identify other aspects of messages that change as you go from talking with an acquaintance to talking with a friend or an intimate?

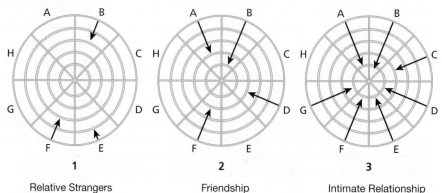

1	2	3
Relative Strangers	Friendship	Intimate Relationship

might have with an acquaintance. Circle 2 represents a more intense relationship, one that has greater breadth and depth; more topics are discussed and to deeper levels of penetration. This is the type of relationship you might have with a friend. Circle 3 represents a still more intense relationship. Here there is considerable breadth (seven of the eight areas are penetrated) and depth (most of the areas are penetrated to the deepest levels). This is the type of relationship you might have with a lover or a parent or child.

Here are some examples of how people communicate as they develop and seek to maintain their relationships, presented in the form of suggestions for more effective interpersonal relationships. As a preface, it should be noted that these messages may be sent over any of the available communication channels. Many relationships develop online (Match.com commercials claim that one out of five relationships begin online), and because online contact is so easy to maintain even when partners are widely separated geographically, a great deal of relationship communication occurs through e-mail, Facebook postings, instant messaging, texting, and tweeting. One behavior that cannot be fully appreciated online is kissing. Kissing, more important to women than to men, is frequently used to maintain, solidify, and strengthen relationships (Wlodarski & Dunbar, 2013).

- **Reach out.** You call just to say, "How are you?" or send cards or letters. Sometimes communication is merely small talk that is insignificant in itself but is engaged in because it preserves contact. Also included would be talking about the honesty and openness in the relationship and talking about shared feelings. Responding constructively in a conflict (even when your partner may act in ways harmful to the relationship) is another type of communicative maintenance strategy (Rusbult & Bunk, 1993).

- **Be nice.** You're polite, cheerful, and friendly; you avoid criticism; and you compromise even when it involves self-sacrifice. This behavior also includes talking about a shared future, for example, talking about a future vacation or buying a house together. It also includes acting affectionately and romantically.

- **Be open.** You engage in direct discussion and listen to the other—for example, you self-disclose, talk about what you want from the relationship, give advice, and express empathy.

- **Give assurances.** You assure the other person of the significance of the relationship—for example, you comfort the other, put your partner first, and express love.

- **Share joint activities.** You spend time with the other—for example, playing ball, visiting mutual friends, doing specific things as a couple (even cleaning the house), and sometimes just being together and talking with no concern for what is done. Controlling (eliminating or reducing) extrarelational activities would be another type of togetherness behavior (Rusbult & Bunk, 1993). Also included here would be ceremonial behaviors, for example, celebrating birthdays and anniversaries, discussing past pleasurable times, and eating at a favorite restaurant.

- **Be positive.** You try to make interactions pleasant and upbeat—for example, holding hands, giving in to make your partner happy, and doing favors. At the same time, you avoid certain issues that might cause arguments.

- **Focus on improving yourself.** For example, you work on making yourself look especially good and attractive to the other person.

- **Be empathic.** This skill is covered in the accompanying Understanding Interpersonal Skills box.

VIEWPOINTS

Growing Similarity

It's been found that couples in long-term relationships resemble each other in facial features more than do couples formed at random. One reason offered (in addition to the obvious one that we select a relationship partner who looks like us to start with) is empathy. People come to have similar facial features because they empathize with each other—they in effect copy each other's facial behaviors (for example, smiling or wrinkling the forehead) and eventually develop greater similarity in facial appearance (Zajonc, Adelmann, Murphy, & Niedenthal, 1987; Dean, 2007). In what other ways (physical and emotional) might couples in long-term relationships come to resemble each other?

Communicating in Deteriorating and Dissolving Relationships

Like communication in developing relationships, communication in deteriorating relationships involves special patterns and special strategies of disengagement.

Recognizing Patterns of Deterioration Communication patterns such as withdrawal and increased negativity, for example, are in part a response to the deterioration; you communicate the way you do because you feel that your relationship is in trouble. However, these patterns are also causative: the communication patterns you use largely determine the fate of your relationship. Here are a few communication patterns that are seen during relationship deterioration.

- *Withdrawal* Nonverbally, withdrawal is seen in the greater space you need and in the speed with which tempers and other signs of disturbance arise when that space

THE CULTURAL MAP Relationship Length

In some cultures, mainly high collectivist cultures, there is great value placed on long-term relationships; relationships that last are viewed positively and relationships that don't last are viewed negatively. Other cultures, mainly high individualist cultures, are more accepting of short-term, temporary relationships.

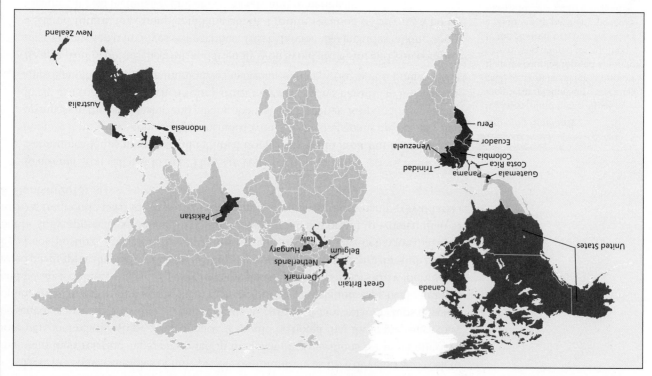

■ These countries are among the most strongly affiliated with individualism. Relationships in individualist cultures are more temporary than long-lasting, and individualist cultures are more accepting of change in relationships. Divorce rates, for example, are generally high in these cultures.

■ These countries are among the most strongly affiliated with collectivism. Relationships in collectivist cultures are more long-lasting than temporary, and, in fact, collectivist cultures often expect relationships to last forever. Divorce rates, as you'd expect, are generally low in these cultures.

How do you feel about long-term versus short-term romantic relationships? What are some of the advantages and disadvantages of long-lasting and of temporary romantic relationships? Are these the same advantages and disadvantages you'd find in friendship relationships?

is invaded. Other nonverbal signs of withdrawal include a decrease in eye contact and touching; less similarity in clothing; and fewer displays of items associated with the other person, such as bracelets, photographs, and rings (Knapp, Vangelisti, & Caughlin, 2014; Miller & Parks, 1982). Verbally, withdrawal is marked by a decreased desire to talk and, especially, to listen. At times, you may use small talk not as a preliminary to serious conversation but as an alternative, perhaps to avoid confronting the serious issues.

- *Depenetration* Recall that when a relationship moves to intimacy, the breadth and depth of communication increases. Conversely, as a relationship begins to deteriorate, the breadth and depth reverse themselves in a process called **depenetration**. For example, while ending a relationship, you might cut out certain topics from your interpersonal communications. At the same time, you might discuss the remaining topics in less depth. In some instances of relational deterioration, however, both the breadth and the depth of interaction increase. For example, when a couple breaks up and each is finally free from an oppressive relationship, they may—after some time—begin to discuss problems and feelings they would never have discussed when they were together. In fact, they may become extremely close friends and come to like each other more than when they were together. In these cases, the breadth and depth of their relationship may increase rather than decrease (Baxter, 1983).

- *Decline in self-disclosure* Self-disclosing communications decline significantly. If the relationship is dying, you may think self-disclosure is not worth the effort. Or you may limit your self-disclosures because you feel that the other person may not accept them or can no longer be trusted to be supportive and empathic.

- *Deception* Deception increases as relationships break down. Sometimes this takes the form of clear-cut lies, which you or your partner may use to avoid arguments over details such as staying out all night, not calling, or being seen in the wrong place with the wrong person. At other times, lies may be used because of a feeling of shame; you may not want the other person to think less of you. One of the problems with deception is that it has a way of escalating, eventually creating a climate of distrust and disbelief.

- *Positive and negative messages* During deterioration, there's an increase in negative messages and a decrease in positive messages. Once you praised the other's behaviors, but now you criticize them. Often the behaviors have not changed significantly; what has changed is your way of looking at them. What once was a cute habit now becomes annoying; what once was "different" now becomes inconsiderate. When a relationship is deteriorating, requests for pleasurable behaviors decrease ("Will you fix me my favorite dessert?") and requests to stop unpleasant or negative behaviors increase ("Will you stop whistling?") (Lederer, 1984). Even the social niceties that accompany requests get lost as they deteriorate from "Would you please make me a cup of coffee, honey?" to "Get me some coffee, will you?" to "Where's my coffee?"

Disengaging from a Relationship Another dimension of communicating in a relationship deterioration focuses on the strategies people use in breaking up a relationship. When you wish to exit a relationship, you need some way of explaining this—to yourself as well as to your partner. You need a strategy for getting out of a relationship that you no longer find satisfying or profitable. A few such strategies are presented in the list that follows (Cody, 1982). As you read the list, note that your choice of a strategy depends on your goal. For example, you're more likely to remain friends if you use de-escalation than if you use justification or avoidance (Banks, Altendorf, Greene, & Cody, 1987).

- *Positive tone* is used to preserve the relationship and to express positive feelings for the other person. For example, "I really care for you a great deal, but I'm not ready for such an intense relationship."

- **Negative identity management** to blame the other person for the breakup and to absolve yourself; for example, "I can't stand your jealousy, your constant suspicions, your checking up on me. I need my freedom."

- **Justification** to give reasons for the breakup; for example, "I'm going away to college for four years; there's no point in not dating others."

- **De-escalation** to reduce the intensity of the relationship. For example, you might avoid the other person, cut down on phone calls, or reduce the amount of time you spend together. Or you might de-escalate to reduce the exclusivity and hence the intensity of the relationship and say, for example, "I'm just not ready for an exclusive relationship. I think we should see other people."

Dealing with a Breakup Regardless of the specific reason for the end of the relationship, relationship breakups are difficult to deal with. They invariably cause stress and emotional problems, and they may actually create as much pain in a person's brain as physical injuries (Eisenberger, Lieberman, & Williams, 2003). Women, it seems, experience greater depression and social dysfunction than men after relationship dissolution (Chung, et al., 2002). Consequently, it's important to give attention to self-repair. Here are a few suggestions to ease the difficulty that is sure to be experienced, whether the breakup is between friends or lovers or occurs because of death, separation, or the loss of affection and connection.

- **Break the loneliness–depression cycle.** Instead of wallowing in loneliness and depression, be active. Engage in social activities with friends and others in your support system. Many people feel they should bear their burdens alone. Men, in particular, have been taught that this is the only "manly" way to handle things. But seeking the support of others is one of the best antidotes to the unhappiness caused when a relationship ends. Tell your friends and family of your situation—in only general terms, if you prefer—and make it clear that you want support. Seek out people who are positive and nurturing. Avoid negative individuals who paint the world in even darker tones. Make the distinction between seeking support and seeking advice. If you feel you need advice, seek out a professional.

- **Take time out.** Resist the temptation to jump into a new relationship while the old one is still warm or before a new one can be assessed with some objectivity. At the same time, resist swearing off all relationships. Neither extreme works well. Also, take time out for yourself. Renew your relationship with yourself. If you were in a long-term relationship, you probably saw yourself as part of a team, as part of a couple. Now get to know yourself as a unique individual—standing alone at present but fully capable of entering a meaningful relationship in the near future.

- **Bolster your self-esteem.** When relationships fail, self-esteem often declines. This seems especially true for those who did not initiate the breakup (Collins & Clark, 1989). You may feel guilty for having caused the breakup or inadequate for not holding on to the relationship. You may feel unwanted and unloved. Your task is to regain a positive self-image. Recognize, too, that having been in a relationship that failed—even if you view yourself as the main cause of the breakup—does not mean that you are a failure. Neither does it mean that you cannot succeed in a new and different relationship. It does mean that something went wrong with this

VIEWPOINTS

Breakup Rules

The more intimate your relationship (and the longer you've been together), the more intimate the method of breaking up needs to be. You cannot announce for the first time that you are divorcing your spouse of 20 years on a Facebook update or on a post-it note you leave on the refrigerator as you're hopping a plane for Tahiti. How would you describe the rules for relationship breakup? Are they the same for online and for face-to-face relationships?

one relationship. Ideally, it was a failure from which you have learned something important about yourself and about your relationship behavior.

- **Remove or avoid uncomfortable relationship symbols.** After any breakup, there are a variety of reminders—photographs, gifts, and letters. Resist the temptation to throw these out. Instead, remove them. Give them to a friend to hold or put them in a closet where you won't see them. If possible, avoid these places you frequented together. These symbols bring back uncomfortable memories. After you have achieved some emotional distance, you can go back and enjoy these as reminders of a once pleasant relationship. Support for this suggestion comes from research showing that the more vivid your memory of a broken love affair—a memory greatly aided by these relationship symbols—the greater your depression is likely to be (Harvey, Flanary, & Morgan, 1986). Additional research shows that remaining friends on Facebook after a breakup obstructs healing and the ability to move on past the broken relationship to another (Marshall, 2012).

- **Become mindful of your own relationship patterns.** Avoid repeating negative patterns. Many people repeat their mistakes. They enter second and third relationships with the same blinders, faulty preconceptions, or unrealistic expectations with which they entered earlier involvements. Instead, use the knowledge gained from your failed relationship to prevent repeating the same patterns. At the same time, don't become a prophet of doom. Don't see in every relationship vestiges of the old. Don't jump at the first conflict and say, "Here it goes all over again." Treat the new relationship as the unique relationship it is. Don't evaluate it through past relationships. Use past relationships and experiences as guides, not filters.

Communicating in Relationship Repair

If you wish to save a relationship, you may try to do so by changing your communication patterns and, in effect, putting into practice the insights and skills learned in this course. First, we'll look at some general ways to repair a relationship; second, we'll examine ways to deal with repair when you are the only one who wants to change the relationship. We can look at the strategies for repairing a relationship in terms of the following six suggestions, whose first letters conveniently spell out the word *REPAIR* (**R**ecognize the problem. **E**ngage in productive communication. **P**ose possible solutions. **A**ffirm each other. **I**ntegrate solutions into everyday behavior. **R**isk giving without promises of reciprocity.), a useful reminder that repair is not a one-step but a multistep process (see Figure 9.3).

Recognize the Problem Your first step is to identify the problem and to recognize it both intellectually and emotionally. Specify what is wrong with your present relationship (in concrete terms) and what changes would be needed to make it better (again, in specific terms). Create a picture of your relationship as you would want it to be, and compare this picture to the way the relationship looks now. Specify the changes that would have to take place if the ideal picture were to replace the present picture.

Also try to see the problem from your partner's point of view and to have your partner see the problem from yours. Exchange these perspectives, empathically and with open minds. Try, too, to be descriptive when discussing grievances, taking special care to avoid such troublesome terms as *always* and *never*. Own your feelings and thoughts; use I-messages and take responsibility for your feelings instead of blaming your partner.

Engage in Productive Communication Interpersonal communication skills such as those discussed throughout the text (for example, other-orientation, openness, confidence, immediacy, expressiveness, and empathy) are especially important during repair and are an essential part of any repair strategy. Here are several suggestions to refresh your memory:

- Look closely for relational messages that help clarify motivations and needs. Respond to these messages as well as to the content messages.
- Exchange perspectives and see the situation as your partner does.
- Practice empathic and positive responses, even in conflict situations.
- Own your feelings and thoughts. Use I-messages and take responsibility for these feelings.
- Use active listening techniques to help your partner explore and express relevant thoughts and feelings.
- Remember the principle of irreversibility; think carefully before saying things you may later regret.
- Keep the channels of communication open. Be available to discuss problems, negotiate solutions, and practice new and more productive communication patterns.

Similarly, the skills of effective interpersonal conflict resolution are crucial in any attempt at relationship repair. If partners address relationship problems by deploying productive conflict resolution strategies, the difficulties may be resolved, and the relationship may actually emerge stronger and healthier. If unproductive and destructive strategies are used, however, then the relationship may well deteriorate further.

Propose Possible Solutions After the problem is identified, examine the possible choices you have for resolving any problems. Look for solutions that enable both of

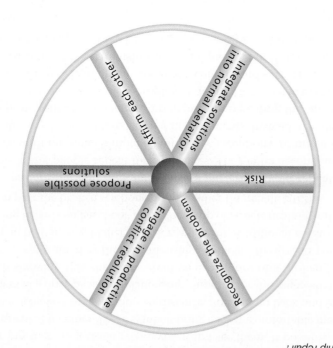

Figure 9.3 The Relationship Repair Wheel

The wheel seems an apt metaphor for the repair process; the specific repair strategies—the spokes—all work together in a constant process. The wheel is difficult to get moving, but once in motion it becomes easier to turn. Also, it's easier to start when two people are pushing, but it is not impossible for one to move it in the right direction. *What metaphor do you find helpful in thinking about relationship repair?*

you to win. Discuss the possible solutions, their pros and cons. Try to avoid "solutions" in which one person wins and the other loses. With such win–lose solutions, resentment and hostility are likely to fester.

Affirm Each Other   Any strategy of relationship repair should incorporate supportiveness and positive evaluations. For example, happy couples engage in greater positive behavior exchange: they communicate more agreement, approval, and positive affect than do unhappy couples (Dindia & Fitzpatrick, 1985). Clearly, these behaviors result from the positive feelings the partners have for each other. It can also be argued, however, that these expressions help to increase the positive regard each person has for the other.

One way to affirm another is to talk positively. Reverse negative communication patterns. For example, instead of withdrawing, talk about the causes of, and the possible cures for, your disagreements and problems. Reverse the tendency to hide your inner self. Disclose your feelings. Compliments, positive stroking, and all the nonverbals that say, "I care," are especially important when you wish to reverse negative communication patterns.

Cherishing behaviors are an especially insightful way to affirm another person and to increase favor exchange (Lederer, 1984). **Cherishing behaviors** are the small gestures you enjoy receiving from your partner (a smile, a wink, a squeeze, a kiss). Cherishing behaviors should be (1) specific and positive, (2) focused on the present and future rather than related to issues about which the partners have argued in the past, (3) capable of being performed daily, and (4) easily executed. People can make a list of the cherishing behaviors they each wish to receive and then exchange lists. Each person then performs the cherishing behaviors desired by the partner. At first, these behaviors may seem self-conscious and awkward. In time, however, they will become a normal part of interaction. Recent research confirms the usefulness of cherishing behaviors delivered by texting. Texting messages of confirmation—*I'm thinking of you, I miss you, How are you? What's up?*—leads to improved relationship satisfaction (Schade, Sandberg, Bean, Busby, & Coyne, 2013; Ni, 2013).

Integrate Solutions   Often solutions that are reached after an argument are followed for only a very short time; then the couple goes back to their previous, unproductive behavior patterns. Instead, integrate the solutions into your normal behavior; make them an integral part of your everyday relationship behavior. For example, make the exchange of favors, compliments, and cherishing behaviors part of your normal relationship behavior.

Risk   Take risks in trying to improve your relationship. Risk giving favors without any certainty of reciprocity. Risk rejection by making the first move to make up or by saying you're sorry. Be willing to change, adapt, and take on new tasks and responsibilities. Risk the possibility that a significant part of the problem is you—that you're being unreasonable, or controlling, or stingy and that this is causing problems and needs to be changed.

Table 9.4 offers a brief summary of communication and relationship stages.

Table 9.4   In a Nutshell   Communication and Relationship Stages

Relationship Stages	Communication
Communicating in development and maintenance	Being at your best and observing all the rules of politeness characterize the developing stages of relationships.
Communicating in deterioration and dissolution	When a relationship deteriorates, communication lessens in quantity and quality.
Communicating in repair	During relationship repair, you attempt to resolve the problems and improve the relationship by, for example, engaging in productive communication, affirming each other, and taking risks.

UNDERSTANDING *INTERPERSONAL SKILLS*

Empathy: Feeling What Another Person Feels From That Person's Point of View

Empathy is feeling what another person feels from that person's point of view without losing your own identity. The first step in empathy, of course, is to understand what the other person is thinking and feeling. To achieve this, you need to put into practice all the skills discussed throughout this text and course; for example, listen carefully to what the speaker is saying and pay close attention to those small nonverbal movements of the face and eyes that often reveal nonverbalized feelings. If you listen carefully, you'll find yourself imitating the expressions of this other person, which will help you feel what the other person is feeling. You'll be less able to do this if you've had Botox injections, however, because you'll be less able to use your facial muscles to echo the expressions of the other (Whitbourne, 2013b).

Empathy enables you to understand emotionally what another person is experiencing. (To sympathize, in contrast, is to feel *for* the person—to feel sorry or happy for the person, for example.) Women, research shows, are perceived as more empathic and engage in more empathic communication than do men (Nicolai & Demmel, 2007). Research also shows that empathy among college students has declined significantly from the 1970s to 2010, despite the great number of social media connections among friends (Konrath, 2012). And, on the more practical side, there is evidence that empathy in the workplace adds to the bottom line; empathic employees are more effective in dealing with customers and are less likely to leave the company, for example (Goleman, 1995a). Given the importance of empathy in the workplace, a mobile app called Translator, is in development and is designed to teach employees how to be more empathic (Zarya, 2017).

Empathy is best expressed in two distinct parts: thinking empathy and feeling empathy (Bellafiore, 2005). In *thinking empathy*, you express an understanding of what the other person means. For example, when you paraphrase someone's comment, showing that you understand the meaning the person is trying to communicate, you're communicating thinking empathy. The second part is *feeling empathy*; here you express your feeling of what the other person is feeling; in other words, you demonstrate a similarity between what you're feeling and what the other person is feeling. Often you'll respond with both thinking and feeling empathy in the same brief response; for example, when a friend tells you of problems at home, you may respond by saying, "Your problems at home do seem to be getting worse. I can imagine that you feel so angry at times."

Communicating with Empathy

Here are a few more specific suggestions to help you communicate both your feeling and your thinking empathy more effectively (Authier & Gustafson, 1982):

- *Be clear.* Make it clear that you're trying to understand, not to evaluate, judge, or criticize.
- *Focus.* Maintain eye contact, an attentive posture, and physical closeness to focus your concentration. Express involvement through facial expressions and gestures.
- *Reflect.* To check the accuracy of your perceptions and to show your commitment to understanding the speaker, reflect back to the speaker the feelings that you think are being expressed. Offer tentative statements about what you think the person is feeling, for example, "You seem really angry with your father" or "I hear some doubt in your voice."
- *Disclose.* When appropriate, use your own self-disclosures to communicate your understanding, but be careful that you don't refocus the discussion on yourself.
- *Address mixed messages.* At times you may want to identify and address any mixed messages that the person is sending as a way to foster more open and honest communication. For example, if your friend verbally expresses contentment but shows nonverbal signs of depression, it may be prudent to question the possible discrepancy.
- *Acknowledge importance.* Make it clear that you understand the depth of a person's feelings.

Sometimes you will want to control your empathy, for example, when you want to remain especially calm and logical in order to help another person. Similarly, a physician often wants to control empathy in order to focus on the medical problem at hand in a dispassionate manner (Goleman, 2013b).

Working with Empathy

Empathy can also yield practical benefits. For example, research shows—from a study in 38 countries—that managers who display empathy toward their employees get higher performance ratings from their supervisors than do those who don't display empathy (Gentry, Weber, & Golnaz, 2007). And empathic physicians enjoy greater patient satisfaction (Swink, 2013). *What pratical benefits might empathy have for you at school and at work?*

Relationship Theories

9.3 Summarize the major theories that explain relationship development, deterioration, and repair (attraction, relationship rules, relationship dialectics, social exchange, equity, and politeness).

Several theories offer insight into why and how you develop and dissolve your relationships (Baxter & Braithwaite, 2008b). Here we'll examine six such theories: attraction, relationship rules, relationship dialectics, social exchange, equity, and politeness, previewed in Figure 9.4.

Attraction Theory

Attraction theory holds that people form relationships with those they consider attractive.

Before reading about the factors that make for attractiveness, examine your attractiveness preferences by rating the following qualities on a 5-point scale in terms of how important each is to you: 5 = Very important; 4 = Important; 3 = Neither important nor unimportant; 2 = Unimportant; 1 = Very unimportant):

_____ 1. Facial appearance

_____ 2. General body structure (weight, height, shape)

_____ 3. Grooming and general cleanliness

_____ 4. Appropriate financial resources

_____ 5. Intelligence

_____ 6. Similarity in religious beliefs

_____ 7. Sense of humor

_____ 8. Positive toward me

_____ 9. Optimistic toward life in general

_____ 10. Honest/ethical

_____ 11. Ambitious

_____ 12. Communicative

_____ 13. Similarity in cultural backgrounds, including race and nationality

_____ 14. Available

_____ 15. Sexual compatibility

There are no correct or incorrect answers, and people are likely to respond to such characteristics very differently. This brief exercise was designed to stimulate you to think in specific terms about the characteristics of another person that are important to you. Those given here are often mentioned in research and theory as being significant in evaluating a potential life partner.

If you're like most people, then you're attracted to others on the basis of these major factors: similarity, proximity, reinforcement, physical attractiveness and personality, socioeconomic and educational status, and reciprocity of liking. As a preface to the discussion of these factors, it's important to recognize the difference between online and face-to-face relationships. Attraction to a person in an online relationship (especially one that is going to stay online) depends on the communicated messages, photos, videos, the responsiveness to your posts, the sense of humor—all of which may have nothing to do with the person's physical appearance. With face-to-face relationships or online relationships that will morph into face-to-face relationships, there is considerable emphasis on the physical qualities of the individual.

Figure 9.4 Relationship Theories

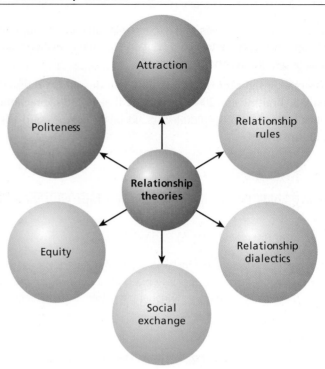

Online Relationships

Among the advantages of online relationships is that they reduce the importance of physical characteristics and instead emphasize factors such as rapport, similarity, and self-disclosure, and in the process promote relationships that are based on emotional intimacy rather than physical attraction (Cooper & Sportolari, 1997). *What do you see as the main advantages of online relationships? The main disadvantages?*

Similarity   If you could construct your mate, according to the **similarity** principle, it's likely that your mate would look, act, and think very much like you (Burleson, Samter, & Luccetti, 1992; Burleson, Kunkel, & Birch, 1994). Generally, people like those who are similar to them in nationality, race, abilities, physical characteristics, intelligence, and attitudes (Pornpitakpan, 2003). A study of 65,000 online daters showed that similarity guided their choices in selecting potential dating partners (Fiore & Donath, 2005; Dean, 2010b). No doubt this counts in great part for the proliferation of dating sites focusing on specific religious or racial groups. There is, however, some evidence that this preference for similarity (at least in facial appearance) only holds for people already in a relationship. Those who are single and perhaps seeking a partner are more apt to favor faces that are dissimilar to their own (Lindová, Little, Havlíček, Roberts, Rubešová, & Flegr, 2016; Dean, 2016a).

Research also finds that you're more likely to help someone who is similar in race, attitude, general appearance, and even first name. Even the same first name or coming from the same state or city is significant (Wyer, 2012). Sometimes people are attracted to their opposites, in a pattern called **complementarity**; for example, a dominant person might be attracted to someone who is more submissive. Generally, however, people prefer those who are similar.

Proximity   If you look around at people you find attractive, you will probably find that they are the people who live or work close to you. People who become friends are the people who have the greatest opportunity to interact with each other. Proximity, or physical closeness, is most important in the early stages of interaction—for example, during the first days of school (in class or in dormitories). The importance of proximity as a factor in attraction decreases, though always remaining significant, as the opportunity to interact with more distant others increases.

Reinforcement If you're like most people, you're attracted to people who give rewards or reinforcements, which can range from a simple compliment to an expensive cruise. You're also attracted to people you reward (Jecker & Landy, 1969; Aronson, Wilson, Akert, & Sommers, 2016). That is, you come to like people for whom you do favors; for example, you've probably increased your liking for persons after buying them an expensive present or going out of your way to do them a special favor. In these situations, you justify your behavior by believing that the person was worth your efforts; otherwise, you'd have to admit to spending effort on people who don't deserve it.

Physical Attractiveness and Personality It's easily appreciated that people like physically attractive people more than they like physically unattractive people. And, consistent with popular stereotypes, men place greater emphasis on physical attractiveness than do women. In one study of heterosexual men and women, 92% of men (but only 84% of women) indicated they wanted a good-looking partner and 80% of men (but only 58% of women) wanted a partner who had a slender body (Dean, 2017; Fales, et al., 2016). What isn't so obvious is that we also feel a greater sense of familiarity with more attractive people than with less attractive people; that is, we're more likely to think we've met a person before if that person is attractive (Monin, 2003). Another not so obvious connection is that attractive students get higher grades than less attractive students and the more attractive also earn higher salaries than their less attractive counterparts (Gordon, Crosnoe, & Wang, 2014). Even the more attractive candidate gets elected more often than the less attractive candidate (White, Kenrick, & Neuberg, 2013).

The perception of physical attractiveness is also influenced by a person's friends. A person with attractive friends (as shown by the photos they post on Facebook) is judged more attractive than that same person with unattractive friends' photos posted (Walther, Van Der Heide, Kim, Westerman, & Tong, 2008). And, perhaps in light of this, there are websites that will write flattering, interesting, and clever status updates for your Facebook wall. After all, if people write flattering, interesting, and clever posts on your wall, then surely you too must be interesting and clever—and deserving of flattery. Even your association with positively reviewed films and television shows has been found to increase your perceived attractiveness rating on OK Cupid (Roper, 2014).

Also, although culture influences what people think is physical attractiveness and what isn't, some research indicates that there are certain facial features that seem to be thought attractive in all cultures—a kind of universal attractiveness (Brody, 1994). Additionally, you probably tend to like people who have a pleasant rather than an unpleasant personality (although people will differ on what is and what is not a pleasant personality).

Socioeconomic and Educational Status Popular belief holds that, among heterosexual men and women, men are more interested in a woman's physical attributes than in her socioeconomic status. And, indeed, research shows that women flirt on the Internet by stressing their physical attributes, whereas men stress their socioeconomic status (Whitty, 2003b). There is interesting evidence that men, too, consider a woman's socioeconomic status in making romantic relationship decisions—but whereas women find higher socioeconomic status more attractive, men find just the opposite. Men report greater likelihood of a romantic relationship with a woman lower in socioeconomic status than they are. Further, men find women with a higher educational level (which is often responsible for the higher socioeconomic status) less likeable and less faithful, and as a result see less likelihood of a romantic relationship with such women (Greitemeyer, 2007).

Reciprocity of Liking   It will come as no surprise that research supports what you already know from your own experience: You tend to be attracted to people you think are attracted to you; you come to like those who you think like you. **Reciprocity of liking**, also known as reciprocity of attraction or reciprocal liking, is seen in a variety of situations. We initiate potential friendships and romantic relationships with people who we think like us, certainly not with those we think dislike us. Group members who are told that certain other members like them will later express greater liking for these members than for others. Public speakers are advised to compliment the audience and express liking for them largely on the theory that this liking will be reciprocated. There is even evidence to show that people like "likers"— people who like others generally— more than they like people who don't express such liking (Eastwick & Finkel, 2009).

However, some research indicates that there is some appeal to uncertainty. For example, when participants viewed Facebook profiles, they indicated a greater attraction to those they were told were attracted to them a lot than to those who they were told were attracted to them an average amount (consistent with the notion of reciprocity). But, they were most attracted to a third group who they were told either liked them a lot or an average amount—indicating that there is some benefit to uncertainty (Whitchurch, Wilson, & Gilbert, 2010; Dean, 2016a).

Relationship Rules Theory

You can gain an interesting perspective on interpersonal relationships by looking at them in terms of the rules that govern them (Shimanoff, 1980). The general assumption of **relationship rules theory** is that friendship and love, in particular, are held together by adherence to certain rules. When those rules are broken, the relationship may deteriorate and even dissolve.

Relationship rules theory helps us clarify several aspects of relationships. First, these rules help identify successful versus destructive relationship behavior. In addition, these rules help pinpoint more specifically why relationships break up and how they may be repaired. Further, if we know what the rules are, we are better able to master the social skills involved in relationship development and maintenance. And because these rules vary from one culture to another, it is important to identify those unique to each culture so that intercultural relationships may be developed and maintained more effectively.

Friendship Rules   One approach to friendship argues that friendships are maintained by rules (Argyle, 1986; Argyle & Henderson, 1984). When these rules are followed, the friendship is strong and mutually satisfying. When these rules are broken, the friendship suffers and may die. For example, the rules for keeping a friendship call for behaviors such as standing up for your friend in his or her absence, sharing information and feelings about successes, demonstrating emotional support for a friend, trusting and offering to help a friend in need, and trying to make a friend happy when you're together. On the other hand, a friendship is likely to be in trouble when one or both friends are intolerant of the other's friends, discuss confidences with third parties, fail to demonstrate positive support, nag, and/or fail to trust or confide in the other. The strategy for maintaining a friendship, then, depends on your knowing the rules and having the ability to apply the appropriate interpersonal skills (Blieszner & Adams, 1992; Trower, 1981).

Romantic Rules   Other research has identified the rules that romantic relationships establish and follow. These rules, of course, vary considerably from one culture to another. For example, the different attitudes toward permissiveness and sexual relations with which Chinese and American college students view dating influence the romantic rules each group will establish and live by (Tang & Zuo, 2000). One researcher identified eight major romantic rules that keep the relationship together—or, when broken, lead to deterioration and eventually dissolution (Baxter, 1986). The general form for each rule is that, if you are in a close relationship, then you should:

1. recognize that each has a life beyond the relationship.
2. have and express similar attitudes and interests.
3. reinforce each other's self-esteem.
4. be real: open and genuine.
5. be faithful to each other.
6. spend substantial time together.
7. obtain rewards commensurate with your investment compared to the other party.
8. experience an inexplicable magic when together.

Family Rules   Family communication research points to the importance of rules in defining and maintaining the family (Galvin, Braithwaite, & Bylund, 2015). Family rules concern three main interpersonal communication issues (Satir, 1983):

- *What you can talk about.* Can you talk about the family finances? Grandpa's drinking? Your sister's lifestyle?
- *How you can talk about something.* Can you joke about your brother's disability? Can you address directly questions of family history or family skeletons?
- *To whom you can talk.* Can you talk openly to extended family members such as cousins and aunts and uncles? Can you talk to close neighbors about family health issues?

All families teach rules for communication. Some of these are explicit, such as "Never contradict the family in front of outsiders" or "Never talk finances with outsiders." Other rules are unspoken; you deduce them as you learn the communication style of your family. For example, if financial issues are always discussed in secret and in hushed tones, then you rather logically infer that you shouldn't tell other, more distant family members or neighbors about family finances.

Like the rules of friends and lovers, family rules tell you which behaviors will be rewarded (and therefore what you should do) and which will be punished (and therefore what you should not do). Rules also provide a kind of structure that defines the family as a cohesive unit and that distinguishes it from other, similar families.

The rules a family develops are greatly influenced by the culture. Although there are many similarities among families throughout the world, there are also differences (Georgas, Mylonas, Bafiti, & Poortinga, 2001). For example, members of collectivist cultures are more likely to restrict family information from outsiders as a way of protecting the family than are members of individualist cultures. But this tendency to protect the family can create serious problems in cases of wife abuse. Many women will not report spousal abuse because of this desire to protect the family image and not let others know that things aren't perfect at home (Dresser, 2005).

Family communication theorists argue that rules should be flexible so that special circumstances can be accommodated; for example, there are situations that necessitate changing the family dinnertime, vacation plans, or savings goals (Noller & Fitzpatrick, 1993). Rules should also be negotiable so that all members can participate in their modification and feel part of family government.

Workplace Rules   Rules also govern your workplace relationships. These rules are usually part of the corporate culture that an employee would learn from observing other employees (especially

---

INTERPERSONAL CHOICE POINT
Virtual Infidelity

You discover that your partner of the last 15 years is being unfaithful with someone online (and in another country), breaking an important but unstated rule of your relationship. You understand that generally such infidelity is seen as a consequence of a failure in communication (Young, Griffin-Shelley, Cooper, O'Mara, & Buchanan, 2000). You want to discover the extent of this online relationship and your partner's intentions in regard to this affair. *What would be an effective way for you to deal with this situation?*

- **a.** Tell you partner what you found and ask to discuss it.
- **b.** Tell your partner to stop.
- **c.** Express your knowledge and disappointment with this affair.
- **d.** Say nothing.
- **e.** Other

those who move up the hierarchy) as well as from official memos on dress, sexual harassment, and the like. Of course, each organization has different rules, so it's important to see what rules are operating in any given situation. Among the rules that you might find are:

- Work hard.
- Be cooperative in teams; the good of the company comes first.
- Don't reveal company policies and plans to workers at competing firms.
- Don't form romantic relationships with other workers.
- Avoid even the hint of sexual harassment.
- Be polite to other workers and especially to customers.

Relationship Dialectics Theory

Relationship dialectics theory argues that someone who is engaged in a relationship experiences internal tensions between pairs of motives or desires that pull him or her in opposite directions. These tensions are much like those you experience in your daily lives. For example, you want to work this summer to earn money to get a new car, but you also want to go to Hawaii and surf for two months. You want both, but you can have only one. In a similar way, you experience tensions between opposites in your relationship desires. Research generally finds three such pairs of opposites (Baxter, 2004; Baxter & Braithwaite, 2007, 2008a; Baxter & Simon, 1993; Rawlins, 1989, 1992).

The tension between *closedness* and *openness* refers to the conflict between openness and privacy. More specifically, it's the conflict between the desire or need to be transparent and to disclose your inner self to the other person and, its opposite, the desire or need to be less transparent and to not disclose your inner self (Baxter & Montgomery, 1998). Another tension that can come under the closeness-openness tension has to do with the conflict between the desire to be in a closed, exclusive relationship and the wish to be in a relationship that is open to different people. This tension manifests itself most during the early stages of relationship development. You like the exclusiveness of your pairing and yet you want also to relate to a larger group. Young heterosexual men, in interacting with women, use a pattern of messages that encourage closeness followed by messages that indicate a desire for distance, followed by closeness messages, followed by distancing messages—a clear example of the tension between the desire for closeness and the desire for autonomy (Korobov & Thorne, 2006).

The tension between *autonomy* and *connection*, which seems to occur more often as the relationship progresses, involves the desire to remain an autonomous, independent individual but also to connect intimately to another person and to a relationship. You want to be close and connected with another person, but you also want to be independent (Sahlstein, 2004). This tension, by the way, is a popular theme in women's magazines, which teach readers to want both autonomy and connection (Prusank, Duran, & DeLillo, 1993).

The tension between *novelty* and *predictability* centers on the competing desires for newness, different experiences, and adventure on the one hand, and for sameness, stability, and predictability on the other. You're comfortable with being able to predict what will happen, and yet you also want newness, difference, and novelty.

Each individual in a relationship may experience a somewhat different set of desires. For example, one

Emotional Relationships

In face-to-face relationships, emotional closeness compromises privacy; the closer you become, the less privacy you have. Research on online relationships, however, indicates that because you're more in control of what you reveal, you can develop close emotional relationships but also maintain your privacy (Ben-Ze'ev, 2003). *Do you find this to be true? If not, how would you express the relationship between emotional closeness and privacy in online and in face-to-face relationships?*

person may want exclusivity above all, whereas that person's partner may want greater openness. There are three main ways that you can use to deal with these tensions.

- *Accept the imbalance.* First, you can simply *accept the imbalance* as part of dating or as part of a committed relationship. You may even redefine it as a benefit and tell yourself something like: "I had been spending too much time at work. It's probably better that I come home earlier and don't work weekends"—accepting the closeness and giving up the autonomy.

- *Exit the relationship.* Second, you can simply *exit the relationship.* For example, if the loss of autonomy is so great that you can't live with it, then you may choose simply to end the relationship and achieve your desired autonomy.

- *Rebalance your life.* A third alternative is to *rebalance your life.* For example, if you find the primary relationship excessively predictable, you may seek to satisfy the need for novelty elsewhere, perhaps with a vacation to exotic places, perhaps with a different partner. If you find the relationship too connected (even suffocating), you may seek physical and psychological space to meet your autonomy needs. You can also establish the balance you feel you need by negotiating with your partner, for example, agreeing that you will take separate vacations or that each of you will go out separately with old friends once or twice a week.

As you can appreciate, meeting your partner's needs while also meeting your own needs is one of the major relationship challenges you'll face. Knowing and empathizing with these tensions and discussing them seem useful (even necessary) tools for relationship maintenance and satisfaction.

Social Exchange Theory

Social exchange theory claims that you develop relationships that enable you to maximize your profits (Chadwick-Jones, 1976; Gergen, Greenberg, & Willis, 1980; Thibaut & Kelley, 1986; Stafford, 2008)—a theory based on an economic model of profits and losses. The theory begins with the following equation: **Profits = rewards − costs**.

- *Rewards* are anything that you would incur costs to obtain. Research has identified six types of rewards in a love relationship: money, status, love, information, goods, and services (Baron & Byrne, 1984). For example, to get the reward of money, you might have to work rather than play. To earn the status of an A in an interpersonal communication course, you might have to write a term paper or study more than you want to.

- *Costs* are what you normally try to avoid, that you consider unpleasant or difficult. Examples might include working overtime; washing dishes and ironing clothes; watching your partner's favorite television show, which you find boring; or doing favors for those you dislike.

- *Profit* is that which results when the costs are subtracted from the rewards (profit = rewards − costs).

Using this basic economic model, social exchange theory claims that you seek to develop the friendships and romantic relationships that will give you the greatest profits, that is, relationships in which the rewards are greater than the costs.

When you enter a relationship, you have in mind a **comparison level**—a general idea of the kinds of rewards and profits that you feel you ought to get out of such a relationship. This comparison level consists of your realistic expectations concerning what you feel you deserve from this relationship. For example, a study of married couples found that most people expect high levels of trust, mutual respect, love, and commitment. Couples' expectations are significantly lower for time spent together, privacy, sexual activity, and communication (Sabatelli & Pearce, 1986). When the rewards that you get equal or surpass your comparison level, you feel satisfied with your relationship.

However, you also have a comparison level for alternatives. That is, you compare the profits that you get from your current relationship with the profits you think you could get from alternative relationships. Thus, if you see that the profits from your present relationship are below the profits that you could get from an alternative relationship, you may decide to leave your current relationship and enter a new, more profitable relationship. And with the Internet providing ready access to literally thousands of alternatives, this type of analysis can get difficult and unwieldy.

Equity Theory

Equity theory uses the ideas of social exchange but goes a step further and claims that you develop and maintain relationships in which the ratio of your rewards relative to your costs is approximately equal to your partner's (Messick & Cook, 1983; Walster, Walster, & Berscheid, 1978). For example, if you and a friend start a business in which you put up two-thirds of the money and your friend puts up one-third, equity would demand that you get two-thirds of the profits and your friend get one-third. In an *equitable relationship,* then, each party derives rewards that are proportional to the costs they each pay. If you contribute more toward the relationship than your partner, then equity requires that you should get greater rewards. If you both work equally hard, then equity demands that you should both get approximately equal rewards. Conversely, inequity exists in a relationship if you pay more of the costs (for example, if you do more of the unpleasant tasks) but your partner enjoys more of the rewards. Inequity also exists if you and your partner work equally hard but your partner gets more of the rewards. In this case, you'd be under-benefited and your partner would be over-benefited.

Much research supports this theory that people want equity in their interpersonal relationships (Hatfield & Rapson, 2007; Ueleke et al., 1983). The general idea behind the theory is that if you are under-benefited (you get too little in proportion to what you put in), you'll be angry and dissatisfied. If, on the other hand, you are over-benefited (you get too much in proportion to what you put in), you'll feel guilty. Some research, however, has questioned this rather neat but intuitively unsatisfying assumption and finds that the over-benefited person is often quite happy and contented; guilt from getting more than you deserve seems easily forgotten (Noller & Fitzpatrick, 1993).

Equity theory puts into clear focus the sources of relational dissatisfaction seen every day. For example, both partners in a relationship may have full-time jobs, but one partner may also be expected to do the major share of the household chores. Thus, although both may be deriving equal rewards—they have equally good cars, they live in the same three-bedroom house, and so on—one partner is paying more of the costs. According to equity theory, this partner will be dissatisfied because of this lack of equity.

Equity theory claims that you develop and maintain relationships that are equitable. You do not develop and may terminate relationships that are inequitable. There's considerable evidence to show that equity leads to satisfying relationships and that a lack of equity leads to dissatisfaction (Marano, 2014). The greater the inequity, the greater the dissatisfaction and the greater the likelihood that the relationship will end.

Politeness Theory

Still another approach to relationships looks at politeness as a major force in developing, maintaining, and deteriorating relationships. **Politeness theory** would go something like this: *Two people develop a relationship when each respects, contributes to, and acknowledges the positive and negative face needs of the other; the same relationship deteriorates when they don't.* Positive face is the need to be thought of highly—to be valued, to be esteemed. In communication terms, respect for positive face entails the exchange of compliments, praise, and general positivity. Negative face is the need to be autonomous—to be in control of one's own behavior, to not be obligated to do something. In communication terms, respect for negative face entails the exchange of permission requests (rather than demands), messages indicating that a person's time is valuable and respected, and few if any imposed obligations. It would also entail providing the other person an easy way out when a request is made.

Relationships develop and are maintained when these needs are met. And relationships deteriorate when the rules of politeness are bent, violated too often, or ignored completely. Relationship repair is encouraged when the rules of politeness are reintroduced. Figure 9.5 depicts a proposed relationship between the levels of politeness and the relationships stages discussed earlier.

Politeness, of course, is not the entire story; it's just a piece. It won't explain all the reasons for relationship development or deterioration, but it explains part of the processes. It won't explain, for example, why so many people stay in abusive and unsatisfying relationships. Its major weakness seems to be that politeness needs for specific individuals are difficult to identify—what is politeness to one person may be perceived as rude or insensitive by another.

And, perhaps not surprisingly, politeness seems to be relaxed as the relationship becomes more intimate. As the relationship becomes more intimate and long-lasting, there is greater license to violate the normal rules of politeness. This may be a mistake, at least in certain relationships. Our needs for positive and negative face do not go away when a relationship becomes more intimate; they're still there. If the definitions of politeness are relaxed by the individuals, then there seems little problem. There is a problem when the definitions—relaxed or original—are not shared by the individuals, when one assumes that something generally considered impolite is okay while the other does not.

When people in relationships complain that they are not respected, are not valued as they used to be when they were dating, and that their relationship is not romantic, they may well be talking about politeness. And so, on the more positive side, politeness theory offers very concrete suggestions for developing, maintaining, and repairing interpersonal relationships: namely, increase politeness by contributing to the positive and negative face needs of the other person.

Breaking up Politely

You want to break up your current romantic relationship of two years. You've fallen in love with someone else. You meet your partner for coffee to reveal your feelings. But, before you can say anything, your partner reveals the desire to break up with you. Inside, you're overjoyed; finally, you're free to pursue your new love. On the other hand, you feel insulted and annoyed that you got dumped; after all, you were a great partner. *What would you most likely say? What would be the most polite reaction in this situation? How would you explain your likely response and the most polite response (if these are different) in terms of positive and negative face?*

Figure 9.5 Politeness and Relationship Stages

Politeness, according to this model, is greatest during the contact stage—you want to put your best foot forward if the relationship is to be established. At involvement the level is still relatively high; you're still on your best behavior. As the relationship becomes intimate, you relax politeness and perhaps moved forward. During dissolution and deterioration, politeness may all but disappear. If you want to repair a relationship, your level of politeness is likely to increase considerably.

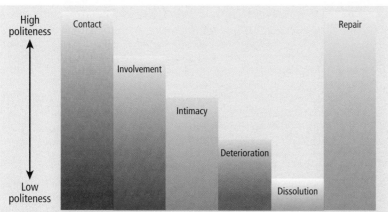

Though each relationship is unique, relationships for many people possess similar characteristics. These general patterns are what these theories try to explain. Taken together, the theories actually illuminate a great deal about why you develop relationships, the way relationships work, the ways you seek to maintain relationships, and the reasons why some relationships are satisfying and others are not. Figure 9.6 compares movement toward and away from intimacy, as seen by the various theories, and offers a nutshell summary of the first two parts of this chapter: Relationship Stages and Relationship Theories.

Figure 9.6   Movement among the Stages as Predicted by Relationship Theories

You move toward intimacy when:	Relationship Stages	You move away from intimacy when:
Attraction Theory Attraction increases: You're attracted to those who are similar, who are nearby, who reinforce you, and who you think are attractive.	Contact	**Attraction Theory** Attraction decreases.
Relationship Rules Theory Rules are followed: When rules are followed, relationships are maintained; when rules are broken, the relationship is in trouble.	Involvement	**Relationship Rules Theory** Rules are broken, disregarded.
Relationship Dialectics Theory Tensions are at acceptable limits: Relationships experience conflicts over, for example, the desire to be free and the desire to be connected.		**Relationship Dialectics Theory** Tensions become too high and unacceptable.
Social Exchange Theory Rewards increase, costs decrease, profits increase: Relationships develop and are maintained when the rewards exceed the costs.	Intimacy	**Social Exchange Theory** Rewards decrease, costs increase, profits decrease.
Equity Theory Equity prevails; each derives rewards in proportion to the costs paid: Relationships are satisfying when each person's rewards are proportional to her or his costs.	Deterioration	**Equity Theory** Inequities exist and grow greater: One person is under-benefited and one person is over-benefited.
Politeness Theory Politeness increases; positive and negative face needs are met: Relationships are satisfying when positive and negative face needs are met.	Dissolution	**Politeness Theory** Politeness decreases; positive and negative face needs are not met or are violated.

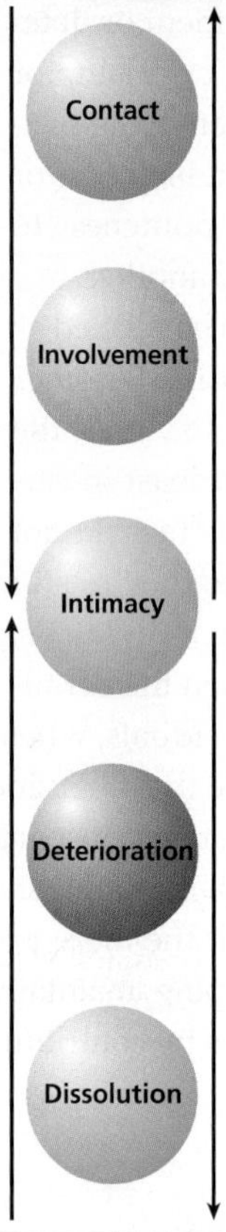

Summary

This chapter introduced interpersonal relationships and focused on the stages you go through in developing and perhaps dissolving relationships, the nature of communication at the various relationship stages, and the various theories of how and why interpersonal relationships develop and dissolve.

Relationship Stages

9.1 Describe the process of relationship development—from contact through (possible) dissolution.

1. At the contact stage of a relationship, you make perceptual contact and later interact with the person.

2. At the involvement stage, you test your potential partner and, if this proves satisfactory, move on to intensifying your relationship.

3. At the intimacy stage, you may make an interpersonal commitment and later enter the stage of social bonding, in which you publicly reveal your relationship status.

4. At the deterioration stage, the bonds holding you together begin to weaken. Intrapersonal dissatisfaction later becomes interpersonal, when you discuss it with your partner and perhaps others.

5. At the repair stage, you first engage in intrapersonal repair, analyzing what went wrong and perhaps what you can do to set things right; later you may engage in interpersonal repair, in which you and your partner consider ways to mend your deteriorating relationship.

6. At the dissolution stage, you separate yourself from your partner and later perhaps separate socially and publicly.

7. A variety of types of movement may be identified: stage movement, turning point movement, and relationship license movement.

Relationship Communication

9.2 Explain the role of communication at the different relationship stages.

8. Communication in developing relationships includes being nice, being open, giving assurances, sharing joint activities, being positive, and improving yourself.

9. Among the communication changes that occur during relationship deterioration are verbal and nonverbal withdrawal, a decline in self-disclosure, an increase in deception, and an increase in negative messages and a decrease in positive messages.

10. General repair strategies include: **R**ecognizing the problem, **E**ngaging in productive communication and conflict resolution, **P**osing possible solutions, **A**ffirming each other, **I**ntegrating solutions into normal behavior, and **R**isking (REPAIR).

Relationship Theories

9.3 Summarize the major theories that explain relationship development, deterioration, and repair (attraction, relationship rules, relationship dialectics, social exchange, equity, and politeness).

11. Attraction theory holds that you develop relationships with those who are similar to you, who are physically close to you, who offer you reinforcement, whom you consider attractive physically and in personality, and who are of a desired socioeconomic and educational level.

12. Relationship rules theory holds that people maintain relationships with those who follow the rules that the individuals have defined as essential to their relationship and dissolve relationships with those who don't follow the rules.

13. Relationship dialectics theory holds that relationships involve tensions between opposing needs and desires, for example, the opposing needs of connection with another person on the one hand and autonomy and independence on the other.

14. Social exchange theory claims that we enter and maintain relationships in which the rewards are greater than the costs. When the costs become greater than the rewards, the relationship deteriorates.

15. Equity theory holds that you develop and maintain relationships in which your ratio of rewards compared to costs is approximately equal to your partner's.

16. Politeness theory holds that you develop and maintain relationships with those who support your positive and negative face needs.

Key Terms

attraction theory

breadth

cherishing behaviors

comparison level

complementarity

contact

costs

depenetration

depth

empathy

equity theory

intimacy

involvement

politeness theory

profits

reciprocity of liking

relationship deterioration

relationship dialectics theory

relationship dissolution

relationship license

relationship repair

relationship rules theory

rewards

similarity

social exchange theory

social penetration theory

turning points

CHAPTER TEN

Interpersonal Relationship Types

Relationships come in different forms. *Interpersonal communication needs to be adjusted to these differences.*

Chapter Topics

Friendship Relationships

Love Relationships

Family Relationships

Workplace Relationships

The Dark Side of Interpersonal Relationships

Learning Objectives

10.1 Define *friendship* and explain how it develops.

10.2 Describe the various types of love.

10.3 Summarize the characteristics of families and distinguish among couple and family types.

10.4 Describe how to create and maintain successful workplace relationships.

10.5 Explain the nature of, and the guidelines for dealing with, jealousy and violence.

This chapter focuses on specific relationship types: (1) friendship, (2) love, (3) family, and (4) workplace relationships, identifying what these are and exploring how interpersonal communication within each of these relationships can be made more effective. We'll also examine the dark side of some relationships in the final section.

All of these relationships can be face-to-face or online or, as is most often the case, some combination. Online relationships have been increasing since the first online dating service was established in 1995. According to one survey, 38 percent of those who identified themselves as "single and looking" used an online dating service (Smith & Duggan, 2013). Social networking sites such as Facebook, Google+, Twitter, Instagram, and Pinterest; professional sites such as LinkedIn; and the dating sites such as Match.com, eHarmony, and OKCupid (and the numerous apps for your phone such as Zoosk, PlentyofFish, and HowAboutWe) make it increasingly easy and interesting to meet new friends and potential romantic partners, to keep in touch with family (websites that provide family hubs are increasing in popularity), and to conduct much of the business of work. As you've no doubt noticed, each type of relationship has both advantages and disadvantages. Here we need to identify just a few of these.

One of the advantages to establishing relationships online (though some may say it's a disadvantage) is that personality outweighs physical appearance. Online communication reveals people's inner qualities first. Rapport and mutual self-disclosure become more important than physical attractiveness in promoting intimacy (Cooper & Sportolari, 1997). And contrary to some popular opinion, online relationships rely just as heavily on the ideals of trust, honesty, and commitment as do face-to-face relationships (Whitty & Gavin, 2001).

Friendship and romantic interaction on the Internet are a natural boon to shut-ins and extremely shy people, for whom traditional ways of meeting others are often difficult. Computer talk is empowering for those with "physical disabilities or disfigurements," for whom face-to-face interactions are often superficial and often end with withdrawal (Bull & Rumsey, 1988; Lea & Spears, 1995). By eliminating the physical cues, computer talk equalizes the interaction and doesn't put the disfigured person, for example, at an immediate disadvantage in a society where physical attractiveness is so highly valued. Online you're free to reveal as much or as little about your physical self as you wish, when you wish.

Another obvious advantage of online relationships is that the number of people you can reach is so vast that it's relatively easy to find someone who matches what you're looking for. The situation is like finding a book that covers just what you need from a library of millions of volumes rather than from a collection of only several hundred or even thousands. In a study of over 19,000 couples who were married between 2005 and 2012, those marriages that started online had higher marital satisfaction and were somewhat less likely to end in divorce than those that started in offline meetings (Cacioppo, Cacioppo, Gonzaga, Ogburn, & Vander-Weele, 2013).

A difference that is often in the news is that of deception. It is a lot easier to lie online than in face-to-face situations. However, most people seem to be relatively truthful in their profiles (Dean, 2010b). As noted elsewhere, women take off a few pounds and men add a bit to their height, but for the most part, the profiles prove accurate (Gibbs, Ellison, & Heino, 2006; Toma, Hancock, & Ellison, 2008). But you really can't tell how much a photo has been enhanced or how long ago the photo was taken. And depending on the technology you're using, you may not be able to hear the person's voice; this too hinders you as you seek to develop a total picture of the other person.

Online, people can present a false self with little chance of detection; minors may present themselves as adults, and adults may present themselves as children in order to conduct illicit sexual communications and perhaps meetings. Similarly, people can present themselves as poor when they're rich or as serious and committed when they're just enjoying the fun and games of this online experience. And they can crowdsource by saying it's for some noble effort when it's actually for totally selfish reasons. Although people can also misrepresent themselves in face-to-face relationships, the fact that it's easier to do online probably accounts for the greater frequency of misrepresentation in computer relationships (Cornwell & Lundgren, 2001).

Friendship Relationships

10.1 Define *friendship* and explain how it develops.

Friendship has engaged the attention and imagination of poets, novelists, and artists of all kinds. On television, friendships have become almost as important as romantic pairings. And friendship also interests a range of interpersonal communication researchers (Samter, 2004). Throughout your life, you'll encounter many people, but out of this wide array you'll develop few face-to-face relationships you would call friendships. Despite the low number of friendships, you may form, however, their importance is great. On social network sites, the number of friends can easily be in the hundreds, even thousands. Of course, different definitions of *friend* are used in each case.

The number of friends you have on your favorite social network site depends on several factors (Awl, 2011): your willingness to make new friends and interact with them, the enjoyment you get from communicating with a wide variety of people, and your time constraints. After all, when you have hundreds of friends, it takes time to read their posts and respond as you might like.

Definition and Characteristics

The type of friendship that we're talking about is the relatively close relationship we have with someone (online or face-to-face) rather than a "friend" who you don't really know but friended because he or she is a friend of a friend of a friend. In this context, **friendship** is an *interpersonal relationship* between two interdependent persons that is *mutually productive* and *characterized by mutual positive regard*.

- *Friendship is an interpersonal relationship.* Communication interactions must have taken place between the people. Further, the relationship involves a "personalistic focus" (Wright, 1978, 1984); friends react to each other as complete persons—as unique, genuine, and irreplaceable individuals.

- *Friendships must be mutually productive.* Friendships cannot be destructive to either person. Once destructiveness enters into a relationship, it really can't be called a friendship. Lover relationships, marriage relationships, parent–child relationships, and just about any other possible relationship can be either destructive or productive, but friendship must enhance the potential of each person and can only be productive. Friendships that are destructive are best viewed as pseudo-friendships.

- *Liking people is essential if we are to call them friends.* Three major characteristics of friendship—trust, emotional support, and sharing of interests (Blieszner & Adams, 1992)—facilitate mutual positive regard. Although mutual liking seems essential for a friendship, the mutuality (the degree of liking) is not necessarily identical. For example, in one study 94 percent of the people surveyed expected their friends to like them in the same way they liked their friends. But, actually, these reciprocity rates ranged from only 34 to 53 percent (Almaatouq, Radaelli, Pentland, & Shmueli, 2016; Murphy, 2016).

In many parts of the world, face-to-face friendships are clearly a matter of choice; you choose—within limits—who your friends will be. And most researchers define friendship as a voluntary relationship of choice (Samter, 2004). But throughout human history, in many parts of the world—for

example, in small villages miles away from urban centers, where people are born, live, and die without venturing much beyond their community—relationships traditionally have not been voluntary. In these settings, you simply form relationships with those in your village. You don't have the luxury of selecting certain people to interact with and others to ignore. You must interact with and form friendships and romantic relationships with members of the community simply because these are the only people you come into contact with on a regular basis (Moghaddam, Taylor, & Wright, 1993). This situation is changing rapidly, however, as Internet use becomes universal. With access to people from all over the world via the Internet, more and more relationships will become voluntary.

Friendship Types

Friendships can be viewed from a variety of perspectives. Here are just a few to give you an idea of the varied types of friends.

- *Functions* One way of looking at friendship types is in terms of the functions they serve. And so, for example, you might classify friends (though not necessarily consciously) according to the purposes of communication identified in Chapter 1: friends that help you learn and stimulate you, friends you can form a close relationship with, friends who will help you in a variety of ways (financially or emotionally, for example), friends who you can influence and get to do the things you want, and friends to play with.

- *Closeness* An obvious way to classify friends is in terms of closeness. For example, you probably have friends who, on closer inspection, you could classify into acquaintances, casual friends, close friends, and intimate friends. Even social media encourages you to classify your friends along this closeness dimension.

- *Communication Media* Another perspective may be in terms of the ways in which you communicate—online, face to face, phone, e-mail, text, or some combination—as well as how frequently you use each medium.

- *Reality Base* Some friendships are real in the sense that both people demonstrate the characteristic you would normally think of when you think of a friend—mutual support, availability, mutual liking, and frequent contact, for example. But, some friendships are less real, for example, the parasocial friendships you might have with a celebrity. Although only you know of this "friendship," it somehow seems real. And then, of course, there is the friendship-of-appearance with, for example, a work colleague you really dislike but with whom you have to work cordially.

- *Interactions* Still another view is to classify friendships according the type of interactions. One time-honored system is to classify friends into three classes: reciprocity, receptivity, and association (Reisman, 1979, 1981).

  - The *friendship of reciprocity* is based on equality: each individual shares equally in giving and receiving the benefits and rewards of the relationship.

  - In the *friendship of receptivity*, one person is the primary giver and one is the primary receiver. This is a positive imbalance because each person (say, teacher and student or doctor and patient) gains something from the relationship.

  - The *friendship of association* is a transitory one, the kind you often have with classmates, neighbors, coworkers, or social media friends or connections.

Two special types of friends need to be singled out for a more complete view of friendship types: the friend with benefits and the frenemy—one that extends and one that contradicts our traditional image of the friend.

Friends with Benefits A **friends with benefits** relationship—which varies greatly from one couple to another—engage in sexual relationships but without any romantic involvement, dating, or the thought of a shared future together (Mongeau, Knight, Williams, Eden, & Shaw, 2013). Only about 15% of friends with benefits relationships develop into something more serious (http://www.inquisitr.com/1982784/new-study-15-percent-friends-with-benefits-relationships-serious/). Although most often portrayed as a cross-sex relationship, it can apply to same-sex as well as opposite sex pairings. This type of relationship has been around probably throughout time, but it has only recently been given a name and today is largely associated with college students. In one study, over 60 percent of college students surveyed reported having had at least one such relationship (Bisson & Levine, 2009).

Among the advantages of such relationships are easy access to sex in a safe and comfortable environment with a trusted friend, freedom from commitment or intense involvement, gaining experience, closeness, and companionship. Among the disadvantages are the possibilities that the friendship will suffer and getting hurt (Weaver, MacKeigan, & MacDonald, 2011). Open, sincere, and direct communication were key factors in ensuring that the relationship has more advantages than disadvantages.

Another type of relationship that is closely akin to friends with benefits is the hookup (made very easy with the numerous websites), where people meet just for sex. These relationships (and some researchers would probably not even consider this a relationship) can morph into friendships and then to friends with benefits.

Frenemies   A **frenemy** is really not a friend in any meaningful sense of the term and yet, because it masquerades as a friend, needs to be noted. A frenemy is an enemy disguised as a friend, someone who appears on the surface to be a friend but on a deeper level is not your friend. And, it's important to note, that these behaviors are repeated; there's a pattern to such behaviors. Any friend can act the frenemy on occasion; the real frenemy does it repeatedly. Here are just a few behaviors commonly associated with the frenemy.

- Unlike a true friend, the frenemy is disconfirming rather than confirming. The frenemy doesn't express happiness or pride in your accomplishments but is often ready to listen to your tales of woe.

- The frenemy frequently criticizes but often under the guise of humor and so you hardly notice it's criticism. And usually the criticism from the frenemy is not constructive; it doesn't help you improve or better yourself in any way. The backhanded compliment is a frequent tool: "Boy, you're looking good; another 15 pounds and you're there."

- The frenemy often discourages friendships with others, often as a way of maintaining control over your relationship and making you more dependent on the frenemy.

- The frenemy is both warm, kind, and understanding and at the same time cold, hurtful, and indifferent. They are bistrategic; they use warmth and similar qualities to keep you a friend but also coldness to hurt and maintain a superior position (Kennedy-Moore, 2014).

- The frenemy will put you down, rather than raise you up. For example, a frenemy might post an unflattering photo of you and when you ask that it be taken down, will tell you something like, "Oh, I think it's cute."

- The frenemy hurts rather than helps. After a true-friend interaction, you generally feel better about yourself; after a frenemy interaction, you generally feel worse. But, there is some evidence that frenemies are at times beneficial, for example, at work where a frenemy can motivate you to do better and to look at other perspectives (Melwani & Rothman, 2015).

Some theorists would argue that you need to get rid of frenemies (something that's not always possible if the frenemy is a work colleague, relative, or neighbor). Others would claim that you should minimize the destructive effects of such relationships

(Weir, 2011). So, if talking about religion results in put-downs, avoid the topic as best you can. If your frenemy is consistently late, plan to use the time to advantage rather than just wait. Still another way to deal with the frenemy is to empathize and come to understand the need he or she has that is leading to this behavior—admittedly a difficult task. And, of course, you can always respond assertively and express your distaste for the backhanded compliment or the frequent criticism.

Friendship Needs

Friendships serve a variety of important needs that most medical professionals recognize as important to both mental and physical health (Mayo Clinic Staff, 2016). On the basis of your experiences or your predictions, you select as friends those who help to satisfy a variety of basic needs. Selecting friends on the basis of need satisfaction is similar to choosing a marriage partner, an employee, or any person who may be in a position to satisfy your needs. For example, depending on your needs, you may look for friends such as these, whether face-to-face or online (Reiner & Blanton, 1997; Wright 1978, 1984):

- *Utility* Someone who may have special talents, skills, or resources that prove useful to you, for example, a person who is especially bright who might assist you in getting a better job or in introducing you to a possible romantic partner. Many of the "friendships" formed on professional social media sites like LinkedIn would be of this type.

- *Affirmation* Someone who affirms your personal value and helps you to recognize your attributes, for example, someone who communicates appreciation for your leadership abilities, athletic prowess, or sense of humor. The friend on Facebook who always comments on your photos and posts would also be serving this affirming function.

- *Ego support* Someone who behaves in a supportive, encouraging, and helpful manner, for example, a person who helps you view yourself as worthy and competent.

- *Stimulation* Someone who introduces you to new ideas and new ways of seeing the world, for example, a person who might bring you into contact with previously unfamiliar people, issues, and experiences. Online friendships with those from other parts of the world or of different religions or cultural traditions regularly serve this function, sometimes without being aware of it.

- *Security* Someone who does nothing to hurt you or to call attention to your weaknesses, for example, a person who is supportive and nonjudgmental.

INTERPERSONAL CHOICE POINT
Asking a Favor

You need to borrow $200 from your work colleague, and you have no idea when you'll be able to pay it back. *In what way would you ask for this loan?*

a. "I need $200 desperately!"

b. "I'm wondering if you could lend me some money?"

c. "You have to lend me $200."

d. Ask a mutual friend to intercede for you.

e. Other

Friendship and Communication

Close and lasting friendships develop over time in stages. At one end of the friendship continuum are strangers, or two persons who have just met or just friended each other, and at the other end are intimate friends. What happens between these two extremes?

As you progress from the initial contact stage to intimate friendship, the depth and breadth of communications increase; you talk about issues that are closer to your inner core. Similarly, the number of communication topics increases as your friendship becomes closer. As depth and breadth increase, so does the satisfaction you derive from the friendship. This increase in depth and breadth can and does occur in all forms of communication—face-to-face as well as online. It's interesting to note that establishing and maintaining friendships are the major reasons for Internet communication (instant messaging and texting, social network sites, and e-mail) among college students and among teens (Knox, Daniels, Sturdivant, & Zusman, 2001; Lenhart, Madden, Macgill, & Smith, 2007). And, of course, these forms of communication promote closeness and intimacy and often encourage online partners to meet face-to-face (Hu, Wood, Smith, & Westbrook, 2004).

We can identify three main stages of friendship development and integrate some of the characteristics of effective interpersonal communication (Johnson, Wittenberg, Villagran, Mazur, & Villagran, 2003). The assumption here is that, as the friendship progresses from initial contact and acquaintanceship through casual friendship, to close and intimate friendship, effective interpersonal communication increases. However, there is no assumption made that close relationships are necessarily the preferred type or that they're better than casual or temporary relationships. We need all types.

Contact   At the contact stage, the characteristics of effective interpersonal communication are usually present to only a small degree. You're guarded rather than open or expressive. Because you don't yet know the other person, your ability to empathize with the other is limited. At this stage, there is little genuine immediacy; you see yourselves as separate and distinct rather than as a unit. Because the relationship is so new and because the people don't know each other very well, the interaction is often characterized by awkwardness—for example, by overlong pauses, uncertainty about topics to be discussed, and ineffective exchanges of sender and receiver roles.

Involvement   In this second stage, there is a dyadic consciousness, a clear sense of "we-ness," of togetherness; communication demonstrates a sense of immediacy. At this stage, you participate in activities as a unit rather than as separate individuals. In the involvement period, the other person can be called "friend"—someone you would go with to the movies, sit with in the cafeteria or in class, ride home with from school, or follow (really follow) on social media. At this friendship stage, you begin to see the qualities of effective interpersonal interaction more clearly. You start to express yourself openly and become interested in the other person's disclosures. Because you're beginning to understand this person, you empathize and demonstrate significant other-orientation. You also demonstrate supportiveness and develop a genuinely positive attitude, both toward the other person and toward mutual communication situations. There is an ease at this stage, a coordination in the interaction between the two persons. You communicate with confidence, maintain appropriate eye contact and flexibility in body posture and gesturing, and use few of the adaptors that signal discomfort.

As friendships develop, whether face-to-face or online, **network convergence** occurs; that is, as a relationship between two people develops, they begin to share their network of other communicators with each other (Parks, 1995; Parks & Floyd, 1996). And this, at least in online friendships, accounts in great part for the enormous number of friends some people have.

Close and Intimate Friendship   At this stage, you and your friend see yourselves more as an exclusive unit, and each of you derives great benefits (for example, emotional support) from the friendship (Hays, 1989). Because you know each other well (for example, you know each other's values, opinions, and attitudes), your uncertainty about each other has been significantly reduced—you're able to predict each other's behaviors with considerable accuracy. This knowledge makes significant interaction management possible, as well as greater positivity, supportiveness, and openness (Oswald, Clark, & Kelly, 2004).

You become more other-oriented and more willing to make significant sacrifices for the other person. You empathize and exchange perspectives a great deal more, and you expect in return that your friend will also empathize with you. With a genuinely positive feeling for this individual, your supportiveness and positive

Closeness Among Friends
Some evidence suggests that close and intimate friends are *less* effective at judging when someone is concealing sadness and anger than are less intimate friends (Sternglanz & DePaulo, 2004). *On the basis of your own experience, how do you see the connection between closeness of a friendship and the ability to decode what another person is feeling?*

stroking become spontaneous. Because you see yourselves as an exclusive unit, equality and immediacy are in clear evidence. You're willing to respond openly, confidently, and expressively to this person and to own your feelings and thoughts. Your supportiveness and positivity are genuine expressions of the closeness you feel for this person. Each person in an intimate friendship is truly equal; each can initiate and each can respond; each can be active and each can be passive; each speaks and each listens.

Friendship, Culture, and Gender

Your friendships and the way you look at friendships are influenced by your culture and your gender. Let's look first at culture.

Culture and Friendships   In the United States, you can be friends with someone yet never really be expected to go out of your way for this person. Many Middle Easterners, Asians, and Latin Americans consider going significantly out of their way an absolutely essential ingredient in friendship; if you're not willing to sacrifice for your friend, then this person is not really your friend (Dresser, 2005).

Generally, friendships are closer in collectivist cultures than in individualist cultures. In their emphasis on the group and on cooperating, collectivist cultures foster the development of close friendship bonds. Members of a collectivist culture are expected to help others in the group. When you help or do things for someone else, you increase your own attractiveness to this person, and this is certainly a good start for a friendship. Of course, the culture continues to reward these close associations.

Members of individualist cultures, on the other hand, are expected to look out for number one—themselves. Consequently, they're more likely to compete and to try to do better than each other—conditions that don't support, generally at least, the development of friendships.

Most people, of course, have both collectivist and individualist values, but they have them in different degrees, and that is what we are talking about here—differences in degree of the collectivist versus the individualist orientation.

Gender and Friendships   Gender also influences your friendships—who becomes your friend and the way you look at friendships. Perhaps the best-documented finding—already noted in our discussion of self-disclosure—is that women self-disclose more than men (e.g., Dolgin, Meyer, & Schwartz, 1991). This difference holds throughout male and female friendships. Male friends self-disclose less often and with less intimate details than female friends do. Men generally don't view intimacy as a necessary quality of their friendships (Hart, 1990).

Women engage in significantly more affectional behaviors with their friends than do males; this difference may account for the greater difficulty men experience in beginning and maintaining close friendships (Hays, 1989). Women engage in more casual communication; they also share greater intimacy and more confidences with their friends than do men. Communication, in all its forms and functions, seems a much more important dimension of women's friendships.

When women and men were asked to evaluate their friendships, women rated their same-sex friendships higher in general quality, intimacy, enjoyment, and nurturance than did men (Sapadin, 1988). Men, in contrast, rated their opposite-sex friendships higher in quality, enjoyment, and nurturance than did women. Both men and women rated their opposite-sex friendships similarly in intimacy. These differences

THE CULTURAL MAP Masculine and Feminine Orientation

Online and face-to-face friendships, romantic relationships, family, and workplace relationships dominate our lives. These relationships are influenced by the masculine-feminine cultural differences. The aggressive, ambitious, and competitive masculine cultural orientation will encourage relationships that are different from what the modest, tender, relationship-focused feminine culture will encourage.

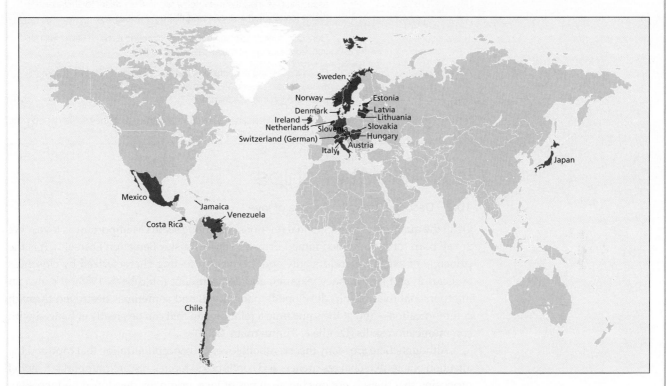

These countries are among the most strongly affiliated with masculine qualities. Masculine cultures emphasize aggressiveness, strength, and success and socialize their members to be assertive, competitive, and ambitious.

These countries are among the most strongly affiliated with feminine qualities. Feminine cultures emphasize modesty, quality of life rather than material success, and a concern for relationships.

Look at your own relationships (friendship and romantic). *Are they mainly with those who have a masculine orientation or mainly with those who have a feminine orientation? If there is a difference, to what do you attribute it?*

may be due, in part, to our society's suspicion of male friendships; as a result, a man may be reluctant to admit to having close relationship bonds with another man. Men's friendships are often built around shared activities—attending a ballgame, playing cards, working on a project at the office. Women's friendships, on the other hand, are built more around a sharing of feelings, support, and "personalism." An important element is similarity in status, in willingness to protect a friend in uncomfortable situations, and in academic major.

As we move further into the twenty-first century, the ways in which men and women develop and maintain their friendships will undoubtedly change considerably—as will all gender-related variables. In the meantime, given the present state of research on gender differences, be careful not to exaggerate and to treat small differences as if they were highly significant. Avoid stereotypes and avoid stressing opposites to the neglect of the huge number of similarities between men and women (Wright, 1988; Deaux & LaFrance, 1998).

Table 10.1 provides a brief summary of this discussion of friendship.

Table 10.1 In a Nutshell Friendship

Aspects of Friendship	Explanations
Definition	Friendship is an interpersonal relationship that is mutually productive and characterized by mutual positive regard.
Types	Among the types of friendship are those of reciprocity, receptivity, and association. A friend-with-benefits relationship refers to a relationship that is friendly (rather than romantic) but involves sex.
Needs served	Generally, friendships serve a variety of needs such as utility, affirmation, ego support, stimulation, and security.
Development	Close and lasting relationships develop in stages, with the communication echoing the relationship stage; intimate communication takes place among intimate friends.
Influences	The types of friendship developed and the needs they serve depend greatly on one's culture and gender.

Love Relationships

10.2 Describe the various types of love.

Of all the qualities of interpersonal relationships, none seems as important as love. "We are all born for love," noted famed British Prime Minister Benjamin Disraeli. "It is the principle of existence and its only end." **Love** is a feeling characterized by closeness and caring and by intimacy, passion, and commitment (Sternberg, 1988). It's also an interpersonal relationship developed, maintained, and sometimes destroyed through communication—and at the same time a relationship that can be greatly enhanced with communication skills (Dindia & Timmerman, 2003).

Although there are many theories about love, the conceptualization that captured the attention of interpersonal researchers and continues to receive research support is a model proposing that there is not one but six types of love, originally developed by John Alan Lee (Kimberly & Werner-Wilson, 2013; Guerrero, Andersen, & Afifi, 2013; Lee, 1976, 1988).

As a preface to this discussion of the types of love, you may wish to respond to the following statements to get an idea of your love style. For each statement, indicate if it is true (T) of your feelings about love or false (F). The discussion following will elaborate on these six styles of love and these statements.

_____ **1.** I value physical attractiveness very highly.

_____ **2.** I would not become romantically involved with someone who was not attractive.

_____ **3.** I don't think love should be too intense; it's best when it's kept light.

_____ **4.** I would not love someone who was not interesting or amusing.

_____ **5.** I seek a love that could be described as peaceful.

_____ **6.** I don't think sex is that important to a love relationship.

_____ **7.** I would only become attracted to someone who would help me in my career.

_____ **8.** I would select a romantic partner who is similar in attitudes and personality to me.

_____ **9.** I think love is either a roller coaster or nothing.

_____ **10.** I see love as total, intense, possessive.

_____ **11.** I think love is a selfless feeling.

_____ **12.** I can love someone who doesn't love me.

INTERPERSONAL CHOICE POINT
From Friendship to Love

You have a great friendship with a colleague at work, but recently these feelings of friendship are turning to feelings of love. *What might you do to move this friendship to love, or at least to discover if the other person would be receptive to this change?*

a. Send flowers with a note.

b. Explain your feelings to the person face-to-face.

c. Ask a third party to find out how this person feels.

d. Ask the person about his or her romantic life.

e. Other

Love Types

Let's look at each of these six types of love, previewed in Figure 10.1.

Eros: Beauty and Sexuality   (Statements 1 and 2 in the self-test) Like Narcissus, who fell in love with the beauty of his own image, **eros** love focuses on beauty and physical attractiveness—sometimes to the exclusion of qualities you might consider more important and more lasting. Also like Narcissus, the erotic lover has an idealized image of beauty that is unattainable in reality. Consequently, the erotic lover often feels unfulfilled. Erotic lovers are particularly sensitive to physical imperfections in the ones they love.

Ludus: Entertainment and Excitement   (Statements 3 and 4 in the self-test) **Ludus** love is experienced as a game, as fun. The better you can play the game, the greater the enjoyment. Love is not to be taken too seriously; emotions are to be held in check lest they get out of hand and make trouble; passions never rise to the point where they get out of control. A ludic lover is self-controlled, always aware of the need to manage love rather than allow it to be in control. Perhaps because of this need to control love, some researchers have proposed that ludic love tendencies may reveal tendencies to sexual aggression (Sarwer, Kalichman, Johnson, Early, et al., 1993). The ludic lover retains a partner only as long as the partner is interesting and amusing. When interest fades, it's time to change partners. Perhaps because love is a game, sexual fidelity is of little importance. In fact, research shows that people who score high on ludic love are more likely to engage in "extradyadic" dating and sex than those who score low on ludus (Wiederman & Hurd, 1999). Ludic lovers also score high on narcissism (Campbell, Foster, & Finkel, 2002).

Storge: Peaceful and Slow   (Statements 5 and 6 in the self-test) **Storge** (a word that comes from the Greek for "familial love") love lacks passion and intensity. Storgic lovers set out not to find lovers but to establish a companionable relationship with someone they know and with whom they can share interests and activities. Storgic love is a gradual process of unfolding thoughts and feelings; the changes seem to come so slowly and so gradually that it's often difficult to define exactly where the relationship is at any point in time. Sex in storgic relationships comes late, and when it comes, it assumes no great importance.

Figure 10.1   Types of Love

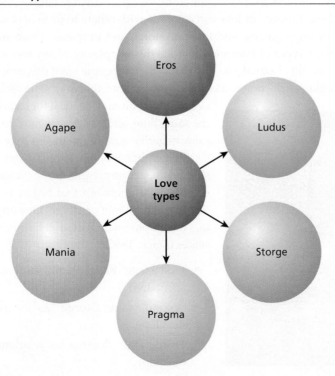

Pragma: Practical and Traditional (Statements 7 and 8 in the self-test) The **pragma** lover is practical and seeks a relationship that will work. Pragma lovers want compatibility and a relationship in which their important needs and desires will be satisfied. They're concerned with the social qualifications of a potential mate even more than with personal qualities; family and background are extremely important to the pragma lover, who relies not so much on feelings as on logic. The pragma lover views love as a useful relationship that makes the rest of life easier. So the pragma lover asks questions about a potential mate such as "Will this person earn a good living?" "Can this person cook?" "Will this person help me advance in my career?" Pragma lovers' relationships rarely deteriorate. This is partly because pragma lovers choose their mates carefully and emphasize similarities. Another reason is that they have realistic romantic expectations.

Mania: Elation and Depression (Statements 9 and 10 in the self-test) **Mania** is characterized by extreme highs and extreme lows. The manic lover loves intensely and at the same time intensely worries about the loss of the love. This fear often prevents the manic lover from deriving as much pleasure as possible from the relationship. With little provocation, the manic lover may experience extreme jealousy. Manic love is obsessive; the manic lover must possess the beloved completely. In return, the manic lover wishes to be possessed—to be loved intensely. The manic lover's poor self-image seems capable of being improved only by love; self-worth comes from being loved rather than from any sense of inner satisfaction. Because love is so important, danger signs in a relationship are often ignored; the manic lover believes that if there is love, then nothing else matters.

Agape: Compassionate and Selfless (Statements 11 and 12 in the self-test) **Agape** is a compassionate, egoless, self-giving love. The agapic lover loves even people with whom he or she has no close ties. This lover loves the stranger on the road even though the two of them probably will never meet again. Agape is a spiritual love, offered without concern for personal reward or gain. This lover loves without expecting that the love will be reciprocated. Jesus, Buddha, and Gandhi preached this unqualified love, agape (Lee, 1976). In one sense, agape is more a philosophical kind of love than a love that most people have the strength to achieve. People who believe in *yuan*, a Chinese concept that comes from the Buddhist belief in predestiny, are more likely to favor agapic (and pragmatic) love and less likely to favor erotic love (Goodwin & Findlay, 1997).

Each of these varieties of love can combine with others to form new and different patterns (for example, manic and ludic or storge and pragma). These six, however, identify the major types of love and illustrate the complexity of any love relationship. The six styles should also make it clear that different people want different things, that each person seeks satisfaction in a unique way. The love that may seem lifeless or crazy or boring to you may be ideal for someone else. At the same time, another person may see these very same negative qualities in the love you're seeking.

Remember, too, that love changes. A relationship that began as pragma may develop into ludus or eros. A relationship that began as erotic may develop into mania or storge. One approach sees this developmental process as having three major stages (Duck, 1986):

- First stage: Eros, mania, and ludus (initial attraction)
- Second stage: Storge (as the relationship develops)
- Third stage: Pragma (as relationship bonds develop)

Romantic Love

When college students were asked to identify the features that characterize romantic love, the five elements most frequently noted were trust, sexual attraction, acceptance and tolerance, spending time together, and sharing thoughts and secrets (Regan, Kocan, & Whitlock, 1998). *How would you characterize love? Do you find that men and women view love differently? If so, in what ways?*

In reading about the love styles, you may have felt that certain personality types are likely to favor one type of love over another. Here are personality traits that research finds people assign to each love style (Taraban & Hendrick 1995). Which set of adjectives would you match with each love style (eros, ludus, storge, pragma, mania, and agape)?

1. inconsiderate, secretive, dishonest, selfish, and dangerous
2. honest, loyal, mature, caring, loving, and understanding
3. jealous, possessive, obsessed, emotional, and dependent
4. sexual, exciting, loving, happy, optimistic
5. committed, giving, caring, self-sacrificing, and loving
6. family-oriented, planning, careful, hard-working, and concerned

Very likely you perceived these personality factors in the same way as did the participants in research from which these traits were drawn: 1 = ludus, 2 = storge, 3 = mania, 4 = eros, 5 = agape, and 6 = pragma. Do note, of course, that these results do not imply that ludus lovers are inconsiderate, secretive, and dishonest. They merely mean that people in general (and perhaps you in particular) *think* of ludus lovers as inconsiderate, secretive, and dishonest.

Love and Communication

How do you communicate when you're in love? What do you say? What do you do nonverbally? According to research, you exaggerate your beloved's virtues and minimize his or her faults. You share emotions and experiences and speak tenderly, with an extra degree of politeness, to each other; "please," "thank you," and similar expressions abound. You frequently use personalized communication, which includes secrets you keep from other people and messages that have meaning only within your specific relationship (Knapp, Ellis, & Williams, 1980; Knapp, Vangelisti, & Caughlin, 2014). You also create and use personal idioms (and pet names): words, phrases, and gestures that carry meaning only for the particular relationship and that say you have a special language that signifies your special bond (Hopper, Knapp, & Scott, 1981). When outsiders try to use personal idioms—as they sometimes do—the expressions seem inappropriate, at times even an invasion of privacy. In online relationships, these romantic messages often move offline or into some private online group.

You engage in significant self-disclosure, and when the self-disclosure is extremely significant, you restrict this to this one person, often offline. There is more confirmation and less disconfirmation among lovers than among either nonlovers or those who are going through romantic breakups. You also use more constructive conflict resolution strategies if you feel your relationship is threatened (Gonzaga, Keltner, Londahl, & Smith, 2001). You're highly aware of what is and is not appropriate to say to the person you love. You know how to reward, but also how to punish, each other. In short, you know what to do to obtain the reaction you want.

Among your most often used means for communicating love are telling the person face-to-face or by telephone (in one survey, 79 percent indicated they did it this way), expressing supportiveness, and talking things out and cooperating (Marston, Hecht, & Robers, 1987). Today, you do the same things but often through instant messaging (IM), Facebook postings, and Twitter; you change your status, post photos of the two of you in romantic settings, or simply post "We in love."

Nonverbally, you also communicate your love. Prolonged and focused eye contact is perhaps the clearest nonverbal indicator of love. So important is eye contact that its avoidance almost always triggers a "What's wrong?" response. You also have longer periods of silence than you do with friends (Guerrero, 1997). In addition, you display affiliative cues (signs that show you love the other person), including head nods, gestures, and forward leaning. And you give Duchenne smiles—smiles that are beyond voluntary control and that signal genuine joy (Gonzaga, Keltner, Londahl, & Smith, 2001).

These smiles give you crow's-feet around the eyes, raise up your cheeks, and puff up the lower eyelids (Lemonick, 2005a).

You eliminate socially taboo adaptors, at least in the presence of the loved one. For example, you curtail scratching your head, picking your teeth, cleaning your ears, and passing wind. These adaptors often return after lovers have achieved a permanent relationship.

You touch more frequently and more intimately (Anderson, 2004; Guerrero, 1997). You also use more tie signs, nonverbal gestures that show that you're together, such as holding hands, walking with arms entwined, kissing, and the like. You may even dress alike; the styles of clothes and even the colors selected by lovers are more similar than those worn by nonlovers. Posting such photos on Instagram, Pinterest, or Flickr or on any social network site communicates more publicly your pairing, your connectedness.

Love, Culture, and Gender

Like friendship, love is heavily influenced by culture and gender (Dion & Dion, 1996; Wood & Smith, 2005). Let's consider first some of the cultural influences on the way you look at love and on the type of love you're seeking or maintaining.

Culture and Love   Although most of the research on the six love styles has been done in the United States, some research has been conducted in other cultures (Bierhoff & Klein, 1991). Here are just a few examples to illustrate that love is seen differently in different cultures. Asians, for example, have been found to be more friendship-oriented in their love style than are Europeans (Dion & Dion, 1993b). Members of individualist cultures (for example, Western Europeans) are likely to place greater emphasis on romantic love and on individual fulfillment. Members of collectivist cultures are likely to spread their love over a large network of relatives (Dion & Dion, 1993a). When compared to their Chinese counterparts, American men scored higher on ludic and agapic love and lower on erotic and pragma love. American men are also less likely to view emotional satisfaction as crucial to relationship maintenance (Sprecher & Toro-Morn, 2002).

One study finds a love style among Mexicans characterized as calm, compassionate, and deliberate (Leon, Philbrick, Parra, Escobedo, et al., 1994). In comparisons between love styles in the United States and France, it was found that people in the United States scored higher on storge and mania than the French; in contrast, the French scored higher on agape (Murstein, Merighi, & Vyse, 1991). In the United States, Caucasian women scored higher on mania than African-American women, whereas African-American women scored higher on agape. Caucasian and African-American men, however, scored very similarly; no statistically significant differences were found (Morrow, Clark, & Brock, 1995).

Gender and Love   Gender also influences love. In the United States, the differences between men and women in love are considered great. In poetry, novels, and the mass media, women and men are depicted as acting very differently when falling in love, being in love, and ending a love relationship. As Lord Byron put it in *Don Juan,* "Man's love is of man's life a thing apart,/'Tis woman's whole existence." Women are portrayed as emotional, men as logical. Women are supposed to love intensely; men are supposed to love with detachment.

Women and men seem to experience love to a similar degree, and research continues to find great similarities between male and female conceptions of love (Fehr & Broughton, 2001; Rubin, 1973). However, women indicate greater love than men do for their same-sex friends. This may reflect a real difference between the sexes, or it may

VIEWPOINTS

Love, Marriage, and Culture

Men and women from different cultures were asked if they would marry a man or a woman who had all the qualities they desired but with whom they were not in love. Fifty percent of the respondents from Pakistan said yes and 49 percent of those from India said yes. At the other extreme were those from Japan (only 2 percent said yes), the United States (only 3.5 percent), and Brazil (only 4 percent) (Levine, Sato, Hashimoto, & Verma, 1994). *How would you answer this question? How is your answer influenced by your culture?*

be a function of the greater social restrictions on men. A man is not supposed to admit his love for another man. Women are permitted greater freedom to communicate their love for other women.

Much research finds that men place more emphasis on romance than women. For example, when college students were asked the question "If a man (woman) had all the other qualities you desired, would you marry this person if you were not in love with him (her)?" Approximately two-thirds of the men responded no, which seems to indicate that a high percentage were concerned with love and romance. However, less than one-third of the women responded no (LeVine, Sato, Hashimoto, & Verma, 1994). Further, when men and women were surveyed concerning their view on love—whether basically realistic or basically romantic—it was found that married women had a more realistic (less romantic) conception of love than did married men (Knapp, Vangelisti, & Caughlin, 2014).

Additional research also supports the view that men are more romantic; for example, "Men are more likely than women to believe in love at first sight, in love as the basis for marriage and for overcoming obstacles, and to believe that their partner and relationship will be perfect" (Sprecher & Metts, 1989). This difference seems to increase as the romantic relationship develops: men become more romantic and women less romantic (Fengler, 1974).

In their reactions to broken romantic affairs, women and men exhibit similarities and differences. For example, the tendency for women and men to recall only pleasant memories and to revisit places with past associations was about equal. However, men engaged in more dreaming about the lost partner and in more daydreaming generally as a reaction to the breakup than did women.

Table 10.2 summarizes the definition, types, communication, and influences on love.

Table 10.2 In a Nutshell Love

Aspects of Love	Explanations
Definition	Love may be viewed as a feeling of closeness and caring and be characterized by intimacy, passion, and commitment.
Types	Among the types of love are eros, ludus, storge, pragma, mania, and agape.
Communication	Communication is likely at its most intimate in a love relationship.
Influences	Your culture and gender influence the type of love that you seek.

Family Relationships

10.3 Summarize the characteristics of families and distinguish among couple and family types.

If you had to define the term **family**, you might reply that a family consists of a husband, a wife, and one or more children. When pressed, you might add that some families also include other relatives—in-laws, brothers and sisters, grandparents, aunts and uncles, and so on. But other types of relationships are, to their own members, families. One obvious example is the family without children—a pattern that has been increasing. Also on the increase is the single-parent family.

Another obvious example is people living together in an exclusive relationship who are not married. For the most part, these cohabitants live as if they were married: there is an exclusive sexual commitment; there may be children; there are shared financial responsibilities, shared time, and shared space. These relationships mirror traditional marriages except that in marriage, the union is recognized by a religious body, the state, or both.

Another example is the gay or lesbian couple who live together—whether as domestic partners or in marriage—in households that have all the characteristics of a family.

The Family Through Time

If you looked at the family from an evolutionary–Darwinian point of view, one research watcher notes, you'd have to conclude that families are inherently unstable and that it's necessity, not choice, that keeps them together. If they had better opportunities elsewhere, many family members would leave immediately (Goleman, 1995b). *What do you see as the greatest advantages of family? What do you see as the greatest disadvantages?*

Many of these couples have children from previous heterosexual unions, through artificial insemination, or by adoption. Although accurate statistics are difficult to secure, primary relationships among gays and lesbians seem more common than the popular media lead us to believe. And, most relationship experts agree, being in a committed relationship is the goal of most people, regardless of affectional orientation (Fitzpatrick & Caughlin, 2002; Kurdek, 2000, 2004; Patterson, 2000).

The communication principles that apply to the traditional nuclear family (the mother–father–child family) also apply to these other kinds of families. In the following discussion, the term **primary relationship** denotes the relationship between the two principal parties—the husband and wife, the lovers, the domestic partners, for example; the term *family* denotes the broader constellation that includes children, relatives, and assorted significant others.

Characteristics of Families

All primary relationships and families have several qualities that further characterize this relationship type: defined roles, recognition of responsibilities, shared history and future, and shared living space.

Defined Roles   Many heterosexual couples divide their roles rather traditionally, with the man as primary wage earner and maintenance person and the woman as primary cook, child rearer, and housekeeper. This is less true among more highly educated couples and those in the higher socioeconomic classes, where changes in traditional role assignments are seen first. However, among gay and lesbian couples, clear-cut, stereotypical male and female roles are not found; they do not conform to traditional "masculine" and "feminine" roles (Cloud, 2008; Peplau, 1988).

Recognition of Responsibilities   Family members see themselves as having certain obligations and responsibilities to one another. For example, individuals have an obligation to help each other financially. There are also emotional responsibilities: to offer comfort when family members are distressed, to take pleasure in their pleasures, to feel their pain, to raise their spirits. Each person in a couple also has a temporal obligation to reserve some large block of time for the other. Sharing time seems important to all relationships, although each couple defines it differently.

Shared History and Future   Primary relationships have a shared history and the prospect of a shared future. For a relationship to become primary, there must be some history, some significant past interaction. This interaction enables the members to get to know each other, to understand each other a little better, and ideally to like and even love each other. Similarly, the individuals view the relationship as having a potential future. Despite researchers' prediction that 50 percent of couples now entering first marriages will divorce (the rate is higher for second marriages) and that 41 percent of all persons of marriageable age will experience divorce, most couples entering a relationship such as marriage view it—ideally, at least—as permanent.

Shared Living Space   In general American culture, persons in primary interpersonal relationships usually share the same living space. When living space is not shared, the situation is generally seen as "abnormal" or temporary, both by the culture as a whole and by the individuals involved in the relationship. Even those who live apart for significant periods probably perceive a shared space as the ideal and, in fact, usually do share some special space at least part of the time. In some other cultures, however, men and women don't share the same living space; the women may live with the children while the men live together in a communal arrangement (Harris, 1993).

Even in the United States, the number of long-distance relationships is not insignificant. For example, the Center for the Study of Long Distance Relationships (www.longdistancerelationships. net) puts the number of married persons who do not share a living space at over 3,500,000, which is 2.9 percent of all U.S. married people. And the number of such relationships is increasing. Approximately 7 million couples (or 14 million people) consider themselves to be in long-distance relationships. It's been estimated that some 75 percent of college students have been, at some point in their lives, a part of a long-distance relationship, and at any one time, some 25 to 50 percent of college students are in long-distance relationships (Stafford, 2004). Long-distance relationships do not seem to have less satisfaction, less commitment, less intimacy, or less durability than shared-space relationships, as long as the individuals are able to get together about once a month (Rohlfing, 1995; Stafford & Merolla, 2007; Jiang & Hancock, 2013).

INTERPERSONAL CHOICE POINT
Maintaining Long-Distance Relationships

You and your romantic partner are going to separate graduate schools—some 2,000 miles apart. You both want your relationship to continue and eventually to be together after completing graduate school. *Among your communication options for keeping in touch and maintaining the relationship, which would you consider the most important?*

   a. Facebook posts and photos
   b. Phone
   c. E-mail
   d. Periodic face-to-face meetings, say, every 3 or 4 months.
   e. Other

Couple Types

Based on responses from more than 1,000 couples to questions concerning their degree of sharing, space needs, conflicts, and the time they spend together, researchers have identified three basic types of primary relationships: traditionals, independents, and separates (Fitzpatrick, 1983, 1988, 1991; Noller & Fitzpatrick, 1993).

Traditional Couples   If you are part of a traditional couple, you tend to agree with statements such as these (taken from Fitzpatrick's [1991; Noller & Fitzpatrick, 1993] Relational Dimensions Instrument):

- We tell each other how much we love or care about each other.
- We eat our meals at the same time every day.
- A woman should take her husband's last name when she marries.

Traditional couples share a basic belief system and philosophy of life. They see themselves as a blending of two persons into a single couple rather than as two separate individuals. They're interdependent and believe that each individual's independence must be sacrificed for the good of the relationship. Traditionals believe in mutual sharing and do little separately. This couple holds to the traditional gender roles, and there are seldom any role conflicts. Research finds that marriages in which traditional gender roles are maintained have higher sexual frequency than those in which these roles are shared (Kornrich, Brines, & Leupp, 2012). Traditionals experience few power struggles and few conflicts in general because each person knows and adheres to a specified role within the relationship. In their communications, traditionals are highly responsive to each other. Traditionals lean toward each other, smile, talk a lot, interrupt each other, and finish each other's sentences.

Independent Couples   If you are an independent, you'll tend to agree with statements such as these:

- In marriage or close relationships, there should be no constraints or restrictions on individual freedom.
- I have my own private work space (study, workshop, utility room, etc.).
- I feel free to interrupt my mate when he or she is concentrating on something if he or she is in my presence.

Couple Combinations

In addition to these three pure types, there also are combinations (Fitzpatrick, 1991). For example, in the separate–traditional couple one individual is a separate and one a traditional. Another common pattern is the traditional–independent, in which one individual believes in the traditional view of relationships and one in autonomy and independence. *How would you describe a previous, current, or hoped-for relationship in terms of traditionals, independents, separates, or some combination?*

Independent couples stress their individuality. The relationship is important but never more important than each person's individual identity. Although independents spend a great deal of time together, they don't ritualize it, for example, with schedules. Each individual spends time with outside friends. Independents see themselves as relatively androgynous—as individuals who combine the traditionally feminine and the traditionally masculine roles and qualities. The communication between independents is responsive. They engage in conflict openly and without fear. Their disclosures are quite extensive and include high-risk and negative disclosures that are typically absent among traditionals.

Separate Couples   If you are a separate, you'll tend to agree with statements such as these:

- If I can avoid arguing about some problems, they will disappear.
- It is better to hide your true feelings in order to avoid hurting your mate.
- In our house, we keep a fairly regular daily time schedule.

Separate couples live together but view their relationship more as a matter of convenience than a result of their mutual love or closeness. They seem to have little desire to be together and, in fact, usually are together only at ritual functions such as mealtime or holiday get-togethers. It's important to separates that each has his or her own physical as well as psychological space. Separates share little; each seems to prefer to go his or her way. Separates hold relatively traditional values and beliefs about gender roles, and each person tries to follow the behaviors normally assigned to each role. What best characterizes this type, however, is that each person sees him- or herself as a separate individual and not as a part of a couple.

Family Types

Families can be classified in any number of ways, for example, according to the number of people in the family, their affectional orientation, and the presence or absence of children or of extended family members. One interesting communication-oriented typology looks at families in terms of conformity and conversation (Arnold, 2008; Galvin, Byland, & Brommel, 2008; Koerner & Fitzpatrick, 1997, 2004).

Conformity orientation refers to the degree to which family members express similar or dissimilar attitudes, values, and beliefs. So we can speak of high-conformity families as those who express highly similar attitudes, beliefs, and values and try to avoid conflict and low-conformity families as those whose members express highly divergent attitudes, beliefs, and values and may frequently engage in conflict interactions. Families high in conformity are likely to be harmonious, with children who are expected to obey their parents, largely without question. Families low in conformity are likely to be less harmonious, with children who are given greater freedom to say or do as they wish.

Conversation orientation refers to the degree to which family members can speak their mind. A family high on conversation orientation encourages members to discuss a variety of issues and to voice their opinions. A family low on conversation orientation discourages discussion and the voicing of opinions.

With these two dimensions in mind, four types of families can be identified as **consensual families**, **protective families**, **pluralistic families**, and **laissez-faire families**:

- *Consensual families:* high in conversation and high in conformity. These families encourage open communication and agreement.

- *Protective families:* high in conformity and low in conversation. These families stress agreement and strive to avoid conflict but with little communication.
- *Pluralistic families:* low in conformity and high in conversation. These family members are encouraged to express different attitudes and points of view and to engage in open communication while being supportive of each other.
- *Laissez-faire families:* low in conformity and low in conversation. These families avoid interaction and communication, and encourage privacy and a "do what you want" attitude.

These family types are simply descriptions and are not meant to be evaluations; no assumption is made that one family type is better or more productive than another. What works for some people does not work for others.

Family and Communication

You know from your own family interactions that technology has greatly changed communication among family members. Cell phones enable parents and children to keep in close touch in case of emergencies or just to chat. College students today stay in closer touch with their parents, in part because of the cell phone but also through e-mail, instant messaging, Facebook, Twitter, Instagram, and a host of other websites.

Another change has been that, in some cases parents and in most cases children, become so absorbed with their online community that they have little time for their biological family members. Sometimes, as in South Korea, Internet use seems to be contributing further to the already significant generational conflict between children and parents (Rhee & Kim, 2004). Similarly, a study on young people (ages 10 to 17) in the United States found that for both girls and boys, those who formed close online relationships were more likely to have low levels of communication with their parents and to be more "highly troubled" than those who don't form such close online relationships (Wolak, Mitchell, & Finkelhor, 2003).

Another interesting change is that, in the case of adopted offspring, discovering birth parents is now a lot easier because of ready access to all sorts of data. Similarly, siblings that have been separated can find one another more easily—a process that may seem relatively unnecessary to most families in the United States but may be extremely important in war-torn countries, where families have been separated through occupation or forced relocation.

With this as a background, let's consider the communication patterns that dominate the family relationship. Four general communication patterns are identified here; each interpersonal relationship may then be viewed as a variation on one of these basic patterns (see Figure 10.2).

The Equality Pattern   The equality pattern probably exists more in theory than in practice, but it's a good starting point for looking at communication in primary relationships. It exists more among same-sex couples than in opposite-sex couples (Huston & Schwartz, 1995). In the equality pattern, each person shares equally in the communication transactions; the roles played by each are equal. Thus, each person is accorded a similar degree of credibility; each is equally open to the ideas, opinions, and beliefs of the other; each engages in self-disclosure on a more or less equal basis. The communication is open, honest, direct, and free of the power plays that characterize so many other interpersonal relationships. In terms of the relationship license noted earlier, there are reciprocal licenses.

Equal relationships also are equitable. According to equity theory, family or relationship satisfaction is highest when there is equity—when each partner gets a proportional share of the costs and the rewards of the relationship. Dissatisfaction over inequities can lead to a "re-balancing of the scales" reaction. For example, an under-benefited

Figure 10.2 Communication Patterns in Couples and Families

This figure represents the four communication patterns discussed in the text in a much simplified form. In (a), equality, there is an equal distribution in terms of communication and decision making; each person sends and receives messages equally; each person has equal authority. In (b), the balanced spilt, each person speaks and listens equally and has equal authority but on different things. In (c), the unbalanced split, one person controls the communication and the decision making more than the other. In (d), monopoly, one person maintains total (or near total) control.

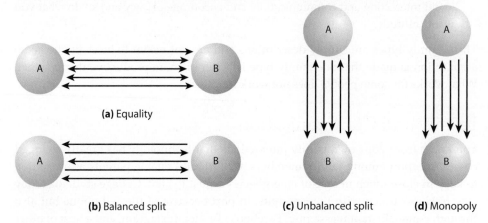

(a) Equality

(b) Balanced split   **(c)** Unbalanced split   **(d)** Monopoly

partner may seek an outside affair as a way to get more relationship benefits—more love, more consideration, more support (Noller & Fitzpatrick, 1993; Walster, Walster, & Traupmann, 1978).

The Balanced Split Pattern   In the balanced split pattern, an equality relationship is maintained but each person has authority over different domains. Each person is seen as an expert or a decision maker in different areas. For example, in the traditional nuclear family, the husband maintains high credibility in business matters and perhaps in politics. The wife maintains high credibility in matters such as child care and cooking. These gender roles are breaking down in many cultures, but they still define many families throughout the world (Hatfield & Rapson, 1996; Hofstede, Hofstede, & Minkov, 2010).

Conflict is generally viewed as nonthreatening by individuals in balanced split families because each has specified areas of expertise. Consequently, the outcome of any conflict is almost predetermined.

The Unbalanced Split Pattern   In the unbalanced split relationship, one person dominates: one person is seen as an expert in more than half the areas of mutual communication. In many unions, this "expertise" equates with control. Thus, in the unbalanced split, one person is regularly in control of the relationship. In some cases, this person is the more intelligent or more knowledgeable, but in many cases, he or she is more physically attractive or earns more. The less attractive or lower-income partner compensates by giving in to the other person, allowing the other to win arguments or to have his or her way in decision making.

The person in control makes more assertions, tells the other person what should or will be done, gives opinions freely, plays power games to maintain control, and seldom asks for opinions in return. The noncontrolling person, conversely, asks questions, seeks opinions, and looks to the other for decision-making leadership.

The Monopoly Pattern   In a monopoly relationship, one person is seen as the authority. This person lectures rather than communicates. Rarely does this person seek others' advice, and he or she always reserves the right to have the final say. The controlling person tells the partner what is and what is not to be. The controlling person talks more frequently and goes off the topic of conversation more than does the noncontrolling partner (Palmer, 1989). The noncontrolling person looks to the other for permission, to voice opinion leadership, and to make decisions, almost as a child looks to an all-knowing, all-powerful parent.

In this type of couple, arguments are few—because both individuals already know who is boss and who will win any argument that may arise. When the authority is challenged, however, there are arguments and bitter conflicts. One reason the conflicts are so bitter is that these individuals have had no rehearsal for adequate conflict resolution. They don't know how to argue or how to disagree agreeably, so their conflict strategies frequently take the form of hurting the other person.

Families, Culture, and Gender

As with friendship and love, families also vary from one culture to another and are viewed differently by men and women.

Culture and Families   In U.S. society, it is assumed in discussions of relationship development—such as the model presented in this text—that you voluntarily choose your relationship partners. You consciously choose to pursue certain relationships and not others. In some cases, however, your husband or wife is chosen to unite two families or to bring some financial advantage to your family or village. An arrangement such as this may have been entered into by your parents when you were an infant or even before you were born. In most cultures, of course, there's pressure to marry "the right" person and to be friends with certain people and not others.

Similarly, U.S. researchers study—and textbook authors write about—how relationships dissolve and how to survive relationship breakups. It's assumed that you have the right to exit an undesirable relationship. But in some cultures, you cannot simply dissolve a relationship once it's formed or once there are children. In Roman Catholicism, once people are validly married, they're always married and cannot dissolve that relationship. In such cultures, more important issues may be "How do you maintain a relationship that has problems?" "What can you do to survive in this unpleasant relationship?" or "How can you repair a troubled relationship?" (Moghaddam, Taylor, & Wright, 1993).

Further, your culture influences the difficulty that you go through when relationships do break up. For example, married persons whose religion forbids divorce and remarriage experience religious disapproval and condemnation as well as the same economic and social difficulties everyone else goes through. In the United States, child custody almost invariably goes to the woman, and this presents an added emotional burden for the man. In Iran, child custody goes to the man, which presents added emotional burdens for the woman. In India, women experience greater difficulty than men in divorce because of their economic dependence on men, cultural beliefs about women, and the patriarchal order of the family. And it was only as recently as 2002 that the first wife in Jordan was granted a divorce. Prior to this, only men had been granted divorces.

Gender and Families   In the United States, both men and women can initiate relationships and both can dissolve them. Both men and women are expected to derive satisfaction from their interpersonal relationships; when that satisfaction isn't present, either person may seek to exit the relationship. In Iran, on the other hand, only the man has the right to dissolve a marriage and does not have to give any reasons.

Gay and lesbian families are accepted in some cultures and condemned in others. In the United States, some states allow same-sex couples to marry legally. In other states, domestic partnerships may be registered, and these grant gay men, lesbians, and (in some cases) unmarried heterosexuals rights that were formerly reserved only for married couples; examples are health insurance benefits and the right to make decisions when one member is incapacitated. In Belgium, the Netherlands, Spain, South Africa, and Canada, same-sex couples can marry; in Norway, Sweden, and Denmark, same-sex relationship partners have the same rights as married partners. In many countries, however, same-sex couples are considered criminals and could face severe punishment, even death in some cultures.

Table 10.3 offers a brief summary of this discussion of families.

Table 10.3   In a Nutshell   Families

Aspects of Families	Explanations
Definition	A family is best defined as a group of people with defined roles, responsibilities toward others in the group, a shared history and future, shared living space (usually), and rules for communicating.
Types of Couples	Among the types of couples are traditional, independent, and separate; each type derives different benefits.
Types of Families	Among the types of families are consensual, protective, pluralistic, and laissez-faire.
Communication	Among the communication patterns that characterize family communication are equality, balanced split, unbalanced split, and monopoly.
Influences	The role and rules of the family vary greatly from one culture to another and are viewed differently by men and women.

UNDERSTANDING *INTERPERSONAL SKILLS*

Supportiveness: Supportive Messages Express Understanding Rather Than Evaluation

Supportiveness in communication is behavior that is descriptive rather than evaluative and provisional rather than certain (Gibb, 1961). Descriptive messages state in relatively objective terms what you see or what you feel—as opposed to evaluative messages, which express your opinions and judgments. Descriptive messages may make others feel supported; judgmental or evaluative messages, on the other hand, may elicit defensiveness. (This doesn't mean that all evaluative communications meet a defensive response, of course. For example, the would-be actor who wants to improve technique often welcomes both positive and negative evaluations.) Similarly, provisional messages express an open-minded attitude and a willingness to hear opposing viewpoints. Certainty messages, on the other hand, tolerate no differences of opinion and are likely to engender defensiveness.

Communicating with Supportiveness

Here are a few suggestions for communicating supportiveness by being descriptive and provisional, which will also increase relationship satisfaction (Cramer, 2004).

- Express your willingness to listen with an open mind and your readiness to consider changing your way of thinking and doing things.
- Ask for the opinions of others, and show that these are important to you. Resist the temptation to focus too much on your own way of seeing things.
- Avoid accusations or blame ("I should have stayed with my old job and not listened to your brother's advice").
- Avoid negative evaluation ("Didn't your sister look horrible in that red dress?").
- Avoid "preaching" ("You need to learn word processing and spreadsheet skills").

Working With Supportiveness

Consider the above suggestions for increasing supportiveness and, consider the situations in which you have recently used or witnessed supportiveness. *In what situations have others responded to you with supportiveness? How was this supportiveness expressed? What situations can you recall in which supportiveness was not used but might have helped?*

Workplace Relationships

10.4 Describe how to create and maintain successful workplace relationships.

The workplace is a context in which all forms of communication take place and all kinds of relationships may be seen. This context is especially influenced by culture—both by the wider culture and by the particular culture of a given workplace. Like all cultures, workplace cultures have their own rituals, norms, and rules for communicating. These rules, whether in an interview situation or in a friendly conversation, delineate appropriate and inappropriate verbal and nonverbal behavior, specify rewards (or punishments for breaking the rules), and tell you what will help you get and keep a job and what won't. For example, the general advice given throughout this text is to emphasize your positive qualities, to highlight your abilities, and to minimize any negative characteristics or failings. But in some organizations—especially within collectivist cultures such as those of China, Korea, and Japan—workers are expected to show modesty (Copeland & Griggs, 1985). If you stress your own competencies too much, you may be seen as arrogant, brash, and unfit to work in an organization where teamwork and cooperation are emphasized.

Whether in a job interview, in the early days on a new job, or in meeting new colleagues, first impressions are especially important because they're so long-lasting and so powerful in influencing future impressions and interactions (Flocker, 2006; Grobart, 2007; Parsons, Liden, & Bauer, 2001). Table 10.4 offers a few guidelines that will help you make a good first impression and should increase your likeability on the job.

When you join an organization, you learn the rules and norms of a culture that is different from, say, the college culture from which you came or from a former organization for which you worked. Put differently, you become acculturated, much as you would if you moved to a foreign country. As you can appreciate, it's essential to learn the organization's culture to know what the rules of the game are, especially the rules of communication. Here we look at a variety of workplace communication patterns and relationships.

Workplace Communication

Communication within the workplace can be described as consisting of four major types: **lateral communication**, **upward communication**, **downward communication**, and **grapevine messages**.

- *Lateral communication* refers to messages between equals—for example, manager to manager, worker to worker. Such messages may move within the same subdivision or department of the organization or across divisions. Lateral communication, for example, is the kind of communication that takes place between two history professors at Illinois State University, between a psychologist at Ohio State and a communicologist at Kent State University, and between a bond trader and an equities trader at a brokerage house.

Table 10.4 How to Be Liked at Work

Strategy	Comments
Look the Part Dress appropriately; even "casual Fridays" have dress codes.	Any drastic deviation from the standard dress for your position may communicate that you don't fit in.
Be Positive Express positive attitudes toward the organization, the job, and your colleagues.	Avoid negative talk and sarcasm (even in humor).
Be Culturally Sensitive Avoid stereotyping and talk that might be considered racist, heterosexist, ageist, or sexist.	You're sure to offend someone with any of these *isms*.
Be Respectful and Friendly Be respectful of other people's time or personal quirks.	At the same time, be available, helpful, and cooperative as appropriate.
Be Interested Focus attention on the other person and really listen.	Express interest in who the person is and what he or she says and does. Maintain eye contact, a pleasant facial expression, an open posture, and relatively close proximity.

- *Upward communication* consists of messages sent from the lower levels of a hierarchy to the upper levels—for example, from line worker to manager or from faculty member to dean. This type of communication usually is concerned with job-related activities and problems; ideas for change and suggestions for improvement; and feelings about the organization, work, other workers, or similar issues.

- *Downward communication* consists of messages sent from the higher levels to the lower levels of the hierarchy—for example, messages sent by managers to workers or by deans to faculty members. Common forms of downward communication include orders; explanations of procedures, goals, and changes; and appraisals of workers.

- *Grapevine messages* don't follow any of the formal lines of communication established in an organization. Much like grapevines, they seem to have a life of their own and go in all different directions. Grapevine messages address topics that you want to discuss in a more interpersonal setting, such as issues that are not yet made public; the *real* relationship among the regional managers; or possible changes that are being considered but not yet finalized, like new rules on personal Internet usage.

Although each of these forms of communication requires somewhat specialized rules and forms, here are a few general communication guidelines:

- *Be respectful of a colleague's time.* This guideline suggests lots of specifics; for example, don't copy those who don't need to be copied; be brief and organized; respond to requests as soon as possible and when not possible, alert the other person that, for example, "the figures will be sent as soon as they arrive, probably by the end of the day." Most important, perhaps, is to be clear. For example, recognize that your own specialty has a technical jargon that others outside your specialty might not know. Clarify when and as needed.

- *Be respectful of a person's territory.* Humans, like animals, are very territorial. This is especially true in the business world where status distinctions are very important and govern the rules of territoriality. For example, don't invade another's office or desk space (personally or even with the scent you wear) and don't overspend your welcome. In brief, treat another's workspace as someone's private territory into which you must be invited.

- *Follow the rules for effective electronic communication,* which will naturally differ from one workplace to another. Generally, look for rules governing the use of e-mails, Internet game playing, cell phones, social networking, and instant messaging.

- *Discard your Facebook grammar, spelling, acronyms, and smiley faces.* These may be seen as not showing sufficient respect for someone high in the company hierarchy. The general suggestion offered for people writing into newsgroups is appropriate here as well; watch how other people write before writing yourself. If you find no guidance here, your best bet is to write as if your e-mail is being graded by your English professor. This means editing for conciseness, proofreading, and spell checking.

- *Use the appropriate medium for sending messages.* Generally, the rule is to respond in kind—for example, if a question is asked in e-mail, answer it in e-mail.

- *Avoid touching except in shaking hands.* Touching is often interpreted as a sexual overture, so it's best avoided on the job. Touching may also imply a familiarity that the other person may not welcome. Your best bet is to avoid initiating touching, but don't be offended if others put their arm on your shoulder or pat you on the back.

- *Be willing to communicate.* Be open to hearing others' comments. Be willing to listen to these messages, even when they're critical, and demonstrate that willingness with appropriate eye contact, posture, and feedback cues. At the same time, when you're offering negative comments, be sure to do so privately to avoid damaging the image of those singled out. Allow the person to save face.

- **Understand the variety of purposes the grapevine serves.** Its speed and general accuracy make it an ideal medium to carry many of the social communications that effectively bind workers together. So listen carefully; it will give you an insider's view of the organization and will help you understand those with whom you work. But treat grapevine information as tentative, as possibly, but not necessarily, true. Although grapevine information is generally accurate, it's often incomplete and ambiguous; it may also contain crucial distortions.
- **Be mindful of all your organizational communications.** The potentially offensive joke that you e-mail a colleague can easily be forwarded to the very people who may take offense.
- **Treat everyone politely, even the newest intern.** Treat that person as if he or she will one day be your boss. He or she may well be.

Networking Relationships

In the popular mind, **networking** is often viewed simply as a technique for securing a job. But it actually has much broader applications; it can be viewed as a process of using other people to help you solve your problems, or at least to offer insights that bear on your problem—for example, how to publish your manuscript, where to look for low-cost auto insurance, how to find an affordable apartment, or how to use Google Drive. At one point, networking took place largely in face-to-face situations, but today networking is largely conducted online—through Facebook and similar sites for things your friends might know or through LinkedIn or similar sites for more professional job-oriented advice and connections. The great value of networking, especially online networking, is that it provides you with quick access to a wealth of specialized information and experts.

Networking comes in at least two forms: informal and formal. Informal networking is what we do every day when we find ourselves in a new situation or are unable to answer questions. For example, if you're new at a school, you might ask someone in your class where to eat, where to shop for new clothes, or who is the best teacher for economics. When you enter a new work environment, you might ask more experienced workers how to perform certain tasks or whom you should approach—or avoid—when you have questions.

Formal networking is the same thing, except that it's much more systematic and strategic. It's the establishment of connections with people who can help you—answer your questions, get you a job, help you get promoted, help you relocate, or accomplish any task you want to accomplish. For example, you might post your question on LinkedIn or seek the advice of those on the site who are experts in your particular field. At the most obvious level, you can network with people you already know. If you review the list of people in your acquaintance, you'll probably discover that you know a great number of people with very specialized knowledge who can be of assistance to you in a wide variety of ways. In some cultures (Brazil is one example), friendships are established in part because of potential networking connections (Rector & Neiva, 1996). You also can network with people who people you know. Thus, you may contact a friend's friend to find out if the firm he or she works for is hiring. Or you may contact people you have no connection with. Perhaps you've read something that someone wrote or you've heard the person's name raised in connection with an area in which you're interested and you want to get more information. With e-mail addresses so readily available, it's now quite common to e-mail individuals who have particular expertise and ask them questions you might have.

INTERPERSONAL CHOICE POINT

Apologizing at Work

You've been very successful in the stock market, so when you got the best tip ever, you shared it with three of your friends at work. Unfortunately, the stock tanked, your colleagues lost several thousand dollars each, and the situation at work is uncomfortable at best. What might you say to these colleagues to help lessen the discomfort everyone is feeling?

a. "That's the breaks. You knew it was risky."
b. "I'm sorry I misled you."
c. "I lost more than all of you."
d. "We'll do better next time."
e. Other

In networking, it's often recommended that you try to establish relationships that are mutually beneficial. Much as others are useful sources of information for you, you're likely to be a useful source of information for others. If you can provide others with helpful information, it's more likely that they will provide helpful information for you. In this way, a mutually satisfying and productive network is established.

Some networking experts advise you to develop files and directories of potentially useful sources that you can contact for needed information. For example, if you're a freelance artist, you might develop a list of people who might be in positions to offer you work or who might lead you to others who offer such work. Authors, editors, art directors, administrative assistants, people in advertising, and a host of others might eventually provide useful leads for such work. Creating a directory of such people and keeping in contact with them on a fairly regular basis can often simplify your obtaining freelance work. Social networking sites such as Plaxo and LinkedIn enable you to do this quickly and easily.

Formal networking requires that you take an active part in locating and establishing these connections. Be proactive; initiate contacts rather than waiting for them to come to you. Of course, this can be overdone; you don't want to rely on people to do work you can easily do yourself. Yet if you're also willing to help others, there is nothing wrong in asking these same people to help you. If you're respectful of their time and expertise, it's likely that your networking attempts will be responded to favorably. Following up your requests with thank-you notes will help you establish networks that can be ongoing, productive relationships rather than one-shot affairs. Table 10.5 summarizes some of these suggestions in terms of politeness, one of the most important qualities of effective networking.

Mentoring Relationships

Mentoring is a partnership in which an experienced individual (the mentor) helps someone who is less experienced (the protégé) learn how to achieve his or her goals (Caproni, 2012; Mullen, 2005). Some organizational experts argue that having a mentor is crucial for rising in a hierarchy and for developing your skills (Dahle, 2004). Mentoring is beneficial to the organization; it improves morale, decreases turnover, and helps position junior members for advancement. Mentoring is also beneficial to the individuals, providing each with new ideas and new perspectives (Metz, 2013). An accomplished teacher, for example, might mentor a younger teacher who has newly

Table 10.5 Social Networking Politeness

Rules of Politeness	The Rule in Operation
Engage in networking feedforward before requesting friendship.	Sending a message complimenting the person's latest post provides some background and eases the way for a friendship request.
Avoid negativity.	Avoid writing negative or embarrassing messages or posting unflattering photos that may generate conflict.
Keep networking information confidential.	It's considered inappropriate and impolite to relay information on Facebook, for example, to those who are not themselves friends.
Be gentle in refusals.	Refuse any request for friendship gently or, if you wish, ignore it. If you're refused, don't ask for reasons; it's considered impolite.
Avoid making potentially embarrassing requests.	Avoid asking to be friends with someone who you suspect may have reasons for not wanting to admit you. For example, your work associate may not want you to see her or his profile.

arrived or who has never taught before (Nelson, Pearson, & Kurylo, 2008). The mentor guides the new person through the organizational maze, teaches the strategies and techniques for success, and otherwise communicates his or her accumulated knowledge and experience to the protégé.

The mentoring relationship provides an ideal learning environment. It's usually a one-on-one relationship between expert and novice, a relationship that is supportive and trusting. There's a mutual and open sharing of information and thoughts about the job. The relationship enables the novice to try new skills under the guidance of an expert, to ask questions, and to obtain the feedback so necessary in learning complex skills. Mentoring is perhaps best characterized as a relationship in which the experienced and powerful mentor empowers the novice, giving the novice the tools and techniques for gaining the same power the mentor holds.

Mentoring is frequently conducted online. One great advantage of e-mentoring is the flexibility it allows for communication. E-mail messages, for example, can be sent and received at times that are convenient for the individuals involved (Stewart, 2006). Because the individuals may be separated geographically, it's possible to have mentor–protégé relationships with people in foreign countries and in widely differing cultures—relationships that would be impossible without online communication. Still another advantage is that persons with disabilities (whether mentor or protégé) who cannot travel easily can still enjoy and profit from e-mentoring relationships (Burgstahler, 2007). The mentoring relationship has been found to be one of the three primary paths for career achievement among African American men and women (Bridges, 1996). And in a study of middle-level managers, those who had mentors and participated in mentoring relationships were found to get more promotions and higher salaries than those who didn't have mentors (Scandura, 1992). More recent research also finds that college students benefit in a variety of ways from having a mentor. At the end of the first year, mentored students had a higher GPA, showed a higher retention rate, and had completed more credits than students who weren't mentored (Campbell & Campbell, 2007).

At the same time, the mentor benefits from clarifying his or her thoughts, seeing the job from the perspective of a newcomer, and considering and formulating answers to a variety of questions. Much as a teacher learns from teaching, a mentor learns from mentoring.

It should also be noted that social networking sites, designed originally as places where people could make new friends and stay in touch with old ones, are increasingly being used for both mentoring and networking. Some sites are "by invitation only" and have been compared to gated communities or exclusive country clubs. These sites seem designed not for friendships but solely for mentoring and networking (MacMillan & Lehman, 2007). For example, Reuters Space is a private online community specifically for hedge fund managers to network, and INmobile is designed for executives in the wireless industry.

Romantic Relationships at Work

Unlike television depictions, in which workers are always best friends who would do anything for one another and in and out of office romances with little difficulty (at least with no difficulty that can't be resolved in 24 minutes), real-life office romance can be complicated. Opinions vary widely concerning workplace romances (Heidel, 2017). Some organizations, on the assumption that romantic relationships are basically detrimental to the success of the workplace, have explicit rules prohibiting romantic involvements. And these rules are becoming stricter (Wilkie, 2013). In some organizations (including the military), members can be fired for such relationships. In other organizations, the prohibitions are unwritten and informal but nevertheless clearly in opposition to office romances. Other organizations have a more lenient policy and recognize that office romances are inevitable. And even the *Huffington Post* says that office romance is "not off-limits" (Paul, 2013).

Advantages of Romance at Work   On the positive side, the work environment seems a perfect place to meet a potential romantic partner. After all, by virtue of the fact that you're working in the same office, probably you are both interested in the same field, have similar training and ambitions, and can spend considerable time together—all factors that foster the development of a successful interpersonal relationship. Also, given that Americans are marrying later in life, they are less likely to meet prospective partners in school; so work seems the logical alternative. Published figures differ about the frequency of office romances. According to a 2009 survey by CareerBuilder.com, 40 percent of U.S. workers said that they had dated a fellow worker, 18 percent reported two or more office romances, and another 12 percent are eager to engage in such relationships (Pearce, 2010). Another survey reported that 58 percent of workers had dated a coworker. Of these, 20 percent admitted to a romantic relationship with a boss and 15 percent to a relationship with someone they supervised (Hemple & Berner, 2007). Even Bill and Melinda Gates met at work.

Office romances can lead to greater work satisfaction. For example, if you're romantically attracted to another worker, it can make going to work, working together, and even working added hours more enjoyable and more satisfying. If the relationship is good and mutually satisfying, the individuals are likely to develop empathy for each other and to act in ways that are supportive, cooperative, and friendly; in short, the workers are more likely to show all the characteristics of effective communication noted throughout this text.

To achieve these advantages, management consultants advise romantic couples at work to, for example (Losee & Olen, 2007; Nemko, 2013):

- Be honest about what you want, for example, a quick office fling or something potentially more permanent.
- Make sure you have enough in common to warrant a relationship.
- Enter relationships with colleagues on the same level rather than with subordinates or superiors.
- Keep your relationship private or as private as you can. Avoid public displays of affection (PDAs).

Disadvantages of Romance at Work   Even when the relationship is good for the two individuals, however, it may not be good for other workers. Seeing the loving couple together every day may generate office gossip that may prove destructive. Others may think the lovers are a team that has to be confronted as a pair, and that you can't criticize one without incurring the wrath of the other.

Workplace romantic relationships may cause problems for management when, for example, a promotion is to be made or relocation decisions are necessary. Can you legitimately ask one lover to move to Boston and the other to move to San Francisco? Will it prove difficult for management to promote one lover who then becomes the supervisor of the other?

The workplace also puts pressure on the individuals. Most organizations, at least in the United States, are highly competitive; one person's success often means another's failure. In this competitive context, the normal self-disclosures that regularly accompany increased intimacy (which often reveal weaknesses, doubts, and misgivings) may actually prove a liability.

Romance in the Workplace

Although most organizations frown on office romance, all the main characters in TV's *Bones* are in romantic relationships with people they work with. And it seems to work well for the individuals and the Jeffersonian Institute (the workplace). How would you describe television's position on romance in the workplace? In what ways does it differ from the real-life workplace?

ETHICS IN INTERPERSONAL COMMUNICATION

Relationship Ethics

The ethical issues and guidelines that operate within a friendship or romantic, family, or workplace relationship can be reviewed with the acronym ETHICS—empathy (Cheney & Tompkins, 1987), talk rather than force, honesty (Krebs, 1989), interaction management, confidentiality, and supportiveness (Johannesen, 2001).

- *Empathy:* People in relationships have an ethical obligation to try to understand what other individuals are feeling as well as thinking from those individuals' points of view.
- *Talk:* Decisions in a relationship should be arrived at by talk rather than by force—by persuasion, not by coercion.
- *Honesty:* Relationship communication should be honest and truthful.
- *Interaction management:* Relationship communication should be satisfying and comfortable and is the responsibility of all individuals.
- *Confidentiality:* People have a right to expect that what they say in confidence will not be revealed to others.
- *Supportiveness:* A supportive and cooperative climate should characterize the interpersonal interactions of people in relationships.

Ethical Choice Point

You're managing a team to select an architect for your company's new office complex. The problem is that Jack doesn't do any work and misses most of the meetings. You spoke with him about it, and he confided that he's going through a divorce and can't concentrate on the project. You feel sorry for Jack and have been carrying him for the last few months, but realize now that you'll never be able to bring the project in on time if you don't replace Jack. Also, you don't want to get a negative appraisal because of Jack. *What would you do in this situation?*

When the romance goes bad or when it's one-sided, there are even more disadvantages. One obvious problem is that it can be stressful for the former lovers to see each other regularly and perhaps to work together. Other workers may feel they have to take sides, being supportive of one partner and critical of the other. This can easily cause friction throughout the organization. In addition, when an office romance breaks up, it's usually the more competent and employable person who leaves for another job, leaving the firm with the less valuable employee and the need to retain someone to take over the departed lover's functions (Jones, 2004). Still another and perhaps more serious issue is the potential for charges of sexual harassment, especially if the romance was between a supervisor and a worker. Whether the charges are legitimate or are the result of an unhappy love affair and unrelated to the organization, management will find itself in the middle, facing lawsuits and time and money lost from investigating and ultimately acting on the charges.

The generally negative attitude of management toward office love affairs and the problems in dealing with the normal stress of both work and romance seem to present significant obstacles to such relationships and to the workplace, so workers are generally advised by management not to romance their colleagues. Friendships, on the other hand, seem the much safer course. Companies often encourage friendships by setting up sports teams, diners, and lounge and exercise areas. In fact, research finds that office friendships increase employees' job satisfaction and commitment to the organization and decrease turnover (Morrison, 2004). And friendships often serve as the basis for productive mentoring and networking.

Table 10.6 provides a brief summary of workplace relationships.

Table 10.6 In a Nutshell Workplace Relationships

Aspects of Workplace Relationships	Explanations
Definition	Workplace communication may be viewed in terms of the direction of the messages: lateral, upward, downward, and grapevine.
Networking	Connections with other people who have useful resources—may be formal or informal.
Mentoring	A partnership between an experienced worker and one who is less experienced, is a relationship that benefits both mentor and protégé.
Romantic relationships at work	Although these have both advantages and disadvantages, they are often prohibited, and most organizations have rather strict rules for what is and what is not acceptable.

The Dark Side of Interpersonal Relationships

10.5 Explain the nature of, and the guidelines for dealing with, jealousy and violence.

In all interpersonal relationships—friendship, love, family, and workplace—there exists the possibility for what has come to be called the dark side of relationships. In any interpersonal interaction, there exists not only the potential for productive and meaningful communication but also the potential for unproductive and destructive communication. Here we consider just a couple of dark sides: jealousy and violence.

Jealousy

Jealousy is similar to envy; in both cases, we experience a negative emotion about our relationship and we often use the terms interchangeably. But they are actually very different. Envy is an emotional feeling that we experience when we desire what someone else has or has more of than we do. And so we might feel envious of a friend who has lots of friends or romantic partners or money when we have significantly less. When we feel envy, we may feel that we are inferior to, or of less importance than, someone else. **Jealousy**, on the other hand, is a form of anger we have when we feel our relationship is in danger due to some rival. Jealousy is a reaction to relationship threat: if you feel that someone is moving in on your relationship partner, you may experience jealousy—especially if you feel that this interloper is succeeding.

Jealousy is not an uncommon reaction and is actually considered a logical reaction to relationship threat (Berscheid, 1983; Knobloch & Schmeizer, 2008). Usually, the rival is a potential romantic partner, but it could also be a close friend or a job that occupies all our partner's time and thoughts. When we feel jealousy, we may feel angry and anxious. As you can expect, the closer a relationship is, the more likely it is that jealousy would be experienced (Attridge, 2013). As you know, jealousy is a big part of social media; with increased use of Facebook comes increased jealousy (Muise, Christofides, & Desmarais, 2009). Among the reasons for this is that, through Facebook, one partner can find out things about the other that might not have been revealed face-to-face. And of course such social media sites provide great opportunities for reconnecting with former romantic partners, which can easily create or increase jealousy (Sarkis, 2011).

The Types of Jealousy   Three types of jealousy are often distinguished: cognitive, emotional, and behavioral (Erber & Erber, 2011):

• *Cognitive jealousy* involves your suspicious thinking, worrying, and imagining the different scenarios in which your partner may be interested in another person.

- **Emotional jealousy** Emotional jealousy involves the feelings you have when you see your partner, say, laughing or talking intimately with a rival, or kissing. Or, perhaps you become jealous if your partner spends too much time on Internet relationships.
- **Behavioral jealousy** Behavioral jealousy refers to what you actually do in response to the jealous feelings and emotions, for example, reading your partner's e-mail, looking on Facebook for incriminating photos, or going through the back seat of the car with the proverbial fine-tooth comb. Sometimes you feel jealousy because of some suspicion that a rival is looking to steal your relationship partner. And so you might conceal your relationship, monopolize your partner's free time, or avoid situations where rivals might be present—strategies referred to as *mate guarding* (Buss, 2000; Erber & Erber, 2011).

Much research has reported that heterosexual men and women experience jealousy for different reasons that are rooted in our evolutionary development (Buller, 2005; Buss, 2000; Buunk & Dijkstra, 2004). Basically, research finds that men experience jealousy from their partner being *physically* intimate with another man, whereas women experience jealousy from their partner being *emotionally* intimate with another woman. The evolutionary reason given is that men provided food and shelter for the family and would resent his partner's physical intimacy with another because he would then be providing food and shelter for another man's child. Women, because they depended on men for food and shelter, became especially jealous when their partner was emotionally intimate with another because this could mean he might leave her and she'd thus lose the food and shelter protection.

Not all research supports this finding and not all theory supports this evolutionary explanation (Harris, 2003). For example, among Chinese men, only 25 percent reported physical infidelity was the more distressing, while 75 percent reported emotional infidelity to be more distressing.

Another commonly assumed gender difference is that jealous men are more prone to respond with violence. This assumption, however, does not seem to be the case; men and women apparently are equally likely to respond with violence (Harris, 2003).

Dealing with jealousy So what do you do when you experience jealousy (short of violence)? Communication researchers find several popular but generally negative interactive responses (Dindia & Timmerman, 2003; Guerrero, Andersen, Jorgensen, Spitzberg, & Eloy, 1995). You may:

- nonverbally express your displeasure, for example, cry or express hurt.
- threaten to become violent or actually engage in violence.
- be verbally aggressive, for example, be sarcastic or accusatory.
- withdraw affection or be silent, sometimes denying that anything is wrong.

On the more positive side are responses known as integrative communication: messages that attempt to work things out with your partner, such as self-disclosing your feelings, being honest, practicing effective conflict management, listening actively—in short, all the skills we talk about in this text.

Violence

This dark side is perhaps most obvious in the various forms of relationship violence.

INTERPERSONAL CHOICE POINT

Dealing with Jealousy

Your romantic partner of the last 6 months has recently been showing signs of jealousy with absolutely no cause. This is making you feel uncomfortable and is restricting your enjoying other friends and activities that don't include your partner. You want to continue this relationship but you want the jealousy to stop. *What are some of the things you might say?*

a. Explain that there is no cause for jealousy and hope your partner believes you and changes.
b. Give an ultimatum—either the jealousy stops or you're moving on.
c. Say nothing; the jealousy will likely get less and eventually go away.
d. Give up your other friends and activities that don't include your partner.
e. Other

Before reading about this important but often-neglected topic, examine your present relationship for **relationship violence** by responding to the following questions, drawn from a variety of sources, for example, the websites of SUNY at Buffalo Counseling Services; the American College of Obstetricians and Gynecologists; Women's Heath Care Physicians; and the University of Texas at Austin, Counseling and Mental Health Center.

Do either of you:

1. _____ get angry to the point of making the other person fearful?
2. _____ engage in behavior that could be considered humiliating to the other person?
3. _____ verbally abuse the other?
4. _____ threaten the other with violence?
5. _____ engage in slapping, hitting, or pushing the other?
6. _____ throw things in anger?
7. _____ make accusations of sexual infidelity?
8. _____ force the other to have sex?
9. _____ use abusive sexual terms in reference to the other?

These nine items are all signs of a violent relationship (it only takes one to make a relationship violent). Items 1 to 3 are examples of verbal or emotional abuse, 4 to 6 of physical abuse, and 7 to 9 of sexual abuse—all of which are explained more fully in the text. If any of these questions describes your relationship, you may wish to seek professional help (which is likely available on your campus). Additional suggestions are offered in the text and are readily available online.

Types of Relationship Violence Three types of relationship violence may be distinguished: verbal or emotional abuse, physical abuse, and sexual abuse (Rice, 2007).

- **Verbal or emotional abuse** may include humiliating you; engaging in economic abuse such as controlling the finances or preventing you from working; and/or isolating, criticizing, or stalking you. Some research shows that people who use verbal or emotional abuse are more likely than others to escalate to physical abuse (Rancer & Avtgis, 2006).
- **Physical abuse** includes threats of violence as well as pushing, hitting, slapping, kicking, choking, throwing things at you, and breaking things.
- **Sexual abuse** involves touching that is unwanted, accusations of sexual infidelity without reason, forced sex, and references to you in abusive sexual terms.

Table 10.7 offers a brief comparison and summary of violent and nonviolent relationships (utexas.edu/student/cmhc/booklets/relavio/relaviol.html). A great deal of research has centered on trying to identify the warning signs of relationship violence. Here, for example, are a few signs compiled by the State University

Table 10.7 Violent and Nonviolent Relationships

Violent Relationships	Nonviolent Relationships
Emotional abuse	Fairness: you look for resolutions to conflict that will be fair to both of you.
Control and isolation	Communication that makes the partner feel safe and comfortable expressing him- or herself.
Intimidation	Mutual respect, mutual affirmation, and valuing of each other's opinions.
Economic abuse	The partners make financial decisions together.
Threats	Accountability—each person accepts responsibility for his or her behavior.
Power over the other	Responsibilities are distributed fairly.
Sexual abuse	Trust and respect for what each person wants and doesn't want.

of New York at Buffalo; you might want to use this list to start thinking about your own relationship or those that you know of (ub-counseling.buffalo.edu/warnings/shtml).

It may be a warning sign if your partner:

- belittles, insults, or ignores you.
- controls pieces of your life, for example, the way you dress or who you can be friends with.
- gets jealous without reason.
- can't handle sexual frustration without anger.
- is so angry or threatening that you've changed your life to avoid provoking additional anger.

As you might expect, there are a variety of consequences to relationship violence: physical injuries, psychological injuries, and economic "injuries" (cdc.gov/ncic/factsheets/ipvfacts.htm). Perhaps the image that comes most quickly to mind when the issue of relationship violence comes up is that of physical violence, and that element is certainly a big part of overall relationship violence. Physical injuries may range from scratches and bruises to broken bones, knife wounds, and central nervous system damage. The results of such injuries can range from minor to death.

Even when physical injuries are relatively minor, however, psychological injuries may be major and may include, for example, depression; anxiety; fear of intimacy; and, of course, low self-esteem. In fact, relationship violence often attacks self-esteem to the point where the victims come to believe that the violence against them was and is justified.

In addition to the obvious physical and psychological injuries, consider the economic impact. It's been estimated that, in the United States, relationship violence costs approximately $6.2 billion for physical assaults and almost $500 million for rape. Interpersonal violence also results in lost days of work. The Centers for Disease Control estimates that interpersonal violence costs the equivalent of 32,000 full-time jobs in lost work each year in the United States. Additional economic costs are incurred when interpersonal violence prevents women from maintaining jobs or continuing their education.

Dealing with Relationship Violence Whether you're a victim or a perpetrator of relationship violence, it is important to seek professional help (and, of course, the help of friends and family where appropriate). In addition, here are several additional suggestions (utexas.edu/student/cmhc/booklets/relavio/relaviol.html).

If your partner has been violent:

- Realize that you're not alone. There are other people who suffer similarly, and there is a mechanism in place to help you.
- Realize that you're not at fault. You did not deserve to be the victim of violence.
- Plan for your safety. Violence, if it occurred once, is likely to occur again, and part of your thinking needs to be devoted to your own safety.
- Know your resources—the phone numbers you need to contact for help, and the locations of money and a spare set of keys.

If you are the violent partner:

- Realize that you are not alone and that help and support are available.
- Know that you can change. It won't necessarily be quick or easy, but you can change.
- Own your own behaviors; take responsibility. This is an essential step if any change is to occur.

Relationship violence is not an inevitable part of interpersonal relationships; in fact, it occurs in a minority of relationships. Yet it's important to know that there is the potential for violence in all relationships, as there is the potential for friendship, love, support, and all the positive things we look for in relationships. Knowing the difference between productive and destructive relationships seems the best way to make sure that your own relationships are as you want them to be.

Table 10.8 offers a brief summary of jealousy and relationship violence.

Table 10.8 In a Nutshell Two Dark Sides of Interpersonal Relationships

Dark Side	Types	Remedies or Strategies
Jealousy, a reaction to relationship endangerment or threat	Cognitive Emotional Behavioral	Communicate to work things out with your partner; for example, self-disclose your feelings, be honest, practice effective conflict management, and listen actively.
Relationship violence, the use of abusive language or actual physical or sexual abuse	Verbal/emotional Physical Sexual	Know that help is available and that you're not at fault. Plan for your safety and have ready access to resources such as a spare set of keys and a phone.

Summary

This chapter explored some major kinds of interpersonal relationships, specifically, friendship, love, family, and workplace relationships. In addition, it explored some of the dark sides of relationships, namely relationship jealousy and violence.

Friendship Relationships

10.1 Define *friendship* and explain how it develops.

1. Friendship is an interpersonal relationship between two persons that is mutually productive and is characterized by mutual positive regard.

2. One classification of the types of friendships identified friendships of (1) reciprocity, which is characterized by loyalty, self-sacrifice, mutual affection, and generosity; (2) receptivity, which is characterized by a comfortable and positive imbalance in the giving and receiving of rewards, and each person's needs are satisfied by the exchange; and (3) association, which is a transitory relationship more like a friendly relationship than a true friendship. Still another type is the friends-with-benefits relationship in which there is sexual intimacy but not romantic intimacy.

3. Friendships serve a variety of needs and give us a variety of values, among which are the values of utility, affirmation, ego support, stimulation, and security.

4. Friendships develop in stages over time, from strangers at one end of the continuum to close and intimate ("best") friends at the other.

5. Friendships are influenced by culture and gender. For example, friendship demands vary between collectivist and individualist cultures. Women share more and are more intimate with same-sex friends than are men. Men's friendships are often built around shared activities rather than shared intimacies. Online friends resemble face-to-face friends in the needs that they serve, but they are often more diverse.

Love Relationships

10.2 Describe the various types of love.

6. Love is a feeling that may be characterized by closeness and caring and by intimacy, passion, and commitment.

7. Among the types of love: (1) Eros love focuses on beauty and sexuality, sometimes to the exclusion of other qualities; (2) ludus love is seen as a game and focuses on entertainment and excitement; (3) storge love is a kind of companionship, peaceful and slow; (4) pragma love is practical and traditional; (5) mania love is obsessive and possessive, characterized by elation and depression; and (6) agape love is compassionate and selfless, characterized as self-giving and altruistic.

8. Verbal and nonverbal messages echo the intimacy of a love relationship. With increased intimacy, you share more, speak in a more personalized style, engage in prolonged eye contact, and touch each other more often.

9. Culture and gender impact on love. For example, members of individualist cultures tend to place greater emphasis on romantic love than do members of collectivist cultures. In terms of gender differences, men generally score higher on erotic and ludic love, whereas women score higher on manic, pragmatic, and storgic love. Men also generally score higher on romanticism than women.

Family Relationships

10.3 Summarize the characteristics of families and distinguish among couple and family types.

10. Among the characteristics of families are: defined roles (members understand the roles each of them serves), recognition of responsibilities (members realize that each person has certain responsibilities to the relationship), shared history and future (members have an interactional past and an anticipated future together), and shared living space (generally, members live together).

11. Couple types have been classified into (1) traditionals, who see themselves as the blending of two people into a single couple; (2) independents, who see themselves as primarily separate individuals and see their individuality as more important than the relationship or the connection between the individuals; and (3) separates, who see their relationship as a matter of convenience rather than of mutual love or connection.

12. Family types have been classified into (1) consensual families: high in conversation and high in conformity, (2) protective families: high in conformity and low in conversation, (3) pluralistic families: low in conformity and high in conversation, and (4) laissez-faire families: low in conformity and low in conversation.

13. Among the prominent communication patterns in families are: (1) equality, in which each person shares equally in the communication transactions and decision making; (2) balanced split, in which each person has authority over different but relatively equal domains; (3) unbalanced split, in which one person maintains authority and decision-making power over a wider range of issues than the other; and (4) monopoly, in which one person dominates and controls the relationship and the decisions made.

14. Families vary from one culture to another and are influenced in varied ways by new technologies.

Workplace Relationships

10.4 Describe how to create and maintain successful workplace relationships.

15. Workplace communication may be viewed in terms of the direction of the messages sent: lateral, upward, downward, and grapevine.

16. Networking helps you expand your areas of expertise and enables you to secure information bearing on a wide variety of problems you want to solve and questions you want to answer.

17. Mentoring relationships help you learn the ropes of an organization through the experience and knowledge of someone who has gone through the processes you'll be going through.

18. Although romantic relationships in the workplace have a variety of benefits, they are often frowned upon and often entail a variety of problems that would not arise in other contexts.

The Dark Side of Interpersonal Relationships

10.5 Explain the nature of, and the guidelines for dealing with, jealousy and violence.

19. Jealousy is a fear of losing a relationship and is often combined with anger.

20. Relationship violence may consist of verbal or emotional, physical, or sexual abuse and has wide-ranging effects.

Key Terms

agape
conformity orientation
consensual families
conversation orientation
downward communication
eros
family
frenemy
friends with benefits
friendship
grapevine messages

independent couples
jealousy
laissez-faire families
lateral communication
love
ludus
mania
mentoring
network convergence
networking
pluralistic families

pragma
primary relationship
protective families
relationship violence
separate couples
storge
supportiveness
traditional couples
upward communication

CHAPTER ELEVEN

Interpersonal Conflict and Conflict Management

Conflict can often have positive consequences. *Using appropriate conflict management strategies can help.*

Chapter Topics

Preliminaries to Interpersonal Conflict

Principles of Interpersonal Conflict

Conflict Management Strategies

Learning Objectives

11.1 Define *interpersonal conflict*, some popular myths, and some issues that create conflict.

11.2 Describe the major principles of interpersonal conflict.

11.3 Describe the influences on, and the strategies for, effective conflict management.

This chapter addresses interpersonal conflict, one of the most important topics in the study of interpersonal communication. As you'll see in this chapter, an understanding of interpersonal conflict and the skills for effective conflict management are essential to all forms of interpersonal interaction. After introducing a few preliminary concepts, this chapter focuses on the principles of conflict, and the strategies for managing interpersonal conflict effectively.

Preliminaries to Interpersonal Conflict

11.1 Define *interpersonal conflict*, some popular myths, and some issues that create conflict.

Before considering the stages and strategies of conflict management, we need to define exactly what we mean by interpersonal conflict, some of the myths surrounding this concept, and some of the issues around which conflict often centers.

Definition of Interpersonal Conflict

You want to go to the movies with your partner. Your partner wants to stay home. Your insisting on going to the movies interferes with your partner's staying home, and your partner's determination to stay home interferes with your going to the movies. Your goals are incompatible; if your goal is achieved, your partner's goal is not. Conversely, if your partner's goal is achieved, your goal is not.

As this example illustrates, **interpersonal conflict** is disagreement between or among connected individuals—friends, lovers, colleagues, family members—who perceive their goals as incompatible (Jandt, 2017; Cahn & Abigail, 2007; Folger, Poole, & Stutman, 2016; Hocker & Wilmot, 2007). More specifically, conflict occurs when people are:

- *interdependent* (they're connected in some significant way); what one person does has an impact or an effect on the other person.
- *mutually aware that their goals are incompatible;* if one person's goal is achieved, then the other person's goal cannot be achieved. For example, if one person wants to buy a new car and the other person wants to pay down the mortgage, there is conflict. Note that this situation would not pose a conflict if the couple had unlimited resources, in which case they could buy the car *and* pay down the mortgage.
- *perceived as interfering with the attainment of the other's goals.* For example, you may want to study, but your roommate may want to party; the attainment of either goal would interfere with the attainment of the other goal.

One of the implications of the concept of interdependency is that the greater the interdependency, (1) the greater the number of issues on which conflict can center, and (2) the greater the impact of the conflict and the conflict management interaction on the individuals and on the relationship. As interdependency increases, so do breadth (the number of topics) and depth (the level to which topics are penetrated). When you think about it this way, it's easy to appreciate how important understanding interpersonal conflict and mastering the strategies of effective conflict management are to your relationship life. Figure 11.1 illustrates the idea that as interdependency increases so does the breadth and depth of conflict.

Figure 11.1 Conflict and Interdependency

The depth and breadth of conflict and its resolution depend on the degree of interdependence between the individuals.

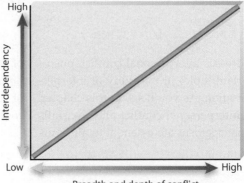

Myths about Interpersonal Conflict

One of the problems many people have in dealing with conflict is that they may be operating on the basis of false assumptions about what conflict is and what it means.

Think about your own assumptions about interpersonal and small-group conflict, which were probably derived from the communications you witnessed in your family and in your social interactions. For example, do you think the following are true or false?

1. Conflict is best avoided. Time will generally solve any problem; most difficulties blow over given time.
2. If two people experience relationship conflict, it means their relationship is in big trouble; conflict is a sign of a deeply troubled relationship.
3. Conflict damages an interpersonal relationship.
4. Conflict is destructive because it reveals our negative selves—our pettiness, our need to be in control, our unreasonable expectations.
5. In any conflict, there has to be a winner and a loser. Because goals are incompatible, someone has to win and someone has to lose.

Each of these statements is false and, as we'll see in this chapter, these myths can easily interfere with your dealing effectively with conflict. To explain briefly: (1) Avoiding conflict prevents differences and disagreements from ever getting resolved. (2) Conflict is inevitable; conflict is a sign of disagreement, not necessarily major relationship problems. (3) Conflict, when it is appropriately managed, can actually improve a relationship. (4) Conflict can be constructive, especially when both individuals approach it logically and with consideration for each other. (5) Conflict does not mean that someone has to lose and someone has to win; both can win.

It's not so much the conflict that creates problems as the way in which you approach and deal with the conflict. Some ways of approaching conflict can resolve difficulties and differences, and can actually improve a relationship. Other ways can hurt the relationship; they can destroy self-esteem, create bitterness, and foster suspicion. Your task, therefore, is not to try to create relationships that will be free of conflict but rather to learn appropriate and productive ways of managing conflict so that neither person emerges a loser.

Interpersonal Conflict Issues

Interpersonal conflicts cover a wide range of issues (Canary, 2003). Such conflicts may focus on goals to be pursued (for example, parents and child disagree on what college the child should attend or what romantic partner he or she should get involved with); on the allocation of resources such as money or time (for example, partners differ on how to spend their money); on decisions to be made (for example, spouses argue about whether to save or splurge after one receives a bonus); or on behaviors that are considered appropriate or desirable by one person but inappropriate or undesirable by the other (for example, two people disagree over whether one of them was flirting or drinking or not working as hard on the relationship).

An interesting way of looking at conflict issues is in terms of content and relationship, concepts introduced in Chapter 1. **Content conflict** centers on objects, events, and persons in the world that are usually external to the people involved in the conflict. These include the millions of issues that you argue and fight about every day—the merits of a particular movie, what to watch on television, the fairness of the last examination, who should get promoted, the way to spend your savings.

Relationship conflicts are equally numerous and are concerned with the relationships between the individuals—with issues such as who's in charge, the equality or lack of it in the relationship, and who has the right to establish rules of behavior.

Examples of relationship conflicts include those involving a younger brother who does not obey his older brother, two partners who each want an equal say in making vacation plans, or a mother and daughter who each want to have the final word concerning the daughter's lifestyle.

Relationship conflicts are often hidden and disguised as content conflicts. Thus, a conflict over where you should vacation may, on the content level, center on the advantages and disadvantages of Mexico versus Hawaii. On a relationship level, however, it may center on who has the greater right to select the place to vacation, who should win the argument, or who is the decision maker in the relationship.

Couple Conflicts   In a study on the issues argued about by gay, lesbian, and heterosexual couples, researchers found that respondents identified six major issues that were almost identical for all couples (Kurdek, 1994). These issues are arranged here in order, with the first being the one mentioned most often. As you read this list and the remaining lists, ask yourself how many of these issues lead to interpersonal conflict in your own life and especially how you deal with them.

- intimacy issues, such as affection or sex
- power issues, such as excessive demands or possessiveness, lack of equality in the relationship, friends, or disagreements over how to spend leisure time
- personal flaws issues, such as drinking or smoking, personal grooming, or driving style
- personal distance issues, such as frequent absence or heavy school or job commitments
- social issues, such as politics and social policies, parents, or personal values
- distrust issues, such as relationship with previous lovers or lying

In another study—this one on same-sex and opposite-sex friends—the four issues most often argued about were shared living space or possessions, violations of friendship rules, the sharing of activities, and disagreement about ideas (Samter & Cupach, 1998). And, another set of conflict issues is identified by the eHarmony.com website: Free time, money, household responsibilities, politics, sex, children and pets, religion, jealousy, and stress.

Workplace Conflicts   In the workplace, conflicts are especially important because of their potential negative effects such as personnel leaving the job (necessitating new recruitment and retraining), low morale, and a lessening desire to perform at top efficiency. In workplace settings, the major sources of conflict among top managers revolved around the issue of executive responsibility and coordination. Other conflicts focused on differences in organizational objectives, on how resources were to be allocated, and on what constituted an appropriate management style (Morrill, 1992; Miller & Reznik, 2009).

Workplace conflicts, according to another study, center on issues such as these (Psychometrics, 2010):

- personality differences and resulting clashes, 86 percent
- ineffective leadership, 73 percent
- lack of openness, 67 percent
- physical and emotional stress, 64 percent
- differences in values and resulting clashes, 59 percent

Social Allergen Conflicts   Another class of issues that can lead to conflict in any relationship is that of social allergens (Cunningham, 2009). A **social allergen** is a personal habit of a friend or romantic partner that you find annoying, unpleasant, distasteful, impolite, inconsiderate, uncouth, or just plain bothersome.

Much like an allergen such as poison ivy irritates you physically, social allergens irritate you psychologically, emotionally, interpersonally. Physical allergies begin with a mild physical reaction and then, upon repeated contact, with reactions that are more and more severe. Similarly, a social allergen—for example, not calling when you're going to be late—may at first be treated as a simple personality quirk. But when it occurs repeatedly over time, it's no longer just a quirk; it's a major annoyance.

Each person, of course, will have his or her own list of what constitutes social allergens. One researcher found that men and women identified different types of allergens. For example, the allergens that men complained about women included: using the silent treatment, bringing up old grievances, being too critical, and being stubborn. Women, on the other hand, complained about men forgetting dates of important events such as birthdays or anniversaries, not working hard enough, burping and flatulence, and looking too much at other women (Cunningham, 2009; Eccles, 2009). Here are a few additional ones mentioned in the many websites that discuss this issue: leaving wet towels on the bathroom floor, not capping the toothpaste tube, blowing one's nose at the dinner table, commanding rather than asking, picking one's nose, leaving toe nail clippings on the floor, smoking, drinking, working on Facebook, or talking on the phone too much.

Online Conflicts   In large part, the same conflicts you experience in face-to-face relationships can also arise in online communication. Yet there are a few conflict issues that seem to be unique to electronic communication, whether via e-mail, on social networking sites such as Facebook, in texts, or on blog posts, for example. For the most part, such conflict results when people violate the rules of Internet courtesy, for example, sending commercial messages to those who didn't request them often creates conflict. Sending someone unsolicited mail (spamming or spimming), repeatedly sending the same mail, or posting the same message in lots of newsgroups, even when the message is irrelevant to the focus of one or more groups, also create conflict. Still another potential cause of such conflict occurs when posting an unflattering photo or comment on social network sites.

Some online conflicts are purposely started by **trolling**, intentional behaviors that are designed to upset another person by, for example, posting upsetting text, photos, or videos. Revenge websites, where someone seeks revenge on say a past relationship partner by posting unflattering or compromising photos and comments (that may or may not be true), seem the extreme.

Another online conflict issue—though certainly not limited to online interactions—is bullying which we discuss in detail in Chapter 12. Online bullying, or **cyberbullying**, takes the same form as face-to-face bullying: gossiping, treating others as inferior, verbal insults, and excessive blaming, for example.

Flaming, especially common in newsgroups, is sending messages that personally attack another user, often with language that is insulting and profane. Flaming frequently leads to flame wars, in which everyone in the group gets into the act and attacks other users. Generally, flaming and flame wars prevent us from achieving our goals and so are counterproductive.

Table 11.1 provides a brief summary of these preliminaries to interpersonal conflict.

Conflict Issues

How do interpersonal conflicts portrayed in popular culture compare to the conflicts people face in real life? Are they similar? If not, how are they different? How would you compare the conflict resolution strategies people use in television dramas and sitcoms to those they use in real life?

Table 11.1 In a Nutshell Preliminaries to Interpersonal Conflict

Preliminaries	Explanations
Nature of Interpersonal Conflict	Interpersonal conflict is a disagreement between connected individuals who perceive their goals as incompatible.
Myths about Interpersonal Conflict	Among the myths interfering with effective conflict management are the beliefs that conflict is bad and that it is best avoided.
Issues in Interpersonal Conflict	Interpersonal conflict focuses on a wide variety of issues, for example, intimacy, power, personal flaws, personal distance, social issues, and distrust issues.

Principles of Interpersonal Conflict

11.2 Describe the major principles of interpersonal conflict.

The importance and influence of conflict in all interpersonal relationships can be best appreciated if we understand some fundamental principles of this particular form of interaction. Here we look at (1) the inevitability of conflict, (2) conflict's positive and negative aspects, (3) cultural and gender influences, (4) differing styles of conflict and their consequences, and (5) conflict management as a multistep process.

Conflict Is Inevitable

Conflict is part of every interpersonal relationship, whether between parents and children, brothers and sisters, friends, lovers, or coworkers. The very fact that people are different, have had different histories, and have different goals invariably produces differences. If the individuals are interdependent, as discussed earlier (see Figure 11.1), these differences may well lead to conflicts—and if so, the conflicts can focus on a wide variety of issues and can be extremely personal.

And, of course, some people have greater tolerance for disagreement. Consequently, they are more apt to let things slide and not become emotionally upset or hostile than are those with little tolerance for disagreement (Teven, Richmond, & McCroskey, 1998; Wrench, McCroskey, & Richmond, 2008).

Conflict Can Have Negative and Positive Effects

Even though interpersonal conflict is inevitable, the way you deal with conflict is crucial because conflict can have both negative and positive effects, depending on how it is handled.

Negative Effects Among the disadvantages of conflict is that it often leads to increased negative feelings. Many conflicts involve unfair fighting methods and focus largely on hurting the other person. If this happens, negative feelings are sure to increase. Conflict may also deplete energy better spent on other areas, especially when unproductive conflict strategies are used.

At times, conflict may lead you to close yourself off from the other individual. When you hide your feelings from your partner, you prevent meaningful communication and interaction; this, in turn, creates barriers to intimacy. Because the need for intimacy is so strong, one possible outcome is that one or both parties may seek intimacy elsewhere. This often leads to further conflict, mutual hurt, and resentment—all of which add heavily to the costs carried by the relationship. As the costs increase, the rewards may become more difficult to exchange. Here, then, is a situation in which costs

---

INTERPERSONAL CHOICE POINT

Escalating to Relationship Conflict

Your own interpersonal conflicts often start as content conflicts but quickly degenerate into relationship conflicts; it goes from "you didn't call when you said you would" to "you obviously don't care about our relationship"—and that's when things get ugly. *What might you do to keep conflicts and their resolution focused on content and not escalate to relationship conflict?*

a. Explain the distinction between content and relationship conflicts.

b. Avoid responding to relationship conflicts.

c. Keep the conflict focused on content.

d. Let the conflict escalate; your partner isn't going to change.

e. Other

increase and rewards decrease, a scenario that often results in relationship deterioration and eventual dissolution.

Positive Effects   Among the advantages of conflict is that it forces you to examine a problem and work toward a potential solution. If you use productive conflict strategies, your relationship is likely to become stronger, healthier, and more satisfying than it was before. Even angry discussions in which you voice your unwillingness to accept certain behaviors can be beneficial (McNulty & Russell, 2010).

Conflict often prevents hostilities and resentments from festering. Say that you're annoyed at your partner, who comes home from work and then talks on the phone with colleagues for two hours instead of giving that time to you. If you say nothing, your annoyance is likely to grow. Further, by saying nothing you implicitly approve of such behavior, so it's likely that the phone calls will continue. Through your conflict and its resolution, you each let your needs be known: your partner needs to review the day's work to gain assurance that it's been properly completed, and you have a need for your partner's attention. If you both can appreciate the legitimacy of these needs, then you stand a good chance of finding workable solutions. Perhaps your partner can make the phone calls after your attention needs are met. Perhaps you can delay your need for attention until your partner gets closure about work. Perhaps you can learn to provide for your partner's closure needs and in doing so get your own attention needs met.

Consider, too, that when you try to resolve conflict within an interpersonal relationship, you're saying that the relationship is worth the effort; otherwise, you'd walk away. Although there may be exceptions—as when you confront conflict to save face or to gratify some ego need—confronting a conflict often indicates concern, commitment, and a desire to protect and preserve the relationship.

VIEWPOINTS

Online And Face-To-Face Conflicts
One study found that, generally at least, people are more positive in dealing with conflict in face-to-face situations than in online communication (Zornoza, Ripoll, & Peiró, 2002). *Do you notice this in your own interactions? If so, why do you think it's true? In what ways might you make your online conflicts more positive?*

Conflict Is Influenced by Culture and Gender

As is true with all communication processes, conflict is influenced by the culture of the participants—and especially by their beliefs and values about conflict—and by their gender.

Cultural Influences   Culture influences the topics people fight about, the nature of their conflict, the conflict strategies they use, and the norms of the organization regarding conflict.

Topics   Culture influences the topics people fight about as well as what are considered appropriate and inappropriate ways of dealing with conflict. For example, cohabiting 18-year-olds are more likely to have conflict with their parents over their living style if they live in the United States than if they live in Sweden, where cohabitation is much more accepted. Similarly, male infidelity is more likely to cause conflict among American couples than among southern European couples. The topics of conflicts also depend on whether the culture is collectivist or individualist. In collectivist cultures, conflicts are more likely to center on violations of collective or group norms and values. Conversely, in individualist cultures, conflicts are more likely to come up when individual norms are violated (Ting-Toomey, 1985).

Nature of Conflict   Cultures also differ in how they define what constitutes conflict. For example, in some cultures it's quite common for women to be referred to negatively and to be seen as less than equal. To most people in the United States, this would constitute a clear basis for conflict. To some Japanese women, however, this isn't uncommon and isn't perceived as abusive (Tanikawa, 1996). Further, Americans and Japanese differ in their views of the aim or purpose of conflict. The Japanese see conflicts and their resolution in terms of compromise; Americans, on the other hand, see conflict in terms of winning (Gelfand, Nishii, Holcombe, Dyer, Ohbuchi, et al, 2001). African Americans and European Americans engage in conflict in very different ways (Hecht, Jackson, & Ribeau, 2003; Kochman, 1981). The issues that cause and aggravate conflict, the conflict strategies that are expected and accepted, and the attitudes toward conflict vary from one group to the other.

Conflict Strategies   Each culture seems to teach its members different views of conflict strategies (Tardiff, 2001). In one study, African American females were found to use more direct controlling strategies (for example, assuming control over the conflict and arguing persistently for their point of view) than did white females. White females, on the other hand, used more solution-oriented conflict styles than did African American females. African American and white men were similar in their conflict strategies; both avoided or withdrew from relationship conflict, preferring to keep quiet about their differences or make them seem insignificant (Ting-Toomey, 1986). Another example of this cultural influence on conflict is seen in the tendency of members of collectivist cultures to avoid conflict more, and to give greater importance to saving face, than members of individualist cultures (Cai & Fink, 2002; Dsilva & Whyte, 1998; Haar & Krabe, 1999; Oetzel & Ting-Toomey, 2003).

Organizational Norms   As in the wider culture, the cultural norms of organizations influence the types of conflicts that occur and the ways in which they may be dealt with. In some work environments, for example, the expression of conflict with high-level management is not tolerated; in others, it might be welcomed. In individualist cultures, there is greater tolerance for conflict within organizations, even when it may involve different levels of the hierarchy. In collectivist cultures, there is less tolerance. And, of course, culture influences how conflicts are resolved. For example, American managers (members of an individualistic culture) deal with workplace conflict by seeking to integrate the demands of the different sides; everyone's demands are important. Chinese managers (members of a collectivist culture) are more likely to call on higher management to make decisions for the benefit of the group as a whole (Tinsley & Brett, 2001).

Gender Influences   Research finds significant gender differences in interpersonal conflict (Kr#løkke & Sørensen, 2006; Wood, 2010). For example, men are more apt to withdraw from a conflict situation than are women. It's been argued that this may be because men become more psychologically and physiologically aroused during conflict (and retain this heightened level of arousal much longer) than do women, and so may try to distance themselves and withdraw from the conflict to prevent further arousal (Goleman, 1995b; Gottman & Carrere, 1994). Another position argues that men withdraw because the culture has taught men to avoid conflict. Still another position claims that withdrawal is an expression of power.

Women, on the other hand, want to get closer to the conflict; they want to talk about it and resolve it. Even adolescents reveal these differences. In research on boys and girls ages 11 to 17, boys withdrew more than girls (Heasley, Babbitt, &

VIEWPOINTS

Gender Differences

Research findings show that when wives discuss problems and possible solutions, conflict resolution is more likely to occur and more likely to be more satisfying. But, it doesn't seem to work for husbands, who are often accused of proposing solutions without thinking through the problem (Bloch, 2013). *Do you find this to be true in your own experience? If so, why do you think this is so?*

Burbach, 1995; Lindeman, Harakka, & Keltikangas-Jarvinen, 1997). Other research has found that women are more emotional and men are more logical when they argue. Women have been defined as conflict "feelers" and men as conflict "thinkers" (Sorenson, Hawkins, & Sorenson, 1995). Another difference is that women are more apt to reveal their negative feelings than are men (Canary, Cupach, & Messman, 1995; Schaap, Buunk, & Kerkstra, 1988).

It should be mentioned, however, that some research fails to support these stereotypical gender differences in conflict style—the differences that cartoons, situation comedies, and films portray so readily and so clearly. For example, several studies dealing with both college students and men and women in business found no significant differences in the ways men and women engage in conflict (Canary & Hause, 1993; Gottman & Levenson, 1999; Canary, Cupach, & Messman, 1995; Gamble & Gamble, 2014).

Conflict Styles Have Consequences

The way in which you engage in conflict has consequences for the resolution of the conflict and for the relationship between the conflicting parties. Conflict researchers identify five styles of engaging in conflict (Thomas & Kilmann, 1977, 2002; Blake & Mouton, 1984). As you read through the following descriptions of these **conflict styles**, try to identify your own often-used conflict style as well as the styles of those with whom you have close relationships.

Competing—I Win, You Lose   The **competing style** represents great concern for your own needs and desires and little for those of others. As long as your needs are met, the conflict has been dealt with successfully (for you). In conflict motivated by competitiveness, you are likely to be verbally aggressive while blaming the other person.

This style represents an "I win, you lose" philosophy. With this philosophy, you attempt to manage the conflict so that you win and the other person loses. As you can tell, this style might be appropriate in a courtroom or in buying a car, two situations in which one person benefits from the other person's losses. But in interpersonal situations, this philosophy can easily lead to resentment in the person who lost, which in turn can easily morph into additional conflicts. Further, the fact that you win and the other person loses probably means that the conflict really hasn't been resolved, just concluded (for now).

Avoiding—I Lose, You Lose   Using the **avoiding style** suggests that you are relatively unconcerned with your own or with the other's needs or desires. The avoider shrinks from any real communication about the problem, changes the topic when the problem is brought up, and generally withdraws from the scene both psychologically and physically.

As you can appreciate, this style does little to resolve any conflicts and may be viewed as an "I lose, you lose" philosophy. Interpersonal problems rarely go away of their own accord; rather, if they exist, they need to be faced and dealt with effectively. The avoidance philosophy just allows the conflict to fester and probably to grow, only to resurface in another guise.

Accommodating—I Lose, You Win   In the **accommodating style**, you sacrifice your own needs for the sake of the needs of the other person. Your major purpose is to maintain harmony and peace in the relationship or group. The accommodating style may help you attain the immediate goal of maintaining peace and perhaps satisfying the other person, but it does little to meet your own needs—which are unlikely to go away.

Accommodating represents an "I lose, you win" philosophy. And although this style may make your partner happy (at least on this occasion), it's not likely to prove a lasting resolution to an interpersonal conflict. You'll eventually sense the unfairness and inequity inherent in this approach to conflict, and you may easily come to resent your partner and perhaps even yourself.

Collaborating—I Win, You Win   In the **collaborating style**, your concern is with both your own and the other person's needs. Often considered the ideal, collaborating takes time and a willingness to communicate, and especially to listen to the perspectives and needs of the other person.

Ideally, collaborating allows each person's needs to be satisfied, an "I win, you win" situation. This is obviously the style that you want to use in most of your interpersonal conflict. Collaborating promotes resolutions in which both people get something.

Compromising—I Win and Lose, You Win and Lose   The **compromising style** is in the middle; there's some concern for your own needs and some concern for the other's needs. Compromising is the kind of strategy you might refer to as meeting each other halfway, horse trading, or give and take. This strategy is likely to result in maintaining peace, but there also will be dissatisfaction over the inevitable losses that have to be endured.

Compromising could be called an "I-win-and-lose and you-win-and-lose" strategy. There are lots of times when you can't both get exactly what you want. For example, you can't both get a new car if the available funds allow for only one. Still, you might

THE CULTURAL MAP   Success

One of the major differences between individualistic and collectivist cultures is the way in which *success* is defined. In individualistic cultures, success is winning, beating the others, and coming out on top. In collectivist cultures, success is contributing to the group's goals, and being an effective member of a team.

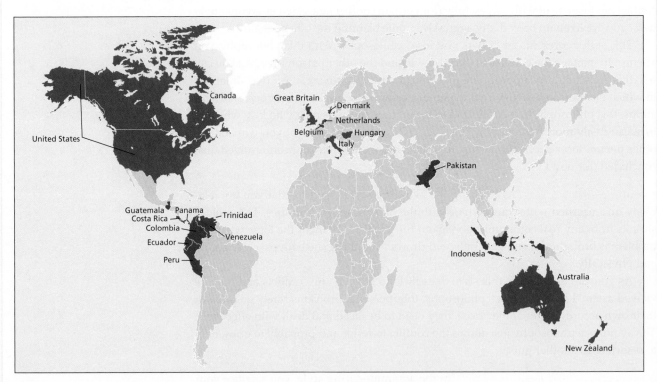

■ These countries are among the most strongly affiliated with individualism. In high individualist cultures, the individual's goals are given the highest priority, and success is measured by the extent to which you surpass other members of your group.

■ These countries are among the most strongly affiliated with collectivism. In high collectivist cultures, the group's goals are given the highest priority, and success is measured by your contributions to the group as a whole.

What is success to you right now? What qualities or achievements would contribute most to your definition of success? In visualizing your successful self, are you more likely to behave as would an individualist or as a collectivist?

each get a better car than what you now have—so you would win something but not everything. You wouldn't get a new car, and the same would be true of your partner.

Conflict Management Is a Multistep Process

Conflict is best understood and managed when viewed as a multistep process. And although every conflict is different, the steps depicted in Figure 11.2, are common to most. In the discussion of each step, suggestions for effective conflict management are offered. More conflict management strategies are covered later in this chapter.

Step 1. Set the Stage   First, try to fight in private. If the conflict begins on a social media site, take the fight offline. When you air your conflicts in front of others, you create a variety of other problems. You may not be willing to be totally honest when third parties are present or when others are reading your posts. You may feel you have to save face and therefore must win the fight at all costs. This leads you to use strategies that win the argument but leave the conflict unresolved. You also run the risk of

Figure 11.2   Stages in Conflict Management

This model provides one way of viewing and talking about the steps or stages involved in conflict management.

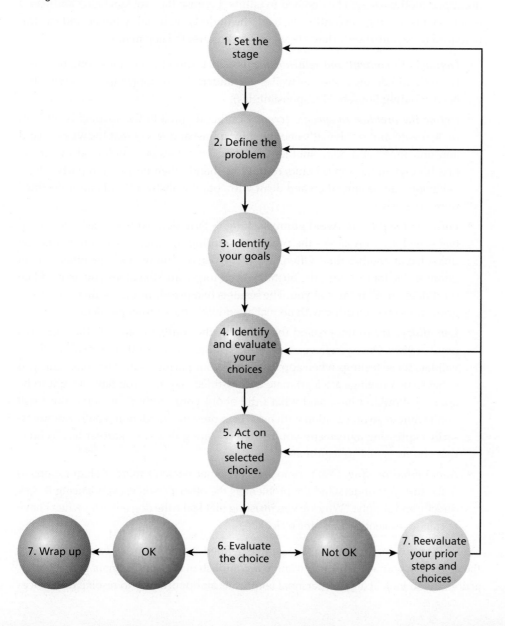

embarrassing your partner in front of others, and his or her embarrassment may turn into resentment and hostility. Finally, on social media, you run an additional risk of having your posts circulated and even quoted back to you long after the conflict is settled.

Be sure you're each ready to fight. Although conflicts arise at the most inopportune times, you can choose the time to resolve them. Confronting your partner when she or he comes home after a hard day of work may not be the right time for resolving a conflict. Make sure you're both relatively free of other problems and ready to deal with the conflict at hand.

Fight about problems that can be solved. Fighting about past behaviors or about family members or situations over which you have no control solves nothing; instead, it creates additional difficulties. Any attempt at resolution will fail, because the problems are incapable of being solved. Often such conflicts are concealed attempts at expressing frustration or dissatisfaction.

Step 2. Define the Conflict   Once you've set the stage, you need to define the conflict. You need to know what you're fighting about. Sometimes people in a relationship become so hurt and angry that they lash out at the other person just to vent their own frustration. The problem at the center of this kind of conflict, for example, the uncapped toothpaste tube, is merely an excuse to express anger. Any attempt to resolve the uncapped toothpaste will be doomed to failure, because the problem being addressed is not what is causing the conflict. Instead, the underlying hostility, anger, and frustration need to be addressed. Here are several techniques to keep in mind.

- *Define both content and relationship issues.* Define the obvious content issues (who should do the dishes) as well as the underlying relationship issues (who has been avoiding household responsibilities).
- *Define the problem in specific terms.* Conflict defined in the abstract is difficult to deal with and resolve. It's one thing for a husband to say that his wife is "cold and unfeeling" and quite another to say that she does not call him at the office, kiss him when he comes home, or hold his hand when they're at a party. These behaviors can be agreed on and dealt with, but the abstract "cold and unfeeling" remains elusive.
- *Focus on the present.* Avoid **gunnysacking** (a term derived from the large burlap bag called a gunnysack)—the practice of storing up grievances so they may be unloaded at another time. Often, when one person gunnysacks, the other person gunnysacks; for example, the birthdays you forgot and the times you arrived late for dinner are all thrown at you. The result is two people dumping their stored-up grievances on each other with no real attention to the present problem.
- *Empathize.* Try to understand the nature of the conflict from the other person's point of view. Once you have empathically understood the other person's feelings, validate those feelings when appropriate. If your partner is hurt or angry and you believe such feelings are legitimate and justified, say so: "You have a right to be angry; I shouldn't have said what I did about your mother. I'm sorry. But I still don't want to go on vacation with her." In expressing validation, you're not necessarily expressing agreement; you're merely stating that your partner has feelings that you recognize as legitimate.
- *Avoid mind reading.* Don't try to read the other person's mind. Ask questions to make sure you understand the problem as the other person is experiencing it. Ask directly and simply: "Why are you insisting that I take the dog out now, when I have to call three clients before nine o'clock?"

Step 3. Identify your Goals   Once you've defined the problem, you need to identify the goals. Ask yourself what you want to accomplish in this conflict management interaction. If you look at an interpersonal conflict as an opportunity to resolve differences and disagreements, it will be easy to identify your goals. Do you want to avoid breaking up? Do you want to have greater freedom to see others? Do you want to kiss and make up? These goals will help you move to the next step.

Step 4. Identify and Evaluate your Choices   In most conflicts, you have choices as to how you might consider resolving the problems. Identify and evaluate these choices. For example, you might brainstorm by yourself or with your partner. Try not to inhibit or censor yourself or your partner as you generate these potential solutions. Once you have proposed a variety of choices, look especially for those that will enable each party to win—to get something he or she wants. Avoid win–lose solutions, in which one person wins and one loses.

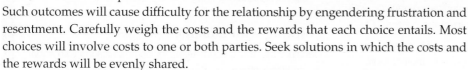

VIEWPOINTS

Conflict Style Changes

What changes would you like to see your relational partners (friends, family members, romantic partners, work colleagues) make in their own conflict management? What might you do to improve your own ways of dealing with conflict?

Such outcomes will cause difficulty for the relationship by engendering frustration and resentment. Carefully weigh the costs and the rewards that each choice entails. Most choices will involve costs to one or both parties. Seek solutions in which the costs and the rewards will be evenly shared.

Using a specific example will help us work through the remaining steps in the conflict management process. In this example, the conflict revolves around Pat's not wanting to socialize with Chris's friends. Chris is devoted to these friends, but Pat actively dislikes them. Chris thinks they're wonderful and exciting; Pat thinks they're unpleasant and boring.

For example, among the choices that Pat and Chris might identify are these:

1. Chris should not interact with these friends anymore.
2. Pat should interact with Chris's friends.
3. Chris should see these friends without Pat.

Clearly choices 1 and 2 are win–lose solutions. In choice 1, Pat wins and Chris loses; in 2, Chris wins and Pat loses. Choice 3 has some possibilities. Both might win and neither must necessarily lose. This potential choice, then, needs to be looked at more closely.

Step 5. Act on the Selected Choice   You might want first to "act" on the choice mentally. How does it feel now? How will it feel tomorrow? Are you comfortable with it? In the previous example, will Pat be comfortable when Chris socializes with these friends alone? Some of Chris's friends are attractive; will Pat be jealous? Will Chris give people too much to gossip about? Will Chris feel guilty? Second, act on the choice. Put the chosen choice into operation (as a temporary measure, if you prefer).

Step 6. Evaluate the Choice   The next step is to evaluate the choice once it has been put into operation. How did it work? Did the choice resolve the conflict? Is the situation better now than it was before? Pat and Chris now need to share their perceptions of this possible solution. Would they be comfortable with this solution on a monthly basis? Is the solution worth the costs each will pay? Are the costs and rewards evenly distributed? Might other solutions be more effective?

If the selected choice works, then you move to the last step. If the selected choice doesn't work, then you need to re-enter the conflict resolution process at some point— perhaps you need to redefine the problem or look for other possible choices.

Critical-thinking pioneer Edward deBono (1987) suggests that in analyzing problems, you use six "thinking hats" as a way of seeking different perspectives. With each hat you look at the problem from a different angle.

UNDERSTANDING *INTERPERSONAL SKILLS*

Equality: An Attitude and a Pattern of Behavior in Which Each Person Is Treated as Interpersonally Equal

In interpersonal communication, the term **equality** refers to an attitude or approach that treats each person as an important and vital contributor to the interaction. In any situation, of course, there is some inequality; one person is higher in the organizational hierarchy, more knowledgeable, or more interpersonally effective. Despite this fact, an attitude of superiority is to be avoided. Interpersonal communication is generally more effective when it takes place in an atmosphere of equality.

Communicating with Equality

Here are a few suggestions for communicating equality in all interactions, and especially in those involving conflict:

- **Avoid "should" and "ought" statements.** Avoid statements such as "You really should call your mother more often" or "You should learn to speak up." These statements put the listener in a one-down position.
- **Request rather than demand.** Make requests (especially courteous ones) and avoid making demands (especially discourteous ones).

- **Avoid interrupting.** This signals an unequal relationship and implies that what you have to say is more important than what the other person is saying.
- **Acknowledge the other person's contributions.** Do this before expressing your own. Saying, "I see," "I understand," or "That's right" lets the other person know you're listening and understanding.
- **Remain culturally sensitive.** Recognize that different cultures treat equality very differently. In low-power-distance cultures, there is greater equality than in high-power-distance cultures, in which status differences greatly influence interpersonal interactions.

Working with Equality

Consider the above suggestions for communicating with equality, and think about your interpersonal interactions over the last few days. In what ways did you express equality? *In what ways were you treated with equality? Can you identify situations in which you or the other person could have expressed greater equality? Would this have made a difference in the interaction?*

- *The fact hat* focuses attention on the facts and figures that bear on the problem. For example, how can Pat learn more about the rewards that Chris gets from the friends? How can Chris learn why Pat doesn't like these great friends?
- *The feeling hat* focuses attention on the emotional responses to the problem. How does Pat feel when Chris goes out with these friends? How does Chris feel when Pat refuses to meet them?
- *The negative argument hat* asks you to become the devil's advocate. How may this relationship deteriorate if Chris continues seeing these friends without Pat or if Pat resists interacting with Chris's friends?
- *The positive benefits hat* asks you to look at the upside. What are the opportunities that Chris's seeing friends without Pat might yield? What benefits might Pat and Chris get from this new arrangement?
- *The creative new idea hat* focuses on new ways of looking at the problem. In what other ways can Pat and Chris look at this problem? What other possible solutions might they consider?
- *The control of thinking hat* helps you analyze what you're doing; it asks you to reflect on your own thinking. Have Pat and Chris adequately defined the problem? Are they focusing too much on insignificant issues? Have they given enough attention to possible negative effects?

Step 7. Wrap it up   Even after the conflict is resolved, there is still work to be done. Often, after one conflict is supposedly settled, another conflict will emerge—because, for example, one person feels that he or she has been harmed and needs to retaliate in order to restore a sense of self-worth (Kim & Smith, 1993). So, it's especially important that the conflict be resolved and not be allowed to generate other, perhaps more significant conflicts.

Learn from the conflict and from the process you went through in trying to resolve it. For example, can you identify the fight strategies that merely aggravated the situation? Do you or your partner need a cooling-off period? Can you tell when minor issues are going to escalate into major arguments? Does avoidance make matters worse? What issues are particularly disturbing and likely to cause difficulties? Can they be avoided?

Keep the conflict in perspective. Be careful not to blow it out of proportion to the extent that you begin to define your relationship in terms of conflict. Avoid the tendency to see disagreement as inevitably leading to major blowups. Conflicts in most relationships actually occupy a very small percentage of the couple's time, and yet in recollection they often loom extremely large. Also, don't allow the conflict to undermine your own or your partner's self-esteem. Don't view yourself, your partner, or your relationship as a failure just because you had an argument or even lots of arguments.

Attack your negative feelings. Negative feelings frequently arise after an interpersonal conflict. Most often they arise because one or both parties used unfair fight strategies to undermine the other person—for example, personal rejection, manipulation, or force. Resolve to avoid such unfair tactics in the future, but at the same time let go of guilt and blame toward yourself and your partner. If you think it would help, discuss these feelings with your partner or even a therapist. Apologize for anything you did wrong. Your partner should do likewise; after all, both parties are usually responsible for the conflict (Coleman, 2002).

Increase the exchange of rewards and cherishing behaviors to demonstrate your positive feelings and to show you're over the conflict and want the relationship to survive and flourish.

Table 11.2 summarizes the principles of conflict.

Table 11.2 In a Nutshell Principles of Interpersonal Conflict

Principle	Description
Conflict is inevitable.	All interpersonal relationships experience conflict at some time and to some degree.
Conflict can have negative and positive effects.	Conflict can be good and it can be bad; it depends largely on how the conflict is managed.
Conflict is influenced by culture and gender.	Cultures vary widely in what they fight about and in how they engage in conflict, as do men and women.
Conflict styles have consequences.	Competing, avoiding, accommodating, collaborating, and compromising all have different effects.
Conflict management is a multistep process.	One set of steps for conflict management includes: set the stage, define the conflict, identify your goals, identify and evaluate your choices, act on the chosen choice, evaluate the choice, accept or reject the choice, and wrap it up.

Conflict Management Strategies

11.3 Describe the influences on, and the strategies for, effective conflict management.

In managing conflict, you can choose from a variety of strategies, which we will explore next. First, however, realize that the strategies you choose will be influenced by a variety of factors, such as (1) the goals to be achieved, (2) your emotional state, (3) your cognitive assessment of the situation, (4) your personality and communication competence, (5) your family history, and (6) your culture (Koerner & Fitzpatrick, 2002). Understanding these factors may help you select strategies that are more appropriate and more effective. Research finds that using productive conflict strategies can have lots of beneficial effects, whereas using inappropriate strategies may be linked to poorer psychological health (Neff & Harter, 2002; Weitzman, 2001; Weitzman & Weitzman, 2000).

- *Goals* The short-term and long-term goals you wish to achieve influence what strategies seem appropriate to you. If you merely want to salvage this evening's date, you may want to simply "give in" and basically ignore the difficulty. On the other hand, if you want to build a long-term relationship, you may want to analyze the cause of the problem fully and to seek strategies that enable both parties to win.

- *Emotional state* Your feelings influence your strategies. You're unlikely to select the same strategies when you're sad as when you're angry. You choose different strategies when you're seeking to apologize than when you're looking for revenge.

- *Cognitive assessment* Your attitudes and beliefs about what is fair and equitable influence your readiness to acknowledge the fairness in the other person's position. Your own assessment of who (if anyone) is the cause of the problem also influences your conflict style. You may also assess the likely effects of your various options. For example, what do you risk if you fight with your boss by using blame or personal rejection? Do you risk alienating your teenager if you use force?

- *Personality and communication competence* If you're shy and unassertive, you may be more likely to try to avoid conflict than to fight actively. If you're extroverted and have a strong desire to state your position, then you may be more likely to fight actively and argue forcefully. And, of course, some people have greater tolerance for disagreement and consequently are more apt to let things slide and not become emotionally upset or hostile than are those with little tolerance for disagreement (Teven, Richmond, & McCroskey, 1998; Wrench, McCroskey, & Richmond, 2008).

- *Family history* The topics you choose to fight about, and perhaps your tendencies to obsess or to forget about interpersonal conflicts, are likely influenced by your family history and the way conflicts were handled as you grew up. Awareness of these influences is a first step in reversing any negative tendencies.

- *Culture* Like the family you grew up in influences your approach to conflict, so does the general cultural in which you grew up. Some cultures, as we note later, emphasize the importance of face-saving more than others and this naturally makes a difference in the way you think about and pursue interpersonal conflict situations.

The following discussion identifies strategies, in addition to those you've already encountered, detailing both the unproductive and destructive strategies that you'll want to avoid and the productive and constructive strategies that you'll want to use. It's important to see at the outset that the strategic choices you make (and do realize that you do have choices, something people frequently try to deny) greatly affect both the specific interpersonal conflict and your relationship as a whole. For example, refusal messages, insults, accusations, and commands are likely to lead to conflict as well as to add to existing conflicts, delaying and perhaps preventing effective conflict management (Canary, Cody, & Manusov, 2003).

Before reading about the various conflict management strategies, examine your interpersonal conflict behavior by responding to the following statements with true (T) if this is a generally accurate description of your interpersonal conflict behavior and false (F) if the statement is a generally inaccurate description of your behavior.

_____ 1. I strive to seek solutions that benefit both of us.

_____ 2. I look for solutions that give me what I want.

_____ 3. I confront conflict situations as they arise.

_____ 4. I avoid conflict situations as best I can.

_____ 5. My messages are basically descriptive of the events leading up to the conflict.

_____ 6. My messages are often judgmental.

_____ 7. I take into consideration the face needs of the other person.

_____ 8. I advance the strongest arguments I can find, even if these attack the other person.

_____ 9. I center my arguments on issues rather than on personalities.

_____10. I use messages that may attack a person's self-image if this helps me win the argument.

These questions were designed to sensitize you to some of the conflict strategies to be discussed in this section of the chapter and previewed in Figure 11.3. As you'll see, if you answered true (T) to the odd-numbered statements (1, 3, 5, 7, and 9) and false (F) to the even-numbered statements (2, 4, 6, 8, and 10), you'd be following the guidelines offered by communication researchers and theorists. As you think about your responses and read the text discussion, ask yourself what you can do to improve your own conflict management skills.

Win–Lose and Win–Win Strategies

As indicated in the discussion of conflict styles, when you look at interpersonal conflict in terms of winning and losing, you get four basic types: (1) A wins, B loses; (2) A loses, B wins; (3) A loses, B loses; and (4) A wins, B wins.

Obviously, win–win solutions are the most desirable. Perhaps the most important reason is that win–win solutions lead to mutual satisfaction and prevent the resentment that **win–lose strategies** often engender. Looking for and developing **win–win strategies** makes the next conflict less unpleasant; it becomes easier to see the conflict as "solving a problem" rather than as a "fight." Still another benefit of win–win solutions is that they promote mutual face-saving; both parties can feel good about themselves.

Figure 11.3   Some Conflict Management Strategies

Finally, people are more likely to abide by the decisions reached in a win–win outcome than they are in win–lose or lose–lose resolutions.

Win–win solutions, in which you and the other person both win, are almost always better. Too often, however, we fail even to consider the possibility of win–win solutions and what they might be. Take an interpersonal example: Let's say that I want to spend our money on a new car (my old one is unreliable), but you want to spend it on a vacation (you're exhausted and feel the need for a rest). Through our conflict and its resolution, ideally, we learn what each really wants and may then be able to figure out a way for each of us to get what we want. I might accept a good used car, and you might accept a less expensive vacation. Or we might buy a used car and take an inexpensive road trip. Each of these win–win solutions will satisfy both of us; each person wins, both of us get what we wanted.

Avoidance and Active Fighting Strategies

Avoidance of conflict may involve actual physical flight, for example, leaving the scene of the conflict (walking out of the apartment or going to another part of the office), falling asleep, or blasting the stereo to drown out all conversation. It may also take the form of emotional or intellectual avoidance, whereby you leave the conflict psychologically by not dealing with the issues raised. As avoidance increases, relationship satisfaction decreases (Meeks, Hendrick, & Hendrick, 1998). Sometimes avoidance is a response to demands—a conflict pattern known as *demand–withdrawal*. Here one person makes demands and the other person, unwilling to accede to the demands, withdraws from the interaction (Canary, Cupach, & Messman, 1995; Guerrero, Andersen, & Afifi, 2007; Sagrestano, Heavey, & Christensen, 2006). This pattern is obviously unproductive, but either individual can easily break it—either by not making demands or by not withdrawing and instead participating actively in conflict management.

Although avoidance is generally an unproductive approach, this does not mean that taking time out to cool off is not a useful first strategy. Sometimes it is. When conflict is waged through e-mail or some social network site, for example, this is an easy-to-use and often effective strategy. By delaying your response until you've had time to think things out more logically and calmly, you'll be better able to respond constructively, to address possible resolutions to the conflict, and get the relationship back to a less hostile stage. And there is some research that shows that as couples age, although they continue to experience the demand–withdrawal pattern, they avoid the conflict rather than confront it (Holley, Haase, & Levenson, 2013). And it seems to work for them. Similarly, in many cultures (and in many specific conflict encounters), avoidance—especially avoiding conflict in public—may be a face-saving strategy and may prove useful in resolving conflict and in preserving the relationship (Cai & Fink, 2002; Jandt, 2017).

Nonnegotiation is a special type of avoidance. Here you refuse to direct any attention to managing the conflict or to listen to the other person's argument. At times, nonnegotiation takes the form of hammering away at your own point of view until the other person gives in.

Another unproductive conflict strategy is the use of silencers. **Silencers** are conflict techniques that literally silence the other individual. Among the wide variety of silencers that exist, one frequently used technique is crying. When a person is unable to deal with a conflict or when winning seems unlikely, he or she may cry and thus silence the other person. Another silencer consists of feigning extreme emotionalism—yelling and screaming and pretending to be losing control. Still another is developing some physical reaction—headaches and shortness of breath are probably the most popular. One of the major problems with silencers is that you can never be certain whether they're strategies to win the argument or real physical reactions to which you should pay attention. Either way, however, the conflict remains unexamined and unresolved.

Instead of avoiding the issues or resorting to nonnegotiation or silencers, consider taking an active role in your interpersonal conflicts. If you wish to resolve conflicts, you need to confront them actively. Involve yourself on both sides of the communication exchange. Be an active participant as a speaker and as a listener; voice your own feelings and listen carefully to your partner's feelings.

An important part of active fighting involves taking responsibility for your thoughts and feelings. For example, when you disagree with your partner or find fault with her or his behavior, take responsibility for these feelings. Say, for example, "I disagree with. . ." or "I don't like it when you. . . ." Avoid statements that deny your responsibility, such as "Everybody thinks you're wrong about. . ." or "Chris thinks you shouldn't. . . ."

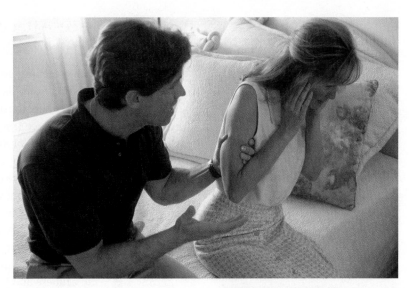

Force and Talk Strategies

When confronted with conflict, many people prefer not to deal with the issues but rather to force their position on the other person. The force may be emotional or physical. In either case, however, the issues are avoided, and the person who "wins" is the one who exerts the most force. This is the technique of warring nations, children, and even some normally sensible adults. It seems also to be the technique of those who are dissatisfied with the power they perceive themselves to have in a relationship (Ronfeldt, Kimerling, & Arias, 1998).

In one study, more than 50 percent of single and married couples reported that they had experienced physical violence in their relationship. If we add symbolic violence (for example, threatening to hit the other person or throwing something), the percentages are above 60 percent for singles and above 70 percent for married people (Marshall & Rose, 1987). In other research, 47 percent of a sample of 410 college students reported some experience with violence in a dating relationship (Deal & Wampler, 1986). In most cases, the violence was reciprocal—each person in the relationship used violence.

The only real alternative to force is talk. For example, the qualities of openness, positiveness, and empathy are suitable starting points. In addition, be sure to listen actively and openly. This may be especially difficult in conflict situations; tempers may run high, and you may find yourself being attacked or at least disagreed with. Here are some suggestions for talking and listening more effectively in the conflict situation:

- *Act the role of the listener.* Also, think as a listener. Turn off the television, stereo, or computer; face the other person. Devote your total attention to what the other person is saying. Make sure you understand what the person is saying and feeling. One way to make sure is obviously to ask questions. Another way is to paraphrase what the other person is saying and ask for confirmation: "You feel that if we pooled our money and didn't have separate savings accounts, the relationship would be more equitable. Is that the way you feel?"

- *Express your support or empathy.* for what the other person is saying and feeling: "I can understand how you feel. I know I control the finances and that can create a feeling of inequality." If appropriate, indicate your agreement: "You're right to be disturbed."

- *State your thoughts and feelings.* on the issue as objectively as you can; if you disagree with what the other person said, then say so: "My problem is that, when we did have equal access to the finances, you ran up so many bills that we still haven't recovered. To be honest with you, I'm worried the same thing will happen again."

Sara and Margaret, both in their early 20s, want to get married. Both sets of parents are adamantly opposed to same-sex marriage, however, and want Sara and Margaret to stop seeing each other and enter "reparative" therapy. *What might Sara and Margaret do to deal with this conflict?*

a. Discover exactly why the parents object and confront the specific objectives.

b. Explain how they feel.

c. Just do it.

d. Present evidence that "reparative" therapy is a hoax.

e. Other

Face-Attacking and Face-Enhancing Strategies

Face-attacking strategies are those that attack a person's positive face (for example, comments that criticize the person's contribution to a relationship or any of the person's abilities) or a person's negative face (for example, making demands on a person's time or resources or comments that attack the person's autonomy). **Face-enhancing strategies** are those that support and confirm a person's positive (praise, a pat on the back, a sincere smile) or negative face (giving the person space and asking rather than demanding), for example.

Cultures vary widely in the importance they place on face-saving. In the United States and generally among individualist cultures, face saving is important but not as important as in other cultures. Among the Chinese and generally among collectivist cultures, for example, face-saving is extremely important and much more important than winning an argument or proving your point (Jandt, 2017).

One popular but destructive face-attacking strategy is **beltlining** (Bach & Wyden, 1968). Much like fighters in a ring, each of us has a "beltline" (here, an emotional one). When you hit below this emotional beltline, you can inflict serious injury. When you hit above the belt, however, the person is able to absorb the blow. With most interpersonal relationships, especially those of long standing, you know where the beltline is. You know, for example, that to hit Kristen or Matt with the inability to have children is to hit below the belt. You know that to hit Jack or Jill with the failure to get a permanent job is to hit below the belt. This type of face-attacking strategy causes all persons involved added problems.

Another such face-attacking strategy is blame. Instead of focusing on a solution to a problem, some members try to affix blame on the other person. Whether true or not, blaming is unproductive; it diverts attention away from the problem and from its potential solution and it creates resentment that is likely to be responded to with additional resentment. The conflict then spirals into personal attacks, leaving the individuals and the relationship worse off than before the conflict was ever addressed.

Strategies that enhance a person's self-image and that acknowledge a person's autonomy will not only be polite, they're likely to be more effective than strategies that attack a person's self-image and deny a person's autonomy. Even when you get what you want, it's wise to help the other person retain positive face because it makes it less likely that future conflicts will arise (Donahue & Kolt, 1992).

Instead of face-attacking, try face-enhancing strategies:

- Use messages that enhance a person's self-image.
- Use messages that acknowledge a person's autonomy.
- Compliment the other person even in the midst of a conflict.
- Make few demands; respect another's time; and give the other person space, especially in times of conflict.
- Keep blows to areas above the belt.
- Avoid blaming the other person.
- Express respect for the other's point of view, even when it differs greatly from your own.

Your Conflict Behaviors

Take a good look at your own conflict behaviors. *What changes would you make? What conflict skills and strategies would you seek to integrate into your own interpersonal conflict resolution behavior?*

Verbal Aggressiveness and Argumentativeness Strategies

An especially interesting perspective on conflict has emerged from work on verbal aggressiveness and argumentativeness (Infante, 1988; Infante & Rancer, 1982; Infante & Wigley, 1986; Rancer & Avtgis, 2006). Understanding these concepts will help you understand some of the reasons things go wrong and some of the ways in which you can use conflict actually to improve your relationships.

Verbal Aggressiveness   **Verbal aggressiveness** is an unproductive conflict strategy in which one person tries to win an argument by inflicting psychological pain and attacking the other person's self-concept. It's a type of disconfirmation (and the opposite of confirmation) in that it seeks to discredit the individual's view of self. Aggressiveness:

- is destructive; the outcomes are negative in a variety of communication situations (interpersonal, group, organizational, family, and intercultural).
- leads to relationship dissatisfaction because it attacks another's self-concept.
- may lead to relationship violence.
- damages organizational life and demoralizes workers on varied levels.
- prevents meaningful parent–child communication and makes corporal punishment more likely.
- decreases the user's credibility, in part because it's seen as a tactic to discredit the opponent rather than address the argument.
- decreases the user's power of persuasion.

Character attack, perhaps because it's extremely effective in inflicting psychological pain, is the most popular tactic of verbal aggressiveness. Other tactics include attacking the person's abilities, background, and physical appearance; cursing; teasing; ridiculing; threatening; swearing; and using various nonverbal emblems (Infante, Sabourin, Rudd, & Shannon, 1990).

Some researchers have argued that "unless aroused by verbal aggression, a hostile disposition remains latent in the form of unexpressed anger" (Infante, Chandler, & Rudd, 1989). There is some evidence to show that people in violent relationships are more often verbally aggressive than people in nonviolent relationships (Sutter & Martin, 1998).

Because verbal aggressiveness does not help to resolve conflicts, results in loss of credibility for the person using it, and actually increases the credibility of the target of the aggressiveness, you may wonder why people act aggressively (Infante, Hartley, Martin, Higgins, et al., 1992; Infante, Riddle, Horvath, & Tumlin, 1992; Schrodt, 2003).

Communicating with an affirming style (for example, with smiles, a pleasant facial expression, touching, physical closeness, eye contact, nodding, warm and sincere voice, vocal variety) leads others to perceive less verbal aggression in an interaction than communicating with a nonaffirming style. The assumptions people seem to make is that if your actions are affirming, then your messages are also, and if your actions are nonaffirming, then your messages are also (Infante, Rancer, & Jordan, 1996).

Argumentativeness   Contrary to popular usage, the term **argumentativeness** refers to a quality to be cultivated rather than avoided.

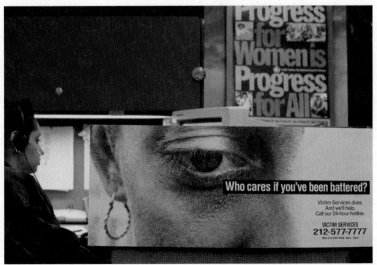

Argumentativeness is your willingness to argue for a point of view, your tendency to speak your mind on significant issues. It's the preferred alternative to verbal aggressiveness (Infante & Rancer, 1996; Rancer & Avtgis, 2006). Among the distinguishing characteristics of argumentativeness that separate it from aggressiveness are that it:

- is constructive; the outcomes are positive in a variety of communication situations (interpersonal, group, organizational, family, and intercultural).
- leads to relationship satisfaction.
- may prevent relationship violence, especially in domestic relationships.

VIEWPOINTS

Gender, Argumentativeness, and Aggressiveness

Men generally score higher both in argumentativeness and in verbal aggressiveness than women. Men are also more apt to be perceived (by both men and women) as more argumentative and verbally aggressive than women (Nicotera & Rancer, 1994; Rancer & Avtgis, 2006). *Why do you think this is so?*

- enhances organizational life; for example, subordinates prefer supervisors who encourage argumentativeness.
- enhances parent–child communication and enables parents to gain greater compliance.
- increases the user's credibility; argumentatives are seen as trustworthy, committed, and dynamic.
- increases the user's power of persuasion in varied communication contexts; argumentatives are more likely to be seen as leaders.

ETHICS IN INTERPERSONAL COMMUNICATION

Ethical Fighting

This section focuses on conflict management strategies and attempts to point out the differences between effective and ineffective conflict management. But communication strategies also have an ethical dimension, and it is important to look at the ethical implications of conflict resolution strategies. Now that you've read this section, consider the ethical dimension for each strategy and indicate how you would answer each of these questions:

- Does conflict avoidance have an ethical dimension? For example, is it unethical for one relationship partner to refuse to discuss disagreements?
- Can the use of physical force to influence another person ever be ethical? Can you identify a situation in which it would be appropriate for someone with greater physical strength to overpower another to compel the other to accept his or her point of view?
- Are face-detracting strategies inherently unethical, or might it be appropriate to use them in certain situations? Can you identify such situations?
- What are the ethical implications of verbal aggressiveness?

Ethical Choice Point

At your high-powered and highly stressful job, you sometimes smoke pot, though illegal in your state. This happens several times a month, but you don't use drugs at any other times. Your relationship partner—who you know hates drugs and despises people who use any recreational drug—asks you if you take drugs. Because it's such a limited use, and because you know that admitting this will cause a huge conflict in a relationship that's already having difficulties, you wonder if, ethically, you can lie about this. *What would you do?*

Strategies for Cultivating Argumentativeness   The following are some suggestions for cultivating argumentativeness. Ideally, most of these guidelines are already part of your interpersonal behavior (Infante, 1988; Rancer & Avtgis, 2006). If any are not part of your conflict behavior, consider how you can integrate them.

- *Treat disagreements as objectively as possible.* Avoid assuming that, because someone takes issue with your position or your interpretation, he or she is attacking you as a person.

- *Attack the argument, not the person.* Avoid attacking the other person rather than the person's arguments, even if this would give you a tactical advantage. Center your arguments on issues rather than personalities.

- *Reaffirm the other person's sense of competence.* Compliment the other person as appropriate.

- *Avoid interrupting.* Allow the other person to state her or his position fully before you respond.

- *Stress equality.* Stress equality, and stress the similarities that you have with the other person (see the Understanding Interpersonal Skills box). Stress your areas of agreement before attacking the disagreements.

- *Express interest.* Express interest in the other person's position, attitude, and point of view.

- *Remain dispassionate.* Avoid presenting your arguments too emotionally. Avoid using a loud voice or interjecting vulgar expressions, which prove offensive and eventually ineffective.

- *Allow the other person to save face.* Never humiliate the other person. Argue politely and respectfully.

Table 11.3 summarizes these five conflict management strategies.

Table 11.3   In a Nutshell Conflict Management Strategies

Effective Strategies	Ineffective Strategies
Win–Win. Try for strategies in which both individuals win.	**Win–Lose.** Avoid, as much as possible, strategies that result in one person losing.
Active Fighting. Participate in the expression of disagreement and in your willingness to resolve the problem.	**Avoidance.** Removing yourself from the problem may be useful if it is temporary, but it doesn't work as a long-term solution.
Talk. Open and honest communication is almost always helpful.	**Force.** Force only enables you to control behavior; it doesn't gain you agreement.
Face-Enhancing. Politeness softens most conflict strategies.	**Face-Attacking**. These strategies are likely to cause resentment and hostility.
Argumentativeness. Argue for or against a point of view.	**Verbal Aggressiveness.** Avoid attacking the person.

Summary

This chapter examined the nature of interpersonal conflict, the principles governing interpersonal conflict, and several unproductive and productive conflict management strategies.

Preliminaries to Interpersonal Conflict

11.1 Define *interpersonal conflict*, some popular myths, and some issues that create conflict.

1. Interpersonal conflict is a disagreement between connected individuals who each want something that is incompatible with what the other wants.

2. Myths about conflict (for example, that it is best avoided or that it's necessarily destructive) can often get in the way of effective conflict management.

3. Interpersonal conflicts arise from a variety of issues, including intimacy issues such as sex and affection, power issues such as possessiveness or lack of equity, and personal flaws issues such as drinking or smoking.

Principles of Interpersonal Conflict

11.2 Describe the major principles of interpersonal conflict.

4. Interpersonal conflict is inevitable; it's a fact of all relationships.

5. Conflict may have both negative and positive effects.

6. Conflict is influenced by both culture and gender.

7. Conflict may be pursued with different styles, each of which has different consequences.

8. Conflict management is aided when it follows a logical pattern such as setting the stage, defining the conflict, identifying your goals, identifying and evaluating your choices, acting, evaluating, accepting or rejecting, and wrapping it up.

Conflict Management Strategies

11.3 Describe the influences on, and the strategies for, effective conflict management.

9. Among the influences on the way you think about and approach conflict and conflict management are your goals, emotional state, cognitive assessment, personal and communication competence, family history, and culture.

10. Seek out win–win solutions. Remember that both parties can win.

11. Become an active participant in the conflict; don't avoid the issues or the arguments of the other person.

12. Use talk to discuss the issues rather than trying to force the other person to accept your position.

13. Try to enhance the face, the self-esteem, of the person you're arguing with; avoid strategies that may cause the other person to lose face.

14. Argue the issues, focusing as objectively as possible on the points of disagreement; avoid being verbally aggressive or attacking the other person.

Key Terms

accommodating style	content conflict	relationship conflict
argumentativeness	cyberbullying	silencers
avoidance	equality	social allergen
avoiding style	face-attacking strategies	trolling
beltlining	face-enhancing strategies	verbal aggressiveness
collaborating style	flaming	win–lose strategies
competing style	gunnysacking	win–win strategies
compromising style	interpersonal conflict	
conflict styles	nonnegotiation	

CHAPTER TWELVE

Interpersonal Power and Influence

Power comes in many forms. *Learning to use it can make life a lot easier.*

Chapter Topics

Principles of Power and Influence

Relationship, Person, and Message Power

Misuses of Power

Prosocial Communication

Learning Objectives

12.1 Describe the major principles of interpersonal power and influence.

12.2 Describe the types of power that reside in the relationship, in the person, and in the message and some of the ways to resist power and influence.

12.3 Explain sexual harassment, bullying, and power plays as misuses of power.

12.4 Define *prosocial communication* and identify some influences on such communication and some effects.

This chapter discusses interpersonal communication power. Power influences what you do, when you do it, and with whom you do it. It influences your choice of friends, your romantic and family relationships, and your workplace relationships. Power makes men appear "sexy" to women as well as to other men (Martin, 2005). Power also influences how successful you feel your relationships are and how personally satisfying they are (Marano, 2014). Here we examine the key principles of power; the kinds of power in the relationship, in the person, and in the message; and three misuses of power: sexual harassment, bullying, and power plays. We conclude with a discussion of prosocial communication.

Principles of Power and Influence

12.1 Describe the major principles of interpersonal power and influence.

Power is the ability of one person to influence what another person thinks or does. You have power over another person to the extent that you can influence what this person thinks or what this person does. Conversely, another person has power over you to the extent that he or she can influence what you think or do. The following principles, previewed in Figure 12.1, explain how power operates interpersonally and offer insight into how you can manage power more effectively.

Some People Are More Powerful Than Others

In the United States, all people are considered equal under the law and therefore equal in their entitlement to education, legal protection, and freedom of speech. But all people are not equal when it comes to just about everything else. Some are born into wealth, others into poverty. Some are born physically strong, good-looking, and healthy; others are born weak, less attractive, and with a variety of inherited illnesses.

Power is asymmetrical: if one person has greater power, the other person must have less. If you are stronger than another person, then this person is weaker than you. If you are richer, then the other person must be poorer. In any one area—for example,

Figure 12.1 Six Principles of Power

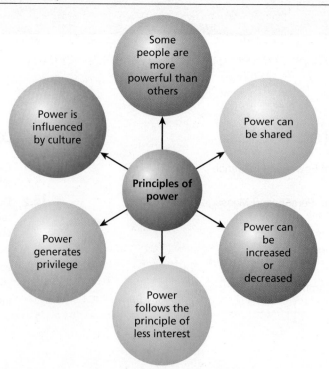

strength or financial wealth—one person has more and, inevitably and by definition, the other person has less (is weaker or poorer).

Some people are born into power, and some of those who are not born powerful learn to become powerful. In short, some people have power and others don't. Of course, the world is not quite that simple; some people exert power in certain areas of life, some in others. Some exert power in many areas, some in just a few.

An important element of power today is social media power, and the Internet includes a wealth of sites that will analyze and graph your social media power. Sites such as Klout, Twenty Feet, Crowdbooster, Tweet-stats, and My Web Career, as well as the analyses available on a regular blog (as well as on social media sites such as Facebook), make it easy to track social media influence. Although such detailed information is designed for, and of most interest to, those in marketing, advertising, or some business venture, it has become part of the interpersonal fabric of our society as well. These sites use information largely from your Facebook, Twitter, and LinkedIn accounts, though new sources are explored and added regularly. They track an amazing array of data that many people would never think of. Among the measures of power and influence tracked by these sites are:

VIEWPOINTS

People with Power
Research shows that people with lots of power are less compassionate toward the hardships of those with less power than are those who themselves have little power. Also, those high in power pay less attention (in conversations, for example) to those with little power than in the opposite situation (Goleman, 2013a). *Why do you think this is so?*

- How many friends do you have? How many followers do you have?

- How many people have accessed your post? From what part of the world are they?

- How often do you post? How many comments or "likes" do you generate? How many are from different people? How many are from powerful people?

- How often do you tweet? How many of your tweets are retweeted? How many generate replies? How many @ mentions do you get?

- How have your statistics changed over time? Do you have more or fewer followers? Are you being retweeted more or less often?

Power Can Be Shared

Some people would argue that power should be guarded—that by sharing it with others, you dilute your own power. Thus, the research scientist who wants to maintain the power advantage should not reveal successful research strategies to his or her assistants because that would make them more powerful and the scientist less powerful, at least by comparison.

Another position would argue that by sharing your power, by empowering others, you actually grow in power. For adherents of this view, empowerment is not just an altruistic gesture on the part of, say, one relationship partner or a company's management; rather, it is a basic philosophy. According to this philosophy, empowered people are more likely to take a more personal interest in the relationship or in the job. Empowered people are proactive; they act and do not merely react. They're more likely to take on decision-making responsibilities, are willing to take risks, and are willing to take responsibility for their actions—all attributes that make relationships and business exciting and productive. In an interpersonal relationship (though the same would apply to a multinational organization), two empowered partners are more likely to meet effectively the challenges and difficulties most relationships encounter. And when power is shared in a relationship, the relationship proves more satisfying and is less likely to break up than a relationship in which one person has a disproportionate share of the power (Marano, 2014).

Should you wish to empower others (your relational partner, an employee, another student, a sibling) so that they gain increased control over themselves and their environment, there are a variety of useful strategies:

- *Raise the person's self-esteem.* Resist faultfinding; it doesn't really benefit the faultfinder and certainly doesn't benefit the other person. Faultfinding disempowers others. Any criticism that is offered should be constructive. Be willing to offer your perspective—to lend an ear to a first-try singing effort or to read a new poem. Also, avoid verbal aggressiveness and abusiveness. Resist the temptation to win an argument with unfair tactics—tactics that are going to hurt the other person.
- *Be open, positive, empathic, and supportive.* Treat the other person with an equality of respect. Be attentive and listen actively; this tells the other person that he or she is important. After all, what greater praise could you pay than to give another person your time and energy?
- *Share skills and decision making.* Be willing to relinquish control and allow the other person the freedom to make decisions. Encourage growth in all forms, academic and relational.

Power Can Be Increased or Decreased

Although people differ greatly in the amount of power they wield at any time and in any specific area, everyone can increase their power in some ways. You can lift weights and increase your physical power. You can learn the techniques of negotiation and increase your power in group situations. You can learn the principles of communication and increase your persuasive power.

Another way to increase power is with what has come to be called **power priming**. For example, in one study of students from three different universities practicing interviewing, one group was told to imagine a time when they were especially powerful and the other group to imagine a time when some person had power over them. Those who power-primed (those who imagined a time when they had power) were much more successful according to the interviewers (who did not know who had been primed); interviewers perceived them as more confident and more persuasive. In another study, voices of those who were power-primed varied less in pitch but more in volume than those who were not power-primed and were perceived to be more authoritative (Galinsky & Kilduff, 2013).

Power can also be decreased. The most common way to lose power is by trying to control another's behavior unsuccessfully. For example, the person who threatens you with punishment and then fails to carry out the threat loses power. Another way to lose power is to allow others to control you, for example, to allow others to take unfair advantage of you. When you don't confront these power tactics of others, you lose power yourself.

Power Follows the Principle of Less Interest

In any interpersonal relationship, the person who holds the power is the one less interested in, and less dependent on, the rewards and punishments controlled by the other person. If, for example, Pat can walk away from the rewards Chris controls or can suffer the punishments Chris can mete out, Pat controls the relationship. If, on the other hand, Pat needs the rewards Chris controls or is unable or unwilling to suffer the punishments Chris can administer, Chris maintains the power and controls the

---

INTERPERSONAL CHOICE POINT
Increasing Power

In your weekly meetings at work, the supervisor who serves as group leader consistently ignores your cues that you want to say something. When you do manage to say something, no one seems to react or take any note of your comments. You're determined to change this situation. *What might you do to increase your interpersonal power and influence in such meetings?*

- **a.** Voice agreement with your supervisor at the first opportunity.
- **b.** Reduce the number of times you talk; use only your best stuff.
- **c.** Interrupt a relatively low-power individual.
- **d.** Stand up when you speak.
- **e.** Other

relationship. Put differently, Chris holds the relationship power to the degree that Chris is not dependent on the rewards and punishments under Pat's control.

The more a person needs a relationship, the less power that person has in it. The less a person needs a relationship, the greater is that person's power. In a love relationship, for example, the person who maintains greater power is the one who would find it easier to break up the relationship. The person who is unwilling (or unable) to break up has less power precisely because he or she is dependent on the relationship and the rewards provided by the other person.

And, it should be added, if you perceive your partner as having greater power than you, you are probably more likely to avoid confrontation and to refrain from criticism (Solomon & Samp, 1998).

Power Generates Privilege

When one person has power over another person, the person with power is generally assumed to have certain privileges—many of which are communication privileges. And the greater the power difference, the greater is the license of the more powerful individual. Sometimes we're mindful of the privilege or license that comes with power. Most often, however, we seem to operate mindlessly, with no one questioning the power structure.

For example, a supervisor or boss can enter a subordinate's office, but the subordinate cannot enter a supervisor's office—at least, not without being asked. Very likely, this power relationship is played out mindlessly by both the supervisor and the subordinate. Similarly, a teacher may invade a student's personal space and lean over the student's desk to inspect his or her work, but a student can't do that to a teacher.

Touch is another privilege. Generally, in any hierarchically organized group, higher-ups can touch those lower than they are. So, a supervisor may touch the arm or rearrange the collar of a subordinate, but the other way around would seem unnatural in any hierarchical organization or culture. The general may touch the corporal, but not the other way around. The doctor may put his or her arm on a patient, but the patient would not do that to a doctor. When such touching is inappropriate or too intimate, it can often be construed as sexual harassment (Chillot, 2013).

Those with power also have the privilege of having the final word, whether in an argument or a discussion. The person with power, for example, is the one who normally wins an argument or whose thoughts and statements are given the most weight in a discussion.

Still another privilege is that those with power can break the rules; those with little power must follow the rules. The supervisor may be late for a meeting or conference call, but the subordinates must be on time lest they be seen as violating the rules of the organization.

Power Is Influenced by Culture

Cultures differ in the amount of power distance or discrepancy that exists between people and in the attitudes that people have about power, its legitimacy, and its desirability (Hofstede, 1983). In many Asian, African, and Arab cultures (as well as in many European cultures, such as Italian and Greek), for example, there is a great power distance between men and women. Men have the greater power, and women are expected to recognize this and abide by its implications. Men, for example, make the important decisions and have the final word in any difference of opinion (Hatfield & Rapson, 1996).

THE CULTURAL MAP   High- and Low-Power Distance

Cultures differ greatly in power distance, the degree of discrepancy between those with power and those without power.

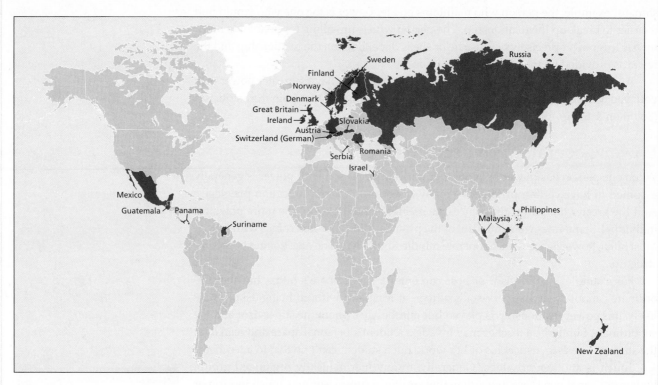

In high-power distance countries such as these, there is great discrepancy between those with and those without power. In the workplace, managers will turn to their superiors and to formal rules in deciding what to do. There is also a very clear distinction between white- and blue-collar workers; white-collar workers are considered more important, whereas blue-collar workers are considered less important.

In low-power distance countries such as these, there is little discrepancy between those with and those without power. Workplace managers rely on their own experiences and consult with subordinates in making decisions. There is also less distinction between blue- and white-collar workers; both are highly valued.

How would you describe the power distance in your various classes? Do your classes differ in power distance? How would you describe the power distance at your workplace? In your family?

In the United States, the power distance between men and women is undergoing considerable changes. In many families, men still have the greater power. Partly because they earn more money, they also make the more important decisions. As economic equality becomes more a reality than an ideal, however, this power difference may change. In contrast, in Arab cultures the man makes the more important decisions not because he earns more money but because he is the man—and men are simply given greater power.

Some cultures perpetuate the power difference by granting men greater educational opportunities. For example, although college education for women is taken for granted in the United States, it's the exception in many other cultures throughout the world.

In some Asian cultures, persons in positions of authority—for example, teachers—have unquestioned power. Students do not contradict, criticize, or challenge teachers. In other cultures, students are expected to interact critically with the material and develop interpretations of their own. As you can appreciate, this difference can easily create problems in many multicultural classrooms.

Table 12.1 summarizes the principles of interpersonal power.

Table 12.1 In a Nutshell Principles of Power

General Principle	More Specifically
Some people are more powerful than others.	Some people have more means of influence at their disposal than do others.
Power can be shared.	Power is not necessarily reduced when it's shared; often it's increased.
Power can be increased or decreased.	Power isn't fixed; it increases or decreases on the basis of your own communication.
Power follows the principle of less interest.	Power is held by the person who is less interested in the relationship, the person who can walk away more easily.
Power generates privilege.	The more powerful person can do more things and break more rules than the less powerful.
Power Is Influenced by Culture	The meaning and effects of power differences vary greatly from one culture to another.

Relationship, Person, and Message Power

12.2 Describe the types of power that reside in the relationship, in the person, and in the message and some of the ways to resist power and influence.

For convenience, we can consider these strategies under three headings that are particularly appropriate to an interpersonal communication analysis of power: (1) power in the relationship, (2) power in the person, and (3) power in the message. In the final section in this part of the chapter, we address the issue of resisting power and influence, or what is commonly called compliance-gaining.

Power in the Relationship

The bases of relationship power, research shows, can be conveniently classified into six types: referent, legitimate, expert, information or persuasion, reward, and coercive (French & Raven, 1968; Raven, Centers, & Rodrigues, 1975; Raven, Schwarzwald, & Koslowsky, 1998). Each of these types of power offers a way of exerting influence or gaining compliance.

Before reading about these types of power, consider your interpersonal power by responding to the following statements. Respond on a 5-point scale in terms of how accurately each statement describes you (5 = very accurate).

_____ 1. People wish to be like me or to be identified with me. For example, high school football players may admire the former professional football player who is now their coach and may want to be like him.

_____ 2. My position is such that I often have to tell others what to do. For example, a mother's position demands that she tell her children what to do, a manager's position demands that he or she tell employees what to do, and so on.

_____ 3. Other people realize that I have expertise in certain areas of knowledge. For example, a doctor has expertise in medicine, so others turn to the doctor to tell them what to do. Someone knowledgeable about computers similarly possesses expertise.

_____ 4. People realize that I possess the communication ability to present an argument logically and persuasively. For example, a competent and persuasive leader will be given greater power than one less competent.

_____ **5.** People see me as having the ability to give them what they want. For example, employers have the ability to give their employees higher pay, longer vacations, and better working conditions.

_____ **6.** People see me as having the ability to administer punishment or to withhold things they want. For example, employers have the ability to reduce voluntary overtime, to shorten vacation time, or to fail to improve working conditions.

These statements refer to the six major types of power discussed in this section. Low scores (say, 1s and 2s) indicate that you believe you possess little of the types of power indicated; high scores (4s and 5s) indicate that you believe you possess a great deal of those types of power. Keep your responses in mind as you read about these six types of power.

Referent Power   If you can establish **referent power** over others (item 1 in the self-test) and make others wish to be like you or to be identified with you, you'll more easily gain their compliance. Referent power is the kind of power an older brother may have over a younger brother because the younger brother wants to be like him. The assumption made by the younger brother is that he will be more like his older brother if he believes and behaves as his brother does. Once he decides to do so, it takes little effort for the older brother to exert influence over, or gain compliance from, the younger sibling.

Referent power depends greatly on attractiveness and prestige; as they increase, so does identification and consequently your power to gain compliance. When you are well-liked and well-respected, are of the same gender as the other person, and have the same attitudes and experiences as the other person, your referent power is especially great.

Legitimate Power   If you are seen as having **legitimate power** over others (item 2 in the self-test)—if others believe you have the right, by virtue of your position, to influence or control their behavior—they'll logically be ready to comply with your requests. Legitimate power stems from our belief that certain people should have power over us, that they have a right to influence us because of who they are. Legitimate power usually derives from the roles that people occupy. Teachers are often perceived to have legitimate power—and this is doubly true for religious teachers. Parents are seen as having legitimate power over their children. Employers, judges, managers, doctors, and police officers are others who hold legitimate power in different areas.

Expert Power   You have **expert power** over others (item 3 in the self-test) when you are seen as having expertise or knowledge. Your knowledge—as perceived by others—gives you expert power. Usually expert power is subject-specific. For example, when you're ill, you're influenced by the recommendation of someone with expert power related to your illness—say, a doctor. But you would not be influenced by the recommendation of someone to whom you don't attribute illness-related expert power—say, the mail carrier or a plumber. You give the lawyer expert power in matters of law and the psychiatrist expert power in matters of the mind, but ideally you don't interchange them.

Your expert power increases when you're seen as unbiased and as having nothing to gain personally from influencing others. It decreases when you're seen as biased or as having something to gain from influencing others.

Information or Persuasion Power   You have **information or persuasion power** over others (item 4 in the self-test) when others see you as having the ability to communicate logically and persuasively.

Gender and Influence
Research findings suggest that women have greater difficulty influencing others by communicating competence and authority than do men. Men, on the other hand, have greater difficulty influencing others using referent power (Carli, 1999). *What would you suggest that men do to increase referent power and women do to increase expert and legitimate power?*

If others believe that you have persuasive ability, then you have persuasion power—the power to influence others' attitudes and behavior. If you're seen as possessing significant information and the ability to use that information to gain compliance by presenting a well-reasoned argument, then you have information power.

Reward Power   You have **reward power** over others (item 5 in the self-test) if you have the ability to reward people. Rewards may be material (money, corner office, jewelry) or social (love, friendship, respect). If you're able to grant others some kind of reward, you have control over them to the extent that they want what you can give them. The degree of power you have is directly related to the perceived desirability of the reward. Teachers have reward power over students because they control grades, letters of recommendation, social approval, and so on. Students, in turn, have reward power over teachers because they control social approval, student evaluations of faculty members, and various other rewards. Parents control rewards for children—food, television privileges, rights to the car, curfew times, and the like—and thus possess reward power.

Coercive Power   You have **coercive power** over others (item 6 in the self-test) when you have the ability to gain compliance by administering punishments or removing rewards if others fail to yield to your influence. Usually, if you have reward power, you also have coercive power. Teachers may not only reward with high grades, favorable letters of recommendation, and social approval but may also punish with low grades, unfavorable letters, and social disapproval. Parents may deny as well as grant privileges to their children and hence they possess coercive as well as reward power.

People rarely use only one base of power to influence others; they usually use multiple power bases. For example, if you possess expert power, it's likely that you also possess information power and perhaps legitimate power as well. If you want to gain the compliance of another person, you probably use all three bases of power rather than relying on only one. As you can appreciate, certain individuals have numerous power bases at their disposal, whereas others seem to have few to none, which brings us back to our first principle: some people are more powerful than others.

Sometimes, attempts to gain the compliance of others through these power bases may backfire. At times, **negative power** operates, where your use of power exerts the opposite of what you intended. Each of the six power bases may, at times, have this negative influence. For example, negative referent power is evident when a son rejects his father's influence and becomes his exact opposite. Negative coercive power may be seen when a child is warned against doing something under threat of punishment and then does exactly what he or she was told not to do.

VIEWPOINTS

Power on the Job

Coercive and legitimate powers have a negative impact when supervisors exercise these powers on subordinates in business settings (Richmond, McCroskey, & McCroskey, 2005). And additional research suggests that effective leaders avoid threats and minimize status differences (Yukl, 1989). Ineffective leaders, instead, exercised power in manipulative, arrogant, and domineering ways. *Does your experience support this?*

Power in the Person

Personal power depends on a variety of factors. In many cultures, as already noted, power is granted to the male, not the female. In some cultures, there is a caste system—though generally outlawed but often practiced in custom—where you are born into a certain caste and are granted or denied power depending on the caste. In some cultures, education, occupation, and financial status will determine your power as it does your socioeconomic status in the United States. And, as illustrated in the chapter opening photo, the physically strong and exceptionally capable are accorded more power than the physically weak or average individual.

Most relevant to interpersonal communication is the power that comes from your credibility. **Credibility** refers to the degree to which others see you as believable and hence influential (not to the way you see yourself). Credibility is not something you have or don't have in any objective sense; rather, it's a function of what other people think of you. If others see you as competent and knowledgeable, of good character, and charismatic or dynamic, they will find you credible and see you as having personal power. As a result, you'll be more effective in influencing their attitudes, beliefs, values, and behavior.

Before reading any further, examine your credibility by considering how true or false the following statements are. Visualize how you think an important group of people (for example, your social network friends, school friends, family, neighbors, or coworkers) see you when you interact interpersonally.

1. People generally see me as knowledgeable.
2. People see me as experienced.
3. People see me as informed about what I'm discussing.
4. I'm seen as fair when I talk about controversial issues.
5. People see me as concerned with who they are and what they want.
6. People see me as consistent over time.
7. People view me as an assertive individual.
8. I'm seen as enthusiastic.
9. People would consider me active rather than passive.

These statements focused on the three qualities that confer credibility—your perceived competence, character, and charisma—and is based on a large body of research; for example, McCroskey (2007); Riggio (1987).

Power in the Media

How is interpersonal power illustrated on television and in movies? For example: (1) Do male and female characters wield the same types of power? (2) Do the storylines in sitcoms and dramas reward the exercise of some types of power and punish the exercise of other types?

Competence   Your perceived competence is the knowledge and expertise that others see you as possessing (statements 1–3 in the self-test). This is similar to expert and information power. The more knowledge and expertise others see you as having, the more likely they will believe you. Similarly, you're likely to believe a teacher or doctor if you think he or she is knowledgeable on the subject at hand.

Character   People see you as credible if they perceive you as being someone of high moral character, someone who is honest, and someone they can trust (statements 4–6 in the self-test). If others feel that your intentions are good for them (rather than for your own personal gain), they'll think you are credible and they'll believe you.

Charisma   Charisma is a combination of your personality and dynamism as seen by other people (statements 7–9 in the self-test). If you are seen as friendly and pleasant rather than aloof and reserved, a dynamic rather than a hesitant and nonassertive speaker, you're likely to be seen as more credible.

Here are a few ways you can enhance your credibility:

- ***Express your expertise when appropriate.*** But don't overdo it.
- ***Stress your fairness.*** Everyone likes people who play fair and think about others fairly.
- ***Express concern for others.*** This shows your noble side and reveals a part of you that says you have character.

- *Stress your concern for enduring values.* This shows consistency and good moral character.
- *Demonstrate a positive outlook.* Positive people are more likely to be believed and to be thought of highly than are negative people.
- *Be enthusiastic.* Enthusiasm helps to demonstrate your charisma.

Power in the Message

You can communicate power much as you communicate any other message. Here we consider power in the message; specifically, how you can communicate power through verbal messages, nonverbal messages, and listening.

Verbal Messages   A great deal of research has addressed the question of the verbal messages that communicate power. Combining these research efforts, we can identify a variety of dos and don'ts (Guerrero, Andersen, & Afifi, 2007; Dillard & Marshall, 2003; Johnson, 1987; Kleinke, 1986; Molloy, 1981). First, here are some suggestions for exerting power and influence and persuading others:

- *Direct request* This is the most common compliance-gaining strategy used by both men and women and is generally the strategy of those in power ("Can you get me a cup of coffee?" or "Please call for reservations").
- *Bargaining or promising* These involve agreeing to do something if the other person does something ("I'll clean up if you cook" or "We'll go out tomorrow; I want to watch the game tonight").
- *Ingratiation* Here you act especially kindly; you try to ingratiate yourself so that eventually you'll get what you want ("You're such a great cook" [*I don't want to cook tonight*] or "You write so well" [*I hope you'll edit my term paper*]).
- *Manipulation* In manipulation you make the other person feel guilty or jealous enough to give you what you want ("Everyone else has an iPhone" [*and you won't have to feel guilty for depriving me*] or "Pat called and asked if I'd go out this weekend" [*unless you finally want to spend time together*]).
- *Threatening* This involves warning the other person that unpleasant things will happen if you don't get what you want ("I'll leave if you continue smoking" [*so stop smoking if you don't want me to leave*] or "If you don't eat your veggies, you won't get any ice cream" [*so finish your broccoli*]).

Hesitations, intensifiers, disqualifiers, tag questions, self-critical statements, slang expressions, and **vulgar expressions** are some verbal messages that seem to weaken power and influence.

- *Hesitations* For example, hesitations such as "I *er* want to say that *ah* this one is *er* the best, *you know*?" make you sound unprepared and uncertain.
- *Overusing intensifiers* Too many intensifiers (for example, "Really, this was the greatest; it was truly phenomenal") make everything sound the same and don't allow you to intensify what should be emphasized.
- *Disqualifiers* For example, disqualifiers, such as "I didn't read the entire article, but . . . " or "I didn't actually see the accident, but . . . " signal a lack of competence and a feeling of uncertainty.
- *Tag questions* For example, tag questions such as "That was a great movie, wasn't it?" "She's brilliant, don't you think?" ask for another's agreement and therefore may signal your need for agreement and your own uncertainty.
- *Self-critical statements* For example, self-critical statements such as "I'm not very good at this" or "This is my first interview." signal a lack of confidence and may make public your own inadequacies.
- *Slang and vulgar expression* For example, slang expressions such as "No problem" and "my bad" and vulgar expressions, signal low social class and hence little power.

Nonverbal Messages Much research has focused on the nonverbal factors related to your ability to persuade and influence others (Burgoon, Guerrero, & Floyd, 2010). For example, clothing and other artifactual symbols of authority help people to influence others. Research shows that others are influenced more easily by someone in, for example, a respected uniform (such as that of police officer or doctor) than by someone in civilian clothes.

Affirmative nodding, facial expressions, and gestures help you express your concern for the other person and for the interaction, and thus help you establish your charisma—an essential component of credibility. Self-manipulations (playing with your hair or touching your face, for example) and backward leaning damages your persuasiveness.

Here are some popular suggestions for communicating power nonverbally, most of which come from Lewis (1989). As you read this list, try to provide specific examples of these suggestions and how they might work in business, at home, or at school.

- *Respond in kind.* For example, if someone raises an eyebrow as a way of acknowledging you, you are expected to do the same.
- *Avoid adaptors.* Avoid self and object adaptors, for example, scratching your head, especially when you wish to communicate confidence and control.
- *Send a consistent message.* Be especially careful that your verbal and nonverbal messages don't contradict each other.
- *Remain comfortable and mobile.* For example, when sitting, select chairs you can get in and out of easily; avoid deep plush chairs that you will sink into and will have trouble getting out of.
- *Touch.* Research shows those who touch others (on the upper arm is a safe place) are perceived as having greater power than those who avoid touch (Summerhayes & Suchner, 1978; Dean, 2011a).
- *Exercise a strong handshake.* To communicate confidence with your handshake, exert more pressure than usual and hold the grip a bit longer than normal.
- *Dress conservatively.* Other things being equal, dress relatively conservatively if you want to influence others; conservative clothing is usually associated with power and status. Trendy and fad clothing usually communicates a lack of power and status.
- *Use facial expressions and gestures as appropriate.* These help you express your concern for the other person as well as your comfort and control of the communication situation.
- *Walk slowly and deliberately.* To appear hurried is to appear without power, as if you were rushing to meet the expectations of another person who had power over you.
- *Maintain eye contact.* People who maintain eye contact are judged to be more at ease and less afraid to engage in meaningful interaction than those who avoid eye contact. Be aware, however, that in some contexts, if you use excessive or protracted direct eye contact, you may be seen as exercising coercive power (Aquinis & Henle, 2001). When you break eye contact, direct your gaze downward; otherwise, you'll communicate a lack of interest in the other person.
- *Watch your distance.* Maintain reasonably close distances between yourself and those with whom you interact. If the distance is too far, you may be seen as fearful or uninvolved. If the distance is too close, you may be seen as pushy or overly aggressive.

Visual Dominance

You can also signal power through visual dominance behavior (Exline, Ellyson, & Long, 1975). For example, the average speaker maintains a high level of eye contact while listening and a lower level while speaking. When powerful individuals want to signal dominance, they may reverse this pattern. They may, for example, maintain a high level of eye contact while talking but a much lower level while listening. *In what specific communication situations would visual dominance behavior prove effective?*

Another way of looking at power in the message is to examine the various **compliance-gaining strategies** that make use of verbal, nonverbal, and listening skills. As you might expect, a great deal of research has been done on this topic that is so important to advertisers, politicians, and just about anyone who wants to exert influence over others. One of the most interesting studies—in terms of its methodology and in terms of its conclusions—was that done by Robert Cialdini, who actually took jobs with various organizations that were in the business of gaining compliance (for example, he worked in sales, advertising, and public relations) and analyzed the techniques used. His research offers a six-part system of compliance-gaining strategies (Kenrick, Neuberg, & Cialdini, 2007):

- *Reciprocation* If you can show that you did someone a similar favor, it will be easier to get that person to comply with your request now.
- *Commitment* If you can get people to make an initial commitment, they're more likely to make subsequent commitments.
- *Authority* If you can get others to see you as authoritative, you're that much closer to gaining compliance.
- *Social validation* If you can make people believe that many others have done what you're requesting, they will more likely follow.
- *Scarcity* If you can make people believe that what you are selling, say, is scarce or rare, they'll be more apt to buy it.
- *Liking* If you can make yourself likeable, you'll find it easier to gain compliance; after all, everyone is more apt to do what a friend requests than what an enemy requests.

Listening   Much as you can communicate power and authority through words and through nonverbal expression, you also communicate power through listening. Throughout your listening, you're communicating messages to others, and these messages comment in some way on your power. Table 12.2 identifies some of the differences between powerful and powerless listeners.

Table 12.2   Powerful and Powerless Listening

Powerful Listening	Powerless Listening
• **Listen actively.** They focus and concentrate (with no real effort) on what is being said, especially on what people say they want or need (Fisher, 1995).	• **Listen passively.** They may appear to be thinking about something else and only pretending to listen, and they rarely refer to what the other person has said when they do respond.
• **Respond visibly but in moderation.** An occasional nod of agreement or a facial expression that says, "That's interesting," is usually sufficient.	• **Respond with too little or too much reaction.** This is likely to be perceived as evidence of powerlessness. Too little response says you aren't listening, and too much response says you aren't listening critically.
• **Give back-channeling cues**—head nods and brief oral responses that say, "I'm listening, I'm following you"—when appropriate.	• **Give no back-channeling cues.** The speaker comes to wonder if you are really listening.
• **Maintain more focused eye contact.**	• **Make little eye contact.** Letting your eyes roam all around the room.
• **Use few or no adaptors.** This makes the listener appear in control of the situation and comfortable in the role of listener.	• **Use adaptors**—playing with hair or a pencil. These give the appearance of discomfort and hence powerlessness.
• **Maintain an open posture.** Resist covering your abdomen or face with your hands.	• **Maintain a defensive posture,** with, for example, arms crossed. This often communicates a feeling of vulnerability and hence powerlessness.
• **Avoid interrupting** the speaker in conversations or in small-group situations, which conforms to the rules of politeness and hence communicates power.	• **Complete the speaker's thoughts** (or what the listener thinks are the speaker's thoughts). This violates conversational politeness and thereby communicates powerlessness.

ETHICS IN INTERPERSONAL COMMUNICATION

The Ethics of Compliance-Gaining Strategies

The strategies of influence discussed in this chapter describe various techniques that people often use and that prove effective in their efforts to influence others. But is it ethical to use some of these approaches? For example:

1. Is it ethical to get people to make a small commitment as a preface to (and solely for the purpose of) asking them to make a major commitment? Would it be ethical to ask for a donation of $1 to gain the person's commitment in order to ask for a much larger donation later?

2. Is it ethical to make yourself likeable when your goal is to influence another's behavior? Would it be ethical to compliment your Facebook friends in order to get them to comment favorably on your status updates?

Ethical Choice Point

Because you've fallen behind schedule, you need your colleague's help to complete your current project on time. You wonder if it would be ethical to give your colleague an expensive watch that she's been wanting, then ask for her help a few days later. You figure that if she accepted the watch, she'd find it difficult not to reciprocate and help you with your project. *What would you do in this situation? What would be the ethical course of action?*

Resisting Power and Influence

Let's say that someone you know asks you to do something you don't want to do, such as lend this person your term paper so he or she can copy it and turn it in to another teacher. Research with college students shows that there are four principal ways of resisting influence (McLaughlin, Cody, & Robey, 1980; O'Hair, Cody, & O'Hair, 1991).

In **negotiation**, you attempt to accommodate to each other or to compromise in some way. In using this strategy to resist complying, you might, for example, offer to meet the request halfway in a kind of compromise ("I'll let you read my paper but not copy it"), or you might offer to help the person in some other way ("If you write a first draft, I'll go over it and try to make some comments"). If the request is a romantic one—for example, a request to go away for a ski weekend—you might resist by discussing your feelings and proposing an alternative, for example, "Let's double-date first."

In **nonnegotiation**, you resist compliance without any attempt to compromise; you simply state your refusal to do as asked without any qualification. You might simply say, "No, I don't lend my papers out."

In **justification**, you resist compliance by giving reasons why you should not comply. You offer some kind of justification for not doing as requested. For example, you might justify your refusal by citing a negative consequence if you complied ("I'm afraid that I'd get caught, and then I'd fail the course") or a positive consequence of not complying ("You'll really enjoy writing this paper; it's a lot of fun").

In **identity management**, you resist by trying to manipulate the image of the person making the request. You might do this negatively or positively. In **negative identity management**, you might portray the person as unreasonable or unfair and say, for

INTERPERSONAL CHOICE POINT
Refusing a Request

Your classmate wants to use a term paper you wrote for another class. *What might you say to refuse the request and yet not alienate your classmate?*

a. "No, I can't. Sorry."

b. "I can't find the paper. I think I deleted it."

c. "It would be better for you if I didn't help; my paper wasn't that good."

d. "You'd be better off doing it yourself. It's a useful skill to learn."

e. Other

UNDERSTANDING *INTERPERSONAL SKILLS*

Interaction Management: Your Ability to Carry on an Interpersonal Interaction Smoothly and Effectively

Interaction management skills represent the techniques and strategies by which you regulate and carry on interpersonal interactions (Spitzberg & Hecht, 1984). Effective interaction management results in an interaction that's satisfying to both parties. Neither person feels ignored or on stage; each contributes to, benefits from, and enjoys the interpersonal exchange.

Communicating with Interaction Management

Of course, this entire text is devoted to the effective management of interpersonal interactions. Here, however, are a few specific suggestions that are related to power:

- *Maintain your role as speaker or listener* and pass the opportunity to speak back and forth—through appropriate eye movements, vocal expressions, and body and facial gestures. This shows that you're in control of, and comfortable in, the interaction.
- *Keep the conversation fluent,* avoiding long and awkward pauses. Powerful people always have something to say. For example, it's been found that patients are less satisfied with their interaction with their doctor when the silences between their comments and the doctor's responses are overly long (Rowland-Morin & Carroll, 1990).
- *Communicate with verbal and nonverbal messages* that are consistent and reinforce each other. Avoid sending mixed messages or contradictory signals—for example, a nonverbal message that contradicts the verbal message. These messages signal indecision and hence a lack of power.
- *Be especially sensitive to the other person's conversational cues,* for example, to end the conversation, to want to say something, to want you to expand on something you said.

Working with Interaction Management

After reading the above skills for effective interaction management, consider how effective you are as an interaction manager. Try to identify two or three areas of interaction management in which you might improve your skills.

example, "That's really unfair of you to ask me to compromise my ethics." Or you might tell the person that it hurts that he or she would even think you would do such a thing. In **positive identity management**, you resist complying by making the other person feel good about him- or herself. For example, you might say, "You know this material much better than I do; you can easily do a much better paper yourself."

Table 12.3 summarizes the discussion of relationship, person, and message power, and some ways for resisting compliance and the influence of power.

Table 12.3 In a Nutshell Relationship, Person, and Message Power, and Resistance

Power in the Relationship	Power in the Person	Power in the Message	Resisting Power
Referent, for example, being a model that others want to follow	**Competence**, for example, knowledge and expertise	**General verbal strategies**, for example, direct request or bargaining	**Negotiation,** for example, attempt to compromise
Legitimate, for example, your position gives power	**Character**, for example, honesty and trustworthiness	**Specific language choices**, for example, avoiding hesitations and disqualifiers	**Nonnegotiation,** for example, simply refuse to comply
Expert, for example, your knowledge and experience	**Charisma**, for example, being friendly and dynamic	**Nonverbal messages**, for example, maintaining eye contact and reasonably close distance	**Justification,** for example, give reasons for noncompliance
Information/Persuasion, for example, your ability to present a persuasive case		**Listening**, for example, listening actively and giving back-channeling cues	**Identity management**, for example, depicting the other person as unreasonable or as more than competent to do it alone
Reward, for example, your ability to give others what they want			
Coercive, for example, your ability to administer punishment or withhold reward			

Misuses of Power

12.3 Explain sexual harassment, bullying, and power plays as misuses of power.

Although it would be nice to believe that power is usually wielded for the good of all, power is often used selfishly and unfairly. Here are three instances when power is used unfairly: sexual harassment, bullying, and the use of power plays.

Sexual Harassment

One type of unfair use of power is **sexual harassment**, a form of behavior that violates Title VII of the Civil Rights Act of 1964, as amended by the Civil Rights Act of 1991. Sexual harassment takes place in a variety of settings: the workplace, the school, and the general social world.

Although we focus here on sexual harassment, there are actually a variety of other forms that harassment can take. All of these are power-driven and are communicated through a variety of verbal and nonverbal messages. The harassments highlighted in Table 12.4 seem to be the most important in terms of type, and they highlight the person most commonly harassed (equalityhumanrights.com, print.employment. findlaw.com, eeoc.gov/types/religion). But nothing in this table should imply that harassment isn't at times perpetuated by the group that is usually harassed.

Table 12.4 Types of Harassment in Addition to Sexual Harassment

Types of Harassment	Examples
Race and color harassment Harassment of another person because of that person's race or color, most often applied to minority and immigrant groups.	Using derogatory names or racial slurs; talking in stereotypes; acting superior and treating others as inferiors (for example, as less intelligent, less ethical, or less "civilized").
Affectional orientation harassment Harassment based on a person's affectional orientation and generally directed at gay men and lesbians, transvestites, and transsexuals.	Using derogatory names, imitating stereotypical mannerisms, threatening the person with outing, excluding same-sex partners from important functions.
Age harassment Harassment generally directed against older persons but often also against the young.	Not promoting or not including individuals in social functions because of age (either too old or too young).
Religious harassment Harassment (sometimes referred to as creed harassment) that is based on a person's religious affiliation or religious beliefs, often directed at atheists.	Making offensive and stereotypical religious jokes; making fun of religious customs, symbols, or clothing; not accommodating to one religion while accommodating to others.
Academic harassment Harassment in the form of statements or actions by senior faculty members that interfere with a junior colleague's development, or statements or actions by a faculty member that interfere with students' ability to perform effectively.	Discriminating in counseling, being less attentive to, or supportive of, junior faculty members; grading students unfairly.
Status harassment Harassment in the organizational setting, generally directed by those with power against those with less power; often takes the form of insulting comments to, or treatment of, workers by managers.	Criticizing publicly; giving unfair salary increases or withholding them; forcing workers to do unethical things (for example, pad an expense account); making insulting or sarcastic comments.
Disability harassment Harassment against persons with disabilities, most often directed at persons with visual or hearing impairment or with physical, speech, or language disabilities.	Failing to adjust communications to the person with the disability; using language that demeans the person; intruding on physical aids (for example, leaning on a person's wheelchair).
Attractiveness harassment Harassment directed at people low in attractiveness, often used against persons because of their weight or their lack of interpersonal popularity or physical attractiveness.	Using derogatory names, especially adjectives that highlight, for example, overweight; excluding people from gatherings or from trendy clubs because they're not attractive enough.
Citizenship harassment Harassment based on a person's citizenship, generally directed against a person who is not a citizen.	Denying financial loans or medical benefits; using derogatory names.
Veteran harassment Harassment based on a person's veteran status, used both against those who are veterans and those who aren't.	Using derogatory names for veterans that refer to wartime actions; using offensive names for those who have avoided military service.

Defining Sexual Harassment The U.S. Equal Employment Opportunity Commission (EEOC) defines sexual harassment as follows:

> Unwelcome sexual advances, requests for sexual favors, and other verbal or physical conduct of a sexual nature constitute sexual harassment when this conduct explicitly or implicitly affects an individual's employment, unreasonably interferes with an individual's work performance, or creates an intimidating, hostile, and offensive work environment.

As you can see from this definition, sexual harassment falls into two general categories: *quid pro quo* (a Latin term meaning "something for something") and the creation of a **hostile environment harassment**.

In *quid pro quo* harassment, employment opportunities (as in hiring and promotion) are dependent on the granting of sexual favors. Conversely, quid pro quo harassment also involves situations in which reprisals and various negative consequences can result from the failure to grant such sexual favors. Put more generally, quid pro quo harassment occurs when employment consequences (positive or negative) hinge on a person's response to sexual advances.

Hostile environment harassment is a much broader term and includes all sexual behaviors (verbal and nonverbal) that make a worker uncomfortable. For example, putting sexually explicit pictures on the bulletin board, using sexually explicit screen savers, telling sexual jokes and stories, and using sexual and demeaning language or gestures all constitute sexual harassment. "Sexual harassment," notes one team of researchers, "refers to conduct, typically experienced as offensive in nature, in which unwanted sexual advances are made in the context of a relationship of unequal power or authority. The victims are subjected to verbal comments of a sexual nature, unconsented touching and requests for sexual favors" (Friedman, Boumil, & Taylor, 1992). Attorneys note that, under the law, "sexual harassment is any unwelcome sexual advance or conduct on the job that creates an intimidating, hostile or offensive working environment" (Petrocelli & Repa, 1992).

Recognizing Sexual Harassment To determine whether behavior constitutes sexual harassment and to assess your own situation objectively rather than emotionally, ask yourself the following questions (VanHyning, 1993):

1. Is it real? Does this behavior have the meaning it seems to have?
2. Is it job related? Does this behavior have something to do with, or will it influence the way you do, your job?
3. Did you reject this behavior? Did you make your rejection of unwanted messages clear to the other person?
4. Have these types of messages persisted? Is there a pattern, a consistency to these messages?

If you answered yes to all four questions, then the behavior is likely to constitute sexual harassment (VanHyning, 1993).

Keep in mind three additional facts that are often misunderstood. First, both men and women may engage in sexual harassment. Although most cases brought to public attention are committed by men against women, women may also harass men. And, of course, harassment may be committed by men against men and by women against women. Second, anyone in an organization can be guilty of sexual harassment. Although most cases of harassment involve harassment of subordinates by persons in

Harassment on Campus

How would you describe the types of online and offline harassment that college students experience?

authority, this is not a necessary condition. Coworkers, vendors, and even customers may be guilty of sexual harassment. Third, sexual harassment, although most often discussed in a workplace context, is not limited to business organizations but can and does occur in schools; in hospitals; and in social, religious, and political organizations.

Avoiding Behaviors Associated with Sexual Harassment   Three suggestions will help you avoid committing sexual harassment (Bravo & Cassedy, 1992):

1. Begin with the assumption that coworkers are not interested in your sexual advances, sexual stories and jokes, or sexual gestures.

2. Listen and watch for negative reactions to any sex-related discussion. Use the suggestions and techniques discussed throughout this text (for example, perception checking and critical listening) to become aware of such reactions. When in doubt, find out; ask questions, for example.

3. Avoid saying or doing anything that you think your parent, partner, or child would find offensive in the behavior of someone with whom she or he worked.

Responding to Sexual Harassment   Should you encounter sexual harassment and feel the need to do something about it, consider these suggestions, which are recommended by workers in the field (Bravo & Cassedy, 1992; Petrocelli & Repa, 1992; Rubenstein, 1993):

1. *Talk to the harasser.* Tell this person, assertively, that you do not welcome the behavior and that you find it offensive. Simply informing Fred that his sexual jokes aren't appreciated and are seen as offensive may be sufficient to make him stop this joke telling. In some instances, unfortunately, such criticism goes unheeded, and the offensive behavior continues.

2. *Collect evidence.* Perhaps seek corroboration from others who have experienced similar harassment at the hands of the same individual, and/or create a log of the offensive behaviors.

3. *Begin with appropriate channels within the organization.* Most organizations have established channels to deal with such grievances. This step, in most cases, eliminates any further harassment. In the event that it doesn't, you may consider going further.

4. *File a complaint.* You'll find a wealth of organization and government agencies with whom you can file on the Internet. A more extreme response is to take legal action.

5. *Don't blame yourself.* Like many who are abused, you may tend to blame yourself, feeling that you're responsible for being harassed. You aren't; however, you may need to secure emotional support from friends or perhaps from a trained professional.

Bullying

Bullying, whether in a close relationship, the workplace, or the playground, consists of abusive acts repeatedly committed by one person (or group) against another. Bullying is behavior that has become a pattern; it's repeated frequently rather than being an isolated instance. On the playground, bullying often involves physical abuse; in the workplace bullying is generally verbal.

Types of Bullying   Here are some of the types of bullying found in various interpersonal interactions.

- Gossiping about someone; making others the butt of jokes.
- Treating others as inferior, for example, frequently interrupting them or otherwise not giving their ideas due attention.
- Excluding members from social functions.

INTERPERSONAL CHOICE POINT
Harassing Behavior

You notice that your colleague at work is being sexually harassed by a supervisor, but she says nothing. You bristle inside each time you see this happen. *What might you do that might help end this harassment?*

a. Talk with your colleague.

b. Talk with your supervisor.

c. Write an anonymous note to the harasser threatening exposure.

d. Do nothing; you'll only hurt yourself. Remember the old adage, "No good deed goes unpunished."

e. Other

- Verbal insults; name-calling.
- Negative facial expressions, sneering, avoiding eye contact.
- Excessive blaming.
- Being supervised (watched, monitored) more closely than others.
- Being unnecessarily criticized, often with shouting and in public.

Sometimes, bullying is part of the organization's culture; for example, first-year interns in a law office are treated unfairly and often abused by their superiors. Sometimes it's perpetrated by a group who, for instance, bully the newcomers or those who do less creative jobs.

The problem with bullying from the employer's point of view is that it reduces productivity and hurts the bottom line. If one or even a few workers are bullied, they're probably not going to be as productive as they would be if they weren't bullied. It is also likely to lead to workers leaving the company—after the company has trained them but before they have become productive team members—with the added cost of hiring and training new people (and perhaps attendant lawsuits).

A special type of bullying is **cyberbullying**, which can take place through any electronic communication system—Facebook, Twitter, e-mail, instant messages, blog posts—and can take the form of sending threatening messages or images, posting negative comments, revealing secrets, or lying about another person. Among the reasons that cyberbullying is so important is that it can occur at any time; the messages, photos, and videos can be distributed quickly and widely; the bully can hide behind false names or remain completely anonymous; and attacks—because they occur electronically—are often crueler than those made in face-to-face attacks (Hinduja & Patchin, 2010).

According to a Washington State Department of Labor & Industries report, victims of bullying may suffer significant mental and physical problems, including high stress, financial problems, reduced self-esteem, and sleep and digestion disturbances. And recent research finds that the mental scars that bullying creates are still detectable even after 40 years (Takisawa, Maughan, & Arseneault, 2014).

From the point of view of the worker being bullied, it obviously creates an uncomfortable atmosphere—perhaps a desire to avoid going into work, perhaps a preoccupation with the bullying rather than the job. And this is likely to spill over into the person's private life; after all, it would be strange if bullying at work did not create problems with other aspects of life. And although the bullies probably derive some personal satisfaction from their wielding power over someone else, they too are likely to fail to be as productive as they might be and may well be personally troubled. From an ethical point of view, bullying destroys a person's right to personal dignity and freedom from intimidation and is therefore unethical. And yet bullying is not illegal in the United States unless it involves harassment based on a person's gender or race, for example.

Dealing with Bullying   Among the actions recommended for combating bullying are these:

1. Workers and organizations need to be clear about their opposition to bullying, and that it doesn't profit anyone and will not be tolerated. Accusations of bullying will be investigated promptly and fairly.

2. If possible and there is no danger (physical or institutional), sometimes confronting the bully assertively (not aggressively) will be enough—"I don't like it when you make fun of the way I dress and I want you to stop—it's not funny and it just makes me feel bad."

3. Taking action when you or someone else is bullied. This suggestion is not always easy to implement, especially if the bullying is part of

VIEWPOINTS

Cyberbullying

In one survey, 32 percent of online teens reported having experienced harassment and bullying (Lenhart, 2007); in another survey, 26 percent of teems reported bullying via their cell phones (Lehnart, Ling, Campbell, & Purcell, 2010). *What's been your experience with cyberbullying? In what ways might it be discouraged?*

the corporate culture or is your boss (one report notes that 81 percent of bullies are bosses (itstime.com/print/jul2005p.htm). But well-kept records of such incidents will often convince even the most reluctant manager about what is happening.

Power Plays

Following Claude Steiner (2004), **power plays** are patterns (not isolated instances) of behavior that are used repeatedly by one person to take unfair advantage of another person. Power plays aim to deny you the right to make your own choices and come in a variety of forms. In responding to such power plays, you generally have three choices:

- *Ignore it.* This is the strategy that many people use simply to avoid an argument or confrontation. The problem with this choice is that it enables the behavior to continue and to become an even more entrenched pattern of behavior.

- *Neutralize it.* In this strategy, you confront the behavior as if it's an isolated instance; you ignore the fact that this behavior is repeated frequently and has become a pattern. The problem with this choice is that it does nothing to prevent future occurrences of the power play.

- *Cooperate.* In this strategy, you confront the power play as a pattern of behavior and seek to accomplish three things: (1) express your feelings (for example, tell the person that you are angry, annoyed, or disturbed by his or her behavior), (2) describe the behavior to which you object (for example, tell the person—in language that describes rather than judges or evaluates—the specific behavior to which you object, such as reading your e-mail or posting embarrassing photos on Facebook), and (3) state a cooperative response that you both can live with comfortably (for example, tell the person what you want: "I want you to stop posting photos of me on Facebook").

Let's look at a few of the major types, identified by Steiner, to see how power plays are used and how they can be identified and responded to effectively.

Nobody Upstairs One type is the **nobody upstairs** power play. In this power play, the individual refuses to acknowledge your request, regardless of how or how many times you make it. One common form is the refusal to take no for an answer. Sometimes nobody upstairs takes the form of pleading ignorance of common socially accepted (but unspoken) rules, such as rules about not posting unflattering photos or not reading another's e-mail: "I think the photos are cute" or "Don't you want me to read your e-mail?"

A cooperative response to nobody upstairs might go something like this: "I'm angry (*statement of feelings*) that you persist in reading my e-mail. You've opened my mailbox four times this past week (*description of the behavior to which you object*). I want you to allow me to open my own mail. If there is anything in it that concerns you, I'll let you know (*statement of cooperative response*).

You Owe Me In **you owe me**, others unilaterally do something for you and then demand something in return. They remind you of what they did for you and use this to get you to do what they want. This type of power play is often seen in the person who buys someone an expensive gift and then asks for something in return—for example, buying your date an expensive dinner and expecting sex in return.

A cooperative response to you owe me might go something like this: "I'm angry that you're doing this to me (*statement of feelings*). I'm disturbed that when you want me to do something, you start by reminding me of my obligations to you (*description of the behavior to which you object*). Please don't do things for me and expect something in return. I don't want to feel obligated or guilty about not paying you back for what you have done for me (*statement of cooperative response*).

Yougottobekidding In **yougottobekidding**, one person attacks the other by saying "You've got to be kidding" or some similar phrase, not out of surprise (which is fine) but out of a desire to put your ideas down: "You can't be serious." "You can't mean that." "You didn't say what I thought you said, did you?" "You can't honestly believe that." The intention here is to express utter disbelief in the other's statement so that you make the statement and the person seem inadequate or stupid.

In a cooperative response to yougottobekidding, you might say: "I'm annoyed and feel like an idiot (*statement of feelings*) when you say things like "you can't be serious" or "You've got to be kidding" when I offer an opinion (*statement of behavior to which you object*). I'd much prefer that you take issue with what I say and tell me why you disagree with me rather than simply dismiss it by telling me I have to be kidding" (*statement of cooperative response*).

Metaphor   **Metaphor** is a power play that is sometimes difficult to identify as a power maneuver. For example, consider the situation in which one member of a group is going out with someone another member doesn't like and responds with such comments as "How can you go out with her; she's a real dog" or "How can you date him; he's a pig." *Dog* and *pig* are metaphors, figures of speech in which one word is used in the place of another. In this case, *dog* and *pig* are used in place of the persons referred to, with the intention of associating the most obvious characteristics of these animals (ugliness, sloppiness, or worse) with the person. The object here is to put the individual down and not allow you a chance to defend him or her. After all, it's difficult to defend dating a dog or a pig.

The three-part cooperative strategy to metaphor might go something like this: "I resent your calling Pat a pig; I'm very attracted to Pat and think we have a good thing together (*statement of feelings*). You use this term repeatedly (*behavior to which you object*), but I want you to refer to Pat as Pat (*statement of cooperative response*).

Thought Stoppers   The **thought stopper** is a power play designed to stop your thinking and especially stop you from expressing your thoughts. Thought stoppers may take a number of different forms. Perhaps the most common is the interruption. Before you can finish your thought, the other person interrupts you and either completes it or goes off on another topic. Another thought stopper is the use of extremely strong language or profanity or raising one's voice to drown out everything else. Regardless of the specific form, the thought stopper shifts the speaker role from you to the other person.

A cooperative response might go something like this: "I get frustrated when you interrupt me before I've had a chance to complete my thoughts (*statement of feelings*). You do this repeatedly (*statement of behavior to which you object*). Please let me complete my thoughts and I'll let you complete yours" (*statement of cooperative response*).

Table 12.5 summarizes these three examples of the misuse of power: sexual harassment, bullying, and power plays.

Table 12.5   In a Nutshell   Three Types of the Misuse of Power

Misuse of Power	Types	Responses (What to do? What are your available choices?)
Sexual Harassment	• Quid pro quo • Hostile environment	• Talk • Collect evidence • Follow channels • File complaint • Don't blame yourself
Bullying	• Making others the butt of jokes • Treating others as inferior • Excluding members from social functions • Verbal and nonverbal insults • Excessive blaming	• Workers and organizations need to understand that accusations of bullying will be investigated. • Sometimes confronting the bully assertively (not aggressively) is enough. • Take action when you or someone else is bullied.
Power Plays	• Nobody upstairs • You owe me • Yougottobekidding • Metaphor • Thought stoppers	• Express your feelings. • Describe the behavior to which you object. • State a cooperative response that you both can live with comfortably

Prosocial Communication

12.4 Define *prosocial communication* and identify some influences on such communication and some effects.

In Chapter 10 we looked at the dark side of interpersonal relationships (jealousy and relationship violence) and, in this chapter, we looked at the misuses of power (sexual harassment, bullying, and power plays), also "dark" sides. As a counterpoint to these "dark" sides we need also to highlight the more positive side of interpersonal communication and relationships or what we might call *prosocial communication*. And, it seems, a nice way of ending a book on interpersonal communication. Here we consider the nature of prosocial communication, the factors that influence or inhibit such communication, some examples of prosocial communication, and some of its potential effects.

The Nature of Prosocial Communication

Prosocial communication is communication that benefits another individual, group, society, or the entire species in some way. The communication may be verbal or nonverbal or, as usual, some combination of verbal and nonverbal messages.

A simple smile, compliment, or helpful advice would be examples of prosocial communication benefiting another individual's self-esteem or future behavioral choices. A phone call or text to report a crime or a person in need of medical attention would also be examples of prosocial communication. The publication of research is another example of prosocial communication because it advances our knowledge of some topic in some way. And, to the extent that knowledge is beneficial, the publication of research is prosocial. Speeches or posts espousing accepted values in a culture—whether they be equality, democracy, freedom of speech—would be considered examples of prosocial communication benefiting the larger social group.

As you might expect the definition of prosocial communication will vary with the culture. And so, while supporting gay rights or women's rights in some cultures would be considered prosocial, it would not be in others. And the same is true with a wide variety of religious, political, and social issues.

On the Internet both crowdsourcing and crowdfunding are examples of prosocial communication (Sproull, Conley, & Moon, 2004). When you help another person find the right plumber or get opinions on different graduate schools (as you would in responding to a crowdsourcing request), you're engaging in prosocial communication. Similarly, when you send in a donation for a particular project (as you would in responding to a crowdfunding request you perceive to be legitimate), you're engaging in a prosocial act. Also needed to be included here are the numerous prosocial communication options for comments on posts, photos, and status updates.

Factors Influencing Prosocial Communication

A wide variety of factors can be identified that may influence prosocial communication. Some factors encourage and others inhibit the expression of prosocial communication.

One factor is that of *similarity*. You're more apt to engage in prosocial communication with those who are similar to you than with those who are different—whether in sex, in age, in culture, or in religion—than you are with those who are unlike you. Dissimilarity often reduces the likelihood of prosocial communication.

Your *relationship bonds* will influence your prosocial communication. You're more likely to engage in prosocial communication with those you are friends with or those you love. With enemies or with disliked others, prosocial communication is likely to be inhibited.

When someone engages in prosocial communication that benefits you, you're more likely to reciprocate and return prosocial communication. This is simply another example of the law of *reciprocity*—you're apt to engage in behavior that is similar to the behavior of others; you tend to give back what you are given. You can look at this law from a different angle: You engage in prosocial behavior because you know that the law of reciprocity will operate and that the person you are helping will help you at some later time.

Your history of *reinforcement* will influence your prosocial communication, as it will any form of communication. If you've been rewarded for prosocial communication, you'd be more likely to continue to engage in and even increase such communication. If you were punished for it or if it was ignored, you'd likely decrease such communication.

Similarly, the *expectation of reward* will influence your prosocial communication. We live in a world that, at least on the surface, rewards prosocial communication. Those who engage in prosocial communication seem to be liked more than those who don't. And so, you might engage in prosocial communication because you anticipate that it will lead others to reward you in some way, perhaps to like you more.

Your *personality* affects your communication and certain personality traits, for example, altruism, will encourage prosocial communication and other personality traits, for example, selfishness, will likely lead to less such communication.

The *teachings* of your culture and with those with whom you come into contact will influence your prosocial communication. Your culture has taught you about the rules for prosocial communication and you likely follow these unconsciously internalized rules. In addition to the rules of the culture, you also learn to engage in prosocial communication from parents, from teachers, and from peers. You may be praised by your parents for saying nice things about your kid sister or notice that those who engage in prosocial communication seem to be liked more than those who don't.

And, because culture influences the *gender* roles you learn, your gender will also influence prosocial communication. Generally, though keep in mind that gender differences are rapidly changing, research finds that both genders engage in prosocial communication equally but in different ways. Women seem to engage in more prosocial verbal communication while men are more likely to engage in more prosocial nonverbal communication (Diekman & Eagly, 2000). For example, a man is more likely to go into a burning building to rescue someone or to break up a fight and a woman is more likely to express positive feelings and give compliments.

One additional factor should be noted and that is the situation that arises when you're in a crowd and someone is in need of help. Research shows that in these situations, you are *less likely* to help. This tendency is referred to as the **bystander effect** (Darley & Latane, 1968). The idea here is that people feel they needn't do anything because someone else in the crowd is likely to do it. A related factor influencing whether or not you offer to act prosocially is your view of the crowd. When you make your decision to act or not to act (that is, to help the person in need or do nothing), you may take your cues from the crowd and if the crowd does nothing, then you figure you shouldn't either. Appropriately enough, this tendency is referred to as **pluralistic ignorance** (Latane & Darley, 1970; Fisher, et al., 2011).

Examples of Prosocial Communication

Throughout your course and this textbook, numerous examples of prosocial communication have been identified. Here are just ten to remind you of the varied ways in which following the principles of interpersonal communication may lead to prosocial communication.

- *Communicating with cultural sensitivity* People benefit in their self-view when their cultural beliefs are understood and respected.

- *Listening empathically* When you listen empathically, you're performing a prosocial communication act by providing a supportive and understanding ear.

- *Responding appropriately to the emotional expression of others* When you offer comfort and support to the grief stricken, you're performing a prosocial communication act.

- *Confirming* Communications that acknowledge the importance and contributions of another are likely to have a beneficial effect while disconfirming messages are likely to yield no such benefits and perhaps a variety of negative responses.

INTERPERSONAL CHOICE POINT
Giving Prosocial Communication

One of your close friends has been having a pretty awful time; failed two courses, lost a great part-time job, and was dumped by a long-time romantic partner. Your friend calls you in an extremely depressed state, tells you all this, and pauses, waiting for you to say something. What would be an appropriate prosocial response?

a. These things happen to all of us; you'll get over it. Don't worry about it.

b. You need to study more; you're always partying.

c. You seem like you're really hurting.

d. Why are you so depressed? I failed three courses and that job was a real dead end.

e. Other

- *Advising* When you offer advice, assuming it is asked for, you are performing a prosocial communication act by sharing what you know or think with another person in an effort to comfort or reassure them.

- *Complimenting* When you compliment someone for a job well done or for looking good, you're performing a prosocial communication act by helping the other person to feel more positively.

- *Mentoring/Sharing* When you mentor someone, you're performing a prosocial communication act by sharing with them your expertise and experience—making them more efficient workers or better speakers, for example. Teaching in all its forms would be included here.

- *Communicating politely* When you respect a person's need for both positive and negative face, you're engaging in prosocial communication.

- *Argue fairly and constructively* When you engage in conflict fairly and constructively you show respect and confirm the other person. So, when you're argumentative rather than aggressive, you're engaging in prosocial communication.

- *Responding to the dark side of interpersonal communication* When you confront bullying or sexual harassment constructively (and safely) you're performing a prosocial communication function.

Effects of Prosocial Communication

Prosocial communication most obviously has an effect on the other person. As the examples given previously illustrate, prosocial communication benefits other people by making them feel better about themselves or enabling them to do something more effectively or more efficiently.

But, your prosocial behavior also has an effect on you; you feel better about yourself for having done something good for someone else. In fact, there is considerable research showing that personal pleasure and happiness often comes from helping others (https://thinklivebepositive.wordpress.com/category/helping-others-makes-you-happy/). There is even research that shows that people who help others live longer and have greater mating success and more sexual relationships (Hilbrand, Coall, Gerstof, & Hertwig, 2016; Arnocky, Piche, Albert, Ouellette, & Baclay, 2016; Dean, 2016b).

And, in many ways, prosocial communication benefits the society as a whole when, for example, you campaign for clean water or when you argue against injustice. Even when you mentor a young person, for example, you're influencing the larger society by helping this person do a better job—be a better bus driver (benefiting the passengers), or teacher (benefiting students), or store clerk (making life easier for harried customers). Each act has ripple effects and prosocial communication has positive ripple effects.

Table 12.6 provides a brief summary of prosocial communication.

Table 12.6 In a Nutshell Prosocial Communication

The Nature of Prosocial Communication	Prosocial communication is communication that benefits another individual, group, society, or the entire species in some way.
Factors Influencing Prosocial Communication	Prosocial communication is influenced by a wide variety of factors such as similarity, relationship bonds, your history of reinforcement, and your personality.
Examples of Prosocial Communication	Examples of prosocial communication include listening empathically, confirming, complimenting, and mentoring/sharing.
Effects of Prosocial Communication	Prosocial communication has effects on others but also on oneself.

Summary

This chapter discussed the principles of power and influence; power in the relationship, in the person, and in the message; and some of the misuses of power and how to deal with them, namely sexual harassment, bullying, and power plays. It concluded with a discussion of prosocial communication.

Principles of Power and Influence

12.1 Describe the major principles of interpersonal power and influence.

1. Some people are more powerful than others; some are born to power, others learn it.

2. Power can be shared. Empowering others enables them to gain power and control over themselves and over the environment. Empowering others has numerous advantages; for example, empowered people are more proactive and more responsible. Empowering others involves strategies such as being positive, avoiding verbal aggressiveness and abusiveness, and encouraging growth.

3. Power can be increased or decreased; power is never static.

4. Power follows the principle of less interest; generally, the less interest, the greater the power.

5. Power generates privilege.

6. Power is influenced by culture; it has a cultural dimension. Power is distributed differently in different cultures.

Relationship, Person, and Message Power

12.2 Describe the types of power that reside in the relationship, in the person, and in the message and some of the ways to resist power and influence.

7. Power in the relationship may be viewed in terms of six types of power: referent (B wants to be like A), legitimate (B believes that A has a right to influence or control B's behavior), expert (B regards A as having knowledge), information or persuasion (B attributes to A the ability to communicate effectively), reward (A has the ability to reward B), and coercive (A has the ability to punish B).

8. Power in the person may derive from personal credibility (a combination of perceived competence, character, and charisma).

9. Power in the message involves powerful speech, powerful nonverbal messages, and powerful listening styles.

10. Among the strategies of resisting power and influence are negotiation, nonnegotiation, justification, and identity management.

Misuses of Power and Influence

12.3 Explain sexual harassment, bullying, and power plays as misuses of power.

11. Sexual harassment occurs when employment opportunities are made dependent on sexual favors and/or a hostile environment is created.

12. Bullying consists of repeated abusive acts by one person or group against another, often by the more powerful against the less powerful.

13. Power plays are patterns of behavior designed to take advantage of another person (including nobody upstairs, you owe me, yougottobekidding, metaphor, and thought stopper). Possible responses to a power play include ignoring it, treating it as an isolated instance, and—the recommended response—cooperating.

Prosocial Communication

12.4 Define *prosocial communication* and identify some influences on such communication and some effects.

14. Prosocial communication is communication that benefits another individual, group, society, or the entire species in some way.

15. Prosocial communication is influenced by a wide variety of factors such as similarity, relationship bonds, your expectation of reward, your teachings, and your personality.

16. Prosocial communication has effects on others but also on oneself.

Key Terms

bullying
bystander effect
coercive power
compliance-gaining strategies
credibility
cyberbullying
disqualifiers
expert power
hesitations
hostile environment harassment
identity management
information or persuasion power
intensifiers

interaction management
justification
legitimate power
metaphor
negative identity management
negative power
negotiation
nobody upstairs
nonnegotiation
pluralistic ignorance
positive identity management
power
power plays

power priming
prosocial communication
referent power
reward power
self-critical statements
sexual harassment
slang expressions
tag questions
thought stopper
vulgar expressions
yougottobekidding
you owe me

Glossary

Here are the definitions of the key terms in the study of interpersonal communication. When a related key term is referenced in a definition, it appears in italic.

A

abstraction The degree to which a concept or term is general or specific; in communication, it refers to the level of generality or specificity of a term.

accent Variations in pronunciation; the emphasis or stress on various syllables.

accommodating style A conflict management style in which you sacrifice your own needs for the sake of the needs of the other person.

acculturation The process by which one culture is modified or changed through contact with or exposure to another culture.

active listening The process by which a listener expresses his or her understanding of the speaker's total message, including the verbal and nonverbal, and the thoughts and feelings.

adaptors Nonverbal behaviors that, when engaged in, either in private or in public, serve some kind of need and occur in their entirety—for example, scratching one's head until the itch is relieved.

advice Messages that tell another person what he or she should do.

affect displays Movements of the facial area that convey emotional meaning, such as anger, fear, and surprise.

affinity-seeking strategies Behaviors designed to increase interpersonal attractiveness.

affirmation The communication of support and approval.

agape A love that is compassionate and selfless.

ageism Discrimination based on age, usually against older people.

ageist language Language that discriminates based on the age of the person.

allness The illogical assumption that all can be known or said about a given person, issue, object, or event.

ambiguity The condition in which a message or relationship may be interpreted as having more than one meaning.

ambiguity tolerance A characteristic of culture referring to the degree to which members of a culture feel comfortable with ambiguity and uncertainty.

anger communication: An expression of anger; distinguished from *angry communication*.

anger A generally unproductive emotion of strong feelings of displeasure, annoyance, or hostility.

anonymous messages Messages that are unsigned; the author is unknown or hidden. Opposite of *onymous messages*.

apology An expression of regret or sorrow for having done what you did or for what happened.

argumentativeness The willingness to argue for a point of view, to speak one's mind. Distinguished from *verbal aggressiveness*.

artifactual communication Messages that are conveyed by objects made by human hands. Art, color, clothing, jewelry, hairstyle, and smell would be examples of artifactual messages.

assertiveness A willingness to stand up for your rights but with respect for the rights of others.

asynchronous communication Communication in which the individuals send and receive messages at different times (as in e-mail communication). The opposite of *synchronous communication*.

attraction theory A theory holding that you develop relationships on the basis of similarity, proximity, reinforcement, physical and personality attractiveness, socioeconomic and educational status, and reciprocity of liking.

attribution of control An impression formation process in which you evaluate behavior on the basis of the degree of control one had.

avoidance An unproductive conflict strategy in which you take mental or physical flight from the actual conflict.

avoiding style A conflict management style that suggests that you are relatively unconcerned with your own or with the other's needs or desires.

B

back-channeling cues Responses a listener makes to a speaker (while the speaker is speaking) but that do not ask for the speaking role, for example, interjections such as "I understand" or "You said what?"

backhanded compliment An insult masquerading as a compliment.

beltlining An unproductive conflict strategy in which one person hits the other at a vulnerable level—at the level at which the other person cannot withstand the blow.

blended emotions Emotions that are combinations of the primary emotions; for example, disappointment is a blend of surprise and sadness.

blind self In the Johari window model, this self represents all the things about yourself that others know but of which you're ignorant.

boundary markers A marker that sets boundaries around or divides one person's territory from another's—for example, a fence.

breadth The number of topics about which individuals in a relationship communicate.

bullying A pattern of abusive behavior (verbal or nonverbal) repeatedly committed by one person (or group) against another.

bystander effect The phenomenon that when in a crowd a person will just stand by and do nothing to help a victim.

C

central marker A marker or item that is placed in a territory to reserve it for a specific person—for example, the sweater thrown over a library chair to signal that the chair is taken.

channel The vehicle or medium through which signals are sent, for example, the vocal–auditory channel.

cherishing behaviors Small behaviors you enjoy receiving from others, especially from your relational partner—for example, a kiss before you leave for work.

choice points Moments when you have to make a choice about whom you communicate with, what you say, what you don't say, how you phrase what you want to say, and so on.

chronemics The study of the communicative nature of time, of how a person's or a culture's treatment of time reveals something about the person or culture; often divided into psychological and cultural time.

cisgender An adjective describing people whose sex and gender identity are similar. Opposed to *transgender*.

civil inattention Polite ignoring of others (after a brief sign of awareness) to avoid invading their privacy.

closed-mindedness An unwillingness to receive certain communication messages.

code-switching Using different language styles depending on the situation; changing from one language or style to another, often in the same sentence.

coercive power Power derived from an individual's ability to punish or to remove rewards from another person.

cognitive labeling theory A theory of emotions that holds that emotional feelings begin with the occurrence of an event; you respond physiologically to the event, then you interpret the arousal (in effect, you decide what it is you're feeling), and then you experience (give a name to) the emotion.

collaborating style A conflict management style in which your concern is with both your own and the other person's needs.

collectivist culture A culture in which the group's goals are given greater importance than the individual's and in which, for example, benevolence, tradition, and conformity are given special emphasis. Opposite of *individualist culture*.

color communication The use of color to communicate different meanings; each culture seems to define the meanings that colors communicate somewhat differently.

comparison level A general idea of the kinds of rewards and profits that you feel you ought to get out of a relationship.

competence "Language competence" is a speaker's ability to use the language; it is knowledge of the elements and rules of the language. "Communication competence" generally refers both to the knowledge of communication and to the ability to engage in communication effectively.

competing style A conflict management style that represents great concern for your own needs and desires and little for those of others.

complementarity A principle of attraction holding that you are attracted by qualities that you do not possess or wish to possess, and to people who are opposite or different from yourself. Opposite of *similarity*.

complementary relationship A relationship in which the behavior of one person serves as the stimulus for the complementary behavior of the other; in complementary relationships, behavioral differences are maximized.

compliance-gaining strategies Behaviors designed to gain the agreement of others, to persuade others to do as you wish.

compliment A message of praise, flattery, or congratulations.

compromising style A conflict management style that is in the middle; there's some concern for your own needs and some concern for the other's needs.

confirmation A communication pattern that acknowledges another person's presence and indicates an acceptance of this person, this person's self-definition, and the relationship as defined or viewed by this other person. Opposite of *rejection* and *disconfirmation*.

conflict styles The approach to conflict resolution, for example, competing, avoiding, accommodating, collaborating, and compromising.

conformity orientation The degree to which family members express similar or dissimilar attitudes, values, and beliefs.

connotation The feeling or emotional aspect of a word's meaning; generally viewed as consisting of evaluation (for example, good–bad), potency (strong–weak), and activity (fast–slow) dimensions. Opposite of *denotation*.

consensual families Families who encourage open communication and agreement; high in conversation and high in conformity.

consistency A tendency to maintain balance in your perception of messages or people; because of this process, you tend to see what you expect to see and to be uncomfortable when your perceptions run contrary to expectations.

contact The first stage in relationship development, consisting of perceptual contact (you see or hear the person) and interactional contact (you talk with the person).

content conflict Interpersonal conflict that centers on objects, events, and persons that are usually external to the parties involved in the conflict. Opposite of *relationship conflict*.

content dimension Reference to the real or outside world rather than to the relationships between the individuals. See also *relationship dimension*.

context The physical, psychological, social, and temporal environment in which communication takes place.

conversation orientation The degree to which family members can speak their mind.

conversation Two-person communication, usually following five stages: opening, feedforward, business, feedback, and closing.

conversational maxims Principles that participants in conversation follow to ensure that the goal of the conversation is achieved.

conversational turns The process of passing the speaker and listener roles back and forth during conversation.

cooperation An interpersonal process by which individuals work together for a common end; the pooling of efforts to produce a mutually desired outcome.

costs Anything that you normally try to avoid—things you consider unpleasant or difficult. See also *rewards*.

credibility Techniques by which you seek to establish your competence, character, and charisma.

credibility strategies Techniques by which you seek to establish your competence, character, and charisma.

critical listening Listening that is logical and dispassionate; listening that is open but that evaluates and judges what is being said.

cultural assimilation The process by which people leave behind their culture of origin and take on the values and beliefs of another culture, as when, for example, immigrants give up their native culture to become members of their new adopted culture.

cultural display rules Rules that identify what are and what are not appropriate forms of expression for members of the culture.

cultural display Sign that communicates a person's cultural identification, such as clothing or religious jewelry.

cultural identifiers The terms used to talk about cultural identifications, for example, race or religion.

cultural sensitivity An attitude and way of behaving in which you're aware of and acknowledge cultural differences.

culture The lifestyle of a group of people; their values, beliefs, artifacts, ways of behaving, and ways of communicating. Culture includes everything that members of a social group have produced and developed—their language, ways of thinking, art, laws, and religion—and that is transmitted from one generation to the next through communication rather than genes.

culture shock The reactions people experience at being in a culture very different from their own and from what they are used to.

cyberbullying A form of bullying that can take place through any electronic communication system—Facebook, Twitter, e-mail, instant messages, blog posts—and can take the form of sending threatening messages or images, posting negative comments, revealing secrets, or lying about another person.

D

deception bias The assumption that the messages will be lies. Opposite of *truth bias*.

decoding The act of understanding messages, for example, listening or reading. The opposite of *encoding*.

denotation The objective or descriptive aspect of a word's meaning; the meaning you'd find in a dictionary. Opposite of *connotation*.

depenetration A reversal of penetration; a condition in which the breadth and depth of a relationship decrease.

depth The degree to which the inner personality—the inner core of an individual—is penetrated in interpersonal interaction.

dialect Variations in a language, mainly in grammar and semantics; dialects are mutually intelligible, unlike different languages, which are mutually unintelligible.

dialogue A form of communication in which each person is both speaker and listener; communication characterized by involvement, concern, and respect for the other person. Opposite of *monologue*.

disclaimer Statement that asks the listener to receive what you say without its reflecting negatively on you.

disconfirmation The process by which someone ignores or denies the right of another individual even to define him- or herself. Opposite of *rejection* and *confirmation*.

disinhibition effect The tendency to disclose more in certain situations than in others; usually used to refer to the tendency to be more uninhibited in online messaging.

display rules Rules or customs (of a culture or an organization) that govern what is and what is not appropriate communication.

disqualifiers Statements that claim some lack of responsibility and signal a lack of competence and a degree of uncertainty.

downward communication Communication sent from the higher levels of a hierarchy to the lower levels—for example, messages sent by managers to workers or from deans to faculty members.

Duchenne smile A genuine smile, as opposed to a **smile** that is faked.

E

ear marker A marker that identifies an item as belonging to a specific person—for example, a nameplate on a desk or initials on an attaché case.

effect The outcome or consequence of an action or behavior; communication is assumed always to have some effect.

emblems Nonverbal behaviors that directly translate words or phrases—for example, the signs for *okay* and *peace*.

emoji Icons illustrating varied emotions.

emoticon Visual representation of emotion produced by a short sequence of keyboard characters.

emotional appeals Persuasive tactics directed at arousing emotional responses.

emotional blackmail A message threatening punishment for noncompliance that takes the form of "If you don't do what I ask, you'll suffer," for example.

emotional communication The expression of feelings—for example, feelings of guilt, happiness, or sorrow.

emotional contagion The process by which the strong emotions of one person are taken on by another person; the assumption that, like the flu, emotions may be contagious.

emotional labor the effort required to manage your emotional expressions.

emotions The feelings we have—for example, our feelings of guilt, anger, or love.

empathic listening Listening to understand what a person means and what a person is feeling.

empathy A quality of interpersonal effectiveness that involves sharing others' feelings; an ability to feel or perceive things from others' points of view.

encoding The act of producing messages, for example, speaking or writing. The opposite of *decoding*.

enculturation The process by which culture is transmitted from one generation to the next.

equality An attitude that recognizes that each individual in a communication interaction is equal, that no one is superior to any other; encourages supportiveness. Opposite of *superiority*.

equilibrium theory A theory of proxemics holding that intimacy and physical closeness are positively related; as a relationship becomes more intimate, the individuals maintain shorter distances between themselves.

equity theory A theory claiming that people experience relational satisfaction when there is an equal distribution of rewards and costs between the two persons in the relationship.

eros A type of love that emphasizes beauty and sexuality.

ethics The branch of philosophy that deals with the rightness or wrongness of actions; the study of moral values; in communication, the morality of message behavior.

ethnic identity The commitment to the beliefs and philosophy of one's culture; the degree to which a person identifies with his or her cultural group.

ethnocentrism The tendency to see others and their behaviors through your own cultural filters, often as distortions of your own behaviors; the tendency to evaluate the values and beliefs of your own culture more positively than those of another culture.

evaluating One of the stages in the process of listening in which you make a judgment about the speaker or the message.

excuse An explanation designed to lessen the negative consequences of something done or said.

expectancy violations theory A theory of proxemics holding that people have a certain expectancy for space relationships. When that is violated (say, a person stands too close to you or a romantic partner maintains abnormally large distances from you), the relationship comes into clearer focus and you wonder why this "normal distance" is being violated.

expert power Power that a person has because others believe the individual to have expertise or special knowledge.

expressiveness A quality of interpersonal effectiveness that consists of genuine involvement in speaking and listening, conveyed verbally and nonverbally.

extensional orientation A point of view in which primary consideration is given to the world of experience and only secondary consideration is given to labels. Opposite of *intensional orientation*.

eye avoidance The lack of eye contact.

eye communication Messages sent by eye movements and pupil dilation and constriction.

F

face-attacking strategies Strategies that attack a person's positive face (for example, comments that criticize the person's contribution to a relationship or the person's ability) or a person's negative face (for example, making demands on a person's time or resources that attack the person's autonomy).

face-enhancing strategies Strategies that support and confirm a person's positive face (praise, a pat on the back, a sincere smile) or negative face (giving the person space and asking rather than demanding).

facial feedback hypothesis The hypothesis or theory that your facial expressions can produce physiological and emotional effects via a feedback mechanism.

fact–inference confusion A misevaluation in which a person makes an inference, regards it as a fact, and acts upon it as if it were a fact.

family A group of people with defined roles, recognition of mutual responsibilities, a shared history and future, shared living space (usually), and rules for communicating.

feedback Information that is given back to the source. Feedback may come from the source's own messages (as when you hear what you are saying) or from the receiver(s)—in forms such as applause, yawning, puzzled looks, questions, letters to the editor of a newspaper, or increased or decreased subscriptions to a magazine. See also *negative feedback, positive feedback*.

feedforward Information that is sent before a regular message, telling the listener something about what is to follow; messages that are prefatory to more central messages.

feminine culture A culture that encourages both men and women to be modest, oriented to maintaining the quality of life, and tender. Feminine cultures emphasize the quality of life and so socialize their people to be modest and to emphasize close interpersonal relationships. Opposite of *masculine culture*.

flaming The use of insulting and often profane messages online.

flexibility The ability to adjust communication strategies and skills on the basis of the unique situation.

formal time Temporal divisions that are measured objectively, such as seconds, minutes, hours, days, weeks, months, and years.

frenemy An enemy who appears on the surface to be a friend.

friends with benefits A relationship between friends that involves sex but no real romantic commitment.

friendship An interpersonal relationship between two persons that is mutually productive, established and maintained through perceived mutual free choice, and characterized by mutual positive regard.

fundamental attribution error The tendency to overvalue and give added weight to the contribution of internal factors (i.e., a person's personality) to behavior, and to undervalue and give less weight to the contribution of external factors (i.e., the situation the person is in or the surrounding events).

G

gender The cultural roles of "masculine" and "feminine" that are learned from one's culture. See also *sex*.

gender display rules cultural rules governing emotional expression that differ for men and for women.

gender identity A person's self-perception as a male, female, neither, or both.

gossip Oral or written communication about someone not present, some third party, usually about matters that are private to this third party.

grapevine messages Organizational messages that don't follow any of the formal lines of communication established in an organization; rather, they cross organizational lines.

gunnysacking An unproductive conflict strategy of storing up grievances—as if in a gunnysack—and holding them in readiness to dump on the other person in the conflict.

H

halo effect The tendency to generalize a person's virtue or expertise from one area to other areas.

haptics The study of touch or tactile communication.

hesitations Verbal expressions such as "er" or "ah" that signal a lack of preparation and certainty.

heterosexist language Language that denigrates lesbians and gay men.

hidden self In the Johari window model, this self contains all that you know of yourself that you keep secret.

high-context culture A culture in which much of the information in communication messages is left implied; it's "understood." Much information is considered to be in the context or in the person rather than explicitly coded in the verbal messages. Collectivist cultures are generally high context. Opposite of *low-context culture*.

high-power-distance culture A culture in which power is concentrated in the hands of a few, and there's a great difference between the power held by these people and the power of the ordinary citizen. See also *low-power-distance culture*.

home field advantage The increased power that comes from being in your own territory.

home territories Territory in which an individual has a sense of intimacy and over which he or she exercises control—for example, a teacher's office.

hostile environment harassment A type of sexual harassment in which verbal and nonverbal messages about sex make a worker uncomfortable.

I

identity management The process you go through to communicate the impression you want the other person to have of you. Some writers use the terms *self-presentation* or *impression management*.

illustrators Nonverbal behaviors that accompany and literally illustrate verbal messages—for example, upward movements of the head and hand that accompany the verbal "It's up there."

image-confirming strategies Techniques you use to communicate or to confirm your self-image, the image you want others to see.

I-messages Messages in which the speaker accepts responsibility for personal thoughts and behaviors and states his or her point of view explicitly. Opposite of *you-messages*.

immediacy A quality of interpersonal effectiveness that conveys a sense of contact and togetherness, a feeling of interest in, and liking for, the other person.

impostor phenomenon The tendency to disregard outward signs of success and to consider oneself an "impostor," a fake, a fraud, one who doesn't really deserve to be considered successful.

impression formation The process by which you perceive another person and ultimately come to some kind of evaluation or interpretation of this person.

impression management The process you go through to communicate the impression you want the other person to have of you. Some writers use the terms *self-presentation* or *identity management*.

independent couples Couples for whom the relationship is important but never more important than each person's individual identity.

indiscrimination A misevaluation that results when you categorize people, events, or objects into a particular class and respond to them only as members of the class; a failure to recognize that each individual is unique.

individualist culture A culture in which the individual's rather than the group's goals and preferences are given greater importance. Opposite of *collectivist culture*.

indulgence A cultural orientation that emphasizes the gratification of desires and a focus on having fun and enjoying life. Opposite of *restraint*.

inevitability A principle of communication holding that communication cannot be avoided; all behavior in an interactional setting is communication.

influencing strategies Strategies designed to influence the attitudes or behaviors of others.

informal time Temporal divisions that are approximate and that are referred to with general terms, for example, *forever, immediately, soon, right away, as soon as possible*.

information or persuasion power Power that a person has because others see that individual as having significant information and the ability to communicate logically and persuasively.

insulation A reaction to territorial encroachment in which you erect some sort of barrier between yourself and the invaders, such as a stone wall around your property, an unlisted phone number, or caller ID.

intensifiers Adjectives or adverbs that emphasize extremes, too many of which signal a lack of power.

intensional orientation A point of view in which primary consideration is given to the way things are labeled and only secondary consideration (if any) to the world of experience. Opposite of *extensional orientation*.

interaction management A quality of interpersonal effectiveness in which the interaction is controlled and managed to the satisfaction of both parties; effectively managing conversational turns, fluency, and message consistency.

intercultural communication Communication that takes place between persons of different cultures or between persons who have different cultural beliefs, values, or ways of behaving.

interpersonal communication Communication between two persons or among a small group of persons and distinguished from public or mass communication; communication of a personal nature and distinguished from impersonal communication; communication between or among connected persons or those involved in a close relationship.

interpersonal conflict Disagreement between two connected persons.

interpersonal time A wide variety of time-related elements that figure into interpersonal interaction, for example, the time you wait for an appointment, the time you devote to a relationship, the time it takes to respond to another's message.

interpretation–evaluation A step in perception that is influenced by experiences, needs, wants, values, and beliefs about the way things are or should be.

interruptions Verbal and nonverbal attempts to take over the role of the speaker.

intimacy The closest interpersonal relationship; usually characterizes close primary relationships.

intimate distance The closest distance in proxemics, ranging from touching to 18 inches.

involvement The second stage in relationship development in which you further advance the relationship, first testing each other and then intensifying your interaction.

irreversibility A principle of communication holding that communication cannot be reversed; once something has been communicated, it cannot be uncommunicated.

J

James–Lange theory A theory of emotions in which you experience emotions in the following way: (1) An event occurs. (2) You respond physiologically. (3) You experience an emotion; for example, you feel joy or sadness.

jealousy A reaction (consisting of feelings, thoughts, and behaviors) to a physical or emotional threat to one or more of your significant relationships.

justification A strategy to resist compliance by giving reasons why you should not comply.

K

kinesics The study of the communicative dimensions of facial and bodily movements.

L

laissez-faire families Families who avoid interaction and communication, encourage privacy, and maintain a "do what you want" attitude; low in confirmation and low in conversation.

lateral communication Messages between equals—manager to manager, worker to worker.

legitimate power Power a person possesses because others believe he or she has a right—by virtue of his or her position—to influence or control their behavior.

linguistic collusion A response to territorial encroachment in which you speak in a language or jargon that the "invaders" don't understand and thus exclude them from the interaction. See also *withdrawal, turf defense,* and *insulation*.

listening An active process of receiving aural stimuli consisting of five stages: receiving, understanding, remembering, evaluating, and responding.

long-term memory Memory that is (theoretically) unlimited in storage capacity and that holds information for long periods of time. Opposite of *short-term memory*.

long-term orientation A cultural orientation that promotes the importance of future rewards; for example, members of these cultures are more apt to save for the future and to prepare for the future academically. Opposite of *short-term orientation*.

love A relationship with another person in which you feel closeness, caring, warmth, and excitement.

low-context culture A culture in which most of the information in communication is explicitly stated in the verbal message rather than being left implied or assumed to be "understood." Low-context cultures are usually individualist cultures. Opposite of *high-context culture*.

low-power-distance culture A culture in which power is relatively evenly distributed throughout the citizenry. See also *high-power-distance culture*.

ludus A type of love that stresses entertainment and excitement.

lying The act of sending messages with the intention of giving another person information you believe to be false.

M

mania A type of love characterized by elation and depression, extreme highs and extreme lows.

manner maxim A principle of conversation that holds that speakers cooperate with listeners by being clear and by organizing their thoughts into meaningful and coherent patterns.

markers Devices that signify that a certain territory belongs to a particular person. See also *boundary marker, central marker,* and *earmarker*.

masculine culture A culture that views men as assertive, oriented to material success, and strong; such a culture views women, on the other hand, as modest, focused on the quality of life, and tender. Masculine cultures emphasize success and so socialize their people to be assertive, ambitious, and competitive. Opposite of *feminine culture*.

mentoring The process by which an experienced individual (mentor) helps to train a less experienced person referred to as a mentee or, more often, a protégé.

messages Any signal or combination of signals that serves as a stimulus for a receiver. See also *stimulus*.

meta-advice Advice about advice; for example, suggesting that one seek more expert advice.

metacommunication Communication about communication.

metamessages Messages that make reference to other messages, such as "Did I make myself clear?" or "That's a lie."

metaphor In language, metaphor refers to the figure of speech in which two unlike things are compared. **In the discussion of power, a** *power play* that relies on negative metaphors to criticize or put down another person.

mindfulness A state of awareness in which you are conscious of the logic and rationality of your behaviors and of the logical connections existing among elements.

mindlessness A lack of conscious awareness of the logic or reasons behind your thoughts or behaviors.

monochronic time orientation A view of time in which things are done sequentially; one thing is scheduled at a time. Opposite of *polychronic time orientation*.

monologue A form of communication in which one person speaks and the other listens; there's no real interaction among participants. Opposite of *dialogue*.

N

negative face The desire to be autonomous, to have the right to do as you wish.

negative identity management A strategy for resisting power and influence in which you portray the person as unreasonable. Opposite of *positive identity management*.

negative power Power that has the opposite effect to that which is intended.

negotiation A strategy for resisting compliance in which you attempt to accommodate or compromise in some way.

network convergence The blending or sharing of one individual's circle of friends with another person's circle of friends.

networking Connecting with people who can help you accomplish a goal or help you find information related to your goal; for example, to your search for a job.

nobody upstairs A *powerplay*, in which one person simply refuses to comply with reasonable requests by ignoring them.

noise Anything that interferes with receiving a message as the source intended the message to be received. Noise is present in communication to the extent that the message received is not the message sent.

nonnegotiation An unproductive conflict strategy in which an individual refuses to discuss the conflict or to listen to the other person; a strategy to resist compliance without any attempt to compromise; you simply state your refusal to do as asked without any qualification.

nonverbal communication Communication without words; communication by means of space, gestures, facial expressions, touching, vocal variation, or silence, for example.

O

oculesics The study of the messages communicated by the eyes.

olfactory communication Communication by smell.

onymous messages Messages that are signed; the author is identified. Opposite of *anonymous messages*.

open self In the Johari window model, this self represents all the information, behaviors, attitudes, feelings, desires, motivations, and ideas that you and others know.

other-orientation A quality of interpersonal effectiveness involving attentiveness, interest, and concern for the other person.

overattribution The tendency to attribute to one or two characteristics most or even all of what a person does.

owning feelings The process of taking responsibility for your own feelings instead of attributing them to others.

P

paralanguage The vocal but nonverbal aspects of speech. Paralanguage consists of voice qualities (for example, pitch range, resonance, tempo); vocal characterizers (laughing or crying, yelling or whispering); vocal qualifiers (intensity, pitch height); and vocal segregates ("uh-uh" meaning "no," or "sh" meaning "silence").

perception The process by which you become aware of objects and events through your senses.

perception checking The process of verifying your understanding of some message, situation, or feeling.

perceptual accentuation A process that leads you to see what you expect or want to see—for example, seeing people you like as better looking and smarter than people you don't like.

personal distance The second closest distance in proxemics, ranging from 18 inches to 4 feet.

personality theory A theory of personality, complete with rules about what characteristics go with what other characteristics, that you maintain and through which you perceive others.

phatic communication Communication that is primarily social; communication designed to open the channels of communication rather than to communicate something about the external world. "Hello" and "How are you?" in everyday interaction are examples.

physical noise Interference that is external to both speaker and listener and that interferes with the physical transmission of a signal or message.

physiological noise Interference within the sender or receiver of a message, such as visual impairments, hearing loss, articulation problems, and memory loss.

pitch In relation to voice qualities, the highness or lowness of the vocal tone.

pluralistic families Families whose members are encouraged to express different attitudes and points of view and to engage in open communication while being supportive of each other.

pluralistic ignorance The tendency to take your cues from the crowd; if the crowd does nothing, so will you.

polarization A form of fallacious reasoning in which only two extremes are considered; also referred to as black-and-white or either/or thinking or as a two-valued orientation.

politeness Civility, consideration, refinement, respect, and regard for others as expressed verbally and nonverbally; interaction that follows the socially accepted rules for interpersonal interaction.

politeness strategies Strategies that are often used to make ourselves appear likeable, in terms of negative and positive types.

politeness theory A theory holding that perceived politeness leads to relationship development and maintenance and impoliteness leads to deterioration.

politeness Civility, consideration, refinement, respect, and regard for others as expressed verbally and nonverbally; interaction that follows the socially accepted rules for interpersonal interaction.

polychronic time orientation A view of time in which several things may be scheduled or engaged in at the same time. Opposite of *monochronic time orientation*.

positive face The desire to be viewed positively by others, to be thought of favorably.

positive identity management A strategy for resisting power and influence in which you make the other person feel good about him- or herself. Opposite of *negative identity management*.

power The ability to influence or control the behavior of another person; A has power over B when A can influence or control B's behavior; an inevitable part of interpersonal relationships.

power distance The degree to which differences in power exist among a people.

power plays A consistent pattern of behavior in which one person tries to control the behavior of another.

power priming Recalling instances of being in power that seem to transfer to current behavior.

pragma A type of love that is practical and traditional.

primacy effect Giving more importance to that which occurs first instead of that which occurs last or more recently. Opposite of *recency effect*.

primacy–recency Impression formation processes referring to the influence of first perceptions (primacy) and of last perceptions (recency). See *primacy effect, recency effect*.

primary emotions Basic emotions; usually identified as joy, acceptance, fear, surprise, sadness, disgust, anger, and anticipation.

primary relationship The relationship between two people that they consider their most (or one of their most) important, for example, the relationship between husband and wife or domestic partners.

primary territories Areas that you consider your exclusive preserve—for example, your room or office.

profits The result of the rewards or benefits one derives from a relationship minus the costs.

prosocial communication Communication that benefits another individual, group, society, or the entire species in some way. The communication may be verbal or nonverbal or, as usual, some combination of verbal and nonverbal messages.

protection theory A theory of proxemics holding that people establish a body-buffer zone to protect themselves from unwanted closeness, touching, or attack.

protective families Families who stress agreement and strive to avoid conflict but with little communication.

proxemic distances The distance we maintain between each other in our interactions.

proxemics The study of the communicative function of space; the study of how people unconsciously structure their space—the distance between people in their interactions, the organization of space in homes and offices, and even the design of cities.

psychological noise Mental interference in the speaker or listener, such as preconceived ideas, wandering thoughts, biases and prejudices, closed-mindedness, and extreme emotionalism.

psychological time An emphasis on, or orientation toward, past, present, or future time; varies from person to person.

public distance The farthest distance in proxemics, ranging from 12 feet to 25 feet or more.

public territories Areas that are open to all people—for example, restaurants or parks.

punctuation The breaking up of continuous communication sequences into short sequences with identifiable beginnings and endings or stimuli and responses.

Pygmalion effect The condition in which you make a prediction of success, act as if it is true, and thereby make it come true (for example, acting toward students as if they'll be successful influences them to become successful); a type of self-fulfilling prophecy.

Q

quality maxim A principle of conversation that holds that speakers cooperate with listeners by saying what they think is true and by not saying what they think is false.

quantity maxim A principle of conversation that holds that speakers cooperate with listeners by being only as informative as necessary to communicate their intended meanings.

R

race A group of people that have common heredity and can be distinguished from others by their common physical/genetic traits.

racist language Language that denigrates, demeans, or is derogatory toward members of a particular ethnic group.

rate In relation to voice qualities, the speed at which you speak, generally measured in words per minute.

recall The perception stage that involves accessing the information stored in memory.

receiving A stage in listening involving the hearing of, and attending to, the message.

recency effect Giving more importance to that which occurs last or more recently instead of that which occurs first. Opposite of *primacy effect*.

reciprocity of liking The tendency to like those who we think like us.

reciprocity The tendency to respond in ways similar to the other person, to give back what you're given.

referent power Power that a person possesses because others desire to identify with or be like that individual.

regulators Nonverbal behaviors that regulate, monitor, or control the communications of another person.

rejection A response to an individual that acknowledges the person but expresses disagreement. Opposed to *confirmation* and *disconfirmation*.

relation maxim A principle of conversation that holds that speakers cooperate with listeners by talking about what is relevant and by not talking about what isn't relevant.

relationship conflict Interpersonal conflicts that center on the connection or relationship between people rather than events or people external to them. Opposite of *content conflict*.

relationship deterioration The stage of a relationship during which the connecting bonds between the partners weaken and the partners begin drifting apart.

relationship dialectics theory An explanation of the conflicting motives that people in close relationships often experience.

relationship dimension The dimension of messages that comments on the relationship between the speakers rather than on matters external to them. See also *content dimension*.

relationship dissolution The termination or end of an interpersonal relationship.

relationship license Permission to violate some relationship expectation, custom, or rule.

relationship repair That stage of relationships in which one or both parties seek to resolve problems.

relationship rules theory A theory that holds that people maintain relationships with those who follow the rules the individuals have defined as essential to their relationship and dissolve relationships with those who don't follow the rules.

relationship violence Generally considered to consist of verbal or emotional abuse, physical abuse, or sexual abuse.

remembering A stage in listening referring to the retention of what you hear.

remote audience Those people who receive your message although they were not your intended audience.

responding Listening stage that occurs in two phases: responses you make while the speaker is talking (immediate feedback) and responses you make after the speaker has stopped talking (delayed feedback).

restraint A cultural orientation that fosters the curbing of immediate gratification and regulates it by social norms. Opposite of *indulgence*.

reverse halo effect ("horns" effect) The tendency to judge a person you know to have several negative qualities also to have other negative qualities (that you have not observed); also known as the horns effect. See also *halo effect*.

reward power Power derived from an individual's ability to give another person what that person wants or to remove what that person wants removed.

rewards: Anything that you want, that you enjoy, and that you'd be willing to incur costs to obtain.

rule of contrast A principle of perception that holds that items that are very distinct from each other are seen as separate and not belonging to the same group.

rule of proximity As a principle of perception, the tendency to perceive people or events that are physically close as belonging together or representing some unit; physical closeness—one of the qualities influencing interpersonal attraction.

rule of similarity A principle of attraction holding that you're attracted to qualities similar to your own and to people who are similar to you. Opposite of *complementarity*.

S

schema A way of organizing your perceptions. See *schemata*.

schemata Ways of organizing perceptions; mental templates or structures that help you organize the millions of items of information you come into contact with every day as well as those you already have in memory; general ideas about groups of people or individuals, about yourself, or about types of social roles. The word *schemata* is the plural of *schema*.

script A type of schema; an organized body of information about some action, event, or procedure. A script provides a general idea of how some event should play out or unfold, the rules governing the events and their sequence.

secondary territories An area that does not belong to you but that you've occupied and that is therefore associated with you—for example, the seat you normally take in class.

selective attention The tendency to attend to those things that you want to see or that you expect to see.

selective exposure The tendency to expose your senses to certain things and not others, to actively seek out information that supports your beliefs and to actively avoid information that contradicts these beliefs.

selective perception The tendency to perceive certain things and not others; includes selective attention and selective exposure.

self-awareness The degree to which you know yourself.

self-concept Your self-image, the view you have of who you are.

self-critical statements Statements that reflect negatively on the self.

self-deprecating strategies Techniques you use to signal your inability to do some task or your incompetence in order to encourage another to help you out.

self-destructive beliefs Beliefs that create problems; often beliefs that are unrealistic and set goals that are impossible to achieve.

self-disclosure The process of revealing something about yourself to another; usually refers to information that you'd normally keep hidden.

self-esteem The value (usually, the positive value) you place on yourself; your self-evaluation.

self-fulfilling prophecy The situation in which you make a prediction or prophecy and fulfill it yourself. For example, expecting a person to be hostile, you act in a hostile manner toward this person and, in doing so, elicit hostile behavior in the person, thus confirming your prophecy that the person will be hostile.

self-handicapping strategies Techniques you use to excuse possible failure, for example, setting up barriers or obstacles to make the task impossible so that, when you fail, you won't be blamed or thought ineffective.

self-monitoring strategies Manipulating the image you present to others in interpersonal interactions to create the most favorable impression of yourself.

self-serving bias A bias that operates in the self-attribution process, leading you to take credit for the positive consequences of your behaviors and to deny responsibility for the negative consequences.

semantic noise Interference created when a speaker and listener have different meaning systems; such noise can include language or dialectical differences, the use of jargon or overly complex terms, or ambiguous or overly abstract terms whose meanings can be easily misinterpreted.

separate couples Couples who live together but view their relationship more as a matter of convenience than a result of their mutual love or closeness.

sex The biological distinction between males and females; the genetic distinction between men and women. See also *gender*.

sexist language Language derogatory to members of one gender, generally women.

sexual harassment Unsolicited and unwanted verbal or nonverbal sexual messages.

short-term memory Memory that is very limited in capacity; contains information that is quickly lost if it is not passed on to *long-term memory*.

short-term orientation A cultural dimension in which people look more to the past and the present; these cultural members spend their resources for the present and want quick results from their efforts. Opposite of *long-term orientation*.

signal The information you hear that you find useful.

signal-to-noise ratio A measure of the relationship between meaningful information (signal) and interference (noise).

silence The absence of vocal communication; often misunderstood to refer to the absence of communication.

silencers Unproductive conflict strategies (such as crying) that silence your opponent.

similarity A principle of attraction holding that you're attracted to qualities similar to your own and to people who are similar to you. Opposite of *complementarity*.

slang expressions Language used by special groups, often not considered standard in general society.

small talk Noncontroversial talk that is usually short in duration and often serves as a polite way of introducing one's self or a topic.

smiley A typed symbol or icon that expresses an emotional state.

social allergen A habit of a friend or romantic partner that you find uncouth, impolite, or unpleasant and that often leads to interpersonal conflict.

social distance The next-to-farthest distance in proxemics, ranging from 4 feet to 12 feet; the distance at which business is usually conducted.

social exchange theory A theory hypothesizing that you cultivate profitable relationships (those in which your rewards are greater than your costs) and that you avoid or terminate unprofitable relationships (those in which your costs exceed your rewards).

social penetration theory A theory concerned with relationship development from the superficial to the intimate levels (depth) and from few to many areas of interpersonal interaction (breadth). See also *depenetration*.

source–receiver A communication term that emphasizes that both functions are performed by each individual in an interpersonal message.

spiral of silence A theory that argues that you're more likely to voice agreement than disagreement.

static evaluation An orientation that fails to recognize that the world is constantly changing; an attitude that sees people and events as fixed rather than as ever changing.

stereotype In communication, a fixed impression of a group of people through which we then perceive specific individuals. Stereotypes are most often negative but may also be positive.

storge A type of love that is peaceful and slow.

strategic ambiguity Deliberate ambiguity designed to achieve a variety of specific purposes.

strategic emotionality Using emotions (for example, crying, ranting, screaming, and threatening to commit self-harm) for one's personal ends.

supportiveness An attitude of an individual or an atmosphere in a group that is characterized by openness, absence of fear, and a genuine feeling of equality. Opposite of *defensiveness*.

symmetrical relationship A relation between two or more persons in which one person's behavior serves as a stimulus for the same type of behavior in the other person(s)—for example, a relationship in which anger in one person encourages anger in the other, or in which a critical comment by one person leads the other to respond in kind.

synchronous communication Communication that takes place in real time; sending and receiving take place at the same time (as in face-to-face communication). The opposite of *asynchronous communication*.

T

tactile communication Communication by touch; communication received by the skin.

tag questions Questions that ask for agreement.

temporal communication The messages that your time orientation and treatment of time communicate.

territorial encroachment The trespassing on, use of, or appropriation of one person's territory by another.

territoriality A possessive or ownership reaction to an area of space or to particular objects.

thought stopper A *power play* designed to stop your thinking and especially stop you from expressing your thoughts.

touch avoidance The tendency to avoid touching and being touched by others.

traditional couples Couples who share a basic belief system and philosophy of life; they see themselves as a blending of two persons into a single couple rather than as two separate individuals.

transactional perspective A view of communication as an ongoing process in which all elements are interdependent and influence one another.

transgender An adjective describing people whose sex and gender identity are different. Opposed to *cisgender*.

trolling The purposeful act of starting arguments by using inflammatory messages online.

truth bias The assumption most people operate under that the messages they hear are truthful. Opposite of *deception bias*.

turf defense   A response to territorial encroachment in which you defend the territory against invasion, sometimes with something as simple as saying, "This is my seat," or you might start a fight as nations do. See also *withdrawal, insulation,* and *linguistic collusion.*

turning points   Significant relationship events that have important consequences for the individuals and the relationship and may turn its direction or trajectory.

U

understanding   A stage in listening involving deciphering meaning from the message you hear.

unknown self   In the Johari window model, this self represents truths about yourself that neither you nor others know.

unrepeatability   A characteristic of communication referring to the fact that all communication acts are unique and can never be repeated exactly.

upward communication   Communication sent from the lower levels of a hierarchy to the upper levels—for example, from line worker to manager or from faculty member to dean.

V

ventilation hypothesis   The assumption that expressing emotions (that is, giving vent to the emotions) lessens their intensity.

verbal aggressiveness   A method of arguing in which one person attacks the other person's self-concept.

verbal messages   Messages that are sent using words.

volume   In relation to voice qualities, the relative loudness of the voice.

vulgar expressions   Language that is considered obscene by the general culture.

W

win–lose strategies   Conflict management strategies that seek a resolution in which one person wins and the other loses.

win–win strategies   Conflict management strategies that seek a resolution in which both parties win.

withdrawal   A response to territorial encroachment by which you leave the scene, the country, home, office, or classroom. See also *turf defense, insulation,* and *linguistic collusion.*

Y

you owe me   A *power play* in which someone does something for you and then demands that you do something in return because "you owe me."

yougottobekidding   A *power play* that criticizes another's idea with phrases such as "you can't be serious" or "you've? got to be kidding."

References

A

AARP (2014). Age discrimination. *AARP Bulletin*, 36 (January/February).

Abel, G. G., & Harlow, N. (2001). *The stop child molestation book.* Xlibris. Retrieved from www.stopchildmolestation.org/pdfs/study.pdf

Acor, A. A. (2001). Employers' perceptions of persons with body art and an experimental test regarding eyebrow piercing. Ph.D. dissertation, Marquette University. *Dissertation Abstracts International: Second B: The Sciences and Engineering* 61, 3885.

Adams-Price, C. E., Dalton, W. T., & Sumrall, R. (2004). Victim blaming in young, middle-aged, and older adults: Variations on the severity effect. *Journal of Adult Development* 11 (October), 289–295.

Afifi, W. A. (2007). Nonverbal communication. In *Explaining communication: Contemporary theories and exemplars* (pp. 39–60), B. B. Whaley & W. Samter (eds.). Mahwah, NJ: Erlbaum.

Afifi, W. A., & Johnson, M. L. (2005). The nature and function of tie-signs. In *The sourcebook of nonverbal measures: Going beyond words* (pp. 189–198), V. Manusov (ed.). Mahwah, NJ: Erlbaum.

Al-Simadi, F. A. (2000). Detection of deception behavior: A cross-cultural test. *Social Behavior & Personality* 28, 455–461.

Alessandra, T. (1986). How to listen effectively. *Speaking of success* (Video Tape Series). San Diego, CA: Levitz Sommer Productions.

Allen, J. L., Long, K. M., O'Mara, J., & Judd, B. B. (2003). Verbal and nonverbal orientations toward communication and the development of intracultural and intercultural relationships. *Journal of Intercultural Communication Research* 32, 129–160.

Almaatouq A., Radaelli L., Pentland, A., & Shmueli, E. (2016) Are You Your Friends' Friend? Poor Perception of Friendship Ties Limits the Ability to Promote Behavioral Change. PLoS ONE 11(3): e0151588. doi:10.1371/journal.pone.0151588

Alpert, K. (2013). Ten tips to writing a kickass online dating profile. Retrieved from http://www.chicagonow.com/baby-sideburns/2013/09/online-dating-profile

Alsop, R. (2004). How to get hired: We asked recruiters what M.B.A. graduates are doing wrong. Ignore their advice at your peril. *Wall Street Journal* (September 22), R8.

Altman, I. (1975). *The environment and social behavior.* Monterey, CA: Brooks/Cole.

Altman, I., & Taylor, D. (1973). *Social penetration: The development of interpersonal relationships.* New York, NY: Holt, Rinehart & Winston.

Amante, C. (2013). Emotional contagion in seduction and socializing. Retrieved from http://www.girlschase.com/content/emotional-contagion-seduction-and-socializing

Amato, P. R. (1994). The impact of divorce on men and women in India and the United States. *Journal of Comparative Family Studies* 25, 207–221.

Amble, B. (2005). Corporate culture encourages lying. http://www.management-issues.com.

Andersen, P. A. (1991). Explaining intercultural differences in nonverbal communication. In *Intercultural communication: A reader*, 6th ed., (pp. 286–296), L. A. Samovar & R. E. Porter (eds.). Belmont, CA: Wadsworth.

Andersen, P. A. (2004). *The complete idiot's guide to body language.* New York, NY: Penguin Group.

Andersen, P. A., & Bowman, L. L. (1999). Postiions of power: Nonverbal influence in organizational communication. In L. K. Guerrero, J. A. DeVito, & M. L. Hecht (Eds.), *The nonverbal communication reader: Classic and contemporary readings* (2nd ed., pp. 317–334). Prospect Heights, IL: Waveland.

Andersen, P. A., & Leibowitz, K. (1978). The development and nature of the construct touch avoidance. *Environmental Psychology and Nonverbal Behavior* 3, 89–106.

Anderson, I. (2004). Explaining negative rape victim perception: Homophobia and the male rape victim. *Current Research in Social Psychology* 10 (November), np.

Anderson, K. J. (1998). Meta-analysis of gender effects on conversational interruption: Who, what, when, where, and how. *Sex Roles* 39 (August), 225–252.

Andrews, P. W., Gangestad, S. W., Miller, G. F., Haselton, M. G., Thornhill, R., & Neale, M. C. (2008). Sex differences in detecting sexual infidelity: Results of a maximum likelihood method for analyzing the sensitivity of sex differences to underreporting. *Human Nature* 19 (4), 347–373.

Angier, N. (1995a). Powerhouse of senses: Smell, at last, gets its due. *New York Times* (February 14), C1, C6.

Angier, N. (1995b). Scientists mull role of empathy in man and beast. *New York Times* (May 9), C1, C6.

Angier, N. (2010). Just don't call me. *New York Times* (August 29), Weekend, p. 3.

Aquinis, H., & Henle, C. A. (2001). Effects of nonverbal behavior on perceptions of a female employee's power bases. *Journal of Social Psychology* 141 (August), 537–549.

Aral, S. (2013). What would Ashton do—and does it matter? *Harvard Business Review* 91, 25–27.

Argyle, M. (1986). Rules for social relationships in four cultures. *Australian Journal of Psychology* 38, 309–318.

Argyle, M. (1988). *Bodily communication,* 2nd ed. New York, NY: Methuen.

Argyle, M., & Dean, J. (1965). Eye contact, distance and affiliation. *Sociometry* 28, 289–304.

Argyle, M., & Henderson, M. (1984). The rules of friendship. *Journal of Social and Personal Relationships* 1, 211–237.

Argyle, M., & Ingham, R. (1972). Gaze, mutual gaze, and distance. *Semiotica*, 1, 32–49.

Armour, S. (2003). Cupid finds work as office romance no longer taboo. *USA Today* (February 11), Money Section, 1.

Arnocky, S., Piché, T., Albert, G., Ouellette, D. and Barclay, P. (2016), Altruism predicts mating success in humans. *British Journal of Psychology*. doi:10.1111/bjop.12208

Arnold, L. B. (2008). *Family communication: Theory and research.* Boston, MA: Allyn & Bacon.

Aronson, E., Willson, T. D., & Akert, R. M. (2013). *Social psychology*, 8th ed. Boston, MA: Pearson.

Aronson, J., Cohen, J., & Nail, P. (1998). Self-affirmation theory: An update and appraisal. In *Cognitive dissonance theory: Revival with revisions and controversies*, E. Harmon-Jones & J. S. Mills (eds.). Washington, DC: American Psychological Association.

Aronson, E., Wilson, T. D., Akert, R., & Sommers, S.R. (2016). *Social psychology*, 9th ed. Hoboken, NJ: Pearson.

Asch, S. (1946). Forming impressions of personality. *Journal of Abnormal and Social Psychology* 41, 258–290.

Ashcraft, M. H. (1998). *Fundamentals of cognition.* New York, NY: Longman.

Aspinwall, L. G., & Taylor, S. E. (1993). Effects of social comparison direction, threat, and self-esteem on affect, evaluation, and expected success. *Journal of Personality and Social Psychology* 64, 708–722.

Attridge, M. (2013). Jealousy and relationship closeness. SageOpen. http://sgo.sagepub.com/content/3/1/2158244013476054.figures-only doi: 10.1177/2158244013476054

Aune, K. S. (2005). Assessing display rules in relationships. In *The sourcebook of nonverbal measures: Going beyond words* (pp. 151–162), V. Manusov (Ed.). Mahwah, NJ: Lawrence Erlbaum.

Authier, J., & Gustafson, K. (1982). Microtraining: Focusing on specific skills. In *Interpersonal helping skills: A guide to training methods, programs, and resources* (pp. 93–130), E. K. Marshall, P. D. Kurtz, and Associates (eds.). San Francisco, CA: Jossey-Bass.

Awl, D. (2011). *Facebook me! A guide to socializing, sharing, and promoting on Facebook*, 2nd ed. Berkeley, CA: Peachpit Press.

Axtell, R. E. (2007). *Essential do's and taboos: The complete guide to international business and leisure travel.* Hoboken, NJ: Wiley.

Ayres, J. (1983). Strategies to maintain relationships: Their identification and perceived usage. *Communication Quarterly* 31, 62–67.

B

Babcock, J. C, Waltz, J., Jacobson, N. S., & Gottman, J. M. (1993). Power and violence: The relation between communication patterns, power discrepancies, and domestic violence. *Journal of Marriage and the Family* 60 (February), 70–78.

Bach, G. R., & Wyden, P. (1968). *The intimate enemy.* New York, NY: Avon.

Bacon, B. (2004). *Meet me don't delete me: Internet dating: I've made all the mistakes so you don't have to.* Burbank, CA: Slapstick Publications.

Bailenson, J. N., Blascovich, J., Beall, A. C., & Loomis, J. M. (2001). Equilibrium theory revisited: Mutual gaze and personal space in virtual environments. *Presence: Teleoperators and Virtual Environments* 10 (December), 583–595.

Bailey, J., Steeves, V., Burkell, J., & Regan, P., Negotiating with gender stereotypes on social networking sites: From "Bicycle Face" to Facebook (2013). *Journal of Communications Inquiry*, 37, 91–112.

Baker, A. (2002). What makes an online relationship successful? Clues from couples who met in cyberspace. *CyberPsychology and Behavior* 5 (August), 363–375.

Balswick, J. O., & Peck, C. (1971). The inexpressive male: A tragedy of American society? *The Family Coordinator* 20, 363–368.

Banks, S. P., Altendorf, D. M., Greene, J. O., & Cody, M. J. (1987). An examination of relationship disengagement: Perceptions, breakup strategies, and outcomes. *Western Journal of Speech Communication* 51, 19–41.

Barbato, C. A., & Perse, E. M. (1992). Interpersonal communication motives and the life position of elders. *Communication Research* 19, 516–531.

Barker, L. L. (1990). *Communication,* 5th ed. Upper Saddle River, NJ: Prentice-Hall.

Barna, L. M. (1997). Stumbling blocks in intercultural communication. In *Intercultural communication: A reader,* 7th ed. (pp. 337–346), L. A. Samovar & R. E. Porter (eds.). Belmont, CA: Wadsworth.

Barnlund, D. C. (1989). *Communicative styles of Japanese and Americans: Images and realities.* Belmont, CA: Wadsworth.

Baron, R. (1990). Countering the effects of destructive criticism: The relative efficacy of four interventions. *Journal of Applied Psychology* 75 (3), 235–245.

Baron, R. A., & Byrne, D. (1984). *Social psychology: Understanding human interaction*, 4th ed. Boston, MA: Allyn & Bacon.

Barrett, L., & Godfrey, T. (1988). Listening. *Person Centered Review* 3 (November), 410–425.

Barta, P. (1999, December 16). Sex differences in the inferior parietal lobe. *Cerebral Cortex*. Retrieved from www.wired.com/news/technology/0,1282,33033,00.html

Bartholomew, K. (1990). Avoidance of intimacy: An attachment perspective. *Journal of Social and Personal Relationships* 7, 147–178.

Basso, K. H. (1972). To give up on words: Silence in Apache culture. In *Language and social context*, Pier Paolo Giglioli (ed.). New York, NY: Penguin.

Bateson, G. (1972). *Steps to an ecology of mind.* New York, NY: Ballantine.

Baumeister, R. F., Bushman, B. J., & Campbell, W. K. (2000). Self-esteem, narcissism, and aggression: Does violence result from low self-esteem or from threatened egotism? *Current Directions in Psychological Science* 9 (February), 26–29.

Bavelas, J. B. (1990). Can one not communicate? Behaving and communicating: A reply to Motley. *Western Journal of Speech Communication* 54, 593–602.

Baxter, L. A. (1983). Relationship disengagement: An examination of the reversal hypothesis. *Western Journal of Speech Communication* 47, 85–98.

Baxter, L. A. (1986). Gender differences in the heterosexual relationship rules embedded in break-up accounts. *Journal of Social and Personal Relationships* 3, 289–306.

Baxter, L. A. (2004). Relationships as dialogues. *Personal Relationships* 11 (March), 1–22.

Baxter, L. A., & Braithwaite, D. O. (2007). Social dialectics: The contradiction of relating. In *Explaining communication: Contemporary theories and exemplars* (pp. 275–292), B. B. Whaley & W. Samter (eds.). Mahwah, NJ: Erlbaum.

Baxter, L. A., & Braithwaite, D. O. (2008a). Relational dialectics theory. In *Engaging theories in interpersonal communication: Multiple perspectives* (pp. 349–362), L. A. Baxter & D. O. Braithwaite (eds.). Los Angeles, CA: Sage.

Baxter, L. A., & Braithwaite, D. O., eds. (2008b). *Engaging theories in interpersonal communication: Multiple perspectives.* Los Angeles, CA: Sage.

Baxter, L. A., & Bullis, C. (1986). Turning points in developing romantic relationships. *Human Communication Research* 12, 469–493.

Baxter, L. A., and Montgomery, B. M. (1998). A guide to dialectical approaches to studying personal relationships, Dialectical Approaches to Studying Personal Relationships pp. 1-15 (Eds.) Barbara Montgomery & Leslie Baxter. Mahwah, NJ: Erlbaum.

Baxter, L. A., & Simon, E. P. (1993). Relationship maintenance strategies and dialectical contradictions in personal relationships. *Journal of Social and Personal Relationships* 10, 225–242.

Baxter, L. A., & Wilmot, W. W. (1984). Secret tests: Social strategies for acquiring information about the state of the relationship. *Human Communication Research* 11, 171–201.

Beach, W. A. (1990). On (not) observing behavior interactionally. *Western Journal of Speech Communication* 54, 603–612.

Beard, A. (2014). Mindfulness in the age of complexity: Interview with Ellen Langer. *Harvard Business Review* 94 (3), 68–73.

Beatty, M. J., Rudd, J. E., & Valencic, K. M. (1999). A re-evaluation of the verbal aggressiveness scale: One factor or two? *Communication Research Reports* 16, 10–17.

Beilock, S. L., & Goldin-Meadow, S. (2010). Gesture changes thought by grounding it in action. *Psychological Science* 21, 1605–1610. doi:10.1177/0956797610385353

Bell, R. A., & Buerkel-Rothfuss, N. L. (1990). S(he) loves me, s(he) loves me not: Predictors of relational information-seeking in courtship and beyond. *Communication Quarterly* 38, 64–82.

Bell, R. A., & Daly, J. A. (1984). The affinity-seeking function of communication. *Communication Monographs* 51, 91–115.

Bellafiore, D. (2005). *Interpersonal conflict and effective communication.* Retrieved from http://www.drbalternatives.com/articles/cc2.html

Ben-Ze'ev, A. (2003). Primacy, emotional closeness, and openness in cyberspace. *Computers in Human Behavior* 19 (July), 451–467.

Bennett, M. (1990). Children's understanding of the mitigating function of disclaimers. *Journal of Social Psychology* 130, 29–37.

Berg, J. H., & Archer, R. L. (1983). The disclosure-liking relationship. *Human Communication Research* 10, 269–281.

Berger, C. R., & Bradac, J. J. (1982). *Language and social knowledge: Uncertainty in interpersonal relations.* London: Edward Arnold.

Berger, C. R., & Calabrese, R. J. (1975). Some explorations in initial interaction and beyond: Toward a theory of interpersonal communication. *Human Communication Research* 1, 99–112.

Berger, P. L., & Luckmann, T. (1980). *The social construction of reality.* New York, NY: Irvington.

Bernstein, W. M., Stephan, W. G., & Davis, M. H. (1979). Explaining attributions for achievement: A path analytic approach. *Journal of Personality and Social Psychology* 37, 1810–1821.

Berrett, D. (2013, September 18). Employers and public favor graduates who can communicate, survey finds. *The Chronicle of Higher Education* (September 18). https://chronicle.com/article/EmployersPublic-Favor/141679/

Berry, J. N. III (2004). Can I quote you on that? *Library Journal* 129, 10.

Berry, J. W., Poortinga, Y. H., Segall, M. H., & Dasen, P. R. (1992). *Cross-cultural psychology: Research and applications.* Cambridge: Cambridge University Press.

Berscheid, E. (1983). Emotion. In *Close relationships* (pp. 110–168), Kelley, H., Berscheid, E., Christensen, A., Harvey, J. H., Huston, T. L., Levinger, G., & Peterson, D. R. (eds.). New York, NY: Freeman.

Berscheid, E., & Reis, H. T. (1998). Attraction and close relationships. In *The handbook of social psychology*, 4th ed., Vol. 2 (pp. 193–281), D. Gilbert, S. Fiske, & G. Lindzey (eds.). New York, NY: W. H. Freeman.

Bersin, J. (2013). The 9 hottest trends in corporate recruiting. Retrieved from http://www.forbes.com/sites/joshbersin/2013/07/04/the-9-hottest-trends-in-corporate-recruiting/

Bierhoff, H. W., & Klein, R. (1991). Dimensionen der Liebe: Entwicklung einer Deutschsprachigen Skala zur Erfassung von Liebesstilen. *Zeitschrift for Differentielle und Diagnostische Psychologie* 12, 53–71.

Bishop, J. E. (1993). New research suggests that romance begins by falling nose over heels in love. *Wall Street Journal* (April 7), B1.

Bisson, M. A., & Levine, T. R. (2009). Negotiating a friends with benefits relationship. *Archives of Sexual Behavior* 39, 66–73.

Black, H. K. (1999). A sense of the sacred: Altering or enhancing the self-portrait in older age? *Narrative Inquiry* 9, 327–345.

Blake, R. R., & Mouton, J. S. (1984). *The managerial grid III*, 3rd ed. Houston, TX: Gulf Publishing.

Blieszner, R., & Adams, R. G. (1992). *Adult friendship.* Thousand Oaks, CA: Sage.

Bloch, L. (2013). The strongest emotion: The impact of emotion and communication on marriage. Retrieved December 6, 2013, from http://www.psychologytoday.com/blog/the-strongest-emotion/201311/happy-wife-happy-life

Blumstein, P., & Schwartz, P. (1983). *American couples: Money, work, sex.* New York, NY: Morrow.

Bochner, A. (1984). The functions of human communication in interpersonal bonding. In *Handbook of rhetorical and communication theory* (pp. 544–621), C. C. Arnold & J. W. Bowers (eds.). Boston, MA: Allyn & Bacon.

Bochner, S. (1994). Cross-cultural differences in the self-concept: A test of Hofstede's individualism/collectivism distinction. *Journal of Cross-Cultural Psychology* 25, 273–283.

Bochner, S., & Hesketh, B. (1994). Power distance, individualism/collectivism, and job-related attitudes in a culturally diverse work group. *Journal of Cross-Cultural Psychology* 25, 233–257.

Bodon, J., Powell, L., & Hickson III, M. (1999). Critiques of gatekeeping in scholarly journals: An analysis of perceptions and data. *Journal of the Association for Communication Administration* 28 (May), 60–70.

Bok, S. (1978). *Lying: Moral choice in public and private life.* New York, NY: Pantheon.

Bok, S. (1983). *Secrets.* New York, NY: Vintage.

Bombari, D., Mast, M. S., Brosch, T., & Sander, D. (2013). How interpersonal power affects empathic accuracy: Differential roles of mentalizing *vs.* mirroring?

Bond, Jr., C. F., & Atoum, A. O. (2000). International deception. *Personality & Social Psychology Bulletin* 26 (March), 385–395.

Boneva, B., Kraut, R., & Frohlich, D. (2001). Using e-mail for personal relationships: The difference gender makes. *American Behavioral Scientist* 45, 530–549.

Borden, G. A. (1991). *Cultural orientation: An approach to understanding intercultural communication.* Upper Saddle River, NJ: Prentice-Hall.

Bowen, F., & Blackmon, K. (2003). Spirals of silence: The dynamic of diversity on organizational voice. *Journal of Management Studies* 40 (September), 1393–1417.

Bower, B. (2001). Self-illusions come back to bite students. *Science News* 159, 148.

Bower, S. A., & Bower, G. H. (2005). *Asserting yourself: A practical guide for positive change.* Cambridge, MA: DaCapo Press.

Brashers, D. E. (2007). A theory of communication and uncertainty management. In *Explaining communication: Contemporary theories and exemplars* (pp. 201–218), B. B. Whaley & W. Samter (eds.). Mahwah, NJ: Erlbaum.

Bravo, E., & Cassedy, E. (1992). *The 9 to 5 guide to combating sexual harassment.* New York, NY: Wiley.

Bridges, C. R. (1996). The characteristics of career achievement perceived by African American college administrators. *Journal of Black Studies* 26, 748–767.

Britnell, A. (2004). Culture shock-proofing. *Profit* 23 (November), 79–80.

Briton, N. J., & Hall, J. A. (1995). Beliefs about female and male nonverbal communication. *Sex Roles* 32, 79–90.

Brody, J. F. (1994). Notions of beauty transcend culture, new study suggests. *New York Times* (March 21), A14.

Brody, L. R. (1985). Gender differences in emotional development: A review of theories and research. *Journal of Personality* 53 (June), 102–149.

Brooks, D. (2014). The existential anguish of the tattoo. *New York Times Magazine* (February 16), 44–45.

Brown, C. T., & Keller, P. W. (1979). *Monologue to dialogue: An exploration of interpersonal communication,* 2nd ed. Upper Saddle River, NJ: Prentice-Hall.

Brown, P., & Levinson, S. C. (1987). *Politeness: Some universals of language usage.* Cambridge: Cambridge University Press.

Brownell, J. (2013). *Listening: Attitudes, principles, and skills,* 5th ed. New York, NY: Routledge.

Bruneau, T. (1985). The time dimension in intercultural communication. In L. A. Samovar & R. E. Porter (Eds.), *Intercultural communication: A reader* (4th ed., pp. 280–289). Belmont, CA: Wadsworth.

Bruneau, T. (1990). Chronemics: The study of time in human interaction. In J. A. DeVito & M. L. Hecht (Eds.), *The nonverbal communication reader* (pp. 301–311). Prospect Heights, IL: Waveland Press.

Buber, M. (1958). *I and thou,* 2nd ed. New York, NY: Scribner's.

Bugental, J., & Zelen, S. (1950). Investigations into the "self-concept." I. The W-A-Y technique. *Journal of Personality* 18, 483–498.

Bull, R., & Rumsey, N. (1988). *The social psychology of facial appearance.* New York, NY: Springer-Verlag.

Buller, D. B., LePoire, B. A., Aune, R. K., & Eloy, S. (1992). Social perceptions as mediators of the effect of speech rate similarity on compliance. *Human Communication Research* 19, 286–311.

Buller, D. J. (2005). *Adapting minds: Evolutionary psychology and the persistent quest for human nature.* Cambridge, MA: MIT Press.

Bullock, B. E., & Toribio, A. J. (2012). *The Cambridge handbook of linguistic code-switching.* Cambridge, UK: Cambridge University Press.

Bumby, K. M., & Hansen, D. J. (1997). Intimacy deficits, fear of intimacy, and loneliness among sexual offenders. *Criminal Justice and Behavior* 24, 315–331.

Bunz, U., & Campbell, S. W. (2004). Politeness accommodation in electronic mail. *Communication Research Reports* 21 (winter), 11–25.

Burgoon, J. K. (1991). Relational message interpretations of touch, conversational distance, and posture. *Journal of Nonverbal Behavior* 15, 233–259.

Burgoon, J. K. (2005). Measuring nonverbal indicators of deceit. In V. Manusov, V. (Ed.) (2005). *The sourcebook of nonverbal measures: Going beyond words* (pp. 237–250). Mahwah, NJ: Lawrence Erlbaum.

Burgoon, J. K., & Bacue, A. E. (2003). Nonverbal communication skills. In *Handbook of communication and social interaction skills* (pp. 179–220), J. O. Greene & B. R. Burleson (eds.). Mahwah, NJ: Lawrence Erlbaum.

Burgoon, J.,K., Buller, D. B., & Woodall, W. G. (1996). *Nonverbal communication: The unspoken dialogue* (2nd ed.). New York, NY: McGraw-Hill.

Burgoon, J. K., & Hoobler, G. D. (2002). Nonverbal signals. In *Handbook of Interpersonal Communication,* 3rd ed. (pp. 240–299), M. L. Knapp & J. A. Daly (eds.). Thousand Oaks, CA: Sage.

Burgoon, J. K., Berger, C. R., & Waldron, V. R. (2000). Mindfulness and interpersonal communication. *Journal of Social Issues* 56, 105–127.

Burgoon, J. K., Guerrero, L. K., & Floyd, K. (2010). *Nonverbal Communication.* Boston, MA: Allyn & Bacon.

Burgstahler, S. (2007). Managing an e-mentoring community to support students with disabilities: A case study. *Distance Education Report* 11 (July), 7–15.

Burleson, B. R. (2003). Emotional support skills. In *Handbook of communication and social interaction skills* (pp. 551–594), J. O. Greene & B. R. Burleson (eds.), Mahwah, NJ: Erlbaum.

Burleson, B. R., Holmstrom, A. J., & Gilstrap, C. M. (2005). 'Guys can't say *that* to guys': Four experiments assessing the normative motivation account for deficiencies in the emotional support provided by men. *Communication Monographs* 72 (December), 468–501.

Burleson, B. R., Kunkel, A. W., & Birch, J. D. (1994). Thoughts about talk in romantic relationships: Similarity makes for attraction (and happiness, too). *Communication Quarterly* 42 (summer), 259–273.

Burleson, B. R., Samter, W., & Luccetti, A. E. (1992). Similarity in communication values as a predictor of friendship choices: Studies of friends and best friends. *Southern Communication Journal* 57, 260–276.

Bushman, B. J., & Baumeister, R. F. (1998). Threatened egotism, narcissism, self-esteem, and direct and displaced aggression: Does self-love or self-hate lead to violence? *Journal of Personality and Social Psychology* 75, 219–229.

Buss, D. M. (2000). *The dangerous passion: Why jealousy is as necessary as love and sex.* New York, NY: Free Press.

Buss, D. M., Shackelford, T. K., Kirkpatrick, L. A., Choe, J. C., Lim, H. K., Hasegawa, M., Hasegawa, T., & Bennett, K. (1999). Jealousy and the nature of beliefs about infidelity: Tests of competing hypotheses about sex differences in the United States, Korea, and Japan. *Personal Relationships* 6, 125–150.

Butler, P. E. (1981). *Talking to yourself: Learning the language of self-support.* New York, NY: Harper & Row.

Buunk, B. P., & Dijkstra, P. (2004). Gender differences in rival characteristics that evoke jealousy in response to emotional versus sexual infidelity. *Personal Relationships* 11 (December), 395–408.

Byers, E. S., & Demmons, S. (1999). Sexual satisfaction and sexual self-disclosure within dating relationships. *Journal of Sex Research* 36, 180–189.

C

Cacioppoa, J. T., Cacioppoa, S., Gonzagab, G. C., Ogburnc, E. L., & VanderWeelec, T. J. (2013). Marital satisfaction and break-ups differ across on-line and off-line meeting venues. *Proceedings of the National Academy of Sciences* PNAS 2013 110 (25, June 3) 10135–10140. doi:10.1073/pnas.1222447110

Cacioppo, J. T., Cacioppo, S., Gonzaga, G. C., Ogburn, E. L., & VanderWeele, T. J. (2013). Marital satisfaction and break-ups differ across on-line and off-line meeting venues. *Proceedings of the National Academy of Sciences* 110, 10135-10140. http://www.pnas.org/content/110/25/10135.full.pdf

Cahn, D. D., & Abigail, R. A. (2007). *Managing conflict through communication*, 3rd ed. Boston, MA: Allyn & Bacon.

Cai, D. A., & Fink, E. L. (2002). Conflict style differences between individualists and collectivists. *Communication Monographs* 69 (March), 67–87.

Callan, V. J. (1993). Subordinate–manager communication in different sex dyads: Consequences for job satisfaction. *Journal of Occupational & Organizational Psychology*, 66 (March), 1–15.

Camden, C., Motley, M. T., & Wilson, A. (1984). White lies in interpersonal communication: A taxonomy and preliminary investigation of social motivations. *Western Journal of Speech Communication* 48, 309–325.

Campbell, T. A., & Campbell, D. E. (2007). Outcomes of mentoring at-risk college students: Gender and ethnic matching effects. *Mentoring and Tutoring* 15 (May), 135–148.

Campbell, W. K., Foster, C. A., & Finkel, E. J. (2002). Does self-love lead to love for others? A story of narcissistic game playing. *Journal of Personality and Social Psychology* 83 (August), 340–354.

Canary, D. J. (2003). Managing interpersonal conflict: A model of events related to strategic choices. In *Handbook of communication and social interaction skills* (pp. 515–550), J. O. Greene & B. R. Burleson (eds.). Mahwah, NJ: Lawrence Erlbaum.

Canary, D. J., & Cupach, W. R., & Messman, S. J. (1995). *Relationship conflict: Conflict in parent-child, friendship, and romantic relationships* Newbury Park, CA: Sage.

Canary, D. J., & Hause, K. S. (1993). Is there any reason to research sex differences in communication? *Communication Quarterly* 41, 129–144.

Canary, D. J., & Stafford, L. (1994). Maintaining relationships through strategic and routine interaction. In *Communication and relational maintenance,* D. J. Canary & L. Stafford (eds.). New York, NY: Academic Press.

Canary, D. J., Cody, M. J., & Manusov, V. L. (2003). *Interpersonal communication: A goals-based approach,* 3rd ed. Boston, MA: St. Bedford/St. Martins.

Canary, D. J., Cupach, W. R., & Messman, S. J. (1995). *Relationship conflict: Conflict in parent-child, friendship, and romantic relationships.* Thousand Oaks, CA: Sage.

Canary, D. J., Stafford, L., Hause, K. S., & Wallace, L. A. (1993). An inductive analysis of relational maintenance strategies: Comparisons among lovers, relatives, friends, and others. *Communication Research Reports* 10, 5–14.

Cappella, J. N., & Schreiber, D. M. (2006). The interaction management function of nonverbal cues. In *The Sage handbook of nonverbal communication* (pp. 361–379), V. Manusov & M. L. Patterson (eds.). Thousand Oaks, CA: Sage.

Caproni, P. J. (2012). *Management skills for everyday life: The practical coach.* Upper Saddle River, NJ: Prentice-Hall.

Carey, B. (2005). Have you heard? Gossip turns out to serve a purpose. *New York Times* (August 16), F1, F6.

Carli, L. L. (1999). Gender, interpersonal power, and social influence. *Journal of Social Issues* 55 (spring), 81–99.

Carlock, C. J., ed. (1999). *Enhancing self-esteem,* 3rd ed. Philadelphia, PA: Accelerated Development, Inc.

Carmeron, H., & Xu, X. (2011). Representational gesture, pointing gesture, and memory recall of preschool children. *Journal of Nonverbal Behavior* 35, 155–171. doi: 10.1007/s10919-010-0101-2

Carroll, D. W. (1994). *Psychology of language,* 2nd ed. Pacific Grove, CA: Brooks/Cole.

Carson, J. W., Carson, K. M., Gil, K. M., & Baucom, D. H. (2004). Mindfulness-based relationship enhancement. *Behavior Therapy* 35 (summer), 471–494.

Cashdan, E. (2001). Ethnocentrism and xenophobia: A cross-cultural study. *Current Anthropology* 42, 760–765.

Castleberry, S. B., & Shepherd, C. D. (1993). Effective interpersonal listening and personal selling. *Journal of Personal Selling and Sales Management* 13, 35–49.

Cawthon, S. W. (2001). Teaching strategies in inclusive classrooms with deaf students. *Journal of Deaf Studies and Deaf Education* 6, 212–225.

Chadwick-Jones, J. K. (1976). *Social exchange theory: Its structure and influence in social psychology.* New York, NY: Academic Press.

Chan, D., K., & Cheng, G. H. (2004). A comparison of offline and online friendship qualities at different stages of relationship development. *Journal of Social and Personal Relationships* 21 (June), 305–320.

Chaney, R. H., Givens, C. A., Aoki, M. F., & Gombiner, M. L. (1989). Pupillary responses in recognizing awareness in persons with profound mental retardation. *Perceptual and Motor Skills* 69, 523–528.

Chang, H., & Holt, G. R. (1996). The changing Chinese interpersonal world: Popular themes in interpersonal communication books in modern Taiwan. *Communication Quarterly* 44, 85–106.

Chanowitz, B., & Langer, E. (1981). Premature cognitive commitment. *Journal of Personality and Social Psychology* 41, 1051–1063.

Chapdelaine, R. F., & Alexitch, L. R. (2004). Social skills difficulty: Model of culture shock for international graduate students. *Journal of College Student Development* 45 (March–April), 167–184.

Chen, G. (1992). Differences in self-disclosure patterns among Americans versus Chinese: A comparative study. Paper presented at the annual meeting of the Eastern Communication Association, Portland, ME.

Cheney, G., & Tompkins, P. K. (1987). Coming to terms with organizational identification and commitment. *Central States Speech Journal* 38, 1–15.

Cherulnik, P. D. (1979). Sex differences in the expression of emotion in a structured social encounter. *Sex Roles* 5 (August), 413–424.

Childress, H. (2004). Teenagers, territory and the appropriation of space. *Childhood: A Global Journal of Child Research* 11 (May), 195–205.

Chillot, R. (2013, April). The power of touch. *Psychology Today* 46, 53–61.

Cho, H. (2000). Asian in America: Cultural shyness can impede Asian Americans' success. *Northwest Asian Weekly* 19 (December 8), 6.

Christians, C. G., & Traber, M., eds. (1997). *Communication ethics and universal values.* Urbana, IL: University of Illinois Press.

Chua, A. (2011a). *Battle Hymn of the Tiger Mother.* New York: Penguin Books.

Chua, A. (2011b). Why Chinese mothers are superior. *Wall Street Journal.* Retrieved April 3, 2014, from http://online.wsj.com/news/articles/SB10001424052748704111504576059713528698754

Chung, L. C., & Ting-Toomey, S. (1999). Ethnic identity and relational expectations among Asian Americans. *Communication Research Reports* 16 (spring), 157–166.

Chung, M. C., Farmer, S., Grant, K., Newton, R., Payne, S., Perry, M., Saunders, J., Smith, C., & Stone, N. (2002). Gender differences in love styles and post traumatic reactions following relationship dissolution. *European Journal of Psychiatry* 16 (October–December), 210–220.

Cialdini, R. (2013). The uses (and abuses) of influence. *Harvard Business Review* (July–August), 76–81.

Ciccarelli, S. K., & White, J. N. (2017). *Psychology: An exploration,* 5th ed. Hoboken, NJ: Pearson.

Clance, P. (1985). *The Impostor Phenomenon: Overcoming the fear that haunts your success.* Atlanta: Peachtree Publishers.

Clayton, R. B., Nagurney, A., & Smith, J. R. (2012). Cheating, breakup, and divorce: Is Facebook use to blame? *Cyberpsychology, Behavior, and Social Networking* 16, 717–720.

Clement, D. A., & Frandsen, K. D. (1976). On conceptual and empirical treatments of feedback in human communication. *Communication Monographs* 43, 11–28.

Cline, M. G. (1956). The influence of social context on the perception of faces. *Journal of Personality* 2, 142–185.

Cloud, J. (2008). Are gay relationships different? *Time* (January), 78–80.

Coates, J., & Sutton-Spence, R. (2001). Turn-taking patterns in deaf conversation. *Journal of Sociolinguistics* 5 (November), 507–529.

Coats, E. J., & Feldman, R. S. (1996). Gender differences in nonverbal correlates of social status. *Personality and Social Psychology Bulletin* 22 (October), 1014–1022.

Cody, M. J. (1982). A typology of disengagement strategies and an examination of the role intimacy, reactions to inequity, and relational problems play in strategy selection. *Communication Monographs* 49, 148–170.

Cody, M. J., & Dunn, D. (2007). Accounts. In *Explaining communication: Contemporary theories and exemplars* (pp. 237–256), B. B. Whaley and W. Samter (eds.). Mahwah, NJ: Erlbaum.

Cohen, J. (2002). An e-mail affliction: The long goodbye. *New York Times* (May 9), G6.

Cohen, J. (2003). Parasocial breakups: Measuring individual differences in responses to the dissolution of parasocial relationships. *Mass Communication and Society* 6, 191–202.

Cohen, J. (2004). Parasocial break-up from favorite television characters: The role of attachment styles and relationship intensity. *Journal of Social and Personal Relationships* 21 (April), 187–202.

Coleman, P. (2002). *How to say it for couples: Communicating with tenderness, openness, and honesty.* Upper Saddle River, NJ: Prentice-Hall.

Colley, A., Todd, Z., Bland, M., Holmes, M., Khanom, N., & Pike, H. (2004). Style and content in e-mails and letters to male and female friends. *Journal of Language and Social Psychology* 23 (September), 369–378.

Collins, J. E., & Clark, L. F. (1989). Responsibility and rumination: The trouble with understanding the dissolution of a relationship. *Social Cognition* 7, 152–173.

Collins, N. L., & Miller, L. C. (1994). Self-disclosure and liking: A meta-analytic review. *Psychological Bulletin* 116 (November), 457–475.

Comer, L. B., & Drollinger, T. (1999). Active empathic listening and selling success: A conceptual framework. *Journal of Personal Selling and Sales Management,* 19, 15–29.

Comstock, J. (2012, December). The underrated sense. *Psychology Today* 45, 46–47.

Conlin, M. (2002). Watch what you put in that office e-mail. *Business Week* (September 9), 114–115.

Conniff, K., & Nicks, D. (2014). The new habits of highly successful digital daters. *Time* 183 (February 17), 40–45.

Constantine, M. G., Anderson, G. M., Berkel, L. A., Caldwell, L. D., & Utsey, S. O. (2005). Examining the cultural adjustment experiences of African international college students: A qualitative analysis. *Journal of Counseling Psychology* 52 (January), 57–66.

Cooley, C. H. (1922). *Human nature and the social order,* rev. ed. New York, NY: Scribner's.

Cooper, A., & Sportolari, L. (1997). Romance in cyberspace: Understanding online attraction. *Journal of Sex Education and Therapy* 22, 7–14.

Coover, G. E., & Murphy, S. T. (2000). The communicated self: Exploring the interaction between self and social context. *Human Communication Research* 26, 125–147.

Copeland, L., & Griggs, L. (1985). *Going international: How to make friends and deal effectively in the global marketplace.* New York, NY: Random House.

Cornwell, B., & Lundgren, D. C. (2001). Love on the Internet: Involvement and misrepresentation in romantic relationships in cyberspace vs. realspace. *Computers in Human Behavior* 17, 197–211.

Counts, D. A., Brown, J. K., & Campbell, J. C. (1992). *Sanctions and sanctuary: Cultural perspectives on the beating of wives.* Boulder, CO: Westview Press.

Cramer, D. (2004). Emotional support, conflict, depression, and relationship satisfaction in a romantic partner. *Journal of Psychology: Interdisciplinary and Applied* 138 (November), 532–542.

Crampton, S. M., Hodge, J. W., & Mishra, J. M. (1998). The informal communication network: Factors influencing grapevine activity. *Public Personnel Management* 27 (winter), 569–584.

Crohn, J. (1995). *Mixed matches: How to create successful interracial, interethnic, and interfaith relationships.* New York, NY: Fawcett.

Croucher, S. M. (2013). The differences in verbal aggressiveness between the United States and Thailand. *Communication Research Reports* 30, 264–269.

Cross, E. E., & Madson, L. (1997). Models of the self: Self-construals and gender. *Psychological Bulletin* 122, 5–37.

Crusco, A. H., & Wetzel, C. G. (1984). The Midas touch: The effects of interpersonal touch on restaurant tipping. *Personality and Social Psychology Bulletin* 10, 512–517.

Cuddy, A. (2015). *Presence: Bringing your boldest self to your biggest challenges.* New York, NY: Little, Brown and Company.

Cunningham, M. R. (2009). Social allergies. In *Encyclopedia of human relationships.* H. T. Reis & S. Sprecher (eds.). Thousand Oaks, CA: Sage.

D

Dahle, C. (2004). Choosing a mentor? Cast a wide net. *New York Times* (July 25), BU 9.

Dainton, M., & Stafford, L. (1993). Routine maintenance behaviors: A comparison of relationship type, partner similarity, and sex differences. *Journal of Social and Personal Relationships* 10, 255–272.

Damasio, A. (2005). *Descartes' error: Emotion, reason, and the human brain.* New York, NY: Penguin.

Darley, J. M., & Latane, B. (1968). Bystander intervention in emergencies: Diffusion of responsibility. *Journal of Personality and Social Psychology* 8, 377–383.

Darwin, C. (1872). *The expression of the emotions in man and animals.* Chicago, IL: University of Chicago Press (reprinted 1965).

Davis, K. (1980). Management communication and the grapevine. In *Intercom: Readings in organizational communication* (pp. 55–66), S. Ferguson & S. D. Ferguson (eds.). Rochelle Park, NJ: Hayden Books.

Davis, M. S. (1973). *Intimate relations.* New York, NY: Free Press.

Davitz, J. R. (ed.). (1964). *The communication of emotional meaning.* New York, NY: McGraw-Hill.

deBono, E. (1987). *The six thinking hats.* New York, NY: Penguin.

DeFrancisco, V. (1991). The sound of silence: How men silence women in marital relations. *Discourse and Society* 2, 413–423.

DePaulo, B. M. (1992). Nonverbal behavior and self-presentation. *Psychological Bulletin* 111, 203–212.

DePaulo, B. M., Lindsay, J. J., Malone, B. E., Muhlenbruck, L., Charlton, K., & Cooper, H. (2003). Cues to deception. *Psychological Bulletin* 129, 74–118.

DeVito, J. A. (1989). *The nonverbal communication workbook.* Prospect Heights, IL: Waveland Press.

DeVito, J. A. (2003a). MEDUSA messages. *Etc: A Review of General Semantics* 60 (fall), 241–245.

DeVito, J. A. (2003b). SCREAM before you scream. *Etc: A Review of General Semantics* 60 (spring), 42–45.

DeVito, J. A. (2012). *50 communication strategies.* Bloomington, IN: iUniverse.

DeVito, J. A. (2014). *The nonverbal communication book.* Dubuque, IA: Kendall-Hunt.

Deal, J. E., & Wampler, K. S. (1986). Dating violence: The primacy of previous experience. *Journal of Social and Personal Relationships* 3, 457–471.

Dean, J. (2007). Getting closer: The art of self-disclosure. Retrieved from http://www.spring.org.uk/2007/02/getting-closer-art-of-self-disclosure.php

Dean, J. (2010a). Twitter: 10 psychological insights (August 10). Retrieved November 7, 2013, from http://www.

spring.org.uk/2010/08/twitter-10-psychological-insights.php

Dean, J. (2010b). Online dating: 10 psychological insights. Accessed December 21, 2013, from http://www.spring.org.uk/2010/09/online-dating-10-psychological-insights.php

Dean, J. (2010c). Gesturing while talking influences thoughts. Retrieved from http://www.spring.org.uk/2013/11/gesturing-while-talking-influences-thoughts.php

Dean, J. (2011a). 10 psychological effects of nonsexual touch. Retrieved from http://www.spring.org.uk/2011/04/10-psychological-effects-of-nonsexual-touch.php

Dean, J. (2011b). 10 hidden benefits of smiling. Retrieved December 22, 2013, from http://www.spring.org.uk/2011/06/10-hidden-benefits-of-smiling.php

Dean, J. (2011c). Six memory myths. Retrieved December 22, 2013, from http://www.spring.org.uk/2011/08/memory-test-whats-your-score.php

Dean, J. (2013). High emotional intelligence dramatically improves decision-making. Retrieved from http://www.spring.org.uk/2013/12/high-emotional-intelligence-dramatically-improves-decision-making.php

Dean, J. (2014a). How many basic emotions are there? Fewer than previously thought. Retrieved from http://www.spring.org.uk/2014/02/how-many-basic-emotions-are-there-fewer-than-was-previously-thought.php

Dean, J. (2014b). Blue light can improve alertness and attention day or night. Retrieved from http://www.spring.org.uk/2014/02/blue-light-can-improve-alertness-and-attention-day-or-night.php

Dean, J. (2016a). 9 new facts about attraction we learned in 2016. Psyblog http://www.spring.org.uk/2016/12/attraction-9-scientific-facts-we-learned-in-2016.php

Dean, J. (2016b). Why helping others will change your life. Psyblog http://www.spring.org.uk/2016/12/helping-others-makes-you-live-longer.php.

Dean, J. (2017). http://www.spring.org.uk/2016/06/people-find-essential-long-term-partner.php

Deaux, K., & LaFrance, M. (1998). Gender. In *The handbook of social psychology*, 4th ed., Vol. 1 (pp. 788–828), D. Gilbert, S. Fiske, & G. Lindzey (eds.). New York, NY: Freeman.

Delia, J. G. (1977). Constructivism and the study of human communication. *Quarterly Journal of Speech* 63, 66–83.

Delia, J. G., O'Keefe, B. J., & O'Keefe, D. J. (1982). The constructivist approach to communication. In *Human communication theory: Comparative essays* (pp. 147–191), Frank E. X. Dance (ed.). New York, NY: Harper & Row.

Dell, K. (2005). Just for dudes. *Time* (February 14), B22.

Dereshiwsky, M. I., Moan, E. R., & Gahungu, A. (2002). Faculty perceptions regarding issues of civility in online instructional communication. *USDLA Journal* 16, No. 6 (June).

Derlega, V. J., Winstead, B. A., Greene, K., Serovich, J., & Elwood, W. N. (2004). Reasons for HIV disclosure/nondisclosure in close relationships: Testing a model of HIV-disclosure decision making. *Journal of Social and Clinical Psychology* 23 (December), 747–767.

Derlega, V. J., Winstead, B. A., Wong, P. T. P., & Hunter, S. (1985). Gender effects in an initial encounter: A case where men exceed women in disclosure. *Journal of Social and Personal Relationships* 2, 25–44.

Desar, L. (2013). Hiding in plain sight. *Psychology Today* 46 (December), 18.

Dewey, J. (1910). *How we think.* Boston, MA: Heath.

DiBaise, R., & Gunnoe, J. (2004). Gender and culture differences in touching behavior. *Journal of Social Psychology* 144 (February), 49–62.

Diekman, A. B., & Eagly, A. H. (2000). Stereotypes as dynamic constructs: Women and men of the past, present, and future. *Personality and Social Psychology* 26, 1171–1188.

Dillard, J. P., & Marshall, L. J. (2003). Persuasion as a social skill. In *Handbook of communication and social interaction skills* (pp. 479–514), J. O. Greene & B. R. Burleson (eds.). Mahwah, NJ: Lawrence Erlbaum.

Dillard, J. P., Anderson, J. W., & Knobloch, L. K. (2002). Interpersonal influence. In *Handbook of interpersonal communication*, 3rd ed. (pp. 425–474), M. L. Knapp & J. A. Daly (eds.). Thousand Oaks, CA: Sage.

Dillard, J. P., ed. (1990). *Seeking compliance: The production of interpersonal influence messages.* Scottsdale, AZ: Gorsuch Scarisbrick.

Dindia, K., & Baxter, L. A. (1987). Strategies for maintaining and repairing marital relationships. *Journal of Social and Personal Relationships* 4, 143–158.

Dindia, K., & Fitzpatrick, M. A. (1985). Marital communication: Three approaches compared. In *Understanding personal relationships: An interdisciplinary approach* (pp. 137–158), S. Duck & D. Perlman (eds.). Thousand Oaks, CA: Sage.

Dindia, K., & Timmerman, L. (2003). Accomplishing romantic relationships. In *Handbook of communication and social interaction skills* (pp. 685–721), J. O. Greene & B. R. Burleson (eds.). Mahwah, NJ: Erlbaum.

Dion, K. K., & Dion, K. L. (1993a). Individualistic and collectivist perspectives on gender and the cultural context of love and intimacy. *Journal of Social Issues* 49, 53–69.

Dion, K. K., & Dion, K. L. (1996). Cultural perspectives on romantic love. *Personal Relationships* 3, 5–17.

Dion, K. L., & Dion, K. K. (1993b). Gender and ethnocultural comparisons in styles of love. *Psychology of Women Quarterly* 17, 464–473.

Dion, K., Berscheid, E., & Walster, E. (1972). What is beautiful is good. *Journal of Personality and Social Psychology* 24, 285–290.

Dixson, B. J. W., Sulikowski, D., Gouda-Vossos, A., Rantala, M. J. and Brooks, R. C. (2016), The masculinity paradox: facial masculinity and beardedness interact to determine women's ratings of men's facial attractiveness. *Journal of Evolutionary Biology*, 29: 2311–2320. doi:10.1111/jeb.12958

Doherty, R. W., Orimoto, L., Singelis, T. M., Hatfield, E., & Hebb, J. (1995). Emotional contagion: Gender and occupational differences. *Psychology of Women Quarterly* 19, 355–371.

Dolgin, K. G., Meyer, L., & Schwartz, J. (1991). Effects of gender, target's gender, topic, and self-esteem on disclosure to best and middling friends. *Sex Roles* 25, 311–329.

Donahue, W. A. (with Kolt, R.). (1992). *Managing interpersonal conflict.* Thousand Oaks, CA: Sage.

Dorland, J. M., & Fisher, A. R. (2001). Gay, lesbian, and bisexual individuals' perception: An analogue study. *Counseling Psychologist* 29 (July), 532–547.

Dosey, M., & Meisels, M. (1976). Personal space and self-protection. *Journal of Personality and Social Psychology* 38, 959–965.

Douglas, W. (1994). The acquaintanceship process: An examination of uncertainty, information seeking, and social attraction during initial conversation. *Communication Research* 21, 154–176.

Dovidio, J. F., Gaertner, S. E., Kawakami, K., & Hodson, G. (2002). Why can't we just get along? Interpersonal biases and interracial distrust. *Cultural Diversity and Ethnic Minority Psychology* 8, 88–102.

Doyle, A. (2016). Top 10 communication skills for workplace success: Employers look for these communication skills. (https://www.thebalance.com/communication-skills-list-2063779).

Drass, K. A. (1986). The effect of gender identity on conversation. *Social Psychology Quarterly* 49, 294–301.

Dresser, N. (2005). *Multicultural manners: Essential rules of etiquette for the 21st century*, rev. ed. New York, NY: Wiley.

Drews, D. R., Allison, C. K., & Probst, J. R. (2000). Behavioral and self-concept differences in tattooed and nontattooed college students. *Psychological Reports* 86, 475–481.

Dreyfuss, H. (1971). *Symbol sourcebook.* New York, NY: McGraw-Hill.

Drummond, K., & Hopper, R. (1993). Acknowledgment tokens in series. *Communication Reports* 6, 47–53.

Dsilva, M., & Whyte, L. O. (1998). Cultural differences in conflict styles: Vietnamese refugees and established residents. *The Howard Journal of Communication* 9, 57–68.

Duck, S. (1986). *Human relationships.* Thousand Oaks, CA: Sage.

Duke, M., & Nowicki, S., Jr. (2005). The Emory dyssemia index. In *The sourcebook of nonverbal measures: Going beyond words* (pp. 35–46), V. Manusov (ed.). Mahwah, NJ: Erlbaum.

Dunbar, N. E., & Burgoon, J. K. (2005). Measuring nonverbal dominance. In *The sourcebook of nonverbal measures: Going beyond words* (pp. 361–374), V. Manusov (ed.). Mahwah, NJ: Erlbaum.

Dunbar, R. I. M. (2004). Gossip in evolutionary perspective. *Review of General Psychology* 8 (June), 100–110.

Duncan, B. L., & Rock, J. W. (1991). *Overcoming relationship impasses: Ways to initiate change when your partner won't help.* New York, NY: Plenum Press/Insight Books.

Duncan, S. D., Jr. (1972). Some signals and rules for taking speaking turns in conversation. *Journal of Personality and Social Psychology* 23, 283–292.

Dunn, D., & Cody, M. J. (2000). Account credibility and public image: Excuses, justifications, denials, and sexual harassment. *Communication Monographs* 67 (December), 372–391.

Durst, U. (2003). Evidence for linguistic relativity. *Pragmatics and Cognition* 11, 379–386.

Duval, T. S., & Silva, P. J. (2002). Self-awareness, probability of improvement, and the self-serving bias. *Journal of Personality and Social Psychology* 82, 49–61.

Dwyer, K. K. (2005). *Conquer your speech anxiety: Learning how to overcome your nervousness about public speaking*, 2nd ed. Belmont, CA: Wadsworth.

E

Eastwick, P. W. & Finkel, E. J. (2009). Reciprocity of liking. In H. T. Reis & S. Sprecher (eds.), *Encyclopedia of human relationships* (pp. 1333–1336). Thousand Oaks, CA: Sage.

Eccles, A. (2009). You're driving me crazy! *Psychology Today* 42, 66–75.

Eden, D. (1992). Leadership and expectations: Pygmalion effects and other self-fulfilling prophecies in organizations. *Leadership Quarterly* 3, 271–305.

Eder, D., & Enke, J. L. (1991). The structure of gossip: Opportunities and constraints on collective expression among adolescents. *American Sociological Review* 56, 494–508.

Edstrom, A. (2004). Expression of disagreement by Venezuelans in conversation: Reconsidering the influence of culture. *Journal of Pragmatics* 36 (August), 1499–1508.

Edwards, R., & Bello, R. (2001). Interpretations of messages: The influence of equivocation, face-concerns, and ego-involvement. *Human Communication Research* 27, 597–631.

Ehrenhaus, P. (1988). Silence and symbolic expression. *Communication Monographs* 55, 41–57.

Einhorn, L. (2006). Using e-prime and English minus absolutisms to provide self-empathy. *Etc.: A Review of General Semantics* 63 (April), 180–186.

Einstein, E. (1995). Success or sabotage: Which self-fulfilling prophecy will the stepfamily create? In D. K. Huntley (Ed.), *Understanding stepfamilies: Implications for assessment and treatment.* Alexandria, VA: American Counseling Association.

Eisenberg, E. (2007). *Strategic ambiguities: Essays on communication, organization, and identity.* Thousand Oaks, CA: Sage.

Eisenberger, N. I., Liberman, M. D., & Williams, K. D. (2003). Does rejection hurt? An fMRI study of social exclusion. *Science* 302 (October), 290–292.

Ekman, P. (1985). *Telling lies: Clues to deceit in the marketplace, politics, and marriage.* New York, NY: Norton.

Ekman, P., & Friesen, W. V. (1969). The repertoire of nonverbal behavior: Categories, origins, usage, and coding. *Semiotica* 1, 49–98.

Ekman, P., Friesen, W. V., & Ellsworth, P. (1972). *Emotion in the human face: Guidelines for research and an integration of findings.* New York, NY: Pergamon Press.

Elfenbein, H. A., & Ambady, N. (2002). Is there an in-group advantage in emotion recognition? *Psychological Bulletin* 128, 243–249.

Ellis, A. (1988). *How to stubbornly refuse to make yourself miserable about anything, yes anything.* Secaucus, NJ: Lyle Stuart.

Ellis, A., & Harper, R. A. (1975). *A new guide to rational living.* Hollywood, CA: Wilshire Books.

Ellis, K. (2004). The impact of perceived teacher confirmation on receiver apprehension, motivation, and learning. *Communication Education* 53 (January), 1–20.

Elmes, M. B., & Gemmill, G. (1990). The psychodynamics of mindlessness and dissent in small groups. *Small Group Research* 21, 28–44.

Emmers-Sommer, T. M. (2004). The effect of communication quality and quantity indicators on intimacy and relational satisfaction. *Journal of Social and Personal Relationships* 21 (June), 99–411.

Emmert, P. (1994). A definition of listening. *Listening Post,* 51, 6.

Entis, L. (2013). The Facebook test. *Psychology Today* 44 (December), 19.

Epstein, R. (2005). The loose screw awards: Psychology's top 10 misguided ideas. *Psychology Today* (February), 55–62.

Epstein, R. M., & Hundert, E. M. (2002). Defining and assessing professional competence. *JAMA: Journal of the American Medical Association* 287, 226–235.

Erber, R., & Erber, M. W. (2011). Intimate relationships: Issues, theories, and research (2nd ed.). Boston, MA: Allyn and Bacon.

Erceau, D., & Guéguen, N. (2007) Tactile contact and evaluation of the toucher. *Journal of Social Psychology* 147, 441–444.

Esen, S. (2016). Code switching: Definition, types and examples. *Owlcation* [https://owlcation.com/humanities/Code-Switching-Definition-Types-and-Examples-of-Code-Switching], accessed March 11, 2017.

Exline, R. V., Ellyson, S. L., & Long, B. (1975). Visual behavior as an aspect of power role relationships. In *Nonverbal communication of aggression*, P. Pliner, L. Krames, & T. Alloway (eds.). New York, NY: Plenum Press.

F

Fales, M. R., Frederick, D. A., Garcia, J. R., Gildersleeve, K. A., Haselton, K. M. G., & Fisher, H. E. (2016). Mating markets and bargaining hands: Mate preferences for attractiveness and resources in two national U.S. studies. *Personality and Individual Differences* 88, 78–87.

Fagan, J., & Barnett, M. (2003). The relationship between maternal gatekeeping, paternal competence, mothers' attitudes about the father role, and father involvement. *Journal of Family Issues* 24 (November), 1020–1043.

Faigley, L. (2009). *The Penguin handbook*, 3rd ed. New York, NY: Longman.

Fan, R., Zhao, J., Chen, Y., Xu, K. (2013). Anger is more influential than joy: Sentiment correlation in Weibo. Retrieved February 2, 2014, from http://scholar.google.com/citations?view_op=view_citation&hl=en&user=myZ8_DUAAAAJ&citation_for_view=myZ8_DUAAAAJ:blknAaTinKkC

Feeley, T. H., & deTurck, M. A. (1995). Global cue usage in behavioral lie detection. *Communication Quarterly* 43, 420–430.

Fehr, B. (2004). Intimacy expectations in same-sex friendships: A prototype interaction-pattern model. *Journal of Personality and Social Psychology* 86 (February), 265–284.

Fehr, B., & Broughton, R. (2001). Gender and personality differences in concepts of love: An interpersonal theory analysis. *Personal Relationships* 8, 115–136.

Feiler, B. (2016, October 2). The art of condolence. The New York Times, Sunday Styles, 2.

Fengler, A. P. (1974). Romantic love in courtship: Divergent paths of male and female students. *Journal of Comparative Family Studies* 5, 134–139.

Fernald, C. D. (1995). When in London: Differences in disability language preferences among English-speaking countries. *Mental Retardation* 33, 99–103.

Ferraro, G. (2005). *Cultural dimension of international business,* 5th ed. Upper Saddle River, NJ: Prentice-Hall.

Fesko, S. L. (2001). Disclosure of HIV status in the workplace: Considerations and strategies. *Health and Social Work* 26 (November), 235–244.

Festinger, L. (1954). A theory of social comparison processes. *Human Relations* 7, 117–140.

Fife, E. M. (2007). Male friendship and competition: A dialectical analysis. *Ohio Communication Journal* 45, 41–64.

Finn, J. (2004). A survey of online harassment at a university campus. *English* 19 (April), 468–483.

Fiore, A. T., & Donath, J. S. (2005). Homophily in online dating: When do you like someone like yourself? ACM Digital Library. Retrieved December 22, 2013, from http://dl.acm.org/citation.cfm?id=1056919

Fischer, A. H. (1993). Sex differences in emotionality: Fact or stereotype? *Feminism & Psychology* 3, 303–318.

Fisher, C. (1998). Mood and emotions while working—missing pieces of job satisfaction. *School of Business Discussion Papers.* http://works.bepress.com/cynthia_fisher/3

Fisher, D. (1995). *People power: 12 power principles to enrich your business, career, and personal networks.* Austin, TX: Bard & Stephen.

Fitzpatrick, M. A. (1983). Predicting couples' communication from couples' self-reports. In *Communication yearbook 7* (pp. 49–82), R. N. Bostrom (ed.). Thousand Oaks, CA: Sage.

Fitzpatrick, M. A. (1988). *Between husbands and wives: Communication in marriage.* Thousand Oaks, CA: Sage.

Fitzpatrick, M. A. (1991). Sex differences in marital conflict: Social psychophysiological versus cognitive explanations. *Text* 11, 341–364.

Fitzpatrick, M. A., & Caughlin, J. P. (2002). Interpersonal communication in family relationships. In *Handbook of interpersonal communication,* 3rd ed. (pp. 726–777), M. L. Knapp & J. A. Daly. (eds.). Thousand Oaks, CA: Sage.

Fitzpatrick, M. A., Jandt, F. E., Myrick, F. L., & Edgar, T. (1994). Gay and lesbian couple relationships. In *Queer words, queer images: Communication and the construction of homosexuality* (pp. 265–285), Ringer, R. J. (ed.). New York, NY: New York University Press.

Flocker, M. (2006). *Death by Power Point: A modern office survival guide.* Cambridge, MA: DaCapo Press.

Floyd, J. J. (1985). *Listening: A practical approach.* Glenview, IL: Scott, Foresman.

Floyd, K., & Mikkelson, A. C. (2005). In *The sourcebook of nonverbal measures: Going beyond words* (pp. 47–56), V. Manusov (ed.). Mahwah, NJ: Erlbaum.

Folger, J. P., Poole, M. S., & Stutman, R. K. (2009). *Working through conflict: A communication perspective,* 6th ed. Boston, MA: Allyn & Bacon.

Folger, J. P., Poole, M. S., & Stutman, R. K. (2016). *Working through conflict: Strategies for relationships, groups, and organizations.* (7th ed.). London: Routledge.

Forbes, G. B. (2001). College students with tattoos and piercings: Motives, family experiences, personality factors, and perception by others. *Psychological Reports* 89, 774–786.

Ford, S. (2003). "Dear Mr. Shawn": A lesson in e-mail pragmatics (netiquette). *TESOL Journal* 12 (spring), 39–40.

Foster, D. (2004). Standing on ceremony. *National Geographic Traveler* 21 (May–June), 97–99.

Fox, A. B., Bukatki, D., Hallahan, M., & Crawford, M. (2007). The medium makes a difference: Gender similarities and differences in instant messaging. *Journal of Language and Social Psychology* 26, 389–397.

Franklin, C. W., & Mizell, C. A. (1995). Some factors influencing success among African-American men: A preliminary study. *Journal of Men's Studies* 3, 191–204.

Franklin, R. (2002). Office romances: Conduct unbecoming? *Business Week Online* (February 14), np.

Fraser, B. (1990). Perspectives on politeness. *Journal of Pragmatics* 14, 219–236.

Freedman, J. (1978). *Happy people: What happiness is, who has it, and why.* New York, NY: Ballantine.

French, J. R. P., Jr., & Raven, B. (1968). The bases of social power. In *Group dynamics: Research and theory*, 3rd ed. (pp. 259–269), D. Cartwright & A. Zander (eds.). New York, NY: Harper & Row.

Frentz, T. (1976). A general approach to episodic structure. Paper presented at the Western Speech Association Convention, San Francisco. Cited in Reardon (1987).

Friedman, J., Boumil, M. M., & Taylor, B. E. (1992). *Sexual harassment.* Deerfield Beach, FL: Health Communications, Inc.

Frith, H., & Gleeson, K. (2004). Clothing and embodiment: Men managing body image and appearance. *Psychology of Men and Masculinity* 5(1), 40–48.

Frone, M. R. (2000). Interpersonal conflict at work and psychological outcomes: Testing a model among young workers. *Journal of Occupational Health Psychology* 5, 246–255.

Fu, H., Watkins, D., & Hui, E. K. P. (2004). Personality correlates of the disposition towards interpersonal forgiveness: Chinese perspective. *International Journal of Psychology* 39 (August), 305–316.

Fukushima, S. (2000). *Requests and culture: Politeness in British English and Japanese.* New York: Peter Lang.

Fuller, D. (2004). Electronic manners and netiquette. *Athletic Therapy Today* 9 (March), 40–41.

Furlow, F. B. (1996). The smell of love. *Psychology Today* 29, 38–45.

G

Galinsky, A. D., Kilduff, G. J. (2013). Be seen as a leader: A simple exercise can boost your status and influence. *Harvard Business Review* 91, 127–130.

Galvin, K., Braithwaite, D., & Byland, C. L. (2015). *Family communication: Cohesion and change* (9th ed.). New York, NY: Taylor & Francis.

Galvin, K. M., Bylund, C. L., & Brommel, B. J. (2008). *Family communication: Cohesion and change*, 7th ed. Boston, MA: Allyn & Bacon.

Gamble, T. K., & Gamble, M. W. (2003). *The gender communication connection.* Boston, MA: Houghton Mifflin.

Gamble, T. K., & Gamble, M. W. (2014). *The gender communication connection.* Armonk, NY: M. E. Sharp.

Gamson, J. (1998). Publicity traps: Television talk shows and lesbian, gay, bisexual, and transgender visibility. *Sexualities* 1 (February), 11–41.

Gao, G., & Gudykunst, W. B. (1995). Attributional confidence, perceived similarity, and network involvement in Chinese and American romantic relationships. *Communication Quarterly* 43, 431–445.

Gattis, K. S., Berns, S., Simpson, L. E., & Christensen, A. (2004). Birds of a feather or strange birds? Ties among personality dimensions, similarity, and marital quality. *Journal of Family Psychology* 18 (December), 564–574.

Gelfand, M. J., Nishii, L. H., Holcombe, K. M., Dyer, N., Ohbuchi, K., & Fukuno, M. (2001). Cultural influences on cognitive representations of conflict: Interpretations of conflict episodes in the United States and Japan. *Journal of Applied Psychology* 86, 1059–1074.

Gelles, R., & Cornell, C. (1985). *Intimate violence in families.* Thousand Oaks, CA: Sage.

Gentry, W. A., Weber, T. J., & Golnaz, S. (2007). *Empathy in the workplace: A tool for effective leadership.* Center for Creative Leadership. Retrieved December 24, 2013, from http://www.ccl.org/leadership/pdf/research/EmpathyInTheWorkplace.pdf

Georgas, J., Mylonas, K., Bafiti, T., & Poortinga, Y. H. (2001). Functional relationships in the nuclear and extended family: A 16-culture study. *International Journal of Psychology* 36, 289–300.

George, J. F., & Robb, A. (2008). Deception and computer-mediated communication in daily life. *Communication Reports* 21, 92–103.

Gergen, K. J., Greenberg, M. S., and Willis, R. H. (1980). *Social exchange: Advances in theory and research.* New York, NY: Plenum Press.

Gibb, J. (1961). Defensive communication. *Journal of Communication* 11, 141–148.

Gibbs, J., Ellison, N., & Heino, R. (2006). Self-presentation in online personals: The role of anticipated future interaction, self-disclosure, and perceived success in Internet dating. *Communication Research* 33 (2), 152.

Gibbs, N. (2005). Parents behaving badly. *Time* (February 21), 40–49.

Giles, D. C. (2001). Parasocial interaction: A review of the literature and a model for future research. *Media Psychology* 4, 279–305.

Giles, D. C., & Maltby, J. (2004). The role of media figures in adolescent development: Relations between autonomy, attachment, and interest in celebrities. *Personality and Individual Differences* 36 (March), 813–822.

Giles, H. (2008). Communication accommodation theory. In *Engaging theories in interpersonal communication: Multiple perspectives* (pp. 161–174), L. A. Baxter & D. O. Braithwaite (eds.). Los Angeles, CA: Sage.

Giles, H., & Ogay, T. (2007). In *Explaining communication: Contemporary theories and exemplars* (pp. 293–310), B. B. Whaley, & W. Samter (eds.). Mahwah, NJ: Erlbaum.

GLAAD Media Reference Guide, 2016 (http://www.glaad.org/sites/default/files/GLAAD-Media-Reference-Guide-Tenth-Edition.pdf).

Gladstone, G. L., & Parker, G. B. (2002). When you're smiling, does the whole world smile with you? *Australasian Psychiatry* 10 (June), 144–146.

Goffman, E. (1967). *Interaction ritual: Essays on face-to-face behavior.* New York, NY: Pantheon.

Goffman, E. (1971). *Relations in public: Microstudies of the public order*. New York, NY: Harper Colophon.

Goldin-Meadow, S., Nusbaum, H., Kelly, S. D., & Wagner, S. (2001). Gesture—psychological aspects. *Psychological Science* 12, 516–522.

Goldsmith, D. J. (2007). Brown and Levinson's politeness theory. In *Explaining communication: Contemporary theories and exemplars* (pp. 219–236), B. B. Whaley & W. Samter (eds.). Mahwah, NJ: Erlbaum.

Goldsmith, D. J. (2008). Politeness theory. In *Engaging theories in interpersonal communication: Multiple perspectives* (pp. 255–268), L. A. Baxter & D. O. Braithwaite (eds.). Los Angeles, CA: Sage.

Goldsmith, D. J., & Fulfs, P. A. (1999). "You just don't have the evidence": An analysis of claims and evidence. In *Communication yearbook, 22* (pp. 1–49), M. E. Roloff (ed.). Thousand Oaks, CA: Sage.

Goldstein, N. J., Martin, S. J., & Cialdini, R. B. (2008). *Yes! 50 scientifically proven ways to be persuasive*. New York, NY: Free Press.

Goleman, D. (1992). Studies find no disadvantage in growing up in a gay home. *New York Times* (December 2), C14.

Goleman, D. (1995a). *Emotional intelligence*. New York, NY: Bantam.

Goleman, D. (1995b). For man and beast, language of love shares many traits. *New York Times* (February 14), C1, C9.

Goleman, D. (2013a). Rich people just care less. *New York Times* (October 5), Opinionator, http://opinionator.blogs.nytimes.com/2013/10/05rich-people-just-care-less/

Goleman, D. (2013b). The focused leader. *Harvard Business Review* 91 (December), 51–60.

Gonzaga, G. C., Keltner, D., Londahl, E. A., & Smith, M. D. (2001). Love and the commitment problem in romantic relationships and friendships. *Journal of Personality and Social Psychology* 81 (August), 247–262.

Gonzalez, A., & Zimbardo, P. G. (1985). Time in perspective. *Psychology Today* 19, 20–26.

Goodwin, R., & Findlay, C. (1997). "We were just fated together" . . . Chinese love and the concept of *yuan* in England and Hong Kong. *Personal Relationships* 4, 85–92.

Goodwin, R., & Gaines, S. O., Jr. (2004). Relationships beliefs and relationship quality across cultures: Country as a moderator of dysfunctional beliefs and relationship quality in three former Communist societies. *Personal Relationships* 11 (September), 267–279.

Gordon, A. (2010). Facing up to fatigue. *Psychology Today* (July/August), 29.

Gordon, R. A., Crosnoe, R., & Wang, X. (2014). *Physical attractiveness and the accumulation of social and human capital in adolescence and young adulthood: Assets and distractions*. Hoboken, NJ: Wiley-Blackwell.

Gordon, T. (1975). *P.E.T.: Parent effectiveness training*. New York, NY: New American Library.

Gosling, S. D., Ko, S. J., Mannarelli, T., & Morris, M. E. (2002). A room with a cue: Personality judgments based on offices and bedrooms. *Journal of Personality and Social Psychology* 82 (March), 379–398.

Gottman, J. M., & Carrere, S. (1994). Why can't men and women get along? Developmental roots and marital inequities. In D. J. Canary and L. Stafford (eds.). *Communication and relational maintenance* (pp. 203–229), San Diego, CA: Academic Press.

Gottman, J. M., & Levenson, R. W. (1999). Dysfunctional marital conflict: Women are being unfairly blamed. *Journal of Divorce and Remarriage* 31, 1–17.

Gould, S. J. (1995). No more "wretched refuse." *New York Times* (June 7), A27.

Grace, S. L., & Cramer, K. L. (2003). The elusive nature of self-measurement: The self-construal scale versus the twenty statements test. *Journal of Social Psychology* 143 (October), 649–668.

Graham, E. E., Barbato, C. A., & Perse, E. M. (1993). The interpersonal communication motives model. *Communication Quarterly* 41, 172–186.

Graham, J. A., & Argyle, M. (1975). The effects of different patterns of gaze, combined with different facial expressions, on impression formation. *Journal of Movement Studies* 1, 178–182.

Graham, J. A., Bitti, P. R., & Argyle, M. (1975). A cross-cultural study of the communication of emotion by facial and gestural cues. *Journal of Human Movement Studies* 1, 68–77.

Graham, J. L. & Hernandez Requejo, W. (2008). *Global negotiation: The new rules*. New York, NY: Macmillan.

Grandey, A. A. (2000). Emotion regulation in the workplace: A new way to conceptualize emotional labor. *Journal of Occupational Health and Psychology* 5 (January), 95–110.

Grant, A. (2013). Why some people have no boundaries online. *The Huffington Post*. Retrieved 8/28/15 from http://www.huffingtonpost.com.

Greene, J. O. (2003). Models of adult communication skill acquisition: Practice and the course of performance improvement. In *Handbook of communication and social interaction skills* (pp. 51–92), J. O. Greene & B. R. Burleson (eds.). Mahwah, NJ: Erlbaum.

Greene, J. O., & Burleson, B. R. (eds.). (2003). *Handbook of communication and social interaction skills*. Mahwah, NJ: Erlbaum.

Greene, K., Derlega, V., & Mathews, A. (2006). Self-disclosure in personal relationships. In *Cambridge Handbook of Personal Relationships* (pp. 409–427) A. L. Vangelisti & D. Perlman (eds.). Cambridge: Cambridge University Press.

Greengross, G., & Miller, G. F. (2008). Dissing oneself versus dissing rivals: Effects of status, personality, and sex on the short-term and long-term attractiveness of self-deprecating and other-deprecating humor. *Evolutionary Psychology* 6, 393–408.

Greif, E. B. (1980). Sex differences in parent-child conversations. *Women's Studies International Quarterly* 3, 253–258.

Greitemeyer, T. (2007). What do men and women want in a partner? Are educated partners always more desirable? *Journal of Experimental Social Psychology* 43 (March), 180–194.

Grice, H. P. (1975). Logic and conversation. In *Syntax and semantics, Vol. 3, Speech acts* (pp. 41–58), P. Cole & J. L. Morgan (eds.). New York, NY: Seminar Press.

Grobart, S. (2007, January). Allow me to introduce myself (properly). *Money, 36,* 40–41.

Gross, S. J. (2006). How to raise your self-esteem. *Psych Central*. Retrieved December 28, 2013, from http://psychcentral.com/lib/how-to-raise-your-self-esteem/000737

Gross, T., Turner, E., & Cederholm, L. (1987). Building teams for global operation, *Management Review* (June), 32–36.

Guéguen, N. (2003). Help on the Web: The effect of the same first name between the sender and the receptor in a request made by e-mail. *Psychological Record* 53 (summer), 459–466.

Guéguen, N., & Fischer-Lokou, J. (2004). Hitchhikers smiles and receipt of help. *Psychological Reports* 94, 756–760.

Guéguen, N., & Jacob, C. (2004). The effect of touch on tipping: An evaluation in a French bar. *International Journal of Hospitality Management* 24 (June), 295–299.

Gu, Y. (1990). Polite phenomena in modern Chinese. *Journal of Pragmatics* 14, 237–257.

Gudykunst, W. B. (1989). Culture and the development of interpersonal relationships. In *Communication yearbook 12* (pp. 315–354), J. A. Anderson (ed.). Thousand Oaks, CA: Sage.

Gudykunst, W. B. (1991). *Bridging differences: Effective intergroup communication.* Newbury Park, CA: Sage.

Gudykunst, W. B. (1993). Toward a theory of effective interpersonal and intergroup communication: An anxiety/uncertainty management (AUM) perspective. In *Intercultural communication competence*, R. L. Wiseman (ed.). Thousand Oaks, CA: Sage.

Gudykunst, W. B. (1994). *Bridging differences: Effective intergroup communication,* 2nd ed. Thousand Oaks, CA: Sage.

Gudykunst, W. B., & Kim, Y. W. (1992). *Communicating with strangers: An approach to intercultural communication,* 2nd ed. New York, NY: Random House.

Gudykunst, W. B., & Ting-Toomey, S. (with Chua, E.) (1988). *Culture and interpersonal communication.* Thousand Oaks, CA: Sage.

Gudykunst, W. B., ed. (1983). *Intercultural communication theory: Current perspectives.* Thousand Oaks, CA: Sage.

Gueguen, N., Fischer-Lokou, J., & Lamy, L. (2013). Compliments and receptivity to a courtship request: A field experiment. *Psychological Reports* 112, 239–242.

Guerin, B. (2003). Combating prejudice and racism: New interventions from a functional analysis of racist language. *Journal of Community and Applied Social Psychology* 13 (January), 29–45.

Guerrero, L. K. (1997). Nonverbal involvement across interactions with same-sex friends, opposite-sex friends, and romantic partners: Consistency or change? *Journal of Social and Personal Relationships* 14, 31–58.

Guerrero, L. K., & Andersen, P. A. (1991). The waxing and waning of relational intimacy: Touch as a function of relational stage, gender and touch avoidance. *Journal of Social and Personal Relationships* 8, 147–165.

Guerrero, L. K., & Hecht, M. L., eds. (2008). *The nonverbal communication reader: Classic and contemporary readings,* 3rd ed. Prospect Heights, IL: Waveland Press.

Guerrero, L. K., Andersen, P. A., & Afifi, W. A. (2007). *Close encounters: Communication in relationships,* 2nd ed. Thousand Oaks, CA: Sage.

Guerrero, L. K., Andersen, P. A., & Afifi, W. A. (2013). *Close encounters: Communication in relationships,* 4th ed. Thousand Oaks, CA: Sage.

Guerrero, L. K., Andersen, P. A., Jorgensen, P. F., Spitzberg, B. H., & Eloy, S. V. (1995). Coping with the green-eyed monster: Conceptualizing and measuring communicative response to romantic jealousy. *Western Journal of Communication* 59, 270–304.

Guerrero, L. K., Eloy, S. V., & Wabnik, A. I. (1993). Linking maintenance strategies to relationship development and disengagement: A reconceptualization. *Journal of Social and Personal Relationships* 10, 273–282.

Guerrero, L. K., Jones, S. M., & Boburka, R. R. (2006). Sex differences in emotional communication. In *Sex differences and similarities in communication*, 2nd ed. (pp. 241–262), K. Dindia & D. J. Canary (eds.). Mahwah, NJ: Erlbaum.

Gunaydin, G., Selcuk, E., & Zayas, V. (2017). Impressions based on a portrait predict, 1-month later, impressions following a live interaction. *Social Psychological and Personal Sciences* 8, 36–44.

H

Haake, M., Hansson, K., Gulz, A., Schötz, S, & Sahlén, B. (2013). The slower the better? Does the speaker's speech rate influence children's performance on a language comprehension test? International Journal of Speech-Language Pathology 16, 181-190.

Hochschild, A.R. (1983). The managed heart: Commercialization of human feeling. Berkeley: University of California Press.

HBR Spotlight. (2013). Women in the workplace: A research roundup. *Harvard Business Review* 91 (September), 89.

Haar, B. F., & Krabe, B. (1999). Strategies for resolving interpersonal conflicts in adolescence: A German-Indonesian comparison. *Journal of Cross-Cultural Psychology* 30, 667–683.

Haferkamp, N., Eimler, S. C., Papadakis, A., & Kruck, J. V. (2012). Men Are from Mars, Women Are from Venus? Examining gender differences in self-presentation on social networking sites. *Cyberpsychology, Behavior, and Social Networking.* February 2012, 15(2): 91–98. doi:10.1089/cyber.2011.0151

Haga, Y. (1988). Traits de langage et caractère japonais. *Cahiers de Sociologie* Économique et Culturelle 9, 105–109.

Haidar-Yassine, H. (2002). Internet friendships: Can virtual be real? *Dissertation Abstracts International: Section B: The Sciences & Engineering* 63 (5-B), 2651.

Hall, E. T. (1959). *The silent language.* Garden City, NY: Doubleday.

Hall, E. T. (1963). System for the notation of proxemic behavior. *American Anthropologist* 65, 1003–1026.

Hall, E. T. (1966). *The hidden dimension.* Garden City, NY: Doubleday.

Hall, E. T. (1976). *Beyond culture.* Garden City, NY: Anchor Press.

Hall, E. T., & Hall, M. R. (1987). *Hidden differences: Doing business with the Japanese.* New York, NY: Anchor Books.

Hall, J. A. (1984). *Nonverbal sex differences.* Baltimore, MD: Johns Hopkins University Press.

Hall, J. A. (2006). Women's and men's nonverbal communication: Similarities, differences, stereotypes, and origins.

In *The Sage handbook of nonverbal communication* (pp. 201–218), V. Manusov & M. L. Patterson (eds.). Thousand Oaks, CA: Sage.

Hall, J. K. (1993). Tengo una bomba: The paralinguistic and linguistic conventions of the oral practice Chismeando. *Research on Language and Social Interaction* 26, 55–83.

Hamilton, D. R. (2011). Emotional contagion: Are your feelings "infecting" others? *HuffPost Healthy Living*. Retrieved from http://www.huffingtonpost.com/david-r-hamilton-phd/emotional-contagion_b_863197.html

Hamlin, J. K., Wynn, K., & Bloom, P. (2007). Babies prefer helpful to unhelpful social types. *Nature* 450 (November), 557–559.

Hample, D. (2004). Arguing skills. In *Handbook of communication and social interaction skills* (pp. 439–477), J. O. Greene & B. R. Burleson (eds.). Mahwah, NJ: Erlbaum.

Han, S., & Shavitt, S. (1994). Persuasion and culture: Advertising appeals in individualistic and collectivistic societies. *Journal of Experimental Social Psychology* 30, 326–350.

Haney, W. (1973). *Communication and organizational behavior: Text and cases*, 3rd ed. Homewood, IL: Irwin.

Harris, C. R. (2003). A review of sex differences in sexual jealousy, including self-report data, psychophysiological responses, interpersonal violence, and morbid jealousy. *Personality and Social Psychology Review* 7, 102–128.

Harris, M. (1993). *Culture, people, nature: An introduction to general anthropology*, 6th ed. Boston, MA: Allyn & Bacon.

Hart Research Associates. (2010). Raising the bar: Employers' views on college learning in the wake of the economic downturn: A survey among employers conducted on behalf of the Association of American Colleges and Universities. Washington, DC.

Hart, F. (1990). The construction of masculinity in men's friendships: Misogyny, heterosexism and homophobia. *Resources for Feminist Research* 19, 60–67.

Hart, R. P., Carlson, R. E., & Eadie, W. F. (1980). Attitudes toward communication and the assessment of rhetorical sensitivity. *Communication Monographs* 47, 1–22.

Harvey, J. H., Flanary, R., & Morgan, M. (1986). Vivid memories of vivid loves gone by. *Journal of Social and Personal Relationships* 3, 359–373.

Harvey, J. C., & Katz, C. (1985). *If I'm So Successful, Why Do I Feel Like a Fake: The Impostor Phenomenon*. New York, NY: St. Martin's Press.

Hasart, J. K., & Hutchinson, K. L. (1993). The effects of eyeglasses on perceptions of interpersonal attraction. *Journal of Social Behavior and Personality* 8, 521–528.

Hasegawa, T., & Gudykunst, W. B. (1998). Silence in Japan and the United States. *Journal of Cross-Cultural Psychology* 29, 668–684.

Hatfield, E., & Rapson, R. L. (1996). *Love and sex: Cross-cultural perspectives*. Boston, MA: Allyn & Bacon.

Hatfield, E., & Rapson, R. L. (2007). Equity theory. In *Encyclopedia of Social Psychology*, R. Baumeister & K. D. Vohs (eds.). Los Angeles: Sage.

Haugh, M. (2004). Revisiting the conceptualization of politeness in English and Japanese. *Multilingua* 23, 85–109.

Havlena, W. J., Holbrook, M. B., & Lehmann, D. R. (1989). Assessing the validity of emotional typologies. *Psychology and Marketing* 6 (summer), 97–112.

Hayakawa, S. I., & Hayakawa, A. R. (1989). *Language in thought and action*, 5th ed. New York, NY: Harcourt Brace Jovanovich.

Hays, R. B. (1989). The day-to-day functioning of close versus casual friendships. *Journal of Social and Personal Relationships* 6, 21–37.

Heasley, J. B. S., Babbitt, C. E., & Burbach, H. J. (1995). The role of social context in students' anticipatory reaction to a "fighting word." *Sociological Focus* 27, 281–283.

Heath, W. P., Stone, J., Darley, J. M., & Grannemann, B. D. (2003). Yes, I did it, but don't blame me: Perceptions of excuse defenses. *Journal of Psychiatry and Law* 31 (summer), 187–226.

Hecht, M. L., Jackson, R. L., & Ribeau, S. (2003). *African American communication: Exploring identity and culture*, 2nd ed. Mahwah, NJ: Erlbaum.

Heidel, J. A. (2017). Romance in the workplace: The good, the bad, and the ugly. *Career Intelligence.com* [http://career-intelligence.com/romance-in-the-workplace-the-good-the-bad/} Accessed March 11, 2017.

Helgeson, V. S. (2009). *Psychology of gender* (3rd ed.). Upper Saddle River, NJ: Prentice-Hall.

Hellweg, S. A. (1992). Organizational grapevines. In *Readings in organizational communication* (pp. 159–172), K. L. Hutchinson (ed.). Dubuque, IA: William. C. Brown.

Helsper, E., & Whitty, M. (2010) Netiquette within married couples: Agreement about acceptable online behavior and surveillance between partners. *Computers in Human Behavior* 26 (5), 916–926.

Hempel, J., & Berner, R. (2007). File office romance under "ok." *Bloomberg Businessweek* Retrieved from http://www.businessweek.com/debateroom/archives/2007/05/file_office_rom.html

Hendrick, C., & Hendrick, S. (1990). A relationship-specific version of the love attitudes scale. In *Handbook of replication research in the behavioral and social sciences* (special issue), J. W. Heulip (ed.), *Journal of Social Behavior and Personality* 5, 239–254.

Hendrick, C., Hendrick, S., Foote, F. H., & Slapion-Foote, M. J. (1984). Do men and women love differently? *Journal of Social and Personal Relationships* 1, 177–195.

Henley, N. M. (1977). *Body politics: Power, sex, and nonverbal communication.* Upper Saddle River, NJ: Prentice-Hall.

Hensley, W. E. (1996). A theory of the valenced other: The intersection of the looking-glass-self and social penetration. *Social Behavior and Personality* 24, 293–308.

Hertenstein, M. J., Holmes, R., McCullough, M., & Keltner, D. (2009). The communication of emotion via touch. *Emotion* 9, 566–573.

Herz, R. (2008). *The scent of desire: Discovering our enigmatic sense of smell.* New York: Harper Perennial.

Hess, E. H. (1975). *The tell-tale eye.* New York, NY: Van Nostrand Reinhold.

Hess, E. H., Seltzer, A. L., & Schlien, J. M. (1965). Pupil response of hetero- and homosexual males to pictures of men and women: A pilot study. *Journal of Abnormal Psychology* 70, 165–168.

Hess, U., Kappas, A., McHugo, G. J., Lanzetta, J. T., et al. (1992). The facilitative effect of facial expression on the self-generation of emotion. *International Journal of Psychophysiology* 12, 251–265.

Hewitt, J. P. (1998). *The myth of self-esteem: Finding happiness and solving problems in America.* New York, NY: St. Martin's Press.

Hewitt, J. P., & Stokes, R. (1975). Disclaimers. *American Sociological Review* 40, 1–11.

Hewlett, S. A., Marshall, M., & Sherbin, L. (2013). How diversity can drive innovation. *Harvard Business Review* https://hbr.org/2013/12/how-diversity-can-drive-innovation.

Hilton, L. (2000). They heard it through the grapevine. *South Florida Business Journal* 21 (August), 53.

Hilbrand, S., Coall, D. A., Gerstorf, D., & Hertwig, R. (2016). Caregiving within and beyond the family is associated with lower mortality for the caregiver: A prospective study. *Evolution and Human Behavior* DOI: http://dx.doi.org/10.1016/j.evolhumbehav.2016.11.010.

Hinduja, S., & Patchin, J. W. (2010). Cyberbullying: Identification, prevention, and response. Retrieved from http://www.cyberbullying.us

Hirofumi, A. (2003). Closeness and interpersonal outcomes in same-sex friendships: An improvement of the investment model and explanation of closeness. *Japanese Journal of Experimental Social Psychology* 42 (March), 131–145.

Hocker, J. L., & Wilmot, W. W. (2007). *Interpersonal conflict*, 7th ed. New York, NY: McGraw Hill.

Hoffmann, G. (2005). Rhetoric of Bush speeches: Purr words and snarl words. *Etc: A Review of General Semantics* 62 (April), 198–201.

Hofstede, G. (1983). National culture revisited. *Behavior Science Research* 18, 285–305.

Hofstede, G. (1997). *Cultures and organizations: Software of the mind.* New York, NY: McGraw-Hill.

Hofstede, G. (2000). Masculine and feminine cultures. *Encyclopedia of psychology,* Vol. 5 (pp. 115–118), A. E. Kazdin (ed.). Washington, DC: American Psychological Association and Oxford University Press.

Hofstede, G., ed. (1998). *Masculinity and femininity: The taboo dimension of national cultures.* Thousand Oaks, CA: Sage.

Hofstede, G., Hofstede, G. J., & Minkov, M. (2010). *Cultures and organizations: Software of the mind.* 3rd ed. New York, NY: McGraw-Hill.

Hogue, M. E., McDuff, D. J., & Picard, R. W. (2012). Exploring temporal patterns in classifying frustrated and delighted smiles. *IEEE Transactions on Affective Computing.*

Hoft, N. L. (1995). *International technical communication: How to export information about high technology.* New York, NY: Wiley.

Holden, J. M. (1991). The most frequent personality priority pairings in marriage and marriage counseling. *Individual Psychology Journal of Adlerian Theory, Research, and Practice* 47, 392–398.

Hollenbaugh, E. E., & Everett, M. K. (2013). The effects of anonymity on self-disclosure in blogs: An application of the online disinhibition effect. *Journal of Computer-Mediated Communication* 18, 283–302. doi: 10.1111/jcc4.12008

Holley, S. R., Haase, C. M., & Levenson, R. W. (2013). Age-related changes in demand-withdrawal communication behaviors. *Journal of Marriage and Family* 75 (4), 822–836. doi 10.1111/jomf.12051

Holmes, J. (1995). *Women, men and politeness.* New York, NY: Longman.

Hopper, R., Knapp, M. L., & Scott, L. (1981). Couples' personal idioms: Exploring intimate talk. *Journal of Communication* 31, 23–33.

Hornsey, J. J., Bath, M. T., & Gunthorpe, S. (2004). "You can criticize because you care": Identity attachment, constructiveness, and the intergroup sensitivity effect. *European Journal of Social Psychology* 34 (September–October), 499–518.

Hosman, L. A. (1989). The evaluative consequences of hedges, hesitations, and intensifiers: Powerful and powerless speech styles. *Human Communication Research* 15, 383–406.

How Americans Communicate (1999). Retrieved from http://www.natcom.org/Research/Roper/how_Americans_communicate.htm

How interpersonal power affects empathic accuracy: Differential roles of mentalizing vs. mirroring? *Frontiers in Human Neuroscience* 7 (July 19). doi: 10.3389/fnhum.2013.00375. Retrieved December 24, 2013, from http://www.ncbi.nlm.nih.gov/pmc/articles/PMC3715694/

Howard, P. E. N., Rainie, L., & Jones, S. (2001). Days and nights on the Internet: The impact of a diffusing technology. *American Behavioral Scientist* 45, 383–404.

Hu, Y., Wood, J. F., Smith, V., & Westbrook, N. (2004). Friendships through IM: Examining the relationship between instant messaging and intimacy. *Journal of Computer-Mediated Communication* 10 (November), np.

Huang, C. L., & Yang, S. C. (2013). A Study of online misrepresentation, self-disclosure, cyber-relationship motives, and loneliness among teenagers in Taiwan. *Journal of Educational Computing Research* 48, 1–18.

Hughes, S. M., Mogilski, J. K., & Harrison, M. A. (2014). The perception and parameters of intentional voice manipulation. *Journal of Nonverbal Behavior,* 38 (1), 107-127.

Hunt, M. O. (2000). Status, religion, and the "belief in a just world": Comparing African Americans, Latinos, and whites. *Social Science Quarterly* 81 (March), 325–343.

Hurley, D. (2014). Breathing in vs. spacing out: Is mindfulness always best? *New York Times Magazine* (January 19), 14–15.

Huston, M., & Schwartz, P. (1995). The relationships of lesbians and gay men. In *Under-studied relationships: Off the beaten track* (pp. 89–121), J. T. Wood, & S. Duck (eds.). Thousand Oaks, CA: Sage.

I

Imwalle, D. B., & Schillo, K. K. (2004). Masculinity and femininity: The taboo dimension of national cultures. *Archives of Sexual Behavior* 33 (April), 174–176.

Infante, D. A. (1988). *Arguing constructively.* Prospect Heights, IL: Waveland Press.

Infante, D. A., & Rancer, A. S. (1982). A conceptualization and measure of argumentativeness. *Journal of Personality Assessment* 46, 72–80.

Infante, D. A., & Rancer, A. S. (1996). Argumentativeness and verbal aggressiveness: A review of recent theory and research. In *Communication yearbook 19* (pp. 319–351), B. R. Burleson (ed.). Thousand Oaks, CA: Sage.

Infante, D. A., & Wigley, C. J. (1986). Verbal aggressiveness: An interpersonal model and measure. *Communication Monographs* 53, 61–69.

Infante, D. A., Chandler, T. A., & Rudd, J. E. (1989). Test of an argumentative skill deficiency model of interspousal violence. *Communication Monographs* 56, 163–177.

Infante, D. A., Hartley, K. C., Martin, M. M., Higgins, M. A., Bruning, S. D., & Hur, G. (1992). Initiating and reciprocating verbal aggression: Effects on credibility and credited valid arguments. *Communication Studies* 43, 182–190.

Infante, D. A., Rancer, A. S., & Jordan, F. F. (1996). Affirming and nonaffirming style, dyad sex, and the perception of argumentation and verbal aggression in an interpersonal dispute. *Human Communication Research* 22, 315–334.

Infante, D. A., Rancer, A. S., & Womack, D. F. (2003). *Building communication theory,* 4th ed. Prospect Heights, IL: Waveland Press.

Infante, D. A., Riddle, B. L., Horvath, C. L., & Tumlin, S. A. (1992). Verbal aggressiveness: Messages and reasons. *Communication Quarterly* 40, 116–126.

Infante, D. A., Sabourin, T. C., Rudd, J. E., & Shannon, E. A. (1990). Verbal aggression in violent and nonviolent marital disputes. *Communication Quarterly* 38, 361–371.

Infante, D. A., Rancer, A. S., & Avtgis, T. A. (2010). *Contemporary communication theory.* Dubuque, IA: Kendall Hunt.

Ingegneri, R. (2008). How should you handle tattoos and body piercing during a job interview. http://ezinearticles.com/?expert=Rachel_Ingegneri.

Innis, L. (2013). The Facebook test. *Psychology Today* 46 (December), 19.

Isay, J. (2014). *Secrets and lies: Surviving the truths that change our lives.* New York, NY: Penguin/Random House.

Iverson, J. M., & Goldin-Meadow, S., eds. (1999). *The nature and functions of gesture in children's communication.* San Francisco, CA: Jossey-Bass.

Ivy, D. K., & Backlund, P. (2000). *Exploring gender-speak: Personal effectiveness in gender communication,* 2nd ed. New York, NY: McGraw-Hill.

J

Jörn, R. (2004). How to overcome ethnocentrism: Approaches to a culture of recognition by history in the twenty-first century. *History and Theory* 43 (December), 118–129.

Jack, R. E., Garrod, O. G. B., & Schyns, P. G. (2014). Dynamic facial expressions of emotion transmit an evolving hierarchy of signals over time. *Current Biology* 24, 187–192.

Jackson, L. A., & Ervin, K. S. (1992). Height stereotypes of women and men: The liabilities of shortness for both sexes. *Journal of Social Psychology* 132, 433–445.

Jacobson, D. (1999). Impression formation in cyberspace: Online expectations and offline experiences in text-based virtual communities. *Journal of Computer Mediated Communication* 5, np.

Jain, R. (2010). 4 ways social media is changing your relationships. Retrieved from http://www.socialmediaexaminer.com/4-ways-social-media-is-changing-your-relationships/

Jaksa, J. A., & Pritchard, M. S. (1994). *Communication ethics: Methods of analysis,* 2nd ed. Belmont, CA: Wadsworth.

Jambor, E., & Elliott, M. (2005). Self-esteem and coping strategies among deaf students. *Journal of Deaf Studies and Deaf Education* 10 (winter), 63–81.

Jandt, F. (2016). *An Introduction to Intercultural Communication,* 8th ed. Thousand Oaks, CA: Sage.

Jandt, F. E. (2017). *Conflict and communication.* Thousand Oaks, CA: Sage.

Janus, S. S., & Janus, C. L. (1993). *The Janus report on sexual behavior.* New York, NY: Wiley.

Jaworski, A. (1993). *The power of silence: Social and pragmatic perspectives.* Thousand Oaks, CA: Sage.

Jecker, J., & Landy, D. (1969). Liking a person as a function of doing him a favor. *Human Relations* 22, 371–378.

Jiang, C., & Hancock, J. T. (2013). Absence makes the communication grow fonder: Geographic separation, interpersonal media, and intimacy in dating relationships. *Journal of Communication* 63, 556–577. doi: 10.1111/jcom.12029

Johannesen, R. L. (2001). *Ethics in human communication,* 5th ed. Prospect Heights, IL: Waveland Press.

Johnson, A. J., Wittenberg, E., Villagran, M. M., Mazur, M., & Villagran, P. (2003). Relational progression as a dialectic: Examining turning points in communication among friends. *Communication Monographs* 70 (September), 230–249.

Johnson, C. E. (1987). An introduction to powerful and powerless talk in the classroom. *Communication Education* 36, 167–172.

Johnson, M. P. (1973). Commitment: A conceptual structure and empirical application. *Sociological Quarterly* 14, 395–406.

Johnson, M. P. (1982). Social and cognitive features of the dissolution of commitment to relationships. In *Personal relationships 4: Dissolving personal relationships* (pp. 51–73), S. Duck (ed.). New York, NY: Academic Press.

Johnson, M. P. (1991). Commitment to personal relationships. In *Advances in personal relationships, Vol. 3* (pp. 117–143), W. H. Jones, & D. Perlman (eds.). London: Jessica Kingsley.

Johnson, R. (2017). What are the benefits of effective communication in the workplace? *Chron,* http://smallbusiness.chron.com/benefits-effective-communication-workplace-20198.html, accessed March 11, 1917.

Johnson, S. D., & Bechler, C. (1998). Examining the relationship between listening effectiveness and leadership emergence: Perceptions, behaviors, and recall. *Small Group Research* 29, 452–471.

Johnson, S. M., & O'Connor, E. (2002). *The gay baby boom: The psychology of gay parenthood.* New York, NY: New York University Press.

Joiner, T. E. (1994). Contagious depression: Existence, specificity to depressed symptoms, and the role of reassurance seeking. *Journal of Personality and Social Psychology* 67, 287–296.

Joinson, A. N. (2001). Self-disclosure in computer-mediated communication: The role of self-awareness and visual anonymity. *European Journal of Social Psychology* 31, 177–192.

Jones, B. C., DeBruine, L. M., Little, A. C., Burriss, R. P., & Feinberg, D. R. (2007). Social transmission of face preferences among humans. *Proceedings of the Royal Society* 274 (March 22), 899–903.

Jones, C., Berry, L., & Stevens, C. (2007). Synthesized speech intelligibility and persuasion: Speech rate and non-native listeners. *Computer Speech and Language* 21 (October), 641–651.

Jones, D. (2004). Cupid lurks in cubicles, so what's a worker to do? *USA Today* (April 2), Money Section, 5.

Jones, S. (2005). The touch log record: A behavioral communication measure. In *Applications of nonverbal communication* (pp. 67–82), R. E. Riggio & R. S. Feldman (eds.). Mahwah, NJ: Erlbaum.

Jones, S., & Yarbrough, A. E. (1985). A naturalistic study of the meanings of touch. *Communication Monographs* 52, 19–56.

Joseph, S. (2013). *What doesn't kill us: The new psychology of post-traumatic growth*. New York, NY: Basic Books.

Jourard, S. M. (1968). *Disclosing man to himself*. New York, NY: Van Nostrand Reinhold.

Jourard, S. M. (1971). *Self-disclosure*. New York, NY: Wiley.

Judge, T. A., & Cable, D. M. (2004). The effect of physical height on workplace success and income. *Journal of Applied Psychology* 89, 428–441.

K

Kallos, J. (2005). *Because netiquette matters! Your comprehensive reference guide to e-mail etiquette and proper technology use.* Philadelphia, PA: Xlibris Corporation.

Kanemasa, Y., Taniguchi, J., Daibo, I., & Ishimori, M. (2004). Love styles and romantic love experiences in Japan. *Social Behavior and Personality: An International Journal* 32, 265–281.

Kanner, B. (1989). Color schemes. *New York Magazine* (April 3), 22–23.

Kapoor, S., Wolfe, A., & Blue, J. (1995). Universal values structure and individualism–collectivism: A U.S. test. *Communication Research Reports* 12, 112–123.

Katz, S. (2003). *Down to earth sociology: Introductory readings,* 12th ed. (pp. 313–320), J. W. Henslin (ed.). New York, NY: Free Press.

Kearney, P., Plax, T. G., Richmond, V. P., & McCroskey, J. C. (1984). Power in the classroom IV: Alternatives to discipline. In *Communication Yearbook 8* (pp. 724–746), R. N. Bostrom (ed.). Thousand Oaks, CA: Sage.

Kearney, P., Plax, T. G., Richmond, V. P., & McCroskey, J. C. (1985). Power in the classroom III: Teacher communication techniques and messages. *Communication Education* 34, 19–28.

Keating, C. F. (2006). Why and how the silent self speaks volumes: Functional approaches to nonverbal impression management. In *The Sage handbook of nonverbal communication* (pp. 321–340), V. Manusov & M. L. Patterson (eds.). Thousand Oaks, CA: Sage.

Kellerman, K., & Cole, T. (1994). Classifying compliance gaining messages: Taxonomic disorder and strategic confusion. *Communication Theory* 1, 3–60.

Kennedy-Moore, E., & Watson, J. C. (1999). *Expressing emotion: Myths, realities, and therapeutic strategies.* New York, NY: Guilford Press.

Kennedy, C. W., & Camden, C. T. (1988). A new look at interruptions. *Western Journal of Speech Communication* 47, 45–58.

Kennedy-Moore, E. (2014). Frenemies. *Psychology Today* [https://www.psychologytoday.com/blog/growing-friendships/201404/frenemies]

Kenrick, D. T., Neuberg, S. L., and Cialdini, R. B. (2007). *Social psychology: Goals in interaction,* 4th ed. Boston, MA: Allyn & Bacon.

Keyes, R. (1980). *The height of your life.* New York, NY: Warner Books.

Kim, M., & Sharkey, W. F. (1995). Independent and interdependent construals of self: Explaining cultural patterns of interpersonal communication in multi-cultural organizational settings. *Communication Quarterly* 43, 20–38.

Kim, S. H., & Smith, R. H. (1993). Revenge and conflict escalation. *Negotiation Journal* 9, 37–43.

Kim, Y. Y. (1988). Communication and acculturation. In *Intercultural communication: A reader* (4th ed., pp. 344–354), L. A. Samovar & R. E. Porter (eds.). Belmont, CA: Wadsworth.

Kimberly, C., & Werner-Wilson, R. (2013). From John Lee to John Gottman: Recognizing intra- and interpersonal differences to promote marital satisfaction. *Journal of Human Sciences and Extension* 1, 32–46.

Kindred, J., & Roper, S. L. (2004). Making connections via instant messaging (IM): Student use of IM to maintain personal relationships. *Qualitative Research Reports in Communication* 5, 48–54.

Kirn, W. (2005). It's a glad, sad, mad world. *Time* (January 17), A65–A67.

Kleinke, C. L. (1986). *Meeting and understanding people.* New York, NY: W. H. Freeman.

Kleinke, D. L., & Dean, G. O. (1990). Evaluation of men and women receiving positive and negative responses with various acquaintance strategies. *Journal of Social Behavior and Personality* 5, 369–377.

Kluger, J. (2005). The funny thing about laughter. *Time* (January 17), A25–A29.

Kluger, J. (2008). Why we love. *Time* (January 28), pp. 54–61.

Knapp, M. L. (1978). *Social intercourse: From greeting to goodbye.* Boston, MA: Allyn & Bacon.

Knapp, M. L. (2008). *Lying and deception in human interaction.* Boston, MA: Pearson.

Knapp, M. L., & Hall, J. (2002). *Nonverbal behavior in human interaction,* 3rd ed. New York, NY: Holt, Rinehart & Winston.

Knapp, M. L., Hall, J. A., & Horgan, T. G. (2014). *Nonverbal communication in human interaction,* 8th ed. Boston, MA: Wadsworth.

Knapp, M. L., & Taylor, E. H. (1994). Commitment and its communication in romantic relationships. In *Perspectives on close relationships* (pp. 153–175), A. L. Weber & J. H. Harvey (eds.). Boston, MA: Allyn & Bacon.

Knapp, M. L., Ellis, D., & Williams, B. A. (1980). Perceptions of communication behavior associated with relationship terms. *Communication Monographs* 47, 262–278.

Knapp, M. L., Vangelisti, A., & Caughlin, J. P. (2014). *Interpersonal communication and human relationships,* 7th ed. Boston, MA: Pearson.

Knobloch, L. K., & Carpenter-Theune, K. E. (2004). Topic avoidance in developing romantic relationships. *Communication Research* (April), 173–205.

Knobloch, L. K., & Solomon, D. H. (1999). Measuring the sources and content of relational uncertainty. *Communication Studies* 50 (winter), 261–278.

Knobloch, L. K., & Solomon, D. H. (2005). Measuring conversational equality at the relational level. In *The sourcebook of nonverbal measures: Going beyond words* (pp. 295–304), V. Manusov (ed.). Mahwah, NJ: Erlbaum.

Knobloch, L. K., Haunani, D., & Theiss, J. A. (2006). The role of intimacy in the production and perception of relationship talk within courtship. *Communication Research* 33 (August), 211–241.

Knobloch, L. K., Schmeizer, B. (2008). Using the emotion-in-relationships model to predict features of interpersonal influence attempts. *Communication Monographs* 75, 219–247.

Knox, D., Daniels, V., Sturdivant, L., & Zusman, M. E. (2001). College student use of the Internet for mate selection. *College Student Journal* 35, 158–160.

Kochman, T. (1981). *Black and white: Styles in conflict.* Chicago, IL: University of Chicago Press.

Koerner, A. F., & Fitzpatrick, M. A. (2002). You never leave your family in a fight: The impact of family of origin on conflict behavior in romantic relationships. *Communication Studies* 53 (fall), 234–252.

Koerner, A. F., & Fitzpatrick, M. A. (2004). Communication in intact families. In A. L. Vangelisti (eds), *Handbook of family communication* (pp. 177–195). Mahwah, NJ: Erlbaum.

Koerner, A. F., & Fitzpattrick, M. A. (1997). Family type and conflict: The impact of conversation orientation and conformity orientation on conflict in the family. *Communication Studies,* 48, 59–76.

Koklitz, T. A., & Arkin, R. M. (1982). An impression management interpretation of the self-handicapping strategy. *Journal of personality and Social Psychology* 43, 492–502.

Kollock, P., & Smith, M. (1996). Managing the virtual commons: Cooperation and conflict in computer communities. In *Computer-mediated communication: Linguistic, social, and cross-cultural perspectives* (pp. 109–128), S. Herring (ed.). Amsterdam: John Benjamins.

Konrath, S. (2012). The empathy paradox: Increasing disconnection in the age of increasing connection. In *Handbook of research on technoself: Identity in a technological society* (pp. 204–228), R. Luppicini (ed.). Hershey, PA: IGI Global.

Koppelman, K. L., with Goodhart, R. L. (2005). *Understanding human differences: Multicultural education for a diverse America.* Boston, MA: Allyn & Bacon.

Korda, M. (1975). *Power! How to get it, how to use it.* New York, NY: Ballantine.

Kornrich, S., Brines, J., & Leupp, K. (2012). Egalitarianism, housework, and sexual frequency in marriage. *American Sociological Review* 78, 26–50.

Korobov, N., & Thorne, A. (2006). Intimacy and distancing: Young men's conversations about romantic relationships. *Journal of Adolescent Research* 21, 27–55.

Korzybski, A. (1933). *Science and sanity.* Lakeville, CT: The International Non-Aristotelian Library.

Kouchaki, M., & Smith, I. H. (2013). The morning morality effect: The influence of time of day on unethical behavior. *Psychological Science* 24.

Kposowa, A. J. (2000). Marital status and suicide in the National Longitudinal Mortality Study. *Journal of Epidemiology and Community Health,* 54 (April), 254–261.

Kramer, R. (1997). Leading by listening: An empirical test of Carl Rogers's theory of human relationship using interpersonal assessments of leaders by followers. *Dissertation Abstracts, International Section A. Humanities and Social Sciences* 58, 514.

Kraut, R., Patterson, M., Lundmarle, V., Kiesler, S., Mukopadhyay, & Scherlis, W. (1999). Internet paradox. *American Psychologist* 53, 1017–1031.

Kreamer, A. (2011). *It's always personal.* New York, NY: Random House.

Krebs, G. L. (1989). *Organizational communication,* 2nd ed. Boston, MA: Allyn & Bacon.

Krippendorff, K. (1993). Major metaphors of communication and some constructivist reflections on their use. *Cybernetics and Human Knowing* 2, 3–25.

Krivonos, P. D., & Knapp, M. L. (1975). Initiating communication: What do you say when you say hello? *Central States Speech Journal* 26, 115–125.

Kroløkke, C., & Sørensen, A. S. (2006). *Gender communication theories and analyses: From silence to performance.* Thousand Oaks, CA: Sage.

Kromberg, J. (2013). The 5 stages of grieving the end of a relationship. Retrieved December 23, 2012, from http://www.psychologytoday.com/blog/inside-out/201309/the-5-stages-grieving-the-end-relationship

Kubler-Ross, E. (1969). *On death and dying: What the dying have to teach doctors, nurses, clergy and their own families.* New York: Simon & Schuster.

Kurdek, L. A. (1994). Areas of conflict for gay, lesbian, and heterosexual couples: What couples argue about influences relationship satisfaction. *Journal of Marriage and the Family* 56, 923–934.

Kurdek, L. A. (1995). Developmental changes in relationship quality in gay and lesbian cohabiting couples. *Developmental Psychology* 31, 86–93.

Kurdek, L. A. (2000). Attractions and constraints as determinants of relationship commitment: Longitudinal evidence from gay, lesbian, and heterosexual couples. *Personal Relationships* 7, 245–262.

Kurdek, L. A. (2004). Are gay and lesbian cohabitating couples really different from heterosexual married couples? *Journal of Marriage and Family,* 66 (November), 880–900.

L

Lachnit, C. (2001). Giving up gossip. *Workforce* 80 (July), 8.

Laing, M. (1993). Gossip: Does it play a role in the socialization of nurses? *Journal of Nursing Scholarship* 25, 37–43.

Lancer, D. (2013). Low self-esteem is learned. *Psych Central*. Retrieved December 28, 2013, from http://psychcentral.com/lib/low-self-esteem-is-learned/00018092

Lane, R. C., Koetting, M. G., & Bishop, J. (2002). Silence as communication in psychodynamic psychotherapy. *Clinical Psychology Review* 22 (September), 1091–1104.

Langer, E. J. (1989). *Mindfulness*. Reading, MA: Addison-Wesley.

Lantz, A. (2001). Meetings in a distributed group of experts: Comparing face-to-face, chat and collaborative virtual environments. *Behaviour and Information Technology* 20, 111–117.

Lanzetta, J. T., Cartwright-Smith, J., & Kleck, R. E. (1976). Effects of nonverbal dissimulations on emotional experience and autonomic arousal. *Journal of Personality and Social Psychology* 33, 354–370.

Lapowsky, I. (2014, February). The lost art of tough love. *Inc.*, 46–47.

Laroche, C., & deGrace, G. R. (1997). Factors of satisfaction associated with happiness in adults. *Canadian Journal of Counseling* 31, 275–286.

Larsen, R. J., Kasimatis, M., & Frey, K. (1992). Facilitating the furrowed brow: An unobtrusive test of the facial feedback hypothesis applied to unpleasant affect. *Cognition and Emotion* 6, 321–338.

Latané, B., & Darley, J. M. (1970). *The unresponsive bystander: Why doesn't he help?* New York: Appleton-Century-Crofts.

Lau, I., Chiu, C., & Hong, Y. (2001). I know what you know: Assumptions about others' knowledge and their effects on message construction. *Social Cognition* 19, 587–600.

Lauer, C. S. (2003). Listen to this. *Modern Healthcare* 33 (February 10), 34.

LeVine, R., & Bartlett, K. (1984). Pace of life, punctuality, and coronary heart disease in six countries. *Journal of Cross-Cultural Psychology* 15, 233–255.

LeVine, R., Sato, S., Hashimoto, T., & Verma, J. (1994). Love and marriage in eleven cultures. Unpublished manuscript. California State University, Fresno. Cited in Hatfield & Rapson (1996).

Lea, M., & Spears, R. (1995). Love at first byte? Building personal relationships over computer networks. In *Understudied relationships: Off the beaten track* (pp. 197–233), J. T. Wood & S. Duck (eds.). Thousand Oaks, CA: Sage.

Leathers, D., & Eaves, M. H. (2008). *Successful nonverbal communication: Principles and applications*, 4th ed. Boston, MA: Allyn & Bacon.

Leavitt, H. J. (2005). *Top down: Why hierarchies are here to stay and how to manage them more effectively*. Cambridge, MA: Harvard Business School Publishing.

Lederer, W. J. (1984). *Creating a good relationship*. New York, NY: Norton.

Lee, H. O., & Boster, F. J. (1992). Collectivism-individualism in perceptions of speech rate: A cross-cultural comparison. *Journal of Cross-Cultural Psychology* 23, 377–388.

Lee, J. (2005). Romance beckons (in case you missed it). *New York Times* (February 23), B4.

Lee, J. A. (1976). *The colors of love*. New York, NY: Bantam.

Lee, J. A. (1988). Forbidden colors of love: Patterns of love and gay liberation. In *Gay relationships* (pp. 11–32), J. P. DeCecco (ed.). San Francisco, CA: Haworth Press.

Lee, R. M. (2005). Resilience against discrimination: Ethnic identity and other-group orientation as protective factors for Korean Americans. *Journal of Counseling Psychology* 52 (January), 36–44.

Lee, T. M. C., Liu, H. L., Tan, L. H., Chan, C. C. H., Mahankali, S., Feng, C. M., et al. (2002). Lie detection by functional magnetic resonance imaging. *Human Brain Mapping* 15, 157–164.

Leech, G. (1983). *Principles of pragmatics*. London: Longman.

Lemonick, M. D. (2005a). A smile doesn't always mean happy. *Time* (January 17), A29.

Lemonick, M. D. (2005b). Stealth attack on evaluation. *Time* (January 31), 53–54.

Lenhart, A. (2007). Cyberbullying. Pew Research Internet Project. Retrieved from http://www.pewinternet.org/2007/06/27/cyberbullying/

Lenhart, A., & Madden, M. (2007). Social networking websites and teens: An overview. *Pew Internet & American Life Project*. Retrieved from www.pewinternet.org

Lenhart, A., Ling, R., Campbell, S., & Purcell, K. (2010). Teens and mobile phones. Pew Research Internet Project. Retrieved from http://www.pewinternet.org/2010/04/20/teens-and-mobile-phones/

Lenhart, A., Madden, M., Macgill, A. R., & Smith, A. (2007). Teens and social media: The use of social media gains a greater foothold in teen life as they embrace the conversational nature of interaction online media. *Pew Internet & American Life Project*. Retrieved from http://www.pewinternet.org

Leon, J. J., Philbrick, J. L., Parra, F., Escobedo, E., et al. (1994). Love styles among university students in Mexico. *Psychological Reports* 74, 307–310.

Leonhardt, D. (2011). A better way to measure Twitter influence. *New York Times Magazine* (March, 27), 18.

Leung, K. (1987). Some determinants of reactions to procedural models for conflict resolution: A cross-national study. *Journal of Personality and Social Psychology* 53, 898–908.

Leung, S. A. (2001). Editor's introduction. *Asian Journal of Counseling* 8, 107–109.

Lev-Ari, S. & Keysar, B. (2010). Why don't we believe non-native speakers? The influence of accent on credibility. *Journal of Experimental Social Psychology*, 46, 1093–1096.

Levine, D. (2000). Virtual attraction: What rocks your boat. *CyberPsychology and Behavior* 3, 565–573.

Levine, M. (2004). Tell the doctor all your problems, but keep it to less than a minute. *New York Times* (June 1), F6.

Levine, T. R., Beatty, M. J., Limon, S., Hamilton, M. A., Buck, R., & Chory-Assad, R. M. (2004). The dimensionality of the verbal aggressiveness scale. *Communication Monographs* 71 (September), 245–268.

Levine, T. R., Kim, R. K., Park, H. S., & Hughes, M. (2006). Deception detection accuracy is a predictable linear function of message veracity base-rate: A formal test of Park and Levine's probability model. *Communication Monographs* 73, 243–260.

Levine, T. R., Serota, K. B., Carey, F., & Messer, D. (2013). Teenagers lie a lot: A further investigation into the prevalence of lying. *Communication Research Reports* 30, 211–220.

Lewin, K. (1947). *Human relations.* New York, NY: Harper & Row.

Lewick, R. J., Polin, B., Lount, Jr., R. B. (2016). An exploration of the structure of effective apologies. http://www.spring.org.uk/2016/04/how-to-make-perfect-apology.php.

Lewis, D. (1989). *The secret language of success.* New York, NY: Carroll & Graf.

Lewis, P. H. (1995). The new Internet gatekeepers. *New York Times* (November 13), D1, D6.

Li, H. Z. (1999). Communicating information in conversations: A cross-cultural comparison. *International Journal of Intercultural Relations* 23 (May), 387–409.

Li, M., Li, J, Cham, D. K. S., & Zhang, B. (2016). When love meets money: priming the possession of money influences mating strategies. Front. Psychol., 21, March 206. http://dx.doi.org/a0.3389/fpsyg.2016.00387

Lindblom, K. (2001). Cooperating with Grice: A cross-disciplinary metaperspective on uses of Grice's cooperative principle. *Journal of Pragmatics* 33, 1601–1623.

Lindeman, M., Harakka, T., & Keltikangas-Jarvinen, L. (1997). Age and gender differences in adolescents' reactions to conflict situations: Aggression, prosociality, and withdrawal. *Journal of Youth and Adolescence* 26, 339–351.

Lindová J, Little, A. C, Havlíček, J., Roberts, S. C., Rubešová, A., & Flegr, J. (2016). Effect of partnership status on preferences for facial self-resemblance, *Frontiers in Psychology*, 7:869. doi: 10.3389/fpsyg.2016.00869

Loftus, E. F. (2004). Memories of things unseen. *Current Directions in Psychological Science* 13, 145–147.

Losee, S., & Olen, H. (2007). *Office mate: Your employee handbook for finding—and managing—romance on the job.* New York, NY: Adams Media.

Lount, R. B., Jr., Zhong, C. B., Sivanathan, N., & Murnighan, J. K. (2008). Getting off on the wrong foot: The timing of a breach and the restoration of trust. *Personality and Social Psychology Bulletin*, 34, 1601–1612.

Lu, L., & Shih, J. B. (1997). Sources of happiness: A qualitative approach. *Journal of Social Psychology* 137, 181–188.

Lubin, J. S. (2004). How to stop the snubs that demoralize you and your colleagues. *Wall Street Journal* (December 7), B1.

Luft, J. (1984). *Group processes: An introduction to group dynamics,* 3rd ed. Palo Alto, CA: Mayfield.

Lukens, J. (1978). Ethnocentric speech. *Ethnic Groups* 2, 35–53.

Lurie, A. (1983). *The language of clothes.* New York, NY: Vintage.

Luscombe, B. (2008). Why we flirt. *Time* (January 28), 62–65.

Lustig, M. W., & Koester, J. (2010). *Intercultural competence: Interpersonal communication across cultures,* 7th ed. Boston, MA: Allyn & Bacon.

Lustig, M. W., Koester, J., & Halualani, R. (2018). *Intercultural competence: Interpersonal communication across cultures,* 8th ed. Hoboken, NJ: Pearson.

Lyman, S. M., & Scott, M. B. (1967). Territoriality: A neglected sociological dimension. *Social Problems* 15, 236–249.

Lyons, A., & Kashima, Y. (2003). How are stereotypes maintained through communication? The influence of stereotype sharedness. *Journal of Personality and Social Psychology* 85 (December), 989–1005.

M

Ma, K. (1996). *The modern Madame Butterfly: Fantasy and reality in Japanese cross-cultural relationships.* Rutland, VT: Charles E. Tuttle.

MacLachlan, J. (1979). What people really think of fast talkers. *Psychology Today* 13, 113–117.

MacMillan, D., & Lehman, P. (2007, November 15). Social networking with the elite. *Business Week.* Retrieved from www.businessweek.com

Mackey, R. A., Diemer, M. A., & O'Brien, B. A. (2000). Psychological intimacy in the lasting relationships of heterosexual and same-gender couples. *Sex Roles* 43, 201–227.

Madon, S., Guyll, M., & Spoth, R. L. (2004). The self-fulfilling prophecy as an intrafamily dynamic. *Journal of Family Psychology* 18, 459–469.

Mahaffey, A. L., Bryan, A., & Hutchison, K. E. (2005). Using startle eye blink to measure the affective component of antigay bias. *Basic and Applied Social Psychology* 27 (March), 37–45.

Main, F., & Oliver, R. (1988). Complementary, symmetrical, and parallel personality priorities as indicators of marital adjustment. *Individual Psychology Journal of Adlerian Theory, Research, and Practice* 44, 324–332.

Malandro, L. A., Barker, L. L., & Barker, D. A. (1989). *Nonverbal communication,* 2nd ed. New York, NY: Random House.

Manusov, V. (ed.) (2005). *The sourcebook of nonverbal measures: Going beyond words.* Mahwah, NJ: Erlbaum.

Mao, L. R. (1994). Beyond politeness theory: "Face" revisited and renewed. *Journal of Pragmatics* 21, 451–486.

Marano, H. E. (2004). Unconventional wisdom. *Psychology Today* 37 (May/June), 10–11.

Marano, H. E. (2008). The making of a perfectionist. *Psychology Today* 41 (March/April), 80–86.

Marano, H. E. (2014). Love and power. *Psychology Today* 47 (January/February), 54–61, 78.

Marsh, P. (1988). *Eye to eye: How people interact.* Topside, MA: Salem House.

Marshall, E. (1983). *Eye language: Understanding the eloquent eye.* New York, NY: New Trend.

Marshall, L. L., & Rose, P. (1987). Gender, stress, and violence in the adult relationships of a sample of college students. *Journal of Social and Personal Relationships* 4, 229–316.

Marshall, T. C. (2012). Facebook surveillance of former romantic partners: Associations with postbreakup recovery and personal growth. *Cyberpsychology, Behavior, and Social Networking* 15, 521–526. doi: 10.1089/cyber.2012.0125

Marston, P. J., Hecht, M. L., & Robers, T. (1987). True love ways: The subjective experience and communication of romantic love. *Journal of Personal and Social Relationships* 4, 387–407.

Martin, G. N. (1998). Human electroencephalographic (EEG) response to olfactory stimulation: Two experiments using the aroma of food. *International Journal of Psychophysiology* 30, 287–302.

Martin, J. L. (2005). Is power sexy? *American Journal of Sociology* 111 (September), 408–446.

Martin, J. S., & Chaney, L. H. (2008). *Global business etiquette: A guide to international communication and customs.* Westport, CT: Praeger.

Martin, M. M., & Anderson, C. M. (1995). Roommate similarity: Are roommates who are similar in their communication traits more satisfied? *Communication Research Reports* 12, 46–52.

Martin, M. M., & Anderson, C. M. (1998). The cognitive flexibility scale: Three validity studies. *Communication Reports* 11 (winter), 1–9.

Martin, M. M., & Rubin, R. B. (1994). A new measure of cognitive flexibility. *Psychological Reports* 76, 623–626.

Martin, M. M., & Rubin, R. B. (1998). Affinity-seeking in initial interactions. *Southern Communication Journal* 63, 131–143.

Marwell, G., & Schmitt, D. R. (1967). Dimensions of compliance-gaining behavior: An empirical analysis. *Sociometry* 39, 350–364.

Marwell, G., & Schmitt, D. R. (1990). An introduction. In *Seeking compliance: The production of interpersonal influence messages* (pp. 3–5), J. P. Dillard (ed.). Scottsdale, AZ.: Gorsuch Scarisbrick.

Maslow, A., & Mintz, N. L. (1956). Effects of esthetic surroundings: I. Initial effects of three esthetic conditions upon perceiving energy and well-being in faces. *Journal of Psychology* 41, 247–254.

Masuda, T., Ellsworth, P. C., Mesquita, B., Leu, J., Tanida, S., & van de Veerdonk, E. (2008). Placing the face in context: Cultural differences in the perception of facial emotion. *Journal of Personality and Social Psychology* 94, 365–381.

Matsumoto, D. (1991). Cultural influences on facial expressions of emotion. *Southern Communication Journal* 56, 128–137.

Matsumoto, D. (1994). *People: Psychology from a cultural perspective.* Pacific Grove, CA: Brooks/Cole.

Matsumoto, D. (1996). *Culture and psychology.* Pacific Grove, CA: Brooks/Cole.

Matsumoto, D. (2006). Culture and nonverbal behavior. In *The Sage handbook of nonverbal communication* (pp. 219–236), V. Manusov & M. L. Patterson (eds.). Thousand Oaks, CA: Sage.

Matsumoto, D. (2009). Culture and emotional expression. In *Understanding culture: Theory, research, and application* (pp. 263–279), R. S. Wyer, C. Chiu, & Y. Hong (eds.). London: Psychology Press.

Matsumoto, D., & Kudoh, T. (1993). American-Japanese cultural differences in attributions of personality based on smiles. *Journal of Nonverbal Behavior* 17, 231–243.

Matsumoto, D., & Yoo, S. H. (2005). Culture and applied nonverbal communication. In *Applications of nonverbal communication* (pp. 259–277), R. E. Riggio & R. S. Feldman (eds.). Mahwah, NJ: Erlbaum.

Matsumoto, D., Yoo, S. H., Hirayama, S., & Petrova, G. (2005). Development and validation of a measure of display rule knowledge: The display rule assessment inventory. *Emotion* 5, 23–40.

Mawi, N. H. M., Redzuan, M., & Hamsan, H. (2012). Inter-relationship between emotional intelligence and personal trait of educator leaders. *International Journal of Academic Research in Business and Social Sciences* 2, 223-237.

Maynard, H. E. (1963). How to become a better premise detective. *Public Relations Journal* 19, 20–22.

Mayo Clinic Staff (2016). Friendships: Enrich your life and improve your health. http://www.mayoclinic.org/healthy-lifestyle/adult-health/in-depth/friendships/art-20044860 (accessed March 11, 2017).

McBroom, W. H., & Reed, F. W. (1992). Toward a reconceptualization of attitude-behavior consistency. Special Issue. Theoretical advances in social psychology. *Social Psychology Quarterly* 55, 205–216.

McCroskey, J. C. (1998). *Why we communicate the ways we do: A communibiological perspective.* Boston, MA: Allyn & Bacon.

McCroskey, J. C. (2007). *An introduction to rhetorical communication*, 9th ed. Boston, MA: Allyn & Bacon.

McCroskey, J. C., & Wheeless, L. (1976). *Introduction to human communication.* Boston, MA: Allyn & Bacon.

McDevitt, M., Kiousis, S., & Wahl-Jorgensen, K. (2003). Spiral of moderation: Opinion expression in computer-mediated discussion. *International Journal of Public Opinion Research* 15 (winter), 454–470.

McDonald, E. J., McCabe, K., Yeh, M., Lau, A., Garland, A., & Hough, R. L. (2005). Cultural affiliation and self-esteem as predictors of internalizing symptoms among Mexican American adolescents. *Journal of Clinical Child and Adolescent Psychology* 34 (February), 163–171.

McFedries, P. (2010). *Twitter, tips, tricks, and tweets*, 2nd ed. Hoboken, NJ: Wiley.

McGill, M. E. (1985). *The McGill report on male intimacy.* New York, NY: Harper & Row.

McGinley, S. (2000). Children and lying. *The University of Arizona College of Agriculture and Life Sciences* (http://www.ag.arizona.edu/pubs/general/resrpt2000/childrenlying.pdf).

McKelway, D. (2013). Funding for Facebook friends? Retrieved from http://www.foxnews.com/politics/2013/12/17/sen-coburn-wastebook-extravagant-government-spending-amid-claims-cupboard-is/

McLaughlin, M. L. (1984). *Conversation: How talk is organized.* Thousand Oaks, CA: Sage.

McLaughlin, M. L., Cody, M. L., & Robey, C. S. (1980). Situational influences on the selection of strategies to resist compliance-gaining attempts. *Human Communication Research* 1, 14–36.

McNamee, S., & Gergen, K. J., eds. (1999). *Relational responsibility: Resources for sustainable dialogue.* Thousand Oaks, CA: Sage.

McNatt, D. B. (2001). Ancient Pygmalion joins contemporary management: A meta-analysis of the result. *Journal of Applied Psychology* 85, 314–322.

McNulty, J. K., & Russell, V. M. (2010). When "negative" behaviors are positive: A contextual analysis of the long-term effects of problem-solving behaviors on changes in relationship satisfaction. *Journal of Personality and Social Psychology* 98, 587–604.

Mealy, M., Stephan, W., & Urritia, C. (2007). The acceptability of lies: A comparison of Ecuadorians and Euro-Americans. *International Journal of Intercultural Relations* 31, 689–702.

Medora, N. P., Larson, J. H., Hortascu, N., & Dave, P. (2002). Perceived attitudes towards romanticism: A cross-cultural study of American, Asian-Indian, and Turkish young adults. *Journal of Comparative Family Studies*, 33 (spring), 155–178.

Meeks, B. S., Hendrick, S. S., & Hendrick, C. (1998). Communication, love and relationship satisfaction. *Journal of Social and Personal Relationships* 15, 755–773.

Mehl, M. R., Vazire, S., Ramirez-Esparza, N., Slatcher, R. B., & Pennebaker, J. W. (2007). Are women really more talkative than men? *Science* 6 (July), 82.

Mehu, M., Grammer, K., Dunbar, R. I. M. (2007). Smiles when sharing. *Evolution & Human Behavior* 28, 415–422.

Melwani, S., & Rothman, N. (2015). Research: Love-hate relationships at work might be good for you. *Harvard Business Review* [https://hbr.org/2015/01/research-love-hate-relationships-at-work-might-be-good-for-you].

Merton, R. K. (1957). *Social theory and social structure.* New York, NY: Free Press.

Messick, R. M., & Cook, K. S., eds. (1983). *Equity theory: Psychological and sociological perspectives.* New York, NY: Praeger.

Messmer, M. (1999). Skills for a new millennium: Accounting and financial professionals. *Strategic Finance Magazine* (August), 10ff.

Metts, S., & Cupach, W. R. (2008). Face theory. In *Engaging theories in interpersonal communication: Multiple perspectives* (pp. 203–214), L. A. Baxter & D. O. Braithwaite (eds.). Los Angeles, CA: Sage.

Metts, S., & Planalp, S. (2002). Emotional communication. In *Handbook of interpersonal communication*, 3rd ed., (pp. 339–373), M. L. Knapp & J. A. Daly (eds.). Thousand Oaks, CA: Sage.

Metz, D. (2013). The value of mentoring. Retrieved from http://www.pcma.org/be-in-the-know/pcma-central/pcma-news/news-landing/2013/04/12/the-value-of-mentoring#.Ur8J_RDt8E

Midooka, K. (1990). Characteristics of Japanese style communication. *Media, Culture and Society* 12, 477–489.

Miller, C. W., & Reznik, R. (2009). Social allergens in the workplace: Exploring the impact of emotion, perception of the allergen, and repair work on confrontation frequency and relational well-being. Paper presented at the annual meeting of the NCA 95th Annual Convention, Chicago Hilton & Towers, Chicago, IL. Online PDF. Retrieved December 12, 1013 from http://citation.allacademic.com/meta/p315255_index.html

Miller, G. R. (1978). The current state of theory and research in interpersonal communication. *Human Communication Research* 4, 164–178.

Miller, G. R. (1990). Interpersonal communication. In *Human communication: Theory and research* (pp. 91–122), G. L. Dahnke & G. W. Clatterbuck (eds.). Belmont, CA: Wadsworth.

Miller, G. R., & Parks, M. R. (1982). Communication in dissolving relationships. In *Personal relationships 4. Dissolving personal relationships* (pp. 127–154), S. Duck (ed.). New York, NY: Academic Press.

Mintz, N. L. (1956). Effects of esthetic surroundings: II. Prolonged and repeated experience in a beautiful and ugly room. *Journal of Psychology* 41, 459–466.

Mitro, S., Gordon, A. R., Olsson, M. J., & Lundström, J. N. (2012). The smell of age: Perception and discrimination of body odors of different ages. *PLoS ONE*, 7, e38110.

Moghaddam, F. M., Taylor, D. M., & Wright, S. C. (1993). *Social psychology in cross-cultural perspective.* New York, NY: W. H. Freeman.

Molloy, J. (1981). *Molloy's live for success.* New York, NY: Bantam.

Monahan, J. L. (1998). I don't know it but I like you. *Human Communication Research* 24, 480–500.

Mongeau, P. A., Knight, K., Williams, J., Eden, J., & Shaw, C. (2013). Identifying and explicating variation among friends with benefits relationships. *Journal of Sex Research* 50 (1), 37–47.

Mongeau, P. A., & Henningsen, M. L. M. (2008). Stage theories of relationship development. In *Engaging theories in interpersonal communication: Multiple perspectives* (pp. 363–375), L. A. Baxter & D. O. Braithwaite (eds.). Los Angeles, CA: Sage.

Monin, B. (2003). The warm glow heuristic: When liking leads to familiarity. *Journal of Personality and Social Psychology* 85 (December), 1035–1048.

Monk, A., Fellas, E., & Ley, E. (2004). Hearing only one side of normal and mobile phone conversations. *Behaviour & Information Technology* 23 (September–October), 301–306.

Moon, D. G. (1996). Concepts of "culture": Implications for intercultural communication research. *Communication Quarterly* 44, 70–84.

Morahan-Martin, J., & Schumacher, P. (2003). Loneliness and social uses of the Internet. *Computers in Human Behavior* 19 (November), 659–671.

Moran, R. T., Abramson, N. R., & Moran, S. V. (2014). *Managing cultural differences: Global leadership strategies for cross-cultural business success,* 9th ed. New York: Butterworth-Heinemann.

Morand, D. (1995). Cited in When style is vile, *Psychology Today* (March), 16.

Morgan, R. (2008, March 16). A crash course in online gossip. *New York Times*, Styles, p. 7.

Morreale, S. P., & Pearson, J. C. (2008). Why communication education is important: The centrality of the discipline in the 21st century. *Communication Education* 57 (April), 224–240.

Morreale, S. P., Osborn, M. M., & Pearson, J. C. (2000). Why communication is important: A rationale for the centrality of the study of communication. *Journal of the Association for Communication Administration* 29 (January), 1–25.

Morreale, S. P., Valenzano, J. M., & Bauer, J. A. (2016). Why communication education is important: A third study on the centrality of the discipline's content and pedagogy, *Communication Education* 65, 1–21.

Morrill, C. (1992). Vengeance among executives. *Virginia Review of Sociology* 1, 51–76.

Morris, D. (1977). *Manwatching: A field guide to human behavior.* New York, NY: Abrams.

Morris, D. (2002). *Peoplewatching.* New York, NY: Vintage.

Morrison, E. W., Chen, Y., & Salgado, S. R. (2004). Cultural differences in newcomer feedback seeking: A comparison of the United States and Hong Kong. *Applied Psychology: An International Review* 53 (January), 1–22.

Morrison, R. (2004). Informal relationships in the workplace: Associations with job satisfaction, organizational commitment and turnover intentions. *New Zealand Journal of Psychology* 33, 114–128.

Morrow, G. D., Clark, E. M., & Brock, K. F. (1995). Individual and partner love styles: Implications for the quality of romantic involvements. *Journal of Social and Personal Relationships* 12, 363–387.

Mosteller, T. (2008). *Relativism: A guide for the perplexed.* London: Continuum.

Motley, M. T. (1990a). On whether one can(not) not communicate: An examination via traditional communication postulates. *Western Journal of Speech Communication* 54, 1–20.

Motley, M. T. (1990b). Communication as interaction: A reply to Beach and Bavelas. *Western Journal of Speech Communication* 54, 613–623.

Mottet, T., & Richmond, V. P. (1998). Verbal approach and avoidance items. *Communication Quarterly* 46, 25–40.

Mrazek, M. D., Franklin, M. S., Phillips, D. T., Baird, B., & Schooler, J. W. (2013). Mindfulness training improves working memory capacity and GRE performance while reducing mind wandering. *Psychological Science* 24, 776–781.

Muise, A., Christofides, E., & Demarais, S. (2009). More information than you ever wanted: Does Facebook bring out the green-eyed monster of jealousy? *Cyberpsychology & Behavior* 12, 441–444.

Mullany, L. (2004). Gender, politeness and institutional power roles: Humor as a tactic to gain compliance in workplace business meetings. *Multilingua* 23, 13–37.

Mullen, C. A. (2005). *Mentorship primer.* New York, NY: Peter Lang.

Murphy, K. (2016, August 7). Do your friends actually like you? New York Times, Week in Review, 7.

Murstein, B. I., Merighi, J. R., & Vyse, S. A. (1991). Love styles in the United States and France: A cross-cultural comparison. *Journal of Social and Clinical Psychology* 10, 37–46.

Myers, S. A., & Zhong, M. (2004). Perceived Chinese instructor use of affinity-seeking strategies and Chinese college student motivation. *Journal of Intercultural Communication Research* 33 (September–December), 119–130.

N

Nabi, R. L., Prestin, A., & So, J. Facebook friends with (health) benefits? Exploring social network site use and perceptions of social support, stress, and well-being. *Cyberpsychology, Behavior, and Social Networking* 16, 721–727. doi: 10.1089/cyber.2012.0521

Nauert, R. (2015). Negative effects of sexism. *Psych Central.* Retrieved on April 10, 2017, from https://psychcentral. com/news/2010/03/19/negative-effects-of-sexism/ 12252.html

Neff, K. D., & Harter, S. (2002). The authenticity of conflict resolutions among adult couples: Does women's other-oriented behavior reflect their true selves? *Sex Roles* 47 (November), 403–417.

Neher, W. W., & Sandin, P. (2007). *Communicating ethically.* Boston, MA: Allyn & Bacon.

Nelson, P. E., Pearson, J. C., & Kurylo, A. (2008). Developing an intellectual communication. In *Getting the most from your graduate education in communication: A student's handbook,* S. Morreale & P. Arneson (eds.). Washington, DC: National Communication Association.

Nemko, M. (2013). Top 5 keys to mixing work and romance. Retrieved from http://career-advice.monster.com/in-the-office/work-life-balance/Top-5-Keys-Mixing-Work-and-Romance/article.aspx

Neugarten, B. (1979). Time, age, and the life cycle. *American Journal of Psychiatry* 136, 887–894.

Neuliep, J. W., & Grohskopf, E. L. (2000). Uncertainty reduction and communication satisfaction during initial interaction: An initial test and replication of a new axiom. *Communication Reports* 13 (summer), 67–77.

Neuliep, J. W., & McCroskey, J. C. (1997). The development of a U.S. and generalized ethnocentrism scale. *Communication Research Reports* 14, 385–398.

Ng, S. H., He, A., & Loong, C. (2004). Tri-generational family conversations: Communication accommodation and brokering. *British Journal of Social Psychology* 43 (September), 449–464.

Ni, P. (2013). How texting can improve or ruin your relationship happiness. Retrieved from http://www.psychologytoday. com/blog/communication-success/201311/how-texting-can-improve-or-ruin-your-relationship-happiness

Nicholas, C. L. (2004). Gaydar: Eye-gaze as identity recognition among gay men and lesbians. *Sexuality and Culture: An Interdisciplinary Quarterly* 8 (winter), 60–86.

Nicolai, J., & Demmel, R. (2007). The impact of gender stereotypes on the evaluation of general practitioners' communication skills: An experimental study using transcripts of physician–patient encounters. *Patient Education and Counseling* 69 (December), 200–205.

Nicotera, A. M., & Rancer, A. S. (1994). The influence of sex on self-perceptions and social stereotyping of aggressive communication predispositions. *Western Journal of Communication* 58, 283–307.

Nie, J., & Sundar, S. S. (2013). Who would pay for Facebook? Self-esteem as a predictor of user behavior, identity construction and valuation of virtual possessions. In *Proceedings of INTERACT 2013, Part III, LNCS 8119* (pp. 726–743), P. Kotzé et al. (eds.).

Niemeier, S., & Dirven, R. (eds.). (2000). *Evidence for linguistic relativity.* Philadelphia, PA: John Benjamins.

Noble, B. P. (1994). The gender wars: Talking peace. *New York Times* (August 14), p. 21.

Noelle-Neumann, E. (1973). Return to the concept of powerful mass media. In *Studies in broadcasting: An international annual of broadcasting science* (pp. 67–112), H. Eguchi & K. Sata (eds.). Tokyo: Nippon Hoso Kyokai.

Noelle-Neumann, E. (1980). Mass media and social change in developed societies. In *Mass communication review yearbook*, Vol. 1 (pp. 657–678), G. C. Wilhoit & H. de Bock (eds.). Thousand Oaks, CA: Sage.

Noelle-Neumann, E. (1991). The theory of public opinion: The concept of the spiral of silence. *Communication yearbook/14* (pp. 256–287), J. A. Anderson (ed.). Thousand Oaks, CA: Sage.

Noller, P., & Fitzpatrick, M. A. (1993). *Communication in family relationships.* Upper Saddle River, NJ: Prentice-Hall.

Norton, M. I., Frost, J. H., & Ariely, D. (2007). Less is more: The lure of ambiguity, or why familiarity breeds contempt. *Journal of Personality and Social Psychology* 92 (January), 97–105.

O

O'Hair, D., Cody, M. J., & McLaughlin, M. L. (1981). Prepared lies, spontaneous lies, Machiavellianism, and nonverbal communication. *Human Communication Research* 7, 325–339.

O'Hair, D., Cody, M. J., Goss, B., & Krayer, K. J. (1988). The effect of gender, deceit orientation and communicator style on macro-assessments of honesty. *Communication Quarterly* 36, 77–93.

O'Hair, M. J., Cody, M. J., & O'Hair, D. (1991). The impact of situational dimensions on compliance-resisting strategies: A comparison of methods. *Communication Quarterly* 39, 226–240.

Oatley, K., & Duncan, E. (1994). The experience of emotions in everyday life. *Cognition and Emotion* 8, 369–381.

Ober, C., Weitkamp, L. R., Cox, N., Dytch, H., Kostyu, D., & Elias, S. (1997). *American Journal of Human Genetics* 61, 494–496.

Oberg, K. (1960). Cultural shock: Adjustment to new cultural environments. *Practical Anthropology* 7, 177–182.

Oetzel, J. G., & Ting-Toomey, S. (2003). Face concerns in interpersonal conflict: A cross-cultural empirical test of the face negotiation theory. *Communication Research* 30 (December), 599–624.

Okrent, D. (2005). Numbed by the numbers, when they just don't add up. *New York Times* (January 23), Section 4, 2.

Olson, E. (2002). Switzerland tells its men: Wash that pot! Mop that floor! *New York Times* (April 6), A14.

Olson, E. (2006). Better not miss the bus. *New York Times* (April 6), G1–G2.

Onishi, N. (2005). In Japan crash, time obsession may be culprit. *New York Times* (April 27), A1, A9.

Oswald, D. L., Clark, E. M., & Kelly, C. M. (2004). Friendship maintenance: An analysis of individual and dyad behaviors. *Journal of Social and Clinical Psychology* 23 (June), 413–441.

Owen, J., & Fincham, F. D. (2009). Effects of gender and psychosocial factors on "friends with benefits" relationships among young adults. *Archives of Sexual Behavior.* doi: 10.1007/s10508-010-9611-6

Owens, T. J., Stryker, S., & Goodman, N. (eds.). (2002). *Extending self-esteem research: Sociological and psychological currents.* Cambridge, MA: Cambridge University Press.

P

Palmer, M. T. (1989). Controlling conversations: Turns, topics, and interpersonal control. *Communication Monographs* 56, 1–18.

Parker, J. G. (2004). Planning and communication crucial to preventing workplace violence. *Safety and Health* 170 (September), 58–61.

Parker, R. G., & Parrott, R. (1995). Patterns of self-disclosure across social support networks: Elderly, middle-aged, and young adults. *International Journal of Aging and Human Development* 41, 281–297.

Parks, M. R. (1995). Webs of influence in interpersonal relationships. In *Communication and social influence processes* (pp. 155–178), C. R. Berger & M. E. Burgoon (eds.). East Lansing, MI: Michigan State University Press.

Parks, M. R., & Floyd, K. (1996). Making friends in cyberspace. *Journal of Communication* 46, 80–97.

Parsons, C. K., Liden, R. C., & Bauer, T. N. (2001). Personal perception in employment interviews. In M. London (Ed.), *How people evaluate others in organizations* (pp. 67–90). Mahwah, NJ: Lawrence Erlbaum.

Pasley, K., Kerpelman, J., & Guilbert, D. E. (2001). Gendered conflict, identity disruption, and marital instability: Expanding Gottman's model. *Journal of Personal and Social Relationships* 18, 5–27.

Passel, J. S., Wang, W., & Taylor, P. (2010). One-in-seven new U.S. marriages is interracial or interethnic. *Pew Research Social & Demographic Trends.* Retrieved December 21, 2013, from http://www.pewsocialtrends.org/2010/06/04/marrying-out/

Patterson, C. (2000). Family relationships of lesbians and gay men. *Journal of Marriage and the Family* 62, 1052–1067.

Paul, A. M. (2001). Self-help: Shattering the myths. *Psychology Today* 34, 60ff.

Paul, M. (2013). Should you date your coworker? Retrieved from http://www.huffingtonpost.com/the-levo-league/dating-coworker_b_2689019.html

Pearce, J. A. (2010). What execs don't get about office romance. *MITSloan Management Review* http://sloanreview.mit.edu/article/what-execs-dont-get-about-office-romance/

Pearson, J. C. (1993). *Communication in the family*, 2nd ed. Boston, MA: Allyn & Bacon.

Pearson, J. C., & Spitzberg, B. H. (1990). *Interpersonal communication: Concepts, components, and contexts*, 2nd ed. Dubuque, IA: William C. Brown.

Pearson, J. C., Turner, L. H., & Todd-Mancillas, W. (1991). *Gender and communication*, 2nd ed. Dubuque, IA: William C. Brown.

Pearson, J. C., West, R., & Turner, L. H. (1995). *Gender and communication*, 3rd ed. Dubuque, IA: William C. Brown.

Penfield, J., ed. (1987). *Women and language in transition.* Albany, NY: State University of New York Press.

Pennebacker, J. W. (1991). *Opening up: The healing power of confiding in others.* New York, NY: Morrow.

Peplau, L. A. (1988). Research on homosexual couples: An overview. In *Gay relationships* (pp. 33–40), J. DeCecco (ed.). New York, NY: Harrington Park Press.

Peterson, C. C. (1996). The ticking of the social clock: Adults' beliefs about the timing of transition events. *International Journal of Aging and Human Development* 42, 189–203.

Petrocelli, W., & Repa, B. K. (1992). *Sexual harassment on the job.* Berkeley, CA: Nolo Press.

Petty, R. E., & Wegener, D. T. (1998). Attitude change: Multiple roles for persuasion variables. In *The handbook of social psychology,* 4th ed., Vol. 1 (pp. 323–390), D. T. Gilbert, S. T. Fiske, & G. Lindzey (eds.). New York, NY: McGraw-Hill.

Pinker, S. (1994). *The language instinct: How the mind creates language.* New York, NY: Morrow.

Plaks, J. E., Grant, H., & Dweck, C. S. (2005). Violations of implicit theories and the sense of prediction and control: Implications for motivated person perception. *Journal of Personality and Social Psychology* 88 (February), 245–262.

Plutchik, R. (1980). *Emotion: A psycho-evolutionary synthesis.* New York, NY: Harper & Row.

Pollack, A. (1996). Happy in the East (^—^) or smiling (:—) in the West. *New York Times* (August 12), D5.

Popkin, H. A. S. (2013) As your social media emotions go viral, anger spreads the fastest. Retrieved from http://www.nbcnews.com/technology/your-social-media-emotions-go-viral-anger-spreads-fastest-4B11186087

Pornpitakpan, C. (2003). The effect of personality traits and perceived cultural similarity on attraction. *Journal of International Consumer Marketing* 15, 5–30.

Porter, R. H., & Moore, J. D. (1981). Human kin recognition by olfactory cues. *Physiology and Behavior* 27, 493–495.

Porter, S., Brit, A. R., Yuille, J. C., & Lehman, D. R. (2000). Negotiating false memories: Interviewer and rememberer characteristics relate to memory distortion. *Psychological Science* 11 (November), 507–510.

Powell, M. (2005). *Behave yourself!: The essential guide to international etiquette.* Guilford, CT: Globe Pequot.

Prosky, P. S. (1992). Complementary and symmetrical couples. *Family Therapy* 19, 215–221.

Prusank, D. T., Duran, R. L., & DeLillo, D. A. (1993). Interpersonal relationships in women's magazines: Dating and relating in the 1970s and 1980s. *Journal of Social and Personal Relationships* 10, 307–320.

Psychometrics (2010). Warring egos, toxic individuals, feeble leadership. Retrieved from http://www.psychometrics.com/docs/conflictstudy_09.pdf on May 11, 2012.

Puentes, J., Knox, D., & Zusman, M.E. (2008). Participants in "friends with benefits" relationships. *College Student Journal* 42 (1), *176–180.*

R

Rabinowitz, F. E. (1991). The male-to-male embrace: Breaking the touch taboo in a men's therapy group. *Journal of Counseling and Development* 69, 574–576.

Radford, M. H., Mann, L., Ohta, Y., & Nakane, Y. (1993). Differences between Australian and Japanese students in decisional self-esteem, decisional stress, and coping styles. *Journal of Cross-Cultural Psychology* 24, 284–297.

Raes, F., Griffith, J. W., Van der Gucht, K., & Williams, J. M. G. (2013). School-based prevention and reduction of depression in adolescents: A cluster-randomized controlled trial of a mindfulness group program. *Mindfulness* (March). doi: 10.1007/s12671-013-0202-1

Rahman S. A., Flynn-Evans, E. E., Aeschbach, D., Brainard, G. C., Czeisler, C. A., & Lockley, S. W. (2014). Diurnal spectral sensitivity of the acute alerting effects of light. *Sleep* 37, 271–281.

Rancer, A. S. (1998). Argumentativeness. In *Communication and Personality: Trait Perspectives* (pp. 149–170), J. C. McCroskey, J. A. Daly, M. M. Martin, & M. J. Beatty (eds.). Cresskill, NJ: Hampton Press.

Rancer, A. S., & Avtgis, T. A. (2006). *Argumentative and aggressive communication: Theory, research, and application.* Thousand Oaks, CA: Sage.

Raney, R. F. (2000). Study finds Internet of social benefit to users. *New York Times* (May 11), G7.

Rappaport, H., Enrich, K., & Wilson, A. (1985). Relation between ego identity and temporal perspective. *Journal of Personality and Social Psychology* 48, 1609–1620.

Rapsa, R., & Cusack, J. (1990). Psychiatric implications of tattoos. *American Family Physician* 41, 1481–1486.

Raven, B. H., Schwarzwald, J., & Koslowsky, M. (1998). Conceptualizing and measuring a power/interaction model of interpersonal influence. *Journal of Applied Social Psychology* 28, 307–332.

Raven, B., Centers, C., & Rodrigues, A. (1975). The bases of conjugal power. In *Power in families* (pp. 217–234), R. E. Cromwell & D. H. Olson (eds.). New York, NY: Halsted Press.

Rawlins, W. K. (1983). Negotiating close friendship: The dialectic of conjunctive freedoms. *Human Communication Research* 9, 255–266.

Rawlins, W. K. (1989). A dialectical analysis of the tensions, functions, and strategic challenges of communication in young adult friendships. In *Communication yearbook 12,* (pp. 157–189), J. A. Andersen (ed.), Thousand Oaks, CA: Sage.

Rawlins, W. K. (1992). *Friendship matters: Communication, dialectics, and the life course.* Hawthorne, NY: Aldine DeGruyter.

Rawlins, W. K. (2008). *The compass of friendship: Narratives, identities, and dialogues.* Thousand Oaks, CA: Sage.

Read, A. W. (2004). Language revision by deletion of absolutisms. *ETC: A Review of General Semantics* 61 (December), 456–462.

Reardon, K. K. (1987). *Where minds meet: Interpersonal communication.* Belmont, CA: Wadsworth.

Reasoner, R. (2010). The true meaning of self-esteem. Retrieved from http://www.self-esteem-nase.org/what.php

Rector, M., & Neiva, E. (1996). Communication and personal relationships in Brazil. In *Communication in personal relationships across cultures* (pp. 156–173), W. B. Gudykunst, S. Ting-Toomey, & T. Nishida (eds.). Thousand Oaks, CA: Sage.

Reed, M. D. (1993). Sudden death and bereavement outcomes: The impact of resources on grief, symptomatology and detachment. *Suicide and Life-Threatening Behavior* 23 (fall), 204–220.

Regan, P. C., Durvasula, R., Howell, L., Ureno, O., & Rea, M. (2004). Gender, ethnicity, and the developmental timing of first sexual and romantic experiences. *Social Behavior and Personality: An International Journal* 32 (November), 667–676.

Regan, P. C., Kocan, E. R., & Whitlock, T. (1998). Ain't love grand! A prototype analysis of the concept of romantic love. *Journal of Social and Personal Relationships* 15, 411–420.

Rehman, A. A. (2007) *Dubai & Co.: Global strategies for doing business in the Gulf states.* New York, NY: McGraw-Hill.

Reiner, D., & Blanton, K. (1997). *Person to person on the Internet.* Boston, MA: AP Professional.

Reisenzein, R. (1983). The Schachter theory of emotion: Two decades later. *Psychological Bulletin* 94, 239–264.

Reisman, J. (1979). *Anatomy of friendship.* Lexington, MA: Lewis.

Reisman, J. M. (1981). Adult friendships. In *Personal relationships. 2: Developing personal relationships* (pp. 205–230), S. Duck & R. Gilmour (eds.). New York, NY: Academic Press.

Remland, M. S. (2006). Uses and consequences of nonverbal communication in the context of organizational life. In *The Sage handbook of nonverbal communication* (pp. 501–519), V. Manusov & M. L. Patterson (eds.). Thousand Oaks, CA: Sage.

Rhee, K. Y., & Kim, W-B (2004). The adoption and use of the Internet in South Korea. *Journal of Computer Mediated Communication* 9 (July) 4.

Rhee, S., Chang, J., & Rhee, J. (2003). Acculturation, communication patterns, and self-esteem among Asian and Caucasian American adolescents. *Adolescence* 38 (winter), 749–768.

Rice, M. (2007). Domestic violence. *National Center for PTSD Fact Sheet.* Retrieved from www.ncptsd.va.gov/ncmain/ncdocs/fact_shts/fs_domestic_violence.html

Rich, A. L. (1974). *Interracial communication.* New York, NY: Harper & Row.

Richards, I. A. (1951). Communication between men: The meaning of language. In *Cybernetics, Transactions of the Eighth Conference*, Heinz von Foerster (ed.).

Richards, I. A. (1968). The secret of "feedforward." *Saturday Review* 51 (February 3), 14–17.

Richmond, V. P., & McCroskey, J. C. (1984). Power in the classroom II: Power and learning. *Communication Education* 33, 125–136.

Richmond, V. P., McCroskey, J. C., & McCroskey, L. L. (2005). *Organizational communication for survival: Making work, work.* Boston, MA: Allyn & Bacon.

Richmond, V. P., Davis, L. M., Saylor, K., & McCroskey, J. C. (1984). Power strategies in organizations: Communication techniques and messages. *Human Communication Research* 11, 85–108.

Richmond, V. P., McCroskey, J. C., & Hickson, M. L. (2012). *Nonverbal behavior in interpersonal relations*, 7th ed. Boston, MA: Allyn & Bacon.

Richmond, V. P., Smith, R., Heisel, A., & McCroskey, J. C. (2001). Nonverbal immediacy in the physician/patient relationship. *Communication Research Reports* 18, 211–216.

Riggio, R. E. (1987). *The charisma quotient.* New York, NY: Dodd, Mead.

Riggio, R. E., & Feldman, R. S. (eds.). (2005). *Applications of nonverbal communication.* Mahwah, NJ: Erlbaum.

Rime, B. (2007). Interpersonal emotion regulation. In *The handbook of emotion regulation* (pp. 466–478), J. J. Cross (ed.). New York: Guilford Press.

Rivlin, G. (2005). Hate messages on Google site draw concern. *New York Times* (February 7), C1, C7.

Robbins, S. P., & Hunsaker, P. L. ((2009). *Training in interpersonal skills*, 5th ed. Boston, MA: Allyn & Bacon.

Roeher Institute (1995). *Harm's way: The many faces of violence and abuse against persons with disabilities.* North York, Ontario: Roeher Institute.

Rogers, C. (1970). *Carl Rogers on encounter groups.* New York, NY: Harrow Books.

Rogers, C., & Farson, R. (1981). Active listening. In *Communication: Concepts and Processes,* 3rd ed. (pp. 137–147), J. DeVito (ed.). Upper Saddle River, NJ: Prentice-Hall.

Rohlfing, M. E. (1995). "Doesn't anybody stay in one place anymore?" An exploration of the under-studied phenomenon of long-distance relationships. In *Under-studied relationships: Off the beaten track* (pp. 173–196), J. T. Wood & S. Duck (eds.). Thousand Oaks, CA: Sage.

Rokach, A. (1998). The relation of cultural background to the causes of loneliness. *Journal of Social and Clinical Psychology* 17, 75–88.

Rokach, A., & Brock, H. (1995). The effects of gender, marital status, and the chronicity and immediacy of loneliness. *Journal of Social Behavior and Personality* 19, 833–848.

Roloff, M. E., & Solomon, D. H. (2002). Conditions under which relational commitment leads to expressing or withholding relational complaints. *International Journal of Conflict Management* 13, 276–291.

Ronfeldt, H. M., Kimerling, R., & Arias, I. (1998). Satisfaction with relationship power and the perpetration of dating violence. *Journal of Marriage and the Family* 60 (February), 70–78.

Roper, C. (2014). The data miner's guide to romance. *Wired* 22 (February), 76–81.

Rosen, E. (1998). Think like a shrink. *Psychology Today* (October), 54–59.

Rosenbaum, M. E. (1986). The repulsion hypothesis. On the nondevelopment of relationships. *Journal of Personality and Social Psychology* 51, 1156–1166.

Rosengren, A., Orth-Gomér, K., Wedel, H., & Wilhelmsen, L. (1993). Stressful life events, social support, and mortality in men born in 1933. *British Medical Journal* (October 19). Cited in Goleman (1995a).

Rosengren, A., Orth-Gomer, K., Wedel, H., & Wilhelmsen, L. (1993). Stressful life events, social support, and mortality in men born in 1933. *British Medical Journal*, 307, 1102–1105

Rosenthal, R. (2002). The Pygmalion effect and its mediating mechanism. In *Improving academic achievement: Impact of psychological factors on education* (pp. 25–36), J. Aronson (ed.). San Diego, CA: Academic Press.

Rosenthal, R., & Jacobson, L. (1992). *Pygmalion in the classroom: Teacher expectations and pupils' intellectual development* (Rev. ed.). Norwalk, CT: Crown House.

Rosh, L., & Offermann, L. (2013, October). Be yourself, but carefully: How to be authentic without oversharing. *Harvard Business Review* 91, 135–139.

Rowland-Morin, P. A., & Carroll, J. G. (1990). Verbal communication skills and patient satisfaction: A study of doctor–patient interviews. *Evaluation and the Health Professions* 13, 168–185.

Ruben, B. D. (1985). Human communication and cross-cultural effectiveness. In *Intercultural communication: A reader,* 4th ed. (pp. 338–346), L. A. Samovar & R. E. Porter (eds.). Belmont, CA: Wadsworth.

Rubenstein, C. (1993). Fighting sexual harassment in schools. *New York Times* (June 10), C8.

Rubin, D. C., Groth, E., & Goldsmith, D. J. (1984). Olfactory cues of autobiographical memory. *American Journal of Psychology* 97, 493–507.

Rubin, R. B., & Graham, E. E. (1988). Communication correlates of college success: An exploratory investigation. *Communication Education* 37, 14–27.

Rubin, R. B., & Martin, M. M. (1994). Development of a measure of interpersonal communication competence. *Communication Research Reports* 11, 33–44.

Rubin, R. B., & McHugh, M. (1987). Development of parasocial interaction relationships. *Journal of Broadcasting and Electronic Media* 31, 279–292.

Rubin, Z. (1973). *Liking and loving: An invitation to social psychology.* New York, NY: Holt, Rinehart & Winston.

Rusbult, C. E., & Buunk, B. P. (1993). Commitment processes in close relationships: An interdependence analysis. *Journal of Social and Personal Relationships* 10, 175–204.

Rushe, R. H. (1996). Tactics of power and influence in violent marriages. *Dissertation abstracts international: Section B: The Sciences and Engineering* (University of Washington), 57, 1453.

Ryan, R. M., & Ryan, W. S. (2012, April 27). Homophobic? Maybe you're gay. *New York Times*, SR, 12.

Rydell, R. J., McConnell, A. R., & Bringle, R. G. (2004). Jealousy and commitment: Perceived threat and the effect of relationship alternatives. *Personal Relationships* 11 (December), 451–468.

S

Sabatelli, R. M., & Pearce, J. (1986). Exploring marital expectations. *Journal of Social and Personal Relationships* 3, 307–321.

Sabourin, M. (2007). The assessment of credibility: An analysis of truth and deception in a multiethnic environment. *Canadian Psychology* 48, 24–31.

Sagrestano, L. M., Heavey, C. L., & Christensen, A. (2006). Individual differences versus social structural approaches to explaining demand–withdrawal and social influence behaviors. In *Sex differences and similarities in communication*, 2nd ed. (pp. 379–395), K. Dindia & D. J. Canary (eds.). Mahwah, NJ: Erlbaum.

Sagula, D., & Rice, K. G. (2004). The effectiveness of mindfulness training on the grieving process and emotional well-being of chronic pain patients. *Journal of Clinical Psychology in Medical Settings* 11 (December), 333–342.

Sahlstein, E. M. (2004). Relating at a distance: Negotiating being together and being apart in long-distance relationships. *Journal of Social and Personal Relationships* 21 (October), 689–710.

Samter, W. (2004). Friendship interaction skills across the life span. In *Handbook of communication and social interaction skills* (pp. 637–684), J. O. Greene & B. R. Burleson (eds.). Mahwah, NJ: Lawrence Erlbaum.

Samter, W., & Cupach, W. R. (1998). Friendly fire: Topics variations in conflict among same- and cross-sex friends. *Communication Studies* 49, 121–138.

Sanders, J. A., Wiseman, R. L., & Matz, S. I. (1991). Uncertainty reduction in acquaintance relationships in Ghana and the United States. In *Cross-cultural interpersonal communication* (pp. 79–98), S. Ting-Toomey & F. Korzenny (eds.). Thousand Oaks, CA: Sage.

Santora, J. C. (2007). Assertiveness and effective leadership: Is there a tipping point? *Academy of Management Perspectives* 21, 84–86.

Sapadin, L. A. (1988). Friendship and gender: Perspectives of professional men and women. *Journal of Social and Personal Relationships* 5, 387–403.

Sarkis, S. (2011). Does Facebook increase jealousy? Retrieved from http://www.psychologytoday.com/blog/here-there-and-everywhere/201110/does-facebook-increase-jealousy

Sarwer, D. B., Kalichman, S. C., Johnson, J. R., Early, J., et al. (1993). Sexual aggression and love styles: An exploratory study. *Archives of Sexual Behavior* 22, 265–275.

Satell, G. (2015). Why communication is today's most important skill. *Forbes* http://www.forbes.com/sites/gregsatell/2015/02/06/why-communication-is-todays-most-important-skill/#72685c0b3638, accessed January 28, 2017.

Satir, V. (1983). *Conjoint family therapy*, 3rd ed. Palo Alto, CA: Science and Behavior Books.

Savage, N. (2013, April 29). Artificial emotions: How long until a robot cries? Retrieved from http://nautil.us/issue/1/what-makes-you-so-special/artificial-emotions?

Savitsky, K., Epley, N., & Gilovich, T. (2001). Do others judge us as harshly as we think? Overestimating the impact of our failures, shortcomings, and mishaps. *Journal of Personality and Social Psychology* 81 (July), 44–56.

Scandura, T. (1992). Mentorship and career mobility: An empirical investigation. *Journal of Organizational Behavior* 13, 169–174.

Schaap, C., Buunk, B., & Kerkstra, A. (1988). Marital conflict resolution. In *Perspectives on marital interaction* (pp. 203–244), P. Noller & M. A. Fitzpatrick (eds.). Philadelphia, PA: Multilingual Matters.

Schachter, S. (1971). *Emotion, obesity and crime.* New York, NY: Academic Press.

Schade, L. C., Sandberg, J., Bean, R., Busby, D., & Coyne, S. (2013). Using technology to connect in romantic relationships: Effects on attachment, relationship satisfaction, and stability in emerging adults. *Journal of Couple & Relationship Therapy: Innovations in Clinical and Educational Interventions* 12, 314–338.

Schegloff, E. (1982). Discourses as an interactional achievement: Some uses of "uh huh" and other things that come between sentences. In *Georgetown University roundtable on language and linguistics* (pp. 71–93), Deborah Tannen (ed.). Washington, DC: Georgetown University Press.

Scheufele, D. A., & Moy, P. (2000). Twenty-five years of the spiral of silence: A conceptual review and empirical outlook. *International Journal of Public Opinion Research* 12 (spring), 3–28.

Schmidt, T. O., & Cornelius, R. R. (1987). Self-disclosure in everyday life. *Journal of Social and Personal Relationships* 4, 365–373.

Schoeneman, T. J., & Rubanowitz, E. E. (1985). Attributions in the advice columns: Actors and observers, causes and reasons. *Personality and Social Psychology Bulletin* 11, 315–325.

Schott, G., & Selwyn, N. (2000). Examining the "male, antisocial" stereotype of high computer users. *Journal of Educational Computing Research* 23, 291–303.

Schrodt, P. (2003). Students' appraisals of instructors as a function of students' perceptions of instructors' aggressive communication. *Communication Education* 52 (April), 106–121.

Schumann, K., & Ross, M. (2010). Why women apologize more than men: Gender differences in thresholds for perceiving offensive behavior. *Psychological Science* 21, 1649–1655. doi: 10.1177/0956797610384150.

Schutz, A. (1999). It was your fault! Self-serving biases in autobiographical accounts of conflicts in married couples. *Journal of Social and Personal Relationships* 16, 193–208.

Schwartz, E. (2005). Watch what you say. *InfoWorld* 27 (February 28), 8.

Schwartz, M., and the Task Force on Bias-Free Language of the Association of American University Presses (1995). *Guidelines for bias-free writing*. Bloomington, IN: Indiana University Press.

Scott, M. L., & Lyman, S. M. (1968). Accounts. *American Sociological Review* 33, 46–62.

Seiter, J. S. (2007). Ingratiation and gratuity: The effect of complimenting customers on tipping behavior in restaurants. *Journal of Applied Social Psychology* 37 (March), 478–485.

Seiter, J. S., & Sandry, A. (2003). Pierced for success? The effects of ear and nose piercing on perceptions of job candidates' credibility, attractiveness, and hirability. *Communication Research Reports* 20 (fall), 287–298.

Seiter, J. S., & Weger, H., Jr. (2010). The effects of generalized compliments, sex of server, and size of dining party on tipping behavior in restaurants. *Journal of Applied Social Psychology* 40, 1–12.

Serewicz, M. C. M., & Petronio, S. (2007). Communication privacy management theory. In *Explaining communication: Contemporary theories and exemplars* (pp. 257–274), B. B. Whaley & W. Samter (eds.). Mahwah, NJ: Erlbaum.

Severin, W. J. & Tankard, J. W., Jr. (2001). *Communication theories: Origins, methods, and uses in the mass media*. Boston, MA: Allyn & Bacon.

Shaw, L. H., & Grant, L. M. (2002). Users divided? Exploring the gender gap in Internet use. *CyberPsychology & Behavior* 5 (December), 517–527.

Sheese, B. E., Brown, E. L, & Graziano, W. G. (2004). Emotional expression in cyberspace: Searching for moderators of the Pennebaker disclosure effect via e-mail. *Health Psychology* 23 (September), 457–464.

Shelton, J. N., & Richeson, J. A. (2005). Intergroup contact and pluralistic ignorance. *Journal of Personality and Social Psychology* 88 (January), 91–107.

Sheppard, J. A., & Strathman, A. J. (1989). Attractiveness and height: The role of stature in dating preferences, frequency of dating, and perceptions of attractiveness. *Personality and Social Psychology* 15, 617–627.

Shibazaki, K., & Brennan, K. A. (1998). When birds of different features flock together: A preliminary comparison of intra-ethnic and inter-ethnic dating relationships. *Journal of Social and Personal Relationships* 15, 248–256.

Shimanoff, S. (1980). *Communication rules: Theory and research*. Thousand Oaks, CA: Sage.

Shirley, J. A., Powers, W. G., & Sawyer, C. R. (2007). Psychologically abusive relationships and self-disclosure orientations. *Human Communication* 10, 289–302.

Short, J., Williams, E., & Christie, B. (1976). *The social psychology of telecommunication*. London: Wiley.

Siavelis, R. L., & Lamke, L. K. (1992). Instrumentalness and expressiveness: Predictors of heterosexual relationship satisfaction. *Sex Roles* 26, 149–159.

Siegert, J. R., & Stamp, G. H. (1994). "Our first big fight" as a milestone in the development of close relationships. *Communication Monographs* 61, 345–360.

Silverman, T. (2001). Expanding community: The Internet and relational theory. *Community, Work and Family* 4, 231–237.

Simons, D. J., & Chabris, C. F. (2011). What people believe about how memory works: A representative survey of the U.S. population. *PLoS ONE* 6 (8), e22757 doi: 10.1371/journal.pone.0022757

Singelis, T. M. (1994). The measurement of independent and interdependent self-construals. *Personality and Social Psychology Bulletin* 20, 580–591.

Singh, N., & Pereira, A. (2005). *The culturally customized web site*. Oxford, UK: Elsevier Butterworth-Heinemann.

Sizemore, D. S. (2004). Ethnic inclusion and exclusion. *Journal of Contemporary Ethnography* 33 (October), 534–570.

Skinner, M. (2002). In search of feedback. *Executive Excellence* (June), 18.

Slade, M. (1995). We forgot to write a headline. But it's not our fault. *New York Times* (February 19), 5.

Smith, A. (2014). 6 new facts about Facebook. http://www.pewresearch.org/fact-tank/2014/02/03/6-new-facts-about-facebook/

Smith, A., & Duggan, M. (2013). Online dating & relationships. *Pew Internet and American Life Project*. Retrieved from http://pewinternet.org/Reports/2013/Online-Dating/Summary-of-Findings.aspx

Smith, A., & Williams, K. D. (2004). R U There? Ostracism by cell phone text messages. *Group Dynamics* 8 (December), 291–301.

Smith, B. (1996). Care and feeding of the office grapevine. *Management Review* 85 (February), 6.

Smith, C. S. (2002). Beware of green hats in China and other cross-cultural faux pas. *New York Times* (April 30), C11.

Smith, D. (2003, December 2). Doctors cultivate a skill: Listening. *New York Times*, p. 6.

Smith, M. H. (2003). Body adornment: Know the limits. *Nursing Management* 34 (February), 22–23.

Smith, R. (2004). The teaching of communication skills may be misguided. *British Medical Journal* 328 (April 10), 1–2.

Smith, S. M., & Shaffer, D. R. (1991). Celerity and cajolery: Rapid speech may promote or inhibit persuasion through its impact on message elaboration. *Personality and Social Psychology Bulletin* 17 (December), 663–669.

Smith, S. M., & Shaffer, D. R. (1995). Speed of speech and persuasion: Evidence for multiple effects. *Personality and Social Psychology Bulletin* 21 (October), 1051–1060.

Snyder, C. R. (1984). Excuses, excuses. *Psychology Today* 18, 50–55.

Snyder, C. R., Higgins, R. L., and Stucky, R. J. (1983). *Excuses: Masquerades in search of grace.* New York, NY: Wiley.

Snyder, M. (1992). A gender-informed model of couple and family therapy: Relationship enhancement therapy. *Contemporary Family Therapy: An International Journal* 14 (February), 15–31.

Solomon, C., & Schell, M. S. (2009). *Managing across cultures: The seven keys to doing business with a global mindset.* New York, NY: McGraw-Hill.

Solomon, D. H., & Samp, J. A. (1998). Power and problem appraisal: Perceptual foundations of the chilling effect in dating relationships. *Journal of Social and Personal Relationships* 15, 191–209.

Solomon, G. B., Striegel, D. A., Eliot, J. F., Heon, S. N., et al. (1996). The self-fulfilling prophecy in college basketball: Implications for effective coaching. *Journal of Applied Sport Psychology* 8, 44–59.

Sommer, K. L., Williams, K. D., Ciarocco, N. J., & Baumeister, R. F. (2001). When silence speaks louder than words: Explorations into the intrapsychic and interpersonal consequences of social ostracism. *Basic and Applied Social Psychology* 23, 225–243.

Sommers, S. (1984). Reported emotions and conventions of emotionality among college students. *Journal of Personality and Social Psychology* 46, 207–215.

Sorenson, P. S., Hawkins, K., & Sorenson, R. L. (1995). Gender, psychological type and conflict style preference. *Management Communication Quarterly* 9, 115–126.

Spencer, T. (1993). A new approach to assessing self-disclosure in conversation. Paper presented at the Annual Convention of the Western Speech Communication Association, Albuquerque, New Mexico.

Spencer, T. (1994). Transforming relationships through everyday talk. In *The dynamics of relationships: Vol. 4. Understanding relationships*, S. Duck (ed.). Thousand Oaks, CA: Sage.

Spett, M. (2004). Expressing negative emotions: Healthy catharsis or sign of pathology? Retrieved from http://www.nj-act.org/article2.html

Spitzberg, B. H. (1991). Intercultural communication competence. In *Intercultural communication: A reader* (pp. 353–365), L. A. Samovar & R. E. Porter (eds.). Belmont, CA: Wadsworth.

Spitzberg, B. H., & Cupach, W. R. (1989). *Handbook of interpersonal competence research.* New York, NY: Springer-Verlag.

Spitzberg, B. H., & Hecht, M. L. (1984). A component model of relational competence. *Human Communication Research* 10, 575–599.

Sprecher, S. (1987). The effects of self-disclosure given and received on affection for an intimate partner and stability of the relationship. *Journal of Social and Personal Relationships* 4, 115–127.

Sprecher, S. (2001). Equity and social exchange in dating couples: Associations with satisfaction, commitment, and stability. *Journal of Marriage and the Family* 63 (August), 599–613.

Sprecher, S., & Hendrick, S. S. (2004). Self-disclosure in intimate relationships: Associations with individual and relationship characteristics over time. *Journal of Social and Clinical Psychology* 23 (December), 857–877.

Sprecher, S., & Metts, S. (1989). Development of the "Romantic Beliefs Scale" and examination of the effects of gender and gender-role orientation. *Journal of Social and Personal Relationships* 6, 387–411.

Sprecher, S., & Toro-Morn, M. (2002). A study of men and women from different sides of earth to determine if men are from Mars and women are from Venus in their beliefs about love and romantic relationships *Sex Roles* 46 (March), 131–147.

Sproull, L., Conley, C., & Moon, J. Y. (2005). Prosocial behavior on the net. In Yair Amichai-Hamburger (ed.), *The Social Net: Human Behavior in Cyberspace*, 139–162. Oxford: Oxford University Press.

Srivastava, K., & More, A. T. (2010). Some aesthetic considerations for over-the-counter (OTC) pharmaceutical products. *International Journal of Biotechnology* 11 (3/4), 267. doi:10.1504/IJBT.2010.036600

Stafford, L. (2004). *Maintaining long-distance and cross-residential relationships.* Mahwah, NJ: Erlbaum.

Stafford, L. (2008). Social exchange theories. In *Engaging theories in interpersonal communication: Multiple perspectives* (pp. 377–390), L. A. Baxter & D. O. Braithwaite (eds.). Los Angeles, CA: Sage.

Stafford, L., & Merolla, A. J. (2007). Idealization, reunions, and stability in long-distance dating relationships. *Journal of Social and Personal Relations* 24, 37–54.

Stafford, L., Kline, S. L., & Dimmick, J. (1999). Home e-mail: Relational maintenance and gratification opportunities. *Journal of Broadcasting and Electronic Media* 43, 659–669.

Stein, M. M., & Bowen, M. (2003). Building a customer satisfaction system: Effective listening when the customer speaks. *Journal of Organizational Excellence* 22 (summer), 23–34.

Stein, S. J., & Book, H. E. (2011). *The EQ edge: Emotional intelligence and your success.* Hoboken, NJ: Wiley.

Steiner, C. (1981). *The other side of power.* New York, NY: Grove.

Steiner, C. M. (2004). The other side of power [http://www.emotional-literacy.com/osp1.htm].

Stephan, W. G., & Stephan, C. W. (1985). Intergroup anxiety. *Journal of Social Issues* 41, 157–175.

Stephen, R., & Zweigenhaft, R. L. (1986). The effect of tipping of a waitress touching male and female customers. *Journal of Social Psychology* 126 (February), 141–142.

Stephens-Davidowitz, S. (2014). Google, tell me. Is my son a genius? *New York Times* (January 19), SR 6–7.

Stephens, G. K., & Greer, C. R. (1995). Doing business in Mexico: Understanding cultural differences. *Organizational Dynamics* 24, 39–55.

Stern, R., & Divecha, D. (2015, May/June). The empathy trap. *Psychology Today* 48, 31–34.

Stern, S. R., & Willis, T. J. (2007). What are teenagers up to online? In *20 questions about youth and the media* (pp. 211–224) S. R. Mazzarella (ed.). New York, NY: Peter Lang.

Sternberg, R. J. (1986). A triangular theory of love. *Psychological Review* 93, 119–135.

Sternberg, R. J. (1988). *The triangle of love: Intimacy, passion, commitment.* New York, NY: Basic Books.

Sternberg, R. J., & Weis, K. (2008). *The new psychology of love.* New Haven, CT: Yale University Press.

Sternglanz, R. W., & DePaulo, B. (2004). Reading nonverbal cues to emotions: The advantages and liabilities of relationship closeness. *Journal of Nonverbal Behavior* 28 (winter), 245–266.

Stevanoni, E., & Salmon, K. (2005). Giving memory a hand: Instructing children to gesture enhances their event recall. *Journal of Nonverbal Behavior* 29, 217–233.

Stewart, L. P., Cooper, P. J., & Stewart, A. D. (with Friedley, S. A.). (2003). *Communication and gender*, 4th ed. Boston, MA: Allyn & Bacon.

Stewart, S. (2006). A pilot study of email in an e-mentoring relationship. *Journal of Telemedicine and Telecare* 12 (October), 83–85.

Strassberg, D. S., & Holty, S. (2003). An experimental study of women's Internet personal ads. *Archives of Sexual Behavior* 32 (June), 253–260.

Strecker, I. (1993). Cultural variations in the concept of "face." *Multilingua* 12, 119–141.

Suler, J. (2004). The online disinhibition effect. *CyberPsychology and Behavior* 7 (June), 321–326.

Summerhayes, D. L., & Suchner, R. W. (1978). Power implications of touch in male-female relationships. *Sex Roles* 4, 103–110.

Sunnafrank, M., & Ramirez, A. (2004). At first sight: Persistent relational effects of get-acquainted conversations. *Journal of Social and Personal Relationships* 21 (June), 361–379.

Surowiecki, J. (2005). *The wisdom of crowds.* New York, NY: Doubleday.

Sutcliffe, K., Lewton, E., & Rosenthal, M. M. (2004). Communication failures: An insidious contributor to medical mishaps. *Academic Medicine* 79 (February), 186–194.

Sutter, D. L., & Martin, M. M. (1998). Verbal aggression during disengagement of dating relationships. *Communication Research Reports* 15, 318–326.

Sutton, R. M., Hornsey, M. J., & Douglas, K. M. (2012). *Feedback: The communication of praise, criticism, and advice.* New York, NY: Peter Lang.

Swink, D. F. (2013). I don't feel your pain: Overcoming roadblocks to empathy. Retrieved from http://www.psychologytoday.com/blog/threat-management/201303/i-dont-feel-your-pain-overcoming-roadblocks-empathy

T

Taddicken, M. (2013). The "Privacy Paradox" in the social web: The impact of privacy concerns, individual characteristics, and the perceived social relevance on different forms of self-disclosure. *Journal of Computer-Mediated Communication.* Article first published online: 18 DEC 2013. doi: 10.1111/jcc4.12052

Takizawa R., Maughan, B., & Arseneault, L. (2014). Adult health outcomes of childhood bullying victimization: evidence from a five-decade longitudinal British birth cohort. *American Journal of Psychiatry* 171, 777–784.

Talwar, V., Murphy, S. M., & Lee, K. (2007). White lie-telling in children for politeness purposes. *International Journal of Behavioral Developmet* 31, 1–11.

Tang, S., & Zuo, J. (2000). Dating attitudes and behaviors of American and Chinese college students. *The Social Science Journal* 37 (January), 67–78.

Tanikawa, M. (1996, September 8). Clubs where, for a price, Japanese men are nice to women. *New York Times, Style* 1, 8. http://www.nytimes.com/1996/09/08/style/clubs-where-for-a-price-japanese-men-are-nice-to-women.html.

Tannen, D. (1990). *You just don't understand: Women and men in conversation.* New York, NY: Morrow.

Tannen, D. (1994a). *Gender and discourse.* New York, NY: Oxford University Press.

Tannen, D. (1994b). *Talking from 9 to 5.* New York, NY: Morrow.

Tannen, D. (2006). *You're wearing that? Understanding mothers and daughters in conversation.* New York, NY: Random House.

Taraban, C. B., & Hendrick, C. (1995). Personality perceptions associated with six styles of love. *Journal of Social and Personal Relationships* 12, 453–461.

Tardiff, T. (2001). Learning to say "no" in Chinese. *Early Education and Development* 12, 303–323.

Tata, J. (2000). Toward a theoretical framework of intercultural account-giving and account evaluation. *International Journal of Organizational Analysis* 8, 155–178.

Tavris, C. (1989). *Anger: The misunderstood emotion*, 2nd ed. New York, NY: Simon & Schuster.

Teven, J. J., Richmond, V. P., & McCroskey, J. C. (1998). Measuring tolerance for disagreement. *Communication Research Reports* 15, 209–221.

Thelen, M. H., Sherman, M. D., & Borst, T. S. (1998). Fear of intimacy and attachment among rape survivors. *Behavior Modification* 22, 108–116.

Thibaut, J. W., & Kelley, H. H. (1959). *The social psychology of groups.* New York, NY: Wiley. Reissued (1986). New Brunswick, NJ: Transaction Books.

Thomas, K. W., & Kilmann, R. H. (1977). Developing a forced-choice measure of conflict handling behavior: The model instrument. *Educational and Psychological Measurement* 37, 309–325.

Thomas, K. W., & Kilmann, R. H. (2002). *Thomas-Kilmann conflict mode instrument.* Mountain View, CA: CPP, Inc.

Thomlison, D. (1982). *Toward interpersonal dialogue.* New York, NY: Longman.

Thompson, C. A., & Klopf, D. W. (1991). An analysis of social style among disparate cultures. *Communication Research Reports* 8, 65–72.

Thompson, C. A., Klopf, D. W., & Ishii, S. (1991). A comparison of social style between Japanese and Americans. *Communication Research Reports* 8, 165–172.

Thompson, M. (2013). Five reasons why people code-switch. Northeast Public Radio, http://www.npr.org/sections/codeswitch/2013/04/13/177126294/five-reasons-why-people-code-switch, accessed March 11, 2017.

Thorne, B., Kramarae, C., & Henley, N. (eds.). (1983). *Language, gender and society*. Rowley, MA: Newbury House.

Tidd, K. L., & Lockard, J. S. (1978). Monetary significance of the affiliative smile: A case for reciprocal altruism. *Bulletin of the Psychonomic Society* 11, 34–346.

Tierney, P., & Farmer, S. M. (2004). The Pygmalion process and employee creativity. *Journal of Management* 30 (June), 413–432.

Ting-Toomey, S. (1981). Ethnic identity and close friendship in Chinese-American college students. *International Journal of Intercultural Relations* 5, 383–406.

Ting-Toomey, S. (1985). Toward a theory of conflict and culture. *International and Intercultural Communication Annual* 9, 71–86.

Ting-Toomey, S. (1986). Conflict communication styles in black and white subjective cultures. In *Interethnic communication: Current research* (pp. 75–88), Y. Y. Kim (ed.). Thousand Oaks, CA: Sage.

Tinsley, C. H., & Brett, J. M. (2001). Managing workplace conflict in the United States and Hong Kong. *Organizational Behavior and Human Decision Processes* 85, 360–381.

Tolhuizen, J. H. (1986). Perceiving communication indicators of evolutionary changes in friendship. *Southern Speech Communication Journal* 52, 69–91.

Tolhuizen, J. H. (1989). Communication strategies for intensifying dating relationships: Identification, use, and structure. *Journal of Social and Personal Relationships* 6, 413–434.

Toma, C. L., Hancock, J. T., Ellison, N. B. (2008). Separating fact from fiction: An examination of deceptive self-presentation in online dating profiles. *Personality and Social Psychology Bulletin* 34, 1023–1026.

Tracy, J. L., & Beall, A. T. (2011). Happy guys finish last: The impact of emotion expressions on sexual attraction. *Emotion* 2011. doi: 10.1037/a0022902

Trager, G. L. (1958). Paralanguage: A first approximation. *Studies in Linguistics* 13, 1–12.

Trager, G. L. (1961). The typology of paralanguage. *Anthropological Linguistics* 3, 17–21.

Trower, P. (1981). Social skill disorder. In *Personal Relationships* 3 (pp. 97–110), S. Duck & R. Gilmour (eds.). New York, NY: Academic Press.

Tsiantar, D. (2005). The cost of incivility. *Time* (February 14), B5.

Tyler, J. J., Feldman, R. S., & Reichert, A. (2006). The price of deceptive behavior: Disliking and lying to peole who lie to us. *Journal of Experimental Social Psychology* 42, 69–77.

Tynes, B. M. (2007). Internet safety gone wild? Sacrificing the educational and psychosocial benefits of online social environments. *Journal of Adolescent Research* 22, 575–584.

U

Ueleke, W., et al. (1983). Inequity resolving behavior as a response to inequity in a hypothetical marital relationship. *A Quarterly Journal of Human Behavior* 20, 4–8.

Unger, F. L. (2001). Speech directed at able-bodied adults, disabled adults, and disabled adults with speech impairments. *Dissertation Abstracts International: Second B: The Sciences and Engineering*, 62, 1146.

V

Vaidis, D. C., & Haimi-Falkowicz, S. G. (2008). Increasing compliance with a request: Two touches are more effective than one. *Psychological Science* 103, 88–92.

Vainiomaki, T. (2004). Silence as a cultural sign. *Semiotica* 150, 347–361.

Valkenburg, P. M., & Peter, J. (2007). Online communication and adolescent well-being: Testing the stimulation versus the displacement hypothesis. *Journal of Computer-Mediated Communication* 12, article 2. Retrieved May 28, 2008, from http://jcmc.indiana.edu/vol12/issue4/Valkenburg.html

Valkenburg, P. M., Peter, J., & Schouten, A. P. (2006). Friend networking sites and their relationhip to adolescents' well-being and social self-esteem. *CyberPsychology & Behavior* 9, 584–590.

VanHyning, M. (1993). *Crossed signals: How to say no to sexual harassment*. Los Angeles, CA: Infotrends Press.

Varenik, T. (2010). How tattoos and body piercing affect your career. Retrieved from http://www.resumark.com/blog/tatiana/how-tattoos-and-body-piercing-affect-your-career

Varma, A., Toh, S. M., & Pichler, S. (2006). Ingratiation in job applications: Impact on selection decisions. *Journal of Managerial Psychology* 21, 200–210.

Veenendall, T. L., & Feinstein, M. C. (1995). *Let's talk about relationships: Cases in study*. Prospect Heights, IL: Waveland Press.

Velting, D. M. (1999). Personality and negative expectations: Trait structure of the Beck Hopelessness Scale. *Personality and Individual Differences* 26, 913–921.

Victor, D. (1992). *International business communication*. New York, NY: HarperCollins.

Vonk, R. (2002). Self-serving interpretations of flattery: Why ingratiation works. *Journal of Personality and Social Psychology* 82 (April), 515–526.

von Tetzchner, S., & Jensen, K. (1999). Interacting with people who have severe communication problems: Ethical considerations. *International Journal of Disability, Development and Education* 46 (December), 453–462.

Voo, J. (2007). How to handle an office romance. Retrieved from http://www.cnn.com/2007/living/worklife/08/29/office.romance/index.html

Vrij, A., & Mann, S. (2001). Telling and detecting lies in a high-stakes situation: The case of a convicted murderer. *Applied Cognitive Psychology*, 15 (March–April), 187–203.

W

Waddington, K. (2004). Psst—spread the word—gossiping is good for you. *Practice Nurse* 27, 7–10.

Wade, C., & Tavris, C. (2007). *Psychology*, 9th ed. Upper Saddle River, NJ: Prentice-Hall.

Wade, N. (2002). Scent of a man is linked to a woman's selection. *New York Times* (January 22), F2.

Walfisch, T., Van Dijk, D., & Kark, R. (2013). Do you really expect me to apologize? The impact of status and gender on the effectiveness of an apology in the workplace. *Journal of Applied Social Psychology* 43, 1446–1458.

Walsh, D. G., & Hewitt, J. (1985). Giving men the come-on: Effect of eye contact and smiling in a bar environment. Perceptual and Motor Skills, 61(3, Pt 1), 873–874 http://dx.doi.org/10.2466/pms.1985.61.3.873

Walster, E., Walster, G. W., & Berscheid, E. (1978). *Equity: Theory and research.* Boston, MA: Allyn & Bacon.

Walster, E., Walster, G. W., & Traupmann, J. (1978). Equity and premarital sex. *Journal of Personality and Social Psychology* 36, 82–92.

Walther, J. B. (2008). Social information processing theory. In *Engaging theories in interpersonal communication: Multiple perspectives* (pp. 391–404), L. A. Baxter & D. O. Braithwaite (eds.). Los Angeles, CA: Sage.

Walther, J. B., & Parks, M. R. (2002). Cues filtered out, cues filtered in: Computer-mediated communication and relationships. In *Handbook of interpersonal communication,* (pp. 529–563), M. L. Knapp & J. A. Daly (eds.). Thousand Oaks, CA: Sage.

Walther, J. B., Van Der Heide, B., Kim, S., Westerman, D., & Tong, S. T. (2008). The role of friends' appearance and behavior on evaluations of individuals on Facebook: Are we known by the company we keep? *Human Communication Research* 34, 28–49. doi: 10.1111/j.1468-2958.2007.00312.x

Walther, J. D. (1992). Interpersonal effects in computer-mediated interaction: A relational perspective. *Communication Research* 19, 52–90.

Wan, C. (2004). The psychology of culture shock. *Asian Journal of Social Psychology* 7 (August), 233–234.

Wang, W. (2015). Interracial marriage: Who is "marrying out"? *Pew Research Center* http://www.pewresearch.org/fact-tank/2015/06/12/interracial-marriage-who-is-marrying-out/.

Ward, C., Bochner, S., & Furnham, A. (eds.). (2001). *The psychology of culture shock.* Hove, UK: Routledge.

Ward, S. F. (2003). Lawyers in love. *ABA Journal* 89 (September), 37.

Watzlawick, P. (1977). *How real is real? Confusion, disinformation, communication: An anecdotal introduction to communications theory.* New York, NY: Vintage.

Watzlawick, P. (1978). *The language of change: Elements of therapeutic communication.* New York, NY: Basic Books.

Watzlawick, P., Beavin, J. H., & Jackson, D. D. (1967). *Pragmatics of human communication: A study of interactional patterns, pathologies, and paradoxes.* New York, NY: Norton.

Watzlawick, P., Weakland, J. H., & Fisch, R. (2011). *Change: Principles of problem formation and problem resolution.* New York, NY: W. W. Norton.

Weathers, M. D., Frank, E. M., & Spell, L. A. (2002). Differences in the communication of affect: Members of the same race versus members of a different race. *Journal of Black Psychology* 28, 66–77.

Weaver, A. D., MacKeigan, K. L., & MacDonald, H. A. (2011). Experiences and perceptions of young adults in friends with benefits relationships: A qualitative study. *Canadian Journal of Human Sexuality* 20, (1–2), n.p. Retrieved February 22, 2013, from Biomedsearch.com

Weigel, D. J., & Ballard-Reisch, D. S. (1999). Using paired data to test models of relational maintenance and marital quality. *Journal of Social and Personal Relationships* 16, 175–191.

Weinberg, H. L. (1959). *Levels of knowing and existence.* New York, NY: Harper & Row.

Weir, K. (2011). Fickle friends: How to deal with frenemies. *Scientific American* https://www.scientificamerican.com/article/fickle-friends/.

Weitzman, P. F. (2001). Young adult women resolving interpersonal conflicts. *Journal of Adult Development* 8, 61–67.

Weitzman, P. F., & Weitzman, E. A. (2000). Interpersonal negotiation strategies in a sample of older women. *Journal of Clinical Geropsychology* 6, 41–51.

Wert, S. R., & Salovey, P. (2004). A social comparison account of gossip. *Review of General Psychology* 8 (June), 122–137.

Wertz, D. C., Sorenson, J. R., & Heeren, T. C. (1988). Can't get no (dis)satisfaction: Professional satisfaction with professional-client encounters. *Work and Occupations* 15, 36–54.

Westwood, R. I., Tang, F. F., & Kirkbride, P. S. (1992). Chinese conflict behavior: Cultural antecedents and behavioral consequences. *Organizational Development Journal* 10, 13–19.

Wheeless, L. R., & Grotz, J. (1977). The measurement of trust and its relationship to self-disclosure. *Human Communication Research* 3, 250–257.

Whitbourne, S. K. (2013a). 8 behavioral catchphrases: Cool ideas in the quest to understand behavior. *Psychology Today* 46, 48–49.

Whitbourne, S. K. (2013b). Uh, thanks? *Psychology Today* 46, 19.

Whitchurch, E. R., Wilson, T. D., & Gilbert, (2010). "He Loves Me, He Loves Me Not . . . " Uncertainty can increase romantic attraction, *Psychological Science* 22, 172-175. Doi: 10.1177/0956797610393745

White, A. E., Kenrick, D. T., & Neuberg, S. L. (2013). Beauty at the ballot box: Disease threats predict preferences for physically attractive leaders. *Psychological Science* 24, 2429–2436. doi:10.1177/0956797613493642

Whitty, M. T. (2003a). Cyber-flirting: Playing at love on the Internet. *Theory and Psychology* 13 (June), 339–357.

Whitty, M. T. (2003b). Logging onto love: An examination of men's and women's flirting behaviour both offline and on the Internet. *Australian Journal of Psychology* 55, 68–72.

Whitty, M., & Gavin, J. (2001). Age/sex/location: Uncovering the social cues in the development of online relationships. *CyberPsychology and Behavior* 4, 623–630.

Wiederman, M. W., & Hurd, C. (1999). Extradyadic involvement during dating. *Journal of Social and Personal Relationships* 16, 265–274.

Wilkie, D. (2013). Forbidden love: Workplace-romance policies now stricter. Retrieved from http://www.shrm.org/hrdisciplines/employeerelations/articles/Pages/Forbidden-Love-Workplace-Romance-Policies-Stricter.aspx

Wilkins, B. M., & Andersen, P. A. (1991). Gender differences and similarities in management communication: A meta-analysis. *Management Communication Quarterly* 5, 6–35.

Willis, F.N. & Hamm, H.K. J. (1980). The use of interpersonal touch in securing compliance. *Nonverbal Behavior* 5, 49. doi:10.1007/BF00987054

Willis, J., & Todorov, A. (2006). First impressions: Making up your mind after a 100-ms exposure to a face. *Psychological Science* 17 (July), 592–598.

Willson, R., & Branch, R. (2006). *Cognitive behavioural therapy for dummies*. West Sussex, England: Wiley.

Wilson, S. R., & Sabee, C. M. (2003). Explicating communicative competence as a theoretical term. In *Handbook of communication and social interaction skills* (pp. 3–50), J. O. Greene & B. R. Burleson (eds.). Mahwah, NJ: Erlbaum.

Windy, D., & Constantinou, D. (2005). *Assertiveness step by step*. London: Sheldon Press.

Winquist, L. A., Mohr, C. D., & Kenny, D. A. (1998). The female positivity effect in the perception of others. *Journal of Research in Personality* 32, 370–388.

Witcher, S. K. (1999). Chief executives in Asia find listening difficult. *Asian Wall Street Journal Weekly* 21 (August 9–15), p. 11.

Wlodarski, R., & Dunbar, R. I. M. (2013). Examining the possible functions of kissing in romantic relationships. *Archives of Sexual Behavior*. doi: 10.1007/s10508-013-0190-1

Wolak, J., Mitchell, K. J., & Finkelhor, D. (2003). Escaping or connecting? Characteristics of youth who form close online relationships. *Journal of Adolescence* 26 (February), 105–119.

Wolpe, J. (1958). *Psychotherapy by reciprocal inhibition*. Stanford, CA: Stanford University Press.

Won-Doornink, M. J. (1985). Self-disclosure and reciprocity in conversation: A cross-national study. *Social Psychology Quarterly* 48, 97–107.

Wood, A. F., & Smith, M. J. (2005). *Online communication: Linking technology, identity, and culture*. Mahwah, NJ: Lawrence Erlbaum.

Wood, J. T. (1994). *Gendered lives: Communication, gender, and culture*. Belmont, CA: Wadsworth.

Wood, J. T. (2010). *Gendered lives: Communication, gender and culture*, 2nd ed. Belmont, CA: Wadsworth.

Woodzicka, A. A., & LaFrance, M. (2005). Working on a smile: Responding to sexual provocation in the workplace. In *Applications of nonverbal communication* (pp. 141–160), R. E. Riggio & R. S. Feldman (eds.). Mahwah, NJ: Erlbaum.

Worthington, D. L., & Fitch-Hauser, M. E. (2012). *Listening: Processes, functions, and competency*. Boston, MA: Allyn & Bacon.

Wrench, J. S., McCroskey, J. C., & Richmond, V. P. (2008). *Human communication in everyday life: Explanations and applications*. Boston, MA: Allyn & Bacon.

Wright, J. W., & Hosman, L. A. (1983). Language style and sex bias in the courtroom: The effects of male and female use of hedges and intensifiers on impression formation. *Southern Speech Communication Journal* 48, 137–152.

Wright, J., & Chung, M. C. (2001). Mastery or mystery? Therapeutic writing: A review of the literature. *British Journal of Guidance and Counseling* 29 (August), 277–291.

Wright, K. (2011). A chick critique. *Psychology Today* 44, 54–62.

Wright, P. H. (1978). Toward a theory of friendship based on a conception of self. *Human Communication Research* 4, 196–207.

Wright, P. H. (1984). Self-referent motivation and the intrinsic quality of friendship. *Journal of Social and Personal Relationships* 1, 115–130.

Wright, P. H. (1988). Interpreting research on gender differences in friendship: A case for moderation and a plea for caution. *Journal of Social and Personal Relationships* 5, 367–373.

Wyer, R. S. (2012). Your commute can improve your relationship. *Harvard Business Review* 90, 28–29.

Y

Yap, A. J., (2013, November). Big chairs create big cheats. *Harvard Business Review*. https://hbr.org/2013/11/big-chairs-create-big-cheats

Yau-fair Ho, D., Chan, S. F., Peng, S., & Ng, A. K. (2001). The dialogical self: Converging East–West constructions. *Culture and Psychology* 7, 393–408.

Yela, C. (2000). Predictors of and factors related to loving and sexual satisfaction for men and women. *European Review of Applied Psychology* 50, 235–243.

Yip, J. A., Côté, S. (2013). The emotionally intelligent decision maker: Emotion-understanding ability reduces the effect of incidental anxiety on risk taking. *Psychological Science* 24, 48–55.

Young, K. S., Griffin-Shelley, E., Cooper, A., O'Mara, J., & Buchanan, J. (2000). Online infidelity: A new dimension in couple relationships with implications for evaluation and treatment. *Sexual Addiction and Compulsivity* 7, 59–74.

Yuki, M., Maddux, W. W., Masuda, T. (2007). Are the windows to the soul the same in the East and West? Cultural differences in using the eyes and mouth as cues to recognize emotions in Japan and the United States. *Journal of Experimental Social Psychology* 43, 303–311.

Yukl, G. A. (1989). *Leadership in organizations* (2nd ed.). Albany, NY: State University of New York at Albany.

Yun, G. W., & Park, S. (2011). Selective posting: Willingness to post a message online. *Journal of Computer-Mediated Communication* 16, 201–227.

Z

Zajonc, R. B., Adelmann, P. K.; Murphy, S. T., Niedenthal, P. M. (1987). Convergence in the physical appearance of spouses. *Motivation and Emotion* 11(4): 335–346. http://hdl.handle.net/2027.42/45361

Zakowski, S. G., Harris, C., Krueger, N., Laubmeier, K. K., Garrett, S., Flanigan, R., & Johnson, P. (2003). Social barriers to emotional expression and their relations to distress in male and female cancer patients. *British Journal of Health Psychology* 8, 271–286.

Zarya, V. (2017, May 1). The future of collaboration. *Fortune* 175, 71–72.

Zhang, S., & Merolla, A. (2006). Communicating dislike of close friends' romantic partners. *Communication Research Reports* 23 (3), 179–186.

Zimmer, T. A. (1986). Premarital anxieties. *Journal of Social and Personal Relationships* 3, 149–159.

Zornoza, A., Ripoll, P., & Peiró, J. M. (2002). Conflict management in groups that work in two different communication contexts: Face-to-face and computer-mediated communication. *Small Group Research* 33 (October), 481–508.

Zuckerman, M., Klorman, R., Larrance, D. T., & Spiegel, N. H. (1981). Facial, autonomic, and subjective components of emotion: The facial feedback hypothesis versus the externalizer-internalizer distinction. *Journal of Personality and Social Psychology* 41, 929–944.

Zunin, L. M., & Zunin, H. S. (1991). *The art of condolence: What to write, what to say, what to do at a time of loss.* New York, NY: Harper Perennial.

Zunin, L. M., & Zunin, N. B. (1972). *Contact: The first four minutes.* Los Angeles, CA: Nash.

Credits

Text and Illustrations

Chapter 1   Page 2: Source: Alsop, R. (2004). How to get hired: We asked recruiters what M.B.A. graduates are doing wrong. Ignore their advice at your peril. Wall Street Journal (September 22), R8; **p. 2 (bottom):** Source: Hart Research Associates (2010). Raising the bar: Employers' views on college learning in the wake of the economic downturn: A survey among employers conducted on behalf of the Association of American Colleges and Universities. Washington, D.C; **p. 4:** Source: Messmer, M. (1999). Skills for a new millennium: Accounting and financial professionals. Strategic Finance Magazine (August), 10ff; **pp. 4-5:** Based on Hall, E. T. (1976). Beyond culture. Garden City, NY: Anchor Press; Hofstede, Hofstede & Minkov, 2010 Cultures and Organizations: Software of the Mind, Third Edition, McGraw Hill; and the websites of Culture at Work and Culturally Teaching: Education across Cultures; **p. 10:** Data from CIA, www.cia.gov/library/publications/the-world-factbook/rankorder/2153rank.html and Internet Live Stats, www.internetlivestats.com/internet-users-by-country/); **p. 17:** Emma Lazarus (1883). The New Colossus.

Chapter 2   Page 43: Based on (Hofstede, Hofstede, & Minkov, 2010); **p. 50:** Based on Lukens, J. (1978). Ethnocentric speech. Ethnic Groups 2, 35–53; Gudykunst, W. B. (1991). Bridging differences: Effective intergroup communication. Newbury Park, CA: Sage; Gudykunst, W. B., & Kim, Y. W. (1992). Communicating with strangers: An approach to intercultural communication, 2nd ed. New York, NY: Random House.

Chapter 3   Page 59: Figure: Group Processes: An Introduction to Group Dynamics, 3d ed. by Joseph Luft, 1984, p. 60. Reprinted by permission of Mayfield Publishing Company, Mountain View, CA; **p. 59:** Group Processes: An Introduction to Group Dynamics, 3d ed. by Joseph Luft, 1984, p. 60. Reprinted by permission of Mayfield Publishing Company, Mountain View, CA; **p. 72:** Asch, S. (1946). Forming impressions of personality. Journal of Abnormal and Social Psychology 41, 258–290; **p. 80:** These suggestions were drawn from a variety of websites, such as those of eHarmony, Ask, and from research: Alpert (2013) and Conniff & Nicks (2014).

Chapter 4   Page 100: William James (1890). The Principles of Psychology. New York, H. Holt and Co.; **p. 101:** Based on Galvin, K. M., Bylund, C. L., & Brommel, B. J. (2011). Family communication: Cohesion and change, 8th ed. Boston, MA: Allyn & Bacon; Pearson, J. C. (1993). Communication in the family, 2nd ed. Boston, MA: Allyn & Bacon; **p. 109:** Benjamin Disraeli (1845). Sybil: Or, The Two Nations. Auckland: Floating Press; **p. 110:** Based on Haney, W. (1973). Communication and organizational behavior: Text and cases, 3rd ed. Homewood, IL: Irwin. Weinberg, H. L. (1959). Levels of knowing and existence. New York, NY: Harper & Row; **p. 113:** T.S. Eliot's ""The Cocktail Party"" Faber & Faber, 1974.

Chapter 5   Page 120: Based on Andersen, P. A. (2004). The complete idiot's guide to body language. New York, NY: Penguin Group; Riggio, R. E., & Feldman, R. S. (eds.). (2005). Applications of nonverbal communication. Mahwah, NJ: Erlbaum; **p. 131:** These suggestions were drawn from a variety of sources, including the websites of the Cincinnati Association for the Blind and Visual Impaired, the Association for the Blind of WA, the national Federation of the Blind and the American Foundation for the blind, all accessed October 25, 2013; **p. 136:** Thomas Mann & H T Lowe-Porter. The Magic Mountain, New York: Knopf, 1953; **p. 136:** Max Picard, The World of Silence, Trans. Stanley Godman (Chicago: H. Regnery, 1952); **p. 149:** Based on Hall, E. T., & Hall, M. R. (1987). Hidden differences: Doing business with the Japanese. New York, NY: Anchor Books.

Chapter 7   Page 182: Based on Rime, B. (2007). Interpersonal emotion regulation. In J. J. Cross (Ed.). The handbook of emotion regulation (pp. 466-478). New York: Guilford Press; Dean, 2011; **p. 186:** Reprinted with permission from Annette deFerrari Design; **p. 198:** Based on Plutchik, R. (1980). Emotion: A psycho-evolutionary synthesis. New York, NY: Harper & Row; **p. 199:** Charles Darwin observed in his The Expression of the Emotions in Man and Animals (John Murray, 1872); **p. 202:** Based on Elisabeth Kubler-Ross (1969) in her On Death and Dying. Macmillan Publishers.

Chapter 8   Page 207: These suggestions were drawn from a variety of sources, including the websites of the National Stuttering Association, the National Aphasia Association, the United States Department of Labor, and the American Speech and Hearing Association, all accessed March 7, 2017; **p. 213:** Based on Burgoon, J. K., Guerrero, L. K., & Floyd, K. (2010). Nonverbal Communication. Boston, MA: Allyn & Bacon; Pearson, J. C., & Spitzberg, B. H. (1990). Interpersonal communication: Concepts, com-ponents, and contexts, 2nd ed. Dubuque, IA: William C. Brown; **pp. 226-227:** Based on Snyder, C. R. (1984). Excuses, excuses. Psychology Today 18, 50–55.

Chapter 9   Page 254: Authier, J., & Gustafson, K. (1982). Microtraining: Focusing on specific skills. In Interpersonal helping skills: A guide to training methods, programs, and resources (pp. 93–130), E. K. Marshall, P. D. Kurtz, and Associates (eds.). San Francisco, CA: Jossey-Bass; **p. 259:** Satir, V. (1983). Conjoint family therapy, 3rd ed. Palo Alto, CA: Science and Behavior Books.

Chapter 10   Page 278: Based on Duck, S. (1986). Human relationships. Thousand Oaks, CA: Sage; **p. 280:** Lord Byron in Don Juan New York; London: George Routledge & Son.; **p. 272:** Based on Reiner, D., & Blanton, K. (1997). Person to person on the Internet. Boston, MA: AP Professional; Wright, P. H. (1978). Toward a theory of friendship based on a conception of self. Human Communication Research 4, 196–207; Wright, P. H. (1984). Self-referent motivation and the intrinsic quality of friendship. Journal of Social and Personal Relationships 1, 115–130; **p. 276:** Benjamin Disraeli (1845). Sybil: Or, The Two Nations. Auckland: Floating Press; **p. 279:** Taraban, C. B., & Hendrick, C. (1995). Personality perceptions associated with six styles of love. Journal of Social and Personal Relationships 12, 453–461; **p. 281:** Sprecher, S., & Metts, S. (1989). Development of the "Romantic Beliefs Scale" and examination of the effects of gender and gender-role orientation. Journal of Social and Personal Relationships 6, 387–411; **p. 288:** Based on Cramer, D. (2004). Emotional support, conflict, depression, and relationship satisfaction in a romantic partner. Journal of Psychology: Interdisciplinary and Applied 138 (November), 532–542; **p. 297:** Based on Dindia, K., & Timmerman, L. (2003). Accomplishing romantic relationships. In Handbook of communication and social interaction skills (pp. 685–721), J. O. Greene & B. R. Burleson (eds.). Mahwah, NJ: Erlbaum; Guerrero, L. K., Andersen, P. A., Jorgensen, P. F., Spitzberg, B. H., & Eloy, S. V. (1995). Coping with the green-eyed monster: Conceptualizing and measuring communicative response to romantic jealousy. Western Journal of Communication 59, 270–304; **p. 298:** These questions were drawn from a variety of sources; for example, the websites of SUNY at Buffalo Counseling Services; The American College of Obstetricians and Gynecologists; Women's Heath Care Physicians; and the University of Texas at Austin, Counseling and Mental Health Center; **p. 298:** utexas.edu/student/cmhc/booklets/relavio/relaviol.html; **p. 299:** utexas.edu/student/cmhc/booklets/relavio/relaviol.html

Chapter 11   Page 306: Quote: Warring Egos, Toxic Individuals, Feeble Leadership: A study of conflict in the Canadian workplace; Psychometrics, 2009; **pp. 315-316:** Based on deBono, E. (1987). The six thinking hats. New York, NY: Penguin; **p. 323:** Dominic A. Infante, Teresa A. Chandler & Jill E. Rudd, Test of an argumentative skill deficiency model of interspousal violence, Communication Monographs, Vol.86(2), 1989.

Chapter 12   Page 339: Quote: Kenrick, D. T., Neuberg, S. L., and Cialdini, R. B. (2007). Social psychology: Goals in interaction, 4th ed. Boston, MA: Allyn & Bacon; **p. 343:** Friedman, J., Boumil, M. M., & Taylor, B. E. (1992). Sexual harassment. Deerfield Beach, FL: Health Communications, Inc.; **p. 343:** U.S. Equal Employment Opportunity Commission (EEOC) definition 'Sexual harassment'; **p. 343:** Petrocelli, W., & Repa, B. K. (1992). Sexual harassment on the job. Berkeley, CA: Nolo Press; **p. 344:** Based on Bravo, E., & Cassedy, E. (1992). The 9 to 5 guide to combating sexual harassment. New York, NY: Wiley; **p. 344:** Quote: Based on Bravo, E., & Cassedy, E. (1992). The 9 to 5 guide to combating sexual harassment. New York, NY: Wiley; Petrocelli, W., & Repa, B. K. (1992). Sexual harassment on the job. Berkeley, CA: Nolo Press; Rubenstein, C. (1993). Fighting sexual harassment in schools. New York Times (June 10), C8.

Photo Credits

Chapter 1   Page 1: Image Source/Alamy Stock Photo; **p. 5:** Jelena Aloskina/Shutterstock; **p. 7:** AF archive/Alamy Stock Photo; **p. 8:** Myrleen Pearson/Alamy Stock Photo; **p. 11:** Antonio Guillem Fernández/Alamy Stock Photo; **p. 20:** Joseph DeVito; **p. 22:** Kumar Sriskandan/Alamy Stock Photo; **p. 24:** littleWhale/Shutterstock.

Chapter 2   Page 29: Tom Merton/GettyImages; **p. 32:** MARKA/Alamy Stock Photo; **p. 34:** Paul Thompson Images/Alamy Stock Photo; **p. 35:** Sylvain Grandadam/AgeFotostock; **p. 41:** digital vision/Getty Images; **p. 39:** Alix Minde/PhotoAlto/Alamy; **p. 44:** Thomas Barwick/GettyImages; **p. 48:** AF archive/Alamy Stock Photo; **p. 50:** John Birdsall/The Image Works.

Chapter 3   Page 55: Datacraft Co Ltd/GettyImages; **p. 58:** Image Source/Alamy Stock Photo; **p. 62:** Pixellover RM 6/Alamy Stock Photo; **p. 64:** Tetra Images/Alamy Stock Photo; **p. 70:** michaeljung/Shutterstock; **p. 78:** Marquicio Pagola/Contributor/GettyImages; **p. 82:** John Howard/GettyImages; **p. 84:** Hemis/Alamy Stock Photo.

Chapter 4   Page 87: Agencja Fotograficzna Caro/Alamy Stock Photo; **p. 88:** Tim Larse/AP Photo; **p. 93:** LDprod/Shutterstock; **p. 96:** Photononstop/Photononstop; **p. 98:** Pearson Education; **p. 100:** Jupiterimages/GettyImages; **p. 104:** Kevin Dietsch/Upi/Newscom; **p. 105:** Micheko Productions, Inh. Michele Vitucci/Alamy Stock Photo; **p. 106:** Megapress/Alamy Stock Photo.

Chapter 5   Page 149: michaeljung/Fotolia; **p. 153:** Pearson; **p. 137:** Franz Pfluegl/Shutterstock; **p. 116:** bbtomas/Shutterstock; **p. 120:** Antonello Turchetti/GettyImages; **p. 127:** joSon/GettyImages; **p. 128:** Cultura RM/Alamy Stock Photo; **p. 132:** Blend Images/Alamy Stock Photo; **p. 141:** JGI/GettyImages; **p. 144:** Chris Rout/Alamy Stock Photo.

Chapter 6   Page 157: Wavebreak Media ltd/Alamy Stock Photo; **p. 160:** Wavebreak Media LTD/AgeFotostock; **p. 161:** Everett Collection; **p. 164:** Image Source/Alamy Stock Photo; **p. 165:** Toby Burrows/Getty Images; **p. 170:** ZoneCreative/Shutterstock; **p. 173:** stylephotographs/123rf; **p. 175:** Ben Welsh/age fotostock/Alamy Stock Photo; **p. 178:** Ammentorp Photography/Alamy Stock Photo.

Chapter 7   Page 200: Koji Aoki/Age Fotostock America Inc.; **p. 201:** Iakov Filimonov/Shutterstock; **p. 181:** Iconic Cornwall/Alamy Stock Photo; **p. 183:** Anna Berkut/Alamy Stock Photo; **p. 185:** Dmitriy Shironosov/Alamy Stock Photo; **p. 186:** Blend Images/Alamy Stock Photo; **p. 189:** Alex Segre/Alamy Stock Photo; **p. 190:** Sergey Peterman/Shutterstock; **p. 192:** Fotolia; **p. 194:** Pixland/Getty Images.

Chapter 8   Page 205: fStop Images GmbH/Alamy Stock Photo; **p. 208:** HONGQI ZHANG/123rf gb Ltd; **p. 209:** MBI/Alamy Stock Photo; **p. 214:** SKA/Getty Images; **p. 218:** Blend Images/Alamy Stock Photo; **p. 219:** Atlaspix/Alamy Stock Photo; **p. 224:** svetikd/Getty Images; **p. 228:** JGI/Jamie Grill/Getty Images; **p. 231:** age fotostock/Alamy Stock Photo; **p. 215:** Pixellover RM 1/Alamy Stock Photo.

Chapter 9   Page 246: David J. Green/Alamy Stock Photo; **p. 247:** Hero Images Inc./Alamy Stock Photo; **p. 250:** Joseph DeVito; **p. 256:** Wavebreak Media ltd/Alamy Stock Photo; **p. 263:** ableimages/Alamy Stock Photo; **p. 260:** Galina Barskaya/Fotolia; **p. 236:** Nick Sinclair/Alamy Stock Photo; **p. 241:** PHOVOIR/Alamy Stock Photo; **p. 244:** Antonio Guillem Fernández/Alamy Stock Photo.

Chapter 10   Page 267: Antonello Turchetti/GettyImages; **p. 269:** PhotoAlto/Alamy Stock Photo; **p. 274:** ONOKY -

Index

Note: Italicized letters *f*, *t*, and *b* following page numbers indicate figures, tables, and boxes, respectively.